# Great Garden Sources for Texans

# Great Garden Sources for Texans

# Great Garden Sources for Texans

## A Regional Guide to Designing, Constructing, Planting & Furnishing Your Landscape

by
Nan Booth Simpson, ASLA
&
Patricia Scott McHargue

Portland, Oregon U.S.A.

**Great Garden Sources for Texans**
ISBN 0-9639879-4-1
**Library of Congress Catalog Card Number: 98-61779**

---

### Forewarning

This publication is intended as a general guide. The subject matter deals with hundreds of independent businesses, nonprofit organizations and public agencies which are apt to change at any time. Therefore it is sold as is, and without a warranty of any kind, either express or implied.

Every effort was made to ensure that the information presented was accurate on the date of publication. Businesses do close, locations and hours often change, and companies alter their product mix. Therefore, neither the author nor the publisher shall be liable to the purchaser or any other person or entity with respect to any liability, loss or damage caused or alleged to be caused directly or indirectly by information appearing in this publication.

We neither expressly guarantee, warrant nor endorse the businesses, locations and/or subjects to which this guide provides descriptions and other general information.

---

### Bulk Sales

Copies of this book in case lots are available at discount for fund raising by garden clubs and non-profit organizations. Contact the publisher for more information.

As an environmentally conscious publisher,
we have printed this book on recycled paper.

Graphic Design: Jim Moothart

First Edition

Printed in the United States of America.

Published by:

The **Authors** Communication Team
Post Office Box 25211
Portland, Oregon 97298 U.S.A.
Phone & Facsimile 503/297-0873

# Dedication

This book is dedicated to Lady Bird Johnson. More than any other person in the country, Mrs. Johnson has opened our eyes to the inherent beauty of Texas. Her Wildflower Center has brought worldwide acclaim to this state. Her untiring efforts in the domain of native plants will change, for the betterment of mankind, the way people garden for centuries to come.

# Table of Contents

# Chapter One
## Finding Your Garden Style

## *Chapter Two*

# Sources of Inspiration & Information

## *Chapter Three*

# Garden Construction

## Chapter Four

# Garden Conservation

## Chapter Five

# The Garden's Green Foundation

## Chapter Six

# Naturescaping the Urban Environment

## Chapter Seven

# The Gardener's Garden

## Chapter Eight

# Special Plants for Special Places

## Chapter Nine

# Garden Furniture

## Chapter Ten

# Finishing Touches

# Appendices & Indexes

# Foreword

This book is not intended to collect dust on your bookshelf. Rather, it's meant to be used until it falls apart or is replaced by the next edition. This is a how-to and where-to workbook, a compendium of information for improving your garden and your gardening skills. Reading this book from cover to cover is not required or even recommended. However, we think you'll find each section's introduction filled with practical information and personal insights from the pen of Nan Simpson, an experienced Texas designer/gardener/garden writer. Although this is primarily a sourcebook, the essays are full of timesaving, laborsaving and moneysaving tips.

The listings, which were written primarily by Pat McHargue, are presented to help you choose the most appropriate supplier of goods and services. There is really no single best source for everything. This book can aim you in the right direction, but it's up to you to make the decisions. Don't forget to take this book with you on your travels. Wonderful resources for design inspiration and garden shopping are dotted throughout the state. Visit and learn.

# About the Authors

Nan Booth Simpson, a fifth-generation Texan, is a registered landscape architect who specializes in residential garden design. A member of The American Society of Landscape Architects, she has worked on projects throughout the United States. She holds degrees from Southern Methodist University in Fine Arts and Texas A&M University in Landscape Architecture. She has spent much of her career writing about gardens for such prominent journals as *Southern Living, Southern Accents* and *Garden Design*. She edited *The Naturalist's Garden* for Globe Pequot Press and served as a consultant to *Practical Guide to Garden Design*, in the Time-Life Complete Gardener series. When she lived in Dallas, she served on the Park Board of the City of University Park, which sparked her interest in returning to school to study landscape architecture. During her years in Austin, she founded a garden club and served on the Professional Advisory Board of the Landscape Architecture Department at TAMU. Today, Nan lives with her husband in Portland, Oregon, which she describes as "a lovely place to live, a gardener's paradise, and just a four-hour flight from home."

Patricia Scott McHargue, is an Austinite who majored in English and Classical Civilization at the University of Texas. As a keen gardener and a "wannabe-writer" with an absolute devotion to the intricacies of the English language, she was the obvious choice to serve as copy editor for Nan's previous book, *Great Garden Sources of the Pacific Northwest*. Patricia has contributed to this book by researching and describing sources and acting as the co-editor. Her organizational skills have been honed by work in banking and interior design and years of leadership in such organizations as The Theta Charity Antique Show in Houston, The Junior League of Austin's Christmas Affair and Live Oak Theater of Austin.

# Reader Feedback

A book of this type is an ever-changing database of discovery. Your input can make it better, and your recommendations will most assuredly be considered. If you know of a "Great Garden Source" that doesn't appear in this edition, the authors would like to hear from you. We've reserved a page at the end of the book for your comments and suggestions. Mail, e-mail or FAX us your ideas. Each will be reviewed carefully before the next edition is published.

# Introduction

"It is our hope that
Great Garden Sources for Texans
will serve the inexperienced gardener
as well as the connoisseur."

*....Nan Simpson & Pat McHargue*

# Notes from Nan:

Having grown up in the rolling farmland of Central Texas and practiced landscape architecture throughout the state, it was not an easy decision to move to the Pacific Northwest, far away from family, friends and the land I love. But I had married a man whose roots are as deep in the sodden soil of Oregon as mine are in Texas. Convincing me to relocate in mid-career was made palatable by the reality of jet travel and the promise of a small piece of property. The former makes it possible for me to continue working with my Texas clients; the latter allows me to garden in the most hospitable growing environment in North America.

New to the Northwest, I was eager to find the best sources for the frilly ferns and majestic native conifers that make this landscape wonderful. I searched libraries and bookstores for a comprehensive regional guidebook only to discover that no single publication covered the gamut of garden materials from plants to garden art. So I decided to write a book.

I've been enormously pleased with the response to *Great Garden Sources of the Pacific Northwest*. It was greeted with high critical acclaim in the press, but what has really made me feel terrific is that gardeners have called and written to say that they couldn't do without it! Texas friends who saw the book persuaded me that Texans, often gardening under adverse circumstances, are even more eager for reliable garden information. Thus, *Great Garden Sources for Texans*.

I could never have produced this book without the help and support of my friend and client, Patricia McHargue. An English major, Pat admirably served as Copy Editor for the Northwest book. To this project she has brought her expertise as a writer and her own practical knowledge about gardening in Texas. The two of us embarked on a 5,436-mile journey, visiting hundreds of nurseries and garden shops.

We prevailed upon all of the state's landscape architects, who willingly shared information and advice. While I had expected that most of the places where my fellow professionals trade would be "wholesale only," I've been surprised to learn that some of the best sources are open to the public, if only the public knows where to find them. Gardening friends throughout the state also shared their "secret sources." And often, one source led us to three more!

But just knowing where to shop does not equip garden consumers with everything they should know about *how* to shop. As in the Northwest book, I'm not only sharing garden resources, but also everything I've learned (often the hard way) as a design professional. The trick is selecting the right plant for the right place, the best container for the best effect and the sturdiest landscape materials for the use intended.

You'll find Money-saving Tips sprinkled throughout the text. I've tried to suggest economical ways for you to improve your garden, with enough advice to get you pointed in the right direction and enough horticultural information to ask the right questions. There are hundreds of excellent, highly specialized books that cover every aspect of gardening.

I will be sharing what I know about planting design in the chapters on plant sources. It is not enough to love plants. It is creating a pleasing composition of color and texture that makes a garden. In most cases, I have chosen to use the common names of plants in this text. It was a difficult decision. On the one hand, Latin botanical nomenclature is a universal language. On the other hand, many gardeners are scared off by "*Latinus grandiosus esoterica*." This book is not meant to intimidate novice gardeners. What I hope to convey is that gardening is a life-long avocation. Nobody knows everything there is to know about the vast world of plants.

To avoid unpleasant surprises, one does need to learn something about Latin names, if only to read plant tags. Common names can present problems. A rose is a rose is a rose, but a Rose of Sharon (*Hibiscus syriacus*) is not a rose at all. To compound the confusion, this plant is commonly called "Althaea" in Texas. Furthermore, if you walk into a nursery looking for "hibiscus," you could be directed to a tropical plant or a hardy garden perennial or one of several deciduous shrubs. *Hibiscus* tells us the genus. *Hibiscus syriacus* is the species name for a lovely flowering shrub. *Hibiscus syriacus* '*Albus*' further tells us that the shrub is a white-flowering cultivar.

This book aims to serve both experienced and inexperienced gardeners. Gardening is the #1 hobby in America today! An increasing number of homeowners are no longer satisfied with planting a flat of purple petunias and retiring to the deck with a cold beer. For some, gardening has become a competitive sport! If you are a gardener who would pursue to the ends of the earth a rare Texas native snowbell (*Styrax youngae*), which can only be found in the wild in a few remote sites in Mexico, I've got your source!

I'm fairly certain that the majority of people who will read this book truly enjoy their gardens, but have limited time to spend. Even homeowners who only mow the lawn to keep the neighbors from complaining should find resources within these pages. I've laced the text with timesaving ideas and, hopefully, introduced you to products to make every aspect of gardening easier and more rewarding.

Nobody loves a fabulous garden more than I, but this book is not meant to fuel the fires of guilt or send over-achievers to a chiropractor's office. As a gardener, I fall into a sort of middle ground. My father, a devout grower of beautiful things, once gave me sage advice. When I asked him what to do about crabgrass, he said, "Learn to love it."

I'm less sanguine about volunteer hackberry trees, and I confess to the occasional use of herbicide when confronted with poison ivy, but I'm willing to accept a few serendipitous surprises the birds bring in. I happen to believe gardening should be good for the environment as well as enjoyable for the gardener. And while I'm as guilty as the next person of impulse buying, once I've planted some new "horticultural marvel," I tend to take a laissez faire attitude. If I've carefully chosen its spot, given it reasonable care and it doesn't respond, I figure that the plant didn't "belong." Part of the fun of gardening is experimentation.

Good overall design is another matter. You can consign plant mistakes to a compost pile, but a drainage problem, a misplaced patio or an ugly retaining wall won't simply go away. As a landscape architect, I promise my clients that I'll save them money in the long run by preventing costly mistakes. It only seems fair that I should share the same information with readers.

# Postcard from Pat:

Contributing to this book has taught me a series of lessons. My job was to research, write commentary on sources and edit Nan's text.

**Lesson #1** — You *can* teach an old dog. When Nan asked me to collaborate, I protested, "Not me! I can't even turn on a computer." With a sweet smile and a stern voice she said, "You'll learn." And so I did!. Thanks to my son Scott who tutored me via long distance from midnight until 2 a.m. every night for weeks, I passed "Computer 101." Scott's patience was incredible. Of course, I kept reminding him that I had taught him to tie his own shoes. Pay-back time!

**Lesson #2** — Being an author isn't as glamorous as it sounds. I really can't say I enjoyed the hours I spent in the public library looking up the addresses and phone numbers of companies all over Texas and planning the itinerary for our travels.

**Lesson #3** — What I did enjoy was exploring the state with a dear friend. It' a big place to cover. There was lots of laughter as we spent two hot summer months traveling north to south, east to west and everywhere in between. Actually there were three of us on the road: Nan, me and my new Buick Riviera, "Good Girl." Much to our chagrin, she got all the admiring glances. Truth is, Nan and I looked pretty scuzzy as we hauled our maps, notebooks, ice chests, suitcases and weary bodies into yet another motel. Thelma and Louise. (Without the mayhem, of course, and, unfortunately for me, without Brad Pitt.) What a ride!

**Lesson #4** — People who love gardening are the most generous people in the world. From personal friends who offered to put us up for the night to design professionals who revealed their "secret" sources and nursery owners who spent hours showing us around, all the people we encountered freely shared their expertise and offered us unmitigated encouragement. I hope everyone who reads this book will learn as much as I learned in the process of helping it come to life.

While this is an era for global thinking, there's much to be said for buying locally. It's good for our regional economy. But more importantly, plants grown in Texas are better adapted for our soils and climate than those grown on the East Coast or in California. Don't be afraid to ask the big chain stores where they obtain their plants. Do take a look at some of the "out-of-the-way" suppliers you'll meet in this book.

Please respect the privacy of the sources that are open by-appointment-only or deal strictly by mail-order. Some are one-person operations in residential neighborhoods. Others are large wholesalers who, although they are not set up to meet the public, will sell to homeowners under certain circumstances. A number of the manufacturers listed in this book do not sell directly to the public, but they will happily furnish the name of a dealer in your area. Enjoy gardening in your own backyard. I hope we cross garden paths someday.

# Invitation to Readers

Let us know if you are familiar with other sources that should be included in this book. In three years of research we discovered how many public gardens and garden-related businesses there are in Texas. We were unable to visit every town in the state, and we're certain that we have even missed a few good sources in the cities and towns we did visit. We respected the wishes of those who asked not to be in the book because the owners are getting up in age or they have more business than they can serve.

We've tried diligently to avoid mistakes like the one Nan found in a respected garden book on the subject of manure: "For the same expenditure, far better results may be obtained from the use of domestic humans and commercial fertilizers." **To err is humus.**

# What to Expect from this Book

We hope you'll take time to read the text that precedes the source lists throughout the book. In Chapter One, we've included a brief history of gardening to help you choose your "garden style." Then we discuss the physiography of Texas and divide the state into twelve distinct gardening regions. We think it is folly to attempt to garden without a complete understanding of the soils, climate and native vegetation of your region. Further, we believe that gardeners hold a large responsibility for maintaining the unique biological diversity of each region!

In organizing a book as comprehensive as this, the first question we asked was, "Where do we begin?" After much deliberation, we decided to begin with North and East Texas, which includes three very different garden regions: **Cross Timbers & Grand Prairie** (with Fort Worth as its market center); **Trinity Blacklands** (with Dallas as its market center); and the **Piney Woods** (including Tyler and Nacogdoches) Next, we work our way, clockwise, along the Gulf Coast, which incorporates: **Coastal Prairies & Marshes** (with Houston as its market center); **Coastal Bend** (Corpus Christi and Padre Island); and the **Valley** (from Brownsville to McAllen). Then we go back up through Central Texas: **Rio Grande Plain** (including San Antonio and Laredo); **Central Prairies & Savannas** (including Waco and Bryan/College Station) and the **Hill Country** (with Austin its major market). Finally we cover West Texas: **Red Rolling Plains** (Wichita Falls, Abilene and San Angelo); **High Plains** (Amarillo, Lubbock and Midland); and the **Trans-Pecos** (with El Paso as its major market).

In Chapter Two, we've provided the names and addresses of places to look for design inspiration. We've also provided reading lists, as well some other important sources of information to expand your gardening knowledge. In Chapter Three, we stress Master Planning. Then we discuss the walls, walkways, fences and "follies," garden structures and lighting that are as important to a landscape design as plants. And, we list resources for the materials that go into the "hardscape."

Before getting into plants, Chapter Four takes up sound gardening practices. We're dwelling heavily on the topic of conservation. We've shared practical ways of improving the soil, feeding plants and coping with pests in the most environmentally sensitive manner. The good news is that these techniques can result in reduced garden maintenance! The sources for plants begin in Chapter Five. Before we get into one-stop shopping at the state's great garden centers, we provide basic information about choosing the plants for your garden. For beginners and "old hands" alike, garden centers offer the widest range of products and services.

Specialty nurseries appear in Chapters Six through Eight. Chapter Six is devoted to "naturescaping," the most important new trend in gardening today. The chapter includes discussions on Texas natives, backyard wildlife habitats, wildflower meadows and drought-tolerant plants. Water conservation has been a "hot" issue in environmental circles for years. The summer of '98 served as yet another wake-up call. Hopefully it won't be forgotten. (Water-wise gardening tips that occur throughout this text are summarized on page 166.)

Chapter Seven addresses the more sophisticated levels of planting design and lists specialized sources for flowering shrubs, perennials, bulbs, herbs and other edible plants. Chapter Eight is all about special plants for special places. These are the water gardens, the hanging baskets, tropical plants and "living sculptures" that are used to embellish our gardens, patios and interiors. Few gardeners are aware of the small nurseries in Texas that grow specialized, sometimes rare, plant materials. Many began as backyard hobbies and remain labors of love.

Chapter Nine deals with garden furniture and Chapter Ten addresses the decorative accessories that make a garden both livable and memorable. Basically, the book is arranged in the order in which the work of a landscape architect progresses: planning, constructing and conserving, planting and, finally, embellishing the garden.

In the appendices you'll find a list of landscape architectural firms that are known for their residential designs. Mail-order Shopping Tips contains 25 helpful hints for anyone who has ever perused a plant catalog. We've also included a Glossary that defines words you will encounter in this book and in catalogs. The Geographical Index may help you discover some nearby sources you didn't know existed. It should be especially useful, however, on your travels through Texas.

# Acknowledgments

We want to thank special people who encouraged and guided us through this project. James Parsons of Corpus Christi provided invaluable assistance as copy editor. Texas authors William Welch, Malcomb Beck and Howard Garrett provided advice in their areas of expertise, as well as resources within their respective regions. Landscape architects in all parts of the state freely shared their favorite sources. A few, including Doug Wade in Corpus Christi, Rick White in the Valley, Hal Stringer in Waco and John Troy in San Antonio, spent an inordinate amount of time helping us. Gardening friends throughout the state also offered both inspiration and assistance.

We are particularly grateful to friends who graciously provided room and board during our travels: Kay Tiller in Dallas, Hal Hall in San Angelo, Ann Moore in McAllen and Mollie and Franklin Maresh, on the banks of the Guadalupe. Kay Tiller is our PR Director, and she is doing a marvelous job!

In Houston we sought the advice of Betty Davis, Susu Ross and Bobbie Todd. Our "network" also included Mary Ann Hasie in Lubbock, Mike Reid in Bedford, Evelyn Perdue in Dallas, Marietta Allmond in Galveston, Scott and Joy McHargue in Tyler; Beth Thornton in Longview, Joe Baldwin and Jerry Hollier in Brownsville, Ridge Floyd in Hunt, Jeannette Brown, Fran Ramsey, Martha Grant, Pat Booker, Bill Ater and Phil and Rebecca Hudson in Austin.

Folks at the Texas Parks and Wildlife Department and the Texas Association of Nurserymen were most gracious, as well. And how could we not acknowledge all of the individual nursery professionals, garden shop owners and product manufacturers in Texas? Many not only shared their enthusiasm for the "green industry," but also shared the names of their competitors!

We can't name all of the friends and family members who forgave us when we forgot to return phone calls or failed to write thank-you notes. You know who you are; we hope you know we've appreciated your support. Pat and I both wish we could thank our late fathers, Spencer Scott and Zachary Booth, whose love of all things green and growing inspired our own early gardening efforts.

## Chapter One
# Finding Your Garden Style

*"Gardens were before gardeners, and
but some hours after the earth."*
....*Sir Thomas Browne 1658*

# Don't Generalize about Texas

Movies persist in portraying the state as a barren wasteland, and for people who've never seen beyond DFW Airport, the myth endures. Gardeners I've met in the Pacific Northwest have actually said, "You're from Texas? I'll bet you know all about cactus." And I reply in my very best drawl, "Well, dearie, I've never actually cultivated cacti in my garden..."

Then I begin explaining that dense forests blanket the eastern quarter of the state, that majestic native pines, cypresses and oaks grow beside the sleepy bayous near Houston, and that Austin is set in green hills and surrounded with sparkling lakes. I wax poetic about the 5,000 species of wildflowers in Texas. By the time I've gotten to "lost" maples or the flora of salt marshes, I've lost my audience. (By the way, I do know and grow cacti, but I resent people picturing Texas as a desert.)

During the several years I wrote the Texas Garden Checklist for *Southern Living*, I was reminded every day how diverse this land really is. No one can make general statements in a state characterized by such radically different climate zones, vegetation patterns and soil types. The average annual rainfall ranges from 56 inches in Port Arthur to a mere eight inches in El Paso. Mean minimum January temperature ranges from 24° in Amarillo to a mild 51° in Brownsville. A prescription for amending the soil in San Antonio would be terrible advice for gardeners in Tyler. When it's time to plant lettuce in Lubbock, it's time to harvest in Houston!

The one thing all Texas gardens have in common is intense summer heat. Only the eastern part of the state has an annual average rainfall that exceeds the evaporation caused by heat and drying winds, and even the forested region is subject to occasional droughts. After the months of heat and drought, a "blue norther" can send balmy temperatures plummeting forty degrees in a matter of hours. Then throw in hail and hurricanes. Gardening in Texas requires a good sense of humor!

# Where We've Been

If you are new to Texas, locate the center of the state on a globe and trace with your finger a path around the world at the 32nd parallel. You may be surprised to find that the trip takes you to Casablanca, Tripoli, Tel Aviv, Isfahan, and on around through India and China. While distance from the equator is not the only factor that affects plant life, in terms of climate, the western two-thirds of Texas has more in common with Egypt than England. **For more than a century, Texas gardeners have followed Northern European styles. That's where we made our first mistake!**

## Average Annual Rainfall

1. *More than 56 inches*
2. *45 to 56 inches*
3. *33 to 44 inches*
4. *21 to 32 inches*
5. *Eight to 20 inches*
6. *Less than eight inches*

# Gardening on the Frontier

We can't blame the early settlers. They brought to this vast, virtually vacant land a no-nonsense approach to gardening. On their journey to Texas, homemakers might have stowed a few precious flower seeds and bulbs along with the vegetable seeds, but few ornamental plantings adorned the earliest Texas homes. No matter what the building style, houses were sited to catch prevailing breezes, and the gardens were made for feeding the family. The location of the garden would have been based on soil quality and proximity to water rather than any aesthetic consideration. Impressing the neighbors was not what life on the frontier was all about.

The few exceptions were ante-bellum plantations that were patterned after the gardens of the Old South. Tree-lined entry drives and planting beds edged with clipped boxwoods were somewhat possible in the luxuriant Piney Woods. This garden style was clearly out of the question on the grassland prairies, where unrelenting sun and summer droughts quickly put an end to boxwoods, azaleas and camellias. Even where the growing conditions were right, importing such shrubs was far beyond the means of most early immigrants to Texas.

In 1854, Frederick Law Olmsted, conservationist and social reformer, followed the Old Spanish Road through the hardscrabble countryside of Northeast Texas to San Antonio. He found no evidence of any ornamental gardening until he reached New Braunfels, where he encountered little homesteads lovingly tended by their German owners. Botanist Ferdinand Jakob Lindheimer, who built his home there in 1852, was one of several influential naturalists who studied and appreciated native Texas flora. More than 20 species, including the now-popular perennial, *Gaura lindheimeri*, now bear his name. Regrettably, few people saw the beauty in our native vegetation.

We know that by the mid-1850s, several mail-order nurseries had been established in Texas. Their primary customers seemed to have been the 35,000 German residents eager to put down "roots" in the new towns they were establishing throughout South-central Texas. Of these, only the Otto M. Locke Nursery in New Braunfels remains today (see page 228), but the fruit trees, roses, iris and other ornamental plants these nurseries introduced set new standards for domestic gardening.

Garden historian Dr. William C. Welch noted in a recent article in *Neil Sperry's GARDENS* magazine, "Today as you travel the state you can explore these relatively intact German communities, with their tidy well-planned gardens and family-oriented parks. Take note of the historic plants in cemeteries, the ornate fences, and the orchards and tree-lined streets. Public and private gardens alike have been influenced by this group of settlers." A stroll through the cottage garden of the **Schultz House** preserved in San Antonio's Hemisfair Plaza or the **Steves Homestead** in the "upscale" King William Historic District admirably demonstrate the garden style and range of plants favored by nineteenth-century German gardeners. (Chapter Two lists addresses, phone numbers and hours of operation for the gardens highlighted in this chapter.)

# The Victorian Era in Texas

With the coming of the railroads, Texas communities began growing rapidly. Town gardens quickly evolved into something far more orderly and ornamental than rural landscapes. The advent of dependable water supplies and such "modern conveniences" as lawn mowers and canvas hoses made lawn grasses and elaborate flowerbeds more feasible. As affluence and leisure time increased, the garden began to be seen as a healthful retreat from the vexations of everyday life. The late 19th century was a time of great energy in the field of horticulture in Texas. A now-thriving nursery industry began introducing a wide variety of plant materials for Texas gardens.

Unfortunately, the years in which garden design blossomed in Texas happened to coincide with the Victorian era. The penchant was for sentimental statues and flowerbeds cut into the lawns in the shapes of hearts, circles and fans, brimming with show-stopping "bedding plants." The national press touted "correct taste," and the people who had built fashionable new homes in San Antonio, Galveston, and other prosperous enclaves were not to be outdone. They soon surrounded their residences with tight corsets of shrubbery and dotted the lawns with fanciful pergolas, dovecotes, rose arbors, fountains and fishponds.

The problem with all of this was that the plants native to Texas were forsaken in the effort to be fashionable. Fascination with "exotic" plants was at a zenith as the twentieth century began. City gardens were often designed by nurserymen who were only too happy to import ornamental shrubs and trees from all over the world. In this environment, how could our common native plants compete with such colorful imports as azaleas, hydrangeas or camellias? It's interesting to note that most of the plant materials available, indeed many of the plants we consider as Southern as "grits and gravy," were introductions from China and Japan — gardenias, mimosas, boxwoods, daylilies, althaeas, ligustrum, and flowering quince!

Vestiges of nineteenth-century design ideas remain to this day. Intensively pruned foundation plantings still surround many houses, long after the high foundations of Victorian-era homes have given way to slab construction. And, most of our gardens are still brimming with imported, non-native plants that generally require inordinate quantities of water to survive the summer.

It is in public parks throughout Texas that we see the happiest holdovers from the nineteenth century. However gaudily they may have executed their displays of petunias, marigolds and zinnias, the Victorians pursued city beautification with a passion. Maintenance costs have diminished the exuberance of former times, but brightly colored flowers are still used to create a sense of place, as evidenced by the much-photographed Flower Clock in the new development of Las Colinas between Dallas and Fort Worth.

Devoting a separate section of the garden to roses and planting them in a formal arrangement appears to have been another late-nineteenth-century phenomenon. The American Rose Society, formed in 1899, is responsible for most of the rose displays and test sites we enjoy in parks throughout Texas, most notably in the **Tyler Rose Garden**. Enthusiasm for single-species gardens has inspired other plant societies (chrysanthemum, iris, daylily, canna, etc.) to display their prize-winning blooms in numerous Texas public parks and gardens.

Greenhouses allowed the Victorians to indulge their enthusiasm for palms, bromeliads, cacti, orchids and assorted tropical exotics from all over the world. Such contemporary glass houses as the Lucile Halsell Conservatory at the **San Antonio Botanical Gardens**, the Rainforest Pyramid at **The Moody Gardens** in Galveston, the Conservatory of **The Fort Worth Botanic Garden** continue the tradition of exhibiting horticultural rarities.

# The Days of Grand Estates

After the turn of the century and the discovery of oil, the state's more affluent citizens began building suburban villas in the fashionable new developments of our growing cities. Classical architecture had supplanted fanciful Victorian residential styles throughout the United States as architects, trained at the Ecole des Beaux-Arts in Paris, promoted a new sense of restraint. With this change came a returning taste for a more formal approach to the landscape.

City residences were now sited farther back from the street, surrounded by manicured grass and punctuated with symmetrical arrangements of clipped hedges and obligatory rose gardens. Where the prairie landscape offered neither dramatic

topography nor venerable trees, neoclassical garden style amounted to little more than a "suitable setting." Several notable landscape architects set up practices in Texas during the era, however, and a few Texas gardens compared favorably with any estate garden produced in the country at the time.

In *The Golden Age of American Gardens: Proud Owners, Private Estates, 1890-1940*, Mac Griswold and Eleanor Weller provide details on the development of **Bayou Bend** in Houston's River Oaks. Here, Miss Ima Hogg carved a magnificent fourteen-acre garden out of dense woods. The garden evolved over a period of years with input from several prominent landscape architects, and it draws from several centuries of European garden art. Its formality dissolves into luxuriant naturalism at the property's outer edges. The estate is now open to the public as an arm of the Houston Museum of Fine Arts.

Griswold and Weller also commend the **DeGolyer Estate**, which was designed in the Spanish Colonial style. Very different from Bayou Bend in terrain and flavor, the De Golyer's landscape extended seamlessly out from tile floors to a rolling lawn behind the central portion of the house that commands a breathtaking view of White Rock Lake. Now part of **The Dallas Arboretum and Botanical Society**, its formal side gardens have been restored to reflect the style of the late 1930s, complete with a quatrefoil parterre and a magnolia allée with a large fountain as its focal point.

# The Burgeoning Burbs

Texas has never lacked for land. As families resumed their lives after the Second World War, land developers could afford to be generous. In front of the ranchburger houses in the seamless front yards in the endless tract developments that sprang up around our cities, homeowners happily lined-up little shrubs like soldiers on guard duty. Now everyman had his own half-acre of grass to mow.

By the 1960s another garden style had entered the Texas design vocabulary. California landscape architects had discovered in the gardens of Japan a source of inspiration compatible with contemporary horizontal house-forms. National magazines hailed "outdoor living rooms" composed of free-form patios surrounded by loose, informal plantings. Pools and barbecue pits began to punctuate the huge barren backyards. Never mind that the magazine photos usually included an ocean view (and presumably ocean breezes), we had recognized a style of outdoor living more in keeping with our notions of hospitality.

Texans' willingness to haul in nursery stock from other places continued unabated. Waco's soil too alkaline for azaleas? No problem. Dig a crater, backfill with a few cubic yards of peat moss and *Voila!* Houston's winter too warm for Dutch tulips? Cram them into the refrigerator for a few weeks. Austin's summer too humid for hybrid roses? Spray fungicides twice weekly to prevent powdery mildew. Too little water to run the automatic sprinkler systems needed to keep those huge lawns green? Dam every running stream in the state...

Today, people are taking a hard look at these wasteful ways. We're not only rethinking the way we deal with natural resources, but also developing a new appreciation for the plants that "belong" in this climate. Throughout this book, we'll be talking about maintaining "a sense of place." Lady Bird Johnson once observed that "Texas should look like Texas, and Vermont like Vermont." Within a state as large and diverse as Texas we might add the Piney Woods should look like the Piney Woods and the Trans-Pecos like the Trans-Pecos.

A second factor that is changing the way we design our gardens is economics. Because most new residences are built on small lots and subject to restrictive new building and water-use codes, landscape designers have begun drawing upon previously untapped historical models for inspiration. There's a lot to learn from other cultures and other times.

> "Landscape design may well be recognized as the most comprehensive of the arts... Art is a continuous process. However new the circumstances may be, it is virtually impossible to create a work of art without antecedents."
>
> ....Sir Geoffrey Jellicoe

# What We Can Learn from Others

Societies have always tended to adhere to fixed patterns of architecture that fit their own cultures. Thus, Greek homes were generally all of one type and quite different from typical Chinese homes of the same period. Because of the ephemeral nature of gardens, we have few tangible records. What we know of garden design is deduced from the spacing of ancient buildings, from images on walls, vases and carpets and from literature. There can be no doubt, however, that from the beginning, garden design has fluctuated between polar opposites — ordered, intellectual, symmetrical vs. natural, intuitive and asymmetrical.

Gardens did not originate as aesthetic enterprises. They were necessary to sustain life. However, the garden has always been a place to express spiritual values while providing food for the family and opportunities for recreation and renewal. Rich in symbolism, gardens reflected the needs and dreams of the cultures within which they were made. Gardening remains both art and science.

## Middle Eastern, Greek & Roman Gardens

Gardening began in Mesopotamia. Archeologists have found evidence of large-scale irrigation projects that flourished as early as 6,000 B.C. It may be no accident that the first true gardens documented in Western civilization occurred in hot, dry climates. What could be more primal than the desire for a cool, green oasis in a harsh environment? The Garden of Eden as described in the Old Testament was thought to be in the fertile plain between the Tigris and Euphrates, and sacred texts of ancient Mesopotamian civilizations referred to paradise gardens. The word "paradise" came from Persian to Greek to English. Its original meaning was literally, "a walled enclosure."

A tomb painting at Thebes (circa 1400 B.C.) depicts the home and garden of an official in the court of Amenhotep III. The property, which appears to be similar in size to a city lot in Dallas or Houston, is completely surrounded by high walls that provided shelter from drying winds. From the entrance gate in the center of the front wall, an arbor-shaded path leads to the house, which is sited at the back edge of the property. The garden's two halves are designed as mirror images. Raised planting beds for herbs, vegetables and flowers and rectangular ponds filled with fish and water plants flank the central vine-covered arbor. Fruit trees planted around the outer walls provide additional shade. (What is amazing is how pleasant this simple, elegant plan, drawn 2,400 years ago, would be in a Texas landscape today!)

A recurring design theme throughout Western history has been the square divided into four parts, symbolizing the four corners of the earth and the four rivers of heaven. Generally a fountain stands in the center of the square. This straightforward, symmetrical form is depicted on Persian carpets and seen in the atriums of Pompeii. It appears again in the courtyards of Moorish Spain (the meeting place of Islam and Christian cultures) and in the medieval cloisters and Tudor herbal gardens of Northern Europe.

Orderly geometric forms fit well within the confines of an enclosure. They also provide a sense of comfort in a disorderly world. Throughout most of history, people had good reason to fear the open countryside. Cities, homes and gardens were normally built in a defensive mode. Even large symbolic structures such as Mesopotamian ziggurats or Egyptian tombs, which were built out in vast open space, used mirror-image plantings along the entryways to facilitate a sense of order and provide some sense of enclosure.

Rigid axial geometry extended even into the large parks in the heart of the Persian Empire, where kings and nobles hunted wild animals imported from the far reaches of their domain. These heavily planted open spaces inspired the Greeks to landscape their agoras. But here, we see a change. Because their country's dramatic topography didn't lend itself to symmetry, the Greeks fit their highly geometric architecture within the natural terrain rather than trying to unduly order nature. While the residential gardens of classical Greece would have been enclosed, Greek literature contains numerous references to sacred springs and groves and vistas of mountains and open seas, implying a reverence for the natural environment.

With the Romans came order and planning on a scale never before known. Roman city homes were designed with open interior courtyards where colonnaded covered walkways wrapped around symmetrically arranged planting beds and water features. The country estates, however, represented a new form of residential garden design that took formal, ordered gardens and stretched them out into the open landscape. The ruins of Hadrian's Villa, built in the second century A.D., gives us a glimpse of the long, tree-shaded promenades and parterres (patterned ornamental planting beds meant to be viewed from overlooking windows and terraces) that typified the *villa rustica*. Its 750 acres were organized into architectural "compartments" enclosed with cypress, boxwood and laurel hedges and elegantly ornamented with columns, fountains and statuary.

The Romans may have been the first civilization to design gardens for sheer pleasure. Their villas were replete with pools and bathhouses and outdoor theaters. And, like all people living in hot climates, they enjoyed eating outdoors. Undoubtedly music, dancing and theatricals would have accompanied the meals. Such an embracement of the open countryside was possible only in a society governed by rule of law.

# Medieval European Gardens

Civil disorder reigned after the fall of the Roman Empire, and medieval gardens once again assumed inwardly oriented forms. Monasteries that flourished during this period were built around interior cloister gardens designed in the form of a cross for walking and meditating. Wrapped around the monastery, but within the compound, were "physick" gardens for growing healing herbs and the vegetable plots and orchards necessary to sustain communal life.

As the general public retreated to the protection of castles and fortified cities, gardens existed primarily for such practical purposes as growing medicinal and edible plants. Drawings from the period depict castle gardens replete with poetic touches in the form of pergolas and fountains. Walled cities were tightly packed, however, so the fabled village fairs and major agricultural pursuits took place in fields outside the walls.

Once the need for fortification diminished, towns spread beyond the walls and people once again began enjoying the luxury of little gardens attached to their houses. By the end of the medieval period, gardens had evolved into something quite fanciful with knot patterns, topiaries, mazes and bowling greens.

# Islamic Gardens in Spain

While Christian Europe was still in a period of isolation, Islam, founded in 622 A.D., had spread by 712 from Persia to the Pyrenees. When Moroccans (Moors) conquered the southern half of Spain, they brought with them a joyful appreciation of the outdoors. Based in part on climatic factors and in part on an Islamic imperative for family privacy, even the smallest house was built around an open-air patio. Characterized by colorful decorative flourishes and fragrant plants, these outdoor rooms were central to daily living.

Typically the spaces were symmetrical in design, like the foursquare Persian gardens that preceded them. A fountain customarily stood in the center of crossing paths, which were constructed of unglazed tiles laid in intricate geometric patterns. Ornate iron gates punctuated the thick white stucco outer walls. Inside walls, fountains and shady niches were richly decorated with polychrome glazed tiles (*azulejos*).

It was in the economical use of water that these Moorish gardens excelled. Based on the ideal of an oasis and always audible, the fountains and pools presented water as life-giving, which indeed it was. In this arid climate, planting beds were kept simple in design. Orange trees and palms provided shade, and flowering plants spilled out of containers. By the time that Islam was expelled from Spain in 1492, the Moorish aesthetic was firmly entrenched, and it was this influence that the Spaniards brought to the New World.

# The Renaissance Gardens of Italy and France

The Renaissance not only marked a return to civility in Italy, but also a hunger for the civilization of former times. Italian pleasure gardens were designed as stage sets, recalling the ancient gods with temple buildings, ruins and grottoes. It was a time for re-embracing the world. Copies of Greek and Roman statuary appeared in niches or as the focal point of an axis. Urns, balustrades, columns and topiaries punctuated the landscapes, and here the Roman style of arranging plantings into formal parterres became fashionable again.

By terracing hillsides and utilizing natural springs, the Italians created fantastic water gardens with every form of fountain and water cascading down grand staircases. The best known of the Renaissance country estates, Villa d'Este at Tivoli, is a triumph of hydraulic engineering. According to landscape historians, its water organ produced "such unusual sound effects as the booming of a cannon, the song of birds, the bedlam of exploding fireworks and tunes played on organ pipes."

While this villa's fountains are playful in the extreme, its labyrinthine plantings are rigidly geometrical. Were they not deliciously overgrown today, the square, compartmentalized planting beds would appear as monotonous as they did at the time. Other Italian villas more deftly terraced the landscape, using diagonal sight lines to break up the rigid bilateral symmetry and creating complicated routes for visitors to reach the various focal points.

Where the Italians excelled was in creating gardens that could withstand Italy's dry, hot summers. Floral displays were almost nonexistent. Instead, the sights and sounds in classic Italian gardens were contrived to counteract the effects of scorching sun. Playing against cool stonework, the grays and greens of neatly clipped shrubbery soothe the psyche. Crunchy gravel paths, fragrances of sage, cypress and rosemary and the sound of water augment the cooling effects.

A taste for such formality spread from Italy into northern Europe. Rococo fountains, clipped shrubbery and avenues of trees still defined the sight lines, but where the topography was more level, the gardens became progressively less dramatic. In France, the parterres evolved into baroque *parterres de broderies*, planting beds embroidered with flowers. Visually interconnected and totally symmetrical, these beds were organized within crisply defined boxwood edges. French design reached a preposterous apex at Versailles where gardeners changed the color schemes in the planting beds several times a day for the amusement of the royal family.

# The English Landscape School

The English countryside as we think of it today was "invented" in the eighteenth-century. At the time, most of England's trees had been felled for lumber and the land had been terraced for strip farming. Grand country homes were surrounded by walled gardens to shut out views of mundane agricultural pursuits. Inside were patterned flowerbeds (pale imitations of Renaissance gardens in Italy and France).

Mid-century, the walls came down. Wealthy landholders opened vistas into vast rolling lawns and serpentine ponds surrounded by great sweeps of deciduous trees. Serpentine roads replaced all vestiges of straight lines in the landscape. What the eighteenth-century designers created for their clients was actually no more natural than what they swept away, but the landscape was made to appear natural. Views from the house became all-important. In bringing grass right up to the doorstep, however, the eighteenth-century English landscape designers left the houses looking somewhat austere.

Several factors contributed to this notion of co-opting the countryside. French landscape paintings and newly available Chinese woodcuts had created a romantic vision of nature. But more than just artistic, the naturalistic revolution was a strongly anti-monarchist political statement. It greatly influenced Thomas Jefferson, whose vast greensward at Monticello was the first in America in the style of the English Landscape Gardening School.

Frederick Law Olmsted, who is remembered chiefly as the designer of New York City's Central Park, was the spiritual successor to this soft, pastoral planting style. It must be remembered that English-influenced landscape designers were working with acres and acres of countryside. Few facilities can support vast expanses of mown grass today, but large public parks and well-designed golf courses still exemplify the eighteenth-century ideal of beauty. In these open, rolling landscapes, we can get a feel for the effect of clipped grass, sparkling ponds, swaths of trees and picturesque background vistas that existed in eighteenth-century English landscapes.

The one lasting consequence of the style has been our ubiquitous suburban lawn. Grass takes on an entirely different appearance when the rolling acreage of a country estate is reduced to a small urban plot, but, for better or for worse, manicured front lawns remain as the major cultural holdover from the eighteenth century.

# Gardens of the Old South

Elements of seventeenth-century renaissance design and the naturalistic style eighteenth-century England merged in the gardens of the American South. George Washington's Mount Vernon remains a model of the early plantation landscape. Here, the front of the house overlooks a sweeping lawn that terminates at the soft bank of the Potomac River. The rear garden is as formal as the front is naturalistic. It features a vista across a perfectly symmetrical shield-shaped bowling green flanked by wavy lines of trees. Tucked behind the trees are a grid-plan kitchen garden on one side and boxwood-edged parterres on the other.

As the English style was interpreted throughout Virginia, the Carolinas and Georgia and a simplified French style developed in Louisiana, certain features remained constant. Brick gateposts typically marked the approach roads, which were lined with allées of magnolia or oak trees. Formal parterres traditionally graced the immediate environs, and park-like grass meadows separated the house from surrounding fields and woods.

The Civil War and Victorian taste combined to put an end to many of the formal gardens of the Old South. With the abandonment of the labor-intensive parterres, which had served as a transition between the building with the landscape, nineteenth-century designers began banking plants around the foundations of the houses. Planting beds became increasingly colorful and capricious in shape. Plants came to be prized as "specimens" rather than part of a soothing overall mass.

# Cottage Garden Style

The geometric patterns of medieval cloister gardens never disappeared entirely. Even after walls were no longer necessary for security, farmer's wives continued to grow their herbs, fruits and vegetables behind walls built to keep the livestock out. Out of this tradition came the gardens of colonial America, which typically brimmed with a profusion of fragrant flowers as well as life-sustaining plants enclosed by tidy picket-fences.

Before 1900, English painter-turned-garden designer Gertrude Jekyll led a revolt against imported plants and Victorian garden styles. Her work revived the strong architectural forms of Elizabethan walled gardens, but she softened the walls with unpruned shrubs and profuse perennials. She made the transitions between house and garden in rhythmic stages, connecting different areas of the garden with grassy paths flanked by double flower borders. Her soft, harmonic hues could not have been more different from the bold color contrasts that typified urban Victorian style in this country.

Contemporaneously with the arts and crafts movement, which stressed quality of workmanship, she accented her gardens with simple, classical garden furniture, elaborate pergolas and handsome containers. The English county homes Gertrude Jekyll embellished are mansions by today's standards, but the beguiling charm of the cottage garden lives on at a different scale. Such prolific contemporary English designers as Penelope Hobhouse, Rosemary Verey and Graham Stuart Thomas continue to inspire gardeners on both sides of the Atlantic. At the heart of this garden tradition is a love of old-fashioned plant materials — shrub roses, flowering vines, fruit trees and billowing perennials chosen for texture, color and fragrance.

# The Asian Aesthetic

As previously acknowledged, the Chinese landscape aesthetic indirectly influenced English garden style in the eighteenth-century, and Japanese garden design inspired American designers in this century. The symbolism and complex philosophical premises of two thousand years of garden-making in Asia may escape a Western viewer, but the pure visual impact of an Oriental garden rarely fails to please even the most casual observer.

The Chinese word for landscape is a combination of the characters for mountain and water. Old Chinese art depicts mountains rising above a misty landscape, water cascading into shimmering lakes, craggy coastlines and wooded hillsides. The ancient Chinese saw the workings of universal forces and laws in their landscape, and their naturalistic garden art was based on harmony between opposing forces.

Garden art flowed from China to Japan through Korea in the sixth century. While very different styles evolved out of these different cultures, all Asian gardens use rock and water to represent heaven and earth. Unlike Western landscape painters and garden designers, the Asian artist assumes the human is in the landscape, not viewing it from the outside. Asian gardens point out man's insignificance in relation to the majesty of untamed nature.

While Chinese gardens are rich in complexity, Japanese garden styles have become increasingly simplified over time. The earliest Japanese "paradise gardens" were similar to the Chinese, with elaborate adornment and concern for "correct" placement of stones, streams and waterfalls. Even the plant materials were aligned by rules of compass and astronomical instruments. The idea of a garden used for strolling was adopted in Japan during this first period of garden design, but the strolling gardens we find in Americanized Japanese gardens have more in common with later phases of Japanese garden design.

After Zen Buddhism flowered in the twelfth century, Japanese gardens increasingly focused on miniature landscapes. Simple compositions of rocks, evergreens and ground covers create intriguing textural contrasts. Layered plant materials conform to the contours of the land, framing little vignettes or disclosing vistas that suggest limitless space. The art of bonsai is part of this trend toward miniaturization and understated elegance.

Drinking tea to prevent drowsiness during meditation was elevated to an art form in the sixteenth century. Tranquil tea gardens were designed to inspire deep contemplation. From these gardens evolved utilitarian features such as stone pathways, wash basins and lanterns to light the way at night. The Japanese also made increasing use of evergreen plants and stones employed as sculpture. Boulders were balanced asymmetrically; for example, three small stones might be played against a large one. Rock was also used to represent flowing water, with different sizes of stones suggesting different sounds and velocities.

The Asian garden is composed of asymmetrically balanced interlocking parts, with materials shaped as mirror images of others nearby. Patterns are repeated to create a jigsaw puzzle effect, yet the transitions between the garden's spaces are smooth. Where Western people most often respond to a straight axis (which allows them to know exactly where they are), the gardens in Japan devise ways to create mystery. Plants are used to create a feeling of enclosure; walkways are made difficult to negotiate; hidden secrets are revealed behind each bend in the path. There will be great distances hinted-at and the suggestion of things unsaid, all used to draw the visitor irresistibly into the experience. The French royals who commissioned Versailles would not have understood it at all.

Asian gardens, it must be remembered, are no less man-made than Versailles. Structures, lanterns and bridges are actually used to indicate a *human* presence amid the symbols of heaven and earth. Unlike gardens in Japan, which are generally the creation of a garden master working in a period style, Asian gardens in America appropriate freely from the several schools of garden art. An Asian garden is above all a display of nature's handiwork. For Western man, this includes a lesson in humility. Perhaps, after the environmental disruption created by the industrial revolution is analyzed, modern man may realize what Asian garden-makers have known all along — humans are not the center of the universe.

## Modernist American Gardens

The modernist movement of the 1920's in architecture brought changes in landscape design as well, although the changes were not felt on the residential level until after the Second World War. In 1955 California landscape architect Thomas Church published *Gardens Are for People*. Church's melding of the home's interior and exterior was nothing short of revolutionary. His designs incorporated new materials and addressed new economic realities.

As Church noted in his book, indoor-outdoor living is not a new idea. Urban dwellers living in small homes on small lots are once again inclined to carry some of the functions of the house into the outdoors. Taking cues from the walled gardens of ancient Persia, Egypt and Rome, as well as medieval cloister gardens, modern designers began exploring old ways of preserving privacy. In Japan, they found inspiration for richly textured gardens in tiny spaces and gained respect for fine materials.

With fewer people trained to do garden maintenance (or few people willing to pay garden laborers a living wage), Church and the residential designers that followed him began designing for lower levels of maintenance. Church used flowing swaths of concrete or pavers to replace lawns and elaborate planting beds. He introduced mowing strips and curbs to separate the lawn from planting beds, and he confined unclipped plants within easily accessible raised beds.

As we look at his book today, some of Church's work is a bit dated, especially the photos that include '50s-style garden furniture, but his ideas were truly ahead of their time. As he noted in the second edition of the book, "Art Moderne strangled in the mesh of its own steel tubing... 'Modern' can be revived as an honest word when we realize that modernism is not a goal, but a broad highway."

# Texas Gardens for the 21st Century

Texas design professionals are rediscovering old solutions for new problems. Because building codes requiring standard setbacks waste valuable land in unused front lawns, city planners are exploring historical precedents such as townhouse developments with small private gardens behind the house and common open space nearby. Architects are recognizing that the early settlers had the right idea when they built their houses to capture breezes. Returning to favor are the large windows that provided cross-ventilation, French doors that opened into courtyard gardens, and shady screened porches with ceiling fans.

Landscape architects are putting new emphasis on comfort and function. They are creating visually interesting gardens in less space, making outdoor living areas easier to maintain, furnishing gardens with elegant outdoor furniture, incorporating re-circulating water features and emphasizing hardy plants grown in containers and raised beds.

## Borrowing (Judiciously) from the Past

As popular new housing styles recall traditional architecture, it is increasingly important to understand historic garden styles. However, these styles must be adapted to our climate and needs. For example, the gardens of several historic Texas homes now recreate in modern materials some of the aspects of antebellum southern garden style. The **Texas Governor's Mansion** in Austin, the **McFaddin-Ward House** in Beaumont, and the **Earle-Harrison House** and **Nell Pape Gardens** in Waco offer proof that Greek Revival-style homes can be successfully landscaped with Texas native and hardy adapted plant materials. Galveston's **Ashton Villa** and the **Sam Bell Maxey House** in Paris are examples of high Victorian houses appropriately adorned with low-maintenance plantings. The courtyard of the **McNay Art Museum** in San Antonio gives us a splendid model for sustainable garden architecture of the Spanish Colonial period.

For contemporary houses and somewhat featureless ranch-style houses, there are aspects of Asian gardens we might incorporate. The **Japanese Garden** in the **Fort Worth Botanic Garden** is undoubtedly the most refined work of its kind in the state. Its massive wooden entrance gates open to a partially enclosed courtyard, where a large stone lantern symbolically lights the way. Richly textured ground covers hug the pathways, and layers of evergreen shrubs frame each viewpoint, disclosing tiny vignettes or opening to vistas that suggest limitless space.

It does all of this with a palette of mostly native plants. The garden was created out of an abandoned gravel pit that had been used by a World War I cavalry unit as a disposal area for stable refuse. Its luxuriant plant materials certainly demonstrate the efficacy of good compost! In terms of how to plant a pond edge, frame a view, punctuate with sculpture or create a delicious sense of mystery in your garden, seek enlightenment here.

Two other Texas gardens that take great journeys of the imagination can be found in Houston's new **Japanese Garden** in Hermann Park and in Austin's Taniguchi Oriental Garden in **Zilker Botanical Garden**. The three Asian gardens could not be more different, but in each, the ideals of *wabi* (quietude) and *sabi* (elegant simplicity) are translated into Western experience. These serene gardens offer strolls that reveal vignettes presented as landscape paintings, much as we might translate into our own gardens the scenes we remember from nature walks in the parks and wildlife refuges in our various regions of Texas.

Texas gardeners with small lots can employ optical "tricks" that have been practiced for hundreds of years in Asian gardens. Streams and paths narrow as they get farther away. In the foreground, trees are kept small so they will not disrupt the view; the middle ground is fully developed to create an illusion of distance. Smaller elements and small-leafed plants are placed in the rear to appear diminished. A stone may represent a mountain, a clump of bamboo becomes a forest and a pond may symbolize the ocean. The background (which can simply be treetops "borrowed" from the landscape beyond) is used to suggest unlimited space.

# Taking Cues from Nature

Throughout Texas there are ideas to be drawn from nature. A client once brought me photographs he took of shallow pools at Pedernales Falls State Park. We used the concept to create a re-circulating pond/spa for his tiny garden in suburban Austin. From East Texas woodlands I've borrowed ideas for massing evergreens as visual screens. From observing creek banks I've learned how plants meet the water's edge. From fields of wildflowers I've taken color schemes.

In the face of an exploding population and dwindling resources, it is becoming clear to Texans that working in harmony with the environment makes good sense. As urban sprawl eats away at fertile farm and ranch land and the costs of extending roads and utilities out farther into our counties becomes exorbitant, we've begun accepting houses built on smaller lots and thinking more about using our exterior spaces as additional living space. The high cost of electricity is forcing us to recognize that we cannot depend solely on air conditioning to keep us cool.

In spite of a wet year in 1997, the summer of '98 reminded us (again) of the fact that our water demands will ultimately exceed the capacity of our reservoirs. We're beginning to see the beauty in plants that can survive on scant rainfall. In every region of Texas there are new xeriscape demonstration gardens and nature centers that extol the beauty of our native Texas plants.

The one Texas garden every homeowner should visit for inspiration is the new **Lady Bird Johnson Wildflower Center** in Austin. The September 1995 issue of Landscape Architecture magazine called it, "a tour-de-force of architecture, landscape architecture and even sustainable design. Water and stone are the unifying themes of this ten-building complex on 42 acres, which recalls Spanish mission, German and ranch-style architecture — robustly, artfully hewn in four types of native stone."

The design team (which included Texas landscape architects J. Robert Anderson and Elinor McKinney) handled water on the 42-acre site in several significant ways. One of the most striking of the complex's ten buildings is a tall limestone-clad cylindrical cistern for collecting roof runoff to be used for drip irrigation watering throughout the site. The central theme of the entry court is water, which is played out in charming little ponds, a simple waterfall and a bubbling pool that mimics a spring. Not a drop is wastefully sprayed into the air. A transition area between the courtyard and demonstration gardens features freeform paths of decomposed granite. These paths recall dry streambeds ambling through pastel ribbons of grasses and native flowers. Stormwater filtration ponds surround the parking areas.

Even the attractively composed native plantings in the courtyard beds are arranged according to water requirements. The Center uses neither pesticides nor chemical fertilizers to grow its collection of Hill Country trees, shrubs and wildflowers, and the natural landscape around the center is largely undisturbed. The few trees that had to be removed were ground-up and recycled for mulch on the trails. All stone excavated for the construction was incorporated into the site design.

Of course, the plants that grow here are indigenous to the Austin area. They would not be right for the soils or climates of Dallas, Houston, Tyler or El Paso, each of which has its own store of underutilized native plant materials. Until quite recently few native plants were available in any part of the state. Texas nurserymen resisted experimentation with natives because "the designers were not demanding them." Landscape designers, on the other hand, were hesitant to specify plants that were difficult to obtain. This "Catch-22" situation has been resolved, thanks in large part to the Wildflower Center's efforts to educate the public. Now aware of the advantages of natives over imported plants, homeowners are finding a wide array of hardy indigenous species in their local garden centers.

Another exciting new development is that the Texas Department of Agriculture is widely promoting "TEXAS GROWN" plants. This is good news for gardeners who can now be assured that the plants they buy are acclimated to local climate and soils. The good news for growers is that Texas is now one of the largest horticulture producing states in the country. East Texas is establishing a thriving market in bedding plants. The majority of our trees, shrubs and turf grasses are grown in Central and Southeast Texas, and the Valley is actively employed in the production of palms and tropical houseplants sold throughout the country.

**Just as there is no one plant palette for the entire state, neither can there be one "Texas Garden Style"** for the 21st Century. Each Texas garden can be as colorful and individual as its owner! There should be strong connections between outdoor and indoor living spaces. There should be trees, shade structures and water features to counter the hot summer sun and sufficient shelter from the cold winter winds. In place of expansive grass, there should be planting beds filled with easy-care shrubs and ground covers, wildflower meadows and inviting surfaces built for entertaining and relaxing. Seating areas should be as carefully furnished as any living room and accessorized with cheerful plants spilling out of containers. One can see these solutions in all the best magazines today. Funny thing is, the ancient Egyptians thought of them first....

# Accepting the "Givens"

Texas can be divided into no fewer than twelve distinct regions, each with specific characteristics that play into the subject of Garden Style. Each region has its own combination of factors, including USDA growing zone, physiographic characteristics, soil types, typical native vegetation and range of average annual rainfall, that influence one's choice of landscape materials. Even within the twelve regions, you'll find striking diversity. For example, the city of San Antonio occurs at the junction of three regions, so gardeners in its suburban areas must understand their property's characteristics before choosing plants.

## Vegetation

Environmentally speaking, Texas is a transition zone between the humid eastern and arid western portions of the United States. Moreover, the state spans four USDA Hardiness Zones (based on average lowest winter temperatures) from Zone 9 in the sub-tropical Rio Grande Valley to Zone 6 in the Panhandle where thermometer readings more closely resemble those of Pennsylvania or western Idaho. In this one big state, the national regions designated as Southern Coastal Prairies, Southeastern Pine Forests, Central Hardwoods and Tallgrass Prairies, Great Plains and Southwestern Deserts all merge. These overlapping zones produce a wealth of grasses, wildflowers, shrubs and trees we can proudly call "Texas natives."

# Topography

Elevations in the eastern portion of the state rise almost imperceptibly from sea level along the Gulf Coast to no more than 700 feet along present-day Interstate Highway 35. Just west of this freeway, Texas rises to a level above 1,000 feet. The most dramatic rise occurs along the Balcones Escarpment. This series of fault lines is imperceptible in places, and in other places the escarpment reminded Spanish explorers of balconies, hence its name. The Escarpment runs from Del Rio on the Rio Grande River through Central Texas between Dallas and Fort Worth to the Red River. As one drives from east to west through the Hill Country and Red Rolling Plains of western Texas, the land gradually rises another 2,000 feet.

Toward the Panhandle, the striking Caprock Escarpment marks another sharp rise. In some places it is a thousand-foot-high wall, but in its southern reaches, the boundary between the High Plains and Red Rolling Plains is less well defined. The virtually treeless High Plains region appears to be flat, but it actually rises another 1,000 feet to an elevation of 4,000 feet at the extreme northwest corner of the Panhandle. The area west of the Pecos River Valley is known as the Basin and Range area, punctuated by the Chisos Mountains in the Big Bend and the Guadalupe Range and Davis Mountains. The state's highest spot (8,749 feet) is Guadalupe Peak near the New Mexico border.

# Geology

Geologically, Texas is fascinating. Its history-in-rock explains the wide variety of soil types that are found within its borders. Precambrian rocks more than 600 million years old underlie the entire state. These ancient rocks are exposed in the Llano uplift of Central Texas Hill Country and in the Davis Mountains of the Trans-Pecos. Shallow seas repeatedly covered the state over the eons, depositing sediments that hardened into limestone (the fossil remains of sea creatures), sandstone or shale. Ancient mountains and volcanoes arose only to be weathered and worn down by rivers and streams.

Dinosaurs inhabited present-day Texas during the era between 225 and 130 million years ago. Approximately 140 million years ago, the state was inundated again by shallow seas that deposited the limestone we can see in the eroded canyon walls of the Big Bend National Park and along the Balcones Escarpment. Volcanic eruptions in the Trans-Pecos area ejected volcanic ash and lava, which can be still be found in this arid landscape today.

About 65 million years ago, huge amounts of sand and gravel washed into the Texas panhandle as the Rocky Mountains were forming. Meanwhile, the thick, sandy and clayey soils of East Texas and the Coastal Plains began developing. Deposits in broad, river-fed deltas and marshy lagoons gave rise to luxuriant vegetation. The grasslands began forming some 55 million years ago.

During the past three million years, successive periods of worldwide glaciation caused sea levels to rise and fall. While glaciers never extended as far south as Texas, the Ice Age created a colder more humid climate. The Caprock was formed about two million years ago as the Panhandle area became isolated from Rocky Mountain streams and the heavy flow of alluvial material began to recede. From the lower sections of Texas, rivers carried extensive sand and gravel deposits into the Gulf Coastal Plain. The present day sea level was established only in the past 3,000 years; our beaches and barrier islands have all formed since that time.

# Water Resources

The rivers in Texas flow basically from northwest to southeast. The Canadian River crosses the Panhandle north of Amarillo. The Red River forms the northern border of most of the state. (One of its forks created Palo Duro Canyon.) Both the Canadian and the Red Rivers end up in the Mississippi River system. The Sabine River forms the lower half of the state's eastern boundary line, and the Rio Grande marks the boundary between Texas and Mexico. Between these two "border rivers," nine other rivers (Neches, Trinity, San Jacinto, Brazos, Colorado, Lavaca, Guadalupe, San Antonio and Nueces) rise within the state and funnel into the Gulf of Mexico. Texas rivers and their numerous tributaries have been impounded into 203 reservoirs that provide much of the water we drink and use for irrigation.

# Land Use

Of the state's 170.7 million acres, less than two million are covered with water. Dry ranchland used primarily for grazing accounts for 100 million acres, 36 million acres are utilized as cropland, and forests cover 23 million acres. Aquifers underlie 81% of Texas, and more than half of the state's water comes from these underground water sources. Unfortunately, pumping now exceeds recharge from rain in most years, and Texas will face water shortages as demand increases.

Texas is rapidly becoming urbanized. In the past decade, urban development has increased by half a million acres to a total of 4.8 million acres. Additionally, the state has 69,000 miles of highway, including 3,000 miles of Interstate Highways. Highways require between ten and thirty-five acres per mile. The Texas Department of Transportation has earned a fine reputation as the "nation's largest gardener." Its carefully managed wildflower program has created roadside plantings that are important not only for their incomparable beauty, but also as a natural habitat for birds and small animals. Abundant parks and recreational land account for the remaining land within the state.

# Protecting our Future

Why is it important to understand our cultural and geological history? Without such knowledge, we are likely to continue gardening practices that degrade the larger environment. We are stewards not only of our personal properties, but also of the land we own in common with others — parks, roadsides, and wilderness. As gardeners, we are taking greater responsibility for the way we treat our soil and deal with garden pests. We are learning how to choose plants that conserve precious water and offer food and protection to wildlife. As active citizens, we have the power to encourage and support the public and private organizations that are working to protect this beautiful landscape we call Texas.

> *"I think that I shall never see*
> *A billboard lovely as a tree.*
> *Indeed, unless the billboards fall*
> *I'll never see a tree at all."*
> *....Ogden Nash*

# The Twelve Gardening States of Texas

In organizing this book, Pat and I decided to begin with the Northeast quadrant of the state. Next, we work our way (clockwise) through the regions that border the Gulf Coast. Then we go up through Central Texas and, finally, cover vast West Texas. Throughout the book, we'll be listing garden sources, region-by-region. Within each there are public spaces that illuminate various garden styles and nature trails that provide clues to the plants that "belong" in the area. (Chapter Two begins with addresses, phone numbers and hours of operation for places to visit for inspiration.)

1  *Cross Timbers & Grand Prairie*
2  *Trinity Blacklands*
3  *Piney Woods*
4  *Coastal Prairies & Marshes*
5  *Coastal Bend*
6  *Valley*

7  *Rio Grande Plain*
8  *Central Blacklands & Savannas*
9  *Hill Country*
10  *Red Rolling Plains*
11  *High Plains*
12  *Trans-Pecos*

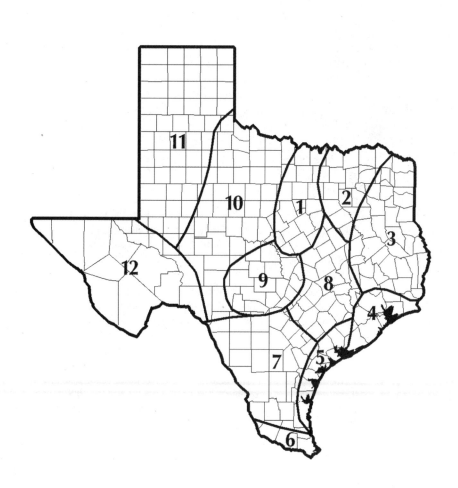

## *Cross Timbers & Grand Prairie*

Between the Red Rolling Plains of West Texas and the Blackland Prairies of Central Texas, two long bands of woodlands once jutted down like fingers through North Texas. A long narrow swath of grassland, The Grand Prairie, cuts through these Western and Eastern Cross Timbers. Fort Worth, the region's major market center, stands on the prairie's western edge. In terms of climate, Fort Worth quite correctly bills itself as "Where the West Begins."

The alternating bands of woodlands and grassland prairie run more or less north-south from the Red River down through Lampasas County and west almost halfway to Abilene. The region includes Gainesville and Denton to the north and the towns of Brownwood, Cisco, Cleburne, Gatesville, Glen Rose, Goldthwaite, Hamilton, Lampasas, Mineral Wells, Stephenville and Weatherford to the south and west of Fort Worth. The Grand Prairie and Eastern Cross Timbers funnel between Dallas and Fort Worth, incorporating the suburban areas as far east as Arlington and the city of Grand Prairie.

The millions of acres of blackjack and post oak that were the Cross Timbers have long since been cut down and converted to farmland. Originally these were very significant physiographic features, forming a natural barrier beyond which the forest fires that roared through the Great Plains could never penetrate. In 1852, Army Captain Randolph Marcy wrote, "At six different points I have found the Cross Timbers with the same peculiarities — the trees standing at such intervals that wagons can pass between them. The soil is thin, sandy and poorly watered. This forms a boundary line between the country suited to agriculture and the great prairies, which for the most part are arid and destitute of timber."

The trees that remain are small and scrubby, commercially useful mainly for firewood and fence posts. Shinnery, blackjack, post and live oaks predominate; where the oaks are thin, thickets of mesquite and cedars have invaded. Sandy loam soils generally underlie these once heavily timbered areas.

The Grand Prairie is of a different character. Its thin, limestone-based soils are rocky and clayey. Here, white chalk hills and dark green cedar breaks stand in bold contrast with the verdant fields that now cover the gently rolling landscape. Before it was put to agricultural uses, such mid-size grasses as big and little bluestem, sideoats grama, indiangrass, Canada wildrye, Texas wintergrass and buffalo grass predominated on the gently rolling prairie. Interspersed among the grasses, such prairie wildflowers as purple coneflower, butterfly weed and Englemann's daisy bloomed in profusion. Nature trails at **Cedar Hill State Park** in Southwestern Dallas County showcase the beauty of this unique area of Texas.

Stands of native trees still occur along the numerous streambeds that run east-west throughout the region. A locale where the Cross Timbers intersects with riverbottom can be seen at the **Fort Worth Nature Center and Refuge** (ten miles northwest of the city). The Grand Prairie widens out south of Fort Worth. One of the best places to experience its distinct environment is at **Cleburne State Park**, ten miles south of Cleburne off Hwy. 67. Here, oak, elm, mesquite, cedar and redbud clothe the chalk hills, and bluebonnets bloom around a spring-fed 116-acre lake. Rare golden-cheeked warblers nest in the thick stands of cedar at **Meridian State Park** in Bosque County, where Western Cross Timbers and Grand Prairie merge in an area called the Comanche Plateau which resembles Hill Country.

At the western edge of the region between Abilene and Fort Worth, a small, scenic formation of hills called the Palo Pintos forms a gentle transition between crosstimbers and prairie. North of these hills, the landscape dissolves into short-grass prairie more typical of the Red Rolling Plains.

Average annual rainfall in the region ranges from about 28 to 33 inches per year. The terrain is primarily adapted to raising livestock and growing grain crops. Farmers produce pecans, peanuts and a variety of fruits and vegetables in the southern reaches of the area. The soils around Stephenville, Graham and Denton have proven to be suitable for prosperous greenhouse and nursery industries. Gardeners in the region must regularly irrigate all but the most hardy native plants.

## Trinity Blacklands

Dallas and its surrounding suburbs (Irving, Farmers Branch, Carrollton, Plano, Richardson, Garland, Mesquite, Lancaster and Duncanville) are located on the western edge of the Trinity Blacklands. McKinney, Dennison, Sherman, Waxahachie, Greenville, Paris and Corsicana also fall within this distinct region of Texas. The Trinity Blacklands region was cotton country in the late 19th and early 20th centuries, but the land that hasn't been paved-over has now been converted to grazing.

Blackland soil is deep, dark and clayey. Farmers and gardeners consider it the best in Texas. The smooth rolling hills of this part of the state have been described as enormous green waves that crest every couple of miles. Originally, the region was a sea of big and little bluestem, Indiangrass and switchgrass. Only one-tenth of one percent remains of this luxuriant grassland.

The thick, four-foot-high grasses were punctuated with tall colorful wildflowers — gayfeathers, coreopsis, butterfly weed cardinal flowers and firewheel. Today the grasses and flowers are found only in pockets left undisturbed by cultivation, but the region's signature trees — hackberries, oaks, pecans, soapberries and cedar elms — still thrive in the bottomlands.

**Pioneer Plaza** in downtown Dallas with its bronze cattle crossing a stream beautifully captures the way the Trinity River landscape might have looked in the early nineteenth century. Remnants of tallgrass prairie can be seen in the hiking trails at the **Heard Natural Science Museum** in McKinney, which also takes you into areas of rich bottomland. Gardeners in the Trinity Blacklands can draw from a wide range of imported and native plant materials, provided that they are willing to keep the soil sufficiently moist through the summer months.

Beneath the rich black clay soil is a limestone base, which means that its pH registers in the alkaline range. Moreover, the clay is subject to deep cracks in dry weather. Rainfall averages 45 inches per year in Paris. One hundred miles southwest of Paris, in Dallas County, the average drops to just under 36 inches. (It's interesting to note that another 30 miles to the west, Fort Worth's average annual rainfall is only 31.3 inches.) The northeastern portion of this region falls within USDA Zone 7; Dallas and the southern counties lie in the upper reaches of Zone 8. Winter ice storms and short periods of 10-degree temperatures sweep down into the region with greater regularity than in the blacklands of Central Texas.

## Piney Woods

Although named for its three species of pine (longleaf, shortleaf and loblolly), the woods were originally replete with venerable deciduous trees as well — beech, elms, hickories, magnolias, maples, oaks and sweet gums. Unlike other urban areas in Texas, visible from miles around, the cities of Tyler, Longview, Marshall, Nacogdoches, Lufkin and Huntsville are tucked into the dense East Texas forests. The region extends from Texarkana south through the **Big Thicket National Preserve**, which is one of four National Forests in East Texas.

As you drive through the Piney Woods, the landscape appears uniformly luxuriant. However, with few exceptions, the second-growth forests that we see today do not contain the rich ecological mix that existed before the first sawmills were built here in the early nineteenth century. By the 1940s almost all of the native forests had been timbered. In many areas, including the National Forests, pine plantations have replaced the mature forests that nurtured a mix of pines and hardwoods and an abundance of wildlife.

Selective breeding has produced fast-growing pines, and while the planted seedlings quickly grow tall, all mature at the same rate. Such a monoculture supports fewer plant and animal species and is more vulnerable to insects and diseases. Where the forests are left natural, a thick understory of dogwood, yaupon holly, paw-paw, plum, cherry laurel and wax myrtle can make these gently rolling woodlands almost impenetrable.

In its natural state, the Piney Woods is far more diverse than it appears. Five major plant communities reflect differences in soils, moisture levels and elevation. The northern portions vary from dry uplands to mesic (moderately moist) upland forests, with swampy areas alongside the creek and river banks. One of the most ethereal landscapes of Northeast Texas can be discovered in **Caddo Lake State Park**. While most Texas lakes are manmade, this one was created by a vast natural log jam. Ultimately the jam was removed, and the Army Corps of Engineers drained the lake in 1873. It was restored on a smaller scale, but it still looks much as it might have in mid-nineteenth-century with dense vegetation that includes lotus and lily pads and hundreds of swampy cypress islands.

Nature trails in **Daingerfield State Park** and the Old Settlers Nature Trail, in **Governor Hogg State Historical Park** at Quitman provide excellent examples of the dry upland landscapes. Farther south, near the center of the Piney Woods, the **Texas State Railroad** between Palestine and Rusk offers an especially fun way to enjoy the scenery. **Mission Tejas State Park** at Weches occupies 363 acres at the northern tip of the Davy Crockett National Forest. And, at **Stephen F. Austin State University Arboretum** in Nacogdoches the region's trees are labeled, and many of the native shrubs and wildflowers are on display, as well as an array of cultivated plants suitable for area gardeners.

The southern forests are more moist than the sandy hills of Northeast Texas. A wealth of garden-worthy plants grow wild in **Martin Dies, Jr. State Park**, which lies in the heart of the Big Thicket between Woodland and Jasper. Although greatly reduced from its original three and a half million acres, the remaining 86,000 acres of the **Big Thicket National Preserve** are the least altered area of the Piney Woods. It was saved from destruction partially because settlers avoided the area (wagons routinely became mired down in its bayous). These swampy bottomlands still nurture bald cypress and water tupelo, beneath which grow numerous rare and endangered species, including orchids and pitcher plants.

Decomposing leaves and an average 46 inches of rainfall each year combine to make the Piney Woods' fertile sandy loam soils register acid on the pH scale. Such acid-loving plants as azaleas and blueberries flourish. In a few areas where the post oak is the dominant native tree species, however, the soils are too sandy to hold moisture and gardening can be more difficult. From a planting perspective, the entire Piney Woods region falls within USDA Zone 8. Winter temperatures will occasionally dip down to into the teens, but compared to most other regions of Texas, gardening is a dream.

## *Coastal Prairies & Marshes*

The upper Gulf coast is the most heavily populated and industrialized area of the state, yet its principal cities, Houston, Galveston and Beaumont, are remarkably green. This topographically flat region is well known for steamy summers and mild winters, both of which make for a most hospitable growing environment. The region as we define it in this book also includes the growing cities that ring Houston: Deerpark, Pasadena and Baytown to the east; Sugar Land, Katy, Rosenberg and Richmond to the south and east, and to the north, The Woodlands, Spring and Conroe. The region extends to the Louisiana border to include Orange and Port Arthur and west through Brazosport (a group name applied to Freeport, Clute, Brazoria and Lake Jackson), which has developed into an important market center.

The Nature Conservancy describes as fragile this "interlocking mosaic of fresh and saltwater wetlands and estuaries, coastal prairies, and near coastal woodlands." The organization has several projects aimed at preserving the dwindling natural resources while creating a balance with such "compatible human activities as rice farming and cattle grazing," which produce the region's primary agricultural income.

The Gulf has inundated Texas many times in geological history. Although it's slowly rising at present, it is too soon to buy ocean-front property in College Station! The last invasion was 40 million years ago. Houston is sinking not because the Gulf is rising, but because so much ground water has been pumped out from beneath it. Slow drainage is a common problem for gardeners throughout the region.

Soils here are mostly clayey and acid, but there are pockets of sandy soil within the region. The clay soils are particularly rich, heavy and nutritious. Live oaks and elms predominate in the slow-draining "gumbo" soils alongside the sluggish bayous, while pines and post oaks are indicators of sand. Beneath the towering live oaks of the coastal woodlands you'll often find a thick understory of tropical-looking palmettos with their beautiful fan-shaped leaves. The live oaks are frequently festooned with long strands of Spanish moss, which is not a parasite, but rather an epiphyte that feeds on dust and rain.

While trees are plentiful, the region's principal vegetation is grass — big and little bluestem, Texas wintergrass and gulf cordgrass on the drylands; saltgrass, sedges and bullrush in the marshes. Where farming and heavy grazing have disrupted the natural composition of species in this fertile region, oak underbrush, mesquite, Macartney rose, ragweed and other weedy plants readily invade.

Barrier islands protect almost the entire Texas Gulf Coast. These huge sandbars created by the accumulation of shells and sand provide shelter for the inland marshes, mudflats and saltflats that nourish everything that lives in the sea. Marsh environments are disappearing at an alarming rate, however. They've been filled in for real estate, decimated by upstream dams that withhold vital fresh water and silt, and used as dumping grounds for chemicals. One of the least-spoiled environments can be experienced at **Sea Rim State Park** between Port Arthur and Sabine where boardwalks allow glimpses into critical marsh ecology.

Just ten miles north of Beaumont, **Village Creek State Park** is an rainforest environment filled with cypress and water tupelo swamps. Several environmentally oriented botanical repositories can be found in the Houston area. **Armand Bayou Nature Center** in Pasadena, the **Mercer Arboretum** in Spring and the **Houston Arboretum** provide miles of nature trails. Southeast of Houston, you'll find bottomland vegetation in **Brazos Bend State Park** and **Varner-Hogg Plantation State Historical Park**.

Rainfall in the Gulf Prairies region varies from an average annual 59.2-inches in Orange County to 43.2-inches in Matagorda County. Rain falls heaviest in July, August and September. Poor drainage aside, from the gardener's standpoint this region has much to offer. Lush ground covers like creeping fig and confederate star jasmine and such exotic flowering shrubs as bottlebrush and pineapple guava, which are marginal in gardens as far north as Austin, can be grown with impunity here in Zone 9. Acid-loving plants — azaleas, magnolias and camellias to name a few — positively thrive.

## *Coastal Bend*

Corpus Christi is the major market center within this region that extends from Port Lavaca to the tip of Padre Island. The cities of Victoria and Kingsville also fall within the maritime influence of the bays and cordgrass marshes that host rich marine life and serve as wintering grounds for numerous species of water birds. Coastal tall grasses, morning glories, sea ox-eyes and beach evening primroses color the landscape here.

The grasslands northeast of Corpus look similar to those of the upper coastal prairies, but the region is far less "green." The more southern Coastal Bend is dryer and warmer, which causes the soil to form layers of highly alkaline caliche (calcium carbonate). Corpus Christi can expect an average of only 30.2 inches of rain each year, which is about the same as Fort Worth, just to put things in perspective. The growing season lasts 309 days, and the January mean minimum temperature is 46°. Freezing temperatures are rare, but they occur often enough to discourage gardeners from planting tropical foliage plants.

The woods, tidal flats and brush of the **Aransas National Wildlife Refuge** provide an ideal habitat for whooping cranes and the people who watch them. Nature trails at the Padre Island National Seashore also offer access to the complicated ecosystems of sand dunes, with their sea oats, soilbind morning glories and beach panic grass. Inland, the **Welder Wildlife Refuge** is a biological crossroads between coastal prairies and South Texas brushland.

The area around Rockport is noted for its sculptural live oaks, shaped by wind and salt spray to appear as if pruned by a Japanese gardener. The biggest live oak in the state grows in **Goose Island State Park**. Wind-blown sand up to 60-feet deep covers the counties south of Corpus Christi. Here, only grasses, prickly pears, the ubiquitous mesquites, and about two people per square mile occupy the land.

Hosts of native and imported plants are available to area gardeners, but the choices are far fewer than in the Houston area because conditions are more harsh in this region of the coast. Such lovely natives as wild rose, huisache and retama (the bane of ranchers) are becoming available as garden plants. The gardener's biggest problems will be keeping enough organic material in the clayey soil to neutralize the alkalinity and getting the standing water out of flat lawns and planting beds after hurricane-force rains.

# Valley

A chain of towns — Brownsville, Harlingen, Pharr, McAllen, Mission and Edinburg — hug the lower Rio Grande River as it makes its way to the Gulf of Mexico. The combination of deep and fertile soil, water available for irrigation, and very mild winters have made the Valley famous for citrus and winter vegetable crops. Homeowners grow palms, rubber trees, philodendrons and scores of other "houseplants" in their gardens and resign themselves to the killing frosts that come along every few years. Within a few months they'll be once again pruning lush vegetation with machetes!

The Valley is not a valley at all, but rather the delta and floodplain of the lower Rio Grande River. Its native plants and animals are more typical of Mexico than of any other part of Texas. However, little native vegetation remains; the land is much too valuable for row crops. Our only native palm, *Sabal texana*, can be found mainly in residential gardens and city parks. In the few places where virgin countryside exists, such trees as anaqua, Texas ebony and Mexican ash offer hospitality to rare birds, and such cats as ocelot and jaguarundi still stalk their prey. Nature trails at the **Sabal Palm Grove Wildlife Sanctuary** in Brownsville (a National Audubon Society property), **Bentsen-Rio Grande Valley State Park** and the **Santa Ana National Wildlife Refuge** provide rare glimpses of the region's natural habitats.

It takes a great deal of water to keep lawns green in the Valley during the hot, windy summer months, so many of the area's native trees — desert olive, mesquite and huisache — actually struggle in irrigated residential landscapes. Other choice native trees such as retama, guayacan, anaqua, Mexican poinciana and Texas ebony are commonly used in the landscape and prized for their flowers. Both the soil and the water are highly alkaline, so gardeners find it necessary to maintain the soil with continuous additions of compost, which also serves to improve the texture of the heavy river soils. Standing water can be a problem during heavy rains, so homeowners may also contend with drainage problems.

So many exotic species thrive in the region that the homeowner's biggest problem may be in achieving a cohesive design plan. Valley gardens are typically a riot of colors. With bananas, bougainvillea, allamanda, oleanders and plumarias part of the plant palette, how could they not be? A visit to one of the region's garden centers listed in Chapter Five will introduce you to plants unimaginable in the rest of the state. Pothos, the world's most hard-to-kill houseplant, is actually grown as a lawn substitute here! The **Gladys Porter Zoo** in Brownsville is the closest thing to a tropical botanical garden that exists in Texas.

# *Rio Grande Plain*

Inland from the Gulf of Mexico, the landscape quickly becomes harsh. Population centers are few and far between in this large, arid region that was once open grassland. San Antonio, Laredo and Del Rio serve as its major market areas. The land is primarily used for grazing, but a number of small farming communities occur along the Rio Grande or in the northern portion of the region along the Nueces and its several tributaries. No river flows through the southern half of the region between the Nueces and Rio Grande.

South Texas is cattle country. It was here that Texas longhorns evolved from wild cattle abandoned by Mexican ranchers when Texas won its independence and the Rio Grande became the boundary between the two countries. The region has been described as a land where every living thing bites, stings or punctures the skin! Its climate is sub-tropical, subject to hard freezes. There's rarely more than 25-inches of rainfall each year, but when rain comes, it often comes in life-threatening torrents. The rains create a colorful show of cactus blossoms and bring life to such wildflowers as prickly poppies and the beautiful gray shrub, cenizo, which is also called a "barometer plant" because it flowers in periods of high humidity.

The Rio Grande Plain is dotted with mesquite and huisache trees and an assortment of thorny shrubs. Cross fencing and the elimination of fire allowed trees and chaparral to muscle-out much of the natural grass. This takeover has not only eliminated grass, but has dried up numerous little streams. However, the brush is a lively plant community, rich in berries and fruits. The legumes — mimosas, acacias, locusts, paloverdes and mesquites — "fix" nitrogen in the soil and bear seeds in pods. The thorn-bearing plants provide protection for small mammals and food for numerous birds and animals. **Choke Canyon State Park** west of Three Rivers and **Falcon State Park** on the southern end of Falcon Reservoir provides trails into ruggedly beautiful brushlands.

San Antonio sits at the northern edge of the Rio Grande Plain. The eastern suburbs of the city juts into Blackland Prairie and its northwest neighborhoods reach into the adjacent Hill Country. The fabulous **San Antonio Botanical Garden** celebrates the area's diversity with plant materials drawn from all three regions. Several acres are devoted to native Texas plantings. Another botanical treasure is San Antonio's Riverwalk, which is lined with semi-tropical plants that could thrive only in the protected environment of a sunken waterway. Within Bexar County there are nine distinct soil types, ranging from black clay to acidic sand. Gardeners are well-advised to test their soils and understand the climate before assuming that "anything grows."

A thriving nursery industry has developed south of San Antonio in the fertile sandy loam soil of the Medina River. The area around Carrizo Springs and Crystal City is known as the "Winter Garden" and famous for its vegetables, especially spinach. Crops are irrigated by underground water drawn from the Carrizo Springs. The beautiful canyons in Uvalde County are formed by four spring-fed rivers flowing off the Balcones Escarpment onto the Rio Grande Plain where bees utilize the fragrant blooms of guajillo (*Acacia berlandieri*) to make the highly prized Uvalde honey.

## *Central Blacklands & Savannas*

The metropolitan areas of Waco and Temple/Belton/Killeen and Bryan/College Station are the largest market areas in this region that also encompasses Brenham, Seguin and Palestine. The southern portion of the region is sparsely dotted with small farming communities, established around the fertile farmland favored by early German immigrants to Texas. Clay soils (Blackland Prairie) and sandy soils (Post Oak Savanna) occur in bands throughout the south-central region of the state.

Technically, a savanna is a grassland; in Texas, Post Oak Savannas are transition zones between dense forest and open grassland. The Crosstimbers of North Texas and the Post Oak Savannas of Central Texas are (or more accurately *were*) an extension of the Central Hardwoods region of the United States. Before settlement, these park-like meadows were almost entirely covered with an evenly spaced tree canopy. Settlers loved the Post Oak Savanna; its trees supplied timber for houses and barns, and its grass easily submitted to the plow.

Like the Trinity Blacklands, the blackland prairies of Central Texas originally hosted tall grasses. Only the riverbottoms were heavily wooded. The entire region has been so altered by the elimination of prairie fires and the conversion to agriculture that it's hard to tell blackland prairie from savanna until you look at the color of the soil. (The Post Oak soils are lighter in color.) Once the most prosperous farmland in Texas, this region has more recently turned to ranching. Gardening can be tricky in post oak country. A water-impervious "clay pan" underlies the soil's loamy surface layers. Dryer than the Piney Woods, the region's annual rainfall ranges from 40-inches in eastern counties down to 32-inches in counties to the west.

The Brazos River flows through the center of the region. Before it was dammed, the river flooded regularly, depositing deep alluvial soil across a wide area. Numerous old channels can still be seen from an airplane. These bottomlands provide a rich environment for a wide range of native shade trees — elms, ashes, pecans, soapberry and a variety of oaks (bur, red, chinquapin). Such flowering trees as Texas redbud, Mexican plum and rusty blackhaw viburnum bloom in the understory.

Many of these same riverbottom species grow among the post oaks in the savanna. Here you'll also spot some of the hardwoods found in the Piney Woods, such as flowering dogwood and sassafras. Wildflowers blanket these gently rolling meadows in spring. Here and there, post oak woodlands are still punctuated by ponds and streams with dense stands of yaupon, dogwood, hawthorn, elm and hackberry.

Little remains, however, of the original character of Central Texas; the grassland was simply too profitable for agriculture. Today's farmers and ranchers accept as a given that they must spend money to root out the briars and mesquites that invaded after the natural grasses were removed.

Two isolated features of Central Texas are unique. The "lost pines" that grow in **Bastrop State Park** are not lost at all; they are merely isolated from their loblolly brothers two hundred miles away in East Texas because a pocket of sandy acidic soil met their conditions for survival. However, **Palmetto State Park** on the San Marcos River south of Luling is truly a strange place. Here, orchids, hibiscus, ferns and wild iris combine with palm-like dwarf palmettos to create an environment that could pass for jungle! "Mud boils" caused by gases rising up from under the swampy ground burp and sigh, and colorful butterflies flit through the thick vegetation.

The dry sandy soils of the Post Oak Savanna are especially good for growing melons and sweet potatoes. They are also hospitable to such wildflowers as wild phlox and blue bells, both of which were shipped to England in the early 19th-century, hybridized, and returned to us as prized garden species! There's probably no better place for viewing spring wildflowers than the back roads of Washington County, in the heart of post oak country. Southwest of Brenham at Round Top, the fantasy landscape of **McAshan Gardens** at Festival Hill is definitely worth a visit.

With summer irrigation, Central Texas gardeners can grow a very wide range of plants, which makes it all the more lamentable that no public botanical garden showcases the region's plants. Nature Trails in heavily wooded **Mother Neff State Park** west of Moody wind past ancient riverbottom oaks and elms, native pecans and old cedars. **Miller Springs Nature Center** near Temple features a restored native prairie and lush bottomlands. **Cameron Park** and **The Sculpture Garden** at The Art Center of Waco (the old Cameron summer home) offer spectacular vistas of the heavily wooded plain where the Brazos and Bosque Rivers converge.

# Hill Country

What Texans commonly call "Hill Country" incorporates two distinct physiographic regions, the eastern portion of the Edwards Plateau and the Llano Uplift (also called the Central Mineral Region), which are underlain by very different rock. Interstate Highway-35 as it passes through Austin, San Marcos and New Braunfels roughly marks the eastern boundary of the Edwards Plateau. Kerrville and Fredericksburg are at its center.

This geologically interesting region is replete with rocky cliffs, springs and sparkling streams. Its meadows and roadsides provide a perfect habitat for wildflowers. Bluebonnets, Indian paintbrush, winecups and lemon mint literally carpet the skimpy soils in spring. Some of the most scenic drives in the state are FM 337 between Leakey and Vanderpool, FM 187 north of Vanderpool (the route to **Lost Maples State Natural Area**) and Devil's Backbone (RM 12) from south of Wimberley to near Blanco. Hill Country vistas along these and other back roads define the Texas Hill Country.

The Edwards Plateau, which now ranges from 1,500 to 3,000 feet above sea level was, for millions of years, the bottom of a shallow sea. The ocean floor kept sinking as sediments piled-up to depths of up to two miles! Limestone holds water like a sponge. Water bubbles out of springs all along the Balcones fault at the eastern edge of the Edwards Plateau. Over the eons, underground water has slowly dissolved the limestone, forming thousands of caves throughout the region.

Highway cuts merely scratch the surface of these deep limestone formations. A unique feature of the Edwards Plateau is the stair-step appearance of the hills. Alternating deposits of soft rock (marl) and solid limestone caused the phenomenon; marl layers erode more readily than the limestone. From the air, the hills resemble contour maps. From the ground, the grasses and other plant life that grows more abundantly in the marl appear as green bands purposefully planted across the hillsides.

Soils in the "Llano Uplift" are sandy and granitic. If you've never been there but have seen a map that labels it thus, you'll be surprised to find that this 70-mile-wide feature is not a mountain, but rather a basin surrounded by rough hills. The "uplift" occurred millions of years ago when molten rock forced up from inside the earth cooled to form a blister on the surface. The surface rock that later covered it eroded away, exposing stone that contains such minerals as gold, silver and gemstones (in insufficient quantity to mine). The area is also called the Central Mineral Region. **Enchanted Rock State Natural Area** is the best-known of the numerous bald granite domes that occur throughout the region. The area's grasses were especially tall and vigorous before overgrazing allowed the colonization of mesquite, whitebrush and shorter grasses.

The Colorado River cuts through the Llano Uplift on its way to the Gulf of Mexico. This formerly flood-prone river has been dammed in its entirety; four of its lakes lie within the Llano Uplift. These dams provide electricity and city water supplies, but they've also covered over thousands of acres of wooded bottomlands. The Pedernales, Guadalupe, Medina, Sabinal, and Frio Rivers rise out of springs in the western edges of the region. Some of the state's best peaches, apples, grapes, pecans and walnuts are produced in the valleys of these clear streams.

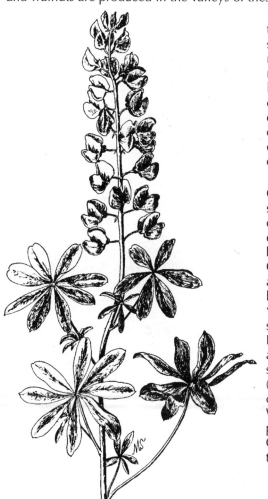

Many of the Hill Country's native trees and shrubs, such as the sycamore-leafed styrax, can be found nowhere else on earth. A surprising number of the natives are evergreen — live oaks, junipers (erroneously called cedars), Texas mountain laurel, evergreen sumac and agarito. Stands of big-toothed maples and bald cypress are hardy remnants of bygone epochs.

The scrubbier live oaks of the Hill Country appear to be a different species from the big moss-laden live oaks of the Gulf Coast, but the only difference is environment. Likewise, bald cypress trees growing beside Hill Country streams are the same species as the ones in Eastern swamps, but here the trees rarely need to develop "knees" for support. However, the shallow soil and lesser rainfall of the Edwards Plateau have forced adaptations that actually resulted in several new species. The cedars (*Juniperus ashei*) are thought to be a cross between Eastern red cedar and Western red cedar. Buckeyes, persimmons and mulberries of the Hill Country are all quite different from their Eastern cousins.

The rich palette of plants and naturally occurring rock for paths and walls make garden design in the region particularly interesting, provided that the gardener accepts alkaline soil as a given. There was so little topsoil at my hilltop home in Austin, I used a jackhammer to fracture the limestone to make planting holes! The good news is that Hill Country soil drains well, unlike the black clay soil to the east. Ferns and wildflowers indigenous to the region can be found growing in the tiniest crevices.

Because Austin is perched at the eastern edge of the Hill Country, the quiet pools, waterfalls, and plants growing beside the hiking trails at **McKinney Falls State Park** east of the city mark a transition zone between Blackland Prairie and Hill Country. The vegetation you'll find at **Wild Basin Wilderness** and the various nature trails in Zilker Park (most famous for its Barton Springs Pool) on the city's west side are clearly the limestone-tolerant species of the Hill Country.

The natural water features at **Westcave Preserve** and nearby Hamilton Pool and **Colorado Bend State Park's** Gorman Falls (near San Saba) showcase lush ferns and other plant life at the water's edge. **Guadalupe River State Park** and adjacent **Honey Creek State Natural Area**, as well as beautiful **Pedernales Falls State Park** are other picturesque areas to explore for landscaping ideas on Hill Country sites.

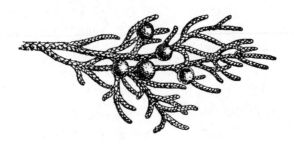

## *Red Rolling Plains*

Wichita Falls, Abilene and San Angelo serve as the major markets within this vast region that spans West Texas from the Red River to a line some 50 miles south of San Angelo. The stark and rugged landscape of this part of Texas may be an acquired taste, but this author finds great beauty here, especially in late spring and early fall when rains green the grasses and brings on bursts of wildflowers. The undulating mid-grass prairies alternate with lacy mesquite groves that may include small junipers and shinnery oaks. The land gradually becomes more rough and broken as you travel west.

Between Abilene and San Angelo, white hills (a northern extension of the limestone of the Edwards Plateau) called the Callahan Divide stand in sharp contrast to the overall reddish color of the landscape. Here, the vegetation includes live oaks and pecans. For thousands of years Buffalo Gap (now a town with a population of 469), provided passage through the divide for the migrating herds. Later it served as a route for cattle trails and wagon trains headed for California.

Red soils are usually visible between the plants that naturally grow throughout most of this region. Islands of sandy soil appear irregularly, usually on high ground. Regional gardeners will find that the sandy loams and clayey soils support a variety of native flora, but visitors will see little in the way of crops except those grown to sustain the abundant livestock. Soils adjacent to streams tend to be gravelly. Because limestone-based soils exist alongside red sand or clay, home owners are well advised to have their soils tested before deciding on the plant materials that will best grow on their properties.

Rainfall varies from about 20 to 27 inches per year. Although the entire region falls within Zone 7, winter temperatures occasionally drop below zero. Summers are extremely hot and dry. For this reason, more and more gardeners here are learning to appreciate such native plants as yucca and beautiful blue-green sand sagebrush. The City of Abilene has done a particularly admirable job of introducing native plants into its public parks and the **Abilene Zoological Gardens**. San Angelo's approach has been quite different; it's city parks focus on the surprisingly verdant Concho River and a series of plant "collections." The **San Angelo Nature Center** is a 260-acre wetland that resulted from an accidental 25-year leak in a dam!

Several of the region's place names recall striking natural features in the landscape. In the northernmost reaches of the Red Rolling Plains at **Copper Breaks State Park** near Quanah, one can enjoy the rugged, scenic beauty of red mesas covered with grasses, mesquite and thick juniper breaks. At Wichita Falls, a wooded walkway provides access to the river, and the new **Wichita Falls Waterfall** recalls the source of the town's name. The town of Big Spring was named for a natural spring that served as the only watering place for herds of bison, antelope and wild horses within a 60-mile radius. Mesquite, shin oak, skunkbush sumac, redberry juniper and various cacti cling to the rocky slopes at **Big Spring State Park**.

## *High Plains*

Lubbock and Amarillo are the major market cities of the prosperous agricultural region commonly referred to as The Panhandle. Midland and Odessa stand on the southern edge of the High Plains, sustained by an oil and ranching economy that has more in common with the adjacent Red Rolling Plains than with the Panhandle. (Midland was so named because it is the half-way point between the 600 miles that separate Fort Worth from El Paso.)

The Panhandle is dotted with farming communities. Seen from an airplane, the land is gridded into squares. Large green circles within the squares are the result of irrigation equipment that water in a circular pattern from a single central source. The colorful canyons that punctuate the landscape are actually fingers of the Red Rolling Plains that extend up onto the featureless High Plains.

With temperatures regularly plunging below zero, winters are hard in this region. Average annual rainfall is between 18 to 20 inches. Because no rivers drain the High Plains, rainwater collects in thousands of shallow playa lakes and filters down into underground aquifers that have provided irrigation water for acres and acres of cotton and wheat since the 1930s. Unfortunately, the water table has rapidly dropped as demand has outstripped inflow. If the trend continues, the High Plains will someday revert to the buffalo grass and other short grasses that once covered this high, dry region of Texas.

A wide range of native wildflowers bloom and grow on the High Plains, but you can forget about incorporating native trees into High Plains gardens. There aren't any. The **Ranching Heritage Center** in Lubbock is a testament to the difficulties pioneers faced in an area devoid of materials for building homes. Supplied with sufficient water, however, the rich, well-drained, loamy soil that is so hospitable to agricultural crops supports a surprising variety of imported trees and shrubs. The **Lubbock Memorial Arboretum** showcases drought-tolerant ornamental plants from several similar warm summer/cold winter regions of the world. Midland's **Sibley Nature Center** draws on a wide range of native shrubs as well as wildflowers suitable for landscaping.

Several highways take you through dramatic Caprock scenery, where Red Rolling Plains meet the High Plains. Highway 207 between Silverton and Claude dips down into Palo Duro Canyon. Near Silverton at Quitaque is the entrance to **Caprock Canyons State Park**, where sparse countryside gives way to bottomlands filled with tall grasses, cottonwoods, plum thickets and hackberries. South of Lubbock on FM 669 between Post and Gail, you'll also encounter some of the state's most dramatic cliff and canyon vistas.

## *Trans-Pecos*

The Pecos River Valley more or less forms the eastern boundary of this region of desert and mountains. El Paso is its major market area, but the towns of Alpine, Fort Stockton, Pecos and Monahans also serve the farmers and ranchers who live in this most sparsely populated part of the state. **Big Bend National Park** at the region's southern tip draws visitors from all over the world to enjoy the spectacular scenery of the River and the Chisos Mountains' diverse flora and fauna. Moist canyons and dry, rocky mountains in the northern reaches also draw numerous nature-loving travelers to the **Guadalupe Mountains National Park**. Between the Chisos and Guadalupe Mountains lie the Davis Mountains. Volcanic in origin, their fertile soils support vegetation different from rest of the Trans-Pecos area.

There are thirty named mountain ranges in the Trans-Pecos. Between the mountains, the terrain is mostly sandy basins and salty playas, which are shallow lakes created when rain leaches salts and other minerals from the mountain walls. After the water evaporates, the playas become salt flats. The dry, hot basins support desert plants and the tough shrubs that are called chaparral. Only a few halophytes (salt-grower) can survive in the playas.

Most of the region falls within the Chihuahuan Desert, but this landscape bears no resemblance to the Sahara. Plant life in the Trans-Pecos is diverse, amazingly abundant and uniformly tough. Average annual rainfall ranges from only 12.2 inches in Pecos County to a mere 7.8 inches in El Paso County. The "rainy season" is July, August and September. The scant rainfall comes in sudden cloudbursts that cause flash floods and quickly runs off.

Lack of moisture and extreme summer heat combine to severely limit agricultural pursuits. Some counties produce no crops at all, but most of the region is suitable for raising cattle, sheep and goats. Where irrigation water is available, apples, pecans, grapes and onions thrive, especially in the sandy loam soils of the Pecos Valley and along the Rio Grande. Pecos is renowned for its cantaloupes. Deep volcanic soils around Marfa and Alpine allow profitable ranching. Spanish mission lands within the city limits of El Paso have been in constant cultivation since 1682. However, rapidly growing El Paso and Juarez, which have a combined population of 1,800,000, are now consuming water much faster than nature can replenish it.

Nature trails, desert gardens and scenic highways at or near several of the region's State Parks offer easy access to the natural wonders of the Trans-Pecos. **Big Bend Ranch State Park** between Presidio and Lajitas can be accessed through **Barton Warnock Environmental Education Center**, where you'll discover a world-renowned desert garden. One hundred miles north, a scenic loop west of Fort Davis (Highways 118 and 166) takes you to McDonald Observatory, Madera Canyon and **Davis Mountains State Park**. The park has nature trails where visitors can experience both grasslands and piñon-juniper-oak woodlands. Nearby is the **Chihuahuan Desert Research Center**, which also offers hiking and nature study. In El Paso, **Franklin Mountains State Park** takes you into the largest urban wilderness park in the nation!

The Monahans Sandhills, unlike true desert dunes, are the remains of a Permian sea that extend into five counties. **Monahans Sandhills State Park** contains one of the largest oak forests in the United States. However; its Havard oaks seldom grow more than waist-high! The Stockton Plateau, which is south of the dunes between the Chisos Mountains and the Pecos River, is technically the westernmost section of the Edwards Plateau and therefore not actually part of the Trans-Pecos. In this area, it's not just the lack of rainfall that limits vegetation to cacti and chaparral, but also the absence of soil.

Where the Pecos and the Rio Grande come together in Val Verde county, cave-dwelling people lived for thousands of years, harvesting wild plants and game, and leaving a record of their lives in cave paintings. Strategic stops for early travelers included Comanche Springs near Fort Stockton, Balmorhea Springs between Pecos and Alpine and Hueco Tanks (now **Hueco Tanks State Park**) near El Paso where natural rock basins store precious water. The muddy mineral-laden Pecos River does not offer particularly good drinking water. Even today Interstate Highway-10 follows the route of reliable water sources west to El Paso (The Pass).

Although it boasts a mild winter climate, gardening is not easy here. Most of the area's soils are extremely alkaline and high in salts due to the scarcity of rainfall, (7.2-inches per year, on average.) Soil types within the Trans-Pecos region range from the sandy, alkaline soils of the basins to the acidic soils of the Davis Mountain area, which weathered from volcanic rock.

Drought resistant vegetation prevails throughout — creosote bush, yucca, cenizo, sand sagebrush, ocotillo and several species of short, sparse grasses. Creosote bushes cover thousands of acres of the landscape, a species that native plant enthusiast Sally Wasowski notes can be pruned into a handsome landscape specimen. The wide range of soil types supports a surprisingly wide variety of native plant life. Bright yellow-blooming broomweed and several other poisonous plants have invaded depleted rangeland. The occasional rains bring out colorful desert marigolds, blackfoot daisies, ocotillo, mountain laurel, a variety of blooming cacti and big, beautiful Chisos bluebonnets. The mountainous areas are clothed in piñon pine, juniper and other Rocky Mountain vegetation not found anywhere else in the state.

Five separate life zones exist in **Big Bend National Park** alone. The scenic drive along The River Road (Texas FM 170), which follows the meanders of the Rio Grande, is among the most spectacular in the nation. FM 170 allows access to small recreation areas along the river and to rafting and canoeing "put-in" and "take-out" points. If you're planning a trip downriver from Colorado Canyon into the canyons in **Big Bend National Park**, the necessary permits must be secured from the National Park Service.

The Guadalupe Mountains are the limestone remains of a Permian sea fossil reef. Within **Guadalupe Mountains National Park**, you'll not only discover four of the highest peaks in the state, but also plant life that includes ponderosa pine, Douglas fir, ferns and abundant spring wildflowers. A stream that flows through McKittrick Canyon nurtures plants from several habitats. The park is not developed as a recreation area, but for serious hikers, it is a joy to behold. Autumn colors are spectacular!

# Chapter Two

# Sources of Inspiration & Information

*"We are the children of our landscape; it dictates behavior and even thought in the measure to which we are responsive to it."*
....*Lawrence George Durrell*

# Public Gardens & Nature Trails to Visit

In the first half of Chapter One we talked about the history of gardening, mentioning public gardens and historic homes throughout the state that provide wonderful sources of inspiration for garden design. In seeking a personal "style," you need not be confined to the landscapes of your own region. A San Antonio homeowner interested in Asian gardens should certainly visit Fort Worth's exquisite Japanese Garden. An art collector from Tyler will appreciate the deft way that sculpture is blended into the natural landscape at the Umlauf Garden in Austin or The Art Center in Waco. A Dallas gardener whose property lends itself to formalism could find no better example than in the gardens of Bayou Bend in Houston.

However, when it comes to plants, every region of the state is distinct, which is why we hope you've read the second half of the previous chapter, or at least the part that applies to the region where you live. It's imperative that you select plant materials well-adapted to the specifics of your own soil, climate and landforms. Native vegetation in your area is the best indicator for which plants will thrive and which won't. For design inspiration, Mother Nature is the best teacher. Notice the variety of colors, forms and textures she has combined. Look closely at the way the stream bends. Study the way the rocks occur (or note the absence thereof)…

In listing places to visit for inspiration, this chapter not only includes botanical gardens where both native and appropriate imported plants are featured, but also selected parks and preserves where gardeners can experience plants growing in natural communities. We've also listed several new Xeriscape gardens that demonstrate water-wise planting. Many of the nurseries we've listed in other chapters of this book also feature display gardens. You'll find them all in the geographical index that begins on page 399. Tuck a copy of the book into the glove box of your car when you travel around Texas. Just look at how much this state has to offer!

## Cross Timbers & Grand Prairie
### Cedar Hill

## Cedar Hill State Park

P.O. Box 2649
Cedar Hill, Texas 75104
☎ 972/291-3900
**Hours** Daily year-round 8 a.m.-10 p.m.
**Admission** $5 per person age 13 and up; children free
**Accessible** Partially

The natural vegetation of the Grand Prairie is showcased at Cedar Hill State Park. Its scenic, rugged hills are covered with cedar elm, honey locust, mesquite, and juniper (cedar) trees, and there are several areas where you'll find remnants of tall-grass prairie replete with wildflowers. Botanists have found species of 80 different plant families within this park. Located in southwestern Dallas County, this 1,810-acre preserve is on the land settled in 1854 by John Anderson Penn. Today, the Penn Farm Agricultural History Center pays tribute to Texas' agrarian heritage and affords a glimpse into the life of North Texas farm families in the 19th century. Interpretive tours of the old farm are scheduled monthly. Activities include nature study on 4.2 miles of hiking/backpacking trails.

*Directions: Located three miles west of Cedar Hill and four miles southeast of Grand Prairie. From US Highway 67, exit FM 1382 and travel 2.5 miles north. From IH-20, exit FM 1382 and travel four miles south.*

### Cleburne

## Cleburne State Park

RR 2, Box 90
Cleburne, Texas 76031
☎ 817/645-4215
**Hours** Daily year-round 8 a.m.-10 p.m.
**Admission** $5 per person age 13 and up; children free
**Accessible** Partially

This Cross Timbers landscape was a favorite hunting ground for Indian tribesmen because the dense woods and plains included several clear-water springs. Later it was a camp site for cowboys on the Chisholm Trail. In 1934, the Civilian Conservation Corps (CCC) began building the dam, buildings, boathouse and water tower in this beautiful valley of springs. You'll enjoy hiking on 2.4 miles of trails, nature study, picnicking and swimming in a spring-fed lake. You can explore the aquatic environment from a paddle boat or canoe, which can be rented during the spring, summer and fall. Interpretive activities include guided trail walks and kid's wilderness survival courses. Juniper (a.k.a. cedar), oak, elm, mesquite, redbud, cottonwood, sycamore, and sumac trees cover the white rocky hills. In early spring, bluebonnets carpet the open fields, and many other varieties of wildflowers bloom throughout the year. The park hosts Wildflower Tours in the spring and Foliage Tours in fall. (Call for dates and times.)

*Directions: Located in Johnson County, ten miles southwest of Cleburne. Take Highway 67 to Park Road 21, then southwest on Park Road 21 for six miles.*

## Fort Worth Botanic Garden and Japanese Garden

*3220 Botanic Garden Drive*
*Fort Worth, Texas 76107*
☎ *817/871-7689 (general info), 817/871-7685 (Japanese Garden)*
**Hours** *Gardens: Daily 8 a.m.-sundown; Conservatory: Mon-Fri 10-9, Sat 10-6, Sun 1-4 (summer) closed at 4 p.m. on weekends during the winter; Japanese Garden: Daily 9-7 (summer); Tues-Sun 10-5 (winter); The Gardens Restaurant: Tues-Sat 11-3, Sun 10-2; Gift Shops: Daily 10-4 (Japanese Garden Shop closed Mondays)*
**Admission** *Free to gardens; Conservatory $1 (adults), $.50 (seniors and children over 4); Japanese Garden: $2-weekdays, $2.50-weekends and holidays (adults), with $.50 discount for seniors; $1 (children 4-12); under 4 free; children under 13 must be accompanied by an adult.*
**Accessible** *Yes to all buildings; portions of the grounds have limited access*

More than a half-million people visit this garden every year! For locals, this is the single best place to see the region's wide range of gardening possibilities, and for gardeners from other parts of the state, it offers a world of design ideas. The Fort Worth Botanic Garden began as a rose display in 1933. Now, the granddaddy of Texas public gardens has grown to an impressive collection of specialty gardens tucked into a 110-acre park-like site. Within the planted gardens and surrounding woodlands, more than 2,500 native and exotic species are waiting to be explored. The main building houses a large conservatory, and behind the building is the Adelaide Polk Fuller Garden, replete with winding paths and attractive garden structures. Highlights to be discovered along the Old Garden Road include a Fragrance Garden designed for the visually impaired. Farther along you'll find the extensive formal European-style rose garden, a naturalistic Perennial Garden, featuring a kitchen herb garden, and so much more… One can easily spend the entire day.

Among the garden's treasures is the 7.5-acre Japanese Garden, where water in all its forms — cascading down a bluff, gurgling over rapids, shimmering in large reflecting pools, or swirling symbolically in raked gravel — is the theme. Schools of gaily colored koi dart through interconnected ponds under the several bridges that crisscross the garden. Each of the many pathways leads to yet another undiscovered pleasure — an island where ducks reside, a teahouse complex, a moon-viewing deck, a five-tiered pagoda.

The garden's labyrinthine paths guide a journey over and around a series of interconnecting ponds. Choose one path and you happen upon a recreation of Kyoto's Ryoan-ji temple garden where 15 rocks rise out of a sea of swirling raked gravel. A different fork in the path leads to a spot where you can rest and ponder an island "inhabited" by graceful bronze cranes. On the distant shore, water cascading down a dark, rugged limestone escarpment calls to mind a mountain spring. The path will disappear enticingly around a corner, then a stone lantern half-hidden in the foliage will mark the beginning of yet another sensory experience.

*Directions: Take IH-30 west from downtown; exit at University Drive. Travel north on University Drive to the main garden entrance.*

## Fort Worth Nature Center and Refuge

*9601 Fossil Ridge Road*
*Fort Worth, Texas 76135*
☎ *817/237-1111*
**Hours** *Tues-Sat 9-5, Sun 12-5; closed major holidays*
**Admission** *Free, donations accepted*
**Accessible** *Partially*

This 3,500-acre sanctuary preserves prairies, riverbottom forest and marshlands much as these habitats existed before European settlement. Twenty-five miles of trails provide opportunity to observe the plant communities of three different North Texas ecosystems. A variety of educational programs for children and adults are held at the Hardwicke Interpretative Center. Memberships are available, and facilities include a natural history library and Nature Center Gift Shop.

*Directions: Take Highway 199 (Jacksboro Highway) northwest of the city. The entrance is four miles beyond Loop 820.*

## Fort Worth Water Gardens

*1501 Commerce Street*
*Fort Worth, Texas*
**Hours** *Daily during daylight*
**Admission** *Free*
**Accessible** *Partially*

"Water does all kinds of funny things — it jumps, it's quiet, it makes noise, it makes films, it goes high, it goes low, it falls down," observed the architect Philip Johnson, who thoroughly explored its capabilities. The only sounds you'll hear in this downtown park are those of children laughing, birds chirping and the music of the water. The several water features here are too large in scale for residential landscape design, but the sights and sounds will make you eager for a fountain, pool or pond in your own backyard. This is an enchanted landscape!

## Fort Worth Museum of Science and History

*1501 Montgomery Street*
*Fort Worth, Texas 76107*
☎ *817/732-1631*
**Hours** *Daily during daylight*
**Admission** *Free*
**Accessible** *Difficult gravel paths*

Between the main parking lot and the rear of the museum, you'll find a testament to the beauty and efficacy of native plants. Arranged into gardens representing West Texas, East Texas, Edwards Plateau and the Gulf Coast. Sally and Andy Wasowski noted in their book, *Native Texas Gardens*, that the East Texas Garden has not fared well, which is not surprising since Fort Worth's average annual rainfall is considerably less than the amount that Tyler normally receives and its soils are completely different. Case closed on the subject of choosing the right plant for the right place!

*Directions: Take IH-30 west from downtown; exit at Montgomery. Travel north about a mile on Montgomery.*

*Meridian*

---

## Meridian State Park

*P.O. Box 188*
*Meridian, Texas 76665*
☎ *817/435-2536*
**Hours** *Daily year-round 8 a.m.-10 p.m.*
**Admission** *$5 per person age 13 and up; children free*
**Accessible** *Partially*

Native Americans still occupied the Bosque River Valley when the Texas-Santa Fe Expedition passed through this site in 1841. This Cross-Timbers landscape remains heavily wooded with Ashe juniper and oak, as well as abundant woody plants and wildflowers. A variety of wildlife and birds, including the endangered Golden-cheeked warbler, may be seen from the five miles of hiking and nature trails (250 yards are paved and accessible to the disabled, with benches along the trail). There are also five miles of scenic paved road for vehicles and biking.

*Directions: Take State Highway 174 from Cleburne, State Highway 144 from Glen Rose or State Highway 6 from Waco. Join State Highway 22 and proceed to the park. Take State Highway 22 from Hillsboro or Hamilton. The park is located about three miles southwest of Meridian off State Highway 22.*

## Trinity Blacklands
### Dallas Metropolitan Area

---

## Dallas Arboretum and Botanical Society

*8525 Garland Road*
*Dallas, Texas 75218-3914*
☎ *214/327-8263; Dallas Blooms hotline: 214/327-4901*
**Hours** *Daily 10-6 (closes at 5p.m. in winter)*
**Admission** *$6 (adults), $5 (seniors), $3 (children 6-12), free under 6*
**Accessible** *Yes, plus tram service for mobility impaired*

To discover the myriad planting possibilities for the Trinity Blacklands one need only to visit the eastern shore of White Rock Lake. Although this magnificent 66-acre garden is relatively new, its designers incorporated two fine residential estates from the 1930s and built upon their existing trees and shrubs to create a very sophisticated landscape. The main entrance leads first to a shady fern dell, then opens into a 6.6-acre color garden aimed to awaken the senses! The historical gardens adjacent to the DeGolyer House remain (see page 11), and the new "A Woman's Garden" has been added on an overlook above the lake.

On the north side of the Camp home, which now serves as headquarters for the Arboretum and Botanical Society, you'll find an informal English-cottage style garden with colorful native and adapted plants and several enticing water features, including Toad Corners Fountain and Water Walls. Adjacent to the south side of the house is a lovely little herb garden. Dallas Blooms, the organization's five-week spring festival attracts thousands of people to see 2,000 varieties of blooming azaleas in what is billed as "the country's largest collection" and participate in a host of related garden activities.

*Directions: From downtown: travel east on IH-30 to the East Grand exit, go north on East Grand, which becomes Garland Road. From Loop 635 E., take the Garland Road exit and travel south approximately five miles.*

## Dallas Horticulture Center

*3601 MLK Boulevard (P.O. Box 152537)*
*Dallas, Texas 75210*
☎ *214/428-7476*
**Hours** *Visitor Center and Conservatory: Tues-Sat 10-5, Sun 1-5; gardens open daily during daylight hours*
**Admission** *Free except for occasional special events*
**Accessible** *Yes*

The second oldest of its kind in Texas, this education-based organization attracts 300,000 visitors annually to its 7.5 acres in Fair Park. Its Community Gardens Program takes horticultural education out into neighborhoods, as well. The Blachly Conservatory houses a rare collection of African flora, including the spectacular succulents from dry regions and, from African forests, the ferns, orchids and palms. The conservatory is filled with live butterflies during the State Fair. Behind the conservatory, 14 theme gardens and several water features are designed to inspire by example. The Benny J. Simpson Texas Native Plant Collection will be seen an even more valued treasure now that we've lost this intrepid collector, educator and writer who spent 35 years championing the beauty and diversity of Texas flora.

*Directions: From downtown, take IH-30 east to the 2nd Avenue exit. Curve to the right, take a left at the second light onto MLK. The Center is just inside the park.*

## Dallas Nature Center

*7171 Mountain Creek Parkway*
*Dallas, Texas 75249*
☎ *972/296-1955*
**Hours** *Daylight, year-round*
**Admission** *$3 donation appreciated; small fee schedule under consideration.*
**Accessible** *Very limited*

Dr. Geoffrey Stanford, a Brit by birth, truly embraced the Texas landscape when he founded this 630-acre preserve. I once heard him make a speech in which he wryly observed that developers name their subdivisions in memory of the trees they cut down. (Oak Hills, Mesquite Ridge, etc.) Here you'll find hiking trails, picnic facilities, a native plant nursery (see page 245) and a summer day camp for children in an environment that needs no euphemisms.

*Directions: Take IH-20 between Dallas and Fort Worth. Exit at Mountain Creek Parkway; go south 2.7 miles.*

## Pioneer Plaza

*Young Street at Griffin Street*
*Dallas, Texas 75201*
**Hours** *Day and night, year-round*
**Admission** *Free*
**Accessible** *Yes*

This work-in-progress is already the largest sculptural group in the world. Only 40 of its intended 70 bronze longhorn steers are cast and in place. Award-winning sculptor Bob Summers of Glen Rose, "to capture the full impact of a trail drive" created the setting, the larger-than-life animals and their attendant cowboys. Located on a historic cattle trail that came into use in 1854, the 4.2-acre site incorporates native trees and grasses, a waterfall and a flowing stream. The landscape architects who worked with the sculptor beautifully captured the grandeur of the grassland prairie as it existed throughout this region of Texas in the 19th century.

*Directions: In downtown, just north of the Dallas Convention Center, next to City Hall.*

### Xeriscape Demonstration Garden

*Water Operations Control Center at White Rock Pump Station*
*2900 White Rock Road*
*Dallas, Texas 75214*
**Hours** *Daily during daylight*
**Admission** *Free*
**Accessible** *Yes*

Where better than at a water station to show how rich and pleasing a water-wise garden can be? The work of landscape designer Bonnie Reese, who happens to be the wife of County Extension Agent Stacey Reese, this garden combines natives with hardy adapted species to attract birds and butterflies and to introduce people to the notion of seasonal appeal with minimal labor. (Bonnie is the author of a book, *Common Sense Landscaping*.) More than 80 plant varieties (most of them are labeled) are combined in a well-organized design plan. The effect perfectly complements the historic red brick building, proving that "wild" plants work well in a "tamed" garden.

## McKinney

### Heard Natural Science Museum & Wildlife Sanctuary

*One Nature Place*
*McKinney, Texas 75069*
☎ *972/562-5566*
**FAX** *972/548-9119*
**Hours** *Mon-Sat 9-5, Sun 1-5; self-guided trails open until 4*
**Admission** *Museum: $3 (adults), $2 (children); free on Monday; all trails free, but register with receptionist upon arrival.*
**Accessible** *Paved trail for wheelchairs*

A new $175,000 native plant demonstration garden is this premier museum's "front yard." Designed by Beth Francell as a master's degree practicum and executed by designer Rosa Finsley of Kings Creek Landscaping, the entry serves both aesthetic and educational purposes. The Heard's wildlife sanctuary is equally instructive to area gardeners who would devote a portion of their property to "naturescaping." Returned as closely as possible to the high grasslands and bottomland woods one would have found here in centuries past, the trails are replete with natural streams, ponds and meadows. Guided trail walks are available on a first come, first served basis on Saturdays at 11:30 and Sundays every half-hour between 1:30 and 3:30. The museum's Native Plant Sale every April attracts an enthusiastic audience; it publishes an extensive list of available plants. Year-round, the Nature Store is well worth a visit. Museum membership rewards participants with an informative newsletter and discounts on merchandise, classes, workshops and field trips.

*Directions: Take U.S. Highway 75 to Exit 38 and follow the signs. The museum is located one mile east of State Highway 5 on FM 1378.*

*Paris*

## Sam Bell Maxey House State Historical Park
*812 South Church Street*
*Paris, Texas 75460*
☎ *903/785-5716*
**Hours** *Grounds open daily year-round, dawn to dusk. House open weekends or by special reservation. Closed Christmas and New Year's Day. Guided tours: Fri 1-5, Sat 8-5, Sun 1-5*
**Admission** *Free to grounds; house tours $5 per person age 13 and up; children free*
**Accessible** *Partially*

Confederate General and U.S. Senator Samuel Bell Maxey and his wife, Marilda, moved into their fashionable High Victorian Italianate style house on the south side of Paris in 1868. It has been restored and furnished to reflect almost 100 years of continuous use by the family. Old oaks and pecans grace the two-acre site, along with crepe myrtles, pears, hackberrys, and dogwoods. Mrs. Maxey's formal garden is maintained today with a display of colorful annuals, and the boxwoods once used to edge the parterres have been transplanted to other areas of the garden, but it's still a good place to get the feel of an "Old South" landscape.

*Directions: Located in the city of Paris on the corner of South Church and Washington Streets.*

## Piney Woods
*Daingerfield*

## Daingerfield State Park
*RR 1, Box 286-B*
*Daingerfield, Texas 75638*
☎ *903/645-2921*
**Hours** *Daily year-round 8 a.m.-10 p.m.*
**Admission** *$2 per person age 13 and up; children free*
**Accessible** *Partially*

Springtime brings breath-taking color to the park's rolling hills as the dogwoods, redbuds and wisteria burst into bloom. In autumn the sweetgum, oak and maple trees produce dazzling shades of red and gold. This 551-acre recreational area in Morris County includes an 80-acre lake and stonework built in the 30's by the CCC. The park offers picnicking, camping, boating, fishing; hiking; and nature study. Tours may be arranged by special request.

*Directions: Located east of Daingerfield on State Highway 49 for two miles to Park Road 17 entrance. From Dallas/Ft Worth take Interstate 30 to Mt. Pleasant and exit on Ferguson Road; follow State Highway 49 to Daingerfield State Park (about 22 miles from IH-30). From Longview, take State Highway 259 to Daingerfield; turn right on State Highway 11 and State Highway 49.*

## Hardin, Jasper & Tyler Counties

### Big Thicket National Preserve

*3785 Milam (administrative office)*
*Beaumont, Texas 77701*
☎ *409/246-2337*
**Hours** *Daily, year around; Information Center open 9-5 except Christmas Day*
**Admission** *Free*
**Accessible** *Partially*

The Big Thicket has been called "The American Ark." Ecologists estimate that it would take about a thousand years for such a forest to regenerate. While only a small portion of the original forest remains, you'll find several distinct plant communities ranging from dry sandhills with shortgrass and prickly pears to cypress bogs and upland forests within this marvelous preserve. Its forests are richly layered, with tall, medium and small trees towering over an understory of shrubs and ground covers (including ferns and mosses) that retain moisture around the tree roots. Nine trails through the preserve range in length from a quarter-mile to 18 miles. There are guided tours and environmental education programs available year-round, including wildflower identification from March through October. The major access point to the forest is from the Visitor Information Center north of Kountze. At the northern edge of one section, the Alabama and Coushatta Indians preserve about four thousand acres on their reservation east of Livingston.

## Karnack

### Caddo Lake State Park

*RR 2 Box 15*
*Karnack, Texas 75661*
☎ *903/679-3351*
**Hours** *Daily year-round 8 a.m.-10 p.m.; Call for dates and prices of scheduled tours*
**Admission** *$2 per person age 13 and up; children free*
**Accessible** *Partially*

Caddo Lake State Park, consists of over seven thousand acres along Little Cypress Bayou, which feeds into Caddo Lake. A sprawling maze of bayous and sloughs, Caddo was the only natural lake in Texas until it was dammed in the early 1900s. Caddo Indian legend attributed its formation to an earthquake, but in fact it was a massive logjam that impounded the water.

Activities include nature study, camping, hiking, swimming, picnicking, fishing, and boating. There's an interpretive center; 1½-miles of hiking trails; a ¾-mile nature trail. According to the Parks and Recreation Department, "naturalists will enjoy the stately cypress trees, the lotus and lily pads, the waterfowl, alligators, turtles, frogs, raccoons, minks, nutrias, beavers and snakes." ("Enjoying" snakes may be what separates naturalists from other folks.) The park offers canoe rentals and pontoon boat tours daily except Wednesday. Tours of the lake are also available through Caddo Lake Steamboat Company (☎ 903/665-1665) and Jefferson Landing Riverboat (☎ 903/665-2222).

*Directions: Travel north of Karnack one mile on State Highway 43 to FM 2198; go east a half-mile to Road 2. The park is 15 miles northeast of Marshall.*

## Marshall

### Starr Family State Historical Park
*407 West Travis Street*
*Marshall, Texas 75670*
☎ 903/935-3044
**Hours** *Grounds open daily year-round during daylight hours. House open Fri & Sat 10-4 Sun 1-5 or by appointment. Closed Thanksgiving, Christmas, and New Year's Day.*
**Admission** *Grounds free; House tours: $3 (adults), $1 (students)*
**Accessible** *Yes*

   This three-acre estate features homes and gardens enjoyed by five generations of a prominent Texas family. Rosemont was built before the Civil War. Maplecroft, built in 1871, is the centerpiece of the compound, which also served as a station for stagecoach lines and railroads and is today listed in the National Register of Historic Places. There are guided and self-guided tours of the houses and extensive gardens, where you'll find majestic east Texas timber, as well as magnificent azaleas, roses, fruit trees, red maples, camellias, dogwoods, wisterias, and other fragrant plants.

*Directions: The park can be reached by exiting Interstate 20 onto US Highway 59 north; then going west on Travis Street to the corner of South Grove Street.*

## Mount Pleasant

### Tankersley Gardens
*IH-30 at Loop 271 (Rt. 7, Box 696)*
*Mt. Pleasant, Texas 75455*
☎ 903/572-0567
**Hours** *Tues-Sat 9-6 (March 1-Oct. 31); by reservation in winter*
**Admission** *$2 (adults); $1 (students); no fee for shopping*
**Accessible** *Yes*

   This five-acre garden is a couple's retirement project — his background was in forestry, and she was a "green thumb" gardener. Annuals and perennials provide the seasonal color amidst flowering shrubs and native trees. A mile-long strolling trail takes visitors over nine foot bridges to a natural island and through an iris field where 125 varieties bloom in spring. The pavilion shop offers potted plants, statuary and garden gifts. The garden's chapel and gazebo make it a popular place for weddings.

## Nacogdoches

### Stephen F. Austin State University Arboretum
*SFASU Campus; P.O. Box 13000*
*Nacogdoches, Texas 75962*
☎ 409/468-4343
**Hours** *Daily year-round, dawn to dusk*
**Admission** *Free*
**Accessible** *Mostly*

   Begun in 1985 as a small planting area beside the Agriculture Building, this facility has quickly risen to national stature under the direction of Dr. David Creech. Through trades with Boston's Arnold Arboretum, the National Arboretum in Washington, DC and North Carolina State University and the gifts of numerous Texas growers, the Arboretum has evolved into an outstanding collection of rare shrubs, vines, ground covers, herbs, herbaceous perennials and, of course, trees. It is arranged as 19 "theme" gardens. The herb garden, maintained by the Herb Society of Deep East Texas, is particularly notable.

*(Listing continued on next page)*

A visitor can easily spend a day exploring the "Asian Valley" with its 40 varieties of Japanese maples, the Texas heritage garden, the "dry" garden that features new plants from western states and Mexico, and the "woodland glen" with its collection of native ferns, hosta and other shade-loving plants. A butterfly garden and an "endangered plants" garden are in the works. A new rock garden just south of the daylily collection displays an array of heat-loving perennials. The arboretum's mission is to promote the conservation, selection and use of native plants, and encourage diversity in the landscape philosophy of Texas. Its new 46-page plant location guide, which sells for $15; should become required reading for East Texas gardeners!

*Directions: On the SFASU Campus, off Wilson Drive between College and Starr Avenue.*

# Newton

## Wild Azalea Canyons Trail

*Newton County Chamber of Commerce*
*P.O. Box 66*
*Newton, Texas 75966*
☎ *409/379-5527*
**Hours** *Daily, dawn to dusk during spring and summer*
**Admission** *Free*
**Accessible** *No*

Trails of varying length allow visitors to walk deep into this forest where Piedmont azaleas (*Rhododendron canescens*) bloom on rocky cliffs under a canopy of long-leaf pines. Begun as a project by the Magnolia Garden Club, this breathtaking wild area is now maintained by the Chamber of Commerce on Temple Inland Forest Products Corporation's private land near the Sabine River. The peak season is in March.

*Directions: Take Texas Highway 87 north from Newton, then 6.7 miles east on FM 1414, then 1.8 miles on unpaved roads. Follow the signs.*

# Quitman

## Governor Hogg Shrine State Historical Park

*RR 3, Park Road 45*
*Quitman, Texas 75783*
☎ *903/763-2701*
**Hours** *Daily year-round 8 a.m.-10 p.m.; museum tours: Fri & Sat 10-4, Sun 1-5*
**Admission** *Grounds free; museum: $3 (adults); $1 (students)*
**Accessible** *Partially*

Named for the state's first Texas-born governor, this small Historical Park includes museums housing items that belonged to the Hogg and Stinson families. Of interest to East Texas gardeners and history buffs alike is the half-mile nature/interpretive trail where the vegetation has remained undisturbed since 1900. Located northwest of Tyler, this area is a transition zone between pine and post oak woodlands. Guided by an informative brochure, you'll visit 23 signed stops and discover a turn-of-the-century iron pony truss bridge along the way. Reservations are required for picnic sites.

*Directions: Located off State Highway 37, about six blocks south of the Wood County Courthouse in Quitman.*

*Rusk/ Palestine*

## Texas State Railroad Historical Park

*P.O. Box 39*
*Rusk, Texas 75785*
☎ *1-800/442-8951(In Texas Only) or 903/683-2561*
**Hours** *Rusk/Palestine State Parks open daily year-round. Railroad offices* **Hours** *Daily 8-5. Trains run weekends-only in spring and fall; Thurs-Sun (June and July). Reservations are recommended!*
**Admission** *Park grounds free; One-way train trip: $10 (adults), $6 (children 12 and under), Round-trip $15 (adults), $9 (children)*
**Accessible** *Yes*

There's probably no more delightful way to introduce your children to East Texas woodlands than aboard a steam engine train chugging through Anderson and Cherokee Counties. Passengers board in either Rusk or Palestine for the 1½- hour, 25-mile trip. Once you've arrived at the opposite station, you'll have an hour to enjoy lunch (there are picnic facilities adjacent to both depots). Then take a short nature hike through the park, enjoy a ride on a paddle boat or browse through the train store before re-boarding for the return trip.

The railroad was restored by the Parks and Wildlife Department and opened to the public in 1976 as part of the nation's Bicentennial Celebration, but trains have been rolling along these tracks since 1896, crossing 24 bridges over rolling hardwood creek bottoms. The countryside is replete with loblolly pine, sweetgum, redbud, cedar-elm, willow, blackjack oak, Spanish mulberry, flatwood plum and osage orange. Flowering dogwoods provide for a spectacular spring excursion during late March and early April, and warm shades of red and gold blanket the woods in November.

*Directions: Located between the Cities of Palestine and Rusk, the railroad is adjacent to US Highway 84.*

## Tyler

## Tyler Municipal Rose Garden

*420 South Rose Park Drive*
*Tyler, Texas 75702*
☎ *903/531-1212*
**Hours** *Mon-Fri 8-5, Sat 9-5, Sun 1-5. Call for extended hours during peak seasons. Gardens are closed periodically to treat pest and disease problems. Museum & gift shop: Tues-Fri 9-4, Sat 10-4, Sun 1:30-4.*
**Admission** *Gardens and building free. Museum: $3.50 (adults), $2 (children 3-11)*
**Accessible** *Almost entirely*

Spring and fall are peak seasons at the nation's largest municipal rose garden, but its daylilies delight in summer and the Vance Burks Memorial Camellia Garden extends this garden's appeal through the winter. What words can describe 30,000 rose bushes representing over 400 varieties of every imaginable color in six acres of terraced beds? The bulk of the collection consists of hybrid teas, floribundas and grandifloras. Of special interest to rosarians is the All American Rose Selection test garden (one of only 24 in the country) where new varieties are evaluated before they can be selected and patented. Our favorite section is the one-acre Heritage Rose and Sensory Garden, which features hardy varieties that date back to 19th century. The nearby perennial border demonstrates plants that combine well with roses. The garden's 15 acres also features a picnic area, fountains and a gazebo. Inside, a gift shop offers potpourris, garden books and other rose-related items. The Rose Museum

*(Listing continued on next page)*

features historical mementos of the sixty-five-year-old Texas Rose Festival, and it maintains a computerized catalog that describes and pictures over 250 rose varieties.

*Directions: From Loop 323: Take Highway 31 (which runs east-west through town) to Rose Park Drive.*

## Weches

### Mission Tejas State Historic Park

*RR 2, Box 108*
*Grapeland, Texas 75844*
☎ *409/687-2394*
**Hours** *Daily year-round 8 a.m.-10 p.m.*
**Admission** *$2 per person age 13 and up; children free*
**Accessible** *Partially*

Situated near the northern end of the Davy Crockett National Forest, Mission Tejas State Historical Park is all rustic beauty and tranquillity beneath the canopy of tall pine trees. The 363-acre park was built in 1934 by the CCC as a representation of the first Spanish mission in the province of Texas. You'll also find a restored 1828 log home, which served as a stopover for immigrants, adventurers, and locals traveling the Old San Antonio Road. Activities include camping; picnicking and hiking along 3.5 miles of trails, plus a large nature pond, which offers an opportunity to explore aquatic life. There's a printed guide to the trees of the Forest Trail. A favorite time to visit is when the dogwoods bloom, usually the last week of March.

*Directions: Located 22 miles northeast of Crockett and 12 miles west of Alto on State Highway 21 in Houston County. The entrance to the park is in Weches, where Park Road 44 intersects with State Highway 21.*

## Woodville

### Martin Dies, Jr. State Park

*RR 4, Box 274*
*Jasper, Texas 75951*
☎ *409/384-5231*
**Hours** *Daily year-round 8 a.m.-10 p.m.*
**Admission** *$2 per person age 13 and up; children free*
**Accessible** *Partially*

Located at the edge of the Big Thicket National Preserve, this 705-acre park showcases genuine old growth forest. Its numerous sloughs are lined with mature cypress, willow, beech, magnolia and sweet bay. In autumn the golden hues of beeches are brilliant against the reds of blackgums, maples and oaks, mixed among the evergreen pines. Three hiking trails provide excellent opportunities to view the flora and such wildlife as woodland warblers, woodpeckers, bluebirds, herons, wood ducks, cranes and alligators. A garden area displays native East Texas plants and medicinal, culinary and fragrant herbs. The park hosts naturalist activities on weekends and canoe trips down the Angelina or Neches River on the third Saturday of each month. Call at least a week in advance to make reservations. You'll also find a Texas State Park Store and Nature Center.

*Directions: Located between Woodville and Jasper off US Highway 190. Turn north on Park Road 48.*

## Coastal Prairies & Marshes
### Beaumont/ Orange/ Port Arthur Area

### Beaumont Botanical Gardens

*Tyrrell Park (P.O. Box 7962)*
*Beaumont, Texas 77726*
☎ *409/842-3135*
**Hours** *Daily, 7:30-dusk*
**Admission** *Free*
**Accessible** *Yes*

   This garden's highlights include a display garden that features sun-loving plants, including an extensive daylily collection. There's a native plant and wildflower garden, herb garden and an informal antique rose garden. You'll also discover a Japanese Garden, several color-coordinated garden areas (green and white, all violet, etc.), waterfall courses and ponds. The Stream Side and Grandmother's Gardens display all manner of shade-loving plants. A new 10,000-square-foot conservatory houses tropical plants from around the world. The Garden Center building is used as a horticultural education facility, and the Beaumont Council of Garden Clubs maintains the gardens. A paved "Friendship Walk" allows easy access, and numerous benches invite a leisurely stay. When you leave, you might want to visit Cattail Marsh, which is located about a mile south of the Botanical Gardens in Tyrrell Park. Billed as Beaumont's best kept secret, this wetlands wildlife refuge features hiking trails where you'll find iris, cattails, arrowhead and other marsh-loving plants providing a home for some 350 species of birds.

*Directions: Turn south off IH-10 at Walden Road exit (west of the city) Follow Walden Road about a mile to the park entrance.*

### McFaddin-Ward House

*1906 McFaddin Avenue*
*Beaumont, Texas 77701*
☎ *409/832-2134*
**Hours** *Daily during daylight*
**Admission** *Free*
**Accessible** *Yes*

   One of the loveliest Texas homes from the era of grand estates is this 1906 Beaux Arts colonial. Early photos show little landscaping on the large, flat site, but Mamie McFaddin Ward, who was only eleven when her parents moved into the home, embellished the gardens throughout her life. A founding member of the Magnolia Garden Club, she planted hundreds of blooming plants, bulbs, trees and shrubs. The house now stands in a sea of azaleas. The rose gardens have been refurbished with 200 new and antique varieties. Family tradition has it that the 100-year-old twin oak trees near the porte cochere were grown from acorns gathered at the Battle of San Jacinto where young William McFaddin served as a guard to the wounded. Many of the original garden ornaments remain intact. You may take a guided tour of the house ($3 per person), but children under eight are not permitted. Children accompanied by an adult are welcome to take a self-guided tour of the carriage house.

*Directions: Exit IH-10 at Calder Avenue and travel east on Calder. Tours begin at the Visitor Center at the corner of Calder and 3rd Street.*

## Pinehurst Gardens

*Old Highway 90*
*Orange, Texas 77630*
☎ *409/833-3536 (Chamber of Commerce) or 409/883-5351 (recorded message)*
*www.pnx.com/pinehurst*
**Hours** *open 2nd & 3rd weekends in March and last two weekends in May*
**Admission** *Free; donations accepted*
**Accessible** *Partially*

Located just four miles west of the Louisiana border and set amid a forest of 100-year-old pine trees, this exquisite private estate is largely unknown to the general public in Texas. It was created by the late Betty and Edgar Brown, whose life-long avocation was the hydridizing of daylilies. Not only did they produce over 600 named varieties and collect over a thousand of the best varieties produced by other hybridizers, but also they created a diversified eleven-acre garden around their collection. In March, during the annual Orange Azalea Trail, the manicured grounds are awash in blooming azaleas, camellias and tens of thousands of colorful daffodils, tulips and hyacinths. In May the vast drifts of daylilies begin a three-month-long show. Paths wrap around shimmering ponds, and the landscape is punctuated with gazebos, benches, a "Walk of Saints," an aviary and a topiary garden that features a giant chessboard. Sections of the garden are devoted to displays of perennials, Asiatic lilies and bearded iris. A national Display Garden of the American Hemerocallis Society, its gates are open to members of the Society during the months of May, June and July.

## Sea Rim State Park

*P. O. Box 1066*
*Sabine Pass, Texas 77655*
☎ *409/971-2559*
**Hours** *Daily year-round 7 a.m.-10 p.m. except during migratory waterfowl season, when part of the park is closed*
**Admission** *$2 per person age 13 and up; children free; hour-long airboat tours by reservation only, additional fees apply*
**Accessible** *Partially*

With over 15,000 acres of marshland and 5.2 miles of shoreline, this park is named for that portion of the seashore where marsh grasses extend into the surf. This biologically-important zone is a prime wintering area for a variety of waterfowl and wetlands wildlife. The marshland waters provide fertile nursery grounds for aquatic life and are essential for the productivity of marine fisheries. People flock here for the birding, beach combing, canoeing and kayaking.

The Harrington Beach Unit features a Visitors' Center with exhibits, observation deck and nature trail (on a boardwalk through the marsh) with a self-guided booklet. The Marshlands Unit, which is accessible only by boat, has observation blinds for bird watching, photography and nature study. Fishing is permitted from dawn to dusk, but swimming is not permitted because alligators ply the waters. Airboat tours and canoe rentals are dependent on marsh water level conditions.

*Directions: Located 20 miles south of Port Arthur on State Highway 87.*

## Village Creek State Park

P.O. Box 8575
Lumberton, Texas 77657
☎ 409/755-7322
**Hours** Daily year-round 8 a.m.-10 p.m.
**Admission** $2 per person age 13 and up; children free
**Accessible** Partially

These 1,004 acres of heavily forested, virtually unspoiled bottomland are located just ten miles north of Beaumont. The park takes its name from a free flowing stream that rises near the Alabama-Coushatta Indian Reservation and runs in a southwesterly direction 63 miles to a junction with the Neches River. Although it floods severely every few years, this is an extremely popular flat water canoe trail within the heart of the Old Texas Big Thicket. The park is a "rain forest" full of cypress swamps, water tupelo swamps, river birch, mayhaw and yaupon trees. Wildlife is also abundant, and birding enthusiasts will enjoy the rain-loving wood ducks, egrets and herons, just to name a few from over 200 species of birds you may encounter along the park's ten miles of hiking trails. Canoe rental is available through Timber Ridge Tours, Kountze, TX (409/246-3107).

*Directions: From Beaumont, take US Highway 69 North; take Mitchell Road exit just before the US Highway 69/96 split. Go approximately .4 mile and turn north on FM 3513. Go approximately two miles and turn East on Alma Drive. Cross the railroad tracks (veer to the left) and go .6 mile to park entrance.*

## Galveston

## Ashton Villa and Harris Park

2328 Broadway
Galveston, Texas 77550
☎ 409/762-3933
**Hours** Garden open during daylight hours; villa open Mon-Sat 10-4, Sun 12-4
**Admission** Garden free; villa tours: $4 (adults), $3.50 (seniors and children 7-18)
**Accessible** Yes

Another grand residential garden to visit on the Upper Gulf Coast is Ashton Villa in Galveston. While simple in design, the garden's plant materials provide a nice base for the handsome Italianate house. Its rose garden has recently been refurbished with old roses set in a sea of rosemary, coreopsis and salvia. Adjacent to the villa, Harris Park is a modern design that alludes to classicism. Within the square block, a central pergola is surrounded by four circular "secret gardens" enclosed in yew hedges. This site is a good place to begin a walking or driving tour of the island. The Galveston Historical Foundation at 2016 Strand offers a free guide to the East End Historical District where huge live oaks line the streets, and palms, ferns, oleanders and other luxuriant plants spill out of the gardens behind intriguing iron fences. No plantings on the island pre-date the disastrous 1900 hurricane, but vegetation positively flourishes in this semi-tropical environment.

## The Moody Gardens

*1 Hope Boulevard*
*Galveston, Texas 77554-8928*
☎ *409/744-4673; 800/582-4673*
**Hours** *Sun-Thurs 10-6, Sat & Sun 10-9 (summer); Daily 10-6 (winter)*
**Admission** *$6*
**Accessible** *Yes*

The late Sir Goeffrey Jellicoe's original intent for The Moody Gardens was to reflect the full scope of his history of garden design, *The Landscape of Man*. Only a small portion of this great landscape architect's vision has been realized. The garden's tropical rainforest is truly spectacular! The ten-story glass pyramid displays over 2,000 plant and animal species from the Americas, Asia and Africa. The structure encloses an acre at its base, and flamingos wade in a pool at the entrance. The garden's paths skirt various waterfalls, cross over streams and wander through thickets of ferns, bromeliads, orchids, bamboo, gingers and palms. Colorful birds and butterflies flit through the tree canopy overhead. Bat caves and a Mayan colonnade are but a few of the surprises contained within this verdant greenhouse.

The grounds that surround the rainforest are lush, but they are given over to more commercial enterprises than Jellicoe might have preferred. His "masterwork" was to have illustrated how "civilizations have assembled, nurtured and integrated plants of all kinds into their various forms of gardens and landscapes." Even if funding for such a grand scheme were available, many horticulturists question whether representative historic gardens (a nineteenth-century English rock garden, for example) could have taken root in Galveston's sandy soil. Staff members offer tram tours of the existing gardens and greenhouses on Fridays at 1 p.m.

*Directions: From IH-45 South, exit 61st Street. Right on 61st and again on Seawall Blvd. Right on 81st to Jones Road. Left on Hope Blvd.*

## Houston Metropolitan Area

## Armand Bayou Nature Center

*8600 Bay Area Boulevard*
*Houston, Texas 77058*
☎ *281/474-3074*
**Hours** *Wed 9-dusk, Thurs & Fri 9-5, Sat dawn-5, Sun noon-dusk*
**Admission** *$2.50 (adults); $1 (seniors and children)*
**Accessible** *Partially*

One doesn't expect to find 2,500 unspoiled acres at the edge of one the country's biggest cities, and certainly it is a surprise to discover three different wild habitats — tallgrass prairie, estuary bayou and bottomland hardwood forest — next door to the bustling Johnson Space Center. At the entrance to this pristine preserve, a lovely wood bridge crosses a pond that absolutely teems with life. From there, you'll find a Visitor's Center where you can get a trail map and perhaps visit the gift shop before exploring this vast and tranquil place. Its Coastal prairie environment is especially valuable because only one-percent of such wilderness remains. Behind the center is a restored farm where volunteers demonstrate pioneer-era skills during summer weekends.

*Directions: From Downtown Houston travel south on IH-45. Exit at Bay Area Boulevard and travel east to the intersection at Red Bluff Road and the Center's entrance.*

## Bayou Bend Collection and Gardens

*1 Westcott Street*
*Houston, Texas 77007-7009*
☎ *713/520-2600*
**Hours** *Tues-Sat 10-4:30, Sun 1-4:30; mansion tours by reservation only*
**Admission** *$3 (age 11 and older)*
**Accessible** *Limited*

Out of wild woodlands on the bank of Buffalo Bayou, the finest private garden in Texas was created in the early years of this century. Among the factors that set Bayou Bend apart is its exceptionally strong overall design. (Also see page 11.) Eight distinctive gardens are woven into the fabric of the landscape here. The dense woods open up to reveal the late Miss Ima Hogg's pink stucco house glistening in a sea of bright green grass. Framing the house at the woodland edges are planting beds drawn in sweeping curves and massed with rich evergreen shrubbery. As you walk through the garden, vistas open and close. Formal fountains, charming statuary and colorfulplantings keep your eye moving from place to place.

A broad terraced lawn behind the house leads to a rectangular pool and arching fountain designed to frame a white marble statue of Diana, goddess of the hunt. Here, the sculpture plays dramatically against a backdrop of dark, columnar clipped hedges. Directly west of the Diana Garden is a parterre where Clio, the muse of history, presides on a central pedestal, encircled by brick walks and beds filled with clipped azaleas and boxwoods. Smaller "outdoor rooms" are tucked into the surrounding woods and designed to be experienced in sequence. Members of the River Oaks Garden Club lovingly maintain Bayou Bend. All tours are self-guided.

*Directions: Take Memorial Drive west from downtown. Turn south on Westcott and park in the free public lot. A suspended footbridge leads to Jones Visitor Center.*

## Cullen Sculpture Garden at MFAH

*Bissonet at Montrose*
*Houston, Texas 77005*
☎ *713/639-7375*
**Hours** *9 a.m.-10 p.m.*
**Admission** *Free*
**Accessible** *Yes*

Created by the famous Japanese-American sculptor Isamu Noguchi and opened to the public in 1986, this one-acre site displays masterworks by nineteenth and twentieth-century sculptors. Works by such luminaries as Matisse, Aristide Maillol, Auguste Rodin, Alberto Giacometti, Frank Stella, Ellsworth Kelly, Louise Bourgeois and Anthony Caro animate the space amid a serene envelope of native trees and shrubs. Dedicated to the trustees of the Museum of Fine Arts, the garden provides a perfect setting for events that benefit the museum.

## Harris County Extension Center Display Garden

*#2 Abercrombie Drive*
*Houston, Texas 77084*
☎ *281/855-5600*
**Hours** *Mon-Fri 7:30-4*
**Admission** *Free*
**Accessible** *Yes*

This test and display site offers a wealth of practical ideas. There's a vineyard, fruit trees, a floral display area that's changed-out seasonally and vegetables growing in waist-high raised beds for the benefit of folks in wheelchairs. Novice gardeners will appreciate that plants are labeled and advice is freely given.

*Directions: From downtown take IH-10 west to Highway 6. Travel three miles north on Highway6. Turn right on Patterson, left at Bear Creek Road. The building faces Bear Creek.*

## Houston Arboretum and Nature Center

*4501 Woodway Drive*
*Houston, Texas 77024*
☎ *713/681-8433*
**Hours** *Daily 8:30-6*
**Admission** *Free*
**Accessible** *Alice Brown Interpretive Trail*

This facility in Memorial Park offers city folk a wonderful way to experience the wonders of nature. The 155-acre wildlife sanctuary offers a wide array of classes for adults, family programs and popular year-round adventures for children. (Membership has its advantages in discounted programs.) Sunday lectures and guided walks that begin at 2 and 3 o'clock are free to the public. Five miles of wooded trails wind under the forest canopy, around ponds, through a swamp and a demonstration prairie. These diverse habitats are a great place to reflect on the complex habitats of the Coastal prairies and marshes. In conjunction with the University of Houston, knowledgeable environmentalists teach classes leading toward the Naturalist Certification Program here. Its Nature Store is a great place to find gifts for fellow gardeners.

*Directions: The park is located just south of the intersection of IH-10 and Loop 610 west of downtown.*

## Houston Garden Center

*1500 Hermann Drive, Hermann Park*
*Houston, Texas 77004*
☎ *713/529-3960*
**Hours** *Mon-Fri 8-8, Sat & Sun 10-8; closed Thanksgiving, Christmas and New Years Day*
**Admission** *Free*
**Accessible** *Yes*

Houston's Hermann Park offers gardeners and nature-lovers much to enjoy within its 440 acres. The Houston Garden Center and Museum of Natural Science stand at the north end of the park, across the street from the monumental equestrian statue of Sam Houston. The Garden Center's All-America Rose Garden displays about 2,500 bushes of 93 varieties, which are at peak in late March/early April and again in late October/early November. The wildflower garden is also at its most colorful in spring and fall. In summer, the Fragrance Garden's 80 herbal species come into their own. (Nationally known herbalist Madalene Hill selected the plants, which are divided into aromatic themes.) Other favorites to be found along the Center's walkways include a Bog Garden that features lilies and iris, a Bulb Garden and a Perennial Garden. An International Sculpture Garden is also tucked into a corner of this showcase for garden plants. The Museum of Natural Science next door is noted for its Cockrell Butterfly Garden, which is filled with a collection of tropical plants that will thrill indoor gardeners. The new Japanese Garden is another *must* while you're in Hermann Park. (See next listing.)

*Directions: From downtown take Fannin south and turn left into the park. The Garden Center is just past the Museum of Natural Science; it has a parking lot.*

## Houston Japanese Garden

*Hermann Park (2999 South Wayside Drive)*
*Houston, Texas 77004*
☎ *713/520-3283*
**Hours** *Daily 10-6 (April-Sept); 10-5 (Oct-March)*
**Admission** *$1.50 (adults); $1.00 (seniors); $.25 (children 3-12); free under 3*
**Accessible** *Yes*

One tends to think of a Japanese garden as venerable, but this very young garden already possesses magical qualities. Constructed under the canopy of mature oak and pine trees, it features winding paths that crisscross interconnected ponds. Crepe myrtles are used in lieu of traditional cherry trees to create breathtaking vistas, especially when viewed through the opened screens of the tea house. A garden for all seasons, its Japanese iris, dogwoods and azaleas provide spring color, and the young Japanese maples color the garden in autumn. Japanese landscape architect Ken Nakajima took a Zen approach to the problems inherent in the site: flat topography, existing tree roots that prevented major changes in grade, and a lack of native weather rock. "I had to induce and create a different concept to design the garden," he noted at its inception. He succeeded admirably. This garden will become even more tranquil with age.

*Directions: Located about a block south of the Sam Houston statue.*

## Mercer Arboretum and Botanic Gardens

*22306 Aldine Westfield Road*
*Humble, Texas 7738-1071*
☎ *281/443-8731*
**Hours** *Daily 8-7 (summer); 8-5 (winter); closed Thanksgiving, Christmas and New Years Day*
**Admission** *Free*
**Accessible** *Yes*

The Mercer has something for everyone with its displays of cultivated and native plants. Close to the Botanic Information Center, its gardens have been filled with pleasing perennial beds. There's an iris bog, a vine garden, herb garden, bamboo collection, fern gardens and a tropical garden that's designed to recall a rainforest. Beyond the ¾-acre lily pond, you'll discover loop trails through unspoiled natural areas. More than simply an outstanding public garden, the Mercer's mission includes education and research. As a participating member of the Center for Plant Conservation, Mercer features one of the nation's first Endangered Species Gardens. It hosts a variety of programs for children, adults and families. Knowledgeable volunteers are heavily involved in its programs and maintenance. A vast expanse of forest on the west side of Aldine Westfield Road is the arboretum with its outdoor classroom, Big Thicket Loop, ponds, bogs and picnic pavilion.

*Directions: From IH-45, take FM 1960 east to Aldine Westfield Road. Turn left (north) to the Mercer entrance.*

## Robert A. Vines Environmental Science Center

*8856 Westview*
*Houston, Texas 77055*
☎ *713/365-4175*
**Hours** *Mon-Fri 8:30 -4:45; Botanical garden open daily, dawn to dusk*
**Admission** *Free*
**Accessible** *Yes*

This resource facility for the Spring Branch School District brings together a five-acre arboretum, a museum of Texas wildlife, a geology hall and an oceanography study center. The botanical garden in front of the building features plant materials drawn from Northern Mexico and all parts of Texas. Mike Anderson and his father-in-law, the late Lynn Lowrey (an important name in Texas native flora), designed this residential-scale display. In addition to serving the district, the Center's programs are open to the public . It hosts seminars, wildflower and bird identification classes in spring and fall and educational field trips to such places as the Galapagos Islands, Hawaii and Central America.

*Directions: Located a mile north of the Katy Freeway (IH-10) between Campbell and Bingle Road.*

## *Richmond*

## Brazos Bend State Park

*21901 FM 762*
*Needville, Texas 77461*
☎ *409/553-5101*
**Hours** *Daily year-round 8 a.m.-10 p.m.*
**Admission** *$2 per person age 13 and up; children free*
**Accessible** *Partially*

With almost 5,000 acres and an eastern boundary that fronts on a 3.2-mile stretch of the Brazos River, this lush park is a combination of upland coastal prairies and numerous swales that become freshwater marshes during periods of heavy rain. Visitors are cautioned to pay due respect to alligators in the floodplains! Big Creek meanders diagonally across the park, with tributary sloughs and bayous and cutoffs called "oxbow lakes." Sycamore, cottonwood and black willow line the creek banks. Picnic areas are sited among huge, moss-draped live oaks, and nature trails run along the lakes and through bottomland forests of pecans and various oak species. Ongoing educational programs every weekend explore a half-mile nature/interpretive trail. An informative booklet explains the flora and fauna of the Creekfield Lake Nature Trail. This pilot project includes a series of panels with tactile bronzes of wetland wildlife for the blind, an accessible boardwalk and observation deck for people with limited mobility and a captioned orientation video for visitors with hearing difficulties.

*Directions: The park may be reached by traveling approximately 20 miles southeast of Richmond on FM 762, or by traveling south from Houston approximately 28 miles on State Highway 288 to Rosharon, then west on FM 1462.*

## West Columbia

### Varner-Hogg Plantation State Historical Park
FM Road #2852; P.O. Box 696
West Columbia, Texas 77486
☎ 409/345-4656
**Hours** Grounds open daily year-round during daylight hours. House open Fri & Sat 10-4 Sun, 1-5 or by appointment. Closed Thanksgiving, Christmas, and New Year's Day.
**Admission** Grounds free; House tours: $3 (adults), $1 (students)
**Accessible** Partially

   Established by Martin Varner, member of Stephen F. Austin's "Old Three Hundred," this property pictures colonial life in the early days of Texas. Varner established the first rum distillery in Texas here in 1829, and Varner Creek was used to transport sugar to market from a mill once located on the site. Later Governor James S. Hogg bought the site. Miss Ima Hogg donated the park to the state, and it includes the completely furnished old plantation manor that was her father's home. You'll see lots of plantation-era flora and pecan orchards within its 65 acres. Other park activities include picnicking and bird watching. The interpretive barn (ca. 1890) is open daily.

*Directions: Located two miles north of West Columbia on FM 2852. From Houston, take State Highway 288 south to State Highway 35. Turn south on State Highway 35 and travel 12 miles to West Columbia. Outside West Columbia take FM 2852 to Park Road 51 (1702 North 13th Street).*

## Coastal Bend
### Corpus Christi

### Corpus Christi Botanical Gardens
8545 South Staples Street
Corpus Christi, Texas 78413
☎ 512/852-2100
**FAX** 512/852-7875
**Hours** Tues-Sun 9-5; call for extended summer hours and holiday schedule
**Admission** $2 (adults); $1.50 (seniors); $1 (children 5-12); free to gallery and gift shop
**Accessible** All buildings

   Blessed with a lovely 180-acre site on Oso Creek, this organization is up and coming. Its new greenhouse is home to the Don Larkin Memorial Orchid collection, which is among the largest in the southwest with 2,100 orchids. The four-winged Exhibit House is surrounded by plumeria. The Sensory Garden focuses on sigh, sound, touch and mobility enhancements. A shady Bird and Butterfly Trail leads to panoramic views from the Birding Tower. The Visitors Center houses gift shop and gallery. Nearby, you'll also find water-wise display beds. For children, there's a self-guided tour that identifies animal tracks and native plants in a treasure hunt format. Near the picnic area, there's a 60-bed children's garden area. The facility hosts seminars, workshops and ecology-oriented group tours.

*Directions: From the downtown bayfront area, take Crosstown Expressway (Texas Highway 286) to South Padre Island Drive, Highway 358). Exit Staples Street and turn right (south). Watch for green signs. Cross Oso Creek to entrance.*

## Museum of Science and History

*1900 North Chaparral*
*Corpus Christi, Texas 78401*
☎ *512/883-2862*
**Hours** *Daily during daylight*
**Admission** *Free*
**Accessible** *Yes*

The new Xeriscape demonstration garden on the museum's west side shows just how colorful a water-wise garden can be! About 100 species of native and adapted plants bloom and grow at this outdoor learning center. The scale of the garden is just right for small city lots, and city officials are hoping people will want to copy its example. Exhibits demonstrate how to conserve water by properly planting, irrigating and mulching. Between the museum and the convention center you'll also find a lovely re-circulating fountain. A smaller version of this water feature would make a nice addition to any home garden.

*Directions: Located just north of the city center near the waterfront.*

## Rockport Area

## Goose Island State Park

*HC 01 Box 105*
*Rockport Texas 78382*
☎ *512/729-2858*
**Hours** *Daily year-round 7 a.m.-10 p.m.*
**Admission** *$2 per person age 13 and up; children free*
**Accessible** *Partially*

The St. Charles and Aransas Bays surround Goose Island State Park's 314 acres. Its prized feature is "Big Tree," named state champion Coastal Live Oak in 1969 and thought to be the second-largest in the nation. The 1,000-year-old tree has a circumference of 35 feet, a crown spread of 90 feet and is 44 feet in height. Activities at the park include picnicking, camping, fishing, boating, swimming in the bay (unsupervised), nature study, wildlife observation and photography, and excellent birding. Guided bird tours are held in April each year. Located directly across St. Charles Bay from the park are the wintering grounds for rare and endangered whooping cranes in the Aransas National Wildlife Refuge.

*Directions: Take State Highway 35 north from Rockport across the Copano Causeway to Park Road 13 (about a half-mile north of the bridge), then two miles east to the park entrance.*

## Hummingbird Demonstration Garden and Wetlands Pond

*404 Broadway (Rockport-Fulton Chamber of Commerce)*
*Rockport, Texas 78382*
☎ *1-800/242-0071 or 512/729-6445*
**Hours** *Daily, year-round*
**Admission** *Free*
**Accessible** *Yes*

This community project was built in cooperation with the Texas Department of Public Transportation. A small garden, it was designed to give homeowners ideas for plantings that attract hummingbirds and butterflies. Colorful stands of firecracker bush, cape honeysuckle, hummingbird bush, Mexican bush sage and other salvias provide the nectar that keeps these fascinating creatures returning every spring. Visit the Chamber of Commerce at the address listed above (across the street from the

Rockport Harbor) to see its native plant garden. Here you can obtain information about the Connie Hager Bird Sanctuary, the annual Hummer/Bird Celebration (held in September) and various boat and bus tours that provide close-up views of coastal terrain and wildlife.

*Directions: The hummingbird garden is located in a public rest area east side of Business Highway 35 N, less than ½ mile north of downtown Rockport.*

## Aransas National Wildlife Refuge

*FM 2040*
*Austwell, Texas 77950*
☎ *512/286-3559*
**Hours** *Daily, sunrise to sunset*
**Admission** *$3 per person or $5 per vehicle with two or more people*
**Accessible** *Partially*

Grasslands, live oak and redbay thickets ringed by brackish tidal marshes provide the perfect haven for about 400 species of birds and animals. Best-known as the wintering grounds for whooping cranes, this refuge has counted more bird species than any other refuge in the country. For a human visitor there's a 16-mile paved road, a Wildlife Interpretive Center, 40-foot observation tower, several miles of walking trails and a picnic area.

*Directions: Between Rockport and Port Lavaca, seven miles southeast of Austwell.*

## Sinton

## Welder Wildlife Refuge

*P.O. Box 1400*
*Sinton, Texas 78387*
☎ *512/364-2643*
**Hours** *Guided tours Thurs 3-5; groups by appointment.*
**Admission** *Free*
**Accessible** *Bus is not accessible, you can follow in your car; restroom is okay*

The Welder Wildlife Foundation is a non-profit institution dedicated to wildlife research and education. The two-hour bus tour offers an overview of the sixteen different plant communities that foster 1,300 native species within 7,800 acres. Its diverse topography and habitats make the refuge a treasure-trove for resident wildlife. The Foundation's property is but a small part of a sprawling ranch that has been owned by the same family since it was established as a Spanish land grant. The land has never been under cultivation. Pristine woodlands border the Aransas River, and former river channels form temporary lakes and marshes on the south end of the property. A biological crossroads, the landscape is part coastal in appearance, while other areas more resemble the native brushlands of the Rio Grande Plain. The tour also includes a visit to the Foundation headquarters and a discussion of the organization's objectives.

*Directions: Located on the east side of the Missouri Pacific railroad tracks on U.S. Highway 77 approximately 7.4 miles northeast of Sinton.*

## The Texas Zoo

*Riverside Park, 110 Memorial Drive*
*Victoria, Texas 77902*
☎ *512/573-7681*
**Hours** *Daily 10-6 (April-Aug); 10-5 (Sept-March); closed Thanksgiving, Christmas*
*and New Years*
**Admission** *$2 (adults), $1.50 (seniors), $1 (children)*
**Accessible** *Yes*

   Dedicated to the conservation, protection and preservation of Texas animal species, this zoo is also doing a wonderful job with a natural setting beside the Guadalupe River. Signage is provided to identify plants, and the plants are matched to the needs of the animals. The Butterfly Garden includes the Mexican milkweed that Monarchs love. The Bird Garden is filled with such shrubs as yaupon holly and American beautyberry, and columbine grows under the canopy of large pecans and oaks. Gardeners will also find joy in Victoria's Rose Gardens in Riverside Park.

*Directions: From Highway 87 south of the business district to Highway 59. Turn left on Stayton Street and follow the signs.*

# Valley
## Brownsville

## Gladys Porter Zoo

*500 Ringgold Street*
*Brownsville, Texas 78520*
☎ *956/546-2177 (recording); 210/546-9453 (education office)*
**Hours** *Daily 9-5; extended summer hours*
**Admission** *$6 (adults); $3 (children 2-13); free under 2*
**Accessible** *Yes; strollers, wheelchairs and wagons are available for rent.*

   All animals live in open exhibits completely surrounded by naturally flowing waterways and a botanical wonderland. Over 250 species of tropical and semi-tropical plants bloom year-round in environments that make every attempt to replicate the animals' native habitats in Africa, Asia, Indo-Australia and Tropical America. Among the botanical treasures are a cactus and succulent garden and a rare Hong Kong orchid tree, which no longer exists in the wild.

*Directions: Off Highway 77/83 at 6th and Ringgold*

## Sabal Palm Audubon Center and Sanctuary

*P.O. Box 5052*
*Brownsville, Texas 78523*
☎ *956/541-8034*
**FAX** *956/504-0543*
**Hours** *Tues-Sun, sunrise to sunset (Oct 1-May 30); Sat and Sun only in summer months;*
*Center open 9-5.*
**Admission** *$3 (adults); $1 (students); free to children 6 and under*
**Accessible** *Partially*

   Cradled in a bend of the Rio Grande, this National Audubon Society property is a remnant of a grove of Texas sabal palms and Texas ebony trees that once extended 80 miles upriver. One half-mile loop trail explores how people traditionally used the plants native to this area. A second half-mile trail take you into a "jungle" of plant, animal and bird species, many of which reach their northernmost limit here and occur nowhere else in the United States. The trails are self-guided, but you can borrow or buy trail maps in the Center, which also contains educational displays, a wildlife viewing area and small gift shop.

*Directions: From U.S. Highway 77/83 in Brownsville, turn left at the end of the freeway onto International Boulevard. After ¾ mile, turn right on Southmost. Continue for six miles to the entrance.*

## Donna/Alamo

### Santa Ana National Wildlife Refuge

*Route 2, Box 202A*
*Alamo, Texas 78516*
☎ 956/787-3079
**Hours** *Daily dawn to dusk; call for seasonal hours for the Visitors Center and guided tours*
**Admission** *Free*
**Accessible** *Partially*

The "Gem of the National Refuge System," these 2000+ acres of subtropical forest and native brushlands on the north banks of the Rio Grande offer insight into the ecology of the region. There are guided walks throughout the year and printed guides to all the trails, one of which is paved and completely accessible. You can visit a Spanish moss forest where such species as cedar elm, sugar hackberry, Rio Grande ash, Texas persimmon and a host of other native trees thrive. A two-mile trail loops down to the river. In winter an accessible tram provides a bird's eye view of the scenery.

*Directions: From Highway 83, take FM 907 south to entrance.*

## Mission

### Bentsen-Rio Grande Valley State Park

*P.O. Box 988*
*Mission Texas 78573-0988*
☎ 956/585-1107
**Hours** *Daily year-round 7 a.m.-10 p.m.*
**Admission** *$2 per person age 13 and up; children free*
**Accessible** *Partially*

Located along the Rio Grande five miles southwest of Mission in Hidalgo County, this 587-acre park provides a chance to study unique birds, animals and plants of the region. Professional naturalists conduct daily, on-site bird watching and wildlife tours in winter. The landscape is typified by subtropical resaca woodlands (low-lying, former river channels, which are partially filled with silt) and brushland composed of thicket-forming thorny shrubs and small trees. The resaca banks support luxuriant stands of cedar elm, anaqua, ebony, hackberry, ash and very large Mexican lead trees. Plants and animals (which are illustrated in a brochure) represent the northernmost extension of the Mexican subtropics. You can study nature on three miles of hiking trails. One takes you through the wilderness; the other goes to the river. Guided tours begin at the group pavilion. Visitors meet in that area at 7:00 a.m. and depart at 7:20 a.m. and are picked up by a bus equipped for disabled persons. Tours last from 6 to 8 hours. (Contact the park at the number above or at ☎ 210/519-6448 for specific fees and details on tours.) Income from tours supports the park's conservation efforts.

*Directions: From Mission, take US Highway 83; continue west on Loop 374 for 2.5 miles, then south on FM 2062 for 2.6 miles, and enter on Park Road 43.*

## Rio Grande Plain
### San Antonio

---

### McNay Art Museum

*6000 North New Braunfels Avenue*
*San Antonio, Texas 78209*
☎ *210/824-5368*
**Hours** *Tues-Sat 10-5, Sun 12-5 except New Years day, July 4th, Thanksgiving and Christmas Day; the grounds close at 7 p.m.*
**Admission** *Free*
**Accessible** *Yes*

This museum's building and grounds are as vibrant as the art on display within. Built in the 1920s by Marion Koogler McNay, the Spanish Colonial-style residence sits on an exquisite 23-acre site. Originally built in the form of a horseshoe, the two-story house wraps around a central courtyard with a reflecting pool built in the shape of the rose window of the Mission San Jose. The original tile remains, including a large peacock wall fresco and the Don Quixote story told in individual tiles.

During her lifetime Mrs. McNay was so fond of the courtyard that she directed visitors through a rear drive so that they might enter the house through the open court. Although it was enclosed by the addition of new galleries in the early 70s, the courtyard remains the museum's focal point. Today it's filled with palms, bougainvillea, ferns, night-blooming jasmine and pots of blooming plants and adorned with sculptures by Barbara Hepworth, Renoir, Charles Umlauf and Ana Hyatt Huntington. Water lilies and goldfish enliven the pool. Mrs. McNay's extensive collection of French Post-Impressionist paintings and early twentieth century art has been broadened by the addition of several other major collections of sculpture and paintings. The impressive Marcia and Otto Koehler Fountain commands the entrance to the museum, and the grounds, which include a Japanese-style garden, are maintained in a way that would make the museum's founder proud.

---

### San Antonio Botanical Gardens

*555 Funston Place*
*San Antonio, Texas 78209*
☎ *210/821-5115*
**Hours** *Tues-Sun 9-6*
**Admission** *$3 (adults), $2 (seniors), $1 (children 3-13)*
**Accessible** *Yes*

No visit to San Antonio would be complete without a visit to this remarkable public garden. Located on a hill near Fort Sam Houston, the 33-acre site is ideal for demonstrating every style of gardening, and San Antonio's mild climate is conducive for particularly luxuriant plant displays. Allow lots of time to stroll! Every detail of the "hardscape" is carefully crafted and worthy of note. A trail map leads you through a connected series of gardens that begin with an appealing fountain and arbor. The paths wind through a series of intimate garden rooms, including fragrant, highly tactile raised beds for the blind. Then an opening in a massive rock wall leads into the fabulous Lucile Halsell Conservatory, a complex of bermed, earth-sheltered limestone and glass greenhouses. Organized around a central outdoor courtyard and pond, the conservatory nurtures all manner of tropical and desert plants.

From here you'll enter a 15-acre expanse of native Texas gardens representing the vegetation of Piney Woods, Hill Country and South Texas Plains, complete with reconstructed homesteads. The pathways encircle a lake and then take you to four thematic formal gardens that demonstrate plants of the Bible, roses, herbs and perennials. All pathways lead back to the entrance and then out to the historic Sullivan Carriage House, which houses a fine gift shop, a tea room and lecture hall. Between this building is an extensive xeriscape demonstration exhibit.

*Directions: From IH-35, exit on New Braunfels Ave. and travel north to Funston. Turn right on Funston.*

## Schultz House

*514 Hemisfair Park*
*San Antonio, Texas 78205*
☎ *210/229-9161*
**Hours** *Daily during daylight for garden viewing; gift shop open Tues-Sat 10-4*
**Admission** *Free*
**Accessible** *Yes*

One of the few remaining examples of German-Texas domestic architecture in downtown San Antonio, this 1893 home is now a gift shop operated by Bexar County Master Gardeners. Surrounding the home is a period garden of the late 1800s and demonstration gardens of native and adapted plants, lovingly tended by Master Gardeners. This garden is just a short stroll from the beautiful Paseo del Rio (Riverwalk), which has become a botanical paradise in the last few years, and a few blocks from the King William Historic District. (See next listing.)

*Directions: Located just north of the Federal Courthouse*

## Steves Homestead

*509 King William Street*
*San Antonio, Texas*
☎ *210/224-6163*
**Hours** *Daily during daylight hours for garden viewing; call for house tour hours*
**Admission** *Grounds free; house tour $2*
**Accessible** *Partially*

The only property in the King William Historic District that's open regularly to the public, this Italian Villa-style home is representative of the eclectic Victorian architecture favored by San Antonio's successful merchant class. The garden's floriferous planting beds and a fountain from the Philadelphia Centennial Exposition of 1876 are original to the house and typical of the period. The entire neighborhood warrants exploration on foot. Colorful plantings literally spill out from the iron fences that surround the sturdily built limestone cottages and mansions of this restored enclave. You can pick up a brochure for a walking tour at the Steves Homestead or at the headquarters of the San Antonio Conservation Society (107 King William Street, across from the gazebo in King William Park).

*Directions: About ½ mile south of the Riverwalk and Hemisfair grounds.*

*Three Rivers*

## Choke Canyon State Park

*P.O. Box 1548*
*Three Rivers, Texas 78071*
☎ *512/786-3868*
**Hours** *Daily year-round 6 a.m.-10 p.m.*
**Admission** *$3 per person age 13 and up; children free*
**Accessible** *Partially*

Choke Canyon State Park, consisting of two units, South Shore and Calliham, is located on the 26,000-acre Choke Canyon Reservoir. Here Indians crossed the Frio River Valley more than 10,000 years ago, following bison and mammoth. Numerous archaic sites in the area have been recorded. Two miles of hiking trails, a mile-long bird trail with feeders and a wildlife educational center that offers educational programs are among the attractions for naturalists. A wide variety of wildlife inhabits the dense thickets of mesquite and blackbush acacia. The reservoir and surrounding terrain are characterized by eroded, gently-rolling brushland crossed by silted stream valleys. The dam is near a 30-million-year-old Gulf shoreline.

*Directions: South Shore Unit is located 3.5 miles west of Three Rivers on State Highway 72. Calliham Unit is located 12 miles west of Three Rivers on State Highway 72 to Tilden.*

*Zapata*

## Falcon State Park

*P.O. Box 2*
*Falcon Heights, Texas 78545*
☎ *956/848-5327*
**Hours** *Daily year-round 6 a.m.-10 p.m.*
**Admission** *$2 per person age 13 and up; children free*
**Accessible** *Partially*

Falcon State Park at the southern end of the International Falcon Reservoir offers 1.75 miles of hiking/nature trails, of which a mile has signs detailing plant life. Mesquite, huisache, wild olive, ebony, cactus and native grasses cover gently rolling hills. Falcon Lake is very popular with bird watchers; varied and interesting bird life consists of common resident birds that range throughout the American Southwest and many of the tropical species for which this is a northernmost outpost.

*Directions: From Zapata, take US Highway 83 to FM 2098, then go southwest for three miles to Park Road 46. From Roma, go 15 miles west on US Highway 83 to FM 2098 to Park Road 46.*

# Central Blacklands & Savannas
## Bastrop

---

## Bastrop State Park

P.O. Box 518
Bastrop, Texas 78602-0518
☎ 512/321-2101
**Hours** *Daily year-round during daylight hours*
**Admission** *$3 per person age 13 and up; children free*
**Accessible** *Partially*

Here's the famous "Lost Pines," a heavily timbered region of loblolly pine and hardwoods which is isolated from the main body of East Texas pines by approximately 100 miles of post oak savanna. The park's 3,500-plus acres provide opportunities for backpacking, camping, picnicking, fishing, swimming, golf, bicycling and hiking. Special tours including a three-hour interpretive bus tour in summer months and the "Houston Toad Tour," a guided night time interpretive trip to study an endangered species. The beautiful Lost Pines, huge live oaks and rugged hills make this park one of the most treasured in Texas. Many species of wildlife scurry through the woods. A checklist of the bird life of Bastrop and nearby Buescher State Park is available at the park headquarters.

*Directions: The park is one mile east of Bastrop on Highway 21. It's also accessible from the east on Highway 71 or by way of Buescher State Park along Park Road 1.*

## Hempstead

---

## Peckerwood Garden Foundation

Route 3, Box 103
Hempstead, Texas 77445
☎ 409/826-3232
**FAX** 409/826-0522
**Hours** *By reservation only (on spring and fall open days)*
**Admission** *$5.00 tax-deductible donation*
**Accessible** *No*

The winter 1998 newsletter of The Garden Conservancy announced the transition of this fabulous private enclave to a public garden. The opening statement read, "For thirty years, Peckerwood Garden, in Hempstead, Texas has been evolving under the expert care of John G. Fairey. Mr. Fairey, whose background in landscape architecture and fine art are evident in the garden's design, is responsible for introducing a wide range of rare, native plants from Mexico to an American audience. The Garden Conservancy is pleased to support [the foundation] in its mission to preserve the garden and increase public awareness of the value and beauty of native plants." Mr. Fairey wrote, "There are many useful ways to describe Peckerwood Garden: it is a collection of more than 3,000 plants, including many rarities; it is a conservation garden containing examples of numerous threatened species, many of which are no longer found in the wild; it is a laboratory garden testing a wide range of "new plants and our Mexican discoveries. It is a garden with a mission to encourage other gardeners to see a beauty in a landscape that is consistent with our plants and climate." Personalized horticultural tours are available year-round for individuals and families and general tours for garden clubs and organized outings (with personnel available to answer questions). Because of the rarity of the plants, several strict rules apply. (No children under 12 are allowed in the nursery or garden, for example.) There is a $50.00 tax-deductible fee to hold the date for tours. Sales from Yucca Do Nursery, Inc. (see page 248) benefit the Peckerwood Garden Conservation Trust.

*Luling*

## Palmetto State Park

*RR 5, Box 201*
*Gonzales, Texas 78629*
☎ *830/672-3266*
**Hours** *Daily year-round 8 a.m.-10 p.m.*
**Admission** *$2 per person age 13 and up; children free*
**Accessible** *Partially*

Palmetto State Park is named for the tropical dwarf sabal palm found here. Diverse flora abounds throughout this unusual botanical area in which the ranges of eastern and western species merge. The San Marcos River runs through this park, which also incorporates a four-acre oxbow lake. Artesian wells produce distinctive, sulfur-laden water. Although there are no tours at this time, there is a mile-long interpretive trail and two miles of hiking trails.

One way to really see the riparian flora is by canoe. You can put in at Luling City Park and travel 14 miles to Palmetto, portaging around one dam along the way; or put in at Palmetto and take out at Slayden bridge, 7.5 miles down river. It's a two-day trip from Luling City Park to Slayden bridge (over-night in Palmetto along the way). Rentals are available at Spencer Canoes (☎ 512/357-6113) in Martindale. Check river conditions and make reservations (☎ 512/389-8900) if you plan to overnight. Take-in and take-out points are limited, mostly bordered by private land. There are no rapids, but there's usually a steady current.

*Directions: Travel ten miles northwest of Gonzales on US 183 to FM 1586, then west on FM 1586 for two miles to Ottine, then south on Park Road 11; or go six miles southeast of Luling on US 183, then southwest on Park Road 11 for two miles.*

*Moody*

## Mother Neff State Park

*Rt. 1, Box 58*
*Moody, Texas 76557*
☎ *254/853-2389*
**Hours** *Daily year-round; no gate*
**Admission** *$2 per person age 13 and up; children free*
**Accessible** *Partially*

The first official state park in Texas, Mother Neff State Park is named for Isabella Eleanor Neff, who donated land along the Leon River to the state in 1916. Her son, Pat Neff, served as Governor from 1921 to 1925. After his mother's death in '21, this gift became the nucleus of the State Park System. In 1935 an excavation unearthed three Indian graves and numerous prehistoric artifacts in the park. The terrain is a mix of prairie land and rugged limestone hills overlooking the rich bottomland of the Leon, which is shaded by pecans, cottonwood, sycamore and several species of oak trees. Wildflowers blanket the park in spring, and its hillsides are covered with dense thickets of cedar and oak. You'll also discover ravines and rock cliffs with a rich array of vegetation and wildlife. Hikers can explore a network of trails through the park. Cultural and natural resource programs and activities are held most weekends.

*Directions: From IH-35, take exit 315 to State Highway 107 west to Moody; continue six miles west on FM 107, then take State Highway 236 for two miles to the park.*

## Temple/ Belton

## Miller Springs Nature Center

P.O. Box 1343
Temple, Texas 76503
☎ 254/298-5720 or 254/939-3551
**Hours** Daily during daylight
**Admission** Free
**Accessible** No

This 266-acre conservation area on the Leon River below Lake Belton Dam was well-known in the time of early settlers, and its rock shelters had been used by Native American long before. Plans for an environmental learning center are still unrealized, but the trails offer a rich mosaic of mixed hardwood forest, limestone cliffs, springs and pools.

*Directions: From IH-35 (traveling south) take Highway 2305 west from Temple. Turn left on Highway 2271. From IH-35 (traveling north) take Highway 317 north from Belton, then left on 2305 and left on 2271. The preserve is north of the spillway.*

## Round Top

## McAshan Gardens of Festival Hill

P.O. Drawer 89
Round Top, Texas 78954
☎ 409/249-3129
**Hours** Gardens open during daylight hours
**Admission** Free; group tours available at a fee for groups
**Accessible** Difficult on gravel paths

More than a mecca for music, the International Festival-Institute is a wonderful, improbable landscape-in-the-works! James Dick's earliest vision for this place included planting more than 18,000 trees on his 100-acre utopia. Now, the site is emerging as a vast romantic landscape painting as eclectic as the Institute's cast of international musicians. In 1993 stonemason Jack Finke began turning "reject" stone salvaged from a quarry near Georgetown into a massive "Roman bridge" and waterfall that spills into a duck pond. As featured in the July 1997 issue of *Country Living*, the site's handsome structures, walls and other robust "follies" now recall Celtic, Roman, Moorish and medieval European architecture. Beautiful old statuary and benches are skillfully woven into the fabric of the landscape, and the mother-daughter culinary team of Madalene Hill and Gwen Barclay has contributed their herb collection to the site. Colorful perennials and roses are combined with fragrant, edible plants in four Mediterranean herb gardens. (Call for information about their workshops and other special events.) Organic in feel and still germinating in the artists' imagination, this landscape will continue to progress as time allows. "Nature is a great teacher," James has been quoted. "That everything is interconnected is her greatest lesson."

*Directions: Round Top is about half way between Austin and Houston on Texas Highway 237 of US 290.*

## Cameron Park

*Cameron Park Drive*
*Waco, Texas 76707*
☎ *254/750-5996 or 1-800/922-6386 (Waco Tourist Information Center)*
**Hours** *6 a.m.-midnight*
**Admission** *Free*
**Accessible** *Partially*

Filled with twisting roads and ancient trees, this large urban park is an under-appreciated Texas treasure. Located just a few blocks west of boring old IH-35 you'll discover dramatic cliffs, scenic overlooks high above the confluence of the Brazos and Bosque Rivers, a wildflower preserve (Miss Nellie's Pretty Place) and Proctor Springs. Another unexpected pleasure is the new Cameron Park Zoo, a 53-acre natural habitat, which occupies the east end of the park. Hiking trails crisscross the park's 416 acres where you'll find lots of scenic spots for picnics. Request a trail map from the Tourist Information Center at the numbers listed above or stop by (it's located on the east side of the freeway at the entrance to Fort Fisher.) You'll pass Indian Spring Park and Waco's answer to the Brooklyn Bridge on your way to Cameron Park. If you have time, stop and take a look at the old suspension bridge.

*Directions: From IH-35 take Exit 335B and travel west on University Parks Drive, which turns into Cameron Park Drive.*

## Earle-Harrison House and Nell Pape Gardens

*1901 North 5th Street*
*Waco, Texas 76708*
☎ *254/753-2032 or 254/752-2667 (Nell Pape Garden Center)*
**Hours** *Gardens open daily, dawn to dusk*
**Admission** *Free*
**Accessible** *Yes*

A winding brick walk invites a stroll through five acres of elegant gardens between two historic homes built during the pre-Civil War era when cotton plantations fueled Waco's economy. A recent work of garden art by landscape architect Hal Stringer, the garden was designed to evoke the graciousness of the Old South. Its rolling lawns are shaded by giant live oaks, and its walkways lead to a lily pond, fountain and handsome double gazebo. Planting beds are filled with old-fashioned flowers, fragrant herbs and vegetables useful to nineteenth-century cooking.

*Directions: Located just south of the Cameron Park Zoo. (North 5th street is parallel to University Parks Drive.)*

## Sculpture Garden at The Art Center of Waco

*1300 College Drive*
*Waco, Texas 76708*
☎ *254/752-4371*
**Hours** *Daily dawn to dusk; Art Center open Tues-Sat 10-5, Sun 1-5*
**Admission** *Free*
**Accessible** *Yes*

Once the William Cameron family's summer home, The Art Center now occupies two and a half acres between Cameron Park and McLennan Community College. Art and nature mix here in a Sculpture Garden that was designed to take advantage of a breathtaking view of the river valley below. A walk through the serene natural settings of both the upper- and lower-level trails introduces you to some thirty works of art, primarily by Texas sculptors. There's a playful spirit to many of the works, and the pieces are carefully placed to surprise and delight visitors. "The Waco Door" a 22-foot-tall monolith by internationally-renowned Waco native Robert Wilson is the garden's signature piece. Hal Stringer laid out the grounds of both the Art Center and the beautifully wooded college campus next door.

*Directions: There is no direct connection from within Cameron Park up to the Art Center, but you can cross a bridge over the Brazos River from Herring Street and turn left onto Lake Shore Drive. From IH-35 traveling north take Exit 338 (traveling south take Exit 339) onto Lake Shore Drive. Turn into McLennan Community College. On campus, take the second left and then the first left.*

## *Hill Country*
### *Austin Metropolitan Area*

### *Austin Area Garden Center/ Zilker Botanical Gardens*

*2220 Barton Springs Road*
*Austin, Texas 78746-5737*
☎ *512/477-8672*
**Hours** *Daily, 7 a.m.-7:30 p.m.*
**Admission** *Free*
**Accessible** *Partially*

The Zilker Botanical Gardens grew out of the cooperative efforts of several local garden clubs, whose members continue to use the Garden Center's facilities for meetings, flower shows and plant sales. Started without any serious funding or cohesive master plan, the gardens have evolved into a remarkably lovely place. The site is spectacular. Highlights include a Japanese Garden literally carved out of a cliff by Isamu Taniguchi, who worked with no salary and no restrictions in his retirement years to create the most tranquil retreat in the city. "It is my desire for the peace of mankind which has endowed this man of old age the physical health and stamina to pile stone upon stone without a day's absence from the work for the last 18 months," he said at its completion in the late 1960s. He maintained his work of art until his death in 1992.

The Rose Garden's Gazebo remains one of Austin's most popular places for outdoor weddings. And, the Xeriscape Demonstration Garden and Douglas Blachly Butterfly Trail are interesting new additions that reflect the spirit of environmentally-conscious Austinites. Before the crash of '84, plans called for greatly enlarging the garden's scope. Now that Austin is booming again, perhaps these ambitious schemes will be revived. FloraRama, the garden's annual spring fund-raiser, is a terrific place to find unusual plants from vendors throughout Texas. The gift shop has wonderful custom-designed tee-shirts, as well as seeds, toys and note cards.

*Directions: From downtown, cross the river on Congress Avenue, turn right on Barton Springs Road and continue past Barton Springs pool.*

## Austin Nature Preserves

2416 Barton Springs Road
Austin, Texas 78746
☎ 512/327-8180 (Austin Nature and Science Center)
**Mailing Address:** 301 Nature Center Drive (78746)
**Hours** Daily dawn to dusk. Some preserves in the system are open by appointment only.
**Admission** Free
**Accessible** No

The Austin Nature and Science Center and Zilker Preserve (at the address above) features a meadow-edged creek, streamside habitats and a high cliff with shallow caves. Foot trails are accessed from Barton Springs Road under the Loop 1 bridge. Here, you can obtain maps to explore Austin's other preserves, which include Mayfield Park, a turn-of-the-century lake cottage retreat with five lily ponds and woodland trails. Bee Creek Nature Preserve showcases a steep ravine with seeps, springs and particularly beautiful flora. Onion Creek Wildlife Sanctuary preserves old pecan groves and rare native Texas Bluegrass growing along the stream banks. The Indiangrass Wildlife Sanctuary in east Travis County, where "East Texas forest meets Blackland Prairie," displays five acres of blooming gayfeather each fall.

*Directions: Two blocks west of the Garden Center entrance; park under the bridge.*

## Lady Bird Johnson Wildflower Center

4801 La Crosse Avenue
Austin, Texas 78739
☎ 512/292-4100 (general information) or 292-4200 (education programs
and volunteer opportunities)
**FAX** 512/292-4630
**Hours** Tues-Sun 9-5:30; Wildflower Café Tues-Sat 10-4, Sun 11-4
**Admission** $4.00 adults, $2.50 seniors & students, children (4 and under) free.
**Accessible** Yes

This is a must-visit for every Texan! The plantings and water features here illustrate just how rich and varied a Hill Country landscape can be. However, the Center's courtyard plantings and two-acres of demonstration gardens are instructional for home gardeners from every region of the state. The planting beds here are on a scale that easily translates to gardens of modest size. For those with large properties to maintain, the Center's stylized meadow, which is planted to create "ribbons of color," and its remnant live oak prairie also provide a model.

One very interesting feature is the Center's rainwater collection system, which uses cisterns and aqueducts to collect and distribute by drip irrigation 250,000 gallons of water into the garden annually. (Although the entire complex consists strictly of Texas natives, the plants do need an occasional drink in the driest months.) The Wildflower Center's purpose is almost entirely education-oriented. Its Clearinghouse contains an extensive research library, database and slide collection of wildflower species. It has compiled lists of recommended species for every region and published bibliographies and fact sheets on numerous subjects, from how to plant a buffalo grass lawn to organizing a community wildflower project.

Over 20,000 members support the Center. Members are admitted free, partake in the workshops and classes and receive the Wildflower newsletter. They also receive a 10% discount at Wild Ideas (the bookstore/gift shop) and enjoy reciprocal benefits at other botanical gardens and arboreta across the country.

*Directions: Take Loop 1 (Mopac) south across the river, past Slaughter Lane. Turn left on La Crosse Blvd.*

## McKinney Falls State Park

*5808 McKinney Falls Parkway*
*Austin, Texas 78744*
☎ *512/243-1643*
**Hours** *Daily year-round 7 a.m.-10 p.m.*
**Admission** *$2 per person age 13 and up; children free*
**Accessible** *Partially*

McKinney Falls State Park was named for Thomas F. McKinney, who came to Texas in the early 1820s as one of Stephen F. Austin's first 300 colonists. Around 1850 McKinney moved to Travis County where he became a prominent breeder of race horses. Preserved in the 640-acre park are the ruins of his trainer's cabin and the stabilized ruins of his own homestead. There's a ¾-mile interpretive hiking trail and 3.7 miles of hike and bike trails. Fees are charged per person for various types of interpretive tours; contact the park for specific information/reservations.

*Directions: The park is located 13 miles southeast of Austin off US Highway 183. Take McKinney Falls Parkway south, off US Highway 183 to the park entrance.*

## Texas Governor's Mansion

*1010 Colorado Street*
*Austin, Texas 78701*
☎ *512/463-5518*
**Hours** *Daily dawn to dusk*
**Admission** *Free*
**Accessible** *Yes*

Originally simple and somewhat utilitarian in design, The Governor's Mansion was redesigned in the 1960's in the garden style of the Old South with formal beds and clipped hedges. Because it occupies one of the most visible square blocks in downtown Austin, the Mansion has been recently updated to reflect a more "politically correct" approach to gardening, to quote County Agent Ted Fisher. The brick walks and walls remain, but many of the high-maintenance plantings have been replaced with Texas natives, antique roses and such tough old-fashioned perennials as daylilies and Louisiana iris. It has been designated a "Wildspace" in cooperation with the Parks and Wildlife Department's backyard habitat program. The Men's Garden Club of Austin maintains a large vegetable and herb garden. All garden trimmings are composted and reused. Groups of ten or more may request a tour of the gardens by appointment. House tours are conducted every 20 minutes, Monday through Friday from 10 until 11:40 a.m.

*Directions: One block south and west of the Capitol.*

## Umlauf Sculpture Garden

*605 Robert E. Lee Road*
*Austin, Texas 78704-1453*
☎ *512/445-5582*
**Hours** *Thurs, Sat & Sun 1-4, Fri 10-4:30*
**Admission** *$2 (general; $1 (student); free to members and children under 6*
**Accessible** *Yes*

Charles Umlauf was already an acclaimed artist when he moved to Austin to teach life drawing and sculpture at the University of Texas in 1941. During his forty years of teaching, he produced works in bronze, stone, wood and terra cotta that brought him international fame. His subject matter was diverse, ranging from lyrical abstractions to detailed figurative pieces (mothers and children are a recurring theme), animals

*(Listing continued on next page)*

and mythological creatures. Here you'll see about 150 of his works strategically placed along the pathways in a shady six-acre garden complete with a re-circulating stream and waterfalls. Volunteers manage and maintain the collection. Austin's Parks and Recreation Department maintains the garden, which is planted with native trees and shrubs.

*Directions: Turn south off Barton Springs Road onto Robert E. Lee.*

---

## Westcave Preserve

*24814 Hamilton Pool Road*
*Round Mountain, Texas 78663*
☎ *830/825-3442*
**Hours** *Sat and Sun only; tours at 10, 12, 2 and 4. Thirty people per tour; no reservations accepted*
**Admission** *Free, donation encouraged*
**Accessible** *No*

Westcave Preserve is a grassland savanna with wildflower meadows and stands of juniper/live oak woodlands. The collapsed roof of a huge limestone cave caused its most interesting feature. Here, a canopy of cypress trees has created a gorgeous natural terrarium. Plan to picnic at nearby Hamilton Pool. (Formerly a privately-owned and somewhat trashy "hippie" hangout, Hamilton Pool is now open daily and well-maintained as a Travis County Park.) Here, a 50-foot waterfall spills into an incredible natural grotto.

*Directions: Take Highway 71 to Hamilton Pool Road. Hamilton Pool is about 13 miles from Highway 71, and Westcave Preserve is one mile beyond.*

---

## Wild Basin Wilderness

*805 South Capitol of Texas Highway*
*Austin, Texas 78746*
☎ *512/327-7622*
**Hours** *Trails open daily, dawn to dusk, office: Mon-Fri 9-4:30, Sat & Sun 9-5*
**Admission** *Free*
**Accessible** *Partially*

Wild Basin is 227 tranquil acres on an escarpment where woodlands meet grasslands. Two and a half miles of trails begin from the Environmental Education Center. Here you can obtain the book, *The Trails of Old Time Texas*. The Easy Access Trail has benches every 300 feet and no steep inclines. However, to fully experience the beauty, wear good walking shoes and explore it all. You'll be rewarded with ponds, a waterfall, wonderful scenic views, wildflowers and a wide variety of Hill Country trees and shrubs. The organization is membership supported; guided tours are available.

*Directions: Located on the east side of Loop 360, 1.5 miles north of Bee Caves Road.*

# Bend

---

## Colorado Bend State Park

*Box 118*
*Bend, Texas 76824*
☎ *915/628-3240*
**Hours** *Daily, year-round, except during public deer hunts (call for dates)*
**Admission** *$3 per person age 13 and up; children free; Gorman Falls tour: $2 (adults) $1 (children), Cave tour: $10 per person.*
**Accessible** *Partially*

Colorado Bend's more than 5,000 acres offer outdoor enthusiasts access to primitive camping, 11.7 miles of hiking trails and eight miles of mountain bike trails. When the water level at Lake Buchanan is normal, ten miles of the river from the park's boat ramp to the lake are navigable. This is a trip on slow moving water through the beautiful canyon lands of the Colorado River. For Texas Conservation Passport holders, observation blinds over a baited site are available for wildlife viewing and photography.

Other day-activities include guided tours to Gorman Falls (an impressive, 60-foot-high waterfall) and wild cave tours. (Both the caves and the fragile environment of the falls are closed except through guided tours.) The fall's travertine formations and associated lush vegetation are exceptionally scenic. Small natural dams have formed quiet clear-water pools, which support a variety of aquatic communities. Birders will enjoy viewing some of 155 species of birds here, including golden-cheeked warblers, black-capped vireos and bald eagles. Plans include development of some areas of the park, but the intent is to retain the park's pristine wilderness.

*Directions: The park is west of Lampasas, southeast of San Saba. From the intersection of US Highways 281 and 183 in Lampasas, take FM 580 west 24 miles to Bend and follow the signs four miles to the park entrance. From San Saba, take US Highway 190 about four miles to FM 580 and follow the signs 13 miles to Bend; follow the signs four miles to the park entrance. The headquarters and main camping are six miles past the entrance on the gravel road (unmarked County Road 257). The access road is subject to flooding.*

## *Boerne*

### *Guadalupe River State Park & Honey Creek State Natural Area*

*3350 Park Road 31*
*Spring Branch, Texas 78070*
☎ *830/438-2656*
**Hours** *Park open daily, year-round Mon-Thurs 8-8, Fri 8 a.m.-midnight, Sun 8 a.m.-10 p.m.; Honey Creek open for guided naturalist tours at 9:00 a.m. Saturdays only. Reservations are not required, but call the State Park to confirm. Access is through the park.*
**Admission** *$4 per person age 13 and up; children free*
**Accessible** *Partially*

Located on the boundary between Comal and Kendall Counties, this 1938-acre park is bisected by the clear waters of the Guadalupe. On its winding path, the river courses over four natural rapids. Two steep limestone bluffs reflect its awesome erosive power. Bottomland trees include sycamore, elm, basswood, pecan, walnut, persimmon, willow, and hackberry. In the uplands away from the river, the limestone terrain is typical of the Edwards Plateau. One area of virgin Ashe juniper woodland provides the perfect nesting habitat for the rare golden-cheeked warbler. In addition to numerous species of birds, the park supports a wide variety of wild animals. Visitors can participate in a multitude of outdoor activities: canoeing, fishing, swimming, tubing and camping. Access to the Guadalupe River is available from the day-use area, which has picnic sites and ample parking. The park offers three miles of hiking trails and a Texas State Park Store, which sells nature items and books for children and adults.

The adjacent Honey Creek State Natural Area, once a 2300-acre ranch, was acquired from the Texas Nature Conservancy in 1985 and opened for guided tours only. Chipped stone tools attest to the use of Honey Creek by early hunter-gatherers, and arrowheads give silent testimony of later tribes. The two-hour, guided interpretive tour introduces history, geology, flora and fauna along two miles of nature trails.

*(Listing continued on next page)*

Ashe juniper, live oak, agarita and Texas persimmon dominate the dry, rocky hills, and a few grasses find enough soil in the cracks to persist. Juniper and baccharis are being removed from the upland flats, and stands of native grasses are increasing. Down in the creek's canyon you'll notice cedar elm and old junipers and the rather abrupt appearance of Spanish oak, pecan, walnut and Mexican buckeye. Finally, the terrain levels out again in the narrow flood plain and the creek itself. Here, the dominant species are sycamore and bald cypress, associated with an assortment of flood plain species. Columbine and maidenhair fern occur along the rock banks and a number of emergent plants are plainly visible in the clear blue-green water. Overall, the property's nine soil types can easily be distinguished by changes in the dominant vegetation. The diverse habitats provide homes for varied and abundant fauna.

*Directions: From IH-35, travel west on State Highway 46 through New Braunfels, eight miles west of US Highway 281. Turn right on Park Road 31. From San Antonio take Highway 281 north 30 miles to Highway 46.*

## Fredericksburg

---

### Enchanted Rock State Natural Area

*RR 4, Box 170*
*Fredericksburg, Texas 78624*
☎ 915/247-3903
**Hours** *Daily year-round; gate closed occasionally due to overcrowding or floods*
**Admission** *$5 per person age 13 and up; children free*
**Accessible** *Partially*

People have been visiting Enchanted Rock for over 11,000 years. This huge, pink granite boulder rises 425 feet above ground, covering 640 acres. It's the second-largest batholith (an underground rock formation uncovered by erosion) in the United States. Tonkawa Indians believed ghost fires flickered at the top and heard weird creaking and groaning, which geologists now say resulted from the rock's heating by day and contracting in the cool night.

The four major plant communities of Enchanted Rock are open oak woodland, mesquite grassland, floodplain and granite rock community. Live oak, post oak and blackjack oak dominate the oak woodland, with black hickory in more moist areas. Common shrubs are Texas persimmon, agarita, white brush and prickly pear. The mesquite grassland, once an area of bluestem, is now covered with non-native grasses and invasive mesquite. Elm, pecan, hackberry, black hickory, soapberry and oak characterize the floodplains. Common shrubs are white buckeye, agarita, Texas persimmon, Roosevelt weed and buttonbush. In spring the bluebonnets, Indian paintbrush, yellow coreopsis, bladderpod and basin bellflower bloom. A bird checklist for the park is available upon request.

Primitive backpacking, camping, hiking, technical and rock climbing, picnicking, geological study, bird watching and star gazing are favored activities in the park's 1,643.5 acres. Enchanted Rock was designated a National Natural Landmark in 1970 and was placed on the National Register of Historic Places in 1984. Do not disturb plant or animal life, geological features, or Indian or historical artifacts — they're protected by law! Rock climbers must check in at headquarters. A four-mile trail for backpacking and day-hiking winds around the granite formations, and a short, steep foot trail leads to the top.

*Directions: The park is 18 miles north of Fredericksburg on Ranch Road 965, or from Llano, take State Highway 16 for 14 miles south and then go west on Ranch Road 965.*

## Johnson City

## Pedernales Falls State Park

*RR 1 Box 450*
*Johnson City, Texas 78636*
☎ *830/868-7304*
**Hours** *Daily year-round Mon-Thurs 8-5, Fri & Sat 8-7, Sun 8-10, except when wildlife management activities require closure of all or part of the park.*
**Admission** *$4 per person age 13 and up; children free*
**Accessible** *Partially*

Although the scenic Pedernales River is the focal point, other areas interest nature lovers. There are 19.8 miles of hiking, mountain biking and equestrian trails, plus another eight miles of backpack trails. Well-marked, they pass through hills dotted with oak and juniper woodlands and provide access to more-heavily-wooded areas of pecan, elm, sycamore, walnut and hackberry in the major drainage ways. Ash, buttonbush and cypress grow on the terrace adjacent to the river. Other activities include camping, picnicking, river swimming, tubing and looking for over 150 species of birds that have been seen in the park. Pedernales Falls, the park's main attraction, can be viewed from a scenic overlook at the north end of the park where the river drops about 50 feet over a distance of 3,000 feet. The falls are formed by the flow of water over the tilted, stair-step effect of layered limestone that belongs to the 300-million-year-old Marble Falls formation and is part of the southwestern flank of the Llano Uplift.

*Directions: Travel nine miles east of Johnson City on FM 2766 or travel 32 miles west from Austin on US Highway 290, then north on FM 3232 for six miles.*

## Kerrville

## Riverside Nature Center

*150 Lemos Street*
*Kerrville, Texas 78028*
☎ *830/257-4837*
**Hours** *Dawn-dusk; 10-2 (office hours)*
**Admission** *Free*
**Accessible** *Yes*

This newly established, self-guided arboretum boasts 100 species of native trees. Signs along the trail identify the trees and provide information about their usefulness to both humans and wildlife. Over 100 native wildflowers bloom in their seasons, and you'll discover more than a dozen different grasses and cacti. Located only a few blocks from the downtown area, this former farm is now a setting for numerous nature classes and field trips. The Center maintains a resource library on Hill Country environmental topics.

### *Vanderpool*

---

## Lost Maples State Natural Area

*HCR 1, Box 156*
*Vanderpool Texas 78885*
☎ *830/966-3413; Fall Hotline: 1-800/792-1112, select 3, then 1 for foliage updates.*
**Hours** *Daily year-round 8 a.m.-10 p.m.*
**Admission** *$5 (Oct & Nov); $4 (Dec-Sept). Prices are per person age 13 and up; children free*
**Accessible** *Partially*

Lost Maples State Natural Area covers over 2,000 scenic acres in Bandera and Real Counties on the Sabinal River. You'll find a half-mile nature trail and 11 miles of hiking trails. Its steep, rugged limestone canyons, springs, plateau grasslands, wooded slopes and clear streams make this a prime example of Hill Country landscape. Its claim to fame is a large, isolated stand of bigtooth maple, which produces spectacular fall foliage. Generally, the leaves turn the last two weeks of October through the first two weeks of November.

Rare species of birds, such as the Green Kingfisher, can be seen year-round. The endangered Black-capped vireo and Golden-cheeked warbler nest and feed in the park in spring and early summer. Archaeological evidence shows that prehistoric peoples used this area at various times. Today's visitors enjoy picnics, nature study, camping, backpacking, photography, bird watching, fishing and swimming. People must stay on designated trails, because maples have a shallow root system, and soil compaction can damage the trees. Also, many natural hazards exist due to the steep, rugged terrain. The less-athletic can drive approximately a mile into the park to view foliage. Parking is limited to 250 cars, and this popular park is often crowded. Schedule trips during the weekdays, if possible.

*Directions: The park is located five miles north of Vanderpool on Ranch Road 187.*

# *Red Rolling Plains*
## *Abilene*

---

## Abilene State Park

*150 Park Road 32*
*Tuscola, Texas 79562*
☎ *915/572-3204*
**Hours** *Daily year-round except Pecan Grove, which is closed Dec & Feb*
**Admission** *$3 per person age 13 and up; children free*
**Accessible** *Partially*

This park is located in the Callahan Divide, in a semi-arid region of short prairie grass, brushland and wooded stream valleys where you'll find mesquite, juniper, cedar, native pecan, elm, live oaks, hackberry, Texas red oak and red bud trees. Wildlife observation and photography are popular pastimes here, and nature trail tours are available on request. The CCC did the original park construction in the early 1930's. A portion of the official Texas longhorn herd now resides at the site. Comanches used the present-day picnic area as a campground.

*Directions: To reach the park, travel 16 miles southwest of Abilene, through Buffalo Gap, on FM 89, then on Park Road 32 to the park entrance.*

# Abilene Zoological Gardens

2050 Zoo Lane
Abilene, Texas 79602
☎ 915/676-6085
**Hours** Daily 9-7 (summer), 9-5 (winter )
**Admission** $3 (adults); $2 (children); free under 3
**Accessible** Yes

This zoo garden offers inspiration to gardeners looking for alternatives to standard annual bedding plants and imported trees and shrubs. Rather than landscape with water-guzzling exotic plants, the city's landscape architects have chosen to focus on plants indigenous to Abilene. Especially interesting is its wetland habitat exhibit, which features native riparian plants. The wildflower/ butterfly exhibit is filled with native cold hardy perennials, including a fine collection of salvias.

*Directions: Near the intersection of Highway 36 and Loop 322 in Nelson Park.*

# McMurry Iris Garden

McMurry University Campus
Abilene, Texas 79605
☎ 915/691-6200
**Hours** Daily, dawn to dark
**Admission** Free
**Accessible** Yes

April is the month to see this collection of iris in bloom. Established in 1963 by Dr. Joe Humphrey, a former professor, the one-acre site displays some 650 varieties. All are catalogued, and some are labeled. We hope the collection will be treasured and preserved.

*Directions: Take First Street west of downtown, and turn left on Sayles Boulevard. The garden is near the intersection of 16th and Sayles.*

## Big Spring

# Big Spring State Park

#1 Scenic Drive
Big Spring, Texas 79720
☎ 915/263-4931
**Hours** Daily year-round 8 a.m.-10 p.m. (summer), 8-8 (winter)
**Admission** $2 per person age 13 and up; children free
**Accessible** Partially

In 1936 the CCC used limestone quarried on the site to build a three-mile drive that loops around the mountain following the ledge of limestone rimrock that caps the bluff. The mortarless masonry retaining walls are made of blocks weighing as much as two tons. From here the views are spectacular. Three ecological regions merge in the area around the park. To the north and east are the Rolling Plains; to the south is the Edwards Plateau; and to the west are the High Plains. The mixing of ecological regions results in a variety of plant and animal life since representatives from each region are often found overlapping in a relatively small area. A nature trail introduces visitors to the park's trees: mesquite, shin oak, skunkbush sumac and redberry juniper. Prickly pear and other cacti are common on the rocky slopes. Views from the loop road attract joggers, walkers and cyclists. Roadrunners of the avian type can often be seen as well, particularly early or late in the day. A small prairie dog town lies in a little valley on the south side of the park. The combined scenic

*(Listing continued on next page)*

drive and paved walking route measures 2.4 miles (the top loop is handicapped-accessible; the lower loop has steeper grades). An elaborate Fourth of July fireworks display is one of the largest in the region.

*Directions: Located off Interstate 20 on FM 700 in Big Spring.*

## Quanah

### Copper Breaks State Park

*RR 2 Box 480*
*Quanah, Texas 79252-9420*
☎ *817/839-4331*
**Hours** *Daily year-round; no gate*
**Admission** *$2 per person age 13 and up; children free*
**Accessible** *Partially*

Copper Breaks State Park consists of almost 2000 acres. Prior to the arrival of early settlers, this region was the realm of the Comanche and Kiowa tribes. Part of the official Texas longhorn herd now resides here. The park boasts rugged, scenic beauty with mixed grass/mesquite-covered mesas and juniper breaks, plus a host of North Texas wildlife. A printed guide to the Juniper Ridge Nature Trail includes 24 "information points." Guided trail tours are available by appointment. Nearby, on State Highway 6 between Quanah and the park, observe the prominent hills to the east that make up Medicine Mound, a ceremonial and religious site of the Comanche. The mounds are on private property, and trespassing is prohibited.

*Directions: The park is located between Quanah and Crowell off State Highway 6.*

## San Angelo

### International Lily Pond

*Civic League Park*
*Harris Avenue at Park Street*
*San Angelo, Texas*
☎ *1-800/375-1206 (Visitors Bureau) or 915/653-1206 (local call)*
**Hours** *Daily, year-round dawn to dusk*
**Admission** *Free; group tours $1 (two-week notice required)*
**Accessible** *Partially*

This noteworthy collection of water lilies in Civic League Park includes the world's largest variety, 'Victoria', which grows up to eight feet in diameter with fragrant flowers 18-inches wide. The pond includes many old favorites along with some rare and endangered varieties. Special lighting allows you to view the night-blooming species. Kenneth Landon, director and chief horticulturists for the collection is available to conduct tours. Nearby (in the same park) is the San Angelo Municipal Rose Garden at Park Street and West Beauregard. The Sunken Garden Park at Avenue D and Abe Street features a fabulous canna collection.

*Directions: Civic League park is three blocks west of Highway 87 in the downtown area. From the rose garden to canna collection, go back to Highway 87 on Beauregard, go south about a mile to Avenue D.*

## San Angelo Nature Center

*7409 Knickerbocker Road*
*San Angelo, Texas 76904*
☎ *915/942-0121*
**Hours** *Wed-Sun 10-4 (summer), Tues-Sat 1-6 (fall, winter and spring); trails open daily during daylight hours*
**Admission** *$2 adults; $1 children*
**Accessible** *Partially*

The Center's nature trails include a walk through an astonishing 260-acre wetland in the midst of semi-desert. It resulted from a serendipitous 25-year leak in the dam! You'll also find a library and a growing display of native trees, shrubs and flowers. With membership you can enjoy free admission, receive the organization's newsletter and take discounts on programs and special events.

*Directions: Take Highway 87 south from the city. Turn right on Knickerbocker Road to the south shore of Lake Nasworthy.*

# Wichita Falls

## Lucy Park and Wichita Falls Waterfall

*P.O. Box 630*
*Wichita Falls, Texas 76307*
☎ *1-800/799-6732 (Visitors Bureau)*
**Hours** *Daily dawn to dusk*
**Admission** *Free*
**Accessible** *Yes*

The new Wichita Falls Waterfall (reminiscent of falls on the Wichita River that washed away in the flood of 1886) cascades down 54-feet of massive red sandstone blocks. It's visible from IH-44, but the more interesting way to experience this impressive water feature is through Lucy Park via a quarter-mile walking trail. From the falls there's also a shady riverside walk to O'Reilly Park. Landscaped, lighted walking trails wind through Lucy Park, where you'll find "Nature Works," an interpretive project with informative signage, a duck pond, and about 30 display planting beds with labeled grasses, shrubs and flowers. The park's numerous trees are tough Texas natives and drought-tolerant species from other similar climates, all planted on this former prairie site.

*Directions: Take Highway 277 (Seymour Highway) west from IH-44. Turn right on Sunset Drive, which takes you into a parking lot for Lucy Park.*

# High Plains
## Amarillo

## Amarillo Botanical Garden

*1400 Streit Drive*
*Amarillo, Texas 79106*
☎ *806/352-6513*
**FAX** *806/352-6227*
**Hours** *Grounds open daily during daylight hours*
**Admission** *Free*
**Accessible** *Partially*

Organized in 1954 by the Council of Garden Clubs, this organization is rapidly advancing with a facility master plan for its 3.3 acres in the Harrington Regional Medical Center. The Harrington Fragrance Garden, Butterfly Demonstration Garden

*(Listing continued on next page)*

and Children's Garden are among the new attractions here. A leader in horticultural therapy, the garden also offers a horticulture library and Lattice Gift Shop. Exhibitions and educational programs are geared to both horticulture and environmental issues.

*Directions: From IH-40 (west of downtown) take the Coulter Street Exit north to Wallace. Turn right on Wallace before High Plains Hospital, right on Hagy Drive, then left on Streit.*

# Hale Center

## Bell Park Cacti Garden

*FM 1424 at FM 1914*
*Hale Center, Texas*
☎ *806/839-2642*
**Hours** *Daily, dawn to dark*
**Admission** *Free*
**Accessible** *Yes*

The late Hershall Bell began this half-acre labor-of-love in the early '60s. More than 350 cacti representing 40 species are on display for all to enjoy.

*Directions: The two roads intersect just west of the Hale Center exit off Highway 27 between Lubbock and Amarillo.*

# Lubbock

## Lubbock Memorial Arboretum

*4111 University Avenue*
*Lubbock, Texas 79413-3231*
☎ *806/797-4520*
**Hours** *Daily dawn to dusk; Interpretative Center open Sat 10-1, Sun 1-4*
**Admission** *Free*
**Accessible** *Yes*

Designed for both pleasure and education, this arboretum in Clapp Park is a pocket of tranquil beauty with paths, vistas and resting sites. In a region that has no native trees or shrubs, it serves as exhibit space for the ornamental plants that can be grown in the area and a laboratory for studying existing plants and evaluating new plants. The 55-acre site is managed by a private foundation and supported by gifts and memberships. Volunteers staff the Arboretum Interpretive Center. It houses a horticulture library, gift shop and meeting spaces where experts regularly present programs on gardening topics. Guided tours are available.

*Directions: From the east side of the Texas Tech campus, take University south to 41st.*

## Ranching Heritage Center

*Texas Tech University*
*Lubbock, Texas 79401*
☎ *806/742-2498*
**Hours** *Tues-Sat 10-5, Sun 1-5*
**Admission** *Free*
**Accessible** *Yes*

Here, it's not the vegetation that surrounds this fascinating collection of old homes and ranch buildings that's memorable, but rather its scarcity. The 1904 Picket and Sotol House was built with the only materials the people had at hand — stalks of sotol and small cedar pickets. It's held together with mud chinking and roofed with grass. The entire 14-acre site provides a poignant reminder of how difficult it might have been to feed a family on the prairies of the High Plains before the discovery of underground water supplies in the early 1900s. The Center's buildings and windmills, which are drawn from numerous locations on the High Plains, speak not only of the early pioneers' isolation and hardships, but also of our present-day dependency on water resources. It's a history lesson every Texan can appreciate.

*Directions: Located next the Texas Tech campus, at the corner of Indiana and 4th Street.*

# Midland

## Sibley Environmental Learning Center

*1307 East Wadley*
*Midland, Texas 79705*
☎ *915/684-6827*
**Hours** *By appointment*
**Admission** *Free*
**Accessible** *Yes, building and ¾-mile trail.*

Knowledgeable naturalist Burr Williams directs the program at this facility that's totally dedicated to southwestern ecology. There are two miles of trails, a pond and a soon-to-be-completed demonstration garden here. He notes that indicator species from four different regions appear in and around the Midland area. Mr. Williams has been a strong advocate for landscaping with native plants for many years. For those who share his dedication, he'll arrange (by appointment) a visit to his own 17 acres of reclaimed prairie.

*Directions: From downtown, go north on Highway 349, turn right (east) on Wadley.*

# Quitaque

## Caprock Canyons State Park

*P.O. Box 204*
*Quitaque, Texas 79255*
☎ *806/455-1492*
**Hours** *Daily year-round; honor box used for collecting fees when office is closed*
**Admission** *$2 per person age 13 and up; children free*
**Accessible** *Partially*

This huge park's scenic canyons were home to Native Americans of several cultures, including the Folsum culture of more than 10,000 years ago. Disappearance of some plant species since that time indicates a gradual drying and warming of the climate. Anglo settlement began in 1874 when cattleman Charles Goodnight bought vast acreage. A railroad was built into this area in 1887, and the town of Quitaque (population, 30) became a regular stage stop. This is where High Plains meets Red Rolling Plains, and the caprock is a vivid red. Most of the broken country is still ranch land. Vegetational communities vary from the sparse badlands (with juniper, mesquite and cacti) to the bottomlands (abound in tall grasses, cottonwoods, plum thickets and hackberries). The pride of Caprock Canyons is its herd of Pronghorn Antelope.

A 64.25-mile multiple-use trail (hike, bike, and equestrian), donated by a railroad entrepreneur, extends the park through Floyd, Briscoe, and Hall counties, crossing 54 bridges and running through the last active railroad tunnel in Texas. At present, only 34 miles are open to the public from Quitaque to South Plains, but the park offers almost 90 miles of multiple-use trails that range from rugged terrain to trails for the disabled. Quitaque Riding Stables (☎ 806/455-1208) offers guided or unsupervised rentals. For boats or bikes, call Big "C" Trading Post, (☎ 806/455-1221). Queen of the Valley, Inc. (☎ 806/983-3693) has a guided, motorized tour of the Quitaque Canyon and Los Lingos Trails on Saturday and Sunday. Other times by reservation.

# Trans-Pecos
## Brewster County

### Big Bend National Park

*P.O. Box 129*
*Big Bend National Park, Texas 79834*
☎ *915/477-2251*
**Hours** *Daily, year around*
**Admission** *$10 per passenger vehicle; $5 for 7-day hiking pass*
**Accessible** *Partially*

Within Big Bend's vast boundaries, you'll discover dramatic desert and mountain scenery and amazingly diverse plant life. Willows and cottonwoods form a ribbon of green along the Rio Grande River. Desert vegetation inhabits the flatlands, and grasslands cover the foothills. Woodlands beginning above the 4,500-feet-level consist mostly of piñon pines, junipers and oaks, but on the high, cool north sides of the Chisos mountains, you'll find trees more typical of the Rocky Mountains. Altogether, it is a fragile environment, easily damaged.

Rules are strict here, and the distances can be forbidding. Three paved roads allow access into the park: Vehicular traffic into the park interior is via a well-maintained gravel road and several miles of designated four-wheel drive trails. Motor homes and large recreational vehicles may not be able to enter backcountry park areas. There are 200 miles of hiking trails and campsite facilities. Headquarters is at Panther Junction, 26 miles from the north entrance, but there are four other Visitors Centers within the park, where road guides, hiking and driving tour maps and information about programs are available. Permits are required for river trips. Chisos Mountain Lodge hosts the park's only restaurant. The National Park Service maintains a very informative Web site.

*Directions: Take US Highway 385 from Marathon to the north entrance. From the west, take Highway 118 from Alpine or Ranch Road 170 from Presidio.*

## Culbertson & Hudspeth Counties

### Guadalupe Mountains National Park

*HC 60 Box 400*
*Salt Flat, Texas 79847*
☎ *915/828-3251*
**Hours** *Daily, year around*
**Admission** *Free*
**Accessible** *No*

A magnificent conifer forest stands here, a remnant of ice-age forests that existed 15,000 years ago when Texas was much cooler and more moist. The most popular destination is McKittrick Canyon, which nurtures conifers from the mountains above, desert plants from below and several plant species that grow nowhere else in the world. In autumn you'll see walnut trees, big-tooth maple and Texas madrone clothed in bright red, yellow and orange foliage. There are 80 miles of trails, but no concessions within this remote park. Hikers are required to bring all their own provisions, including one gallon of water per person per day and suitable clothing for sudden weather changes. Permits are required to use the two campgrounds and ten backcountry campsites. The nearest lodging is 35 miles northeast in Whites City, New Mexico, near Carlsbad Caverns.

## Franklin Mountains State Park

P.O. Box 200
Canutillo, Texas 79835-9998
☎ 915/566-6441
**Hours** *Daily year-round*
**Admission** *$2 per person age 13 and up; children free*
**Accessible** *Partially*

The largest sustained mountain range in Texas rises here to an elevation of 7192', some 3000' above the City of El Paso. For thousands of years, native peoples, soldiers, priests, traders, gold-seekers and adventurers passed through the gap known as Paso del Norte. It was only when developers began carving roads into these almost pristine mountains in the 1970s that the Texas legislature acquired the Franklin Mountains as a state park. To the delight of conservationists across the nation, its scenic, ecological and historic features are now protected, including colorful pictographs and deep mortar pits used by early native groups to grind seeds. This is now the largest urban park in the nation (37-square-miles)!

Year-round running water from natural springs attracts abundant wildlife. Observant visitors may even catch a glimpse of a cougar. The skies are home to Golden Eagles, a variety of hawks and the occasional falcon. At night, bats and owls search for food. Existing vegetation is typical of the Chihuahuan Desert, with lechuguilla, sotol, ocotillo, several yuccas and numerous cacti. This is the only known location in Texas for a number of plant species, including the Southwest barrel cactus. Approximately 20 miles of nature trails and numerous hiking and riding trails are currently accessible. Visitors enjoy interpretive nature tours whenever staff or volunteers are available. Contact the park for information.

Directions: *Take Interstate 10 West following the Rio Grande River to the Anutillo/ Trans-Mountain exit, turn toward the mountains, and the park is located 3.8 miles east of Interstate 10; or take Loop 375/Trans-Mountain Road going west up and over the summit. The entrance is three miles down the road.*

## Hueco Tanks State Historical Park

6900 Hueco Tanks Road No 1
El Paso, Texas 79938
☎ 915/857-1135
**Hours** *Daily year-round 8 a.m.-sunset*
**Admission** *$2 per person age 13 and up; children free*
**Accessible** *Partially*

Large natural rock basins called "huecos" (pronounced like the city of Waco) have furnished trapped rain water to travelers in this arid region of west Texas for millennia. Archaic hunters drew strange mythological designs on the rocks, and more recent Apaches, Kiowas and Comanches left pictographs of their adventures. Later the tanks served as a watering stop for Butterfield Overland Mail Route. Fascinating, diverse plants and animals inhabit this section of the Chihuahuan Desert. Of unusual interest in the rock basins are seasonal explosions of tiny, translucent freshwater shrimps that attract a wide range of hungry wildlife. Activities include nature study, picnicking, camping, hiking, rock climbing and stargazing. Guided tours are held Saturday and Sunday at 10 and 2. Special educational tours are held upon request.

Directions: *The park can be reached by traveling 32 miles northeast of El Paso just off US Highway 62/180, then turning north on Ranch Road 2775.*

## Texas A&M Research Facility at El Paso

*1380 A & M Circle*
*El Paso, Texas 79927*
☎ *915/859-7725*
**Hours** *Mon-Fri 8-5; gardens open daily, dawn to dusk*
**Admission** *Free*
**Accessible** *Weekdays only, when staff is available to open a gate.*

You'll find a broad spectrum of native and adapted plants (about 140 species) suitable for El Paso landscapes in the demonstration gardens here. The organization has seven different turf plots under cultivation, and its gardens exhibit hardscape solutions as well as good mulching techniques.

## Fort Davis

## Chihuahuan Desert Research Institute

*Texas Highway 118 South*
*Fort Davis, Texas 79734*
☎ *915/364-2499*
**Hours** *Mon-Fri 9-5; open Sat & Sun 9-6 (April-Labor Day)*
**Admission** *$2 donation per car*
**Accessible** *Limited*
**Mailing Address:** *P.O. Box 905, Fort Davis, Texas 79734*

The diverse flora of the desert is well-exemplified in the nature trail (a half-mile round-trip descent into Modesta Canyon) and the arboretum and cactus greenhouse at this facility of the Chihuahuan Desert Research Institute. The organization sponsors field trips and seminars to help researchers and naturalists better understand the fragile desert ecology. Seeing such an array of drought-resistant, cold-tolerant plants should provide inspiration to gardeners in the area and awaken Texans who garden in less difficult climes to the inherent beauty and untapped usefulness of native desert plants. (All plants are labeled here.) The Institute's annual Native Plant Sale and pre-sale seminars attract enthusiastic crowds during the third weekend in April. A new bookstore/ gift shop dispenses information and garden-related merchandise. The Institute invites membership and publishes a semiannual magazine, *Chihuahuan Desert Discovery*.

*Directions: Located 3.3 miles south of Fort Davis off Texas Highway 118 to Alpine.*

## Davis Mountains State Park

*P.O. Box 1458*
*Fort Davis Texas 79734*
☎ *915/426-3337*
**Hours** *Daily year-round, no gate*
**Admission** *$3 per person age 13 and up; children free*
**Accessible** *Partially*

The Davis Mountains were formed by volcanic activity around 65 million years ago. Winters are often below freezing in this mile-high landscape, and visitors may be treated to an occasional snowfall. Summer days are hot and dry, but the nights are cool. This scenic northern Chihuahuan Desert landscape is composed of both plains grasslands and piñon-juniper-oak woodlands. Scattered stands of ponderosa and the more common piñon pine, mixed with oak and juniper, cover higher elevations. During wet years, the park abounds in wildflowers. Emory oak is predominant along Keesey Creek. Scarlet bouvardia, little-leaf leadtree, trompillo, evergreen sumac, fragrant sumac, Apache plum, little walnut, tree cholla, Torrey yucca, catclaw acacia and agarito are conspicuous flowering shrubs.

Attractions include scenic drives, two scenic overlooks, and four miles of hiking trails. The northern half of the park, north of State Highway 118, has been designated the Limpia Canyon Primitive Area. A special use area with an entrance fee required, it includes ten miles of backcountry trails with primitive campsites. The interpretive center overlooks the wildlife watering station where scrub jays, white-wing doves, curve-billed thrashers and rock squirrels are among the most common wildlife seen. Montezuma quail are regularly observed in the park. In 1961, the historic ruins of Fort Davis (1854 to 1891) were declared a National Historic Site, and a vast restoration program was initiated.

*Directions: The park is reached by traveling a mile north of Fort Davis on State Highway 17 to State Highway 118N, then west on State Highway 118N for three miles to Park Road 3 entrance.*

## Langtry

### Judge Roy Bean Visitor Center

*P.O. Box 160*
*Langtry, Texas 78871*
☎ *915/291-3340*
**Hours** *Daily 8-5; closed New Years Day, Easter, Thanksgiving, Christmas Eve and Day*
**Admission** *Free*
**Accessible** *Yes*

Commemorating Judge Roy Bean's court, which established "Law West of the Pecos" in 1882, the combined saloon, billiard parlor and courthouse has been embellished with a colorful cactus and native shrub garden. The Texas Department of Transportation supplies a plant list complete with medicinal and other practical uses. From the fishhook cactus that Indians used to catch fish to the creosote bush used for deodorizing the skunk traps and treating arthritis, the plant descriptions are as fascinating as the historical lore that surrounds this place.

*Directions: Langtry is off US Highway 90, about 60 miles northwest of Del Rio. If you get to Langtry (pop. 145), you can't miss it.*

## Monahans

### Monahans Sandhills State Park

*Box 1738*
*Monahans Texas 79756*
☎ *915/943-2092*
**Hours** *Daily year-round 8 a.m.-10 p.m.*
**Admission** *$2 per person age 13 and up; children free. Tour fees apply.*
**Accessible** *Partially*

This park is only a small portion of a dune field that extends about 200 miles from south of Monahans into New Mexico. Fresh water occurs at shallow depths within the dunefield, and most of the dunes are stabilized by vegetation. The most interesting plant you'll find here is Shinoak (*Quercus havardii*). Not a stunted form of a larger tree, this plant usually stands less than four feet tall at full maturity and bears an abundance of large acorns. Park activities include camping, hiking, picnicking, birding and wildlife-watching from the interpretive center windows. There's a dune tour in a 4 x4 utility vehicle and a nature trail tour. Many of the dunes in the park are still active, growing and changing shape in response to seasonal, prevailing winds. Some reach up to 70 feet in height.

*Directions: To reach the park, take IH-20 and exit at Mile Marker #86 to Park Road 41.*

*Presidio*

## Big Bend Ranch State Park

P.O. Box 1180
Presidio, Texas 79845
☎ 915/229-3416 or 512/389-8900 (bus tour reservations)
**Hours** Daily year-round; gate open 8-5
**Admission** $3 per person age 13 and up; children free
**Accessible** Very limited

Embracing some of the most remote and rugged terrain in the Southwest, this park encompasses two mountain ranges containing ancient extinct volcanoes, precipitous canyons, waterfalls and thousands of acres of Chihuahuan Desert wilderness. It's home to diverse and rare species, including Hinckley oaks and mountain lions. Certain areas of the park have limited recreational use and vehicular access. Visitors must contact either Fort Leaton State Historical Park (four miles east of Presidio on FM 170) or Barton Warnock Environmental Education Center (see following listing) to obtain permits, pay user fees and receive instructions for vehicular access into the interior of the park.

Thirty miles of hiking and backpacking trails are accessible at trail heads along FM 170, and opportunities for short hikes abound at several locations along the interior park road. The 19-mile Rancherias Loop Trail is available for serious backpackers. Several short trails are ideal for day-hikes. Plans are for a portion of the Ojito Adentro Trail to be wheelchair accessible. All-day Interpretive bus tours (capacity 22), led by a naturalist, are scheduled for the first and third weekends of every month, departing Fort Leaton and Barton Warnock Center, respectively.

*Terlingua*

## Barton Warnock Environmental Education Center

RR HC 70, Box 375
Terlingua, Texas 79852
☎ 915/424-3327
**Hours** Daily 8-4:30
**Admission** $2.50 (adults); $1.50 (children)
**Accessible** No

Built in 1982 as the Lajitas Museum Desert Gardens, this 99-acre facility was purchased by Texas Parks and Wildlife in October 1990. It was renamed to honor Dr. Barton Warnock. A former chairman of the biology department at Sul Ross State University, his *Wildflowers of the Big Bend Country* remains the definitive guidebook. The Center, which serves as the eastern entrance station to Big Bend Ranch State Park, presents an archeological, historical and natural history profile of the Big Bend region. There's a research library and wonderful display of Chihuahuan Desert plants in a self-guided 2½-acre botanical garden here. The museum is also self-guided, but group tours can be arranged. The sales area contains a wide assortment of books and other informational material. This facility now serves as a Regional Information Center for environmental, history and travel information for all points within a 100-mile radius, including Mexico. While the garden is not yet wheelchair accessible; all buildings have been brought up to ADA standards.

*Directions: The Center is located on FM 170, one mile east of Lajitas.*

# Garden Books & Periodicals

My favorite way to spend a winter evening involves a fireplace and a good garden book. From my armchair, I've visited great gardens all over the world. Long before I was able to spend three weeks crisscrossing the British Isles, Graham Stuart Thomas's *Great Gardens of Britain* transported me there. Griswold and Weller's *The Golden Age of American Gardens* introduced me to hundreds of private gardens in this country that I'd never be able to see; some are not open to the public, others no longer even exist.

My viewpoint was greatly enriched by *The Landscape of Man*, a wonderful history of gardens by Geoffrey and Susan Jellicoe. It describes the climatic, topographical, historical, social, economic and philosophical factors that shaped outdoor spaces from pre-history to modern times. (This is the same Geoffrey Jellicoe who designed the master plan for The Moody Gardens in Galveston.) From Anthony Huxley's *An Illustrated History of Gardening*, I've gained new appreciation for people who created uncommon beauty without the mechanization we employ today.

In terms of design, I was influenced by Thomas D. Church's *Gardens are for People*. I also loved John Brookes' *The Book of Garden Design*, which details the basics of landscape design in simple language and reinforces the text with excellent illustrations. I also pored over *Bold Romantic Gardens: The New World Landscapes of Oehme and van Sweden*. Their book illustrates a new, naturalistic way of planting that incorporates grasses and great drifts of hardy wildflowers. When I look at the pictures, however, I substitute Mexican bush sage for their pink loosestrife and imagine using caladiums where they use hostas.

The problem is that none of these books feature plants that are suitable for Texas landscapes. Design is design, but where plant materials are concerned, we must turn to books written by Texans for Texans. Our hot-summer climate does not lend itself to the lush woodland species you'll see pictured in the books published in New York or Great Britain. Even such excellent books as the *Southern Living Garden Guides* features some plants that are ill-suited to the long periods of drought we routinely experience in our more western climes.

One day in an Austin bookstore I observed a couple mulling over the choices in the gardening section. From the conversation I was overhearing, I could tell they were new to the state, so I stepped in and literally snatched from the woman's hand a book published in New England. I directed the couple, instead, to Neil Sperry's *Complete Guide to Texas Gardening*. It contains the most complete general information on soil types, fertilization needs, pests and diseases common to Texas and lists the plants most often used in Texas landscapes. I also recommended Howard Garrett's *Texas Organic Gardening Book*, which explains in its preface, "Organics is not just a switch of products, but a completely new way of life. It's about understanding and enjoying nature."

I introduced them to *Native Texas Plants, Landscaping Region by Region* by Sally Wasowski and Andy Wasowski, which illustrates with beautiful photographs how to identify and save what already may be on your property and how to build upon it with plants indigenous to your area. I also pointed out a third "must have" book for anyone gardening in limestone, alkaline clay and/or caliche (which describes Austin and more than half of Texas): *Gardening Success with Difficult Soils* by Scott Ogden.

If you're interested in the gardening traditions of Texas, you'll love *The Southern Heirloom Garden* by William C. Welch and Greg Grant. Another book, one that belongs in every gardener's glove box, is Geyata Ajilvsgi's *Wildflowers of Texas*, which is color-coded and very user-friendly. Texas also has its own bird book, *Field*

*Guide to the Birds of Texas*, by the late Roger Tory Peterson, who called Texas "the #1 bird state."

If you are about to undertake garden construction, you'll want to look at the familiar paperback series on outdoor building from Sunset Publishing (*Decks, Fences & Gates, Outdoor Furniture, Walks, Walls and Patio Floors*, etc.). Other publishers, including Time-Life, Ortho, Random House and Penguin, offer highly informative books. They are full of practical advice for do-it-yourself garden designers. Even if you're turning your garden over to a professional, I highly recommend these and other good garden design books as tools for helping you communicate your ideas and personal preferences.

# A Texas Gardener's Library
## General Gardening Encyclopedias
*Howard Garrett's Plants for Texas*, J. Howard Garrett
*Know It and Grow It II*, Dr. Carl Whitcomb
*Neil Sperry's Complete Guide to Texas Gardening*, Neil Sperry
*Sunset National Garden Book*, editors, Lane Publishing Company

## Garden Design
*Accessible Gardening for People with Disabilities*, Janeen R. Adil
*Bold Romantic Gardens*, Wolfgang Oehme & James van Sweden
*Landscape Design...Texas Style*, Howard Garrett
*Landscaping with Native Texas Plants*, Sally Wasowski and Julie Ryan
*Native Texas Gardens: Maximum Beauty Minimum Upkeep*,
  Sally Wasowski and Andy Wasowski
*Native Texas Plants, Landscaping Region by Region*,
  Sally Wasowski and Andy Wasowski
*Planting Design*, Theodore D. Walker
*The Southern Heirloom Garden*, William C. Welch and Greg Grant
*Southern Home Landscaping*, Ken Smith
*The Book of Garden Design*, John Brookes

## Garden Construction
*Pergolas, Arbors, Gazebos and Follies*, David Stevens
*Stonescaping*, Jan Kowalczski Whitner
*The Landscape Lighting Book*, Janet Lennox Moyer
*Trellising*, Rhonda M. Hart

## Garden Conservation
*Common Sense Pest Control*, William Olkowski, Sheila Daar & Helga Olkowski
*The Dirt Doctor's Guide to Organic Gardening*, J. Howard Garrett
*The Garden-Ville Method: Lessons in Nature*, Malcolm Beck
*Howard Garrett's Texas Organic Gardening Book*, J. Howard Garrett
*Neil Sperry's 1001 Most Asked Texas Gardening Questions*, Neil Sperry
*The Pruner's Handbook*, John Malins
*Rodale's Garden Problem Solver*, Jeff Ball & Liz Ball
*Soil Science Simplified*, Helmut Kohnke and D.P. Franzmeier
*Tiny Game Hunting*, Hilary Dole Klein & Adrian M. Wenner

## Naturescaping

*Attracting Birds*, Neal Oldenwald
*Butterfly Gardening for the South*, Geyata Ajilvsgi
*How to Grow Native Plants of Texas and the Southwest*, Jill Nokes
*How to Grow Wildflowers*, Eric A. Johnson and Scott Miller
*Landscaping with Native Plants of Texas and the Southwest*, George O. Miller
*Landscaping with Native Trees*, Guy Sternberg and Jim Wilson
*Legends and Lore of Texas Wildflowers*, Elizabeth Silverthorne
*Native Gardens for Dry Climates*, Sally Wasowski
*Texas Monthly Field Guide to Wildflowers, Trees and Shrubs of Texas*,
   Delena Tull and George Oxford Miller
*Wildflowers of Texas*, Geyata Ajilvsgi
*Wildflowers of the Big Bend Country*, Barton H. Warnock
*Wildflowers of the Big Thicket*, Geyata Ajilvsgi
*Xeriscape Planting Guide*, Denver Water Department

## Trees, Shrubs & Grasses

*A Field Guide to Texas Trees*, Benny J. Simpson
*Antique Roses for the South*, William C. Welch
*Complete Guide to Texas Lawn Care*, Dr. Bill Knoop
*Encyclopedia of Ornamental Grasses*, John Greenlee
*Gardening Success with Difficult Soils*, Scott Ogden
*Manual of Woody Landscape Plants*, Michael Dirr
*Texas Gardener's Guide*, Dale Groom
*Trees, Shrubs and Woody Vines of the Southwest*, Robert Vines

## The Flower Garden

*Garden Bulbs for the South*, Scott Ogden
*Perennial Garden Color*, William C. Welch
*The Complete Guide to Using Color in Your Garden*, David Squires
*The Texas Flowerscaper*, Kathy Huber

## The Edible Landscape

*Commonsense Vegetable Gardening for the South*,
   William D. Adams and Thomas R. LeRoy
*Designing and Maintaining your Edible Landscape Naturally*, Robert Kourik
*Growing Fruits, Berries and Nuts in the South*, Dr. George McEachern
*The Herb Garden Cookbook*, Lucinda Hutson
*Herb Gardening in Texas*, Sol Meltzer
*Landscaping with Herbs*, Jim Wilson
*Southern Herb Gardening*, Madalene Hill and Gwen Barclay
*Texas Gardener's Guide to Growing and Using Herbs*, Diane Morey Sitton
*The Herb Garden Cookbook*, Lucinda Hutson
*The Vegetable Book: A Texan's Guide To Gardening*, Dr. Sam Cotner

## Water Gardens

*Water Features for Small Gardens*, Francesca Greendak
*Water Gardens for Plants and Fish*, Charles B. Thomas

**Houseplants**
*The Indoor Garden Book*, John Brooks
*The New Houseplant Expert*, D. G. Hessayon

**Container Gardening**
*The Book of Container Gardening*, Malcolm Hillier
*The Contained Garden*, David Stevens & Kenneth Beckett
*Landscaping with Container Plants*, Jim Wilson

**Garden Furniture & Accessories**
*Decorating Eden*, Elizabeth Wilkinson and Marjorie Henderson

I can't walk into a bookstore without adding a few more gardening books to my collection. Even for a landscape professional, it's hard to choose from the plethora of titles out there. Over 700 new garden books are published each year, and thousands of older books remain in print because many of the garden "secrets" our grandparents knew are still valid. Only the library stands between me and credit card overload! In most public libraries, however, the gardening collections are limited by lack of funding. The good news is that all libraries have borrowing privileges from other public libraries in the country.

☛**Money-saving tip: Ask your local public library about "inter-library loans," through which you can obtain almost any book in print.**

# Magazines that Celebrate the Texas Landscape

Libraries also offer an economical way to keep up with all the garden-related magazines in print. I take advantage of the library's copies of *Horticulture, Garden Design, Fine Gardening* and *Organic Gardening*, to name a few. As a homesick Texan in the Pacific Northwest, I maintain my subscriptions to several magazines that are filled with information specific to gardening and naturescaping in Texas. These are the four I look forward to receiving each month:

*Neil Sperry's GARDENS*
P.O. Box 864
McKinney, Texas 75070
☎ 972/562-5050

*Texas Highways*
1101 East Anderson Lane
Austin, Texas 78752
☎ 1-800/839-4997

*Texas Gardener*
P.O. Box 9005
Waco, Texas 76714
☎ 817/772-1270

*Texas Parks and Wildlife*
3000 South IH-35, Suite 120
Austin, Texas 78704
☎ 1-800/937-9393

# Personalized Sources of Information

Gardeners learn by seeing, reading and questioning. I've always heard that a green thumb is equal parts knowledge, intuition and luck, but knowledge is the only thing that works for me. Luck I've never trusted, and the kind of intuition that allows a gardener to differentiate between weeds and precious seedlings is built on first-hand experience! Happily, Texas is replete with people trained to answer your gardening questions.

## "Green Industry" Professionals

Professionals in the fields of landscape design, construction, horticulture and maintenance can provide you with expertise that may save you hundreds or thousands of dollars in the long term. If you are building a new home or planning a major landscape renovation, by all means consult a professional. While you own your home, you'll enjoy the benefits of a well designed, constructed and easy-to-maintain garden. When you sell the house, a good landscape will pay another dividend. You can expect to speed up the sale by five to six weeks and recover your investment by as much as 200 percent. Before hiring someone to help with your garden, however, you should know that different types of professionals are trained in different, specific fields. The "green industry" is regulated to an extent by professional organizations, but not all landscape services are regulated.

☛**Money-saving tip: Within every area of "expertise," there are people who don't know what they are doing. No matter what kind of landscape service you employ, ask about credentials, check references and look at examples of their completed work.**

### Selecting a Designer

Among design professionals, landscape architects are the most highly trained. To be able to use the title "landscape architect," one must have graduated from an accredited university program, practiced for a number of years and passed a rigorous exam that covers design, construction techniques, plant materials, history and professional ethics. Most are members of the American Society of Landscape Architects (ASLA).

He or she will be trained to help you maximize the use of your property, which includes planning circulation patterns, designing outdoor living areas and selecting the best plant materials in terms of energy efficiency and environmental sensitivity. Not only is a landscape architect qualified to provide help with aesthetic issues, but also with such matters as building codes, structural details and drainage considerations. Landscape architects can help you prevent such costly mistakes as planting trees too close to the house or creating future maintenance problems.

A number of people who call themselves "landscape designers" are graduates of university programs in landscape architecture who have not yet taken the registration exam. Other designers are self-taught individuals who may have years of practical experience and a real flair for aesthetics. A few of the latter have passed exams to become members of the Association of Professional Landscape Designers (APLD). Their emphasis is usually slanted more toward plant materials than hardscape (the garden's walks, walls, drainage and irrigation systems, outdoor lighting, etc.)

Unfortunately the yellow pages include, under "landscape designers," anyone who can afford to have business cards printed and pay for an ad. If there is major structural work to be done, a difficult site with slopes that will require retaining walls, serious drainage problems or a landscape in need of ecological restoration, you should consult a registered landscape architect.

Some landscape architects and professional landscape designers operate "design/ build" firms, which include both design and construction services. Some firms virtually give away their design services to get the more profitable construction contract. My best advice to homeowners is not to lock yourself into a construction contract that doesn't allow for the process of competitive bids unless you personally know the individual with whom you are dealing and highly respect the company's work. (See section on Landscape Contractors.)

Most landscape architectural firms do not specialize in residential design, but most landscape architects enjoy garden design in addition to their work with larger-scale public and commercial projects. For a list of Texas landscape architects who told us they include residential work among their specialties , see page 391.

## Consulting a Nursery Professional

The Texas Association of Nurserymen (TAN) is composed of the states' wholesale nursery-stock growers, garden center retailers, landscape contractors and designers, maintenance contractors and allied suppliers. The Association certifies nursery personnel through training programs, apprenticeships and examinations. To become a Texas Certified Nursery Professional a person must pass a four-part examination that covers basic principles of plant growth, plant identification, plant disease and insect control, weed control, fertilization and proper use of chemicals. To become a Texas Master Certified Nursery Professional, one must attend classroom training and pass an examination that requires an advanced level of knowledge in these subjects.

Most large garden centers employ Certified Nursery Professionals to give advice on plant selection and answer gardening questions. Some also provide design and landscape installation services. You'll find that many nurseries offer free classes and send out newsletters not only to promote products, but also to keep their customers informed about new developments in the field of horticulture. Ask to be added to the mailing list of every nursery where you trade.

## Hiring a Landscape Contractor

Once the design work is complete, you will probably need the services of a landscape contractor for the construction phase. Landscape architects and designers normally prepare plans and written specifications that allow you to get bids from several different contractors who will pour the concrete, lay the brick, build the deck, supply the plants and do the planting. Often they will recommend several contractors with whom they have worked in the past.

Avoid anyone who calls himself/herself a "landscaper." I wince when I hear this term. Qualified people in the industry refer to themselves as landscape contractors. Most are members of the Texas Association of Landscape Contractors (TALC). The organization can refer you to members in your area (☎1-800/832-6934). Make sure that the person you are dealing with is licensed and bonded. Ask for his/her registration number and confirmation of liability insurance. The best landscape contractors take great pride in their profession and back up their work with years of experience and training. They should be happy to give you references. Take time to call the references and study every detail of the contract before signing it.

You may want your landscape contractor to hire and supervise the work of such specialists as irrigation contractors, lighting contractors, paving and fencing contractors, or you may wish to contract for such work separately. If your renovation only requires new plant materials, garden centers often offer plant installation.

☛**Money-saving tip: Obtain recommendations and interview several firms. The lowest bid is not necessarily the best bid.**

**Calling-in an Arborist**

Trust your valuable trees to an insured, licensed arborist. Maintaining the health and form of your trees may be the best money you invest in your garden. Competent arborists are certified by the International Society of Arboriculture (ISA), and many are also members of the Society of American Foresters and the National Arborist Association. Not only should you expect professional affiliations, but you should also demand that the people to whom you entrust your trees be educated in forestry, horticulture or a related field. Your local extension service may be able to provide you with a list of certified arborists in your area.

Unfortunately, Texas does not have a licensing program for arborists, so anyone who can afford a pick-up truck and chain saw can call himself a "tree trimmer." No matter how desperate you are to get tree work done (like, immediately after a storm), do not even consider hiring some "trimmer" who rings your doorbell or select someone out of the newspaper want-ads. The work of untrained tree-care people can be seen all over Texas in trees that have been topped or otherwise mangled, misshapen and ultimately ruined. At a seminar I attended recently, someone asked how to find a reputable tree company. An experienced arborist answered, "Call a company and ask if they top trees. If they say 'yes,' hang up!"

Taking down a tree that must be removed doesn't require the services of a certified arborist, but it is a dangerous job that is best left to a pro. The International Society of Arboriculture recommends that you negotiate a written contract that specifies how the tree is to be removed, where the wood will be taken and who is liable in case of damage. If you want the stump removed as well, provision for this service should be spelled out in the contract.

☛**Money-saving tip: Because you probably don't have the proper tools and ladders to safely prune your own large trees, a professional arborist will not only prolong the life of your valuable trees, but may also save you from a stay in the hospital.**

# Extension Services & Master Gardener Program

Cooperative Extension Services (so named because they are joint ventures between the United States Department of Agriculture, county governments and land-grant universities) were begun in 1914 for the benefit of farmers. As the population became more urban, the agencies widened their focus to include consumer affairs, food and water quality, home and family issues and gardening. In rural areas the extension agents still concentrate on the needs of farming and ranching families, but urban extension agents are responsible for answering the multitude of horticultural questions asked by homeowners, park departments, schools and city governments. The advice is always free, and most of the services are either free or modestly priced. Look for Cooperative Extension in the phone book under county listings.

☛**Money-saving tip: Cooperative Extension Services are funded by your tax dollars. Tap into this gold mine!**

The task of dispensing information in the large urban counties has become impossible for any County Extension Agent to handle alone. The Master Gardener Program was begun to train enthusiastic laymen to share the work of overburdened County Agents. It has worked beautifully. Master Gardeners now answer garden questions, set up demonstrations, diagnose plant problems and make recommendations for the control of plant diseases, insect infestation and cultural problems. The program requires sixty hours of training and sixty hours of volunteer work the first year; it encourages continued learning and a minimum of twenty-five hours of community service in the following years. Thousands of Master Gardeners in the U.S. and Canada take part in this program today. These volunteers conduct neighborhood clinics during the gardening season. They offer taped messages on subjects ranging from "apple varieties to zoysia grass," participate in question-and-answer newspaper columns and make frequent radio and TV appearances. If a Master Gardener doesn't know the answer to your question, he or she will contact the County Agent, who in turn can seek information from experts at Texas A&M University or draw from a nationwide network of information sources.

Master Composters is a new organization dedicated to organic gardening and urban ecology to promote backyard composting. Its long-term goal is to prevent yard waste from reaching already-overburdened landfills. Like the Master Gardener program, it is staffed by volunteers. It provides demonstration sites and "hotlines." Here's a way to improve your soil and save your tax dollars at the same time!

# Organizations Keeping Texas Clean & Green

## Native Plant Society of Texas

*1111 North IH-35, Suite 212*
*Round Rock, Texas 78664*
☎ *512/238-0695*
**FAX** *512/238-0703*
**Hours** *Mon-Fri 8:30-5*
**Mailing Address** *P.O. Box 891, Georgetown, Texas 78627*

Founded in 1980 to protect the state's botanical legacy, this organization has grown to a network of more than 25 local chapters. Education-based, it promotes the preservation of natural habitats and the use of appropriate native plants in landscaping. Individual chapters hold regularly scheduled meetings, lectures and plant and seed exchanges. Activities include field trips and community work projects, habitat restoration and plant surveys. The statewide annual meetings alternate between the state's different vegetational regions. An informative bimonthly newsletter keeps members up-to-date on local and regional events and publishes feature articles and book reviews. Annual membership is only $20 ($15 for students and seniors).

## Texas Natural Resource Conservation Commission

*P.O. Box 13087*
*Austin, Texas 78711*
☎ *1-800/64-TEXAS*
*www.tnrcc.state.tx.us*

This organization is the best single source for information on recycling and composting. Its program, "Clean Texas 2000" reports that five million tons of yard trimmings and food scraps end up in Texas landfills each year, which costs Texans over $100 million per year! The organization offers free brochures to help gardeners begin composting and mulching and understand low-impact pest management, common-sense watering and other environmentally sound practices. Two bulletins of special interest to would-be composters are: "Containing Compost: Building a Bin or Box for Your Backyard Compost," (TNRCC Pub. No. GI-50) and "Worm Composting" (Pub. No. GI- 219). Send inquiries to the Office of Pollution Prevention & Recycling.

## Texas Nature Conservancy

*P.O. Box 1440*
*San Antonio, Texas 78295-1440*
☎ *210/224-8774*
*www.tnc.org/texas*

The Nature Conservancy maintains 34 preserves throughout the state. Most are not open to the public, but member volunteers are invited to take part in workdays, botanical inventories, field trips and other events. The organization now protects almost a half-million acres of fragile landscape in cooperation with private owners and partnerships with businesses, environmental groups and several governmental agencies. Among the varied ecosystems the Conservancy is safeguarding in Texas are a beech-magnolia forest, tallgrass/blackland prairie, estuarial marshes, Chihuahuan high desert and Tamaulipan shrubland. There are several regional chapters; to learn more about the Conservancy and its properties that are open to the public, contact the state organization.

## Texas Parks and Wildlife Department

*4200 Smith School Road*
*Austin, Texas 78744*
☎ *1-800/792-1112 (general information) or 512/389-8900 (park reservations)*
*www.tpwd.state.tx.us*

Our State Parks play host to over 25 million visitors each year at 114 operational parks! The Department oversees everything from rugged camping sites to elegant historical homes. Here's a great gift idea: a Texas Conservation Passport! At a cost of $50 per year, it opens the gate to all of the system's parks that charge an entrance fee and allows access to special wilderness outings and interpretative tours. Passport holders also receive a newsletter and discounts on *Texas Parks and Wildlife* magazine.

Several of the State Parks sponsor tours, programs and workshops that relate to naturescaping. An excellent statewide program of interest to gardeners and nature enthusiasts is the "Design a Wildscape" guide for creating wildlife habitats in your own backyard. It can be as simple as providing food, water and shelter in a small area of your existing garden or as elaborate as restoring native vegetation throughout your landscape.

The Texas Wildscapes information packet contains booklets on butterfly and hummingbird gardening, a book entitled *The Backyard Naturalist*, information on feeders, nest boxes and regional lists of "wildlife friendly" plants (both Texas natives and hardy adapted plants grown in Texas). You will also get an application for certification. Once certified, you'll receive a weatherproof display sign. For a Texas Wildscapes packet send a $15 check or money order to: **Texas Wildscapes**, Nongame and Urban Program, 4200 Smith School Road, Austin, Texas 78744.

## Useful Wild Plants, Inc.

*2612 Sweeney Lane*
*Austin, Texas 78723*
☎ *512/928-4441*
*www.emultimedia.com/weedfeed*

Scooter Cheatham, Marshall Johnston and Lynn Marshall are in the process of writing a 12-volume book on native plants entitled, *Useful Wild Plants of Texas, the Southeastern and Southwestern United States, Southern Plains and New Mexico.* Their organization's subtitle is "Botany for the Real World," and its tee-shirt is inscribed, "Save the rainforest in your own backyard. Join the Useful Wild Plants of Texas!" Membership entitles you to a newsletter filled with information about native and naturalized plants and the chance to participate in field trips, classes, camp-outs and volunteer work with serious botanists who seem to have a lot of fun.

# Continuing Your Education

Many community colleges, arboreta and nature centers offer horticultural classes. Garden clubs and plant societies host hundreds of lecture series and gardening classes throughout the state. They're eager to share information, and sometimes they'll even find mentors for enthusiastic novices. Watch local newspapers and regional magazines for times and dates. Every major newspaper features garden columns, and almost every "talk-radio" station and TV channel offers a gardening program that allows you to call in with your questions.

The gardener's latest learning tool is the computer. If you're interested in gardening in cyberspace, be aware that many of the plants pictured and the attendant cultural information will not be applicable to Texas soils and climate.

## Here are three great Web sites for Texas gardeners:

## Aggie Horticulture

*http://aggie-horticulture.tamu.edu*

The information server of the Texas Horticulture Program; contains Master Gardener information, links to botanic gardens and arboreta all over the world and images of numerous new ornamental plants.

## Garden Escape

*www.garden.com*

Launched in 1995 and headquartered in Austin, this national on-line shopping service offers 12,000 products. Its information center serves gardeners throughout the country with regional garden tips, chat rooms and "The Garden Doctor," which promises to answer your garden questions within 24 hours. There's also "The Garden Planner," which looks very promising. The pre-designed gardens are not yet Texas-specific, but very competent landscape architects are working to improve the site and provide more services. It's an amazing new world!

## The Virtual Garden

*www.timeinc.com/vg/*

This server operated by Time Warner, Inc.; includes *Southern Living* Magazine, *Sunset* Western Garden series, and an excellent plant selector called the "Complete Garden Encyclopedia."

## Chapter Three

# Garden Construction

*"Nature does not complete things.
She is chaotic. Man must finish,
and he does so by making a
garden and building a wall...
Before I built a wall I'd ask to know
what I was walling in or walling out."*
....Robert Frost

# Before you Begin Your Garden

Whether you're establishing a new landscape or simply improving an existing one, take a hard look at what you've got before spending another penny! Good design is the difference between a yard and a garden. A garden is prime living space, worthy of as much attention as you've given to the arrangement of your home's interior spaces. To achieve a coherent design, you may want to hire a professional garden designer, or you can create your own plan. The process is the same either way.

☛ **Money-saving tip (a.k.a. Rule #1): Plan before you Plant!**

## Think about Function

Professional designers begin the design process by examining how the existing landscape works. Is there adequate space for parking, gardening, outdoor entertaining? A place for children to play? Good circulation? Adequate storage? Sufficient privacy? How does the garden look from inside the house? Is it usable at night? Are there drainage problems? Problems with soil erosion?

While visiting the homes of prospective clients, I've observed people who would never tolerate a cluttered closet or an inefficient kitchen enduring all sorts of inconveniences in the landscape. Sometimes there's no way for guests to get to the rear garden without encountering garbage cans or stepping into a mud puddle. Often the concrete patio poured by the contractor as a "selling feature" is too small for a table and chairs. There's no place to store hoes, hoses, bone meal or barbecue grills. The list goes on.

## Make a "Wish-list"

Family members should discuss how they would like to use their outdoor space... *He has always wanted a greenhouse and a vegetable garden; she dreams of a shady spot to curl up and read; the teenage daughter demands a sunning deck; the ten-year-old son wants a basketball goal and a tree house; the dog needs a place to run.* Everyone will perceive the property in different ways. Often this is where a professional designer is able to serve as family "therapist," asking the right questions and listening carefully. As the various members of the family start expressing their dreams for the property, ideas will begin falling into place.

☛ **Money-saving tip: Don't be afraid to invest in your landscape. According to** *MONEY* **magazine, landscaping has a 100 to 200 percent recovery value.**

## Consider the Climate

Another advantage a professional designer can bring you is familiarity with the region where he or she practices — the USDA Hardiness Zone, average dates of first and last frost, average annual rainfall, humidity levels, wind patterns, sun angles, soil temperatures, etc. Anyone new to gardening in Texas will have a lot to learn about the climate. If you've moved to Dallas from Detroit, for example, Zone 8 might sound like the tropics compared to the winter temperatures you experienced in Zone 5. If you've moved to Abilene from Atlanta (both in Zone 7), you could be tempted to think that the climate will be similar. You would be wrong in both instances. The USDA Hardiness Zone Map, which only addresses average winter temperature, doesn't begin to tell you everything you need to know about Texas weather!

Native Texans know that October through May are the premier months for enjoying outdoor living. Summer days are for hibernating, but no matter how cold the winter months may become, you can also expect a few sunny, seventy-two-degree days, perfect for enjoying your garden. Good regional design accommodates our variable winters and sustained summer heat. For example, an open west-facing deck that would have been delightful in Seattle would be unbearable in San Antonio. In a Texas landscape, a covered terrace with a fireplace to mitigate the occasional winter chill could provide year-around comfort.

# Survey Your Site

The garden plan starts with a drawing of what exists. The tools you'll use include graph paper, an architect's scale and a 50-foot tape for measuring the property. You may have a property survey in your files or be able to obtain one from the city. It will probably be drawn at an engineer's scale (1-inch = 20-feet), but you can have it photo-mechanically enlarged. Or, you can take measurements and draw the house and grounds on a large sheet of ¼-inch graph paper, with each square representing one foot. (If your lot is especially large, make the overall site plan at a smaller scale and then enlarge it for construction drawings and planting plans to the scale of ¼-inch = one foot.

Locate all of the home's windows and doors, noting dimensions on the plan. Draw a north-pointing arrow on the plan and note which direction each side of the house faces. Locate existing trees and shrubs. Check out sun angles and wind patterns, keeping in mind that each side of the house has its own micro climate. Observe the vistas from every direction, and make notes right on the plan... *Nice view to the south, patio bakes in the afternoon sun, unsightly view of the neighbor's boat from the dining room window, wasted space in front, gorgeous tree beside the garage...*

You can use a rod and hand level to determine the slope of the land on a simple site. Assume the elevation of the ground floor of the house to be 100 and set the property elevations accordingly. For example, an elevation of 98 would be two feet below the level of the floor of the house. If the lot is so steeply sloped that you have problems with erosion or so flat that you have potential drainage problems, call a landscape architect to prepare a plan for re-grading the property.

☛ **Money-saving tip: Locate sewer, water, gas and any buried electrical cable lines before even thinking about building anything in the landscape.**

Map both the above-ground and underground utilities, as well as any utility easements. If you don't know where your buried lines run, call the various service companies (gas, telephone, electrical, etc.) to come to your house and mark them.

# The Design Phase

After you have a drawing of what exists and you've analyzed how the garden is functioning, it's time to match your wish-list with the property's potential. Designers call this the "schematic phase." Think of it as "brainstorming." Place a piece of tracing paper over the site plan and sketch-in the various amenities your family members have proposed. (Try lots of different arrangements; tracing paper is cheap!) Every corner of the garden has a personality waiting to be developed, and even the tiniest lot will yield myriad solutions.

## Look at Your Options

In an unused side yard, you may discover the potential for a kitchen garden, a "secret garden" off a bedroom or a place for children to play. You'll want to select the most comfortable spots in the garden for the outdoor living areas, even if that means appropriating part of the front yard. There's no rule that says a patio must open off the back door. An entry courtyard might be an ideal place for dining outdoors or reading the Sunday paper. Perhaps an open spot in the rear garden has potential for a sunning deck. Just for visual pleasure, you might decide to break up an expanse of lawn with a gazebo or a fish pond or to build a rose arbor over a gateway.

☛ **Money-saving tip: It's a lot easier to erase pencil marks on a plan than it is to tear out a misplaced wall or walk!**

Before simply slapping an off-the-shelf fence around the perimeter of your property, consider investing in a decorative fence. You might also want to coordinate your fences with other garden structures. Here, you might save money *and* achieve a more pleasing effect. For example, fence posts can double as supports for an arbor or become part of a covered deck. An enclosed gazebo at the rear corner of a property may serve in lieu of a section of fence. A combination of evergreen shrubs and a lattice summerhouse might be used instead of a fence to screen off an unpleasant view while providing a shady spot to enjoy the outdoors.

☛ **Money-saving tip: Be sure to check your local building codes before designing any landscape construction project!**

You'll also want to look at the landscape's effect on household energy consumption. Evergreen trees and shrubs planted on the north might serve as a windbreak to reduce heat loss in winter. Deciduous trees planted on the south and west sides of the property can help cool your house in summer. In winter, they will lose their leaves, allowing the sunshine in.

You may even consider alterations to the house itself, such as French doors to link the house and garden or floor-to-ceiling windows that frame a section of the garden and visually expand the interior living space. You might build a solarium addition out into the garden or extend the roof line to create a covered outdoor seating area.

## Create "Comfort Zones"

As people rediscover the joy of entertaining and vacationing at home, outdoor living areas have become the most essential elements in the landscape. In selecting a site for a patio or other seating area, consider the comfort of all who will be using the space. You'll want privacy and protection from the wind, sun and rain. You'll also need to consider proximity to running water and electricity, and you may want to provide a phone connection. Covered terraces with ceiling fans are especially nice in this climate, and an outdoor fireplace to warm the "room" on chilly nights may extend your outdoor season throughout the year. (If you install an outdoor fireplace, be sure to consider prevailing breezes to avoid a back-draft of smoke, and be careful of overhanging limbs that could pose a fire hazard.)

☛ **Money-saving tip: Make outdoor living spaces large enough to meet all your needs.**

The mistake most commonly made is providing too little outdoor living space. It's a pity to go to all the trouble and expense of constructing a deck, for example, only to discover that a few more feet would have made the area far more functional. When you're designing a deck or patio, plan the sitting areas as carefully as you would plan the seating arrangement of your family room. Here you won't have to worry about the placement of the TV, but you will want the sitting area to face a pleasant view. You'll want ample room for a sofa or bench and as many chairs as you'll need to accommodate the kind of entertaining your family enjoys.

In addition to the space required for a seating arrangement, allow ample room for walking around and through the outdoor sitting room. If you're designing an outdoor dining room, you'll need a minimum of eight by eight feet for the eating area, plus a spot for a barbecue grill and perhaps a service bar. You'll want a minimum of four feet as a transition area between the cooking and eating areas. You might want to consider built-in benches to define and separate the various spaces.

# Provide Adequate Utility Areas

You'll need to accommodate the "business" end of the garden, and for many homeowners a garden shed is indispensable. Inside this structure, you may want to provide built-in benches and work tables as well as designated space for lawn mowers, wheelbarrows and other tools of the trade. Ideally the shed will have a water source and ample space to organize items by the season in which they will be used. A free-standing structure can also be strategically positioned to screen-off unsightly compost piles, cold frames, trash containers and such garden debris as old pots and garden stakes.

Such utility buildings as sheds and greenhouses take up a considerable amount of space on a small lot, so here's where you may want to get creative. With a bit of imaginative design, a homeowner might extend the eaves of a tool shed to create an arbor-like covered sitting area. The structure's roof could even be designed as a play fort for your children. Or, a greenhouse and garden shed could be combined into a single, handsome structure. Whatever its size, shape and function, a garden building should be incorporated into the landscape as part of an overall plan, and it should be designed to complement the style of the garden and the architecture of the house.

# Connect the Garden with Paths

Walkways are to a garden what hallways are to the house. I like to think of the entry walk as the home's first foyer. It sets the character of the landscape. A plain, straight concrete walk between the street and front door, although quite functional, doesn't hold the same welcoming appeal as a meandering pathway constructed of stone or brick. Walkways not only serve as connectors between the house and street, but also they lead from space to space within the garden. They may delineate between different sections of the landscape or be used to separate the lawn from the planting beds.

Walkways should be large enough for two people to walk abreast or for a gardener to maneuver the wheelbarrow or lawn mower; three and a half feet is considered a minimum width for the garden's major connecting links. For reasons of comfort and practicality, the main passageways should be paved. Pathways that lead to seldom-used portions of the garden or simply allow access within a large planting bed can be constructed of stepping stones, bark or gravel.

Steps require special attention. The proportions of garden steps should be different from indoor stairs. In the landscape, steps are more comfortable with deep treads and low risers (I like them only six inches high and 14-16-inches deep. It's very important to keep the riser heights constant throughout the landscape because unanticipated variations in height can cause people to trip and fall. A single step down also presents a danger in that it may not be immediately obvious. It's better to ramp the grade change if you need only one step down. And, if more than five steps are required, break up the staircase with a landing. All steps should be lighted at night.

# Implementing your Master Plan

Once you've considered all of your options, it's time to settle on a Master Plan. This plan is usually a culmination of weeks or months of exploration. There will have been compromises along the way. As the final blueprint for the garden's future, however, the Master Plan should show every deck, patio, walkway, fence, gazebo, etc. you hope to include in the garden. It should reflect the character of the house and its occupants, the family's needs and the capabilities of the site. If you, like most people, cannot immediately afford every improvement, divide the plan into sections (Phase 1, Phase 2, etc.) and build the garden at a pace and price you can manage.

After the Master Plan is drawn, the designer begins preparing a Grading Plan, and the homeowner starts selecting the materials that will be used in the garden. Once the material choices have been made, the designer can get down to detail in the Construction Drawings. With numerous helpful books and computer programs now on the market, many homeowners are capable of drawing their own design details for decks, walkways, etc.

&#9758; **Money-saving tip: Seek professional help with the design and construction of structures that require complicated calculations and special engineering techniques.**

Be aware that specific technical requirements govern such site amenities as driveways, freestanding masonry walls and retaining walls over three feet in height. The factors that must be considered in the design of a driveway, for example, include angle of slope, turning radius and the weight of the vehicles that will be using it. Walls must be designed to withstand the forces of wind and water.

# Deal with Drainage Problems

Proper grading is vital because Texas weather alternates between frog-choking rain and dust-bowl drought. Finding a way to rapidly carry rainwater away from the house can be a nettlesome problem. If standing water is severe and continual, you'll probably need professional help.

The average homeowner can usually correct minor, recurring puddles in lawn areas or planting beds with a simple subsurface drainage system (often called a "French drain"). It's made by digging a trench 12-inches deep and 12-inches wide, with the bottom of the trench sloping away from the problem area toward a slope or storm drain. Line the trench with a layer of gravel, lay-in a four-inch-diameter perforated PVC pipe wrapped in filter fabric and back-fill with coarse gravel. To drain effectively, the slope of the drain should descend at least an inch per foot. This may be impossible in low-lying areas.

Increasingly, city regulations may require you to retain rainwater on your site rather than discharge it into the storm sewer system. One attractive solution is to construct a dry creek that leads excess water toward a small depression in the lawn that serves as a holding pond. When it isn't carrying water, a rock-lined creek bed can be an attractive landscape feature. Perhaps you'll want to run a flagstone walk beside it, line it with iris and design a bridge to cross it. The "stream bed" can terminate in a "bog garden" filled with plants that can withstand both wet and dry conditions. Artificial berms can be constructed to direct both rainfall and excess irrigation water into these wet/dry planting areas.

If, on the other hand, you are dealing with a steep slope and rapid run-off, you may want to construct a series of steppes or retaining walls. (Farmers in dry climates have used terracing to maximize rainwater for centuries.) Rather than let water rush down a slope, terraces conserve the precious water that falls on your site, releasing it more slowly, allowing it to penetrate the soil and preventing erosion. A French drain at the base of each retaining wall will prevent the soil from becoming waterlogged during periods of heavy rainfall. For more moderate slopes, erosion-control fabric is useful for covering newly-tilled soil until the plants are established.

# Select Appropriate Materials

Once the walls, fences and pathways are drawn, it's time for the homeowner to select the materials that will be used for the landscape project. Whatever the choice of materials, they should complement both the architectural style of the house and the garden you envision. For example, a wood deck or a patio paved with Mexican tile are attractive choices for a contemporary or ranch-style home, while brick or cut stone might be more appropriate for a traditional home and garden. A raised planting bed constructed of rugged rock has a very different feel from a tidy timber box painted the same color as the house. The former suggests big, bold naturalistic plantings; for the latter, I picture a more orderly planting scheme.

The Sunset book, *How to Build Walks, Walls and Patio Floors*, discusses the pros and cons of several different landscape materials. If you're designing your own garden, this book is a good starting point for making decisions. It offers practical information on relative costs and durability of brick, gravel, concrete, asphalt, tile, stone and wood. And, it provides good technical information on grading, drainage and foundation requirements.

Materials can be combined to create interest, but too many materials become confusing. I rarely use more than three. If I want to make a small garden seem larger, I'll often use a single material such as brick for all of the walls, walks and patios. Eventually walkways step up to a porch or transition into a patio or courtyard floor that connects directly into the house. Therefore, the materials you choose and the patterns you create in these transitional areas should be selected with an eye toward unifying the house and garden.

Retaining walls present special design challenges. They can be constructed of timber, stone, brick-faced concrete or concrete block. Freestanding walls require footings that will stand up to wind loads, and retaining walls are subject to tremendous forces of water. Walls of any significant height require reinforced concrete footings, and provision must be made for weep holes to ensure proper drainage. Get professional advice before building any walls over three feet in height.

Brick, stone, concrete and wood are the basic choices for the garden's floors and walls. Each of these materials comes in many forms and colors. Each holds the possibility of an almost infinite number of patterns and textures in the landscape. Consider your options carefully because the cost of garden construction depends not only upon the material you choose, but also the labor involved for installation.

## Poured Concrete

Concrete is the single most overused landscape material because it's durable, relatively inexpensive and easily molded into intricate forms. It may be the only feasible choice if you're dealing with large areas and/or curving shapes. However, large expanses of concrete can appear cold and monotonous. Exposed aggregate concrete is warmer than brush-finished concrete, and, if the concrete is combined with a brick border or stone insets, it takes on an even more friendly feeling.

I'm enthusiastic about the effects that can be achieved with colored, stamped concrete that simulates the feel of cobblestone, slate or brick. It "dresses up" the garden, yet it costs less than half as much as professionally installed natural stone or brickwork. The process is tricky, so it's not a job for amateurs. Ask to see completed examples of the work of companies that pour and form stamped concrete. They operate through trained, local licensed contractors, who serve large geographical areas. (See pages 113 and 114 for sources.)

## Brick, Tile & Concrete Pavers

Brick and concrete pavers are attractive and versatile, but labor-intensive to install. Mortared brick walkways and patios usually require the skills of a mason. The average homeowner can lay a relatively durable walk or patio by placing the brick on a bed of compacted sand, sweeping dry mortar mix between the joints, and moistening with a hose to set the mortar. To hold the loose bricks in place, however, you'll need to install a solid edging, such as mortared brick, treated wood or one of the new plastic or steel edging materials made for the purpose.

Given a choice between natural (fired-clay) brick and concrete pavers, I have generally preferred the look of brick. However, concrete pavers have become increasingly sophisticated in recent years, and the variety of colors and shapes available have made it possible to create remarkably interesting patterns in the landscape. The cost is about the same. If you can find a clay brick that you like, there's no real advantage to using concrete pavers for walkways and patios. However, clay brick used for a driveway requires a reinforced concrete base; interlocking concrete pavers need only a sand base. So, if you want to match the driveway and walkways, concrete pavers would be the more cost-effective choice.

Tile is a great choice for covering an unattractive old entry porch or small concrete terrace, but it's the most expensive material you can choose for large-scale new construction. It runs two to four times more per square foot than brick or concrete pavers, and it must be set on a concrete base. To be suitable for landscape use, the product must be non-skid and frost-proof. Included among the wealth of handsome tile paving materials readily available for Texas gardens are terra cotta clay tiles and quarried stone cut in the form of tiles.

## Natural Stone

Ironically, the biggest difficulty with natural stone is making it appear natural. You'll be more pleased with the results if you choose a stone that harmonizes with the color of the local soil. Limestone "belongs" in the Hill Country, while red sandstone blends better into the landscapes of East Texas and the Red Rolling Plains. Stonework can appear very arbitrary in the Blackland Prairies and coastal regions where there is no native stone.

There's artistry involved in setting stone, but a non-professional can lay it if the pieces are small enough to lift by hand. The book, *Stonescaping: A Guide to Using Stone in Your Garden*, by Jan Kowalczewski Whitner, is an excellent source of information. For ideas on the use of rock in the landscape, also seek-out books on Japanese garden design. Some of the secrets to success include paying attention to the grain of the rock and partially burying boulders, just as they are found in nature.

Weathered stone is generally more attractive and almost always more expensive than freshly cut stone. When I built an extensive limestone patio at my home in Austin, I used an affordable mix of weathered and new stones. The contractor mixed lampblack into the mortar, which unified the surface and created the overall effect of old stonework.

Crushed rock or gravel should not be overlooked as a handsome material for pathways and driveways. It's particularly attractive when contained within bold landscape timbers or used as a filler between stepping stones. The price is right.

Texas native stone of every description is readily available throughout the state. It's expensive to ship, so if you are looking for uncut (random-shaped) flagstone or landscape boulders, begin your search with local dealers. If there is more than one source for decorative rocks and paving stones in your area, visit several before deciding which material to choose. You may be surprised to find great differences in prices and selections. There are several companies in Texas that provide cut stone for special uses such as formally patterned walkways, pool coping and architectural detailing. (See pages 116 and 117.)

## Wood

The appeal of wood is that it blends comfortably with the natural environment and achieves a warmth that no other material can match. At about $10 per square foot, wood decking is comparable to mortared brick or stone work in terms of cost. Wood decking allows you to build out over part of the landscape, in some cases doubling your gardening space, with container gardening on the deck and a shade garden beneath.

However, if you're building an outdoor living area close to ground-level and do not have sufficient space between the ground and decking for good air circulation, choose a material other than wood. You'll see wood decks and walks built right on the ground in some of the national magazines, but it's never an advisable practice. There are, however, new decking materials made from recycled materials (cedar chips, plastics and/or old tires) that would work for such applications. The advantages of using such "lumber" include durability in areas that have unusually high exposure to the elements and ease of maintenance.

Sunset's *How to Plan & Build Decks* is an excellent resource for the do-it-yourself deck builder. Even if you're hiring a contractor to build a deck, you should read the section entitled "Buyer's Guide to Building Materials," which not only explains lumber terminology, but also illustrates various types of substructures and attachment methods. The book's color photographs will spark your imagination, and the section, "Protecting Your Investment," will ensure additional years of enjoyment.

# Prepare for Construction

The final steps in the design process will be the Specifications for Soil Preparation, which we will discuss in Chapter Four, and the Planting Plan, which we'll get to in Chapter Five. Before any soil work or planting begins, complete your construction projects. Believe me, they're *always* messy!

Site preparation is the most time-consuming part of many landscape projects, especially if you are building a walk, patio or garden structure over an existing lawn. Getting rid of grass, especially Bermuda grass, is infinitely more difficult than getting it to grow. You can smother it for a couple of months under black plastic or use herbicide to dispatch it quickly. In either case, it's prudent to remove the dead grass and its tenacious root system with a sod cutter.

If you're laying brick on sand, you'll need to place a barrier beneath the sand to reduce the chance of vegetation growing up between the cracks. A layer of polyethylene or roofing felt will suffice, but a brand-name product designed specifically for the job will be more permanent. There's usually some earth moving involved as well. Walkways should be laid with a slight "crown" along the center or slanted toward a slope to shed water. Where walkways adjoin planting beds, raise the level of the walkway so that soil and mulches won't wash out onto the path every time it rains. All patios must be sloped away from the house.

If you've ever had to tear out a section of driveway to install an irrigation line, you'll appreciate how nice it would have been had someone thought to have cast a piece of open pipe into the concrete form *before* the concrete was poured. Called "sleeves" in the industry, pipes set at intervals under new pavement allow you to decide later whether you want to run electrical or irrigation lines for night lighting and/or a sprinkler system. Pennies spent on plastic pipe can literally save hundreds of dollars!

Expect construction damage. I've seen left-over concrete dumped on tree roots, paint splattered all over hedges and plants trampled to a pulp. If you have valuable trees on your lot and there's going to be major construction, keep all men, machines, materials and portable potties out from under the drip line of the trees at

all times. Build a temporary fence around the trees and rope-off planting areas that are to be protected. Allow no cut or fill around the trees. If it appears that cutting or filling around tree roots will be essential to the completion of your building project, there are ways to minimize damage to the roots. Consult a landscape architect or arborist.

☞ **Money-saving tip: Protect existing plants from construction damage by writing in a dollar amount that will cover the cost of replacement if the contractor does not follow the rules!**

Once you're ready to tackle the project, your local lumber yard or home supply store will be a good source for landscape materials. Every city in Texas has listings in the Yellow Pages for retail suppliers of specialty materials for landscape construction and qualified contractors who can help you implement your plan. We've also listed here several suppliers and manufacturers who can direct you to dealers in your area or ship specialty garden products to your doorstep.

# Sources for Stamped Concrete:

*Bomanite*®

**Bomanite of El Paso**
*1075 Esplanada*
*El Paso, Texas 79932*
☎ *915/584-4888*
**FAX** *915/581-6696*

**Bomanite of Houston, Inc.**
*P.O. Box 925*
*Houston, Texas 77001*
☎ *713/523-6210*
**FAX** *713/523-1163*

**Bomanite of the Valley**
*Rt. 3, Box 242*
*Harlingen, Texas 78552*
☎ *956/428-1300*
**FAX** *956/428-1307*

**Bomanite of West Texas**
*4724 W. Storey*
*Midland, Texas 79703*
☎ *915/520-4028*

**Cactus Concrete**
*8700 Grenada Hills Drive*
*Austin, Texas 78737*
☎ *512/288-3773*
**FAX** *512/288-1991*

**North Texas Bomanite, Inc.**
*2636 Walnut Hill Lane, Suite 316*
*Dallas, Texas 75229*
☎ *972/350-8040 or 1-800/492-2524*
**FAX** *972/484-8466*

For over four decades this company has offered a virtually limitless palette of colors, textures and patterns in its poured-in-place concrete. The six local licensees serve wide areas. They can provide you with samples, color chips, photos, references and technical information. Or you can call the Bomanite® national office in California (☎ 1-800/854-2094) or check out the Web site (www.bomanite.com) for more information.

## Patterned Concrete Industries, Ltd.®

### Patterned Concrete by Rey, Inc.
4205 Prospect Lane
Plano, Texas 75093
☎ 972/964-0411

### Patterned Concrete of Dallas
901 East Highway 121
Lewisville, Texas 75056
☎ 972/434-2507

### Patterned Concrete by Rick Davis
5010 Quail Gate
Spring, Texas 77373
☎ 281/353-0154

### Patterned Concrete of Lubbock
5104 34th Street
Lubbock, Texas 79410
☎ 806/799-8743

### Patterned Concrete of Austin
15909 Booth Circle
Volente, Texas 78641
☎ 512/258-9324

This Oklahoma-based company (☎ 1-800/252-4619), has licensed and trained an international network of contractors to install decorative architectural concrete. Patterned Concrete Industries, Ltd.® offers a wide variety of patterns in both standard and custom colors. The colors are mixed through the concrete to realistically simulate stone or brick.

# Sources for Modular Paving Materials & Retaining Wall Systems:

## D'Hanis Brick & Tile Company
311 East Nakoma
San Antonio, Texas 78216
☎ 210/525-8142 or 1-800/299-9399
**FAX** 210/349-2833 or 1-800/299-9398
**Hours** Mon-Fri 8-5
**Catalog** Free brochure

D'Hanis has been making brick for Texas homes and gardens since 1905. Available in Natural Terra Cotta Red and Mocha Brown, the products are hard-fired at 1,800-degrees F. for exceptional durability. The company's floor tiles, which are sized 4"x8", 8"x8" or 12"x12", are especially attractive for patio and walkway applications because of the low porosity of the product. The surface can be finished with a water-based sealer, or the tile can be used in moderate weathering climates without sealing. The company also produces handsome brick pavers and interlocking pavers in several sizes and finishes. Its five-inch-thick turf pavers for parking areas and driveways are designed with five octagonal holes to protect grass roots and effectively retain moisture. Set vertically, these 8"x8" perforated tiles can be used as a fence material and/or solar screen. Call or fax the company for a free brochure and the name of a nearby dealer.

## *Featherlite Building Products*

P.O. Box 1029
Austin, Texas 78767
☎ 512/472-2424 (corporate office)
**FAX** 512/472-2586
**Hours** Mon-Fri 7:30-5
**Catalog** Free

Featherlite's plants in Abilene, Amarillo, Beaumont, Corpus Christi, Dallas, El Paso, Lubbock, Round Rock and San Antonio produce especially attractive concrete block in split-face and burnished finishes. It's also making new lines of concrete paving stones and retaining wall blocks, which will be available in a wide choice of colors and patterns.

## *Pavestone*

3215 State Highway 360
Grapevine, Texas 76051
☎ 817 481-5802
**FAX** 817/488-3216

13702 Thermal Drive
Austin, Texas 78728
☎ 512/346-7245
**FAX** 512/251-3026

30001 Katy-Brookshire Road
Katy, Texas 77494
☎ 281/391-7283
**FAX** 281/391-7337

**Hours** Mon-Fri 8-5

This Dallas-based national company manufactures concrete pavers in 23 different patterns, with eight monochromatic colors and four production blends. Custom colors are available with a minimum order of 10,000 pavers. Patterns include a paver in the shape of Texas, which makes a playful patio floor in the right setting. More sophisticated forms include Roman Cobble™ and City Stone™. The company has recently introduced a handsome "Designer Series" that features textured finishes and multicolor blends. Round stepping stones and scalloped edgings can also the found in Pavestone's extensive product line.

The company makes a handsome modular block that enables homeowners to build retaining walls that do not require concrete footings or mortar. The retaining walls may be straight, concave, convex or laid as serpentine curves. Made of high strength concrete, these walls are virtually maintenance-free. Attractive capstones also make nice steps. Each retaining wall block weighs 26 pounds; you'll need a licensed civil engineer to design any wall over three feet in height. For simple raised beds or other retaining walls less than two feet high, the company makes a lightweight block. Pavestone products are available through a network of local retail suppliers. Call the branch office nearest you for a free brochure and the name of a supplier in your area. Design and installation guides are available from the manufacturer.

# Sources for Cut or Carved Stone:

## Arte en Cantera

2900 North McColl Road
McAllen, Texas 78501
☎ 956/682-1623
**FAX** 956/682-8252
**Hours** Mon-Sat 8-6
**Accessible** Yes
**Mail Order**
**Catalog** Free

This company imports handsome cantera stone decking materials, balustrades, columns, pool coping and fountains from Guadalajara. Customers select the color and supply the measurements; quarry workers hand-cut and shape the stone to Arte en Cantera's specifications. Owner Ricardo Azubell says, "Cantera stone is both elegant and functional. Ordering the precise stone and making sure it arrives exactly as ordered is our secret to creating beautiful accents and assuring happy customers." The company installs the products throughout South Texas and can ship to you or your contractor in other regions of the state.

## Custom Stone Supply

4433 Terry-O Lane
Austin, Texas 78745
☎ 512/462-3363 or 1-800/273-0136
**FAX** 512/462-3365
**Hours** Mon-Fri 7:30-5:30, Sat 7:30-3
**Accessible** Partially
**Mail Order**
**Catalog** Free brochures

Custom Stone Supply stocks local and imported limestone, sandstone from various regions in the country, slate, schist and granite, including Texas pink. Among the specialty aggregates from different parts of the United States are a colorful Texas "rainbow rock" and black Mexican beach pebbles. The company offers custom milling for architectural and paving purposes, as well as pool coping, boulders and ledge rock. Delivery is available throughout the state.

## Materials Marketing

120 West Josephine
San Antonio, Texas 78212
☎ 210/731-8453
**FAX** 210/733-4658

1801 North Lamar, suite 200
Austin, Texas 78701
☎ 512/328-0225
**FAX** 512/328-0517

3433 West Alabama
Houston, Texas 77027
☎ 713/960-8601
**FAX** 713/960-9163

**Hours** Mon-Fri 8-5, Sat 10-2
**Accessible** All except Houston store; call ahead for portable ramp
**Mail Order**
**Catalog** Free

Materials Marketing is a wonderful source for ceramic, saltillo and cantera stone pavers. The company also carries every imaginable architectural embellishment for the exterior of southwestern-style houses — columns, door and window surrounds and handsome fountains. This is also a good source for imported decorative tile to be used on walls, fountains and outdoor counter tops. (See page 318.)

## San Jacinto Materials

*1423 North San Jacinto*
*San Antonio, Texas 78207*
☎ *210/736-0924*
**FAX** *210/736-6943*
**Hours** *Mon-Fri 8-4*
**Accessible** *Yes*
**Mail Order**
**Catalog** *Free brochure*

This company's artisans make coping, portals, fountains and fireplaces (machine or hand-carved) from sandstone and limestone. (Send drawings and specifications for quotes.) You'll also find a large supply of natural stone for a multitude of landscape uses at this full-service stone yard.

## Texas Quarries

*P.O. Box 820*
*Cedar Park, Texas 78630*
☎ *512/258-1474*
**FAX** *512/258-0808*
**Hours** *Mon-Fri 7:30-5*
**Mail Order**
**Catalog** *Free brochure*

Texas Quarries has been in the limestone fabrication business since 1929. "We can make just about anything — turned columns, coping, balusters, etc." says the manager. Ornate carving is a specialty. The Featherlite division of the company offers 1¼-inch and 2¼-inch thick, random-shaped patio stone. Available in cordova cream or shell, this handsome paving material is finished top and bottom to provide a level walking surface.

# Do Fence Me In

Fences not only serve the functions of privacy and security, but also they make an architectural statement. Often the fence is the strongest visual element in a new landscape. Constructed along the perimeter, a handsome fence provides a nice backdrop for an interesting planting scheme. Sections of fencing within the property can be used to create intimate spaces, separate the garden's functions or allow a new use for a portion of the landscape. For example, you might convert part of an open front yard into an entry court or reclaim a side yard as a secure play area. It must be remembered, however, that a high, tight fence built as a visual screen will also act as a windbreak, which may be an asset or a liability.

In choosing your fence material, consider the architectural style of your home. For a traditional cottage, I might select a wood fence topped with lattice, a picket fence or ornamental iron. I might punctuate this fence with a rose-covered trellis arching over the garden gate. A diagonally patterned wood fence would better serve a contemporary residence, and here, I might incorporate an arbor with strong diagonal bracing. For an Oriental effect, I might select a bamboo fence or an intricate design in wood set off with a handsome roofed gate.

Wood is by far the most commonly used material for fences. Don't settle for a plain, off-the-shelf fence until you've looked at the many textural patterns possible with wood fencing — vertical, horizontal, diagonal, basket weave, lattice and louvered. Attention to detail is what makes each fence special. The Sunset book, *Fences and Gates*, is filled with pictures that inspire creative thinking. I hire a freelance carpenter to build wood fences for my most discriminating clients, but many of the fencing companies listed in the yellow pages are willing to do custom-quality work.

In my professional opinion, a chain-link fence devalues a residential landscape unless it is completely hidden by evergreen shrubs or vines. New vinyl-clad chain link fencing, which is available in black, brown or green, tends to "disappear" within a leafy background. To economically surround a large backyard, I've used brick walls or ornamental iron on the side facing the street and vinyl-coated chain link (screened with plantings) along the sides and back of the property. At about $8 per lineal foot, vinyl chain-link fencing compares favorably to a wood fence, with the added advantage of increased durability.

Ornamental iron fencing, which was widely used around Victorian homes in Texas, is making a strong comeback in garden design today. An airy iron fence is especially nice where you have a view. Because even the simplest ornamental iron fences run close to $30 per lineal foot installed, most people choose iron work only for highly visible portions of the fence. Sections of antique iron fencing can be used as attractive focal points within the garden.

Another increasingly viable option is vinyl fencing. I've used vinyl lattice extensively for fencing and trellis work because it never needs painting and doesn't rot. The lattice is available in a multitude of colors, various thickness, several patterns and different panel widths. It is as attractive as wood lattice and far more durable (albeit more expensive) than the thin wood lattice sold in sheets at building supply stores. Vinyl lattice used atop wood slats "dresses-up" a fence, allows greater air circulation in the garden and provides a place for lacy vines to twine. Call these two national manufacturers for brochures and local sources:
**Cross Vinyl Lattice** (☎ 1-800/521-9878) and **Permalatt, Inc.** (☎ 1-888/457-4342.)

Whatever your fence material, the garden gate should make a good first impression. It should stand out from the pattern of the fence, yet harmonize with the fence design. Often, I'll pick up an architectural detail from the house and repeat it in the gate design. To make the gate even more distinctive, I like to set off the gateposts with finials or lights. It's up to homeowners to know what they want and to demand the highest quality possible within their budget. In fencing, like most other things, you get what you pay for.

Properly designed and built, a wood fence should last without repair for twenty years. Its posts are the critical element for ensuring durability. I use either pressure-treated timbers or metal posts. Be sure the depth of the post hole is sufficiently deep and wide to accommodate a stout concrete footing. Depth of burial should equal one-third of the height of the post above ground (i.e. the post for a six-foot-high fence could be no less than eight-feet-long). The width of the footing should be at least three times greater than the diameter of the post. Set the bottom of the post in four or five inches of gravel so that the wood or metal does not stand in water or come in contact with earth. The concrete is then poured on top of the gravel. The tops of the posts should be slightly pointed, rounded or beveled to shed water.

☛ **Money-saving tip: Before signing a contract for fence installation, ask to see samples of a company's work.**

Beware of mass-market companies that assemble fences with staples rather than ring-shank galvanized nails. If you're building down a slope, insist that the fence be designed to step down in increments, with the top of each section horizontal. (The cheap and easy way is to saw off the tops at an angle.) Be sure that gates are to be constructed with extra-sturdy posts and diagonal bracing; otherwise, they will begin to sag within a few months.

☛ **Money-saving tip: If you're handy with a hammer, you can have a local fence company set the posts and construct the face of the fence yourself.**

Setting the posts is the really backbreaking part of the job. I know a homeowner who completed a decorative double-sided fence in a day with boards purchased pre-cut from a lumber yard. There are a number of books that illustrate various construction methods.

# Rediscover Garden "Follies"

Modern gardeners have fallen in love with romantic garden structures. Arbors, belvederes, bowers, gazebos, grottos, hermitages, kiosks, lathhouses, pagodas, pavilions, pergolas, summerhouses, temples and trellises have played important roles in the landscapes of every culture. These structures remain popular because they are practical! Wonderful vine-covered arbors still provide cooling shade in summer. Pavilions continue to make lovely places to escape for al fresco dining, relaxing or sleeping. Beyond mere shelter, garden "follies" are important focal points.

Today's garden structures can be traditional or contemporary in design. An old-fashioned gazebo might incorporate a spa with benches that double as storage compartments. A summerhouse may include a built-in barbecue grill, a wet bar and under-the-counter refrigerator. A fanciful pergola might be used to camouflage the side of a garage as well as support a flowering vine. Lattice lath houses can be designed to screen off a dog run while providing a place for potting and propagating plants.

You'll find small garden structures, such as trellises and rose arbors in all the home improvement stores and large garden centers. Also, see Regional Resources for Garden Accessories in Chapter Ten, which lists special shops that cater to gardeners' practical and aesthetic needs. The listings that follow include suppliers for pre-fabricated components and/or custom-made garden structures. Most offer free catalogs and ship their products.

# Sources for Garden Structures:

### *Affordable Portable Structures*

*15324 North IH-35*
*Austin, Texas 78728*
☎ *512/251-5757*
**FAX** *512/251-7399*

*5510 Highway 290 West*
*Austin, Texas 78735*
☎ *512/892-0797*
**FAX** *512/891-9280*

*www.affordableportable.com*
**Hours** *Mon-Fri 9-6, Sat 10-4*
**Accessible** *Yes*
**Mail Order**
**Catalog** *Free*

This company's all wood structures can be built on location from a kit or delivered to your property in Central Texas. The Mini is available in sizes ranging from 8'x10' to 10'x16'. The taller Maxi comes in sizes up to 12'x20'. Exteriors are clad in 7/16" hardboard siding covered with two coats of acrylic latex paint, with a choice of 12 colors. The American, which can be ordered with an attached porch and screened windows, would make a wonderful playhouse for children. The company also carries a line of six different gazebos constructed by Amish craftsmen in Lancaster County, Pennsylvania. These structures are made of #1 treated, kiln-dried lumber with shake cedar roofs and handcrafted cupolas. You'll find classic rose arbors, small wood bridges, a line of picnic tables, settees and gliders, and a selection of sturdy, attractive doghouses.

### *Anthony Wood Products*

*113 Industrial Loop*
*Hillsboro, Texas 76645*
☎ *254/582-7225*
**FAX** *254/582-7620*
**Hours** *Mon-Fri 8-5*
**Mail Order**
**Catalog** *$3*
**Mailing Address** *P.O. Box 1081, Hillsboro, Texas 76645*

This an excellent source for the do-it-yourself market. If you're seeking components for building a distinctive wood fence, porch or gazebo, this manufacturing company produces brackets, corbels, fretwork, gable trim and finials in cedar, redwood , poplar and oak. Specializing in traditional Victorian gingerbread, the owners are dedicated to Old World standards of craftsmanship. Anthony Wood Products also offers custom reproduction services to duplicate missing or deteriorated gingerbread.

## Childres Custom Canvas

*711 Highway 67 South*
*Duncanville, Texas 75137*
☎ *972/298-4943 or 1-800/631-2008*
**FAX** *972/709-7453*
**Hours** *Mon-Fri 8-5, Sat 9-1*
**Accessible** *Yes*
**Mail Order**
**Catalog** *Free brochures*

Quality workmanship has earned this company a nationwide customer base for its window awnings, patio covers (stationary or retractable) and free-standing shade covers. Hundreds of designs and colors are available; send your measurements and color preferences, and the company will respond with a marketing package that includes fabric swatches. Most of its residential awnings are made of a marine fabric from *Sunbrella*® that carries a five-year warranty. "Our awning will be so taut and wrinkle-free you can bounce a penny off it," says office manager Lisa Thornton.

## Classic Cottages

*611 North Tumbleweed Trail*
*Austin, Texas 78733*
☎ *512/263-5091*
**FAX** *512/263-5746*
**Hours** *Mon-Sat, by appointment only*
**Accessible** *Yes*
**Mail Order**
**Catalog** *Free brochure*

In every building they create, Kevin and Phyllis Woodworth promise to "bring back the romantic style and character of yesteryear." The storage structures, potting sheds, playhouses and gazebos they build are little gems. Brimming with creativity and enthusiasm, the Woodworths lay claim to over 5,000 original designs in sketch form. You can select from an existing cottage that's ready for delivery or they'll design a building to meet your specific needs and site, customized with special doors, stained glass windows, skylights, decorative trim and more. Inside, you can incorporate practical benches, built-in cabinets and lofts. They'll visit your site if you're in the Central Texas area, but often they communicate with clients by long distance, fax and photos and ship the product to your home. Envisioned as garden "destinations," these theme and traditional buildings really provide something interesting to behold from your kitchen window.

## Texas Great Outdoors

*3425 Airport Freeway*
*Fort Worth, Texas 76111*
☎ *817/831-1614*
**FAX** *817/831-6561*
**Hours** *Mon-Fri 10-5:30, Sat 10-2*
**Accessible** *Partial*
**Mail Order**
**Catalog** *Brochure & price list*

The motto for Texas Great Outdoors is "Unique Concepts In Outdoor Living." This is a group that designs, builds and sells high-quality gazebos, arbors, storage buildings, garden furniture, porch swings and weather vanes. The products are most attractively displayed. The company also builds and installs pool cabanas, sun rooms, water features, redwood decks, spas, iron work, pavers and path lighting. Texas Great Outdoors is definitely worth a visit! Prices are marked down in late spring and again in fall.

*Directions: From Dallas, take the Beech Street exit off Airport Freeway (Highway 121); from Fort Worth, take the Riverside exit. The company is located on the access road on the north side of the Freeway.*

## Vintage Wood Works

*Highway 34 South*
*Quinlan, Texas 75474*
☎ *903/356-2158*
**FAX** *903/356-3023*
**Hours** *Mon-Fri 8-4:30*
**Accessible** *Yes*
**Mail Order**
**Catalog** *$4.95; free product brochures*
**Mailing Address** *P.O. Box R, Quinlan, Texas 75474*

Vintage Woodwork's octagonal, bell-roof gazebo creates a real focal point in the garden. The look is light and lacy, but this 11-foot wide x 11-foot-tall cedar and redwood structure is very substantial. It's made to be easily assembled, and it can be customized with different brackets and spandrels. The company also offers an attractive porch swing. If you're remodeling, its color catalog illustrates Victorian and classical porches enhanced with decorative posts and balustrades, as well as plain exteriors dressed up with handsome screen/storm doors. "We always welcome your calls and letters," reads the catalog introduction, ""Some of you already know exactly what you want. Others, at least from time to time, need a little input from us (or maybe even a lot!)" Most of this woodworking factory's business is mail order (and most of its products are for interior use), but you are welcome to stop by if you're in the area.

*Directions: 30 miles east of Dallas between Greenville and Terrell on Highway 34, about ½ mile south of town.*

## The Wood Factory

*111 Railroad Street*
*Navasota, Texas 77868*
☎ *409/825-7233*
**FAX** *409/825-1791*
**Hours** *Mon-Fri 8-5*
**Accessible** *Yes*
**Mail Order**
**Catalog** *Free brochure*

Remodeling contractor Dean Arnold found an old machine and began making fine copies of Victorian millwork. Now his company has expanded into a custom woodworking shop noted for distinctive millwork. Among the product line you'll find beautifully crafted posts, finials and pickets for traditional wood fences. The parts are fabricated from redwood and pre-sanded for painting. The Wood Factory's brochure also depicts all sorts of gingerbread, entry doors and handsome fixed gables that can be made to fit existing gables. The company offers reprints of several old millwork catalogs. "We could not possibly include all the designs in our catalog that were original to the Victorian period. We pride ourselves on our reputation to match existing porch parts or create a new look for your individual needs," says Dean. He and his wife Kathy are on call to help you achieve that custom look.

# Make Room for a Greenhouse

While the primary appeal of a greenhouse may be to indulge an interest in orchids or cacti, it also allows you to get a head-start on spring or store your patio plants in winter. It may simply be a quiet retreat where rain-or-shine greenery offers solace for the soul. Greenhouses have often been used as visual features in the garden, but tool shed and storage buildings have rarely served any use other than function. Well-designed storage structures may serve as attractive focal points in the garden while addressing more practical functions.

Greenhouses range from a $200 window greenhouse to a $25,000 solarium that may serve as a breakfast room, a spa enclosure or even an entrance hall. There are so many options today! If it's to be attached to your house, you'll want a unit with glass glazing and nicely detailed framing. If it will be screened off from the living areas of the garden, one of the less expensive, more utilitarian fiberglass or plastic models may work well for you. A third option is a well-detailed free-standing greenhouse that functions as focal point in the garden.

One of the best I've ever seen was designed by the co-author of this book. At her previous home, Patricia built a handsome freestanding greenhouse that also housed a small exercise pool and a comfortable sitting area. It provided a cozy place for plants and people in winter, and with its multiple French doors open, the space functioned as part of the garden in summer. Designed to replicate the colonial style of her home, the building was linked to the house by a covered breezeway.

Attached greenhouses are generally less expensive to heat than free-standing models because they share a wall with the house. They are also easier to hook up to utilities. Before you attach a working greenhouse, however, consider the moisture factor and the heat-load on your home furnace.

☛ **Money-saving tip: Be sure to check local building codes before ordering any greenhouse or garden building.**

# Sources for Greenhouses & Solariums:

## Coleman Bright Ideas

4820 S.E. Loop 820
Ft. Worth, Texas 76140
☎ 817/572-0004 or 1-800/880-4820
**FAX** 817/572-2407
**Hours** Mon-Sat 10-6, Sun 1-5
**Accessible** Yes
**Mail Order**
**Catalog** Free

This Fort Worth-based company makes solariums, "sky windows," and window walls that can extend a section of your home into the garden. "With Coleman you are buying direct from the manufacturer." says Mr. Coleman. "Service is provided by our own factory service department with professionally trained, experienced staff. For most companies, building sunrooms is a secondary effort. At Coleman, building the finest Garden Room® addition is our specialty." The company, which has been in business since 1958 also makes attractive patio covers and shade structures.

## The Greenhouse Mall

9900 Ranch Road 620 North
Austin, Texas 78726-2203
☎ 512/250-0000
**FAX** 512/250-0000
**Hours** Mon-Sat 10-6, Sun 12-6 (summer); Mon-Sat 10-5, Sun 12-5 (winter)
**Accessible** Partially (carts available)
**Mail Order**
**Catalog** Free

The Greenhouse Mall an experience to visit. Owner Matt Wiggers may personally escort you through his several acres on a golf cart. The company both manufactures greenhouses and distributes other companies' products, so you'll be able to compare a lot of different models. His catalog not only illustrates the products, but also discusses the pros and cons of various materials that go into greenhouse construction, compares costs, and gives tips on location, temperature, ventilation and general greenhouse management. The company sells a wide variety of accessories, including control panels, exhaust fans, nutrient tanks, coolers, heaters, humidistats, pumps and even plant food. In addition to greenhouses, the company stocks a wide range of outdoor furniture. (See page 357.)

## Pope's Greenhouses

Route 2, Box 132
Canton, Texas 75103
☎ 903/829-5921
**FAX** 903/829-8022
**Hours** Mon-Fri 8-5; by appointment on weekends
**Accessible** Yes
**Mail Order**
**Catalog** Free brochure

These economical greenhouses can be assembled in only a day or two. They're made of galvanized material and designed to be covered with plastic or shade cloth. Available in 12', 16' and 20' widths, the lengths are variable, in 8' increments.

## Rounhouse

*P.O. Box 1744*
*Cleveland, Texas 77328*
☎ *281/593-1118*
**FAX** *281/592-7474*
**Hours** *Mon-Fri 8-4:30*
**Accessible** *Yes*
**Mail Order**
**Catalog** *Free*

A manufacturer of steel-frame, Quonset-style greenhouses for almost 30 years, Rounhouse also sells fans, heaters, cooling systems, shade cloth and ground cloth. These utilitarian structures are available in a wide variety of sizes suitable for commercial growers and serious hobbyists.

*Directions: Go 11.5 miles west of Cleveland on Texas Highway 105.*

## Texas Greenhouse Company, Inc.

*2524 White Settlement Road*
*Ft. Worth, Texas 76107*
☎ *817/335-5447, 654-1379 (metro), 1-800/227-5447*
**FAX** *817/334-0818*
**Hours** *Mon-Fri 8-5*
**Accessible** *Yes*
**Mail Order**
**Catalog** *Free*

In business since 1948, Texas Greenhouse has long been considered a leader in the design and manufacture of graceful curved-glass greenhouses. The company's "American Classic" series features aluminum glazing bars suspended on a galvanized substructure. All are made with double-strength glass throughout and adjustable roof ventilators. Several sizes are available in the freestanding structures, from a 9'x12' model designed for small gardens to spacious units measuring up to approximately 5'x37'. Smaller, all aluminum units are available with glass or twin-wall polycarbonate panels. Texas Greenhouse also makes good looking lean-to structures that can be attached to your house, as well as wall-hung units that serve as bay windows. The free, color catalog includes benches, heating and cooling equipment, roll-up shades and other accessories. All products carry a five-year warranty.

# Plan for Play

In the past thirty years, there has been a revolution in manufactured play equipment. The wonderful structures developed for city parks have finally reached the realm of backyard play. My kids frequently got hurt on the slides, see-saws, monkey bars and merry-go-rounds at school and in the local parks. Especially dreadful were the swings, which came equipped with wooden seats guaranteed to knock out teeth. Beneath all the equipment was a layer of potentially deadly asphalt. Things had to change.

I've always thought my father was lucky to have grown up in the country, where he had access to creeks, trees, hills, rocks and animals. He was smart enough to realize that urban-dwellers have to create settings where kids can build strong bodies and develop imagination. I remember that as a child in Dallas, I was allowed to make playhouses out of cardboard boxes, drag the garden hose to a sandbox to build castles, skate on sidewalks and play hide and seek in the garden shrubbery.

When my three children were small, I turned our entire backyard into a playground. I surrounded the lawn with a curving concrete pathway for tricycles, built a huge sandbox and bought the sturdiest swing set on the market. As they grew older, we built a playhouse with a marvelous "lookout" platform tucked into the branches of an old tree. When they became teenagers, the playhouse became my garden storage shed, and the tricycle-path served as an edging for flowerbeds. Finally sandbox and swings gave way to a swimming pool. (A beautiful garden is one of the few rewards of old age.) I wouldn't trade having provided a special place for my children and their friends to indulge in imaginative play.

Backyard play areas have a great advantage over parks and school yards. At home you can not only provide space for climbing and playing games, but also encourage the messy activities that stimulate creativity. You can include sandboxes (double the fun with a garden hose nearby), outdoor art easels, workbenches with scrap lumber, small garden plots and a section of driveway that's available for chalk drawings and racing toy trucks.

It's up to parents to ensure that home playgrounds are as safe as the ones mandated on public property. Be sure the structures you buy or build are sufficiently sturdy for growing children. What works for a two-year-old may not support the weight of a couple of rowdy eight-year-olds. To prevent eye injury and abrasions, the equipment you buy or build must be constructed with recessed bolts. Do not nail structures together.

The most important factor in playground safety is the surface that's under the play structure. Children *will* fall! All equipment should be installed over a soft cushion of sand, pea gravel or bark chips. Grass (which is pictured in all the catalogs) will not stand up to the foot traffic of children, so the surface around a play structure will quickly turn into hard packed earth, which can be as lethal as concrete. The safety-surfacing under and around any piece of climbing equipment should be at least ten inches deep. It should extend a minimum of six feet beyond the edge of the equipment or the arc of a swinging device.

Regular maintenance is critical. Check the depth and cleanliness of the surfacing material and replenish it as needed to maintain a yielding surface that will absorb the impact of a fall. Keep sandboxes covered when not in use. Check the bolts every few weeks to make sure they remain tight. Keep a close watch for wood splinters, frayed rope or open S-hooks.

In the listings that follow, you will find a number of sources for well-designed structures that incorporate climbing, sliding and swinging activities. Some of the companies offer playhouses for pretend-play and equipment for games, as well.

# Sources for Sports & Play Equipment:

## Backyard Adventures
*14201 IH-27*
*Amarillo, Texas 79119*
☎ *806/622-1220 or 1-800/345-1491*
*FAX 806/622-1515*

### Other Local Dealers:
**Backyard Adventures**
*17148 IH-35*
*Shertz, Texas 78155*
☎ *210/651-9401*
*FAX 210/651-5200*

**Backyard and Patio**
*9520 Summer Bell Lane*
*Houston, Texas 77074*
☎ *713/778-9889*
*FAX 713/778-6006*

**Hours** *Variable; call your nearest dealer*
**Accessible** *Partially*
**Mail Order**
**Catalog** *Free*

**Backyard Adventures of Abilene**
*3382 South 14th*
*Abilene, Texas 79605*
☎ *915/690-1600*

**Backyard Adventures of Lubbock**
*Goodtimes Power Sports*
*4202 West Loop 289*
*Lubbock, Texas 79407*
☎ *806/790-1354*

**Wooden Swing**
*13617 Inwood Road #200*
*Dallas, Texas 75244*
☎ *972/386-6280*
*FAX 972/386-6805*

Owner Charles Sammann says, "As the father of six children, I am keenly aware of children's need for safe, creative, physically stimulating play. We feel that our kid-tested sets are the best in the marketplace. We encourage you to compare our design, function and value." The company builds its products from kiln-dried cedar or redwood, and it uses patented compression clamps to join accessories to platforms. All of its steel components are powder-coated for durability, just like park equipment. The company's best selling model is "Tom's Treehouse," a wood-roofed 5'x5' platform with several optional configurations and accessories built onto it, including swings, inclined ladders, cargo nets and spiral, straight and wave slides. Also pictured in the colorful catalog are playhouses, free-standing swing sets and an "Adventure Ship."

## The Carpenter's Shop

*321 Craig Place (mailing address only)*
*San Antonio, Texas 78212*
☎ *201/736-2883*
**FAX** *201/734-8665*
*www.jhc-carpentry.com*
**Hours** *By appointment only*

On-line you'll discover wonderful tree houses and playhouses made by craftsmen on a working ranch near Boerne. The tree houses are all custom-made, and there are 15 different styles available in the playhouse line. The Victorian model could easily become the focal point of a grandmother's garden! There are also child-size porch swings and a remarkable "Best friends" swing with facing recliners. All the ordering information is on the web, but you can also visit the factory and see sample products. Call for an appointment. (See page 277 for information about the Peaceful Habitations Rose Garden, which is also on the property.)

*Directions: Located about 5½ miles north of Boerne FM 1376, between Boerne and Sisterdale. From San Antonio drive north on IH-10 West. Take Exit 542 and go through Boerne on main street to the 5th stop light. Turn right at the Sisterdale Road Cutoff; go about ½-mile until it runs into Sisterdale Road. Turn right on FM 1376 and go about 5½-miles. Look for the sign for the Peaceful Habitations Rose Gardens on the right just before a deep cut. Turn right at the sign and go another half-mile.*

## Dallas Custom Swings

*11660 Plano Road*
*Dallas, Texas 75243*
☎ *214/341-3727*
**FAX** *214/341-1221*

**Other Local Dealers**

**Custom Swings of Texas**

*2829 West Loop South*
*Houston, Texas 77027*
☎ *713/779-4647*

**Custom Swings of Texas**

*21210 Northwest Freeway*
*Cypress, Texas 77429*
☎ *281/630-7951*

**Hours** *Mon Sat 9-5 (Dallas);*
*Tues-Sat 10-6 (Houston)*
**Accessible** *Partially*
**Mail Order**
**Catalog** *Free*

"When I started Dallas Custom Swings in 1984, I never imagined that my little company would ever grow to reach the position it has now," says Debbie Muse. "When you see our product you'll know why our customers have such fierce loyalty." The structures are constructed of treated Southern yellow pine and finished with Swingseal™ to retard weathering, splitting and splintering. They can be customized from a small, basic fort with sandbox to an elaborate 20'x30' model with every imaginable accessory, from swings to a "Space Walk Bridge." In the right setting, the company's wooden Choo-Choo Train could function as garden art!

## *Gym•N•I Playgrounds*

*1980 IH-35 North*
*New Braunfels, Texas 78130*
☎ *1-800/294-9664*
**FAX** *830/629-9140*
**Hours** *Mon-Fri 8-5, Sat 10-5*
**Catalog** *Free*
**Accessible** *Yes*

This company's equipment ranges from a simple swing set with a platform and slide to a two-platform units that can accommodate eight to ten players. Colorful tent-tops provide shade, and accessory options include a cargo net, fireman's pole, crawl tube, turbo slide, rope ladders and tire swing. For grown-ups, the company also makes lawn swings, picnic tables and benches. Gym•N•I playsets are constructed of #1 Select Wolmanized pine. The wooden components are pre-drilled for easy assembly with rust-resistant, recessed bolts. The products are sold by a network of dealers across Texas and can be delivered and installed for a reasonable fee. Call for the dealer nearest you.

## *Sport Court of Texas*

*10208 Highway 620 North*
*Austin, Texas 78726*
☎ *1-800/880-0234 or 512/335-9779*
**FAX** *512/335-8556*
**Hours** *Mon-Fri 8-5 or by appointment*
**Accessible** *Yes*
**Catalog** *Free brochure and/or video*

One toll-free call to the Austin office can put you in touch with local dealers throughout the state who construct mini-courts for 15 different sports and games. Not only used for paddle tennis and basketball, the courts also facilitate badminton, pickle-ball, shuffleboard, hop-scotch and more. Sizes start at 20'x20' (the most popular is 30'x60'), and all are surfaced with a modular, resilient material that quickly sheds water. They make great play areas for children of all ages. (Tots even use them for tricycles.) The company also offers rebounders for soccer, tennis and softball, plus new backyard putting greens. Designed for healthy family fun, the courts and putting greens are individually customized to fit your lot. Says Greg Dettman, head of the Texas office, "Keeps your kids in your own backyard and keeps the rest of the neighborhood back there with them."

# Light-up the Night

Many homeowners think of outdoor lighting as something reserved for the wealthy, but in fact, you can make a big impact for as little as $200. With a budget of $1,000 you can achieve a truly sophisticated lighting system in an average-size garden. If you consider that lighting adds refinement and value to the house, enhances safety, and extends your hours of enjoyment in the garden, it's a bargain. A few well-placed fixtures allow you to reveal the garden's best features while hiding others. Lighting can make a large garden seem intimate or create an illusion of depth in a small space.

☛ **Money-saving tip: Light only the areas you use at night.**

Painting the landscape with light can create magical effects. Use soft uplighting to display a sculptural plant in silhouette against a wall or to define the trunk and branching pattern of a graceful tree. Employ downlighting to create a dance of shadows on lawn and terraces beneath the tree canopy. Tuck a string of low-voltage lights into ground covers to illuminate pathways and define the edges of planting beds. Mark the entrance to a driveway or frame a garden gate with handsome post lights.

Good lighting design involves controlling not only the direction, but also the color and intensity of the light. It's best done by a professional who is trained to place the right fixtures and the right lamps in the right spot. Twice as many of the wrong fixtures may give half the impact, so assistance from a lighting designer can save you money in the long run. Many of the retail lighting stores listed in this section offer moderately-priced design services.

As a "picture book" source of ideas for how different lighting effects appear at night, the *Ortho* paperback, *How to Design and Install Outdoor Lighting* is top-notch. Even if you're bringing in a professional lighting designer or planning to work with a lighting dealer, the book's color photographs will enable you to visualize and communicate what you want. If you're installing a system yourself, the book contains a wealth of information on planning, installation techniques and maintenance.

For large properties, you may want to consider a commercial-grade line-voltage system that runs on household current. Note, however, that such a system should be laid in metal conduit, which is more expensive to buy and install than plastic. (With plastic conduit there is a dangerous potential for cutting through the conduit with a shovel or spading fork.)

Low-voltage systems eliminate the need for conduit altogether. These systems offer a wider choice of small, unobtrusive fixtures and are more easily moved as the garden grows and changes. The main disadvantage to low-voltage systems is that they cannot be strung more than 50' without losing candlepower at the end of the line. And surprisingly, low-voltage systems are not necessarily less expensive to operate than a well-designed line-voltage system (It's the watts that count.)

Twelve-volt systems available at local hardware stores are safe, easy to install and quite inexpensive. I recently found a kit of four plastic low-voltage pathway lights for $34.99. The same store had attractive shell-shaped cast-metal lights for under $25 apiece and all of the wiring and transformers necessary to devise your own twelve-volt system. Inexpensive kit-form fixtures are better than no lighting at all, but I always suggest to my clients that they buy the highest quality fixtures they can afford and add lighting in phases if necessary.

Be sure any lighting equipment you buy bears a label that indicates approval by Underwriters Laboratory (UL). In terms of durability, I would choose die-cast or heavy-gauge metal over any plastic material. Look for neoprene gaskets. If vandalism might be a problem, buy a fixture with Lexan™ lenses rather than glass. If the fixture is brass, it should be triple-lacquered.

By day you want fixtures that complement the architectural style of the house. At night, the most important visual aspect is the color effect created by the lamp inside the fixture. For natural-looking color in the landscape, fluorescent or halogen lamps (such as MR 16 or PAR 36) are more effective than high-pressure sodium lamps, which have the poorest color-rendering characteristics.

There are a number of "bells and whistles" you can add to a lighting system, including photocells that turn the light on at dusk. You can also get motion detectors that sense intruders or turn lights on as you come in late at night. Many systems come with timers that turn off certain lights at a specified time. For example, you may want the security lighting left on, but choose not to burn decorative lighting all night. Remote controls allow you to turn on security lights from inside.

☛ **Money-saving tip: Try various fixture arrangements before you decide on permanent placement. Get it right the first time!**

If you seek professional help, ask to see several of the firm's completed projects and talk to homeowners who have used their services. Don't be afraid to request a demonstration in your own garden. If you're into doing-it-yourself, take flashlights out in your garden and see what uplighting will do for trees or how a wash of light might enliven a bare wall.

# Sources for Outdoor Lighting:

## *Adkins Reproduction Antique Lighting*
*IH-35*
*Georgetown, Texas 78626*
☎ *512/869-1645*
**FAX** *512/869-1645 (call before sending)*
**Hours** *Mon-Sat 9-5:30, Sun 1-5:30*
**Accessible** *Yes*
**Mail Order**
**Catalog** *$6*
**Mailing Address** *108 Highview, Georgetown, Texas 78628*

Ten pages of this company's catalog are devoted to street lights, post lamps and wall sconces that recall turn-of-the-century Texas, when city streets were illuminated by fancifully shaped fixtures. Reproduced here in cast aluminum, these pieces complement traditional homes, old and new. The 41-page catalog also features old-fashioned mail boxes, street signs and a wide array of garden furnishings, which are further described on page 344 of this book.

*Directions: From the south, take exit 266, 4½ miles north of Georgetown. Coming from the north, take exit 268 and cross over; the company is on the east side of the Interstate.*

## Brandon Industries, Inc.
*1601 West Wilmeth Road*
*McKinney, Texas 75069*
☎ *1-800/247-1274 or 972/542-3000 (local)*
**FAX** *972/542-3000*
*www.brandonmail.com/lights/lights.html*
**Hours** *Mon-Fri 8:30-5*
**Accessible** *Yes*
**Mail Order**
**Catalog** *Free*

Here's another company that manufactures new lights with a historic flavor. Rust proof, durable and reasonably priced, the company's products are shipped by UPS within two weeks. The product line includes classic mailboxes, antique reproduction lamp posts, luminaires, wall sconces and deck lights. For the energy-conscious, high pressure sodium and metal halide options are available.

## Greenlee Landscape Lighting
*1300 Hutton Drive, Suite 110*
*Carrollton, Texas 75006*
☎ *972/466-1133*
**FAX** *972/446-2202*
**Hours** *Mon-Fri 8-5*
**Accessible** *Yes*
**Catalog** *Available through rep*

Greenlee markets its distinctive line-voltage and low-voltage outdoor lighting through local representatives. The company has developed a full line of very high quality outdoor landscape lights, including up-lights, well lights, flood lights, path lights, in-ground units and lighted bollards. Call the factory in Carrollton to find your nearest representative.

## Isaac Maxwell Metalworks
*1009 South Alamo*
*San Antonio, Texas 78210*
☎ *210/227-4752*
**Hours** *By appointment only*
**Accessible** *Yes*
**Mail Order**
**Catalog** *Free brochures and photographs available*

The late architect Isaac Maxwell left "a treasure-trove" of over 1,300 drawings of his designs for intricate metal sconces, post lamps and hanging fixtures, planters and architectural accessories. His wife Judith now directs the work of four craftsmen who are carrying on the production in a workshop where every piece is made entirely by hand. The firm produces lights custom-made to your design, or you can select from a brochure that shows Mr. Maxwell's styles and designs. It also fabricates handsome doors for clients nationwide.

## John Watson Landscape Illumination

1933 Regal Row
Dallas, Texas 75235
☎ 1-800/886-7751
FAX 214/638-1811

1000 North Walnut Avenue, Suite CC
New Braunfels, Texas 78130
☎ 1-800/466-6123 (Central and South Texas)
FAX 210/620-7442

**Hours** Mon-Fri 8-12 & 1-5; evenings Mon-Thurs
**Catalog** Free brochure

John Watson Landscape Illumination is *the* pioneer in landscape lighting. What began over 40 years ago with Mr. Watson's master's thesis as a landscape architectural student at Texas A&M has evolved into a company with an international reputation. Now recognized as an artist in a field that did not exist at the time, his first projects were accomplished with incandescent bulbs in coffee cans. Today the company designs, manufactures and installs outdoor lighting systems that are known for especially soft and subtle effects in the landscape. "We take the black canvas of the night and paint it with light. We meet our clients at their residence or business and work with their particular taste and style to create a unique nighttime environment that will fit into their budget. Our designs combine both security and aesthetic lighting, with a side benefit of low maintenance and energy efficiency. We do our initial visit, design and cost work-up at no charge or obligation." The company has a slide presentation that illustrates how its products and designs can highlight the best aspects of the client's architecture and the landscape. John Watson takes pride in its ability to manufacture to the client's specifications. Eighty percent of its work comes by referral from satisfied customers.

## Lars Stanley — Architects & Artisans

2007 Kinney Avenue
Austin, Texas 78704
☎ 512/445-0444

This firm fabricates handsome metal lighting fixtures in addition to the custom-made garden elements (gates, fountains, etc.) for which it is better known. See complete listing on page 366.

## Luminarios Ceramic Design

346 West Sunset
San Antonio, Texas 78209
☎ 210/824-5572
FAX 210/824-5245
**Hours** Mon-Fri 8-5
**Accessible** Yes
**Mail Order**
**Catalog** Free

This company's ceramic and punched tin lighting fixtures are works of art. The ceramic fixtures are available in unglazed or colored, glazed finishes. The metal fixtures can also be crafted of copper, brass or German silver. Available for wall-mounting or hanging, these handmade fixtures are ideal for porches and entryways where they can be enjoyed up-close. Most have a southwestern flavor, but some are well-suited to contemporary architecture, and others draw upon early Texas and seaside motifs. Owner Rusty Konitz is willing to work directly with a client who wants something distinctive. The Lady Bird Johnson Wildflower Center is among the places you can see this company's handsome product. Luminarios will refer you to the nearest dealer or sell directly to customers in areas where there's no dealer.

## Mel Northey Company

*303 Gulf Bank*
*Houston, Texas 77037*
☎ *1/800-828-0302*
**FAX** *281/445-7456*
**Hours** *Mon-Thurs 9-5, Fri 9-4:30*
**Accessible** *Yes*
**Mail Order**
**Catalog** *Free*

This company advertises its handsome fluted street lamps and wall sconces in trade magazines throughout the country. Graceful posts support a variety of traditional lamp shapes. These cast aluminum fixtures are available in black, dark verde green or white. Among the large line of mailboxes designed to complement the fixtures, the Williamsburg box is particularly handsome. The company also makes a nice Victorian park bench and porch swing.

## Two Hills Studio

*2706 South Lamar Boulevard*
*Austin, Texas 78704*
☎ *512/707-7571 or 1-800/239-5530*
**Hours** *Mon-Fri 8:30-5:30*
**Accessible** *Yes*
**Mail Order**
**Catalog** *$15 (refundable), free brochure*

Two Hills Studio produces an array of handsome handcrafted sconces, lanterns and hanging fixtures. Copper, brass, tin, zinc, glass, mica and mirrors are the craftsmen's media here. "Innovative techniques that we have developed enhance the dramatic play of light and shadow in our fixtures." Custom commissions are welcome.

## Chapter Four

# Garden
# Conservation

*"Nothing endures but change."*
*....Heraclitus c.540 – c.480 B.C.*

# A Plea for Sound Management

More than any other art form, a garden is subject to change — through varying patterns of light each day, from season-to-season and from year-to-year. Unlike the architect's building, the artist's painting or the playwright's words, a garden designer's best efforts exist in a state of evolution. Garden designers don't even live to see their work at full maturity. The sapling I plant today will not become the venerable oak I envision for another seventy-five years. From the moment it is installed, the garden I've designed will either be improving or deteriorating. This is where proper preparation and maintenance come into the picture.

Before listing sources, I've attempted to share everything I've learned about building up the soil, managing pests, pruning properly and conserving water. Please read these sections! I *promise* that sound garden management will ultimately make lighter work of your garden tasks.

# All About Soil

Soil is a combination of weathered rock, air, water, decaying organic matter (humus) and living organisms (microbes). Texas soils range from remarkably rich river valley loams to thin, rocky clays. Most could stand improvement. We are generally dealing with soil that was depleted of nutrients and compacted by farming and ranching long before our home was built on the site. As gardeners we need to be concerned about the soil's depth, texture, chemistry and, finally, its fertility.

☛**Money-saving tip: Improve the soil before thinking about establishing a new landscape or a garden renovation. It's a total waste to put good plants in poor soil!**

In our eagerness to make our gardens lush and green, all our instincts tell us to dash to the garden center and pick up a bag of 10-10-10. STOP! Any experienced gardener can attest to the effectiveness of store-bought fertilizer as a "quick-fix," but we're setting up a vicious cycle when we rely on it to keep plants healthy. The real problem with chemical fertilizer is that microbes can't use it, so they take their nutrients from the humus in the soil. As this organic matter is depleted, microbes begin to disappear.

Microbes and earthworms are essential for "stirring" the soil and helping to make nutrients available. Their digestion of organic materials actually binds soil particles into a crumb-like structure that increases the soil's water-holding capacity. Without humus, water-soluble nitrogen leaches more rapidly into the water table. Additionally, salt residues from some synthetic chemicals tend to build up in the soil. The poorer the soil becomes, the more fertilizer it takes to keep the plants healthy.

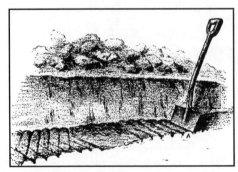

We must treat our topsoil with the respect we would accord any living thing, for that is what it is. Within a handful of healthy soil are millions of living, breathing, growing organisms, 98% of them beneficial to plants. The microorganisms are, of course, invisible, but you can check for life in your soil by just counting the worms. There should be at least five in every cubic foot!

# Soil Depth

The topsoil is very shallow in many areas of the state. (My garden in Austin came with a mere two-inch-deep layer.) Because plants growing in shallow soil require more water and nutrients than those grown in deep soil, Texas homeowners often must import new topsoil before even beginning to garden. In some areas, it's necessary to build raised beds to grow vegetables and/or special ornamental plants such as roses. For these beds, I always recommend a blended soil mix that contains organic matter as well as topsoil.

Whenever you need large quantities of soil or soil mixes, ask a trusted local nursery owner to recommend a reliable source. How you apply the new topsoil is also important. Always break-up the surface of the existing soil and mix-in some of the new soil. Then apply the remainder of the new topsoil or soil mix. This step is especially critical in areas where the existing soil is a hard clay. Otherwise, the plants will remain shallow-rooted or, worse yet, will expire as quickly as a houseplant in a pot without a drainage hole.

☛**Money-saving tip: Be especially wary about the source of any bulk soil you buy. Good gardens have been ruined by a load of soil filled with weed seeds.**

# Soil Texture

Rock weathers into soil in the form of clay (with particles so fine they can only be seen with an electron microscope), silt (intermediate-size particles) and sand (coarse particles). The ideal soil is a soft, crumbly mixture of about 40% sand, 40% silt, 10% clay and 10% organic matter. Soil that's too sandy doesn't retain water; soil that contains too much clay won't drain properly. Squeeze a handful of damp soil. If it will hold together, but not clump into a tight ball, you probably have pretty good soil texture. You can get a better handle on the texture of your soil by performing a couple of easy tests.

---

### The "Mason jar" test for soil texture:

To get a handle on the proportions of sand, silt, clay and organic matter in your soil, take random samples from the areas you're going to plant. Put a cup of dry, pulverized soil, four cups of water and a teaspoon of liquid Ivory detergent in a large jar with a lid. Shake vigorously. The sand will settle to the bottom in about a minute. Mark its level with a crayon. The silt will settle out in about two hours. Mark its level. The clay particles will need a couple of days to settle. The organic matter will rise to the top. Once the water is clear, compare your sample to the ideal proportions listed in the preceding paragraph.

### The "coffee can" test for drainage:

Cut both ends from a one-pound coffee can and force the can into your garden soil to a depth of four inches. (If that's impossible, you know you have a problem!) Fill the rest of the can with water and let it drain through. Then fill it again and measure how long it takes the water level to drop an inch. If it drops immediately, the soil is too sandy and porous; if it takes more than four hours, the soil is too clayey. Your plants are likely to drown from lack of oxygen.

---

Surprisingly, the addition of composted organic matter is the remedy both for soils that are too porous and for those that are too heavy. Clay soils also benefit from the addition of sharp builder's sand or quarter-inch gravel to improve drainage. Enlivening the soil is a labor of love. The project consists of loosening it to improve aeration and amending it with compost to improve structure and fertility. (See pages 141-143 for more about compost.)

# Soil Chemistry: The pH Factor

The pH scale is used to measure soil acidity. The numbers of the scale run from zero (the most acid) to 14 (the most alkaline). The neutral point is 7. Most plants thrive in a slightly acidic environment (6 to 7); some plants such as azaleas absolutely require acidic soil. Acid soils occur mainly in East Texas, where damp conditions and thousands of years of decaying leaves and pine needles have reduced the pH. If the soil is too acid (below 4), it can be neutralized with agricultural limestone or wood ashes. Never use your wood ashes in alkaline soil!

Alkaline soil, which is common in dry climate regions (i.e. most of Texas), is far more difficult to correct than acidic soil. The biggest problem with alkaline soil is that it makes iron and several other important nutrients unavailable to your plants, even when these minerals are present in the soil. Ground sulfur (judiciously applied) can help bring alkaline soil more into the neutral range. Added at the rate of one pound per 100-square-feet, sulfur will lower the pH one point. Exceeding that amount per year is *not* a good idea, and the improvement is only temporary at any rate. Gypsum is often recommended as an additive to alkaline soil, but its primary use is for leaching sodium out of the soil; it should not be applied without a soil test and expert advice.

Sphagnum peat moss is useful for acidifying alkaline soil, but it is too expensive to employ throughout the garden. I've incorporated peat moss into planting holes around acid-loving plants, but having watched clients struggle to grow azaleas in Austin's limestone soil, I'm inclined to confine acid-dependent plants to the eastern region of Texas where the soils naturally accommodate them. By the way, peat moss must be moistened, or it will stay dry in the ground forever. If you're going to use it to acidify soil, mix a "slurry" of peat moss and water in a wheelbarrow before incorporating the product.

Gardeners in the western three-quarters of Texas routinely struggle not only to lower the pH of their soil, but also to compensate for the lack of available iron, which is essential to the production of chlorophyll. The tell-tale symptom of iron starvation is yellowed leaves with dark green veins, so even without the benefit of a soil test, many experienced Texas gardeners add chelated iron every growing season. Again, this is but a temporary "fix." Planting species that prefer, or at least tolerate, alkaline soil is the real solution to gardening with an extremely high pH.

# Soil Fertility

In addition to sunlight, air and water, plants most certainly need nutrients to flourish. Nitrogen, phosphorus and potassium are absolutely essential to plant growth. Plants also use magnesium, calcium and sulfur in relatively large quantities. These are known as "secondary nutrients." Small amounts of iron, zinc, molybdenum, manganese, boron, copper, cobalt and chlorine are also needed for plant growth. These eight elements are called "micronutrients" (or trace elements).

Fertilizer is erroneously called plant food. Plants make their own food from nutrients that are held in the soil. When we fertilize, we are simply adding one or more elements. For an element to be useful, first it must be dissolved, and then it must be absorbed into plant cells by way of complex chemical reactions. Temperature, the availability of water and oxygen and the relative alkalinity or acidity of the soil all greatly affect the chemical processes that allow plants to make food from nutrients. The addition of fertilizer may help plants exist in poor soil, but your long-term strategy should be to build-up the natural health of the soil.

☛**Money-saving tip: Determine what your soil needs before investing in fertilizers or additives.**

Basic soil tests analyze the three primary nutrients: nitrogen, phosphorus and potassium. More sophisticated tests will measure organic matter, secondary nutrients and trace elements. Other tests are available to measure acidity and/or determine if there are toxic substances in your soil. Inexpensive color-chart kits available at local garden centers allow you to measure the presence of the most basic nutrients and test for acidity/alkalinity levels with some degree of accuracy, but professional soil testing is the best way to determine your soil's chemical composition. There are several qualified labs in the state.

# Sources for Soil Testing:

### A&L Plains Agricultural Laboratories

P.O. Box 1590
Lubbock, Texas 77408
☎ 806/763-4278
**FAX** 806/763-2762

Founded in 1971 to serve the agricultural industry, this lab is part of a national company that does comprehensive analyses of soils, plants, water, feed and fertilizers. An extensive 17-page catalog lists the tests available and prices for each.

### Extension Soil Testing Lab

Texas A&M University — Soil & Crop Sciences
College Station, Texas 77843-2474
☎ 409/845-4816

Go to your county extension agent for a form and soil bag to send to the testing lab at Texas A&M University. Costs range from $10 to $30 depending upon the level of testing you want. Extension offices also have information on testing water for various salts.

### Texas Plant Disease Diagnostic Laboratory

Room 101, L.F. Peterson Building
Texas A&M University
College Station, Texas 77843-2131
☎ 409/845-8033
*http://cygnus.tamu.edu/Texlab/tpddl-samples.html*

This lab offers soil testing for nematodes ($15) and plant diagnosis of such diseases as leaf spots, root rots, flower blights and turf problems ($15 per specimen). There are very specific instructions for gathering and submitting samples, which you can access off the web or by writing to the lab.

## Texas Plant and Soil Lab

R.R. 7, Box 213Y
Edinburg, Texas 78539
☎ 956/383-0739
**Hours** Mon-Fri 9-5

If you are unaware that gardening has become chic, consider the fact that this Texas soil testing lab was featured in *Town & Country* magazine! Now operated by Esper K. Chandler, an agronomist and soil scientist, the company began serving citrus farmers in the Valley in 1938. The lab uses a Cation Exchange Capacity testing method that employs carbon dioxide to determine actual nutrient uptake. In addition to data on nutrients, the Standard Topsoil Analysis provides (for $25.95) information on pH, soil texture, humus content and other factors that allow for "the most accurate soil fertilizer recommendations possible." The method works equally well for acid or alkaline soil. "We mimic the plant's method of extracting nutrients from the soil," says Mr. Chandler. The company also offers a basic lawn and garden test ($15) and provides analysis of composts, plants and irrigation water at various prices. Write for information on sample collection and soil sample bags.

# Enhancing Your Soil

Okay, you've gotten the soil tested and found it deficient. Your first reaction may be to pour-on the old fertilizer, but actually that's not the best answer. To prepare your soil to support a community of healthy plants, begin by building-up its organic content. Composted organic material feeds the soil as well as the plants. This miracle material provides a reservoir for nutrients as well as a home to the many beneficial organisms that help decompose dead organic matter. It makes nutrients available to plants, provides aeration and helps regulate moisture retention and soil temperature.

Have you ever noticed that nobody has to fertilize a forest? The fallen leaves and microorganisms that live on the woodland floor continually renew the soil. We do the same when we recycle nature's "waste materials" into nutritious soil amendments and mulches for our planting beds. You can even create a self-mulching lawn! Simply wait to mow until your grass is between two and four inches high. Then mow-off only the top one-third of the grass, and don't rake up the clippings. This way, the clippings will feed your soil, but won't smother the grass.

Organic recycling saves you money, time and effort. The process also benefits your community by saving landfill space, which in turn benefits you as a taxpayer. More directly, the use of compost helps lower your water bill, reduces water pollution and conserves precious water resources. When you use compost as a soil amendment, you'll buy less fertilizer and spend less time fertilizing. When you begin using it as a mulch, you'll water less frequently and eliminate your need for herbicides. Mulches not only help suppress weed seeds, but also make the soil softer, which makes any weeds that do appear easier to pull. Finally, composting allows you to stop buying all those plastic bags you've been using for all those grass clippings and leaves.

# What *is* Compost?

The word "compost" is both a verb and a noun. To compost (*v*) is to expose organic material to bacteria, time, heat and moisture to accelerate natural decomposition. Compost (*n*) is used to describe any organic material (cottonseed meal, blood meal, aged manure, garden debris, etc.) that has been composted. When the mixture breaks down, it forms humus. Although organic matter represents only a small percentage of the overall composition of the soil, the addition of compost will increase the depth and improve the texture of your topsoil. Compost can be used both as a soil amendment/ fertilizer and as a mulch/ top dressing. While only "finished" compost is suitable for use as a soil amendment, partially decomposed materials can be used for mulching.

## How to Make Compost

Libraries and bookstores are replete with books that tell you how to make your own rich compost. Cities are putting out free pamphlets on the subject and setting up demonstration sites. Basically, it's a simple matter of layering brown (shredded leaves) and green (grass clippings) in a well-ventilated bin. Compost bins can be purchased at garden centers or made with lumber, pallets, concrete blocks, wire fencing or other materials. Bins help retain moisture and heat, keep out pests, and keep your yard tidy. Special worm composting bins can be used to compost food scraps and paper, even in an apartment.

The layers should be kept about as moist as a damp sponge and stirred once a month. You can toss-in coffee grounds, tea bags, nutshells, raw vegetable scraps, fruit peelings and other non-fatty kitchen wastes. Many gardeners also add some garden soil and manure to speed decomposition. It's not rocket science.

Composting goes faster when you break everything into small pieces and mix it all together. Try chopping or mashing the food scraps and mowing the leaves before adding them to the pile. (If you have an existing pile that's not breaking down, sift the materials through a 3/8-inch mesh screen. Shred the materials that cannot sift through the screen or start a second pile.) A pile that is composting properly will get about as warm as the hot water in your house (140 F or even higher). Temperatures this high will kill weed seeds and pathogens that cause disease, but allow the beneficial organisms to remain. If you're unsure, use a special compost thermometer to monitor the temperature of your pile.

If the materials stay moist, the mixture should compost within a year without producing an odor or spreading diseases or pests. Avoid meat and dairy products, which cause odors and attract rodents, as well as pet droppings, which can harbor diseases. Don't compost weeds with seeds or any diseased or insect-infested plants. Also avoid treated wood or other materials that may contain preservatives or other toxins.

A bad odor indicates that your compost has too much "fresh" material or is too wet. If your pile is dry, turn it and add water until the whole pile is evenly moist. If it's too damp, turn the pile and add dry leaves or other "dried-out" materials. If your pile is attracting ants, flies or roaches, make sure you bury any food materials under a layer of leaves. You can also use a low-toxicity bait formulation near (but not in) the pile. Any other insects in your pile are probably harmless composters. Should problems persist, bury the compost and start another pile.

One of the funniest stories I've ever heard was told by an extension agent who got a call from an irate gardener saying, "I followed your directions for making compost, and all I got was dirt!" Yes, Virginia, perfect compost looks like rich, friable soil. You'll know when it's ready to use because it will smell pleasantly earthy.

If you can't generate enough compost to meet your garden's needs, call your city's Waste Management Department. The Texas Natural Resources Conservation Commission (TNRCC) has helped 166 cities set up programs to convert yard trimmings into compost. Yard debris makes up at least 15% of all municipal solid waste generated in Texas! (See page 100 for more information about TNRCC programs and publications.) Fifty-seven cities manage home composting programs in conjunction with the TNRCC's Master Composter program, which is successfully diverting over a million pounds of yard trimmings from landfills each year. Large-scale centralized processing of yard trimmings and other organic material has become a big industry in Texas. Many cities have begun their own composting operations; others send the debris to private contractors to turn into compost.

☛**Money-saving tip: If your city has not begun a composting program, demand one!**

In surveying the state of composting in Texas, I learned that there are far too many composting companies to list in this book. I did, however, talk to several of the most respected in the state. I was amazed to find out what kinds of waste products are candidates for recycling! Laredo landscape contractor John Stineff is typical of the numerous Texas entrepreneurs who have realized the potential for converting locally available "discards" into "black gold." He originally began his composting operation, **Lawn Lovers**, to meet the needs of his own clients. Now he's in the business full-scale, producing rich compost and mulch from reject vegetables he gets from local farmers and horse manure from a near-by racing stable, as well as yard debris from area gardeners.

**Silver Creek Materials Recycling** of Fort Worth makes its aerated compost from "uniquely blended ingredients" Not only does it contain lawn waste, but also it's "chockfull of zoo manures, thousands of gallons of out-of-date beer, tons of vegetables, and oceans of soft drinks. This is not the compost your granddad made! We scour the countryside looking for the perfect ingredients to make this remarkably rich work of nature." Founded 1991, Silver Creek is now one of largest operations of its kind in the state. Its Premium Soil Mix, which contains 60% compost, 40% sand and diatomaceous earth, is blended to contribute valuable time-release nutrients and beneficial microorganisms to worn-out soil. The company also sells Texas Pecan Mulch and Native Tree Mulch, which is delivered "slightly moist, with the aroma of a mist-covered meadow."

"The majority of wood we get comes from land clearing and demolition," says Jim Doersam, compost manager of **Texas Organic Products**, in Austin. Other materials the company uses come from a maker of prefabricated homes and from computer companies, who must dispose of massive quantities of pallets. "They grind very nicely," he says. Beverage companys' wastes and shredded paper also go into Texas Organic's compost. More than 50 percent of Austin's dried biosolids are processed at a city waste water treatment facility into a stable organic product called **Dillo Dirt**. These treated biosolids are combined with "bulking agents" such as tree trimmings, yard waste and recycled Christmas trees and then formed into six-foot-high wind rows to create the compost. By reusing lawn debris collected from Austin's "Don't Bag It" and "Curbside Recycling" programs, Texas Organic Products estimates that it diverts more than 70,000 cubic yards of material from local landfills annually, saving valuable space and greatly reducing the cost of solid waste disposal for Austin residents.

**Nature's Way** of Houston also turns yard debris into compost, rich native mulches and several specialized soil mixes. "Our focus is on quality," says John Ferguson. Noting that his company accepts tree-trimmings and grass-clippings from landscape companies and individual homeowners, he explains that his fee is based on processing cost. The cleaner the material, the less the debris costs to process.

(Usually it's about half the cost of taking the material to a landfill.) The trimmings are separated, heated to about 160° and pulverized to produce high-nutrient organic matter. Also in Houston, **Natural Earth Products** makes a soil-less mix of chicken manure, rice hulls, composted pine mulch and masonry sand. Good for loosening Gulf Coast "gumbo" clay, this soil amendment registers a pH between 6.3 and 6.5. The company custom blends soil mixes for customers, and it offers all of its basic ingredients alone.

What I also learned from my research is that no set of standards currently regulates the compost industry, so it's important for homeowners to question suppliers about their methods and finished products before ordering bulk soil compost or soil amendments. Moreover, there are several products out there that I believe should NEVER be incorporated into the soil. Raw manure heads the list. It can burn plants and it's high in salts. Uncomposted wood products are also unsuitable because raw wood ties-up soil nitrogen as it decomposes.

Uncomposted manure is easy to recognize; it has a strong, distinctive odor of ammonia. Avoid it like the plague. One of my clients ordered a load of compost from a "reputable" dealer, but wasn't home when it was delivered. The maintenance person who worked it into her new planting bed noted that it smelled of manure. Sure enough, she had the most astounding crop of weeds within a couple of weeks, and it took months to get rid of them! She and I both learned (the hard way) not to buy soil amendments from unknown sources.

## How to Use Compost

If you're beginning a garden in a new subdivision, spend the first season working lots of composted organic material into the soil, especially in areas where you'll be putting non-native trees, shrubs, lawn grass, flowers and vegetables. (I tilled two truckloads of "store-bought" compost into my planting beds before setting-out a single plant.) When planting a lawn, mix one to two inches of compost into the top six inches of soil. Before establishing a new planting bed, mix a three-inch layer of compost into the top 12 inches of soil. To maintain the lawn or garden, sprinkle-on and water-in a half-inch layer of finished compost once each year.

There's no substitute for good old-fashioned cultivation to bring worn-out, compacted earth back to a healthy state. It takes time and patience. Working the soil on a bare lot in a new subdivision or in a vegetable garden that sits empty over the winter is relatively easy. Here, you can use a mechanical tiller to loosen the soil to a depth of 12 to 18 inches and then fork-in the composted organic matter. (Never cultivate wet soil — you'll eliminate the air spaces and compact it even more. Work from one end of a bed to the other so that you won't step on the soil you've just loosened.)

Building-up the soil in an established bed is more difficult. In this case, you'll need to work carefully around the roots, cultivating the compost into the soil between the plants, by hand if necessary. In spots where you're adding new plants beneath existing shrubs and trees, excavate as large an area as possible and fill with a mix of your garden soil and a good, rich compost.

☞**Money-saving tip: The incorporation of compost will allow you to reduce the amount of fertilizer you'll need.**

In addition to building healthy soil, a second strategy for reducing your dependence on fertilizer is to give serious consideration to the plants you choose. Devote at least part of your garden to plants that are indigenous to your region. (See Chapter 6 for more about natives.) A plant growing in soil that's natural to its needs does not require a lot of supplementary enrichment. As one company that's in the fertilizer business says, "Don't ask a plant to do something it's not genetically designed to do."

# Mulch, Mulch, Mulch

Mulch is any material that's used to blanket the bare earth. Among the materials most commonly used are wood or bark chips, but I won't use wood products that have not undergone a composting process. Not only does raw wood appear unnatural in a refined garden, but (as previously mentioned) it also depletes the soil of nitrogen as it decomposes. Raw grass clippings are also unsuitable because they become compacted. Straw is sometimes recommended as a mulch, but it may contain weed seeds, and cottonseed hulls tend to blow away. Sawdust, peat moss and composted manure are poor mulching materials because they are too fine in texture. They will compact to form a pancake layer that inhibits water penetration. There are also several non-organic mulches on the market.

In my opinion, the best mulches are made from partially decomposed and partially decomposed leaves and grass clippings or commercially available organic matter that has been screened and blended for the purpose. If it's organic, the mulch will also be slowly adding nutrients as it breaks down.

There's so much to recommend mulch! It not only contributes valuable nutrients, but also serves to inhibit nutrient-robbing weeds, insulate the soil from sun and wind, moderate soil temperature, retain moisture and prevent erosion. Mulching is the simplest, most obvious way to conserve plant life, labor and money. What is amazing is that when I began gardening 35 years ago nobody told me about its benefits. These days it's the darling of the gardening world.

Now, I keep my established garden healthy by continually mulching the soil and generally letting the soil feed the plants. I apply a two-inch layer of organic mulch twice each year — in late-fall to protect plant roots from winter cold and in late-spring to preserve soil moisture during periods of heat and drought. By working the old, decomposed mulches into the soil year after year, I've reclaimed some pretty poor patches of earth. (Okay, I'll be honest here. I *hire* someone to do the spade work. My back can't take the strain and my beloved husband has never loved the back end of a garden tool.)

The first year into this approach, apply a slow-release organic fertilizer under the mulch. In subsequent years, you can begin reducing the amount of fertilizer you use. As the mulch breaks down, it is adding nutrients, just as nature replenishes the forest floor. It has been my experience that plants tend to grow at a reasonable rate with this regimen. In the long run, plants are hardier and more pest-resistant if they are not fed excessively or encouraged to put on great spurts of growth. Continue to monitor the pH and fertility, however, and add nutrients as needed to maintain a well-balanced soil.

☛**Money-saving tip: Turn all of your yard wastes into valuable mulch.**

"Store-bought" mulches are pretty pricey. A two-cubic-foot bag of mulch can cost as much as $4.50. Assuming you apply a three-inch layer, one bag will cover only eight square feet. While I was willing to shell-out for bulk compost to get my soil in condition for planting, I've decided that it makes a lot more sense to recycle my yard debris into the mulch I apply twice each year.

Every autumn I shred all my leaves and layer them with grass clippings I "borrow" from a neighbor since I don't have a lawn. I don't put weeds or the remains of my flower garden into my compost bin because I fear that it doesn't get sufficiently hot to kill-off weed seeds and/or plant diseases. Fortunately, the city recycles yard wastes on a large scale, so I send off everything I don't use in my bin, perfectly willing to buy it back (after it has been properly heated) when I need more mulch than my small bin can generate.

I turn the contents of the bin periodically and let the debris decompose for several months before "harvesting" it. Soil tests have indicated that my soil is still a little low in nitrogen and phosphorus, so I add some blood meal and colloidal phosphate into the mix. (The blood meal is high in nitrogen, and the colloidal phosphate is high in both phosphorous and trace elements.) I'm careful not to exceed amounts recommended on the label because I know that even organic products can burn plants if used in excess. I'm not worried, however, if my yard waste is only partially decomposed when I use it as a mulch. It continues decomposing and ultimately becomes incorporated into the soil.

A three-inch layer of mulch is sufficient. Heavy mulch inhibits gas exchanges and prevents rainwater from penetrating the soil. Be aware that any mulch may attract snails and rodents, so keep it an inch or two away from the plant's trunks and low branches. The benefits from mulching your garden far outweigh any problems you may encounter.

If you don't have access to yard waste or simply can't make enough mulch to blanket your planting beds twice each year, buy commercially blended mulch in bulk. Aged hardwood or aged pine-bark mulches are also acceptable. Aged hardwood mulch is quite fibrous, which makes it especially good for slopes. Neither pine nor hardwood mulch has much nutritional value, however, so a slow-release high-nitrogen fertilizer should be applied beneath bark mulch. Pine needles, if you have access to them, are good for mulching acid-loving plants.

# Fertilizers & Soil Additives

Fertilizers, both the synthesized and the commercially produced organic varieties, are labeled according to their content of nitrogen (N), phosphorus (P) and potassium (K). For example, a 10-10-10 contains 10% of each; the other 70% is filler. Plants can't tell the difference between organic and synthesized nutrients. So why are we hearing so much about organic fertilizers these days? Let me explain.

Most synthetic fertilizers are designed to be rapidly absorbed into the roots of the plant, and many of these fast-acting products contain more nitrogen than the plants can actually use. What's not absorbed is flushed out by rain and wasted. Moreover, chemical fertilizers do nothing for microorganisms and earthworms.

The earthworm," says Malcomb Beck in his charming little book of essays, *The Garden-Ville Method: Lessons in Nature*, "is nature's plow, chemist, cultivator, maker, and distributor of plant food. It is very valuable to man as it enriches and aerates the soil. Its tunnels allow rainwater and oxygen to penetrate deeply into the soil, thus promoting the growth of helpful microorganisms." Mr. Beck notes that ammonium sulfate (21-0-0), which is a commonly used lawn and garden fertilizer, has actually been used for the purpose of killing earthworms on golf courses!

Unlike fast-acting chemicals, organic fertilizers are released gradually into the soil, where the plants can extract them as needed. Composted manures, bone meal, blood meal, alfalfa meal, cottonseed meal, kelp meal, fish meal, etc., which are derived from by-products of once living organisms, and rock powders (lava sand, greensand and colloidal phosphate) are all classified as organic. In addition to these products, a number of organic gardeners apply biostimulants, which are formulated to invigorate microbial activity in the soil.

☛**Money-saving tip: Determine what your soil actually needs before investing in fertilizers or additives. Test a small amount in your garden before ordering large quantities of any product.**

Organic fertilizers and additives are more expensive than the synthetic products, and they are generally lower in nutrients per pound, so they must be applied liberally to be effective. What has discouraged a lot of gardeners from "going organic" is that shoveling a truckload of organic material is harder work than hand-broadcasting a granulated fertilizer. For some of us older folks, especially those with a lot of garden to keep, packaged commercial fertilizers have seemed the only feasible choice. Happily, there are now numerous sources for organic fertilizers in easy-to-apply liquid and granular forms.

Howard Garrett's *Texas Organic Gardening Book* provides an excellent list of the various organic fertilizers and biostimulants on the market. It also has a helpful rate-of-application chart. You must use your soil test and your own good common sense, however, to determine which products your plants really need. Going into a garden store to buy "plant food" is not unlike going into a health food store to buy vitamins. The array is overwhelming, and if you ingested one of everything, you would probably die.

☛**Money-saving tip: Stock-up on bagged soil, soil amendments and fertilizers when they are marked-down.**

Just before going to press, I talked to Bill Ater, my friend and gardening guru in Austin. In the heat of August, Bill's garden was thriving. He reported that he had top dressed his plants with "a handful of alfalfa pellets and a handful of organic fertilizer." He also had maintained a monthly regimen of foliar feedings with 2T seaweed and 1T of magnesium mixed into 2 gallons of water. I report this scientifically unproven "formula" because I think we are only beginning to learn all the benefits of organic gardening. I do know that alfalfa pellets contain a hormone that works as a plant growth regulator, so perhaps that is what kept his plants from burning to a crisp in what everyone has assured me was "the worst summer in memory." I think it's important for our research institutes to seriously experiment with the organic prescriptions about which such anecdotal evidence continues to accumulate.

# Sources for Amendments, Mulches & Fertilizers:

## Austin Wood Recycling

4950 FM 1431
Leander, Texas 78641
☎ 512/259-7430
**Hours** Mon-Sat 8-5
**Accessible** Yes

This company's *Native Texas Mulch* has become very popular with Central Texas and Hill Country gardeners. Available locally in bulk or in bags at home improvement stores and nurseries throughout the state, the product is made from hardwood and cedar brush that is brought-in by land developers and individual homeowners. The material is ground, aged for 12 months, then ground again. No trees are cut down to manufacture this rich mulch. Austin Wood Recycling also distributes a "gardener's mix" (a combined soil and mulch) and *Dillo Dirt*, which is made from Austin sewage sludge.

## Back To Earth Resources, Inc.

5307 East Mockingbird Lane, Suite 202 (corporate office)
Dallas, Texas 75206
☎ 214/828-0090 or 1-800/441-2498
**FAX** 214/373-4161
**Hours** Mon-Fri 9-5
**Catalog** Free

Back To Earth Resources manufactures and markets premium composts: cotton burr compost and composted cattle and chicken manure. I have a client who swears by the cotton burr compost. It's available fine-screened and coarse-screened, and it's certified safe for organic gardening. (The product is manufactured near Lubbock, where early freezes naturally defoliate the cotton crops, so the cotton gin by-products used to make *Back To Earth™* are not contaminated with chemical defoliants.) Used as a soil conditioner, it loosens clay soil and, in sandy soil, it improves moisture and nutrient retention. It can be used as a mulching material. The company's manure products are fully composted, and the products contain no filler materials of any kind. Advice is offered in the form of a brochure entitled, "Let's Talk Dirty." The products are available at retail nurseries throughout the state and available in bulk in Lubbock (Sparkman), Carrollton (Southwest Landscape), Terrell (J&T Nursery) and Austin (Garden-Ville). If you cannot find *Back To Earth™*, call the corporate office to get the name of the nearest dealer.

## Badlands & Company

P. O. Box 51831
Midland, Texas 79710
☎ 915/683-4670

*Desert Peat™* is a naturally occurring organic humus soil conditioner that is especially valuable for use in arid and semi-arid areas of the state. High in primary nutrients and micronutrients, it helps retain soil moisture and lowers the alkalinity level of the soil. Contact the company for the name of your nearest distributor.

## Carl Pool Products

P.O. Box 1148
Gladewater, Texas 75647
☎ 1-800/245-7645

This Texas company celebrated its 50th anniversary in 1995, and if you've gardened in this state for long, you probably know Carl Pool products. The company's specialized, 100% water soluble fertilizers are on the shelves of all the best nurseries in Texas. It's original blossom booster, BR-61, has been reformulated to contain more trace elements than any comparable high phosphorus plant food on the market. There are special blends (both liquid and granular) for African violets, azaleas, gardenias and camellias, roses, crepe myrtles, tomatoes, geraniums and mums, house plants, etc., plus Hi-Iron Plant Food and special blends for fruit and nut trees and general landscape use. The folks at Carl Pool have recently introduced *Earth-Safe* Organic products (diatomaceous earth, rock phosphate, bone meal, fish meal, bat guano, seaweed extract, and much more). The products contain no excess salt or other impurities, and the water soluble fertilizers are adaptable to drip or foliar applications. Custom formulations are available. The company packages potting soil, azalea mix, compost and several specialized mulches under the trademark, *Vital Earth Resources*™.

## Garden-Ville

7561 East Evans Road
San Antonio, Texas 78266
☎ 210/651-6115
**FAX** 210/651-9231
**Hours** Mon-Fri 8-5:30,Sat 8-5, Sun 10-4; (Closed Sun in Jan)
**Accessible** Yes

Garden-Ville has been a pioneer in the field of organic gardening, and its products are now available in retail nurseries throughout the state. The company, which was begun by Malcomb and Delphine Beck, takes a problem-solving approach that begins with good soil. The company's environmentally friendly fertilizers and soil amendments work with nature to encourage a healthy, living soil rather than one that is dependent on ever-increasing doses of chemicals. The San Antonio location carries everything for the garden except plants (i.e. soil, soil amendments and a fabulous array of organic supplies). "We stress the importance of quality and durability in all of our products. We would rather sell a customer one turning fork with a lifetime warranty than an inferior one that needs replacing every year. Garden-Ville can supply all of your organic gardening needs," says Mr. Beck. Also see page 155.

## Living Earth Technology Company

5625 Crawford Road (bagging operation)
Houston, Texas 77041
☎ 713/466-7360 or 1-800/665-3826

Living Earth markets hardwood mulch, composted cow manure, organic compost, enriched soil with composts and several specialized growing mixes that have been praised by nursery stock growers, landscape contractors and homeowners. The products are available in bags. Call the number listed above for a dealer in your area. You can also purchase the products in bulk at several locations throughout Texas: (Houston ☎ 713/466-7360, North Houston ☎ 281/537-2377, Richmond ☎ 281/342-6133, The Woodlands ☎ 409/321-4001, Missouri City ☎ 281/499-5641, Dallas ☎ 972/869-4332, Plano ☎ 972/578-7532, Austin ☎ 512/219-5311, Pineland [East Texas] ☎ 1-800/323-4417).

Since the company began its composting operations in 1985, it has seen a complete turn around in public demand for its products. "We were ahead of our time," says Mike Payne. "We have developed a quality line of compost and soil blends that have made us the largest commercial composter, bulk soil and mulch manufacturer in Texas."

## Marshall Distributing Company

2224 East Lancaster
Fort Worth, Texas 76103
☎ 817/536-0066
**FAX** 817/536-1897
**Hours** Mon-Fri 8-5:30
**Accessible** Yes
**Mail Order**
**Catalog** Price lists only

This company has everything an environmentally concerned gardener could ever want. Serving wholesale and retail customers for 51 years, the company offers 200 to 300 natural gardening products, including liquid and dry fertilizers and soil conditioners, compost products, mulches, potting soils, natural herbicides and insecticides, insect traps and beneficial insects. All of the products are packaged in sensible sizes for home gardeners. Says Bobby Spence, "We turn away products the company is not sure about. People from all over the D-FW metroplex come to the retail store, Marshall Grain Co. Folks from other parts of the state can order from us or call for a dealer in their area." The company also carries garden tools, seeds, bat and bird houses, organic pet products and a long list of helpful garden books.

## Medina Agricultural Products

P.O. Box 309
Hondo, Texas
☎ 830/426-3011
**FAX** 830/426-2288
**Hours** Mon-Fri 8-5
**Accessible** Yes
**Mail Order**
**Catalog** Free

Medina's history is long and colorful, checkered with stories of successes and rejections. Medina began taking an "old-fashioned" approach to soil-building at a time when farmers had become totally dependent on chemical fertilizers. Knowing that productive soil required an abundance of beneficial microbes, a country inventor researched methods of developing a product that contained huge quantities of life-giving organisms. "The idea is to duplicate the way the earth developed the soil," explains Stuart Franke, company president and son of the firm's first farmer/backer. "For farmers to be willing to use a product, they have to be able to show practical, profitable results," says Mr. Franke. He notes that the company has grown slowly as more and more people have become loyal to the label and enthusiastic about organic growing. The product line has expanded beyond the original *Medina*® *Soil Activator* to include *Medina*® *Plus*, which is fortified with micronutrients and growth hormones, *Hasta Gro*® (a liquid fertilizer available in formulations for lawns or gardens) and *HuMate Liquid Humus*, which is described as "concentrated compost in a bottle." What began as an inventor's dream has become a growing family business with an impressive family of products. "If you have perfect soil, you don't need us."

## Nature Life, Inc.

P.O. Box 65600-228
Lubbock, Texas 79464
☎ 806/562-3781
**FAX** 806/562-4661
**Hours** Mon-Fri 8-5

Composted cotton burrs from West Texas are the raw materials for this organic soil conditioner. It's higher in nitrogen, phosphorus and potash than manure. Available in bag or bulk, Nature Life is guaranteed to be free of weed seeds, defoliant chemicals and disease organisms. The company's products are sold through retail nurseries and landscape contractors. Royce Acuff says, "We have been active in agriculture for nearly 40 years; consequently the care and use of our land is of primary importance to our business." He notes that with proper use this product will give gardeners rich, mellow soil, and he adds, "Call if you can't find the product in your hometown."

## Nature's Technology, Inc.

P.O. Box 235
Pilot Point, Texas 76258
☎ 940/686-5527
**FAX** 940/686-2527
http://**www**.superbio.com/totalgar.htm
**Hours** Mon-Fri 8-5
**Mail Order**
**Catalog** Free

SuperBio™, a solution of microorganisms, is designed to enhance the work of fertilizers in the soil and to speed the action of decomposition of organic matter in soils and compost piles. Available in various quantities, it can be directly applied to the soil surface with a hose sprayer. One gallon will cover about 24,000 square feet. The company makes several different blends, such as a flower and garden formula that includes seaweed. Other blends introduce trace elements. The company has been in business since 1957, and its products are USDA-approved for bio-remediation projects. If you cannot find SuperBio™ in your local garden center, you can order directly from the company.

## Rohde's Nursery & Nature Store

1651 Wall Street
Garland, Texas 75041
☎ 972/864-1934 or 1-800/864-4445
www.beorganic.com

This excellent all-organic garden center now maintains an on-line catalog for ordering a wide variety of products. You'll find 28 Greensense labels, ranging from blood meal to Vegetable & Flower Food. While most of the goods are for soil improvement, the list includes a trombone sprayer, beneficial nematodes and Solid Water, a product to help keep plant roots moist. See retail store listing on page 188.

### San Jacinto Environmental Supplies

2221-A West 34th Street
Houston, Texas 77018
☎ 713/957-0909 or 1-800/444-1290
*FAX* 713/957-0707
**Hours** Mon-Fri 7-5

This wholesale company manufactures organic fertilizers, amendments and mineralizers. Its *MicroLife*™ products are sold through fine nurseries and landscape contractors in the Gulf Coast area. If you cannot find the products, a call to the company will put you in touch with a retail outlet in the region. Landscape professionals throughout the state can order from the company's catalog. *MicroLife*™ fertilizers contain kelp meal, feather meal, bat guano, fish meal, humates, blood meal, bone meal, rock phosphate, potassium sulfate and magnesium, along with special innoculants. It's available in three different formulas. The company also distributes organic pest controls and a wide range of general landscape supplies.

### Spray-N-Grow, Inc.

P.O. Box 2137
Rockport, Texas 78381
☎ 512/790-0933 or 1-800/323-2363
*FAX* 512/790-9313
*www.spray-n-grow.com*
**Mail Order**
**Catalog** Free

Chemist Bill Muskopf says of the company's signature product, "*Spray-N-Grow* will cause your flowers to bloom more than they ever have before. You'll get more vegetables, fruits, nuts, etc. than you ever have, and you'll have more fun gardening than you ever imagined. *Spray-N-Grow* is a micronutrient complex that utilizes soil nutrients and natural plant qualities to the optimum. It is proven to increase plant production, and you can experience increased yields of 30-200% (based on weight)." His newsletter/catalog is filled with testimonials about this non-toxic liquid fertilizer blend. The company also offers *Bill's Perfect Fertilizer, Coco-Wet* (a coconut oil-based wetting agent), award-winning *Root Guard*, diatomaceous earth, a pyrethrum-based insecticide and a number of labor-saving gardening tools.

### Voluntary Purchasing Groups, Inc.

P.O. Box 460
Bonham, Texas 75418
☎ 903/583-5501
*FAX* 903/583-7124

Voluntary Purchasing Groups, Inc. of Bonham holds trademarks on many familiar garden products, including *ferti·lome*® and *Hi-Yield*®. Begun in 1957 as a co-op, this Texas-based company markets gardening products through locally owned merchants throughout the country. It's new *Natural Guard*® line is promoted to help gardeners work with nature. A ten-page catalog describes composting, introduces the company's organic nutrients, devotes a full page to insect identification (color illustrations of 56 common garden pests) and offers both mechanical and biological controls. If you can't find the products locally, write or call for a free catalog and the name of a local dealer.

### Zipp Industries

P.O. Box 1450
Plainview, Texas 79073
☎ 1-800/247-9722
**FAX** 806/296-1940

"We're hanging in — one of the few manufacturing plants left in Texas," says vice-president Rudy Snyder. Zipp's products are available in garden centers throughout the state under the trade names *Turf Magic*™, *Easy Gro*™ and *Green Charm*™. It also private-labels for Walmart, Wolfe Nurseries and Builder's Square. Basic to the company's fertilizers is a finely ground, quick-dissolving ammonium sulfate. In addition to fertilizers of varying formulations, the company produces specialty plant foods, bone meal and blood meal. Zipp Industries takes pride in the fact that it hires handicapped people to prepare the packaging.

# Managing Pests & Diseases

Those of us who came of age shortly after World War II were promised Nirvana by chemical companies. Soil could be kept forever fertile. Pests would be eliminated. Now, proponents of organic gardening are ready to dispense with all synthesized chemicals. I'm not completely comfortable in either camp. I'm utterly opposed to hiring a "service" that sprays on a regular, whether-it-needs-it-or-not-basis, but I'm not ready to advise my clients that they should never under any circumstances resort to manufactured chemicals. This is a complex subject, and it demands utmost common sense. The benefits must be weighed against the risks.

Recently I received a flyer from a "news service" directed toward garden writers. Under the heading, "A New Image for Pesticides," I found the following sentence: "The term 'pesticides' should be rethought. Indeed it seems, changing the name pesticide to 'a medicine for plants and turf' might go a long way for placing those products in a new light." My first reaction was to laugh, but the subject is far too serious to dismiss lightly. While I cannot argue the industry's assertion that pesticides "have given people safe and dependable food, clean and sanitary homes and hospitals," I cannot agree with the statement: "A parts per trillion measurement of pesticide residue is not a cause for alarm."

Pesticide residue in our soil and water supplies *is* a legitimate concern. Much higher concentrations than mere "parts per trillion" of numerous toxic compounds have been measured in streams throughout the country. The truth is that we don't know all of the long-term hazards to humans. What we do know is that because there are so many of us and because what we use in our gardens does mount up, we should use pesticides only as a last resort. And we should use them with the full knowledge that what poisons "bad" insects also kills the good guys!

While I stated up front that I'm not a certified organic gardener, I've rarely used pesticides. I've always been a lazy gardener, and somehow I just never had time for hauling out the old sprayer. (Ignoring a problem will make it go away. Right?) Well, what I inadvertently discovered is that birds, spiders, toads, wasps and flies would do my work for me! Beneficial insects compare to tigers as efficient predators, and nature strikes a balance in a garden that's friendly to these unsung heroes.

The only time I've ever lost a plant to a "critter" was when snails devoured my hostas. Rather than bring on the snail bait, I figured I shouldn't have planted hostas in Austin in the first place. I've come to believe that pesticides generally worsen our problems. Even such naturally derived insecticides as pyrethrum can be lethal to beneficial insects. I recommend to my clients that they determine the number of pests they can tolerate and their plants can withstand before resorting to poisons. A responsible gardener will accept the fact that a certain amount of damage is normal.

Integrated Pest Management represents the most recent and, in my opinion, most sensible approach to keeping pests at acceptable levels. Good cultural practices are the basis of IPM. It has been wryly observed that the worst plant pest may be the species *Homo sapiens*! Without question, we humans leave our plants susceptible to disease and insect infestation when we fail to maintain healthy soil, forget to keep the garden clean, prune improperly or inappropriately water the garden.

Malcomb Beck's, *The Garden-Ville Method*, has this to say: "Organic growers have the philosophy that plants growing in their preferred environment with soil balanced to suit their needs will be healthy, and healthy plants do not attract destructive insects." Noting that destructive insects act as censors to cut out the unfit and unhealthy plants, Mr. Beck adds, "When insects (and diseases) attack a plant and are able to damage or destroy it, the organic grower asks why and searches for the cause."

Begin any pest management program by identifying what's "bugging" your garden. It may be a bug, but then again it may be one of a hundred plant diseases or it may be stress due to climate extremes or poor maintenance. County extension agents, local nurserymen and Master Gardeners all offer services and publications that help the gardener identify problems.

If you must resort to a management strategy, **look for the least-toxic, most environmentally sound solution**. Don't haul out big guns to attack little problems, or worse yet, "scattershoot." The first line of defense should be mechanical control. These solutions include removing the offenders by hand, pruning out infested leaves or branches (taking care not to butcher the plant), drowning snails in beer (they die happy), and setting out sticky paper or physical barriers such as netting and row covers.

Another promising avenue is biological control, which includes the release of predatory and parasitic insects such as lady beetles, trichogramma wasps and praying mantises. There are two problems associated with purchasing predator insects to patrol your property. First, they may benefit your neighbor's garden more than your own. Second, natural enemies can only be expected to reduce the number of pests. If they eliminated all of their natural meals, the predators themselves would starve to death! More effective perhaps are the several biological agents that keep unwanted insects under control by causing disruption to their mating processes.

Other pest control methods include smothering insects and pathogens with horticultural oils when the plants are dormant or the insects are most vulnerable. Another popular method is the use of insecticidal soaps, which are effective for thinning populations of aphids, mealy bugs, mites, whiteflies and other soft-bodied insects. For these soaps to work, you must make contact with the pest, so it's important to spray the plant thoroughly, including the undersides of the leaves.

Organic gardeners use a variety of non-toxic homemade remedies for controlling pests and diseases. They report some luck controlling fungal diseases with a heaping tablespoon of baking soda and a teaspoon of vegetable oil mixed in a gallon of water. (Recent research at Oregon State University showed that the baking soda/oil spray was not effective against black spot and recommended *Rose Defense*™, which is made of neem oil.) Mulching also helps contain fungal disease by providing a barrier between disease spores from fallen leaves and the soil beneath.

To control sucking insects, one can make a somewhat effective soap with a tablespoon of vegetable oil and a tablespoon of non-phosphate dishwashing detergent in a gallon of water. (Be sure to test it on a leaf or two before widespread spraying; some detergents damage plant foliage.) Another insecticide said to be effective for controlling aphids is made with a cup of rubbing alcohol, a teaspoon of dishwashing soap and a teaspoon of Tabasco.

☛**Money-saving tip: Seek advice on pest control from experts who do not stand to profit from their recommendations.**

Chewing bugs can be discouraged with a garlic-jalapeño pepper mix. Liquefy two bulbs of garlic and two hot peppers in two cups of water in your blender. Strain out the solids and add enough water to make a gallon of concentrate. Add ¼-cup of this mixture to a gallon of water in a sprayer. Hey, if it doesn't work, you can always make pepper jelly....

A number of companies are now producing a wide range of relatively non-toxic pest and disease controls. If you continue to experience an intolerable level of plant damage after you have tried controlling problems without an arsenal of chemicals, only then should you consider purchasing a chemical control. Be sure you are using the right product for the particular pest or disease. Take time to read the label before you buy any product; even "organics" should be handled with caution.

☛**Money-saving tip: Buy the smallest possible quantity of any pesticide, fungicide or herbicide product.**

Chemical companies are becoming increasingly sensitive to ecological concerns, and their labeling is increasingly specific. Follow the instructions and cautions on the label "to-the-letter." Use as little as possible. **Monitor progress**. Document both the treatment and the result. EPA-registered pesticides are required to print storage and disposal information on the labels. Purchase the smallest container available for the use you intend. Mix up only what you need. After applying the chemical, clean out your spray equipment . Fill the sprayer half-full with water, shake and pour the rinse water onto the area where you originally applied the pesticide.

**Don't dispose of unused chemicals in sinks, toilets or storm drains!** Take them to a hazardous waste pick-up point or, if the amount is very small, dilute and pour them into bare soil where the sun and microbes will help break them down. It is okay to dispose of empty bottles (triple rinsed) and bags in the trash, if you first wrap them in layers of newspaper.

# Sources for Pest Management Products:

## ANP Distributors

*3105 Post River Road*
*Cedar Park, Texas 78613*
☎ *512/515-6032*

ANP distributes the products of a company in Georgetown that makes *Moo Dew*™, a manure concentrate. The manufacturer combines the liquid manure with rotenone to make *True Stop*™, a fire ant insecticide, and a similar True Stop™ formulation for controlling whiteflies.

## Biofac Crop Care, Inc.

*P.O. Box 87*
*Mathis, Texas 78368*
☎ *512/547-3259 or 1-800/233-4914*
**FAX** *512/547-9660*
**Mail Order**
**Catalog** *Free*

This company's beneficial insects come in a *BioPac*™ kit that contains ladybugs, trichogrammas, lacewings and praying mantids. The owner, M. A. Maedgen, Jr., suggests serial releases throughout the year because many insects attack only at a certain stage in a pest life cycle. "This assures you of having a constant population of beneficials on your property to ward off migrating populations of pests," he says. "These friendly critters are harmless to people, pets, wildlife, etc." One kit will cover up to a quarter-acre. Each of the predator species, plus several others that are specific to various garden pests, can be purchased individually.

## Garden-Ville

*7561 East Evans Road*
*San Antonio, Texas 78266*
☎ *210/651-6115*

Since 1957, this company has provided alternative solutions to toxic pest control methods for the home and garden. "We believe that the future of gardening will continue to evolve into low toxicity, environmentally friendly methods," says owner Malcomb Beck. The company has come out with a very effective fire ant killer made of dairy cow manure and molasses, among other non-toxic ingredients! Coming soon are all-natural pre-emergent and post-emergent herbicides. Also see page 148.

## Green Light Co.

*P.O. Box 17985*
*San Antonio, Texas 78217-0985*
☎ *210/494-3481*
**FAX** *210/494-5224*

Founded in 1947, this Texas-based company manufactures a broad range of products for the lawn and garden. Its "SafetyPlus" packaging is designed to prevent leaks, odors or accidental ingestion by children. Among the new organic products in the company's line are *Rose Defense*™ (made from harmless neem oil) and *Vegetable Defense*™. The company does not sell directly to the public, but its products are available in garden centers and nurseries throughout the state.

## Indeco Products

P.O. Box 5077
San Marcos, Texas 78666
☎ 512/396-5814 or 1-800/782-7653 ext. 173

Covering plants with *Spunweb* is an excellent way to protect seedlings from birds and varmits and to protect vegetable crops from leaf-eating caterpillars. *Spunweb* products can be found in local nurseries or ordered directly from the manufacturer.

## Kunafin Trichogramma

Route 1, Box 39
Quemado, Texas 78877
☎ 830/757-1181 or 1-800/832-1113
**FAX** 830/757-1468
**Hours** Daily 9-5
**Mail Order**
**Catalog** Free

Frank and Adele Kunafin mass-rear these tiny wasps. They arrive at your home packaged in breathable pouches, ready to rid your orchard or garden of pecan casebearers.

## Organic Solutions Inc.

8023 Vantage Drive, Suite 600 (corporate office)
San Antonio, Texas 78230
☎ 1-800/862-7482 or 210/340-4642
**FAX** 210/340-4844
**Hours** Mon-Fri 8-5
**Mail Order**
**Catalog** Free brochure

The basic ingredient of this company's insecticides is pulverized, fresh-water diatomaceous earth (the fossilized remains of pre-historic, single cell plants), which dispatches insects with razor-sharp particles. The different formulations for vegetable gardens, ornamental gardening and fireant control also contain pyrethrin (derived from an African chrysanthemum) and piperonyl butoxide (sassafras from the ocotea tree). The company also makes flea powders and tick powders for both dogs and cats. Although the products are toxic to fish, they are safe to use with normal precautions. This small company sells through distributors, but will take credit card and ship its products directly to homeowners.

## Pied Piper Traps

445 Garner Adell Road
Weatherford, Texas 76086
☎ 817/682-4663 or 1/800287-2748
**FAX** 817/682-4941
**Mail Order**
**Catalog** Free brochure

After 14 years in the business, this company can provide a trap to catch everything from a rat to a mountain lion! The brochure tells you how to bait and set the traps, as well as how to handle the animal afterwards (very carefully). There's even a trap designed for turtles and another for catching catfish. All in all, there are traps in 20 different styles and sizes, plus carrying cages, rabbit cages, hay racks and saddle racks available from these folks. (*Where was this company when a family of armadillos systematically destroyed my lawn?*)

# The Proper Way to Prune

Pruning is both an art and a science. Unfortunately, few people know how to do it correctly. A drive through any older neighborhood will provide examples of trees topped and shrubs mangled beyond recognition. Such pruning not only leaves the plants looking ugly, it makes them more prone to disease. *Neil Sperry's Complete Guide to Texas Gardening* explains the basics of proper pruning. It's a good place to start learning the terminology and accepted techniques.

When designing a new landscape plan, I promise my clients they'll never have to do much pruning beyond occasional, judicious cuts to thin plants, remove unsafe or unattractive growth and repair damage. How can I make such a promise? By knowing the ultimate size of each plant and choosing the right variety for each situation!

For example, I use dwarf plants beneath windows, select small trees for small gardens, use low-growing plants at the front of a bed and graduate plant heights upward toward the back. I allow just enough space between the plants so that they'll ultimately grow together, but not crowd one another. And, I rarely design clipped hedges. Anything more complicated than an occasional clipped edging is simply too labor-intensive for today's lifestyle. Besides, I prefer a loose, natural look.

☛**Money-saving tip: The least expensive pruning is no pruning at all.**

Before redesigning the planting plan for an older garden, I decide which plants can be saved and which should be removed. Grossly overgrown shrubs cannot simply be cut in half. It's better to take them out and start over, choosing a plant that will not grow too large for the spot.

I thin and head-back shrubs that lack structure, hang over pathways or obscure views. Some large old shrubs, such as photinias, hollies and ligustrum, can be pruned into attractive small trees. If the plant has multiple stems, select a few heavy upright branches to serve as trunks and cut the rest to the ground. Then start at the bottom, exposing each trunk carefully by cutting off lower branches, making the cuts close to the trunk, just outside the rings. Stand back and look, then continue "limbing-up" the lower branches until the overall shape is pleasing. To dress-up the landscape, plant a ground cover under the "new" tree.

☛**Money-saving Tip: Selective pruning can be used to tame a garden of unruly delinquents.**

"Renewal pruning" is another way to rejuvenate plants in an overgrown landscape. This method works well on fountain-shaped shrubs that tend to put on all their growth at the top. I've been known to cut leggy old specimens of abelia, nandina and spiraea all the way to the ground, allowing the entire plant to regenerate from the roots. Thereafter, the homeowner removes a third of the growth each year, cutting out the oldest, woodiest canes. Such pruning forces plants to continually put out new growth from the bottom, keeping the plants fuller and more naturally shaped.

Timing is a critical factor in pruning. Some plants must be pruned during dormancy; others should not be pruned until after flowering. Some plants may be susceptible to fungus if they are pruned during the rainy season. If you are unsure, check with a professional arborist, qualified nurseryman or extension agent before beginning a pruning project.

Always prune with a purpose. Remove rubbing and crossing branches, suckers, weak branches and any broken or diseased limbs. In the latter case, always cut back to healthy wood and disinfect the tool. Use a solution made with one cup of bleach in a gallon of water. Thinning a tree or large shrub is acceptable if it is to provide good air circulation, let more light through the canopy or promote evenly spaced branching patterns. Thinning may also improve a tree's chance of survival in a time of drought, since removing excess foliage reduces water consumption. In wet climates, thinning some shrubbery may help reduce excess dampness around the house foundation.

☛**Money-saving tip: You can add years of life to your tree or shrub with good pruning practices.**

The best pruning removes branches back to the origin of growth. Make the cut almost flush with the branch from which it sprang, cutting just outside the ring that separates the branch from the trunk (called the branch collar). If you're removing a large branch, three cuts are needed to ensure that the bark won't tear. The first cut should be from the bottom, just beyond the place where the final cut will be made. The second should be made from the top to remove the branch. The third and final cut is made to remove the stump just beyond the branch collar.

To head-back growth, make the pruning cut so that the outermost bud left on the branch is pointing in the direction you want the branch to grow. Always cut quickly and cleanly. It's better to perform small annual cuts than to wait until a plant is out of hand and take a chance on hopelessly ruining its shape.

☛**Money-saving tip: A professional arborist may not only prolong the life of your trees, but also save you from a stay in the hospital.**

Most people don't have the proper tools and ladders to safely prune large trees. If a tree must be removed, the International Society of Arboriculture recommends that you negotiate a written contract that specifies how the tree is to be removed, where the wood will be taken and who is liable in case of damage.

☛**Money-saving tip: Topping permanently disfigures a tree, exposing the wood in each growth ring to decay and causing the tree to become hollow over time.**

Never top a tree. Instead of topping, thin the tree to a network of even, regularly spaced branches. If you must reduce the height of a tree, do it over a period of time. There is some disagreement about painting pruning cuts/wounds on trees. I don't ordinarily advocate it, but some experts believe that painting at the time of pruning may be helpful. If the wound isn't painted soon after it occurs, painting is of no value.

Live oaks and red oaks, which are subject to oak wilt in some 60 counties in Texas (mostly located between Dallas/Ft. Worth and San Antonio) should be protected with a wound paint. Dr. David Appel at Texas A&M University, the resident expert on oak wilt, recommends, "All wounding of oaks (including pruning) should be avoided from February through June." (This is the time of year when fungal mats are formed and are attractive to insects, which could vector the oak wilt spores to fresh wounds.) "The least hazardous periods for pruning are during the coldest days in midwinter and extended hot periods in mid- to late summer. Regardless of season, all pruning cuts greater than ½ inch, including freshly cut stumps and damaged surface roots, should be treated immediately with a wound paint to prevent exposure to contaminated insect vectors."

☛**Money-saving tip: Remove a dead or damaged tree *before* it can do damage.**

Dead or unhealthy trees are a liability. It's probably time to bring-in a professional arborist if: 1) the tree is leaning, 2) there's evidence of root rot and/or the trunk has hollows or deep open cracks, 3) there has been improper pruning in the past, or 4) there has been storm damage or construction injury. An arborist is the person most qualified to determine if the tree can be saved. Should the tree pose a danger to a house, power lines, cars or people, let it go and plant a replacement.

# Finding the Best Tools

A beginning gardener need invest in only a few basic tools. The five I use most are a medium-width pointed shovel, a spading fork, weeding hoe, garden rake and trowel. Over the years I've also acquired a flat shovel, leaf rake, edging tool and assorted other devices that promised to make gardening easier. For pruning, I have top-quality hand shears, loppers, a pruning saw and a pole saw.

☛**Money-saving tip: High-quality tools are the most economical in the long run, and the most satisfying to use.**

The more you use a tool, the better it should be. I look for tools that will last a lifetime. Several garden center managers told us that they've quit stocking garden tools because they cannot compete with the large home improvement stores. This is a pity. In their choice of tools, beginning gardeners need the kind of expert advice that's only available from experienced nursery personnel.

Serious gardeners appreciate the difference between an English spading fork that sells for $60 and the Taiwanese-made fork you'll find selling for $15 at the discount stores. The former is made in one piece of solid forged steel. Its tines will not rust or break, and it will penetrate clay soil with greater ease. For my money, it's worth seeking out the best and paying the difference.

You'll find the lowest prices on lawn mowers and power tools at the big hardware chains and home improvement centers, but if you're not the "fix-it" type, don't base your buying decision on price alone. When you shop an independent dealer, you're also buying service. **Turf & Irrigation Hardware**, a large and very complete merchandiser of garden-related products in Corpus Christi, is one of several such stores we visited during our travels through Texas. As owner Herman Johnson says, "We tell our customers the truth, even if it hurts!" Get to know someone like Herman and ask a lot of questions before you invest in garden equipment.

One of the most interesting pieces of literature that has recently crossed my desk was from **Ames Lawn and Garden Tools** of West Virginia. (You can call ☎ 1-800/725-9500 for the nearest local retailer.) This company has introduced a new line of ergonomically engineered shovels, rakes and hoes. Gracefully curved and long-handled, the tools are designed to reduce bending and stooping. They are all made with extra-long cushioned foam grips to lessen hand fatigue.

The best little hand tools I've ever seen are made by Allen Simpson in Ontario, Canada. The company's forks and trowels are made of a rust-free, lightweight aluminum alloy, and they are guaranteed for life. I recently found them at Smith & Hawken, and having gone through a trowel a year, I was attracted like a bear to honey.

A few toll-free calls will bring several rather special catalogs to your mailbox. While only **Teas Nursery** and **Smith & Hawken** have retail stores in Texas (see pages 202 and 352), I'm including some companies outside Texas because they offer a selection of tools and apparel you may not be able to find locally:

**A.M. Leonard,** ☎ 1-800/543-8955

**Brookstone,** ☎ 1-800/926-7000

**Gardener's Supply Company,** ☎ 1-800/955-3370

**Smith & Hawken,** ☎ 1-800/776-3336

**Teas Nursery Company Inc.,** ☎ 1-800/446-7723

**Walt Nicke Company,** ☎ 1-800/822-4114

Fine tools are expensive to replace; treat them like sterling silver. (I have a friend who paints all the handles bright yellow so her tools don't get lost and left out in the garden. Not a bad idea…) Sharp, clean tools make gardening easier, so clean off the soil and/or sap after each use and store your tools in a dry place. Periodically rub linseed oil on wooden handles and sharpen the blades of spades, hoes and pruning tools.

☛**Money-saving tip: Take good care of your tools.**

If you have minimal storage space, rent such items as aerators, chippers, shredders, sod cutters and tillers. There are a number of companies that can supply the large tools you may use only occasionally. Look in the yellow pages under "Rental."

☛**Money-saving tip: Split the cost of rental tools with a neighbor.**

# Dressing for the Sport

Now that health and fitness gurus have finally admitted that gardening is good exercise, it's time we gardeners get serious about our gear. Every well-dressed gardener will need gloves, hats and garden boots. If you are really into making a fashion statement, you'll have elbow-high goatskin gloves and organically grown cotton shirts that say "Save the Earth." But, if you are like me, you've always done your gardening in ratty jeans and paint-spattered tee-shirts. Lately, I've noticed that my jeans are uncomfortable (not enough room to bend and squat). My cloth gloves have developed holes, I've ruined yet another pair of $60 athletic shoes and I've misplaced my straw hat.

This year, I've vowed to get some decent garden apparel. My husband gave me knee-high rubber boots for mucking around in the winter, and for warm weather gardening, I'm planning to get plastic garden clogs. I'm also going to start the season with two new straw hats, a pair of goatskin gloves, kneepads, shatterproof sunglasses and sunscreen, and an apron that holds tools and seed packets!

For gloves, I've found the ultimate selection from **Womanswork** (☎ 1-800/639-2709). Don't let the name deter you, guys; the company also offers gloves for men. But the focus is on apparel for women who aren't afraid of hard work. There are boots, ice treads, kneepads, aprons and even a "bug-baffler" suit in this catalog from Maine! It just puts me in the mood to go split a cord of wood before starting dinner…

# Watering Wisely

There's an old story about a cotton farmer in West Texas whose irrigated fields stretched as far as the eye could see. Right in the middle of the green landscape, visible from the front porch of his comfortable house, was a barren patch of bone-dry soil. Surprised visitors always asked why. "Well, once it was all like that," he replied, "and I don't want to forget."

The summer of 1998 reminded all of us (again) that sustained periods of low rainfall are a way of life in Texas. Folks who weren't around during the Great Drought of the 1950s may have seen for the first time just how devastating a major drought can be. (The Department of Agriculture estimated a loss of $2.4 billion to the economy in '96.) Even in a "normal" year, the gully-washing, frog-choking rains of spring are inevitably followed by long weeks of drought and intense heat.

There are only two sources of water in Texas — lakes and underground aquifers. Both are fed by rain. Until very recently, most Texans designed their landscapes to look like England and simply turned up the volume on the sprinkler systems in summer. No problem. Water was cheap.

New dams and treatment plants, however, do not come cheap. As the population grows, demand for water is increasing dramatically. If we don't learn to conserve, we'll pay dearly. I was living in Austin when the sewer department (unwilling to build additional treatment facilities) began tying its rates to home water consumption. Never mind that water used on the lawn does not go down the drain, the higher our water usage, the higher our sewer bill.

By the time it began costing $250 a month in sewer service to water my average-size suburban lawn, I got the point. Austin had launched a highly successful program to promote low-water-use landscape methods, and my clients and I learned to cope. Expect to abandon water-guzzling landscapes throughout Texas in the coming years, drought or no drought.

## Reducing the Need for Water

Lawns require about four times as much water as planting beds. The single most effective way to reduce water use is to reduce the size of our lawns. Until the early nineteenth century, only the very wealthy could afford great swaths of lawn grass because mowing had to be performed with a scythe, and watering was done by hand. In the twenty-first century, lawns may once again become too expensive to maintain. Already, wise gardeners are questioning the sensibility of pouring not only water, but also fertilizers, herbicides and pesticides into great expanses of lawn.

Grass can be replaced with decking, paved terraces, water features, ground covers and wildflowers. Now, I'm not suggesting that you should plow under *all* of your grass. You may need a section of turf for children to play or for a grown-up game of croquet. You may simply love the texture of a soft green lawn. In the areas where you need mown grass, consider substituting one of the newer, more drought-tolerant varieties. Contact your county agent or a near-by botanical garden for recommendations on the grass best-suited for your area and soil-type. Keep turf areas well aerated to absorb maximum rainwater and free of weeds that would compete for the available moisture.

The second strategy for creating a more drought-enduring garden is to select drought-tolerant shrubs and flowers for your planting beds. Texans have led the nation in converting to water-wise landscapes. Landscape architects and designers have adopted a more naturalistic standard of beauty. County extension services and water districts are busily researching plants that thrive with little supplementary watering. Homeowners are buying into the concept, actively seeking nurseries that supply native and drought-tolerant plants.

The choices in drought-tolerant plants are wider than anyone imagined when the word "xeriscape" was coined a few years ago. My clients didn't want any part of those "zeroscapes," and even I resisted a conversion to dryland gardening, fearing that my design repertoire would be limited to yucca. What I discovered was that a number of lush-looking plants — goldenrain trees, live oaks, magnolias, rock roses, wisteria, coreopsis, iris and many more — made "the list."

Most drought-tolerant plants are native to dry climates. Some evolved in the southwestern United States, and others come to us from wherever in the world climatic conditions have favored adaptation to periods of drought. Researchers are looking closely at plants from South Africa, Australia, the Mediterranean region and portions of South America.

Nature has devised numerous ways for plants to cope with long periods of drought, including a felt-like coat of hair or varnish-like substance on the leaf surface. Silvery leaves reflect rather than absorb sunlight, and small leaves lessen the area of evaporation (pine needles are the ultimate example). You'll find handsome succulents that store moisture in thick stems and leaves and a number of plants that have deep tap roots. Another ploy for survival is to simply go dormant in hot, dry weather.

A visit to regional botanical gardens and nature trails (listed on pages 43-92) will introduce you to a wealth of plants that thrive in dry climates. The particular plants displayed will vary dramatically from region to region. One can't simply drop desert plants into East Texas, where up to 50 inches of rain each year would rot the roots.

A third strategy is to group together plants with similar watering needs, even if that requires some transplanting. For example, mountain laurels are far less thirsty than hydrangeas or roses. If all three shrubs are planted in the same bed, you end up over-watering the drought-tolerant plant to keep the others happy. I would suggest moving thirsty plants to an area that's convenient to water, well-protected from afternoon sun and shielded from drying summer winds.

A fourth design strategy is to add more trees to your landscape. A plant growing in partial shade requires less water than a plant grown in full sun. As the tree canopies spread, fewer sections of your garden will need frequent irrigation. If you're starting a new garden in a sunny, open environment, select your plants from a list of native and other hardy, drought-tolerant species.

Good maintenance is another key component in conserving water. I began this chapter with the importance of good soil. It bears repeating that well-aerated soil absorbs more water than hard, compacted earth. Organic matter mixed into the soil helps retain the moisture. An organic mulch spread on top conserves water by helping to inhibit weeds and reduce evaporation. Remove those water-robbing weeds as soon as they appear.

Make every drop count. More and more homeowners are collecting the rainwater that falls on roofs and washes into storm sewers. A 2,000 square foot roof can produce up to 600 gallons of water from a good rain. There are several ways to make efficient use of your downspouts. The most sophisticated method is to connect the downspouts to storage tanks and use low-pressure drip lines to evenly distribute the water. Large water collection systems may require the help of an engineer or plumber, but do-it-yourself-types can find 55-gallon drums and all the necessary plumbing parts at hardware stores. Check with your local health department before installing a collection system. Because open water sources pose a danger to children and breed mosquitoes, it's imperative to cover all storage tanks.

Another way to use the roof's runoff is to connect perforated pipe to the bottom of the downspouts for watering the plants under the eaves of your house. A fan-shaped section of concrete or brick could also be used beneath each of the downspouts to divert water evenly throughout a planting area. There are hundreds of little ways to conserve water. Use bath water for watering container plants and house plants. (Never use water from the kitchen sink because it may contain harmful bacteria.) Wash the car and the dog on the lawn. Don't over-water anything.

# Watering Efficiently

The question most beginning gardeners ask is: "How often should I water?" The answer is: "Only when the plant needs it!" Water requirements vary with the age of the plantings, soil conditions and the weather. The first few weeks after installation, plants need lots of moisture. It's common practice to build a soil ring just outside the root-ball of each new plant. The ring acts as a reservoir, allowing you to provide extra water for the new plants without over-watering an entire planting bed. The soil ring can be removed when the plant is well-established.

Once your garden is mature, you should be able to determine precisely how much water it needs. One inch of water per week was the old rule-of-thumb, but that may be too much. Different areas of the garden will have different needs, depending upon sun or shade and slope of the land.

Water only when the top four inches of the soil are dry (a bamboo chop-stick makes a dandy soil probe). Chrysanthemums are good "indicator plants." When they wilt, you know the planting bed needs water; the mums will bounce right back. You can test the amount of water your sprinklers are putting out by placing cans in several areas (tuna cans, which are about a inch deep, work well). Run the water for thirty minutes and measure how much water accumulates in each can. Keep records. Pretty soon you'll know how often and how long you must water to keep your plants perky.

☛**Money-saving tip: Learn to water without wasting a drop.**

The best time to water is very early in the morning. From mid-morning on, too much water is lost to evaporation. Watering at night encourages fungi and other pathogens. One long watering is generally better than several short ones. The idea is to encourage deep roots. But, long soakings may exceed the soil's infiltration rate, so keep a watchful eye and shut off the tap if you begin to see any standing water or run-off.

Most old irrigation systems put out more water than the soil can absorb, resulting in big losses to run-off and evaporation. Watering with hoses and portable lawn sprinklers may be even less efficient because the spread is generally uneven, and the spray is thrown high in the air where it evaporates quickly in hot weather. Also, there's a chance of forgetting to turn the water off when you leave to run an errand. (It has happened to me. About the third time I returned to find water running down the street, I solved the problem with a $15 timer.)

The May 1993 issue of *Consumer Reports*, which should be available in most libraries, provides an extensive analysis of garden hoses, soaker-hoses, sprinklers and such watering accessories as timers and couplers. The seven-page article rates different brands for price and performance, and it discusses how different kinds of sprinklers — impulse, rotary, oscillating and traveling — compare in terms of even coverage and speed of water output. In Texas, it's better to deliver large water drops close to the ground rather than shooting fine streams of water high into the air where the moisture will quickly evaporate.

For planting beds, I recommend drip irrigation because these systems deliver water to the plant's root system with almost no evaporation. Additionally, drip irrigation helps promote plant health by keeping the foliage dry, preventing erosion and lessening the leaching of nutrients. Drip irrigation is not as satisfactory as spray heads for watering grass in most soils, but your trees, shrubs, flower beds and container plants can be handled with an easily installed system attached to outdoor faucets.

The investment cost in drip irrigation equipment can be quite low compared to the savings you'll reap. A drip system can cut your water bills in half! I recently bought a 100-foot "sweating hose" at a local hardware store for $32. A drip kit with emitters for 26 plants was priced at $32.99.

In choosing a kit that's right for you, look at the way the water is emitted. Some kits use simple tubing with small, regularly spaced holes. Others contain drip emitters (small plastic devices) installed in solid-wall tubing. A third kind is made of double-walled, flexible tubing that regulates the drip rate and adjusts to a wider range of water pressure. Drip emitter kits allow you to place the drips where you want them. If the system you buy does not contain an anti-siphoning device, be sure to get one. This five-dollar item prevents garden water from back-siphoning into your home water supply, fouling the taste and possibly introducing algae and bacteria.

More sophisticated drip systems can be hooked up to an existing sprinkler system. In the past decade, there has been a lot of improvement in automated sprinkler systems. Fabricated of new high-quality plastics and designed to throw as little water in the air as possible, today's irrigation systems cut down on evaporation. They feature computerized controls that precisely regulate the amount of water that goes to each zone and solenoid electric valves that adjust flow and prevent valves from getting stuck open.

If you're investing in a new automatic irrigation system, insist on separate zones for lawn and planting beds, and be sure that the system can be adjusted for seasonal differences. Consider investing a few extra dollars for rain and moisture sensors, two items that will save considerable water. Learn everything possible about the operation of the system. For future reference, keep an as-built drawing of your system that shows the layout of the lines and the location of each of the heads and valves.

If you have an old system, check its physical condition zone-by-zone at least once a year. Make sure the heads are not too low in the ground and not cockeyed, damaged or dirty. Shrub heads will need extenders if your plants have grown significantly. Look for mist over the sprinkler head, which indicates excessive water pressure.

Make sure all of the valves open and close properly and are not clogged with dirt. Check for line breaks caused by construction or freezes. Run a test of the controller to be sure each station actually runs the length of time for which it is set. Program the system for maximum efficiency. Consider retrofitting old systems with drip lines and "micro sprinkler" heads to avoid over-watering.

# Sources for Irrigation Equipment:

## *Submatic Irrigation Systems*

*P.O. Box 3965*
*Lubbock, Texas 79452*
☎ *1-800/692-4100*
**FAX** *806/745-8010*
**Hours** *Mon-Fri 8-5, Sat 8-12*
**Accessible** *Yes*
**Mail Order**
**Catalog** *Free*

    A pioneer in drip irrigation for more than twenty years, this company has become a leader in do-it-yourself systems for the home gardener. Its comprehensive catalog and free design assistance allow customers to install exactly what their gardens need. For small areas there are kits that start as low as $21.95. One kit is designed especially for pot plants and hanging baskets. In a large garden you can combine the best features of pop-up sprinklers and drip lines. (If your soil and grass type is right for it, drip applications can even work for turf areas.) Timers and valves allow you to fully automate the system. A siphon mixer makes it possible to inject fertilizer through the lines. Most of the company's trade is by mail-order, but you'll find full stocking dealers in Dallas, Houston and Lubbock.

## *Weathermatic*

*P.O. Box 180205*
*Dallas, Texas 75218-0205*
☎ *972/278-6131 or 1-888/4THEPRO*
**FAX** *972/271-5710*
**Hours** *Mon-Fri 8-5*
**Catalog** *Free Brochure*

    For the homeowner who wants a high-quality, professionally designed and installed irrigation system, Weathermatic is an excellent choice. While the company does not sell directly to the public, its products are made in Texas and installed through its "quality contractor program." You can call the company's national office in Dallas or look in the yellow pages for a licensed Weathermatic contractor.

# Summary of Water Conservation Practices

### 1. Develop a Good Design Plan
Appreciate a less manicured, more natural aesthetic.
Add more trees.
Create wind barriers.
Group plants with similar water needs.
Replace unused portions of lawns with ground covers and wildflowers.
Deck or pave-over a portion of the lawn.
Use mulch as a design feature for color and textural contrast.
Control all rainwater falling on the site by carefully grading the slopes.

### 2. Amend the Soil
Add organic matter to maximize its water-holding capacity.
Cultivate to improve penetration and aeration.
Add polymer wetting agents to the soil in container plantings.

### 3. Pick the Right Plants
Select the least water-demanding turf grass available for your region.
Consider slope, exposure and soil type in your choice of plants.
Prefer drought-tolerant species to more thirsty plants.

### 4. Plant Correctly
Plant in early spring or mid-fall to take advantage of rainy seasons.
Make a soil ring around newly-planted trees and shrubs.

### 5. Mulch, Mulch, Mulch

### 6. Water Efficiently
Use a soil probe; water only when the top four inches are dry.
Establish watering priorities.
Convert to drip irrigation wherever possible.
Irrigate with the lowest possible volume to minimize run-off.
Water in early morning to minimize evaporation.
Collect water in covered storage tanks connected to down spouts.

### 7. Maintain the Garden
Aerate the lawn.
Raise the height of the lawn mower.
Judiciously prune trees and shrubs to reduce transpiration.
Fertilize only to keep plants healthy, not to encourage rapid growth.
Minimize competition for water by removing weeds immediately.

## Chapter Five

# The Garden's Green Foundation

*"If a tree dies, plant another in its place."*
....Linnaeus, *Philosophia Botanica, 1750*

# The Planting Plan

If you've recently acquired a home (old or new), take a year to become acquainted with the existing plants before making any big decisions. Walk around each day; observe the patterns of sunlight at different times of the year. After every rain, watch for standing water or rapid runoff. Take photographs of different areas of the garden in each season. Keep a notebook for recording information about the plants you have and jotting down ideas for plants to add. Window shop at area garden centers. If you find a plant you simply can't live without or a friend gives you an unidentified plant from her garden, store it somewhere until you can determine where it would best serve your garden plan. Consider starting your own "nursery" in a garden utility area somewhere out-of-sight.

Your first priority should be the existing trees. If your property has large trees, count yourself blessed and make sure they are healthy. When I bought my home in Austin, I called in a consulting arborist to evaluate the 27 trees I had inherited. Much to my surprise, he found encircling roots that were threatening to choke out a large sycamore that I desperately needed to provide afternoon shade. He also found symptoms of iron deficiency in several live oaks and recommended thinning out a few of the smaller trees to allow the rest of the grove to grow more fully. The tree work was costly, but I considered it money well-spent!

Making the decision to remove a tree is always difficult. Even when you know that a tree is ugly or diseased, it's tempting to wait for an act of God. But if it has brittle branches that may fall onto your roof, messy fruits that make your walkways hazardous or roots that clog your sewer line (weeping willows are infamous for this), you might as well admit the truth and remove it. Plant a good new tree (or trees) that will provide shade and sustenance for the future.

By the time you are ready to start purchasing new plants for your landscape, you will have considered the climate of your region and the specifics of your site — the drainage patterns, soil conditions, and the patterns of sun and shade created by adjacent buildings, trees and fences. Then, the process involves finding the right plants for the right places. Trees and shrubs are major investments.

☛**Money-saving tip: Take it slowly; choose your plants carefully.**

## About Hardiness Zones

In the preceding chapters of this book, we've made several references to USDA (United States Department of Agriculture) Hardiness Zones. In the February 1997 issue of *Neil Sperry's GARDENS*, Gordon Hall wrote, "All of us have those painful little words or phrases that grate on our nerves, as if someone's running fingernails down a chalkboard. 'Hardy' can be one of those words for a horticulturist." He goes on to say, "Plant hardiness refers to the plant's ability to withstand cold. Period. End of definition."

When you see a plant label that says "Zone 8," all you have learned is that the plant can be expected to withstand temperatures down to 10 degrees. The plant should certainly survive the winter in Zone 9 (where average minimum temperatures range from 20 to 30 degrees), but it is a poor candidate for Zone 7 (where the range is from 0 to 10 degrees). As you begin selecting the plants for your landscape, you'll need to be aware of your Zone, but its important here to caution novice Texas gardeners that minimum winter temperatures are the least of your problems.

## Summer Heat AHS Zones

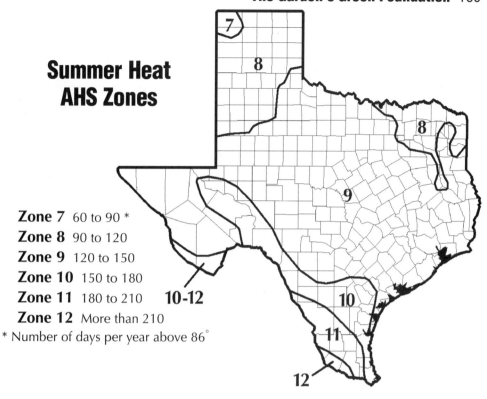

**Zone 7**  60 to 90 *
**Zone 8**  90 to 120
**Zone 9**  120 to 150
**Zone 10**  150 to 180
**Zone 11**  180 to 210
**Zone 12**  More than 210
* Number of days per year above 86°

## Winter Chill USDA Zones

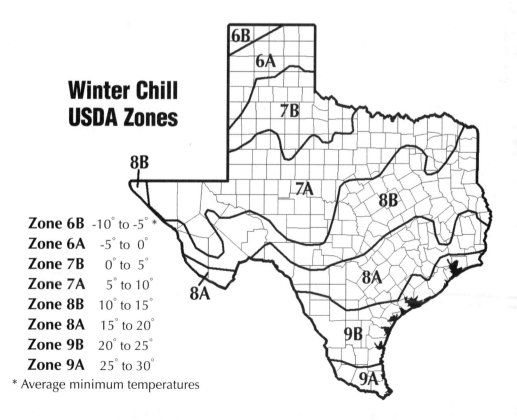

**Zone 6B**  -10° to -5° *
**Zone 6A**  -5° to 0°
**Zone 7B**  0° to 5°
**Zone 7A**  5° to 10°
**Zone 8B**  10° to 15°
**Zone 8A**  15° to 20°
**Zone 9B**  20° to 25°
**Zone 9A**  25° to 30°
* Average minimum temperatures

Camellias are labeled for Zone 7; Fort Worth is in Zone 7. So why are these plants not among the best choices for a garden in Fort Worth? When you read more about camellias, you'll discover that camellias do best in moist, acid soil. OOPS! They prefer sites that are not excessively hot. Oh my! They are susceptible to tea scale, thrips and botrytis. Oh no! Camellias are gorgeous, but are they really worth acidifying soil, adding iron, watering every day in summer, and battling a host of insect and disease problems? Not for *my* money.

I'll cite the low-growing junipers as another example. These plants make dandy ground covers in some regions of the state. They are drought-tolerant and they're "hardy" in Zones 2-6, meaning that they'll withstand the worst winter Texas can offer. This is a plant that requires fast drainage, however. In moist soil and conditions of high humidity, the roots rot and spider mites devour the sap. In either case the needles will quickly resemble little pieces of brown wire. For gardeners in Southeast Texas or along the Gulf Coast, ground cover junipers are simply not an option.

Such plants as tulips and apple trees provide other good examples of plants poorly suited to most areas of Texas because they *require* exposure to a certain number of hours of winter chill to flower. Yes, there are a few apple varieties that will set fruit in Texas. Yes, one can refrigerate tulip bulbs. However, many of the plants that are beloved in northern climes simply do not like our winters, which tend to alternate between warm and cold, or our summers, which I dare not describe in mixed company.

At long last, a new Heat-Zone Map has been developed by the American Horticultural Society. This is big news! I've been saying for years that summer's heat can be as detrimental to plants as winter's cold. Having practiced landscape architecture in Portland and Austin, which are in the same winter-chill zone, USDA Zone 8, I can tell you that only a few plants thrive in both places. The two city's summer zones are very different! It will take several years for all the plants that are commonly grown in the United States are classified by Heat Zone. Unfortunately the new book, *Heat-Zone Gardening* by Dr. H. Marc Cathey, President Emeritus of AHS, contains information that will be misleading to people who are new to Texas gardening.

As you can see from the map on the preceeding page, the major population areas of Texas fall within Heat-Zone 9. If you were to accept the information presented in the book, you might believe that maple and birch trees and such shrubs as rhododendrons, pieris, daphne, witch hazel and sweet bay are viable choices for Central Texas. They aren't! Many of the perennials listed as acceptable for Zone 9 — acanthus, anemones, bergenia, bleeding heart, hostas, peonies and wild ginger, to name a few — are not appropriate for a garden in Austin, no matter how well the plants are sited and tended.

Moreover, some of the plants <u>not</u> listed for Heat-Zone 9 actually perform very well here (in the right conditions). Among these are ajuga, Carolina jessamine, iris, liriope, sedum, crabapples, golden rain tree and deodar cedar! Frankly, I'm stunned by this misinformation. It has to do with the fact that Zone 9 stretches across the country from Southern Georgia to Central California. Moisture and humidity factors make gardening in Georgia quite different from gardening in Texas! It is my hope that before Heat-Zone information is standard on plant labels, the Zones will have been refined to differentiate between eastern and western gardens. In the meantime, Texas gardeners should continue to rely on local sources of information when choosing plants for their gardens.

In creating a plant list for your garden, consider not only the climate of your region, but also the several different microclimates around your home. The north side of the house will be cooler and shadier than the sun-drenched south side. However, because the summer sun actually sets in the northwest, a portion of the north side may get a blast of late afternoon sun. Unless shaded by tree canopy, a fence or a tall building next door, a planting bed on the east side will get full sun until sometime after noon. Therefore, a plant that requires "partial shade" may or may not be a good candidate for an east-facing location.

On the other hand, the east side of your house may provide the perfect environment for such plants as roses and crepe myrtles. Because these plants are susceptible to powdery mildew, they perform best in spots where there is morning sun to dry-off any dew that might collect on the foliage at night. Whole books have been written about the cultural requirements of plants suitable for Texas gardens. I've only space here to remind people who are new to gardening or new to Texas that you must "do your homework" to determine a plant's "suitability" for your particular garden. The Hardiness Zone Maps shown on page 169 are but a starting point.

# Choosing New Trees

Well-placed trees can reduce the cost of heating in winter and provide cooling benefits in summer. You'll want deciduous shade trees on the south and west sides of the house to mitigate summer sun. You may need large evergreen trees or shrubs to serve as windbreaks in winter. A young $100 tree can be expected to mature into a plant with an appraised value of between $1,000 to $10,000. Well-placed trees can reduce the cost of air conditioning by up to 50-percent and lower temperatures by as much as nine degrees. A single large tree releases about 13 pounds of oxygen and removes 26 pounds of carbon dioxide each year. It can mask noise levels with the soothing sound of rustling leaves.

☛**Money-saving tip: Shade trees will significantly appreciate the value of your property.**

Before buying a tree, however, consider its ultimate size and mature form in relation to the size of your house and garden. Does it need lots of open space? How quickly will it grow? Will its roots allow other plants to grow beneath its canopy? Is the wood strong enough to withstand wind?

Many of our most dependable ornamental trees are simply too big for today's urban lots. Small trees such as crepe myrtles, yaupons and flowering fruit trees will be better choices than the oaks or pecans, which need ample growing room. The trees you select to surround your patios or line your walks and driveway should be especially attractive and tidy. What is its branching pattern? Does it flower? Will its form, bark or berries be interesting in winter? Will it drop large seeds or fruit on people, pavement or cars?

Let me tell you about a Deodar cedar purchased about 50 years ago by young couple who thought it would be nice to have a "living Christmas tree." Assured by a store clerk that it would never grow taller than 12 feet, they planted the tree in their small front lawn, unaware that the species' normal mature height is 80 feet, with a 40-foot spread. Its sweeping branches ultimately smothered all the grass and posed a threat to power lines and passing cars. The owners have had the tree topped three times (it's hideously ugly), but the price for removing it is beyond their retirement income.

The moral to the story is that trees are too crucial to the landscape to be chosen indiscriminately. Don't be tempted to plant an inappropriate "gift" tree or to order some fast-growing, weak-wooded species out of the newspaper's Sunday supplement. Your trees will probably outlive you. Seek advice from your extension agent or a trusted nurseryman on the best species for your area.

## Selecting the Shrubs

The garden's shrubbery should be your next priority. Start by re-considering the "foundation plantings." Like most homes built in the '50s, the house I bought in Austin had a row of Burford hollies lined up like soldiers across the front. The planting scheme was boring, and the heavy shrubbery made the low ranch-style structure look squat. Left alone, these plants would have covered the windows, but the previous homeowner had pruned them into tight little boxes in a vain attempt to keep them under control. I dispensed with all of them, and the pair of ubiquitous junipers at the corners of house, too!

Perhaps some of your foundation plants can be salvaged by renewal pruning. (See pages 157-159 for ideas and instructions.) Remove those that aren't worth saving and plant some colorful annuals until you've had time to make a new plan. Garden centers now offer a host of dwarf varieties that will never cover your windows or overgrow the beds. Consider re-drawing the line of the planting beds to make them

deeper or more interesting in shape. In addition to shrubbery, consider richly-textured ground covers and small trees to set off the lines of the house. Start afresh and let the plants retain their soft, natural forms as they mature.

Evergreen shrubs provide the garden's year-around good looks. Such plants as hollies, privets, nandinas and other evergreens appropriate for your growing zone should represent the majority of your selections for privacy screens, accent plants and foundation plantings. However, flowering deciduous shrubs such as roses, spiraea, hydrangeas and flowering quince (a.k.a. japonica) contribute much-needed seasonal color. I prefer to plant deciduous shrubs against a backdrop of evergreens so that they do not create any conspicuous holes in the landscape in winter. Because many of the wonderful old deciduous shrubs tend to become "leggy," I either tuck ground covers at their base or choose the new, more compact varieties of barberry, mock orange, pomegranate and a host of other colorful shrubs.

Avoid "one of everything." Too much variety results in a fidgety-looking landscape. A garden should be like a symphony, with recurring themes. Pick a few of your favorite plants, and mass shrubs of the same variety in groups of three, five or seven for maximum impact. Always buy an uneven number of the same species unless you are using a matching pair to flank a doorway or mark the entrance to some part of the landscape. (Don't ask me why planting in uneven numbers is more visually pleasing, just trust me on this one. It works!)

Be sure to select flowering shrubs that will complement the color of your house. If a client has an orange-tone brick house, I would never plant magenta azaleas anywhere on the property. Likewise, pink brick and red flowers do not make a happy combination. I've often suggested painting a house some shade of white, gray or taupe simply because the client's colorful landscape plantings would play best against a neutral background.

In landscape design, you are painting a picture in three dimensions. Consider the mature form of each plant as well as ultimate size. As I've continuously told my clients, you'll rarely have to prune if you choose plants that fit the spots for which they are intended. Never plant tall shrubs or trees under eaves or power lines, and make sure that broad-branched plants are spaced at proper distances from one another.

When mature, the shrubs should slightly overlap without over-crowding their neighbors. Correct spacing is one of the most difficult aspects of planting design. You'll need to base your decision on each plant's ultimate, unpruned width. For example, if I'm massing a variety of holly that normally spreads to five-feet wide, I space the plants a little less than five feet apart (center-to-center). There are a number of books that specify the height and width of common landscape shrubs. Often the plant tag will provide this information.

☛**Money-saving tip: Don't overplant a new garden.**

Fill-in with annuals for the first few years if a bed full of young plants looks unacceptably skimpy. Eventually the plants will grow together, and the shrub mass will shade out most weeds. Your ultimate goal should be to let the plants do the garden work. Create a canopy if there is none. Mass shade-loving plants beneath the trees and encourage a community of self-sustaining plants. And, if you let the autumn leaves lie where they drop, you'll need little fertilizer and minimal water. Mother Nature has been gardening that way for years!

☛**Money-saving tip: Buy your trees and shrubs from trained nursery personnel.**

Gardeners have developed sophisticated tastes from travel and exposure to books and magazines that picture well-designed gardens from all over the world. Fortunately, garden centers have kept pace by offering a wider variety of plants and new hybrids of old, familiar shrubs and trees. While there is now a wealth of plants from which to choose, the plants you'll find in the marketplace are not all equally easy to grow.

Before you choose the exact species that will go in a specific place, you should be aware that certain varieties are more resistant to pests and disease than others. Unfortunately, some of the state's most beloved plants (azaleas, dogwoods and roses) are the very ones most often brought into the Master Gardener's clinics with problems! Many plants you'll see featured in magazines are not adapted to the western half of Texas at all.

This leads to the next piece of advice... Be prepared to ask intelligent questions about the plants you are considering for your landscape. If the salesperson doesn't seem knowledgeable, ask to speak to the owner or manager. Unlike minimum-wage clerks in the typical discount store, the personnel at reputable garden centers are professional nurserymen (and women). These people will know all about local soil and climate conditions. They'll be qualified to answer your questions, and willing to spend time helping you find the best plants for your specific site. They'll direct you to the varieties that are most resistant to pest and disease problems. They can explain the proper cultural practices that will mean the difference between poor and good performance once the plant is in the ground.

You'll find trees and shrubs offered in garden centers come in three different forms: bare-root (which must be planted while dormant), balled-and-burlapped and container-grown plants. B&B stock is field-grown, dug during the cool months and normally planted soon thereafter. The advantage to container-grown material is that it can be planted at any time. A container-grown plant is generally more expensive, however, and if the plant has been in the container too long, it may be root-bound. I've had equal success with plants sold in all three forms.

☛**Money-saving tip: Learn how to select a healthy plant.**

First, look for supple branches and plump buds that would indicate a young, vigorous tree. Plants should show evidence of recent increase in size. Don't be afraid to pull a plant out into the aisle to inspect it. If a container-grown tree has a stake in it, ask the salesperson to untie it. If the tree bends, the trunk is too weak. Look for healthy leaves and a full branching pattern. A gnarled, misshapen tree that nobody else wants might work as a picturesque focal point, but generally you will want a plant with a consistent shape and evenly spaced branches.

Poor root development and unbalanced or dried-out roots are the most difficult defects to detect when you walk through a nursery, yet the roots are key to the plant's survival. Reject plants that have roots growing out of the container or roots that encircle the trunk. Don't be afraid to ask the salesperson to remove a shrub or tree from its container so that you can inspect for encircling roots. (Once you get the plant home, if you find that it has tightly wound roots, take a spray nozzle, wash the roots and spread them out by hand. Otherwise, they'll continue to grow in circles and the plant will never develop properly.)

☛**Money-saving tip: Shop around. If you're thinking big, ask for a discount or try buying wholesale.**

When you're planting a new landscape or doing major renovation, you may be able to get a discount from your local garden center or deal directly with a wholesale grower. It never hurts to ask. Do what the professionals do: mail or *FAX* a plant list to several suppliers to check on availability and prices. If a grower is adamantly "to the trade only," call a local landscape contractor. Lots of contractors are willing to purchase the plants and deliver them to you for a small up-charge.

☛**Money-saving tip: "Bargain plants" are rarely a bargain.**

# Protecting Your Investment

The major cause of plant loss is due to improper planting. Remove tags, wires and everything else that is not biodegradable. Cut the string from around burlap. Remove the top six-inches of the fabric after the plant is in the hole. If it becomes obvious that the balled and burlapped plant has been grown in heavy clay soil, remove the burlap completely and wash away some of the soil with a spray nozzle as you're backfilling the hole. I've been called to clients' homes to inspect a dead tree as long as two years after it was planted. In digging it up, we discovered that the roots were still growing in the shape of the container or that the burlap was intact, with no roots penetrating the surrounding soil.

Inquire about the mature size of each plant, and be sure that you have selected a good spot for those that will eventually become large. Avoid planting trees under power lines or the eaves of your house. Plant trees and shrubs at a sufficient distance from walls, fences and garden structures to allow for the plant's natural spread.

☛**Money-saving tip: Learn proper planting techniques.**

Avoid planting too deep. There's an old maxim, "Never plant a $50 tree in a $5 hole." The concept is correct, but don't take it too far. Carefully measure the depth and width of the soil in the container. The planting hole should be an inch less deep than the depth of the root ball, but at least twice its width. The shallow depth is critical because the plant will die from lack of oxygen if it is planted too deeply. The width is important because all of the feeding roots are in the top six inches. They'll want plenty of room to spread quickly.

Mix garden soil and composted organic matter (half and half) and fill in around the sides of the plant, gently tamping in the back-fill and moistening the soil as you go. Water thoroughly. If the soil settles, add more back-fill around the edges. Do not pile soil on top of the root ball. Apply a two-inch layer of mulch over the top, but don't place mulch up against the trunk of the plant. Be sure that the dark ring or stain (usually found just above the root ball) remains above the finished ground surface. Never use synthesized nitrogen fertilizer on a newly planted tree or shrub. It may burn the roots.

Stake young trees if they're in a location that is subject to high wind or if the root ball is small in proportion to the height and branching pattern. Three evenly placed stakes work best. Use a soft strapping material or guy wires covered with a piece of

rubber hose to avoid damaging the trunk. Remove the stakes after the first year. Keep the soil moist, but not waterlogged. Build a low mound around the outer rim of the root ball to act as a water-retaining basin. Be sure to remove the ring of soil before spring rains begin.

☛**Money-saving tip: Learn proper maintenance techniques.**

Keep a watchful eye for pests, disease and dieback. Reduction in new shoots and a scarcity of new leaves are reliable clues that the plant needs attention. Mulch trees and shrubs to cut down on climatic stress. (The mulch will also help prevent damage from a lawn mower or string weeder.) Master proper pruning techniques, which we've discussed at length in Chapter Four.

# Adding Seasonal Color

Have you ever noticed that garden centers and home improvement stores place the blooming plants at the front of the store? Color is, for most people, the focus of the garden. Even a novice gardener will want to supplement the landscape's basic greenery with occasional bursts of color. "Bedding plants" provide a simple solution. Widely available in six-packs and flats, annuals are easy to grow and relatively low in cost. They provide a long season of color because they were designed by nature to germinate, sprout leaves, flower, set seed and die within a single growing season. Annuals bloom profusely because they survive only by setting seed in abundance. (Some of the plants we grow as annuals are actually tender perennials and bulbs that cannot survive our winter freezes or summer heat.)

According to the Professional Plant Growers Association, the most popular annuals remain the tried and true impatiens, geraniums, petunias, begonias, pansies, lobelia, marigolds and sweet alyssum. In Texas the list would also have to include such heat-tolerant standards as zinnias, periwinkles, portulaca and verbena. Annuals with colorful foliage — coleus, copper plants, caladiums — are also popular here. For gardeners willing to alternate between "warm-season" annuals and "cool season" annuals, bedding plants provide year-round color. In the past several years Texas gardeners have become increasingly willing to invest in pansies, calendulas, Iceland poppies, snapdragons and flowering kale to enliven the winter landscape.

When designing with flowers, plan your color scheme carefully. Just because impatiens come in 20 colors does not mean you should plant one of every color. Pick a harmonizing scheme of no more than five colors that coordinate with your home's exterior and interior, and repeat that scheme throughout the landscape. To achieve the most impact for your money, avoid "mixed" flats. Plant large drifts of a single color of each species you choose. For example, a flat of lemon-yellow French marigolds, a flat of deep-purple salvia and a half-flat each of white vinca and coral geraniums could be combined to make a spectacular show along an entrance walk or driveway.

To brighten shady areas or play against a dark wall or hedge, let the light colors predominate. To play against a white house or fence, go for maximum impact, but remember to separate and soften bright red and gold with cool blue hues and splashes of gray foliage. Consider unusual color combinations such as lime green with a deep burgundy or a bright salmon with pale blue. Any color scheme is enhanced by the liberal addition of white, which can be used to tie the garden together and can be seen at night.

Annuals have lots of landscape uses beyond the most obvious. Just as nurseries use brilliant color to lure customers, real estate agents routinely ask sellers to plant annuals in front of their houses to make the properties more welcoming. Annuals are wonderful, of course, in containers and hanging baskets. They also make excellent "fillers" in new planting beds and at the base of mature shrubs, where they add a touch of color in mid-summer when few plants are at their peak.

The best thing about annuals is that they can be grown easily and inexpensively from seed. Beginner's mistakes include failing to thin the plants, planting tall varieties in front of the shorter ones, and sowing every tint in the botanist's palette. The second best thing about annuals is that next year you can make a fresh start! And, if you haven't the time or patience to plant from seed, nurseries will have acres of bedding plants awaiting your arrival next spring. Only the most indifferent gardener could resist their appeal.

# Finding a Great Garden Center

When you're establishing a new garden, you'll probably want to start at a nearby garden center. Take a note pad. Jot down the names of the plants you like best. Browse the book section. Peruse the tools. Make friends with the personnel. Establishing a relationship with a garden center is like finding the right medical care for your family. During my adult life, I've lived in four Texas cities and worked as a landscape architect for clients in several others. I know from personal experience how important it is to find a local nurseryman I can trust.

This brings up the subject of discount chains. Patricia and I found a Japanese maple for sale in a large home-improvement chain in Austin. Knowing that its chance for survival in Austin's alkaline soil was akin to "a snowball in hell," I asked to speak to the manager. "Well, you're right," she said when I observed that this species is inappropriate for Austin gardens, "but we have to take what's sent to us by the central purchasing office in [another state]."

The up-side to such mass-market retailers as Lowes and Home Depot is that they have brought large garden centers to some of our smaller cities and new suburbs, where there was little in the way of garden resources. Because these companies buy in volume, the prices there are low, and much of the merchandise is of good quality. Do I frequent discount stores for petunias and packages of bone meal? Of course I do. I've also "snapped-up" some bargains on handsome clay pots, healthy houseplants and lush holiday greenery at these stores.

Do I shop at these places regularly? No way. I not only want a garden center that supplies top-quality plants, but also I want to trade with a firm that employs a knowledgeable staff, a place where I feel comfortable taking a diseased leaf for diagnosis or expect to find guidance on organic fertilizers. Discount chains are certainly not the places that come to mind when I'm about to replace a tree.

I'm troubled by the fact that the big chains have put a lot of "little guys" out of business. When a fine old neighborhood nursery closes, we lose more than just convenience. We lose the years of practical gardening experience the owners and staff had to share. So, the money-saving tip with which I began this chapter (take your time), should be reiterated here. Shop around. It shouldn't take you too long to figure out where the plants are of the highest quality and the personnel most knowledgeable. This chapter lists lots of good garden centers by region. Take a look at several, and find one that's right for you.

# Regional Resources for Your Garden's Green Foundation:
## Cross Timbers & Grand Prairie
### Arlington/ Grand Prairie

## Calloway's Nursery, Inc.

900 Lincoln Square #11
Arlington, Texas 76011
☎ 817/861-1195
FAX 817/275-4803

4940 South Cooper Street
Arlington, Texas 76017
☎ 817/465-2838
FAX 817/465-7791

**Hours** Daily 9-6; generally open until 8 during the holiday season
**Accessible** Yes

Calloway's is synonymous with color — it's where these nurseries really shine — in a profusion of flowering trees and shrubs, herbs, annuals and perennials. With 15 retail stores in the Metroplex, the company uses its great buying power to contract with specialty growers, who may, for example, supply Calloway's with 200,000 pansies in a single weekend! It's the only Texas nursery that gets all of the exclusive new introductions from Blooms of Bressingham. (Varieties best suited for North Central Texas are selected from the collection of this famous English supplier, and then they are grown in Texas specially for Calloway's.) What it does not contract, the company grows on its own. "We guarantee everything, so it must be the finest we can get," explains James Estill, the company's president.

Calloway's produces it's own fertilizers, soil amendments and mulches. Landscaper's Mix (composed of Canadian sphagnum peat moss, perlite and composted bark) is one of the company's most popular products. It also sells fine English garden tools and solid American tools.

The staff is exceptionally well trained. There are 49 Master Certified Nursery Professionals among the personnel you'll meet when you visit one of Calloway's garden centers. "We strongly believe in continuing education, and regularly send our employees to classes and seminars sponsored by the Texas Association of Nurserymen. Our basic philosophy is that we want gardeners to succeed. We do everything we can to ensure the highest quality on our part." (See pages 180, 181 and 185 for other locations.) Ask to be on the mailing list to receive the newsletter.

## Mary Allen's Garden

4808 South Cooper
Arlington, Texas 76017
☎ 817/557-8300
FAX 817/557-8303
**Hours** Thurs-Mon 9-6
**Accessible** Yes

Like Calloways, Mary Allen's is a garden center with multiple locations in the DFW Metroplex. (Arlington has an alphabetical advantage in the area.) Do not let the idea of "chain" deter you in the case of either of these organizations, for both are very attuned to the gardeners they serve. Named for the mother of one of the owners, Mary Allen's is new on the scene, but its staff is comprised of people with strong roots in the "green industry." Some of its stores occupy sites that were formerly Wolfe's Nurseries, and some of Wolfe's staff members are still on-board. However,

While remaining a full-line nursery, there's new emphasis on garden accessories. You'll hear fountains splashing throughout the stores and find an array of containers, garden antiques, teak benches, tables and chairs, as well as several exclusive lines of giftware. Seasonal color is abundant, and within the landscape materials departments, there's new emphasis on native plants and organic supplies. Each store employs Texas Certified Nursery Professionals to guide your gardening efforts.

The late Mary Allen Schultz-Haynes was an enthusiastic gardener, active in garden clubs, and ultimately a national flower show judge. A plaque at each store commemorates this "wonderful and creative lady" and notes that a portion of the profits will be donated in her name for cancer research. Watch for new stores opening in the region, and see pages 182 and 183 for other locations.

## Redenta's Garden

*5111 West Arkansas Lane*
*Arlington, Texas 76016*
☎ *817/451-2149*
**FAX** *817/451-2199*
**Hours** *Mon-Sat 9-6, Sun 10-5 (spring and summer); Mon-Sat 10-5, Sun 11-5 (winter)*
**Accessible** *Yes*

This "100% organic nursery" specializes in perennials, herbs, antique roses and native trees and shrubs. The organic-only policy is in effect throughout Redenta's nurseries in Colleyville and Dallas, as well. These charming, relatively small garden centers carry a fine assortment of Old World garden accessories and planters and a wide selection of gardening books. A special service offered by the company is organic lawn maintenance, a five-times-per-year program that utilizes only non-toxic fertilizers and insect controls. The company's several design consultants specialize in a European approach to landscape design and installation. Ruth Kinler and her staff say, "Gardening should be a personal experience, improving the quality of life!" They are dedicated to spreading the gospel! Customers are encouraged to participate in the numerous free classes and special events that feature recognized experts on diverse gardening topics. The company also publishes an informative newsletter four times a year. See pages 183 and 188 for additional store locations.

## Whipple's Nursery

*625 West Pioneer Parkway (Spur 303)*
*Arlington, Texas 76010*
☎ *817/274-3005*
**Hours** *Mon-Sat 9-6, Sun 10-6; open late in December*
**Accessible** *Yes*

"By maintaining a wide selection of annuals, herbs, perennials and ferns as well as the most sought-after bedding plants," Rebecca and Robert Whipple told us, "we cater to the serious gardener as well as the general public. We try to stock pot sizes that do the plant justice and are economical for the customer." At Whipple's you will also find an extensive selection in the areas of shade and ornamental trees, small and large landscape shrubs and tropicals. The nursery carries tropical hanging baskets, ferns, blooming plants for special holidays and seeds (packaged and bulk). In addition to tools and supplies, you'll find garden furniture, books, gifts and gardening tools and seeds for children. Sales are held most every weekend throughout the year.

## *Cleburne*

---

### Tumbleweed Garden Center

*1521 West Kilpatrick*
*Cleburne, Texas 76031*
☎ *817/641-0817*
**FAX** *817/641-9170*
**Hours** *Tues-Sun 9-6*
**Accessible** *Partially*

A full-service nursery since 1912, Tumbleweed carries a wide variety of plant materials, both outdoors and in its two giant greenhouses. Organic gardening is promoted, and native plants are featured among its offerings. "If we don't have it, we'll try to get it," says owner John Hardee. The company holds seminars and provides landscape estimates and irrigation installation. You'll find a good selection of garden supplies, tools, soil and stone, plus nice gifts and books here.

## *Denton/ Lewisville*

---

### Calloway's Nursery, Inc.

*423 East Round Grove Road (FM 3040)*
*Lewisville, Texas 75067*
☎ *972/315-3133*
**FAX** *972/315-6528*

See complete listing on page 178.

---

### Four Seasons Nursery

*3333 East University*
*Denton, Texas 76208*
☎ *940/566-2172*
**Hours** *Mon-Sat 9-5, Sun 10-5*
**Accessible** *Yes*

This relatively new garden center specializes in natives and plants that are well-adapted to North Texas. All plant material is container-grown, and the vast majority is grown in Texas. "The most diverse soil types in the state of Texas occur within 60 miles of our nursery, so it's important to choose the right plants. We are competitive, but our main emphasis is on quality," say owners Michael Nack and Robert Strawn. Four Season's one-acre-site is brimming with trees (shade and fruit), shrubs, ground covers, seasonal color and herbs. You'll also find tropical houseplants, pest control supplies, soils and amendments, as well as books, wind chimes and birdhouses. Sales are advertised in local newspapers. Staff members welcome groups, speak to garden clubs, and are always accessible for friendly, professional advice.

## *Fort Worth Metropolitan Area*

---

### A&M Greenhouse & Nursery, Inc.

*12809 Gantt Road South*
*Azle, Texas 76020*
☎ *817/444-3848*
**Hours** *Mon-Sat 9-6, Sun 1-6; closed Sundays in winter.*
**Accessible** *Partially*

"What makes us different and attracts our customers is our botanic garden. Our customers can drive in or come by boat!" say Allen and Melody Shelton.

"The landscape serves as our best salesman!" A&M Greenhouse & Nursery is a full-service retail nursery, offering landscape design and installation, irrigation design, installation and repair. The couple host an annual sale in June and offer seminars and tours to garden clubs.

*Directions: From 199, go north on FM 730. Turn right and follow the signs on Peden Road.*

## Archie's Gardenland

*6700 Camp Bowie Boulevard*
*Fort Worth, Texas 76116*
☎ *817/737-6614*
**FAX** *817/737-6640*
**Hours** *Mon-Sat 8:30-6, Sun 10-4 (spring); Mon-Sat 8:30-5:30 (other seasons)*
**Accessible** *Yes*

Archie's is a friendly, family owned and operated garden center that offers landscape design as well. Says owner Rick Archie, "We pride ourselves on good employees, good service and unusual plants. We also stress organic gardening." On our visit, we were pleased to see such a large assortment of trees, shrubs, seasonal color and specialty plants. In addition, you will find materials for garden structures, soil and soil amendments, drip irrigation equipment, pest management supplies, books, tools and gift items. Lectures are held on trees, bonsai, patio gardening and roses, among other topics. These lectures are advertised ahead of time in the newspaper. We were surprised to realize that Archie's, which has an imitate atmosphere, is actually situated on two city blocks.

*Directions: The entrance is located a half-block north of Camp Bowie Blvd.*

## Calloway's Nursery Inc

*2601 South Hulen Street*
*Fort Worth, Texas 76109*
☎ *817/923-0459*
**FAX** *817/923-0374*

*3525 Highway 121 South*
*Grapevine, Texas 76051*
☎ *817/421-6667*
**FAX** *817/421-4285*

See complete listing on page 178.

## Glade Road Garden Center

*1221 West Glade Road*
*Euless, Texas 76039*
☎ *817/283-2781*
**FAX** *817/571-2070*
**Hours** *Mon-Sat 8-6, Sun 9-6*
**Accessible** *Yes*

Glade Road Garden Center is a well maintained, complete garden center with a very large selection of plant materials from natives to water plants. We were really impressed with the bonsai and the tropicals, including what had to be the "largest fiddle leaf fig in captivity!" The nursery publishes an informative newsletter, and it delivers to customers.

*Directions: 200 feet west of Highway 121 in Euless.*

## Hilscher Florist & Garden Center

*5015 East Lancaster*
*Fort Worth, Texas 76103*
☎ *817/536-8369*
**FAX** *817/536-7780*
**Hours** *Mon-Sat 9-5:30, Sun 11-5*
**Accessible** *Yes*

Founded in 1926 in one of the city's old, established neighborhoods, Hilscher's has approximately two and a half acres of shrubs, trees and tropical plants along with seasonal blooming plants. You will also find tools, books and gifts. Steve Hilscher explains, "We are a complete landscape and garden center, from design to installation. All installation is by our own crews, including retaining walls, concrete patios and walks, etc. City bonded, we offer a complete lawn sprinkler system design and installation." Occasionally, the nursery marks-down its garden merchandise. It offers a full-service FTD florist department, with daily delivery in the Metroplex.

## Mary Allen's Garden

*6080 Hulen Road*
*Fort Worth, Texas 76132*
☎ *817/361-7890*
**FAX** *817/361-7884*

See complete listing on page 178.

## McClendon Nursery, Inc.

*2505 Hall Johnson Road*
*Colleyville, Texas 76034*
☎ *817/283-5681*
**FAX** *283-7966*
**Hours** *Mon-Sat 8-5:30, open Sun 12-5 (Feb-May)*
**Accessible** *Yes*

McClendon's has been in the same location since 1962 and is especially well known for its selection of large B&B trees — live oak, red oak, burr oak, bald cypress, slash pine, Japanese black pine, Bradford pear, cherry laurel and crepe myrtles. Says owner, Ronnie McClendon, "If you can't find good quality plants at a good, reasonable price, check with us. If we don't have them, we will try to get them, *if* they are well suited for our area." This complete garden center also carries a wide variety of shrubs, perennials, annuals and hanging baskets, plus a few tropicals. You'll find pots, mulches and garden supplies here as well.

## Redenta's Garden

*6230 Colleyville Boulevard*
*Colleyville, Texas 76034*
☎ *817/488-3525*
**FAX** *817/488-7357*
**Hours** *Mon-Sat 9-6, Sun 10-5 (spring and summer); Mon-Sat 10-5, Sun 12-4 (winter)*
**Accessible** *No*

Redenta's Garden a "100% organic nursery." See complete listing on page 179. Directions Located on the Grapevine Highway at Hall-Johnson Road.

## Weston Gardens In Bloom, Inc.

*8101 Anglin Drive*
*Fort Worth, Texas 76140*
☎ *817/572-0549*
**FAX** *817/572-1628*
**Hours** *Mon-Fri 8-6, Sat 9-5; open Sundays 12-5 (March-June)*
**Accessible** *Partially*

Once upon an early morn (*Pat's best time of day. Not.*) we arrived at Weston Gardens. The excitement of finding such a special place quickly awakened her. We were both soon lulled into a sense of serenity… Weston is no slick nursery; but a gentle, earthy one. Sue and Randy Weston are "one with the ground." The extensive demonstration display gardens that surround their home are like a public botanical garden where all the plants are identified and everything is picture-perfect. There are lily ponds, water falls, fountains and English-style perennial and mixed border gardens. The gardens designed to attract butterflies and hummingbirds are composed of native and highly acclimated plants, and they attest the owners' hands-on approach. "We try new things, but we don't sell them until they are proven. We move things around to determine the right location for them," says Randy. The firm's design services are based on considerable knowledge of cottage-style and mixed border gardens, as well as expertise in the area of water gardening. The company holds seminars as well as a Spring Open House. This is a treat not to be missed!

*Directions: From IH-20, exit at Anglin Drive and go approximately two miles south.*

## Stephenville

## In The Garden

*272 South Belknap*
*Stephenville, Texas 76401*
☎ *254/965-3710*
**Hours** *Mon-Fri 8-5, Sat 8-1*
**Accessible** *Yes*

In The Garden is housed in an old-fashioned seed store in an antique building. In business for 59 years, this nursery carries natives, grasses, annuals, perennials, vegetable starts, hanging baskets and tropicals, as well as seeds in small quantities or bulk. Although you can purchase seeds by mail, you'll find plenty of reasons to visit: materials for walks and patios, greenhouses, soils, pest management supplies and tools, not to mention garden books, furniture and gifts, bird houses and feeders and outdoor fountains! Co-owners Shirley Cox and Geibler Scott feel that the store offers something very special. "Located in the square near the courthouse, the store's fixtures, containers and bins are original to the business." Apart from this nostalgic atmosphere, In The Garden sponsors an heirloom and native plant fair at the local museum and an informative radio program.

## Weatherford

## Stuart Nursery

*2317 Fort Worth Highway*
*Weatherford, Texas 76087*
☎ *817/596-0003*
**FAX** *817/598-0628*
**Hours** *Tues-Sat 8-5, Sun 1-5*
**Accessible** *Yes*

*(Listing continued on next page)*

According to the owners, "We keep basics in stock, but we are always looking for new and different plant material and merchandise." Although the company carries all the familiar plants for North Central Texas, Stuart's specializes in native trees, shrubs and perennials. It offers landscape design and installation and also builds decks. As Paul Simpson and Tommy Cain describe their business, "We try to offer personal and cheerful service to all of our customers!"

# Trinity Blacklands
## Corsicana

## Barlow's Nursery

*700 West 2nd Avenue*
*Corsicana, Texas 75110*
☎ *903/872-0556*
**Hours** *Mon-Sat 8-6 (Feb 20th-Nov 21st); Mon-Sat 8-9 or 10 (Nov 22nd-Dec 20th); Mon-Sat 8-5 (Dec 20th-Feb 19th); closed Thanksgiving, Christmas and New Years Day*
**Accessible** *Partially*

Richard Barlow proudly explains, "We have been a family owned and operated business since 1945. We offer a professional quality and service to our customers and guests." The staff includes two people with horticultural degrees from Texas A&M and two Texas Master Certified Nursery Professionals. Barlow's has summer sales (or as advertised in the local paper). The company is starting an Organic Gardener's Club. Look for the sign: "The Professional Garden Center."

## Dallas Metropolitan Area

## Blooming Colors Nursery & Landscape

*1701 East Beltline Road*
*Coppell, Texas 75019*
☎ *972/393-8660*
**FAX** *972/304-0056*
**Hours** *Mon-Fri 9-7, Sat 9-6, Sun 12:30-6 (March-Oct); Mon-Sat 9-5, Sun 12:30-5 (Nov-Feb)*
**Accessible** *Yes*

We not only found Blooming Colors to be a very neat and attractive nursery, but also much bigger than it looks at first glance. Further expansion is planned for the fall of 1998. Says Barry Johnson, "Our firm is the only true full-service nursery in the area. We carry a complete line of gardening plants and large trees. We specialize in color, and our selection is excellent. Our landscape service gets 90% of its work from customer references! The best value we offer our customers is expert advice and knowledge." You will find seven Certified Nursery Professionals to deliver quality advice. "Our plants sell themselves!" The company has daily sales specials, a big fall clearance sale and offers seminars.

## Calloway's Nursery Inc.

*7410 North Greenville Avenue*
*Dallas, Texas 75231*
☎ *214/363-0525*
**FAX** *214/363-8176*

*8152 Spring Valley Road*
*Dallas, Texas 75240*
☎ *972/994-0134*
**FAX** *972/994-0655*

*14120 Marsh Lane*
*Dallas, Texas 75234*
☎ *972/484-0784*
**FAX** *972/247-6303*

*723 South Cockrell Hill Road*
*Duncanville, Texas 75137*
☎ *972/283-8021*
**FAX** *972/283-3983*

4033 West Airport Freeway
Irving, Texas 75062
☎ 972/258-1312
**FAX** 972/594-6108

4220 North Galloway Road
Mesquite, Texas 75150
☎ 972/686-0048
**FAX** 972/613-0645

1621 Custer Parkway
Plano, Texas 75075
☎ 972/596-5211
**FAX** 972/964-0347

1000 Preston Road
Plano, Texas 75093
☎ 972/964-3084
**FAX** 972/964-3773

2100 North Plano Road
Richardson, Texas 75082
☎ 972/644-0144
**FAX** 972/669-9146

See complete listing on page 178.

## Hawkins Nursery & Landscape Company Inc.

19110 Preston Road
Dallas, Texas 75252
☎ 972/596-5904
**FAX** 972/964-3790
**Hours** Mon-Sat 8-6, Sun 10-6
**Accessible** Partially

As one Dallasite exclaimed, "Everybody in Dallas knows Hawkins!" And well they should. Started by O. T. Hawkins 47 years ago, Hawkins Nursery & Landscape has been in the same location for most of that time. Mr. Hawkins laughingly told us, "We've done some pretty prominent, complicated jobs in our time. We've even planted by helicopter and two-way radio." With the exception of water plants and interior tropicals, you will find everything for the garden here. Hawkins carries some of the largest trees in the Metroplex, with 20,000 ready to plant at all times. In addition, the nursery has "hard goods" for patios, walks and retaining walls, greenhouses, play equipment, soils, drip irrigation, tools, books and furniture. This is a good place to find such uncommon landscape materials as lava rock, rounded pebbles and cypress mulch. Weekly sales ads can be found in the newspaper, as well as general advertising in Neil Sperry's publications. Mr. Hawkins has been a frequent guest on "Inside Dallas" and is a popular speaker at local garden clubs. This is a nursery that, although quite modern, stills embraces the good memories of the past.

## Kings Creek Gardens

813 Straus Road
Cedar Hill, Texas 75104
☎ 972/291-7650
**FAX** 214/293-0920
**Hours** Mon-Wed 8-5, Thurs-Sat 8-6, Sun 12-5
**Accessible** Yes, but paths are gravel in most areas

The word "peaceful" comes to mind first when describing this nursery. Located only 15 minutes south of downtown Dallas, Kings Creek is a world apart. Its weathered building is surrounded by demonstration beds brimming with unusual plant materials. Says Vicki Thaxton, "Our staff consists of real gardeners! We're constantly testing and propagating for customers." The specialties here are natives, herbs, unusual perennials, English and antique roses and aquatic plants. There's also a nice selection of large trees. In this comfortable, naturalistic atmosphere you can

*(Listing continued on next page)*

browse through books or spend time perusing the accessories and twig furniture. Vicki adds, "We want you to visit us for the experience alone — hopefully finding something to add to your own garden. Throughout the year, mailings are sent to customers, inviting them to attend various programs and lectures for inspiration."

*Directions: From Dallas, take IH-35 south to Highway 67 south and exit at FM 1382. Turn right and cross the bridge. After crossing the bridge, stay in the left lane and turn left on Straus. Look for the sign on the right.*

## Mary Allen's Garden

*6615 East Northwest Highway*
*Dallas, Texas 75321*
☎ *214/378-5985*
**FAX** *214/378-5240*

*2100 Alamo Road*
*Richardson, Texas 75080*
☎ *972/671-5752*
**FAX** *972/671-2874*

*7727 South Westmoreland Road*
*Dallas, Texas 75327*
☎ *972/572-8800*
**FAX** *972/572-8806*

*740 Lexington Drive*
*Plano, Texas 75075*
☎ *972/633-0770*
**FAX** *972/633-5465*

See complete listing on page 178.

## Nicholson-Hardie Garden Center

*5725 West Lovers Lane*
*Dallas, Texas 75209*
☎ *214/357-4348*
**FAX** *214/357-7407*

*5060 West Lovers Lane*
*Dallas, Texas 75209*
☎ *214/357-4674*
**FAX** *214/357-4599*
**Hours** *Mon-Sat 9-6, Sun 12-5 (both locations)*
**Accessible** *Yes*

Nicholson-Hardie specializes in top quality merchandise, hard to find perennials and herbs, an extensive selection of indoor color, orchids and tropicals, unique containers, gifts and accessories and top quality (often imported) gardening implements. "Above all, we specialize in success for our customers. Our staff is extremely well-trained in Texas gardening and garden design. We are equipped to help our customers succeed in any gardening endeavor," comments manager John Allen. Nicholson-Hardie has been in business since 1899 and under present ownership since 1974. You will find seeds in bulk as well as packaged seed (wildflower seeds, too), a large assortment of chemical and natural pest controls, and bird feeders, houses and supplies. The company offers lots of seminars, including such topics as organics, cooking with herbs, container gardening and attracting birds. The branch store at 5060 West Lovers Lane specializes in modern and antique roses, small trees (Japanese maples, dogwood, etc.), bonsai, perennials, fountains and statuary. "Again our goal is to sell success," reports manager Bob Wilson. You can attend seminars on modern and antique roses and English gardens (Texas style) here.

## North Dallas Garden Center

*2830 North Josey Lane*
*Carrollton, Texas 75007*
☎ *972/245-8059*
*FAX 972/245-0917*
***Hours** Mon-Sat 8-6, Sun 10-6*
***Accessible** No*

When we visited North Dallas Garden Center, it was a blaze of color! There is plant material in abundance and possibly the largest selections of Jackson & Perkins roses in the Metroplex. According to Paul Rothermel, "We specialize in the hard-to-find and unusual." What impressed us was the extensive array of perennials (all grown on-site) and the water gardens complete with koi.

## North Haven Gardens Inc.

*7700 Northaven Road*
*Dallas, Texas 75230*
☎ *214/363-5316*
*FAX 214/987-1511*
*www.nhg.com*
***Hours** Mon-Sat 9-6, Sun 10-5:30 (April-Oct); Mon-Sat 9-5:30, Sun 10-5 (Nov-Mar)*
***Accessible** Yes*

A family business, North Haven has been serving gardeners from the same location since 1951. With possibly the largest variety of plants available in the Dallas area, it's indeed a "Dallas institution!" Says Joe Steele, "Our staff loves plants and enjoys helping our customers find success with their gardening projects. Many staff members are recognized experts in their fields; we have expertise in all aspects of gardening, including aquatics, begonias, ferns, herbs, Texas natives, orchids, organics, perennials, roses, tropicals and trees." You'll also find a dazzling selection of tools, books and garden gifts and accessories in this very comprehensive garden center.

The Web site includes weekly specials, a calendar of events, newsletter, a garden maintenance checklist and a wealth of good, general gardening information. North Haven offers everyday competitive prices and holds sales for most major holidays. There are free lectures on garden-related topics most weekends, plus "Greenhouse Open House" in February, "Spring Festival" in March, "Herb Festival" four times a year and "Christmas Open House" in November. Other services provided include a full-service florist, a weekly "Cut Flower Happy Hour," delivery and planting or turn-key landscape design and installation. Was it the beautiful color, the sound of trickling water or the friendly, helpful service that impressed us most? We suggest you form your own good impressions.

*Directions: Take North Central Expressway (Highway 75) north from downtown. Exit on Forest Lane to the southbound service road and go west on Northaven to the top of the hill.*

## Puckett's Nursery

*811 East Main Street*
*Allen, Texas 75002*
☎ *972/727-1145*
**FAX** *214/727-2833*
**Hours** *Daily 9-7; 9-5 in winter*
**Accessible** *Yes*

   "We give individual attention to individual needs," says Mark Puckett. What seems to most impress its customers is the extensive variety of plant materials available here. In recent years, the company has begun emphasizing natives and organics. There's also a large selection of books, tools and gift items. Puckett's has a landscape architect and five Texas Certified Nursery Professionals on staff. Sales are held on Memorial Day, 4th of July and Labor Day weekend.

*Directions: From Dallas, take IH-75 north to McDermott or Main Street and go east four miles. It's on the left, next to Braums.*

## Redenta's

*2001 Skillman Street*
*Dallas, Texas 75206*
☎ *214/823-9421*

   See complete listing on page 179.

## Rohde's Nursery & Nature Store

*1651 Wall Street*
*Garland, Texas 75041*
☎ *972/864-1934 or 1-800/864-4445*
**FAX** *972/864-0128*
***www.**beorganic.com*
**Hours** *Mon-Sat 7-30-6, Sun 10-5; closes at 5:30 in winter*
**Accessible** *Yes*
**Mail Order**
**Catalog** *On-line*

   The things that attract birds to a garden are among the elements that attract people to this earth-friendly garden center. Here, you'll find only organic soil amendments and natural pest controls and a palette of plants that's heavily weighted toward natives. Says Gregory Rohde, "We try to carry unusual plant material and offer prices lower than our competitors' on the products normally stocked everywhere. We manufacture our own organic fertilizers and other organic products, so we have an edge." In addition to trees, shrubs and flowers, you'll find garden books, gifts and accessories and products for your pets. This high-quality nursery has been certified as both a Wildlife Habitat and a Butterfly Habitat! Sales are held at the end of seasons, but you must make a donation to the Animal Adoption Center of Garland to qualify for the discounts. Rohde's offers lots in the way of garden advice, seminars and special events. Its on-line catalog contains a wealth of products and information, as well. (See page 150.)

*Directions: From LBJ Freeway, go north on Garland Road to Leon Road; turn right and go one block and turn left on Wall.*

## Southwest Landscape Nursery Company

*2220 Sandy Lake Road*
*Carrollton, Texas 75006*
☎ *972/245-4557*
**FAX** *972/242-5360*
**Hours** *Mon-Sat 8-5:30, open Sun 11-5 (Feb-June and Oct)*
**Accessible** *Yes*

The motto at Southwest Landscape Nursery is "Come to the Farm!" And what a farm it is with 25 acres of trees and shrubs and 13 greenhouses! The sales office is a big red barn, which you cannot miss. This is where you "take a number." As Steve Taber explains, "You may have to wait awhile during peak seasons, but when it's your turn, you get a golf cart and a Texas Certified Nursery Professional, and we are yours, without interruption, for as long as you want." This nursery was started in 1940 and bought by Curtis Taber in 1980. You will find a large selection of plant material, from trees to topiary and from seasonal color to water plants. There are tools, books and decorative structures, as well, but the real specialty is trees. In October and February, the nursery holds a "20% off" sale on trees. During these sales, free guarantee and planting are offered. This is a very large operation and well worth a visit!

## Van Valkenburgh & Vogel

*9923 Denton Drive*
*Dallas, Texas 75220*
☎ *214/351-0321*
**Hours** *Mon-Sat 8-5 or 6*
**Accessible** *Partial*

While it's not a "complete" garden center, Van Valkenburgh & Vogel carries excellent ornamental trees and shrubs, annuals, perennials and bulbs as well as soil, soil amendments and pest management supplies. The firm is best-known for its landscape design and maintenance. As Pat Gilmore says, "We do work the old way, mostly with our hands and old tools. We don't really like power trimmers, blowers or weedeaters, and we only use them if we have to." The company is staffed by very knowledgeable, long-time employees, and most of the new customers at this nursery are referrals. Occasional sales are held, and garden advice is always available.

## Walton's Lawn and Garden Center

*8642 Garland Road*
*Dallas, Texas 75218*
☎ *214/321-2387*
**FAX** *214/321-2405*
**Hours** *Mon-Sat 8:30-6, Sun 11-5*
**Accessible** *Yes*

Located across from the Dallas Arboretum, Walton's is a popular stop for people inspired to beautify their own gardens. It's just brimming with perennials, herbs and bedding plants. We were surprised to find such a wonderful selection of Japanese maples here, but the site *is* deliciously shady. Manager Donna Beeh assured us that these trees thrive in moist Blackland soil, so long as they have protection from afternoon sun. The tree canopy over this nursery ensures pleasant shopping for a full range of landscape plants. You'll also find a lovely gift gallery packed with garden tools, books, furniture and accessories. Sales at Walton's are year-round. Two Certified Nursery Professionals are on staff to provide guidance and answer questions, and the company offers landscape design and installation services.

*Denison/Sherman*

## Gardenland Nursery

*810 Frisco Road*
*Sherman, Texas 75090*
☎ *903/868-1938*
**Hours** *Mon-Sat 8:30-5:30 (Winter close at 5); Spring selling days (April-May) open 1-5*
**Accessible** *Yes*

According to Lynn Low, "We are a "Mom & Pop" year-round horticultural center that was established in 1984 and offers service plus competitive pricing." Lynn is a Texas Certified Professional Nurseryman, and Brenda Low is a professional floral designer. The company offers a large variety of plant material and a full line of organic suuplies, about which they "are gaining knowledge daily." Customers have come to appreciate the seasonal sales and ample garden advice.

## Twin Oaks Landscaping, Inc.

*2107 Highway 691*
*Denison, Texas 75020*
☎ *903/463-2205*
**Hours** *Mon-Sat 8:30-5:30; open Sun 1-5:30 (March-Sept)*
**Accessible** *Yes*

What Luella Graham told us about Twin Oaks was, "We try to handle the highest quality plant materials we can find. We have qualified, well informed sales personnel and feel that our operation is an asset to our community and a pleasant experience for all who shop here." The plant selection is large, and there are water gardening supplies, tools, books, furniture and gift items. Landscape design, irrigation and installation are also available from the experienced staff at Twin Oaks.

## Greenville Area

## Creekside Garden Shop

*2111 Highway 66*
*Caddo Mills, Texas 75135*
☎ *903/527-4731*
**Hours** *Wed-Sat 10-6, Sun 1-6*
**Accessible** *No*

Creekside Garden Shop carries a wide selection of plant material from trees and shrubs, seasonal color and natives to water plants, tropicals and cacti. This nursery also offers outdoor lighting, soil, pest management supplies, tools, garden books, furniture and gifts. Brenda Miles comments, "While we carry the usual, we also offer many unusual items. We are constantly on the lookout for something different for our customers. Shopping at Creekside is a nostalgic experience with a return to old-fashioned service and value." End-of-season clearances are held in late June and mid-November. Seminars and other events are scheduled throughout the year.

*Directions: From IH-30, go north on Highway 36 to Caddo Mills. Turn west on Highway 66.*

## Steve's Nursery

*4386 Highway 34 South*
*Greenville, Texas 75402*
☎ *903/883-2911*
**Hours** *Daily 8-6:30*
**Accessible** *Partially*

Since 1977, Steve's Nursery has provided customers with top quality trees, shrubs, perennials, annuals, vegetables and herbs, as well as seeds, fertilizers, soil amendments and mulches. Here you'll find knowledgeable people ready to offer sound garden advice. Two employees are Texas Certified Nursery Professionals, and two others are Master Certified. Steve Goode comments, "We grow many of the shrubs and roses we sell, which helps keep prices down and quality up. From nearby growers, we regularly receive quality bedding flowers, vegetables, herbs, perennials, flowering shrubs and container-grown trees." December through February the company sells bare-root fruit and pecan trees, which are handled "the old-fashioned way" in large bins of sawdust to keep the roots from drying out. "You choose your trees, and we will prune them and bag them for your trip home," says Steve. For the best-quality roses, the company pots up Jackson & Perkins roses in January for sale in late March, when the plants are established and beginning to bloom. The company also grows antique garden roses and varieties of crepe myrtle that are proven to be hardy and mildew resistant. It manufactures Quonset Greenhouse frames for the home gardener. Mothers Day and Fathers Day specials include hanging baskets and Jackson & Perkins roses.

*Directions: Five miles south of IH-30, across from the Cash Water Tower.*

## Paris Area

## Bratcher's Nursery & Landscaping

*FM 1502*
*Blossom, Texas 75416*
☎ *903/982-5918*
**Hours** *Mon-Sat 9-5:30*
**Accessible** *Yes*
**Mailing Address** *Rt.1, Box 233, Detroit, Texas 75436*

Family owned and operated for 20 years, Bratcher's is a complete garden center that offers friendly, professional service. Landscape design services are available, and the nursery's forte is its large selection of container-grown shade and fruit trees. Other plant materials include shrubs, herbs, seasonal color, seeds, vegetable starts and water plants. Arbors, trellises, statuary, fountains and ponds complement the plant list. Gift items include custom-made gift baskets, books and antiques. Says owner Wynell Bratcher, "Both my husband and I are Texas Certified Nursery Professionals, and our service and low prices make our company 'worth the drive.'"

## Terrell

## J&T Nursery

*5126 West Highway 80*
*Terrell, Texas 75160*
☎ *972/524-0806*
**Hours** *Mon-Sat 8:30-5, Sun 1-4*
**Accessible** *Partially*

*(Listing continued on next page)*

An engineer by training, John Doan emigrated from Viet Nam and found "the work I love" in the landscape business. His two-acre garden center is brimming with shrubs and trees (lots of Texas natives) and all the supplies to keep the garden healthy. Although he carries garden chemicals, he has a large section of organics that includes *Back to Earth™* soil amendments, compost tea, green sand and lava sand. There's a display water garden here, plus all the plants, fountains and supplies for building your own. You'll find over 25 varieties of perennials, plus lots of seasonal color, containers, hanging baskets and carefully tended bonsai. His company also offers landscape design and installation services.

# Piney Woods
## Longview

## Emerald Gardens

*5006 Judson Road*
*Longview, Texas 75605*
☎ *903/663-4757*
**FAX** *903/663-5178*
**Hours** *Mon-Sat 8-6:30, Sun 10-6:30 (spring and summer); Mon-Sat 8-5:30, Sun 10-5 (fall); Mon-Sat 8-5, Sun 10-5 (winter)*
**Accessible** *Yes*

Emerald Gardens is a very pleasant full-service nursery offering consulting, landscaping, garden retail sales and sod sales. Here you will find a good selections in native plant materials, grasses, ornamental trees, bedding plants, water plants, hanging baskets, bonsai, cacti and tropicals. Inside, the store carries garden books, gifts and accessories.

## Plantation Pottery

*3110 North Eastman Road*
*Longview, Texas 75605*
☎ *903/663-3387*
**FAX** *903/663-3078*
**Hours** *Mon-Sat 10-8, Sun 12-6*
**Accessible** *Yes*

Although Plantation Pottery carries everything from pottery to quilts, it is, indeed, a complete garden center with a 10,000-sq.-ft. greenhouse. In this well-maintained environment, you will find lush greenery and healthy bedding plants and ornamentals. Native plants, herbs and perennials are prominently featured. Plantation Pottery occupies three acres of landscaped grounds. Certified Nursery Professional Chris Higgins invites you to relax on nature trails that wind into lovely garden settings. "Fountains bubble, birds sing and our staff is friendly and helpful. We encourage everyone to experience our store."

## Smotherman's Scenery, Inc.

*1122 West Marshall*
*Longview, Texas 75606*
☎ *903/753-4290*
**FAX** *903/753-4473*
**Hours** *Daily 8-5 (winter); Mon-Sat 8-6, Sun 1-5 (other seasons)*
**Accessible** *Yes*

When we queried manager Jack Lewis about Smotherman's specialty, he good-naturedly replied, "We have some of everything and specialize in all of them! If we don't have the plants or the answers for you, we'll find them." Mike Smotherman has owned the nursery for 18 years and prides himself on the "quality of the plants and the personnel." You'll also find a florist and wide selections in the concrete statuary, willow picnic tables and lawn chairs, books, garden tools and gifts at this complete garden center. The company grows many of its plants on 15 acres near Kilgore. Sales are held five or six times a year, and Smotherman's participates in the local spring telethon, "*Live Remote*."

# Lufkin

## Lufkin Farm Nursery

*1217 East Lufkin Avenue*
*Lufkin, Texas 75901*
☎ *409/634-7414*
*FAX 409/634-7948*
**Hours** *Mon-Sat 7-5:30, Sun 1-5 (spring); Mon-Sat 7-5:30 (other seasons)*
**Accessible** *Yes*

"Thirty years and still growing!" As owner Payton Mathis told us, "We're redoing and utilizing more land. In other words, we're 'dressing it up'." Since our impression of Lufkin Farm Nursery was favorable, we can't wait to see the "re-do!" We found an assorted and complete selection of trees, shrubs and plants, all of which "looked happy." This nursery also carries building materials for outdoor structures, play equipment, soils, pest management supplies, drip irrigation equipment, tools, books, furniture, gifts and clay pots. Staff member James Hilliard is a licensed irrigator, and additional services include lawn maintenance, landscaping and sprinkler systems. When asked if Lufkin Farm Nursery specialized, Mr. Mathis replied, "Not really. It used to be vegetables, but now it's just about everything." Sales are held in the fall and spring, and seasonal seminars are held from time to time. The nursery is clean, tidy and well organized, and the plants speak for themselves!

# Nacogdoches

## Cook's Nursery

*Route 14, Box 4150*
*Nacogdoches, Texas 75964*
☎ *409/564-6359*
*FAX 409/569-2533*
**Hours** *Mon-Sat 9-5:30, Sun 1-5*
**Accessible** *Partially*

What we discovered here was "an oasis!" Tucked into the pine forest, about three-quarters of a mile past Loop 224 on Highway 21 West, is the largest retail nursery in the Nacogdoches/Lufkin area. Cook's knowledgeable, experienced staff wants "to help you get things growing." When we visited, the staff was in the process of putting together a comprehensive catalogue and planting guide along with tip sheets. The company carries a large quantity of quality plants, particularly tropical houseplants, unusual perennials, azaleas and shrubs. The atmosphere is most pleasant, and friendly, professional advice is always available. As Mr. Cook says, "If we don't have the answer, we will find it!" In the spring, Cooks holds "orphan sales," and in October there's an Anniversary Sale.

*Tyler*

## Breedlove Nursery & Landscape

*11576 State Highway 64 West*
*Tyler, Texas 75704*
☎ *903/597-7421*
**FAX** *903/597-7423*
**Hours** *Mon-Sat 8-5:30, Sat 9-5*
**Accessible** *Partially*

Breedlove's "roots" go back to 1927. Its founder, Jesse Breedlove, pioneered Tyler's famous rose industry. Today Ray Breedlove, a landscape architect, and Paul and Laurie Breedlove, both horticulturists, manage the nursery and landscape business. The grounds cover four acres and include three display gardens: a formal garden complete with fish pond, a cottage garden, and a Victorian Knot garden. The nursery carries a full line of trees, shrubs, ground covers, seasonal color, herbs and perennials. According to Laurie, "During the Spring Azalea Trail, Breedlove's is a rainbow of color!" The garden center carries fertilizers, chemicals, organics and a refreshing selection of garden gifts. Breedlove's is also known for its "Special Mix," a fertilizer especially for East Texas soil. The company carries extensive lines of statuary, pottery, fountains and planters. As Laurie says, "We love what we do, and it shows!"

## Country Connection Plants & Things

*8111 State Highway 31 East*
*Tyler, Texas 75705*
☎ *903/592-5893*
**Hours** *Mon-Sat 8:30-5:30, Sun 1-5*
**Accessible** *Yes*

We visited Country Connection early one morning and were immediately enchanted with the two-story gray barn, which houses an extensive gift shop. When we walked down into the nursery area, we were even more enchanted! The plants are displayed in a "terraced" landscape that leads to a lovely lake. It's truly like being in a 38-acre garden. The company has a large assortment of trees, shrubs and seasonal color from which to chose, but as owner Bobby Barrow says," We feel our customers keep coming back because the owners are here all the time to welcome them, have a cup of coffee and visit." There are two Certified Nursery Professionals on staff to offer advice on plants and landscaping. They hold an Annual Spring Appreciation Sale on the first of May.

## Thompson-Hills Nursery

*11745 Highway 64 West*
*Tyler, Texas 75704*
☎ *903/597-9951*
**FAX** *903/597-9941*
**Hours** *Mon-Fri 8-6, Sat 8-5:30, Sun 10-5 (spring & summer); Mon-Sat 8-5, Sun 10-5 (fall & winter)*
**Accessible** *Yes*

Thompson-Hills is not just famous in the Tyler area; this nursery enjoys a statewide reputation! In business since 1946, the company specializes in roses, azaleas, native plants and trees. The nursery stock is, of course, extensive, and its staff is friendly and knowledgeable. As owner Laura Miller explains, "Our staff is eager to help any and all with any problem or question." We were very impressed with the selection of pots, statuary and fountains, all of which add to Thompson-Hills' relaxed ambiance.

## Coastal Prairies & Marshes
*Beaumont/ Orange/ Port Arthur Area*

### Al Cook Nursery
*10205 Highway 105*
*Beaumont, Texas 77713*
☎ *409/898-2294*
**FAX** *409/898-2294*
**Hours** *Mon-Sat 9-5:30, Sun 10-5:30*
**Accessible** *Yes*

This large, tidy establishment features six waterfalls and 800-feet of creeks running throughout the property. "We have four greenhouses and a very big selection of quality plants with a knowledgeable staff to answer any questions and offer advice," says Larry Hamlin. With the exception of water plants, almost any other plants or seeds suitable to the area can be found here. In addition, you will find soil and soil amendments, pest management supplies, garden tools and gifts and accessories. Weekly specials are offered, and every Wednesday at Al Cook Nursery is "Ladies' Day" with a 10% discount!

### Beaumont Farmers Market & Gardenworld
*8690 Highway 105*
*Beaumont, Texas 77713*
☎ *409/898-3878*
**FAX** *409/898-4487*
**Hours** *Daily 7 a.m.-10 p.m.*
**Accessible** *Yes*

As Joe Frederick told us, "We opened at our new five-acre location in 1995 and maintain the largest inventory in this three-city area." The company stocks over 1,500 hanging baskets, over 1,500 flats of bedding plants, any kind of fruit tree (over 600 in stock), and over 200 shade trees and ornamentals. You can choose from an inventory of 20,00 shrubs in sizes from one-gallon to 20-gallon pots. Joe also says, "We have the largest inventory of tropical palm trees in stock in the area." Beaumont Farmers Market & Gardenworld holds a sale July 4-20, and the staff is always available to offer garden advice.

### Conway Garden Center
*2690 North Main Street*
*Vidor, Texas 77662*
☎ *409/769-4228*
**Hours** *Mon-Sat 7:30-6 (spring & summer); Mon-Sat 8:30-4:30 (winter)*
**Accessible** *Partially*

Joyce Conway says, "We offer personal service on growing, and we spend time with all of our customers helping them select flowers, shrubs, trees and vegetable plants or seeds best for their area." The company carries a large selection of plant material and will order any item that may not be in stock. You'll find soil and soil amendments, pest management supplies and garden gifts here, too. Conway's holds a "Jump into Spring" and a fall sale.

*Directions: Take IH-10 to the Vidor exit. Turn right on FM North 105 and go two miles to the corner of FM105 and FM 1132.*

## M&D Supply
*4580 College Street*
*Beaumont, Texas 77707*
☎ *409/842-2731 or 1-888/818-4102*
**FAX** *409/842-8361*
**Hours** *Mon-Fri 7:30-8, Sat 7:30-6, Sun 9-5*
**Accessible** *Yes*

"We carry the most unusual and healthy nursery stock in the Golden Triangle, always trying to stock what is new and exciting," says Rick Hamberlin. "We have things that no one else will even try. If we don't have it, we'll get it. We specialize in service, selection and more service." The company staff provides garden advice, seminars and special events.

## Shell Plant Farm
*2680 North 11th Street*
*Beaumont, Texas 77703*
☎ *409/892-0434*
**FAX** *409/892-4959*
**Hours** *Mon-Sat 9-5:30, Sun 12-5*
**Accessible** *Yes*

Kim and Roy Henslee preside over this eleven-acre nursery that has been in the family since 1929. They are both Texas Master Certified Nursery Professionals, and the staff includes three TCNPs, as well. A complete garden center, this company is also a grower, specializing in seasonal color in its nine greenhouses. In addition you'll find lots of shade and fruit trees, shrubs, ground cover, roses, water plants and hanging baskets. "We won't sell a new release until we've tried it. We offer a 90-day, no-hassle guarantee on all our plants. We are involved in the community, and we provide seminars and lectures for garden clubs. Our landscape business is primarily the rejuvenation of older gardens," the Henslees explained. "We are customer-service oriented; we'll even pot your geraniums." They offer good selections in garden supplies here, too.

## Brazosport Area

## Wells Florist, Nursery & Landscape
*Route 1, Box 740*
*Sweeny, Texas 77480*
☎ *409/548-2247*
**FAX** *409/548-7899*
**Hours** *Mon-Sat 8-5*
**Accessible** *Partially*

"This nursery is possibly the largest in Brazoria County, and certainly the oldest (50 years in business)," reports owner Gary Wells. "A very important factor in our success is that 90-95% of the plants are grown on the property and the rest are finished-off here; you can be sure that there will be no plant loss due to acclimatization. Our staff knows what is suitable for the area. We do a lot of landscaping, including consultation and repair." Wells publishes a plant list and will ship to customers. It also carries a large selection of supplies. The nursery has sales in December and March and offers garden advice year round.

*Directions: Located 3½ miles southwest of West Columbia on State Highway 35.*

## Conroe/ Spring/ The Woodlands Area

### Garden World

*1101 IH-45 South*
*Conroe, Texas 77301*
☎ *409/539-6399*
**Hours** *Mon-Sat 8:30-6, Sun 9-6 (summer); Mon-Sat 8:30-5:30, Sun 9-5:30 (winter)*
**Accessible** *Yes*

Garden World is a lovely, complete garden center carrying a wide selection of plant material and a great assortment of containers, baskets, statuary and garden gifts. As Pat and Kay Mathis told us, "Our name, Garden World, best describes our nursery because we have a natural setting of grassy pathways under a canopy of tall trees. The fence line is covered with beautiful antique roses. We have a selection of handmade country-style birdhouses displayed among our hanging baskets. During azalea season, many of our customers bring their children and cameras. We try to please our customers and will make every effort to locate a hard-to-find plant. On the adjoining lot you will find 100-gallon container-grown trees, including palms. We offer landscape design and installation." Garden World always has a 50%-off area and holds an annual anniversary sale in September.

*Directions: Take the Gladstell exit.*

### Teas Nursery Company Inc.

*25598 IH-45 North*
*Spring, Texas 77386 (The Woodlands)*
☎ *281/367-2013*
**FAX** *281/292-4062*

See complete listing on page 202.

### The West Nursery

*8825 IH-45 South*
*Conroe, Texas 77385*
☎ *409/321-2465*
**FAX** *409/273-4077*
**Hours** *Daily 9-5:30*
**Accessible** *Yes*

The selection of trees, shrubs, annuals and perennials is extensive on this eight-acre property. As Bernadette West points out, "We are a 4,000-plant retail center with high quality products and a complete landscaping service." Inside, you will find books, fountains, statuary and garden gifts — there's everything from seeds to tropicals and much more. Sales are held in September, and garden advice is always offered. The West Nursery is also the perfect place to purchase parrots and parrot supplies.

*Galveston/ Galveston Bay Area*

## All Seasons Garden Center

205 North Friendswood Drive
Friendswood, Texas 77546
☎ 281/482-2850
**FAX** 281/482-2731
**Hours** Daily 9-6
**Accessible** Partially

All Seasons is a seven-acre, full-line nursery that specializes in the hard-to-find. Plant materials include shade and fruit trees, shrubs, herbs, ground covers, water plants and tropical houseplants. Quality roses are particular favorites, with between 250 and 300 varieties in stock. Family owned and operated for 15 years, its staff members all have at least nine years of experience. Says owner John Post, "Since we are also growers, we can offer the customer a great selection." Sponsored through a community education program, John lectures on roses and other Gulf Coast plants. Landscape design and friendly advice are always available. Sales are advertised in the local paper.

## Maas Nursery & Landscaping

5511 Todville Road
Seabrook, Texas 77586
☎ 281/474-2488
**FAX** 281/474-4708

1717 2nd Street
Seabrook, Texas 77586
☎ 281/474-4974
**FAX** 281/474-4962

**Hours** Mon-Sat 9-5, Sun 10-5 (both stores)
**Accessible** Partially (gravel paths)

"At Maas Nursery, we specialize in giving our customers a pleasant experience to explore and enjoy," says Jim Maas. "Our out-of-the-way location doesn't lend itself to a quick stop on the way home from work. We therefore cater to the gardener who wants to take more than four or five minutes to shop." (The new second location is conveniently located at the corner of 2nd and Highway 146. It specializes in bedding plants and garden art.) When you visit the original 14 acres, you'll see why he says "We are not just another garden center." Not only does this nursery grow almost every plant that's adapted to this part of Texas, but also it offers fun things to see and do. Maas has live music many weekends in the spring. Local artists carve stone or wood, or paint or throw pots as you watch. Some of the most interesting displays revolve around ethnic and native art from foreign lands. You'll find out about canoes from the Cuna Indians, Indonesian folk art and antique and modern American yard art (furniture and statuary.)

"Our exotic animal compound is very popular with both kids and adults," says Jim. It's a natural environment for all sorts of non-carnivorous animals. We could have anything from rabbits to wallabies to longhorns. Since we rescue, buy, love and sell our animals, the population changes from year to year." The main building is more like a museum than a salesroom. Here you'll find shells, rocks, skulls, artifacts and specimens from all over the world. Unlike a museum, if Maas has it, you can look, touch and buy (almost every item). "If you are interested in an unusual shopping experience, please come visit us. We don't usually have sales, but we definitely offer garden advice."

*Directions: From Houston, take IH-45 to the NASA Road 1 Exit and turn left (east). Cross Highway 146 to the water and turn left on Todville. Go about 3.5 miles and turn right onto Pine Gully Road to the parking lot.*

## Teas Nursery Company Inc.

1445 West Bay Area Boulevard
Webster, Texas 77598
☎ 281/338-2050
See complete listing on page 202.

## Tom's Thumb Nursery & Landscaping

2014 45th Street
Galveston, Texas 77550
☎ 409/763-4713
**FAX** 409/765-9253
**Hours** Mon-Sat 9-6, Sun 10-4
**Accessible** Yes

Tom's Thumb is a family owned business with 25 years of experience assisting island gardeners. According to Peggy Cornelius, "Although we specialize in tropicals and coastal plants, we carry everything from tools to grasses, from trees to vegetable starts and perennials and much more." We were impressed with the company's garden furniture, seaside nautical gifts and large assortment of fountains. According to the locals, "the Christmas store is wonderful!"

## Houston Metropolitan Area

## Buchanan's Native Plants

611 East 11th
Houston, Texas 77008
☎ 713/861-5702
**FAX** 713/861-2063
**Hours** Daily 9-6
**Accessible** Yes

This Houston Heights nursery is a cheery place to linger awhile. Says Donna Buchanan, "We are known for our varied inventory which includes a wide assortment of antique roses, old fashioned perennials, herbs, wildflowers and seasonal color, as well as pond supplies and water lilies. We have three Certified Texas Nursery Professionals on staff who are able to help customers with their most difficult problems, usually recommending natural and organic products as remedies." Buchanan's Native Plants is a complete garden center specializing in plants native to the Texas area, but it also stocks many other hardy, adapted trees, shrubs and ornamentals. The gift shop offers a selection of garden-related books, tools, seeds, and gift items and lots of terra cotta pottery. According to Donna, " We always have something new, and our customers love our two resident cats, Ursula and Mama." Intermittent sales are usually in late summer.

## Condon Gardens

*1214 Augusta Drive*
*Houston, Texas 77057*
☎ *713/782-3992*
**FAX** *713/782-0318*
**Hours** *Mon-Sat 9-5:30, Sun 10-5:30*
**Accessible** *Partially*

Having not visited Condon's in a number of years, we were delighted to recapture the feeling of serenity that's "just a part of Condon's!" This complete, service-oriented garden center has a long-standing reputation for specializing in the unusual. A wide variety of trees, shrubs, annuals and perennials are displayed with originality in a natural 1½-acre setting. A broad selection of antique and modern roses is available, and according to satisfied customers, "represent the highest quality in Houston." Four greenhouses offer a large selection of tropicals and cacti. See information about Stoke's Tropicals on page 330. Amidst the gardens, you'll find fabulous statuary and fountains (some by local artists), all beautifully displayed.

The Patio Shop, a home surrounded by decking, is the hub of the garden center. The topiaries and orchids are found here, in addition to a broad selection of upscale garden gifts, baskets, bonsai supplies, books, cards, furniture, wind chimes, bird feeders and birdhouses. Also to be discovered is a complete line of gardening supplies including wire baskets, hayracks, clay pots, as well as pest controls and fertilizers, with strong emphasis on the organics. Condon Gardens has been in business for 43 years. Seasonal sales/discount coupons are offered in the spring and fall. Knowledgeable staff members are always on hand to offer advice; they're often asked to speak at area garden clubs. This is a real charmer... not to be missed!

## Cornelius Nurseries, Inc.

*2233 South Voss Road*
*Houston, Texas 77057*
☎ *713/782-8640*
**FAX** *713/783-2153*

*1755 F.M. 1960 West*
*Houston, Texas 77090*
☎ *281/444-1210*
**FAX** *281/444-1430*

*1200 North Dairy Ashford*
*Houston, Texas 77079*
☎ *281/ 493-0550*
**FAX** *281/493-6986*

*www.corneliusnurseries.com*
**Hours** *Daily 9-6*
**Accessible** *Mostly*

Cornelius Nurseries has been serving the Houston and Upper Gulf Coast area since 1937. "We pride ourselves on our selection of gardening products that perform for our customers in this area," says Steve Moore, the company's buyer. "Our long suit is the color department. Within this area, we feature new and unusual items for intrepid gardeners, new plant or variety introductions and beautiful bedding plants grown to our specifications. You'll find herbs, vegetables, seasonal specialties, occasion-specific gardening baskets, bulbs and many other related products that encourage success." Because of its affiliation with Turkey Creek, one of the largest wholesale-only nurseries in the state, Cornelius maintains great depth in landscape plant materials. And, its topical plants are spectacular.

The company formulates specialty soil mixes, fertilizers and mulches specifically for the Houston soils. Each of the stores carries an excellent selection of home and garden accessories. We were particularly impressed with the handsome pottery and the garden furniture handmade by Mexican artisans. The stores stock a large selection of books on subjects ranging from gardening advice to beautifully illustrated coffee table conversation pieces. The stores really sparkle at Christmas.

Staff members have worked for many years compiling free information sheets on many Houston-area plants and gardening projects. Other services include delivery, grass pluggers and fertilizer spreaders on loan, landscape design and installation, and business or in-home holiday decorating. "Our goal at Cornelius," says Steve, "is to help you shape your corner of the world." Sales are advertised weekly, and there is a full-time information center staffed with Texas Certified Nursery Professionals to assist customers at each of the stores. Check out the web-site; it lists the weekly specials, provides garden tips and lots more!

## Gateway Ace Hardware and Garden Center

*6860 Telephone Road*
*Houston, Texas 77061*
☎ *713/643-0623*
**FAX** *713/643-5104*
**Hours** *Mon-Fri 7:30-7, Sat 8-6, Sun 10-4 (store); Mon-Sat 9-6, Sun 10-4 (garden center)*
**Accessible** *Partially*

According to manager Eunice Roberts, "The original owners, the Wiatts, spent years building a client base for antique roses, and the new owner, Mr. Humphries, is continuing the tradition, recommending antique roses for their beauty, fragrance, landscape qualities and relative ease of care." The company grows its own, keeps least 100 varieties in stock, and will even special-order, subject to availability. It also carries fine mini-roses, especially in spring, and will also try to find you any of the AARS-winning modern roses. David Austin English roses arrive in February. You will also find tools, books, pest-management supplies, soil and soil amendments. The company hosts well-attended seminars on Saturday mornings in the spring and publishes a newsletter. Watch for periodic sales, promotions and special purchases. Trained and experienced personnel are on hand to help with selections of tropicals, flowering shrubs, trees, native plants and well-adapted annuals and perennials for "the cottage look."

## Glauser McNair Nursery

*1707 Ojeman*
*Houston, Texas 77055*
☎ *713/781-3841*
**FAX** *713/984-9549*
**Hours** *Mon-Fri 8-5, Sat 8-4 (March-May); call for Sat hours from June-Feb*
**Accessible** *Partially*

We so thoroughly enjoyed the serene setting amidst large shade trees and cooing doves that we forgot we were in urban Houston. While Nan was admiring the specimen ornamental and shade trees, natives, grasses, tropicals, annuals and perennials, Pat found the wonderful spider lily she had been seeking for months. Manager Steve Ralya calls Glauser-McNair, "Nature's Best Kept Secret... in the Heart of Spring Branch!" As Mary Ralya told us, "In an industry increasingly dominated by mass-merchandisers and huge, impersonal chain-stores, we strive for friendly, 'old-time' service. From the always helpful staff to the candy jar on the counter, our customers come back time after time for our personalized attention as well as our quality plants."

## RCW Nurseries Inc.

*15809 Tomball Parkway*
*Houston, Texas 77086*
☎ *281/440-5161*
**FAX** *281/440-8158*
**Hours** *Mon-Sat 8-6, Sun 10-5 (March-Oct); Mon-Sat 8-5:30, Sun 10-5 (Nov-Feb)*
**Accessible** *Yes*

What a pleasant surprise it was to find this nursery. Since RCW has its own tree farm, it has created a lovely, shady atmosphere of its own and built a large inventory of shade and flowering ornamental trees for customers. There are also shrubs, perennials, seeds, tools, books, herbs, vegetable starts and water plants to be found in this country-feeling nursery where gardeners are greeted by a fragrant rose garden and large cages of birds and ducks! As customers say, "Not only is the selection great, but this is such a peaceful place to visit." The company offers local delivery, and its trees and shrubs are frequently marked down in late-summer, fall and winter.

## Teas Nursery Company Inc.

*4400 Bellaire Boulevard*
*Bellaire, Texas 77401*
☎ *713/664-4400*
**FAX** *713/295-5170*

*10939 Katy Freeway*
*Houston, Texas 77079*
☎ *713/467-0301*
**FAX** *713/467-5427*

*4545 Beechnut*
*Houston, Texas 77096*
☎ *713/665-6852*
**FAX** *713/665-6234*

**www.**teasnursery.com
**Hours** *Mon-Fri 9-7, Sat & Sun 9-6; opens at 8 on Saturdays in spring*
**Accessible** *Yes*

We had not visited Teas for some years, so we were elated to find the same lovely atmosphere, friendly people and high-quality plants we had remembered from years past. Houston's "super store" for plants, this ten-acre nursery in Bellaire offers over 400 varieties of roses and a broad selection of other plants, including azaleas, crepe myrtles, herbs, orchids, bedding plants, bromeliads, succulents, African violets and much, much more. Houstonians have long appreciated the huge selection of high-quality perennial and seasonal plants at market prices and the great selection of bulbs, which are kept refrigerated to ensure healthy blooms.

A family-owned business established in Raysville, Indiana in 1843, Teas moved to its present location over 90 years ago. A home built on the site in 1910 is available for tours and catered luncheons by appointment, and the 1916 family home serves as a Teas museum and landscape office. In 1998, the company added five new locations (formerly Wolfe Nursery stores) that allow Teas to "reach out" to suburban neighborhoods. In addition to the stores listed here, there's one in Webster/Clear Lake area and another near The Woodlands in Spring. "We've merged the best of two good organizations. It has been very exciting," says Diann Teas. "We continue to enjoy a well-earned reputation as the best nursery in Houston with the highest quality and selection at reasonable prices."

Teas Landscape Services employs landscape architects, designers, installers, and maintenance experts working on interior, exterior, home and business plantscapes. Teas Orchid and Exotic Plant Supply catalog, which has grown to 44 pages, now also includes roses, tools and books. It's mailed to over 50,000 customers each year and provides toll-free ordering service. (See pages 160, 279 and 331.) A separate Selection Guide for roses is filled with information. The company holds a "Back 40" sale in late spring and has summer clearances. Almost every weekend you'll find visiting experts speaking on specific topics. As one of the country's oldest nurseries, Teas is certainly "the grandfather of nurseries in the Houston area!"

## Thompson + Hanson

*2770 Edloe*
*Houston, Texas 77027*
☎ *713/622-3722*
**FAX** *713/622-8083*
**Hours** *Mon-Fri 7-5, Sat & Sun 9-5*
**Accessible** *Yes*

Thompson + Hanson is both a landscape architectural firm and a nursery. Brad Thompson, the nursery manager explains, "Since we are not a huge nursery, we can offer more individualized services to our customers." The company specializes in perennials, tropicals, ferns, ivies and bedding plants, and the quality and selection is all one could want. All of the plants are beautifully maintained. The company carries an unusual selection of pots, ranging from Italian to Chinese. Two people on staff specialize in "custom potting!" There's a limited amount of furniture on display and a number of catalogs from which to order. The company holds sales at the end of the seasons. On our hot-summer-day visit, the shade and ambiance of the water features combined to make Thompson + Hanson a double treat.

# Pasadena/ Baytown Area

## Smith-Barrow Gardens

*8802 Thompson Road*
*Highlands, Texas 77562*
☎ *281/426-3215*
**Hours** *Mon-Sat 9-5 (Jan-June); Mon-Sat 9-3 (July-Dec)*
**Accessible** *Yes*

Smith-Barrow Gardens has been in the same location since 1953, and, as Bernice Smith says, "Our slogan, 'An Old Fashioned Nursery,' means that this is a working operation. We propagate and grow many of our color, vegetable, perennial and tropical house plants from seeds, cuttings or divisions." The nursery is stocked with plants well suited to the area, as well as many unusual plants for collectors. Its service is of the "Mom and Pop" sort, with a personal greeting and friendly, knowledgeable assistance for each customer. Bernice notes, "After 40 years of growing experience, we know the different types of soil that our customers are dealing with — from sandy loam to heavy clay."

## Teas Nursery Company Inc.

*3600 Southeast Beltway 8*
*Pasadena, Texas 77504*
☎ *281/487-9783*
**FAX** *281/487-2344*
See complete listing on opposite page.

## Vaughan's Nursery and Gardens

15647 Avenue C
Channelview, Texas 77530
☎ 281/452-7369
**FAX** 281/457-0344
**Hours** Daily 8-6 (spring and fall); closed Sundays in summer. Closed from Thanksgiving through New Year's Day
**Accessible** Partially

You can find almost any kind of plant material you want at Vaughan's, plus some you hadn't even thought of, from an extensive array of native plants to African violets. You'll find all kinds of environmentally friendly supplies, soils, tools, garden books and gifts. "At Vaughan's Nursery & Gardens, we make gardening a pleasure. We provide friendly service and a garden-like atmosphere where customers can see the plants in action. Everything on display is healthy and adapted to our area. We've established a trustworthy reputation because we don't just sell plants; we teach people how to use them to make their environment more pleasing. We provide safe solutions to garden problems. We're gardeners, too! We take time to visit, to listen to gardeners' problems and successes. We learn from our clients as they learn from us," says owner Maria Vaughan. The nursery hosts seminars and special events and usually holds sales in the fall.

## Rosenberg/ Stafford

## Caldwell Nursery

2436 Band Road
Rosenberg, Texas 77471
☎ 281/342-4016
**FAX** 281/341-7367
**Hours** Mon-Sat 9-5:30, Sun 1-5 (closed Sun mid-June-winter, call for appointment or to check hours)
**Accessible** Partially (some gravel areas)
**Mail Order**
**Catalog** Seed list ($1.00)

This nursery may be "off the beaten path," but it is well worth the trip. A labor of love, its immaculate display gardens are richly textured, soft and naturalistic. Says Cay Dee Caldwell, "I tend to like things overgrown and full." Caldwell specializes in natives, herbs, roses, antique roses, unusual perennials, tropicals, water plants and bog plants. In the past few years the owners have become enthusiastic about named-variety daylilies, and they've begun growing a variety of wetland plants. In an effort to help customers, the Caldwells provide personal, informal signs with accurate knowledge on each plant. According to Cay Dee, "In using texture and contrast plants, we hope to inspire many gardeners to try different natives and perennials. All plants have their own 'uniqueness'...like people, I guess. We don't claim to know everything, but we hope our enthusiasm 'wears off' on our customers." What a delight!

## *Coastal Bend*
### Corpus Christi

## Fox Tree & Landscape Nursery

*5902 South Staples Street*
*Corpus Christi, Texas 78413*
☎ *512/992-6928*
**FAX** *512/ 991-7841*
**Hours** *Mon-Sat 8-7, Sat & Sun 9-6*
**Accessible** *Yes*

The 26 acres of nursery stock and greenhouses here give gardeners a wide range of options. More than 50% of the trees and shrubs are Texas natives, and most of the "seasonal color" is grown on the premises. You'll find landscaping materials from bulk soils to rock, and there's lots of pottery, plus everything you might need in the way of ponds and fountains. The "back 40" is a forest of specimen-size trees, and the company has equipment with which to move and plant them. (The tree service part of the business can also remove your dead or damaged trees when necessary.) There's a designer on staff, and the company offers landscaping and irrigation services.

## Gill Landscape Nursery

*2810 Airline Road*
*Corpus Christi, Texas 78414*
☎ *512/992-9674*
**FAX** *512/992-9796*

*4441 South Alameda*
*Corpus Christi, Texas 78412*
☎ *512/993-4796*
**FAX** *512/993-4796*

**Hours** *Mon-Sat 8-7, Sun 10-6 (Feb-Oct); Mon-Sat 8-6, Sun 10-6 (Nov-Jan)*
**Accessible** *Partially (greenhouse, parking, bedding plants, register & restroom)*

"Friendliest nursery in town! We have the best selection of native plants and Texas Certified Nursery Professionals and Master Certified Professionals to answer your questions regarding plant problems or landscape techniques. Industry reps tell us we have the cleanest facility and healthiest plants of any place they sell to," proudly claims James Gill. The company provides landscape design services. Special orders are welcome, as well as phone orders and in-town delivery service. The selection of perennials is outstanding. To sum it up, says James Gill, "Quality plants, helpful and knowledgeable staff." Gill's on Airline Road offers a pre-Christmas clearance on shrubs and holds seminars in February, May, June and October. Gill's on Alameda is the smaller of the two stores. Located in an old gas station, it specializes in blooming color and "fast-stop shopping." You'll find a complete line of shrubs, tropicals, annuals and perennials, as well as garden supplies and gifts.

## House of Ivy Nursery

*427 Old Robstown Road*
*Corpus Christi, Texas 78408*
☎ *512/882-1433*
**FAX** *512/882-9547*
**Hours** *Mon-Sat 8-5:30*
**Accessible** *Difficult*

House of Ivy provides a very pleasant surprise! From the street, it appears to be a quaint little cottage, but there is really quite a large nursery here. The owner, Helen Philpo, grows about 65% of the plants on the premises and offers a big selection of

*(Listing continued on next page)*

shrubs, trees, specimen plants and perennials. It's fun to just wander about and feel a part of the growing process. House of Ivy has been in this location since 1953, and Helen (a real "green thumb" gardener) says, "Our clientele is loyal because we offer a large selection of unusual, high-quality plants." We paid our visit because the "locals" told us that it was a great place to buy plants and "a little time with Helen is always fun."

## Rockport

### Adams Nursery

*1515 Highway 35 South*
*Rockport, Texas 78382*
☎ *512/729-7111*
**FAX** *512/729-1746*
**Hours** *Mon-Sat 9-5, Sun10-5 spring; Mon-Fri 9-5, Sat 9-1 fall*
**Accessible** *Yes*

At Adams Nursery, you will find two, and soon three, Texas Certified Nursery Professionals who offer advice on dealing with soil conditions, climate and water supply in the area. Says Thelma Adams, "We work with each customer who needs help to make their plantings successful. We love to share our many years of experience (even bad gardening days and stories.) We've helped gardeners from age three to 102, and we feel honored when these same people share their knowledge with us." You'll find tools, books and gifts, as well as a large variety of plant material, water gardening supplies and fish here. And the company definitely carries bulk seed! "We feel our clientele appreciates the service we give, as well as the quality of our stock," she adds. Adams Nursery normally has sales of some sort throughout the year.

## Victoria

### Better Gardens & Landscape

*606 East Mockingbird*
*Victoria, Texas 77904*
☎ *512/573-7434*
**FAX** *512/573-7435*
**Hours** *Mon-Sat 9-6, Sun 12-5*
**Accessible** *Yes*

As Robert L. Rogers reports, "Better Gardens & Landscape is the area's largest retail garden center with emphasis on quality, selection and personal service." This nursery has been serving the Texas Gulf Coast area for over 30 years, offering landscape design and building while emphasizing native color, rock work, waterfalls and special requests. You'll find a large selection of tropicals, annuals and perennials, as well as garden statuary and other accessories here. Better Gardens & Landscape holds late spring and early summer sales.

## Four Seasons Garden Center

*1209 East Salem Road*
*Victoria, Texas 77904*
☎ *512/575-8807*
**FAX** *512/575-4027*
**Hours** *Mon-Sat 8:30-6, Sun 10-6*
**Accessible** *Yes*

Customers agree that Four Seasons is a delightful destination for visiting and shopping. It has a park-like atmosphere, with an arbor and luxuriant display beds year-round. Established in 1984, Four Seasons carries a large selection of natives and hard-to-find heirloom plants. The company carries antique roses from Brenham, and offers large selections of trees, shrubs, herbs, vegetables, bedding plants and everything for the water garden. Its plumerias are propagated on-site. You'll also find a full line of soils, including the nursery's own potting soil, pest controls, fertilizers and quality hand tools from Maine. The gift shop has books, and cut trees are available at Christmas. Owner John Fossati, who holds a degree in horticulture from Texas A&M told us, "We provide friendly service, and offer beautifully displayed plants. We also design and install gardens. Four Seasons is more than just a nursery."

# Valley
### Brownsville/ Harlingen Area

## Bence Nursery

*West Expressway 83 at White Ranch Road*
*Harlingen, Texas 78551*
☎ *956/797-2021*
**FAX** *956/412-2505*
**Hours** *Mon-Sat 8:30-5:30, Sun 12-5*
**Accessible** *Yes*

We were most impressed with Bence Nursery — there was such a "neat and crisp" character about it! The selection and quality of plant material was obvious, and the staff couldn't have been more friendly and helpful. Says owner Linda Bence, "We are a complete garden center with such extras as pottery, concrete benches, statuary, birdbaths, fountains, pots, bulbs, wind chimes, orchids and all kinds of water gardening supplies. We have the Valley's largest landscaping selection and widest variety of plants as well as the most extensive selection of palms." Bence's offers professional design and installation of residential and commercial landscaping services, and holds a Daylily Festival in late spring.

## Gentry's Garden Center

*4580 North Expressway (Highway 77/83)*
*Brownsville, Texas 78526*
☎ *956/350-9805*
**Hours** *Mon-sat 9-6, Sun 12-5*
**Accessible** *Yes*

Manager Joe Flores noted that his surname means flowers in Spanish, "so it makes sense that I should be drawn to this industry!" His wife, Patty Gentry Flores, is doubly blessed because the Gentry name is synonymous with exotic tropicals in South Texas. See page 211 for the wonderful plants her father makes available to gardeners in Laredo. They're all here, too. Joe told us that the company is soon expanding into more varieties of exotic palms. Gentry's maintains landscape design and installation services and offers a complete line of traditional garden center merchandise, including "hard goods."

## Grimsell Seed Company

213 West Monroe Avenue
Harlingen, Texas 78550
☎ 956/423-0370
**FAX** 956/423-1070
**Hours** Mon-Sat 7:30-6, Sun 12-4
**Accessible** Yes

"An oasis amidst the asphalt," Grimsell Seed Company was founded in 1915 by Frank Grimsell. Today his grandson, Donald Giffen, owns and manages the store. Located in downtown Harlingen, its large adjacent display garden projects a feeling far different from one's image of a seed store! Grimsell's has prospered over the years because its well-educated personnel strive to offer the highest level of service and customer attention possible. The company carries a large and varied selection of plant materials (from natives to tropicals) as well as tools, drip irrigation equipment, and pest management supplies. Says Donald Giffen," Customers come from all over the four-county area because of our good service and friendly atmosphere. The 'big calling cards' are our huge inventory of fertilizers formulated for us and sold under the Grimsell label and our vast inventory of garden seeds (package and bulk.)" The long-time motto of Grimsell Seed Company is "Grimsell's has it!" Skilled staff members happily offers advice on plants, plant diseases and maladies, insecticides and anything garden related. The store boasts the tallest freestanding flag pole in Texas!

## Stuart Place Nursery

7701 West Business Highway 83
Harlingen, Texas 78552
☎ 956/428-4439
**FAX** 956/428-3889
**Hours** Mon-Fri 8-5:30, Sat 8-6, Sun 12-5
**Accessible** Yes

Native trees, shrubs, cacti and grasses are in a very special category at this full-range garden center. Owner Glyn Whiddon is both a landscape architect and master certified nursery professional, and he's active in native plant groups in the Valley. He and the other certified nursery professionals on staff bring a wealth of knowledge to the business. "The inventory changes fast," says Mr. Whiddon. "In addition to natives and adapted plants suitable for area landscapes, we carry lots of cycads, palms and exotic tropicals you wouldn't find elsewhere." You'll also find everything for the water garden, including the fish, plus all sorts of containers, statuary and wall ornaments. There are books and supplies to implement the gardening process and a full-service FTD florist shop on-site, as well.

## Tony's Nursery

895 East Los Ebanos Boulevard
Brownsville, Texas 78520
☎ 956/541-5322
**Hours** Mon-Sat 8-6, Sun 9-5
**Accessible** Yes

Tony's is a small, but very nice retail nursery that offers trees, shrubs and tropicals. We observed especially attractive hanging baskets and bedding plants. There are no sales, but Tony's prices are always competitive.

*McAllen/ Mission Area*

## Allen's Garden Center

*1800 East Highway 83*
*Weslaco, Texas 78596*
☎ *956/973-1998*
*FAX 956/973-1999*
**Hours** *Mon-Fri 8:30-5:30, Sat 9-4, Sun 12-5 (Closed Sun in summer)*
**Accessible** *Partially; walkways may be difficult*

Owner Betsy Allen explained, "This nursery was started in the 1930s as Links Nursery, then closed in the late '80s. My partner and I reopened in April 1994." We were enchanted by the lush tropical gardens on the property. Old brick walkways lead through a jungle of exotic trees and shrubs (even champion trees like the "Gru-Gru palm" and a "Brazilian Axe-Breaker tree"). With five ponds brimming with plants and tropical fish, both for show and sale, the company has become known as a mecca for water gardening. You'll find a large variety of plants, tools, books, furniture, gifts, soils and pest management supplies. Betsy comments, "This is a one-of-a-kind garden center, many times compared to a Hawaiian paradise. We welcome all shoppers and nature lovers. Advice is for the asking!"

## Barrera's Nursery

*3501 West Highway 83*
*McAllen, Texas 78501*
☎ *956/686-1706*
*FAX 956/686-1731*
**Hours** *Mon-Sat 9-5:30, Sun 12:30-5; Closed Sun June-Sept*
**Accessible** *Yes*

Established in May of 1940, Barrera's is the oldest retail nursery in the Valley. It has been "in the family" for three generations. Having had occupied several growing places, the nursery is back in its original location. This is a complete garden center carrying tropicals, palms, fruit and shade trees, ornamentals, cement statuary, fertilizers, insecticides and tools. It also offers sprinkler system installation. The Barreras say, "One thing we pride ourselves in is that we tell our customers the truth and offer the best service and information possible. Come see us!" The nursery does have sales, but not at any set time.

## Grand Oak Junction Nursery

*6001 North Tenth*
*McAllen, Texas 78504*
☎ *956/631-6670*
*FAX 956/631-6688*
**Hours** *Mon-Sat 9-6, Sun 12-6*
**Accessible** *Partially*

This full-service nursery provides a most comfortable atmosphere in which to shop. Seasonal color is displayed on tables under the branches of a venerable live oak tree. Grand Oak Junction carries a large supply of plant materials year round, as well as supplies to keep your plants healthy. Certified Nursery Professionals are on staff to assist your needs. You'll find all kinds of trees, vines and shrubs as well as tropicals and indoor plants here. There's also an impressive selection of pottery, statuary, fountains, birdbaths, stepping stones, tables and benches. The gift shop is brimming with accessories for the garden room or covered patio. Judie Geil happily

*(Listing continued on next page)*

remarks, "Things are always changing in the gift shop, so you need to stop by often. There's always a 50%-off room to encourage browsing!" Sales are held at the nursery in June and at Christmas. Advice is also available in the form of a newsletter. The parent company, Earth Irrigation and Landscaping, designs and installs landscaping "to fit your property and lifestyle."

---

## Shary Acres

*3421 North Shary Road*
*Mission, Texas 78572*
☎ *956/581-7783*
**FAX** *956/581-7789*
**Hours** *Mon-Sat 9-5, Sun 12-5*
**Accessible** *Partially*

Our visit to Shary Acres was another pleasant surprise. (*We were generally enthralled with this whole region of Texas!*) The staff here was especially friendly; everything was neat and tidy, and the plants were "happy!" Says Danny Sosebee, "Customers enjoy our lush interior walk filled with three acres of tropical plants. Shary Acres is family owned, and, therefore, customers receive personal help and advice." Although the nursery carries other plants and supplies, its tropicals are the real "eye-catchers!" Certified nursery personnel offer quality landscaping and installation. Since the hot weather and fertile soil in the Rio Grand Valley is ideally suited for the production of ultra-sweet, high quality citrus, Shary Acres has a country store adjacent to the orchards and nursery. During the citrus season, you'll find fresh-picked citrus and delicious, fresh squeezed juices. The company ships citrus throughout the continental United States.

---

## Valley Garden Center

*701 East Highway 83*
*McAllen, Texas 78501*
☎ *956/682-9411*
**FAX** *956/682-5604*
**Hours** *Mon-Sat 8:30-6, Sun 12-5*
**Accessible** *Yes*

"Our stock is maintained year round, not just during the spring and fall planting seasons," Will Klement told us. "We have the best packaged seed selection in the Valley as well as bulk vegetable seeds." Valley Garden Center does indeed have everything, from a large selection of plant materials and water gardening supplies to pottery, books, tools, and even hummingbird and songbird supplies. It also carries unusual and common citrus fruit trees and a good selection of native shrubs and trees. The company offers power lawn care, small engine repairs and lawn sprinkler installation and repair. The "Spring Kick Off Sale" occurs the first or second week of February. Valley Garden Center has two Master Certified and five Texas Certified Nursery Professionals on staff, as well as a Board Certified Entomologist.

---

## Waugh's Nursery & Fruit Ranch

*4616 North Jackson Road*
*McAllen, Texas 78577*
☎ *956/686-5591*
**FAX** *956/686-0994*
**Hours** *Mon-Sat 8:30-6, Sun 1-5*
**Accessible** *Yes*

"Forty-seven years in business means we must be doing something right!" comments Ceciele Waugh Beamsley. "What makes us special is the friendly people who know and care about plants and gardening and who want to help others understand and enjoy them as well." Although Waugh's is a complete garden center, its specialties are tropicals, such as heliconias, bauhinias, bougainvillaea, hibiscus, plumeria, etc. The company also offers an outstanding selection of both culinary and medicinal herbs. Advice is always available to customers, and there's also a daily radio program to keep you informed.

# Rio Grande Plain
## Castroville

### Medina Valley Greenhouses
Old River Road (CR 477)
Castroville, Texas 78009
☎ 210/931-2298
*FAX* 210/538-3704
**Hours** Daily 9-5 except Thanksgiving, Christmas, and New Year
**Accessible** Partially (rough ground and gravel)

Medina Valley Greenhouses, which has been featured in *Texas Monthly* magazine, is a nursery that "specializes in variety." The nursery's motto is "Everything from Cactus to Orchids," and the place is sometimes described as "a school teacher's hobby that got out of hand." Over the years, Mary Burges has enlivened her vacation travels by seeking out beautiful and unusual plants for her collection. Says Mrs. Burges, "They grew and multiplied until I had to open a nursery to take care of the overflow." Mrs. Burges received a special award for her long-time support of the xeriscape concept, a program of water conservation through creative landscaping. Thus, native plants are a specialty, along with other species adapted to the local semi-arid conditions. These range from bedding plants to shrubs to full-sized trees and include both perennials and self-seeding annuals. Many of the plants are also herbs and are useful as well as ornamental.

One room of the greenhouse is devoted to cactus, euphorbias, aloes and other desert plants. The rest are filled with orchids and other tropicals. One whole wall of the main greenhouse is faced with honeycomb rocks planted with orchids, bromeliads, hoyas and ferns to produce a striking rain forest effect. The greenhouse itself is set into the side of a hill to protect it from cold winter winds. Mrs. Burges is a Texas Certified Nursery Professional, ready to give expert advice to the plant shopper, and as she says, "People keep coming back to see what else we have added. The prices are so reasonable at all times that items are rarely marked down." Her monthly news articles appear in four local newspapers.

*Directions: Medina Valley Greenhouses is located just northwest of Castroville on the scenic Old River Road, which is an extension of Mexico Street.*

## Laredo

### Gentry's Laredo Garden Center
3020 Meadow Avenue
Laredo, Texas 78044
☎ 956/722-0555
*FAX* 956/726-9818
**Hours** Daily 9-6
**Accessible** Yes

*(Listing continued on next page)*

"We specialize in tropical and hard-to-find plants," says W. E. Gentry. "We raise many of the plants ourselves because they are usually unavailable from wholesalers." The exotic plant names are reason enough to explore this tropical wonderland. If you're a romantic, you'll want the night-blooming jasmine, night-blooming cereus, Mexican love vine and all three varieties of passion vine! Then there are the flame vines and fireman's caps (you may need one of each), the shaving brushes, royal poincianas, Rangoon creepers, jacarandas, giant thumbergia vines, Easter lily vines, bird of paradise and six varieties of datura! Even well-known tropicals such as plumeria, bougainvillea, hibiscus, oleanders and heliconias can be found in greater profusion than usual in this extraordinary garden center. Oh yes, you'll also find all the familiar garden plants, along with books, pottery, tools and lots more for your landscape here. In addition to the garden center, there's a flower shop, gift shop and pet shop. Tropicals are on sale after the summer season, and garden advice is always freely offered.

## San Antonio Metropolitan Area

### Landscape Marketplace

*1031 Austin Highway*
*San Antonio, Texas 78209*
☎ *210/822-1335*
*FAX 210/826-7152*
*Hours Mon-Sat 9-5:30; open Sundays 10-5 in the spring*
*Accessible Yes*

Family owned and operated, Landscape Marketplace is a nice neighborhood nursery that offers full-scale landscape services including design, installation and consultation. Says Carol Bakke, "Our staff is here to really please you, and the plants that we sell are the best quality in the business! We have a native plant expert on staff and a garden library we are pleased to share." You will find a large selection of trees and shrubs from which to choose, plus seasonal color and house plants.

### Maldonado Nursery & Landscape

*4393 Stahl*                                    *12823 Nacogdoches*
*San Antonio, Texas 78217*            *San Antonio, Texas 78217*
☎ *210/599-1219*                          ☎ *210/599-3358*
*FAX 210/599-9736*

*Hours Mon-Sat 9-6, Sun 10-5*
*Accessible Yes (Stahl), Partially (Nacogdoches)*

Of the two Maldonado nurseries, the Stahl location primarily offers landscape design and installation with a small nursery attached, while the Nacogdoches location is a complete retail nursery. Having been a Texas grower for over a decade, Maldonado's specializes in such trees as live oak and red oak. Diana remarked, "Our trees are the best. People always come back for more!" You will find a selection of native trees and shrubs, lots of seasonal color, seeds, container plants, hanging baskets and tropicals. Maldonado's carries soil and soil amendments at both locations and materials for walks, patios and retaining walls, as well as pest management supplies at the Nacogdoches nursery. Sales are usually held for Mother's Day and Father's Day.

## Milberger Landscape

*3920 North Loop 1604 East*
*San Antonio, Texas 78247*
☎ *210/497-3760*
**FAX** *210/497-3929*
**Hours** *Mon-Sat 9-6, Sun 10-5*
**Accessible** *Yes*

We loved "the feel" of Milberger's, with its weathered wooden buildings and large spreading oak trees. Charles Martelli, the manager, told us: "Milberger's retail nursery specializes in providing the community with the very best available in plants, garden supplies and related services. We strive for the highest quality in plant material assuring the customer the best possible results in their garden and landscape projects." Professional advice on all aspects of plant culture is readily available from a friendly, well trained staff to provide customers with the back-up they need for proper planting. The well-stocked garden center provides all of the aids needed for keeping your garden at peak performance, as well as supplying gift items of special seasonal interest: pottery, books, tools and a large selection of seeds and bulbs. The landscape management department offers turf management, tree and shrub maintenance, chemical programs and irrigation. Milberger's interior foliage department provides consultation, installation, maintenance, leasing, short term rental, seasonal color and florals. The company holds sales throughout the year. According to Mr. Martelli, "We take the same pride in all of our landscape operations regardless of the size of the project. We are just as particular with a small residential renovation as we are with a vast commercial landscape such as Fiesta Texas."

## Rainbow Gardens

*8516 Bandera Road*
*San Antonio, Texas 78250*
☎ *210/680-2394*
**FAX** *210/680-4505*

*2585 Thousand Oaks*
*San Antonio, Texas 78232*
☎ *210/494-6131*

**Hours** *Mon-Sat 9-6, Sun 10-6*
**Accessible** *Yes*

Rainbow Gardens' two locations are every bit as colorful as the name suggests. These nurseries provide a very pleasant shopping atmosphere, complete with encyclopedic descriptive signage for all the plants. The meandering paths are built around large old oak trees, and rest spots are provided throughout the four acres of trees, shrubs and perennials. There are squirrels, rabbits, a pet cat and a peacock, along with a koi pond that delights all ages. And even better, free popsicles during the summer months! The inventory here is extensive. You will find a large variety of plant materials, fountains and statuary, books, furniture, pond supplies and much, much more. We were especially impressed with the excellent water plants and the unusual perennials, many of which are native to the Edwards plateau. In the spring, you'll find over 100 varieties of herbs and display pots of herbs and perennials for customers to "sniff and pinch." Owner Frank Kirby is proud to say, "Rainbow Gardens is devoted to selling quality merchandise at competitive prices. We specialize in customer service, emphasizing a friendly staff and knowledgeable sales personnel." The nurseries offer perennial and shrub sales, spring specials and occasional speakers in the spring.

## Schulz Nursery

*100 West Huebinger*
*Marion, Texas 78124*
☎ *83010/914-2384*
**FAX** *830/420-2386*
**Hours** *Daily 9-6*
**Accessible** *Yes*

Now in its 40th year of business, Schulz Nursery provides a very knowledgeable staff of Texas Certified and Master Certified Nursery Professionals. Along with a complete stock of plant material, this nursery carries soils, pest management supplies, tools, garden books, furniture and gifts. Steve Spalten comments, "We offer exceptional quality at good prices. We grow many of our own products, and we try to carry interesting materials that our competitors don't offer. We also have the best selection of roses in the San Antonio area." Schulz Nursery holds regular seminars on herbs, roses, hummingbirds, African violets, purple martins and turf care. This nursery takes pride in its spring concert series and the award-winning monthly newsletter. "It's a great place to bring your family!"

## Shades of Green

*334 West Sunset Road*
*San Antonio, Texas 78209*
☎ *210/824-3772*
**FAX** *210/826-8797*
**Hours** *Mon-Sat 9-5, Sun 10-4*
**Accessible** *Most areas*

This is a must, an absolute delight! With it boardwalks and brick paths, this complete garden center displays its wares in a way that gives customers ideas and inspiration. The first all-organic nursery in the area, it is involved in environmental issues from wildlife backyard habitats to zero-tolerance for pesticides. The plants are very healthy; the garden-related items are unusual; the garden tools are of the highest quality. We were especially taken with the fabulous house plants. As owner Burt Oatman told us, "I hand-select all the blooming color possible. We are known for our large selection of antique roses and herbs, and we're carrying more and more Texas natives." The knowledgeable staff is friendly and helpful, assisting with design decisions and teaching the public how to replace dependence on toxic chemicals with beneficial insects and other organic pest control measures. Shades of Green offers seminars on some Saturday mornings in the spring and fall and publishes a newsletter. You'll find many handouts, and the staff is most helpful in the advice department.

## Vernon's

*225 Faith*
*San Antonio, Texas 78228*
☎ *210/433-9131*
**Hours** *Mon-Sat 9-6 (closes at 5 in winter), Sun 10-4*
**Accessible** *Yes*

Here's another peaceful place, complete with aviary, under the shade of old pecan trees. Vernon's Nursery has been in business since 1952. Both its grounds and the combined resources of its personnel are extensive. You'll find a vast array of seasonal color, lots of tropicals, trees, shrubs, natives and much, much more. As the staff assured us, "Our plants have to be healthy and sizable before we accept them."

Vernon's carries greenhouses, birdbaths, statuary and a large selection of pots (both terra cotta and white clay.) An added attraction is the company's "home-made" potting soil, which is excellent! Whether you're shopping, browsing or in need of gardening advice, a visit to Vernon's is always a pleasure! "We cater to all of our customers, but we especially love to nurture young green thumbs."

## Wolfe Nursery

*1507 Ruiz Street*
*San Antonio, Texas 78207*
☎ *210/433-9691*
*FAX: 210/433-9623*

*3700 Broadway Street*
*San Antonio, Texas 78209*
☎ *210/822-7311*

*7007 San Pedro Avenue*
*San Antonio, Texas 78216*
☎ *210/342-8291*

*8802 Perrin Beitel Road*
*San Antonio, Texas 78217*
☎ *210/653-9611*

*6714 South Flores Street*
*San Antonio, Texas 78221*
☎ *210/922-4321*

*9455 West IH-10*
*San Antonio, Texas 78230*
☎ *210/641-7559*

*6214 NW Loop 410*
*San Antonio, Texas 78238*
☎ *210/681-5813*

*1134 Pat Booker Road*
*Universal City, Texas 78148*
☎ *210/658-3171*

***Hours*** *Mon-Sat 9-7, Sun 10-6*
***Accessible*** *Yes, all stores*

Wolfe's Nursery is a name familiar to most Texas gardeners. The company grew quite large on its reputation for offering one-stop shopping with good prices, good selection and good quality. When the corporation that owned stores throughout the state went out of business in 1998, George J. Wexler, former president of Texas Nurseryman's Association, bought the San Antonio and Austin stores and will operate as Wolfe's. "The problem with a statewide central buying office," he explains," is that a plant is not a 'commodity'. You can't offer the same merchandise in San Antonio that sells in Houston. Different climates and different soils require different plants." His commitment to professionalism ensures that these well-kept nurseries will continue to serve the needs of area gardeners. You can count on finding healthy trees and shrubs of all sizes and a plethora of seasonal plants here. The stores are well stocked with gardening supplies, books and every accessory for outdoor living except furniture. Austin Area stores are listed on page 225.

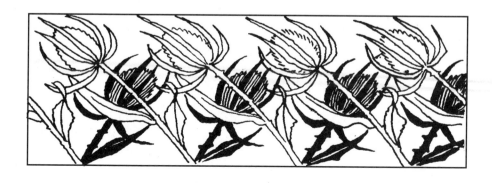

## Central Blacklands & Savannas
### Bryan/ College Station

## Contemporary Landscape Services & Nursery, Inc.

106 North Avenue
Bryan, Texas 77801
☎ 409/846-1448
FAX 409/846-2298
**Hours** Mon-Sat 9-6, call for Sun hours
**Accessible** Yes

"What makes our firm so special is that we have created a whole shopping environment by establishing 'The Garden District' where our customers can not only shop for lawn and garden in our park-like setting, but they can also eat lunch and shop in the other establishments," explains Marilyn Ferguson. "It has been most successful, and having the other businesses here has worked very well for all of us." This establishment offers a great selection of specimen plants, large trees, annuals, perennials, native Texas plants, water gardening plants and interior foliage. The company also carries birdbaths, statuary and fountains, and it maintains a nice gift shop. It's proud to be known as "Your Organic Gardening Headquarters."

## Furrow Building Materials

1501 Highway 6 East Bypass
College Station, Texas 77845
☎ 409/696-9304
FAX 409/693-4017
**Hours** Mon-Fri 7:30-8, Sat 7:30-7, Sun 10-6
**Accessible** Yes

As Piroska Scott told us, "Ours is a customer service store. We carry a very good variety of plants, making sure these plants can be grown in Texas, especially for the 'do-it-yourselfers.' We do on-site estimates for customers so they can be assured they are getting the best plants for their home. We try to keep up with the latest information available." Furrow's keeps most of its products in stock at all times and changes with the season as needed. The company also sponsors and advertises on the Neil Sperry radio show. There is much more offered — books, gifts, tools — just about anything you could need for the garden! Merchandise is constantly marked down as new inventory arrives. Advice from Texas Certified Nursery Professionals is always available, and the nursery holds numerous seminars and special events."

## Plantation Gardens

1804 Southern Plantation Drive
College Station, Texas 77845
☎ 409/690-6045
FAX 409/690-6325
**Hours** Mon-Sat 8:30-6, Sun 11-4 (summer); Mon-Sat 8:30-5:30 (winter)
**Accessible** Partially

Plantation Gardens is a complete garden center, carrying a varied selection of plant material — trees and shrubs (including natives), seasonal color, seeds, water plants and supplies, and tropicals. You will also find stepping stones, soil and soil amendments, pest management supplies, furniture, gifts and accessories. According to owner, Charles King, "We owe our success to a quality product and a helpful, knowledgeable staff."

## Producers Cooperative

*1800 North Texas Avenue*
*Bryan, Texas 77803*
☎ *409/778-6000*
**FAX** *409/778-0243*
**Hours** *Mon-Fri 7:30-5:30*
**Accessible** *Yes*

The name might suggest your typical farm store, but this establishment is a model of everything a garden center should be. The plants and "hard goods" in each department are selectively chosen and carefully tended. Manager Elliott L. Head takes pride in hiring specialists in every area of the operation. There are four Master Certified and two Certified Texas Nursery Professionals on board. The nursery works closely with the extension service and the TAMU Horticulture Department, so even the students who are employed here can call a prof if they're stumped by a question! There's always a big selection of adapted and native shrubs and trees and, in spring, lots of perennials available. The entire greenhouse has recently been devoted to water gardening, so you'll not only find lilies, but also such esoteric offerings as bog plants and submersible grasses. In the supply section you'll find the organic products of *Garden-Ville* and *Medina*, as well as chemicals. "We explain all the alternatives and let customers make their choices." There's an excellent selection of books here, and in the garden accessories department, *Henri* statuary, lots of containers, garden benches and swings. Students will notice a nice selection of houseplants in fall.

## *Elgin*

## Red Barn Nursery of Elgin

*Route 3, Box 442C*
*Elgin, Texas 78621*
☎ *512/281-2276*
**FAX** *512/281/2277*
**Hours** *Daily 9-6 (call for extended hours in summer)*
**Accessible** *All except restrooms*

"The specialty at Red Barn is well adapted, low maintenance drought-resistant natives," says owner Jill Sensiba, a Texas Certified Nursery Professional. "We offer cheerful service as well as healthy plants." In addition to trees, shrubs and seasonal color, you'll find herbs, bulbs, seeds and water plants. Soils, soil amendments, pest control products, trellises, birdhouses and garden art, too. Frequent sales are advertised in local papers; watch for the occasional classes and seminars.

*Directions: From Highway 290, go south one mile on Highway 95.*

*Hallettsville/ Shiner*

---

## Janak Nursery

*Highway 90 A*
*Shiner, Texas 77984*
☎ *512/798-3092*
**Hours** *Mon-Sat 8-5, Sun 10-5; closed Sundays (June-Oct)*
**Accessible** *Yes*

At Janak Nursery, you will find a variety of plants, some of them most unusual. The nursery carries everything from bedding plants to cacti, flowering shrubs, staghorn ferns and fruit trees (including three varieties of the hardy jujube). You'll also find a full line of soils, soil amendments and pest control supplies. The gift shop offers canned jujube delicacies, as well as all kinds of pots and baskets. Garden advice is free, and sales are held in April and May. See page 313 to order jujube trees.

*Directions: Janak Nursery is between Hallettsville and Shiner, six miles west of Hallettsville.*

---

## Jo's Green Hut & Nursery

*Route 4, Box 249B*
*Hallettsville, Texas 77964*
☎ *512/798-2209*
**Hours** *Mon-Fri 8:30-5:30, Sat 8:30-1*
**Accessible** *No*

As Jo Kutac describes her "Green Hut & Nursery, "We have a small retail establishment located next to our home, just 2½ miles west of town. We specialize in individual attention to our customers, whom we also consider our friends. We keep our nursery as neat as we can because it is, in a sense, part of our home's landscape." Along with a nice selection of plant materials, this nursery grows live oak trees in various size containers. You'll also find materials for walks and patios, soils, pest management supplies and concrete statuary.

---

*Hearne*

---

## Four Seasons Garden Center

*1602 Market*
*Hearne, Texas 77856*
☎ *409/279-5640*
**Hours** *Mon-Sat 8-6, Sun 10-6*
**Accessible** *Yes*

As Claudette Freeman told us, "We're a very laid-back nursery. We have no high-pressure salespeople, and we encourage our customers to browse at their own pace. We have many statewide visitors who stop by every time they are in the area. They really like our quality stock, reasonable prices and friendly, professional staff." Four Seasons carries a variety of plants, including natives, cacti, trees and shrubs. You will also find soils, pest management supplies, garden books and tools, and there is always a sale table.

## Madisonville

### Texian Country Nursery & Garden Shop

*Route 1, Box 243*
*Madisonville, Texas 77864*
☎ *409/348-5454*
**Hours** *Wed-Sat 9-6, Sun 2-6*
**Accessible** *Partially*

This is a nursery with a real personal touch. As owner, Margaret Baker says," We design, select or suggest for every project as if it were our own." Texian offers a nice assortment of plant material, especially promoting the concept of xeriscaping and the use of native plants and trees. The nursery carries 96 varieties of antique roses, and the garden shop has wind chimes, birdhouses, garden books, customized gift baskets, arbors and garden art. The owners are happy to give presentations to civic groups, churches, garden clubs or schools as well as advice to customers. They'll even provide delivery within 30 miles.

*Directions: Located on Highway 21, six miles west of Madisonville Square.*

## Seguin

### Gentry's Green Gate Garden Center

*990 South 123 By-Pass*
*Seguin, Texas 78155*
☎ *830/379-8832*
**FAX** *830/379-8926*
**Hours** *Mon-Sat 8-5:30, Sun 9-5*
**Accessible** *Yes*

Gentry's Green Gate occupies a 15-acre site with over three acres of greenhouse space! Five of the greenhouses are open to the public; the others are filled with an array of colorful annuals and perennials in various stages of growth. The company also buys trees, shrubs and tropicals from a select list of vendors. Says owner George Gentry, "Since we grow much of our stock, it is often of better quality and a much lower price." George's family owns nurseries in Laredo and Brownsville, and his decision to purchase this well-established Central Texas nursery ensures that it will continue into the future. The Green Gate also carries a good selection of seasonal stock, including fabulous poinsettias, and lots of garden gifts and accessories. The company doesn't advertise, but "customers come from miles around!" There are occasional sales, but not on any regular basis.

*Directions: Take exit 610 south off IH-10 and continue south about four miles on 123 By-Pass.*

## Temple/ Belton/ Killeen Area

### Cen-Tex Nursery

*3220 FM 2086*
*Temple, Texas 76501*
☎ *254/773-5191*
**FAX** *254/742-2415*
**Hours** *Mon-Sat 8-5:30*
**Accessible** *Partially (gravel surfaces are difficult)*

"We offer a country atmosphere, away from the hustle and bustle of the city, yet we're a pleasant drive away. We try to provide as much personal attention as

*(Listing continued on next page)*

possible to make our customers feel important," comments Alvin D. Simcik, owner and Texas Master Certified Nurseryman. The plants you'll find here are recommended and proven for the area; the owners specialize in natives and stock as many as possible. The recently remodeled selling area is referred to as the "Showroom!" He adds, "People have really enjoyed it because they can look all they want and, when ready to purchase, be helped by one of us." The nursery carries everything needed for planting and maintaining a landscape and offers landscape design and a fertilization program for lawns. The staff mails a monthly newsletter and also presents programs to various service organizations.

*Directions: Take Exit 304 off IH-35 and turn east. Go on Loop 363 about two miles. At the blinking light, turn left on FM 438, go about .9 mile and turn right on FM 2086.*

## Earthscapes

*5317 Loop 205*
*Temple, Texas 76502*
☎ *254/773-4668*
**FAX** *254/773-0816*
**Hours** *Tues-Sat 9:00-5:30, Sun 1-5, closed Mon*
**Accessible** *Yes*

This nursery is owned and operated by Mike and Kay Lynch, both talented landscape architects (Nan's classmates at Texas A&M), who are committed to the highest quality in everything they offer to the public. Earthscapes is an elegant garden center with attractively designed planting displays outdoors and a 12,000-square-foot tropical greenhouse. The indoor showroom is housed in an architecturally attractive building, and the decks, arbors and even the parking area are all designed to provide inspiration for homeowners. In addition to landscape plants, you'll find herbs, garden and nature gift items and an extensive Christmas shop here. Specialties include topiary (indoor and outdoor) and a wide array of perennials and native plants. Earthscapes offers expert advice, great plants and more — gardener's bliss!

*Directions: From IH-35, take West Loop 363 and exit to FM 2305 West. Take the first right to Loop 205.*

## Tem-Bel Nursery & Landscaping

*5300 South General Bruce Drive (IH-35)*
*Temple, Texas 76502*
☎ *254/778-5651*
**FAX** *254/778-0736*
**Hours** *Mon-Fri 9-5:30, Sat 9-5*
**Accessible** *Yes*

Since 1967, Tem-Bel has offered a large variety of plants that do well in the area. Comments David Lockwood, "Our sales staff is knowledgeable, and the plants are well-tended year-round." In addition to trees, shrubs, bedding plants and tropicals, you'll find such accessories as pottery, birdbaths and feeders. Watch for specials in the Saturday newspaper. The company provides design and construction services, including walks and drainage, as well as plant installation.

## Waco

### Westview Nursery & Landscape Company

1136 North Valley Mills Drive
Waco, Texas 76710
☎ 254/772-7890
**FAX** 254/772-7894

10000 Woodway Drive
Waco, Texas 76712
☎ 254/776-2334

**Hours** Mon-Sat 8-6, Sun 12-5 (Valley Mills); Mon-Sat 8:30-5:30 (Woodway)
**Accessible** Yes, both locations

Four generations of the family have been active in this landscape design company/ garden center during its 41-year history. Now headed by landscape architect Eugene Houck, Westview is known as "the place you can get answers." You'll find a lot of everything here. There's always a big selection of trees (shade and fruit) and good choices in shrubs, seasonal color, herbs, ground covers, seeds and indoor plants. The plants are healthy, and the knowledgeable staff is there to lend support. For your walks and walls, there are rocks, gravel and timbers. Finishing touches include fountains, statuary, trellises, arbors, birdhouses and feeders. You'll also find good books and tools here. Shoppers will tell you, "Westview has the best stock in town." Westview provides a fertilizer service (four times per year). Large ads appear in the Waco paper informing customers of sales.

## Hill Country
### Austin Metropolitan Area

### AAA Grass & Landscape, Inc.

5910 Highway 290 West
Austin, Texas 78735
☎ 512/892-3636
**FAX** 512/892-7272
**Hours** Mon-Sat 8-6, Sun 10-4
**Accessible** Yes

AAA is noted for its down-home, comfortable and friendly atmosphere. There are lots of plants here — shrubs and trees, seasonal color, natives, water plants, cacti, tropicals... and, of course, grass. Says Trey Wyatt, "Whether you're looking for a plant to fill an empty spot or to landscape your whole yard, AAA can give you the help you need. You can be sure you'll find your vegetable starts, seeds, tools, materials for walks and patios, soil and soil amendments, pest control supplies, garden accessories, pots and fountains here too. There's a lot to see, so be prepared to stay awhile!" Sales are held weekly during the peak season. Good advice is always available.

### Barton Springs Nursery

3601 Bee Cave Road
Austin, Texas 78746
☎ 512/328-6655
**Hours** Mon-Sat 9-6, Sun 10-6
**Accessible** Yes

This nursery embodies the essence of the "Austin Hill Country!" Last time we visited, Barton Springs was still "a work-in-progress," but the atmosphere at its new upscale location remains as rustic and relaxed as the old place we knew and

*(Listing continued on next page)*

loved. This nursery established its fine reputation by specializing in native Texas and well adapted plants *before* they became popular. Now it lays claim to "the largest selection of perennials in the city of Austin and possibly Texas!" The retail area covers approximately 2½ acres, and it's filled with beautiful display gardens and quiet sitting spaces. You will find all the plant materials that are well suited for Austin gardens, as well as tools, books, soil and soil amendments, pest control supplies, gifts and accessories. Barton Springs Nursery features three garden speakers in the spring (March, April, May) and a Native Plant Week at the end of September.

---

## Gardens

*1818 West 35th Street*
*Austin, Texas 78703*
☎ *512/451-5490*
**FAX** *512/451-4523*
**Hours** *Mon-Sat 9-6, Sun 11-5*
**Accessible** *Yes*

To give you some idea how special this place is, suffice it to say that it has been featured in *Metropolitan Home, Texas Monthly's Domaine, Horticulture, House Beautiful* and in the *New York Times* Home Design section. During its 17 years, Gardens has introduced Texans to more hard-to-find perennials and shrubs than even Nan can name. "We cater to customers who are intensely interested in gardening," says Gary Peese. Inside the garden shop, you'll discover imported seeds from England and Italy, garden books and magazines you can't find anywhere else, an array of fine Italian terra cotta containers and much more. (See page 380 for information about the furniture and accessories.) The knowledgeable staff includes two botanists, one horticulturist, three landscape architects, an architect and several designers. The firm also provides installation and construction. Sales are held in the summer and winter. Ask about scheduled garden tours of homes designed by Gardens.

---

## Garden-Ville of Austin

*8648 Old Bee Cave Road*
*Austin, Texas 78735*
☎ *512/288-6113*
**FAX** *512/288-6114*
**Hours** *Mon-Fri 8-5:30, Sat 8-5, Sun 10-4 (June -Feb);*
*Mon-Fri 8-6, Sat 8-5, Sun 10-5 (March-May)*
**Accessible** *Yes*

John Dromgoole has been dedicated to the organic technique of gardening for the past 27 years. As he can tell you, "In that time I have never lost a tree, shrub, lawn or garden because the organic did not meet certain standards. We have taught literally thousands of gardeners about organics. You, too, can garden organically and successfully." You'll find a great selection of plants, books, tools, soils and organic pest control supplies here. And several new display gardens have made this nursery a destination for gardeners: an herb display by Lucinda Hutson, a vegetable garden designed for photography in *Organic Gardening* and a marvelous orchard. A butterfly garden is in the planning stage. "We will be glad to share our non-toxic approach. You, your neighbors, your pets and your children will all benefit the day you 'go organic,'" says John. There's no lack of advice available at this nursery! John writes for *Texas Gardening Magazine* and also hosts a weekly radio show on KLBJ 590 on Sat 6-8 and Sun 8-10. The company holds sales throughout the year. *Directions: From Loop 1 South, exit Southwest Parkway, go west 4½ miles, turn left on Travis Cook Road, which will dead-end into Old Bee Caves Road.*

## Great Hills Garden Center

*6914 McNeil Drive*
*Austin, Texas 78729*
☎ *512/219-9600*
**FAX** *512/219-6635*
**Hours** *Mon-Sat 9-6, Sun 10-5*
**Accessible** *Yes*

Seasonal color is the draw here. Because Great Hills grows almost all of its own bedding plants, it can offer almost wholesale prices to the public. "We also 'jump-up' last year's plants for a great size and a great price. We have sales year-round," staff members told us. Backed by 11 years of experience in northwest Austin and a stable, knowledgeable staff, this company provides installation services for all available materials.

## Howard Nursery

*111 East Koenig Lane*
*Austin, Texas 78751*
☎ *512/453-3150*
**FAX** *512/453-2068*
**Hours** *Mon-Sat 9-5:30, Sun 10-5*
**Accessible** *Almost completely*

If you "grew-up" in Austin, you know Howard Nursery! Family owned and operated since 1912, it is run by Hank Howard, Jim Howard, Robin Howard Moore and a knowledgeable and helpful staff. In addition to a large selection of annuals, perennials, ground covers, trees and shrubs, you will find a spacious greenhouse full of tropicals, cacti and succulents. There's also a huge selection of ceramic and wicker plant containers. Howard's carries beautiful fountains, wind chimes, sundials, bird feeders and glass gazing balls, as well as organic and chemical fertilizers and pest controls. As Robin Moore will tell you, "We take pride in having quality plants and giving quality help."

## Park Place Gardens

*2710 Hancock Drive*
*Austin, Texas 78731*
☎ *512/458-5909*
**FAX** *512/458-8833*
*www.austingardens.com*
**Hours** *Daily 8:30-6; Closed Thanksgiving day, Christmas day and New Years day*
**Accessible** *Yes*

Don't be misled by your first impression of this converted gas station. It's not only much larger than it looks, but also much more sophisticated! Park Place carries a huge selection of perennials, including many that are hard-to-find. Also expect to see great seasonal bedding plants, specimen trees, rare palms, cactus, herbs, and antique roses. As owner Tom McElhenney told us, "Besides the usual, we specialize in native Texas plants and design." Tom's business card, which looks like a Monopoly card, provides a hint of the whimsy that makes this place so lovable. We never fail to find something unexpected in the way of garden ornaments here, and there's usually a spectacular selection of pottery and fountains, as well. Park Place Gardens holds a sale after Christmas, and garden advice is always available from an exceptionally knowledgeable staff.

## Pots & Plants

5902 Bee Cave Road
Austin, Texas 78746
☎ 512/327-4564
**FAX** 512/328-5965
**Hours** Mon-Sat 9-6, Sun 10-5
**Accessible** Partially

Now, this is a nursery "with an attitude!" You'll know you have arrived when you see a flock of pink plastic flamingos, which, by the way, have been officially proclaimed "Fine Art" by the City of Westlake Hills. According to owner Pat Swanson, "The 'scout bird' usually arrives mid-February, a true harbinger of spring. The rest of the flock arrives about two weeks later." If a laugh is good for the soul, so is the shady, inviting atmosphere at Pots & Plants. You will find natives, antique roses, seasonal color, herbs, tropicals, handmade hanging baskets, topiaries, garden gifts, books, European hand tools, teak furniture and much more. As you must have guessed, we were impressed and delighted! The friendly, professional staff includes a degreed horticulturist, a licensed irrigator and a Texas Master Certified Professional. Pots & Plants offers a wonderful Christmas Tree Program, which includes free delivery and, best of all, free haul-off after the holidays. Be sure to call ahead and get your name on the list.

## Red Barn Garden Centers

13858 Highway 183 North
Austin, Texas 78750
☎ 512/335-8093
**FAX** 512/258-7776

620 West Slaughter Lane
Austin, Texas 78748
☎ 512/280-9898
**FAX** 512/282-9503

**Hours** Daily 9-7
**Accessible** Yes

"Our northside location is a friendly neighborhood nursery in a park-like three-acre setting with pecan trees and lots of shade. The southside store features an 8,000-square-foot, state-of-the-art greenhouse where all flowering plants and tropicals are kept in tip-top shape. Both stores offer a wide selection of plants, good prices and a very knowledgeable staff (six Certified Texas Nursery Professionals and three who are Master Certified," says owner Emily McDaniel. These garden centers carry a large number of natives and perennials. New focus is on increasing the selection of water plants, pond supplies and fountains. There are, of course, tools, books, accessories, soil and soil amendments and pest management supplies. At Red Barn, you will find weekly sales and always friendly, professional advice.

## Sledd Nursery

1211 West Lynn
Austin, Texas 78703
☎ 512/478-9977
**FAX** 512/478-2608
**Hours** Mon-Sat 8:30-5:30, Sun 10-5
**Accessible** Yes

Sledd's has "served three generations of great Austin gardeners!" The clientele is, of course, citywide, but the West Austin crowd is both "legion and loyal." As one customer said, "I go to the grocery store, the drug store, the cleaners, and then I stop at Sledd's!" According to the owner, "Our employees have all been in the nursery business from 10 to 40 years. We not only carry the highest quality plants, but we also offer complete service. We assist in your selection; we deliver, pot or plant and are happy to answer questions and offer advice." Sledd's carries garden related products from pots and baskets to soil amendments, pest management supplies, tools and gifts. Good specials are offered regularly.

## Wolfe Nursery

4715 South Lamar Boulevard
Austin, Texas 78745
☎ 512/892-4926

8701 Research
Austin, Texas 78758
☎ 512/339-6268

1900 South Bell Boulevard
Cedar Park, Texas 78613
☎ 512/331-9510

See complete text on page 215.

# Blanco/ Kendalia

## Little Acres Nursery & Landscape

Route 1, Box 275
Kendalia, Texas 78027
☎ 830/885-7644
**Hours** Mon-Sat 9-5, Sun 10-5
**Accessible** Yes

"From a small sale to a big sale, everybody gets the same service. We treat them right!" says Al Mogavero. In addition to a large selection of trees and shrubs, Little Acres carries herbs and seasonal color. You'll find materials for patios and walks, outdoor lighting, soils, drip irrigation equipment, pest management supplies, tools, books and gifts here.

*Directions: Little Acres is six miles south of Blanco. Take 473 one mile past Kendalia.*

## Main Street Garden Center

500 Main Street (Highway 281)
Blanco, Texas 78606
☎ 830/833-2199
**Hours** Wed-Sat 10-6
**Accessible** Yes

Main Street Garden Center is very obviously a "labor of love!" The brochure puts it this way, "We strive to produce and offer quality plants, seeds, trees, birds and rabbits." Perhaps the first thing to catch your attention will be the aviary in the center of the garden. Under an old native pecan tree, the ringneck doves are cooing and nodding. The gardens are full of beautiful annuals and perennials. Native trees are well represented, including Blanco crabapple, Mexican plum, bur, shumard, live and texana oaks, Texas pistache, Texas ash, vitex and honey locust. Says Debbie Gray," I promote plants that are low maintenance, well adapted and require less water. I often speak on herbs and carry a large selection. Herbs enhance our lives and gardening in general," she observes. You will also find a variety of garden books, tools and gift items here.

## *Fredericksburg*

---

### Dodds Family Tree Nursery

*515 West Main*
*Fredericksburg, Texas 78624*
☎ *830/997-9571*
**FAX** *830/997-9216*
**Hours** *Mon-Sat 8-6, Sun 12-5*
**Accessible** *Yes*

John Dodds describes his nursery as "a very whimsical destination — a must to see in Fredericksburg." What we found was an ever-expanding test garden display area, a fascinating assortment of native plants and perennials that bloom and grow under the 200-foot-tall canopy of a spreading live oak. We really enjoyed our stroll through the place and could have stayed all day. Dodds carries lots of interesting garden items, both hardscape and plant materials. Sales are in late May, and garden advice is always available. The company offers a full-service landscape department and floral division.

---

### Langerhans Florist & Nursery, Inc.

*205 South Elk Street*
*Fredericksburg, Texas 78624*
☎ *830/997-9578*
**Hours** *Mon-Fri 8-5, Sat 9-1*
**Accessible** *No*

Langerhans has been a Fredericksburg institution since 1946. With 12,000-square-feet of greenhouse space, this nursery carries a huge stock of native plants, grasses, ornamental trees and shrubs, lots of seasonal color, container plants, hanging baskets and vegetable starts and seeds. Landscape design services are offered, and Langerhans is known for its patios and waterfalls built of native field stone. Carletta Smith happily reports, "We have excellent personal contact with our customers. We offer gardening, landscaping and maintenance advice on a daily basis." Mid-summer sales feature roses, fruit and nut trees and other plant materials.

## *Georgetown/ Round Rock/ Pflugerville*

---

### Green 'n Growing

*601 West Pecan*
*Pflugerville, Texas 78660*
☎ *512/251-3262*
**Hours** *Mon-Fri 9-6:30, Sat 9-6, Sun 11-5 (daylight saving time); Mon-Sat 9-6, Sun 11-5 throughout the year*
**Accessible** *Difficult*

Green 'n Growing maintains real depth in natives and carries a wide selection of adapted trees, shrubs and seasonal plants, as well. You'll find tools, books, gifts, soils and pest management supplies. This nursery is very attuned to the importance of xeriscape plants and prides itself on the "unusual and hard-to-find." As Rhonda Pfluger assured us, "We have a very knowledgeable sales staff and healthy plants. There is a good selection all year, not just at peak season."

*Directions: From IH-35, exit at 1825. Go east for about three miles.*

## McIntire's Garden Center

303 Leander Road
Georgetown, Texas 78626
☎ 512/863-8243
**FAX** 512/869-0987
**Hours** Mon-Sat 8-6 (March-Dec), 9-5:30 (Jan-Feb), Sun 11-5 (year round)
**Accessible** Yes

Ruby McIntire reports, "We are a complete garden center. In addition to plants, trees, shrubs and other garden-related products, we carry fountains, birdbaths and Christmas trees." The company provides landscape consultation, design and installation, as well as an annual program of Fertilome lawn care and lawn irrigation (design and installation of sprinkler systems.) The staff is friendly and professional. There's a fall sale in October and a spring sale in May. The "Four Star" sales occur in February, April, June and August.

## Murffy's Nursery

901 Sam Bass Road
Round Rock 78681
☎ 512/255-3353
**Hours** Mon-Fri 9-6 (spring & summer) 9-5 (fall and winter), Sat 9-5, Sun 11-4 (spring and summer), by appointment on Sun in fall and winter
**Accessible** Yes

Rosarians from all around the Austin metropolitan area come here for roses. Of the over 250 varieties of roses, about a third are antique and old garden roses. The hybrid varieties arrive bare-root, are planted in a rose mix in a plantable pot to reduce transplant shock, and receive lots of TLC while they live at Murffy's. You'll also be impressed with the selection of water plants, ponds and the lovely water demonstration garden. There's a Texas native section, an array of fruit trees and excellent houseplants, including a wide variety of named orchids, in addition to bedding plants and basic shrubs and trees. "I just love all the advice they've given me over the years," a customer told us while we were waiting to visit with the manager, Laurie Daugherty. This nursery leans heavily towards organic gardening, and we were happy to discover a very impressive array of organic products as well as good pots and tools. We found it an especially pleasant place to visit because the plants are displayed under the shade of large old trees. Owner Claire Smith runs the landscaping division of the company.

## Kerrville

## The Greenery

1245 Bandera Highway
Kerrville, Texas 78028
☎ 830/896-7553
**FAX** 830/896-7266
**Hours** Mon-Sat 8-5, Sun 12-4 (closed Sat after noon and Sun in winter)
**Accessible** Yes

The Greenery carries trees, shrubs, ground covers, natives, tropicals, bedding and blooming plants as well as a good selection of wildflower seeds. It also offers a full-service florist, landscape design and installation as well as year-round maintenance. The owner, John Coleman, who is a Texas Certified Nursery Professional, writes landscaping articles for the local paper and usually teaches adult classes in the evening. He's very willing to provide advice to gardeners.

## The Plant Haus 2

*528 Jefferson Street*
*Kerrville, Texas 78028*
☎ *830/792-4444*
**Hours** *Mon-Sat 8-6, Sun 10-4 (Mar-Oct); Mon-Sat 8-5 (Nov-Feb), Sun 8-5 (Nov & Dec)*
**Accessible** *Yes*
**FAX** *830/792-4442*
See complete listing on opposite page.

## New Braunfels/ Canyon Lake

## Hill Country Nursery

*1398 FM 2673*
*Canyon Lake, Texas 78133*
☎ *210/964-3628*
**FAX** *210/964-3608*
**Hours** *Mon-Sat 9-5:30, Sun 11-5:30*
**Accessible** *Partially (outdoor area)*

When Pat, Mark and Pam Ford opened Hill Country Nursery several years ago, they determined to carry only plants that do well in the area. There are a few exceptions, but the Fords explain, "We make sure our customers know those plants' special needs so that they can be successful with them." The specialty at Hill Country Nursery is water gardening, but there are lots of plants from which to chose, and the owners are always "looking for the unusual." You will also find gift items and handicrafts, as well as books, tools and other garden-related needs, including rental equipment. "We try to manage the nursery with a lot of friendliness, good humor and advice."

*Directions: Take Canyon Lake exit (FM 306) off of IH-35 in New Braunfels. Follow 306 to Canyon Lake and take a left on FM 2673.*

## Otto M. Locke Nursery

*2515 West San Antonio*
*New Braunfels, Texas 78130*
☎ *830/609-4523*
**FAX** *830/620-4965*
**Hours** *Mon-Sat 9-5; Sundays 12-4 (March through June)*
**Accessible** *Yes*

As owner Joe Ed Lyles proudly points out, "Locke's is the oldest nursery in Texas where history, nature and old fashioned service come alive! We have no cash register, no computers and no non-caring sales people." The plant selection includes natives, grasses, trees and shrubs, seasonal color, vegetable starts and seeds, water plants, container plants and hanging baskets. You will also find books, furniture, soil and pest management supplies. Locke's sits on ten acres of tall trees with beautiful display beds and has something else to offer. Your children will be fascinated by the peacocks, pygmy goats, ducks, guineas, squirrels, snapping turtles, iguanas, silky chickens and prairie dog village.

## The Plant Haus

*956 North Walnut*
*New Braunfels, Texas 78130*
☎ 830/629-2401
**FAX** *830/629-0962*
**Hours** *Mon-Sat 8-6, Sun 10-4 (Mar-Oct); Mon-Sat 8-5 (Nov-Feb); open Sun 8-5 (Nov & Dec)*
**Accessible** *Yes*

The Plant Haus is a full-service nursery with two locations in Central Texas. As Weston Pacharzina says, "If you see it and like it, you better take it now, because it won't be here later!" These bright, airy garden centers carry lots of plants native to the Hill Country. Of course, there are ornamental trees and shrubs, annuals, perennials, bulbs, hanging baskets, bonsai, cacti, tropicals, vegetable starts and seeds, as well. Most of the hanging baskets and bedding plants are grown on-site. You can also find materials for walks, patios and retaining walls as well as soil and soil amendments, pest management supplies and garden tools. Both locations carry lots of bird baths and fountains. Over-stock sales on plant materials are held periodically.

## San Marcos

## Garden-Ville of San Marcos

*2212 Ranch Road 12*
*San Marcos, Texas 78666*
☎ 512/754-0060
**FAX** *512/396-2214*
**Hours** *Mon-Sat 8:30-5:30, Sun 12-4; closed the week between Christmas and New Year's Day and on Sundays in January*
**Accessible** *Yes*

Garden-Ville of San Marcos sells and promotes only organic and environmentally sound gardening supplies and products. The plants you'll find here are either native or well adapted to this part of Texas. Says owner Martha Latta, "Our goal is to turn people on to the joys of gardening...naturally!" Her charming little garden center specializes in hard-to-find plants, such as naturalizing bulbs and perennials in 4" pots. It carries an eclectic mix of garden accessories and gift items and takes pride in personalized services such as re-potting plants, diagnosing plant problems, and creating custom gift baskets, arrangements or floral decorations. As a landscape architect, she's able to provide expert design advice. Of course, you can get all the wonderful Garden-Ville organic products here, too. Watch for sales during the month of January and on Labor Day weekend. You'll find fact sheets on many gardening topics and visiting experts several times a year.

## Wimberley

## Natural Gardens

*15401 Ranch Road 12*
*Wimberley, Texas 78676*
☎ 512/847-1239
**FAX** *512/847-7615*
**Hours** *Mon-Sat 9:30-5:30, Sun 10-4*
**Accessible** *Partially*

Natural Gardens is a complete garden center specializing in native and adapted Hill Country plants. As Allan Dyer and John Anderson told us, "Most customers in

*(Listing continued on next page)*

our area have poor, limestone rock and caliche soils so typical to this area and also suffer with an ever-increasing deer population. We offer creative solutions to both. We practice xeriscaping and organic methods at the nursery, as well as in the landscapes we design and install." In addition to a wide selection of plant material, you will find seeds, soils, drip irrigation equipment, pottery, garden books and various other supplies for the home and garden. Natural Gardens offers a comfortable, friendly atmosphere with consultants ready to offer help and suggestions.

## *Red Rolling Plains*
### *Abilene*

### Baack's Landscaping & Nursery

*1842 Matador*
*Abilene, Texas 79605*
☎ *915/692-7763*
**FAX** *915/691-9441*
**Hours** *Mon-Sat 8-5:30; open Sun 1-5 in spring*
**Accessible** *Partially*

Over the years Baack's has established its reputation as a garden center for "the serious gardener," offering hard-to-find selections and wide varieties of well-adapted perennials, herbs and shrubs. It was the first in the area to carry antique roses and David Austin English roses, and it's known throughout the area for zonal geraniums and bougainvilleas. Its award-winning, full-service florist provides area deliveries, and the nursery will also deliver merchandise upon request. Baack's has full landscaping design services available. Sales are held Mother's Day and Memorial Day weekends. Staff members offer seminars on organic gardening, roses, planting container gardens and other areas of interest.

### Garden Place

*4002 North First Street*
*Abilene, Texas 79603*
☎ *915/676-0086*
**FAX** *915/676-8750*
**Hours** *Mon-Sat 9-6, Sun 12-6*
**Accessible** *Yes*

Scott Warren, a Master Certified Nursery Professional, spent quite a bit of time telling us about Garden Place. Its special niche is the promotion of xeriscape plants and all of the organic supplies to keep the garden healthy. The nursery's other specialties are perennials and herbs. In spring you'll find more than 200 perennials and between 50 and 75 different herbs in stock. Trees here range from small to large B&B and container-grown stock. Indoors, there are houseplants, pottery and fountains, books, tools and collectibles.

### Garden World

*2850 South Clack Street*
*Abilene, Texas 79606*
☎ *915/698-2401*
**FAX** *915/698-6739*
**Hours** *Mon-Sat 9-6, Sun 1-6*
**Accessible** *Yes*

Five Certified Texas Nursery Professionals are on duty here to help do-it-yourself gardeners. The company takes pride in the quantity and quality of its plant materials (including natives) and landscape supplies. You'll find soils and mulches, pottery, statuary and fountains, plus a wide variety of houseplants and gifts.

## The Gardens of the Southwest

*5250 South 14th Street*
*Abilene, Texas 79605*
☎ *915-692-1457*
**Hours** *Mon-Sat 8-5*
**Accessible** *Yes*

Our first impression of The Gardens of the Southwest was a lovely surprise in its residential setting. It is set back from the street among beautiful, large trees and raised stone planters. Not a full-scale garden center, The Gardens of the Southwest specializes in specimen trees and shrubs. The trees come in all sizes (both container and B&B) and include native, ornamental and fruit trees. The shrubs are hearty for the area and include interesting conifers. Rodney Fulcher, who is the owner and a Texas Registered Landscape Architect, told us, "I've been in business since 1971 and have done a lot of repeat business... three, four, even five residences for some people. This firm is quality- and customer-oriented, and we're good 'problem solvers!'" You'll find a good selection of garden furniture and accessories here, as well (see page 382). The prices at The Gardens of the Southwest are competitive, and Mr. Fulcher has years of experience to offer. He's a most welcome speaker at area garden clubs.

## *San Angelo*

## Olive's Nursery

*3402 Sherwood Way*
*San Angelo, Texas 76901*
☎ *915/949-3756*
**FAX** *915/949-3758*
**Hours** *Mon-Sat 9-6*
**Accessible** *Yes*

W.E. Olive, grandfather of present owner Tommy Olive, opened Olive Seed Store in 1942 in downtown San Angelo. In 1951 Tommy's father, John, moved the store and started carrying quality nursery stock. "When my mother, Mary, came on board, she brought a flair for color and garden accessories. We try to maintain a setting that's beautiful and comfortable, not a lot of steel and concrete." This complete garden center is also dedicated to keeping the nursery business local. Olive's not only has a very knowledgeable staff but also is competitive in price, even with the chain stores. "Just bring in their ad," he challenges. Long-time customers eagerly await the annual Christmas half-price sale on December 26th. It is also interesting to note that one of the employees, Ken Landon, is a leading hybridizers of water lilies. Olive's newest addition is the water garden display, complete with a waterfall and some "wild life." But Tommy warns, "Please don't bring your boat. The Coast Guard patrols our pond for speeders!"

## Scherz Landscape Co.

*2225 Knickerbocker*
*San Angelo, Texas 76904*
☎ *915/944-0511*
**FAX** *915/949-7224*
**Hours** *Mon-Fri 9-6, Sat 9-5; open Sun 1-5 (March-June)*
**Accessible** *Yes*

This company, established in 1927 by Phillip Scherz, is as "well-rooted in the West Texas soil as the nursery stock we grow and sell." The firm grows 85-90 % of its plant materials, which assures the customer of stock that's acclimated to West Texas growing conditions. Scherz is both a retail and wholesale nursery, and it provides landscape design and construction, with licensed irrigators on staff. Second and third generation family members, as well as landscape architects and graduate horticulturists, all happily to offer assistance. You'll be pleased to find such a large diversity of plant materials and sizes. The stock ranges from trees to seeds, with lots of seasonal color and native plants. Says Kyle Conway, "We have specific interest in growing specimen and unique items that do well in West Texas. We are producers of the "Concho Valley Live Oak" and Scherz Green-Up fertilizer." Look for bargains in September and October. Delivery is provided within 100 miles.

## Wichita Falls Area

## Berend Bros.

*4313 Seymour Highway*
*Wichita Falls, Texas 76309*
☎ *940/691-1141*

*4311 Jacksboro Highway*
*Wichita Falls, Texas 76302*
☎ *940/723-2736*

*IH-44 at Daniels Road*
*Burkburnett, Texas 76354*
☎ *940/569-2272*
**FAX** *940/569-2273*

*Clay at Mason*
*Bowie, Texas 76230*
☎ *940/872-5131*

*Highway 281 South*
*Windthorse, Texas 76389*
☎ *940/423-6223*

**Hours** *Mon-Sat 8-6; open Sundays 11-4 (Wichita Falls & Burkeburnett locations only)*
**Accessible** *Yes*

Founded as a feed store over 60 years ago, this company has developed a strategy that well-serves gardeners in a six-county area of North Central Texas. All of the stores carry plant materials, soils, soil amendments, fertilizers and tools. However, each store is different. Between them, you are sure to find everything you may need. All are within an hour's drive, and there's frequent travel and communication among the staff, which includes five Texas Certified Nursery Professionals and one who is Master Certified. The Jacksboro Highway store is the "showplace," with a degreed horticulturist who specializes in organics. Here you'll find all of the decorative accessories — statuary, fountains, hanging baskets, wind chimes, bird houses, etc., plus garden books and gifts. The Seymour Highway store specializes in the sales and service of lawn equipment. The Windthorse and Bowie locations specialize in seasonal color, and the Burkburnett store carries a large selection of shrubs and trees. The staff is committed to providing all the assistance customers may need. Berend Bros. offers tours and classes for children (complete with activities and books) in conjunction with the schools. What an excellent way to ensure the company's growth for the next 60 years!

## Holt Nursery & Landscape

*3913 Kell Boulevard West*
*Wichita Falls, Texas 76308*
☎ *940/691-4757*
**Hours** *Mon-Fri 8-5:30, Sat 9-5*
**Accessible** *Yes*

"Serving the Wichita Falls area since 1974," Holt Nursery & Landscape carries ornamental trees and shrubs, annuals, perennials and bulbs, fruit trees, vegetable starts, hanging baskets and cacti. The company also provides landscape design, irrigation systems, sodding and hydromulching. Charles Astwood, who received a degree in horticulture from Texas Tech, is there to help with your landscape and irrigation needs.

## Wichita Valley Landscape

*5314 Southwest Parkway*
*Wichita Falls, Texas 76310*
☎ *940/696-3082*
**Hours** *Mon-Fri 8-6, Sat 9-6, Sun 12-6 (Sundays during spring and fall only)*
**Accessible** *Yes*

"What makes Wichita Valley Landscape different from other nurseries in Wichita Falls is that this company specializes in native plants and organic products," says Paul Dowlearn. He's convinced that today's consumer wants low-maintenance landscapes and safe pesticides. "We are constantly bringing in new plant material to experiment with in our area. This makes the business exciting for us and for our customers," he says. "We tend to have what can't be found elsewhere in our town. We're definitely not just another sales-oriented nursery!" The company offers handmade items (as opposed to mass-produced merchandise) and creates its own bonsai, water features and plant arrangements. It has a good collection of garden books and reference materials. He adds, "We especially enjoy working with people who want to develop more natural, easier-to-maintain properties. There are new horizons opening up in this part of the state, and we are proud to be a part of it." Wichita Valley actively supports garden clubs, municipal projects, a chapter of the native plant society and the River Bend Nature Works. "Sales are random because everyday prices are competitive."

# High Plains
## Amarillo

## Coulter Gardens and Nursery

*4200 South Coulter*
*Amarillo, Texas 79109*
☎ *806/359-7432*
**FAX** *806/355-1633*
**Hours** *Daily 9-6; open 9:30-5:30 during the off season*
**Accessible** *Yes*

When you enter the "big red barn," you have the feeling that it goes on and on! Everything you could want can be found in this clean, cheery place. There's a large greenhouse with bedding and container plants, and you'll find a big selection of trees and shrubs drawn from sources throughout the country. We inquired about everything from natives and grasses to water plants and seeds — Coulter's has it! The nursery also carries materials for walks and patios, soil and soil amendments, pest

*(Listing continued on next page)*

management supplies, tools, books, gifts and accessories. Having been in business for 18 years, owners Jim and Warren Reid feel that their clientele is loyal because of the quality of the materials and the helpful customer service. "We think we have the most knowledgeable staff in the Panhandle. This claim is supported by the large number of Texas Certified Nursery Professionals who work here!" Sales are seasonal. Coulter's is a rewarding place to shop for both garden or patio.

## The Gardens at Pete's Greenhouse

*7300 Canyon Drive*
*Amarillo, Texas 79109*
☎ *806/352-1664*
**FAX** *806/352-5609*
**Hours** *Mon-Sat 9-6, Sun 1-5*
**Accessible** *Yes*

When we arrived at The Gardens at Pete's Greenhouse, we thought we had "died and gone to heaven"...or maybe to Europe! The atmosphere here is warm and welcoming with honeysuckle vines and an arborvitae arch through which you pass to the ponds and a charming selection of gifts, furniture and antiques. According to owner Darren Ruthardt, "We go to market every year to find the best selection of indoor and outdoor garden accessories. Our plants are second to none; we're known as the "plant specialist." Because the plant material is grown in nearby White Deer, this nursery can offer a great selection on a daily basis. Inside, there are tools and books, as well as friendly service and advice. What a pretty environment!

## Love & Son, Inc.

*1103 South Ross*
*Amarillo, Texas 79102*
☎ *806/373-9563*
**FAX** *806/373-2509*
**Hours** *Daily 8:30-6 (spring & summer); Mon-Fri 9-5, Sat 9-4 (fall & winter)*
**Accessible** *Yes*

"We're proud of the fact that, in February 1995, we celebrated our 50th anniversary in business," says Ray Love. This fourth-generation business is one of the most complete garden centers in the Panhandle area, and it provides garden design and installation services in addition to its nursery operation. The staff includes a graduate horticulturist, a licensed landscape architect and three licensed irrigators to provide advice as needed. It also has a large floral department. The nursery carries a good selection of large, hardy Texas native trees, such as cedar elms and hackberries, and the staff is willing to special-order almost any plant for customers.

## *Lubbock*

## Holland Gardens

*4315 50th Street*
*Lubbock, Texas 79413*
☎ *806/792-6336*
**FAX** *806/792-7579*
**Hours** *Mon-Sat 9-6; open Sundays 1-5:30 (March-June 15th & Nov-Dec)*
**Accessible** *Yes*

To say that Holland Gardens is a "complete garden center" is understatement! What impressed us is the way this huge establishment is "keeping up with the times." Ann Holland explains, "We offer Texas-tough plants with great signage explaining where and how to plant for this area, particularly stressing the tolerance level for low winter temperatures. With more townhouses and garden homes, we have more types of plants suitable for microclimates such as courtyards. The nursery also offers free classes on such specialized subjects as "No-Till Flower Gardening" and "How To Grow 100 Pounds Of Tomatoes Per Plant." These pre-spring classes emphasize the use of specialized products and non-traditional gardening methods. Realizing that color gardening with perennials and annuals (sold already in bloom, as well as in starter sizes) are very popular, the company's landscaping and design services provide seasonal color, evergreen backdrops and cheerful accents for more pleasurable gardens. In the fall a large display features hay bales, pumpkins, cotton stalks and sunflower heads for bird munching. From October through December, Holland's really glows, with thousands of lights and collection pieces and over 70 themed Christmas trees. It markets outdoor bulbs (clear or jewel-tone) and GPG light clips that are manufactured in Lubbock and shipped worldwide. The nursery has July specials, a store-wide sale December 26 through December 29th, and advice is always free.

## Sparkman's Nursery

*11109 Slide Road*
*Lubbock, Texas 79424*
☎ *806/794-3614*
**FAX** *806/794-4627*
**Hours** *Mon-Sat 8-6, Sun 12-5*
**Accessible** *Partially (greenhouses are gravel)*

Sparkman's is an easy and relaxing place to shop. According to the Sparkmans, "We are the only nursery in this area where a retail customer can find such a large inventory of green goods. Our inventory turns quickly, and this enables us to keep fresh stock on hand at all times." There are 15 acres of trees (many of them very large) and an excellent stock of shrubs, grasses and ground covers. Besides seasonal color, the company also offers a large selection of garden accessories — clay pots, fountains, statuary and planters. You'll find house plants, books, tools, soil amendments, pest control supplies, paving materials, lattice and beautiful, moss-covered landscape boulders here, as well. It has, in fact, almost anything you could want.

## Tom's Tree Place

*5104 34th Street*
*Lubbock, Texas 79410*
☎ *806/799-3677*
**FAX** *806/799-8743*
*www.tomstreeplace.com*
**Hours** *Mon-Sat 8-6*
**Accessible** *Yes*

With three landscape architects and two landscape designers on staff, Tom's Tree Place generates synergy between its nursery, design and installation services. This design-oriented company, established in 1950, is owned and operated by the Scarborough family, which includes their friendly Labradors. According to Alex Scarborough, "We promote natives, and all the plant material here is for outdoor use. With 45 acres of growing space in the Lubbock area, we have a vast selection of specimen trees (the specialty of the nursery)." You'll also find a full line of shrubs and ground covers, as well as seasonal color, seeds and vegetables. We were

*(Listing continued on next page)*

impressed by the garden furniture we found on display here. There were also lots of tools, garden supplies and soil amendments on hand. Customers are encouraged to help themselves to a "prescribed care guide schedule," which contains month-by-month tips. And don't miss the season for Tom's fresh, home-grown pecans!

## *Midland*

### Alldredge Gardens

*3300 North Fairgrounds Road*
*Midland, Texas 79710*
☎ *915/682-4500*
**FAX** *915/687-6876*
**Hours** *Mon-Sat 9-7, Sun 10-6*
**Accessible** *Yes*

The Permian Basin's largest complete garden center, Alldredge's has 11 acres of full-grown balled and burlapped trees, as well as perennials and herbs, all grown on-site. The company provides landscape renovation and installation and stocks paving and retaining wall materials. It also maintains residential and commercial accounts for spraying, feeding and pruning. On staff are five horticulturists, two Master Certified Nursery Professionals, six Texas Certified Professionals and a Landscape Architect. But what "knocked our socks off" was the selection of delightful garden accessories. (Pat had the company ship a wonderful painting on wood to her home in Austin. No problem.) Alldredge's is a most impressive operation and a treat to visit! It holds half-off sales in June and September and offers clinics on a variety of subjects.

### La Casa Verde Nursery, Inc.

*2615 North Midland Drive*
*Midland, Texas 79707*
☎ *915/520-2144*
**FAX** *915/520-2145*
**Hours** *Mon-Sat 9-6, Sun 12-5; closed Christmas Eve through Jan 1*
**Accessible** *Yes*

"We hope to serve you!" is the motto here. Says manager Rick French, "We focus on quality, neatness and service. Since we grow many of our bedding plants, we are able to provide quality care. Our greenhouses are greatly enjoyed by our customers during the 'growing season.' Every customer can be a good friend, and that's the way we treat our customers! If we don't have the answer to your question, we'll do our best to get it for you." He added that La Casa Verde acclimatizes its plants, ensuring a better success rate for the gardener. It also offers complete landscaping services. You can find almost any plant that performs well in the area, plus all the soils, pest management supplies and books needed to improve your garden. There's a good selection of furniture, fountains, statuary and a large supply of clay and concrete pottery. To make a visit to this pretty nursery even more fun, there's always something on sale!

### Manning's Garden Center

*2820 West Golf Course Road*
*Midland, Texas 79701*
☎ *915/682-8533*
**FAX** *915/682-8548*
**Hours** *Mon-Sat 8:30-5:30*
**Accessible** *Partially*

Some of the descriptive comments you'll hear about Manning's Garden Center are, "peaceful, restful atmosphere," "nooks and crannies of interest" and "charming and appealing." We agreed with all of the above! This nursury has been family-owned since the early '40s. Although Manning's is not a large nursery, you'll find a large variety of healthy trees, shrubs and other plants from which to choose. As Tom Manning told us, "We provide an especially good selection of bedding plants, and we assist our customers with a 'color plan' for beds or containers." You will also find the unusual — bromeliads and orchids not found elsewhere, a wonderful selection of baskets (including the larger, moss-lined ones,) and a very creative assortment of gifts and accessories. There are books and tools, as well. Nan "all but swooned" when she discovered that Manning's carries *Alan Simpson* cast aluminum tools! An annual July clearance sale is advertised in the local paper, and Tom often speaks to garden clubs.

## *Trans-Pecos*
### *Alpine*

### Morrison True Value Hardware

*301 North 5th Street*
*Alpine, Texas 79830*
☎ *915/837-2061*
**FAX** *915/837-2092*
**Hours** *Mon-Sat 8-7, Sun 1-5*
**Accessible** *Yes*

Serving as the "shopping headquarters for the Big Bend," Morrison's stocks over 27,000 items. You will find almost anything you need in its garden center, from building materials and plants to books, tools and gifts. As Bob Ward will tell you, "Help is just around the corner!" The plant material includes container-grown trees and shrubs; A particular favorite for fall planting is the elderica pine. A 720-square-foot greenhouse holds colorful year-round bedding and container plants. The "Just Ask" rental department carries tillers, seeder, edgers, aerators and more. Morrison's holds an annual "Start-up Sale" the 2nd Saturday in April, and the bargains are terrific! Someone is always on hand to offer advice.

### *El Paso*

### Black's

*8423 North Loop*
*El Paso, Texas 79907*
☎ *915/591-3333*
**FAX** *915/591-1082*
**Hours** *Daily 9-5:30*
**Accessible** *Yes*

Old pecan trees and huge palms shade a four-acre site where Vicky Black Walker carries-on the traditions of a family nursery begun by her father in 1946. In addition to stocking all the plants that do well in El Paso, Black's packages its own brands of fertilizer to keep them healthy. You'll also find a nice selection of tropical houseplants and containers here.

## Casa Verde Nursery of El Paso

*77 Fountain Street*
*El Paso, Texas 79912*
☎ *915/584-1149*
**Hours** *Mon-Sat 8:30-5:30, Sun 10:30-5 (closed Sun in Jan)*
**Accessible** *Yes*

What a delight! This charming neighborhood nursery not only offers lots of healthy plants, but also it is crammed with a cheerful melange of pots, tools, garden accessories and bird houses. And there's a friendly, knowledgeable staff to assist in your selection. As Lewis Lawrence explains, "Casa Verde has been in this same location for over 27 years, and we've built our business on customer service. We listen to our customers' needs in every area." The nursery offers landscape design, installation and maintenance services, as well. Casa Verde holds sales in January and July.

## Payless Nursery

*8000 Gateway East*
*El Paso, Texas 79907*
☎ *915/592-1894*
**FAX** *915/592-8841*

*338 East Sunset*
*El Paso, Texas 79907*
☎ *915/584-6611*
**Hours** *Daily 8-6 (during daylight savings time); 8-5 (remainder of the year)*
**Accessible** *Yes*

We actually suggested that these lovely garden centers should consider a name-change! Payless Nursery is no second-rate, bargain-basement operation. Rather, its airy display areas are replete with very happy plants, including the biggest and healthiest ferns and spaths we've ever seen. Owner Joyce Watkins says, "Our motto is Helping El Paso Grow." Employees are trained to teach the average gardener how to conquer the harsh climate and poor growing conditions in El Paso. Payless promotes locally made soil amendments such as Ionate Soil Acidifier and discourages the use of chemicals and fertilizers that have a high salt content. She adds, "We strive to offer customers 'one-on-one' attention and to assist them in becoming the best gardeners possible!" The nursery is well-stocked with plants that *will grow* in El Paso, and, yes, the prices are competitive. There are weekly sales, plus in-store and advertised specials. Payless offers periodic seminars as well as a weekly TV show on gardening.

## Chapter Six

# Naturescaping the Urban Environment

*"We have probed the earth, excavated it, burned it, ripped things from it, buried things in it... That does not fit my definition of a good tenant. If we were here on a month-to-month basis, we would have been evicted long ago."*
....*Rose Elizabeth Bird*

# Why We Should Look to Our Own Backyards

Most of us are indignant when we read about the destruction of tropical rain forests. Few of us realize how profoundly urban growth and agricultural activities have impacted our own landscape in the past century and a half. Farmer's plows and free-roaming cattle stripped bare the lush prairie grasses that once covered the western three-quarters of the state, leaving the soil depleted and vulnerable to erosion. The richly layered hardwood and pine forests of eastern Texas have been largely replaced by single-species, same-age pine plantations. Coastal wetlands have been systematically drained to make way for industry and agriculture.

Over four thousand plant species native to the United States are of concern to conservationists, and Texas now ranks third in the country for number of endangered plants. While plant extinction is not a new phenomenon, there is cause for alarm when rare plants face extinction before botanists can fully explore their potential use in the fields of medicine, industry, horticulture and agriculture.

As Richard Phelan wrote in his beautiful book, *Texas Wild*, "We are poor compared with the wealth that might have been ours if we hadn't plundered the land." Noting that the first rule of business is conserve capital, he continues, "we Texans have not just dipped into our natural capital, we have squandered it — forests, grass, water, soil, oil. Not only is Texas poor compared with what might have been, it is getting poorer all the time — being used up, worn out... Mistreated land wears out gradually, unnoticed, the way clock hands move, the way men grow old," he concludes. "And because we don't see it happening, we let it happen."

Before dismissing the text in this chapter as the ravings of an "environmental nut," please believe that I am not condemning growth and development. My concern here is to encourage a new appreciation of our natural botanical heritage. Mankind has taken for granted that plant life, which is necessary to our survival, will continue to flourish no matter how poorly we treat the land. We now know differently. As citizens, property owners and gardeners, we can help repair the damage done by previous generations. I hope to show that by doing so, we stand to reap rewards in terms of both environmental quality *and* economics.

## Nature's Fragile Hold

Anywhere native plant and animal communities have been disturbed, new (introduced) species threaten nature's balance. Nature abhors a vacuum. Where the land has been stripped bare by indiscriminate development, road construction, strip mining, overgrazing or poor farming practices, uninvited plants such as briars, johnsongrass and sandburs muscle-in. Ironically, it has been our farms and ranches that have been most negatively impacted by imported weed species. Millions of dollars have been lost in diminished yields and many more spent trying to deal with non-native species.

I watched as my father worked for twenty years to eradicate mesquite trees on his farm east of Waco. It may come as a surprise to some people that mesquite is not native to Central Texas. This tree came up from Mexico and South Texas with the cattle drives. As the animals ate the beans, mesquite seeds were soon deposited (how shall I put this delicately?) in warm, moist, fertile packages that are perfect environments for germination. Within a few decades the trees spread several hundred miles beyond their normal range.

In the right place, mesquite trees can be valuable garden plants, but farmers and ranchers rightly detest them. Mesquites survive in the wild by sending deep, deep roots in search of water. Zap them in one place and they pop up somewhere else. Daddy did battle with kerosene, dynamite and bulldozers. He didn't live to see mesquite wood prized for the backyard barbecue; he simply knew it as a plant that consumed valuable water and took up space that could be put to use growing grain.

Ranching, as it was practiced in the nineteenth century, profoundly degraded the landscape of Texas. When ranchers overstocked the land, cattle quickly ate the most nutritious grasses to the ground. Then less desirable grasses took over. Bare spots eroded, topsoil blew or washed away, and finally the land produced even weaker grass. Overgrazing was profitable for a few years, but eventually the land supported fewer and fewer cattle.

Part of the problem was that early-day cattle ranching became entrenched on the shortgrass prairies, where the soil was extremely thin and fragile to begin with. Geologists tell us that it takes nature about 100,000 years to weather one inch of limestone into topsoil. With both grass and soil gone from the shortgrass prairies, much of the beef production in Texas has moved to regions of the state where cotton was once the primary crop. To produce cattle feed on farms depleted of nutrients by cotton, ranchers must heavily fertilize the soil, which in turn contributes to the pollution of our waterways. The irony is that the native tallgrasses of Central Texas, which were plowed-up for farming in the nineteenth century, would have been perfectly suited to responsible cattle ranching today.

Plants, like animals, colonize rapidly in areas where they have no natural predators. Once nature's balance has been disturbed, the remedies mankind employs to repair the damage only compound the problems. For example, water hyacinth, which was brought into Texas from Central America to clarify streams, has multiplied rampantly and clogged the very rivers it was meant to improve. We can be grateful that the Texas Highway Department never planted kudzu, "the vine that ate the South." Introduced to Florida for erosion control, kudzu proved ineffective for its intended purpose, but having gained a toehold, it clambers all over southern forests and farms.

One of our own native plants, prickly pear cactus, created havoc when it was introduced in Australia as cattle fodder in the late 1800s. The cows wouldn't eat it, so the fields were plowed under and the cactus cut to shreds. Guess what! Every piece regenerated. Now thousands of acres of Australian ranchland have been ruined. More recently, another of our attractive Texas natives, lantana, has taken over the habitats of numerous species in Hawaii.

The problems caused by the introduction of exotic species extend to wildlife as well. Fire ants, which arrived here by accident, are not only causing problems for humans, but are also contributing to the demise of our native ants, which aerate the soil and serve as important pollinators.

# Hopeful Trends

While observing that our forefather's activities caused ecological imbalances, we have reasons to believe that the participation of an environmentally educated generation will work to bring nature back into harmony in the twenty-first century. There is renewed interest in replanting native shrubs and trees and restoring the grasslands that have been usurped by both weeds and introduced agricultural species. There's new fervor for farming and gardening without the pesticides that pollute our rivers and groundwater supplies. We are finally learning to respect the interdependency of all life forms.

In 1973, the Texas legislature passed the Nongame and Endangered Species Act, which provided funding for management and research programs within the state. The Parks and Wildlife Department now raises funds from the sale of wildlife stamps and posters to purchase land for habitat protection. The program benefits such endangered species as the Attwater's prairie chicken, bald eagles, whooping cranes, reddish egrets and the numerous songbirds that migrate through the state. An integral part of protecting the habitats of birds and animals is restoring the plants that provide them with food and shelter.

According to the *Texas Almanac*, 80% of Texans live in cities of more than 100,000 people! Recently we have begun to value our "urban forests" as major resources. Just as environmental activists are working on regional issues, ordinary citizens are influencing new ways of development within their own cities that preserve larger tracts of open space. We've come to realize that a healthy mature shade tree is worth up to $10,000, and have begun to demand that developers respect the existing vegetation on private lots and public grounds.

People living in manmade landscapes have begun looking at their own backyards more critically. We've discovered that when we cover our properties with non-native lawn grasses and fill our planting beds with an array of imported ornamentals, we not only make more work for ourselves, but we also make our yards uninhabitable to birds, butterflies and other attractive wildlife. Throughout the country, the most important new trend in gardening is the idea of "naturescaping," which is primarily about returning to the species that evolved within the region. Sally and Andy Wasowski's *Native Texas Plants, Landscaping Region by Region* dispelled any lingering notions that incorporating indigenous plants means sacrificing "beauty." Her all-native landscape design plans are truly inspired.

Thousands of gardeners are participating in the new **Texas Wildscapes** program, which encourages homeowners to make their properties more attractive to wildlife. Booklets on butterfly and hummingbird gardening, a book entitled *The Backyard Naturalist*, information on feeders and nest boxes and regional lists of "wildlife friendly" plants are available from the Texas Parks and Wildlife Department. (See page 101 for ordering information.)

Reincorporating the diversity necessary to ensure a sustainable landscape for the twenty-first century can begin with something simple. Plant a few species that produce seeds, nuts and berries as food for wildlife, add native trees to serve as nesting sites and provide water in the form of shallow ponds or birdbaths. If you're buying a new home, look for builders and developers who cater to an environmentally friendly ethic. While it may be cheaper (for the builder) to strip the lot clean, you will save money in landscaping costs, maintenance and water consumption by seeking a builder who is willing to retain as much of the native vegetation as possible.

# To Feed or Not to Feed?

The best way to attract birds to your garden is to provide lots of native plants, especially such berry-laden species as yaupon and possumhaw hollies, flowering dogwood, sumac and American beautyberry. If birds could order a perfect environment, it would also include plenty of fruit trees and big shade trees for nesting, lots of wildflowers and grasses gone-to-seed and a running creek or pond nearby. (Notably absent would be cats, leaf blowers and chemical pesticides.) For much of the year, many birds subsist on the insects that gardeners love to hate, which is one more reason for inviting them to your garden in the first place.

Because birdwatching is such a pleasure, feeding has become a national pastime. Bird shops, specialty catalogs and garden centers are doing a thriving business in feeders and specialized seeds these days. Not all naturalists approve of artificially feeding birds because it encourages dependency on humans. Know that once you start, you'll certainly need to continue the practice, rain or shine. And if you choose to feed, there are a few facts you should keep in mind.

**1.** All-purpose birdseed found in supermarkets doesn't meet the nutritional needs of most birds, so it's better to buy seed from a nature store or specialty catalog. Supply seeds favored by the local bird population.

**2.** Keep the feeders clean. Birds tend to scatter seeds as they eat, so a wire-mesh tray that hangs under the feeder is a worthwhile investment. Because some ground-feeding species will prefer to eat from the tray, it must be cleaned weekly to prevent a build-up of seeds and hulls contaminated with droppings. Throw away any uneaten seeds, wash the feeders and trays in hot soapy water, and rinse with a solution of household bleach and water (about a tablespoon of bleach per gallon). Sterilizing the feeder and tray will prevent spreading any disease that might be brought in by sick birds.

**3.** Hummingbird feeders must be cleaned and refilled twice weekly in hot weather when the sugar-water is prone to fermentation. Glass feeders are especially practical because they can be run through your dishwasher. Always discard any remaining sugar-water and refill the feeder with a fresh solution.

**4.** Birdseed can create a weed problem in your garden, so even if you have trays, you'll need to locate feeders where fallen seeds won't sprout. If you hang the feeder from a tree in a shaded area (where seeds are less apt to germinate), periodically rake or turn the soil underneath the feeder to dispose of the seeds, hulls and droppings. Better yet, locate the feeder over a hard surface that can be swept and hosed-down frequently.

# There's Lots to Love about Natives

Once native plants are well established, they require less water than their non-native counterparts. Natives rarely require fertilizer or pest controls because they have an affinity for the local soils, coping mechanisms to deal with climate extremes and natural resistance to insects and disease.

However, simply calling a plant a "native" is to omit a key question. Native to where? We must go back to the reality of our state's diverse climate zones and soil types. Every region has its own unique set of relationships between different kinds of plants and between plants and animals. Each native plant evolved to fit a narrow range of site-specific variables, which include climate, availability of water, soil chemistry and soil composition.

A fern that grows in the Big Thicket would be a poor choice for a garden in Big Spring! Many of the native shrubs and herbaceous perennials found in East Texas evolved as shade-loving understory plants. Few would survive in an open, sunny location. Our challenge is to match the plant with its normal niche. Not only are plants more likely to thrive where they evolved, but also they appear to "belong." The ancient Greeks had a name for it, *genius loci*, which means "a sense of place."

The Lady Bird Johnson Wildflower Center was founded in 1982 to encourage the propagation and use of "wild" plants in planned landscapes throughout the country. It has been my privilege to interview Mrs. Johnson twice in the past few years. In both conversations Mrs. Johnson referred to the importance of maintaining each region "as the Lord made it." Through the Wildflower Center she has backed-up her conviction with tools that make the idea possible and practical. The organization promotes the use of native plants through programs, research and publications and provides plant lists suitable for every region of the state. Anyone planning a garden anywhere in Texas would be well-advised to obtain a basic plant list from this invaluable source. (See page 76 for information.)

While Mrs. Johnson is identified in the public mind with beautification, she is eager to emphasize that her commitment to native plants is more than pure aesthetics. As Mrs. Johnson puts it, "I think of beautification as making the world more beautiful within the context of what will grow. Native plants are our best hope for ensuring continued habitation of this country, and of the planet."

## The Search for Plants of Our Own

Historically, Texas native plants have been more difficult to obtain than species from China. The horticulturists who promoted natives twenty years ago were real pioneers. The average gardener knew little about the wild plants of Texas, and the wholesale growers avoided investing time in plants for which there was little demand. The few tiny nurseries that were growing natives had very limited supplies. We design professionals were sold on the ecological value of natives, but most of us were unwilling to specify plants that couldn't be found or were too small for landscape use. (Homeowners are not amused when their landscape architect brings in a ten-inch-tall "shade tree.") Until recently, the propagation of native plants remained a lonely and less-than-profitable venture.

New awareness about the advantages of "going native" has turned the growing of native plants into a booming business in this state. Several large-scale wholesale companies are promoting such plants as Texas mountain laurel, Mexican plum, and splendid new varieties of Texas sage. At long last, homeowners are embracing native plants, and neighborhood garden centers are finally making room for them alongside the standard privet, photinia and pyracantha. Homeowners need to keep requesting the natives!

Because it is both unethical and illegal to collect plants from the wild, this chapter features nurseries that have made a commitment to propagating natives from seeds and cuttings or legally digging plants that stand in the way of bulldozers. We are also listing here the regional garden centers that carry significant inventories of suitable native plants.

# Mail-order Sources for Texas Native Plants:

## Bluestem Nursery

*4101 Curry Road*
*Arlington, Texas 76001*
☎ *817/478-6202*
**FAX** *817/572-1289*
**Hours** *By appointment only*
**Accessible** *Partially*
**Catalog** *Free product list*

Bluestem Nursery specializes in containerized native ornamental grasses. Says owner John Snowden, "The best grass for the right job is a native! For shade or for sun, tall or short, ground cover, specimen, drift or screen, we have a grass to fit your needs. Many are also excellent erosion control. We can even beautify drainage ditches!" Wonderful in association with native perennials, these plants are both tough and beautiful. You'll also find a few "well-behaved" non-natives such as *Miscanthus*, *Pennisetum* species and weeping lovegrass, a very attractive African native that performs well throughout Texas. The catalog provides lots of information for selecting the appropriate grasses for your soil and sun conditions and mowing schedule. The company also offers prairie reconstruction and landscape consultation. John participates in special events in concert with local nurseries and is available as a speaker for garden club events. If you call for an appointment, ask for driving directions.

## Dallas Nature Center Nursery

*7171 Mountain Creek Parkway*
*Dallas, Texas 75249-1159*
☎ *972/296-2476*
**FAX** *972/296-2476*
**Hours** *Daily during daylight*
**Catalog** *Free*

"We sell only what we grow (plants) or collect in the wild (seeds) — and only locally native species. Most of what we offer cannot be found elsewhere. Our aim is to make native wildflower enthusiasts, not to make money," states Director Emeritus, Dr. Geoffrey Stanford. Gardeners throughout the Blackland Prairies and Cross Timbers regions of Texas will find here all manner of plants to enrich their landscapes. The staff offers consulting service on how to reconstitute a prairie in a front yard or on a 1,000-acre ranch. (Nan remembers hearing Dr. Stanford deliver a speech in which he observed that subdivisions and shopping centers are often named for the trees that were cut down to build them. It made a strong impression!) See page 47 for information about the center and its activities.

## Desert Moon Nursery

P.O. Box 600
Veguita, New Mexico 78062
☎ 505/864-0614
**Catalog** $1.00

Desert Moon Nursery specializes in native plants of the Southwest, particularly cacti and other succulents. Although visits can be arranged by appointment, this firm is predominantly a grower and mail order company. As Ted Hodoba comments, "Our customers are attracted to our nursery because many of our plants are rare and difficult to find in cultivation. They are also interested in conserving water and are looking for xeriscape plants."

## Mesa Garden

P.O. Box 72
Belen, New Mexico 87002
☎ 505/864-3131
**FAX** 505/864-3124
**Accessible** No
**Catalog** Free

Mesa Garden carries cacti, succulents and dry-land rock garden seeds and plants. This firm is open all year for mail order business and by appointment for visiting.

## Native Ornamentals

P.O: Box 997
Mertzon, Texas 76941
☎ 915/835-2021
**Hours** Mon-Sat 9-6, Sun by appointment
**Accessible** Difficult
**Catalog** $1.00 plant list

Native Ornamentals is a small nursery that grows plants native to the Chihuahuan Desert and Hill Country regions of Texas. Steve Lewis told us, "Our goal is to provide plant materials that are low maintenance and resistant to pest and weather extremes. Speaking of weather extremes, Valorie Lewis recently said that their enterprise had been almost totally wiped out by a hailstorm (grapefruit-size, knee-deep) soon after we visited their place in 1995. Determined to continue making available these beautiful, drought tolerant species, the couple has replaced all the stock. This is good news because about 95% of the species are unknown in the nursery trade — such plants as paper-shell piñon, seven-leaf creeper and unusual strains of desert willow, to mention a few. The plants are small (generally one-gallon containers), but truly rare. Fall sales with 50%-off occur every third year, and programs are available to interested groups statewide.

*Directions: Located off Highway 67. Turn west onto Main Street. Go approximately ½-mile and turn at the sign.*

## Natives of Texas

*6520 Medina Highway*
*Kerrville, Texas 78028*
☎ *830/896-2169*
**FAX** *830/257-3322*
***www.*** *nativesoftexas.com*
**Hours** *Fri & Sat 9-4, Sun 11-4 or by appointment*
**Accessible** *Difficult*
**Catalog** *Free plant list*

Most of Betty Winningham's customers are not local. People come from all over the Hill Country to see the native demonstration garden she and her husband have established on their beautiful ranch and buy the plants she has so lovingly propagated. This retired math teacher "fell in love" with the Texas madrone, and began growing them from seed, two the first year, then ten, then 100… "I killed a few in the learning process," she admits. She has since expanded into a wide range of plants that includes trees and shrubs and lots of native perennials. Among her favorites are the lyre-leaf sage ("a great shade-loving ground cover") and Hill Country penstemon ("it attracts butterflies"). She has learned from experience which plants are not favored by deer and is happy to share all she knows about the cultural requirements of the plants she sells. Her Web site is a delight.

*Directions: Located eleven miles south of Kerrville. Look for the sign on the right side of the road.*

## Plants of the Southwest

*Agua Fria, Route 6, Box 11A*
*Santa Fe, New Mexico 87501*
☎ *505/471-2212 or 1-800/788-7333 (orders only)*
**FAX** *505/438-8800*
***www.*** *plantsofthesouthwest.com*
**Hours** *Mon-Sat 8:30-5:30, Sun 10-5 (April-Oct); Mon-Fri 9-5 (winter)*
**Accessible** *Yes*
**Catalog** *$3.50*

Owner Gail Haggard not only specializes in native plants and traditional vegetables and herbs, but also seeks to promote a caring attitude toward the environment. "We strive to provide caring people with the resources, and perhaps the inspiration, to make bold changes in their relationship with the land and their own perception of beauty. It is a joy to discover the strength and elegance of native plants, for they are the world around us," she told us. Both the Web site and the printed catalog picture stunning wildflowers, as well as trees, shrubs and grasses for ornamental and reclamation uses. "The catalog is presented for joy and independence from expensive watering, fertilizing and Mowing." Most of the plants are available as seeds or as 2¼" container stock. Not all of the stock is suitable for Texas (some are adapted to high altitude gardens), but gardeners in the western two-thirds of Texas will find a wealth of useful, drought-tolerant species available here. Advice and support are always available. When you're in the area you may want to visit the retail stores in Sante Fe (☎ 471-2212) or Albuquerque (☎ 344-8830). Also see pages 271 and 310.

## Rancho Lomitas Native Plants Nursery

P.O. Box 442
Rio Grande City, Texas 78582
☎ 956/486-2576
www.lomitas@vsta.com
**Hours** Daily, by appointment only
**Accessible** Yes
**Catalog** On-line

Benito Trevino, Jr. has created quite a business in native plants suitable for South Texas. Growing over 40,000 seedlings per year, he is supplying trees, shrubs, vines and cacti to ever-expanding retail and wholesale markets. He not only values natives for their usefulness as landscape plants, but also for their traditional roles as medicine and food. His wife has helped generate enthusiasm by joining him on the lecture circuit, making cookies from mesquite bean flour and baking prickly pear cobblers! Among the tough, beautiful plants you'll discover here are anaqua, brasil, Wright acacia, kidneywood, hog plum, wild olive, la coma, coralbean, strawberry cactus, tenaza and allthorn. Call for directions.

## Yucca Do Nursery, Inc.

Route 3, Box 104
Hempstead, Texas 77445
☎ 409/826-4580
**FAX** 409/826-0522
**Hours** Thurs-Sat 9-5 (March-June & Oct-Nov)
**Accessible** No
**Catalog** $4.00; $2.00 seasonal supplements

This nursery received the American Horticultural Society's 1996 Commercial Award, "given to a firm/company whose high standards have made significant contributions to gardening. The award recognizes your outstanding work in collecting seed of rare and endangered plants of Mexico and Texas and reintroducing them into cultivation." This very special nursery is the collaborative effort of John G. Fairey, who teaches design at A&M, and Carl M. Schoenfeld, whose academic background is in architecture and philosophy. Its success can be attributed to their passion for collecting, years of practical gardening experience, and a genuine concern for preserving the survival of little-known species.

The company now offers over 3,000 species of the finest Texas and southeastern natives and their Mexican and Asian counterparts. According to Carl Schoenfeld, "Yucca Do's goal is to provide unusual and rare plants for the collector and discriminating gardener. Over the past decade, we have organized and led numerous plant explorations into the mountains of northern Mexico." These intrepid nurserymen have collected over 300 rare species for testing and are in the process of selecting unusual and outstanding cultivars to be offered in the future. This nursery is the only source in the world for several of the species listed in the catalog. Their trips to Mexico have yielded five new forms of mock orange, a rare variety of sugar maple, a columnar holly, an evergreen clethra and a rare form of podocarpus. Of their forty-five varieties of salvia, nineteen are new to the market. This is where you'll find that elusive native snowbell mentioned in the introduction, as well!

John and Carl are sharing their discoveries with leading botanical gardens and receiving assistance in classifying plants from horticulturists throughout the world. The catalog's plant selections are divided into conifers, trees and shrubs, palms, perennials, woody lilies (which include agave, dasylirion, nolina and yucca), vines, bulbs, cycads and grasses. All plant materials are organically grown. If you plan to visit Yucca Do (and we highly recommend it), ask for directions when you call for an appointment. Peckerwood, the renowned garden that adjoins the nursery, is now open to public by appointment on certain days. (See page 71.)

# Regional Resources for Natives:
## *Cross Timbers & Grand Prairie*

### Bluestem Nursery

*4101 Curry Road*
*Arlington, Texas 76001*
☎ *817/478-6202*
See complete listing on page 245.

### Hickory Hill Herbs & Antique Roses

*307 West Avenue E*
*Lampasas, Texas 76550*
☎ *512/556-8801*
Old roses and native Texas plants share space with the herbs here. See complete listing on page 304.

### Miller Nursery

*1047 Early Boulevard (Highway 377)*
*Early, Texas 76802*
☎ *915/646-2235*
**FAX** *254/968-6903*
**Hours** *Mon-Fri 7-5*
**Accessible** *Yes*

Miller Nursery carries grasses and wildflowers, annuals, perennials and vegetable starts, but the specialty here is native trees and shrubs, which are grown on 140 acres near Stephenville. Trees are available bare root, ball and burlap and container-grown, and the company can transplant trees up to 20 inches in caliper. Among the species you'll find here are Mexican plum, Mexican buckeye, Texas and Mexican redbud, possumhaw, rusty blackhaw viburnum and Texas ash. In spring you'll find over a hundred varieties of perennials. Staff members are happy to give advice when asked.
*Directions: Located just across the river on the east side of Brownwood, Texas.*

### Redenta's Garden

*5111 West Arkansas Lane*
*Arlington, Texas 76016*
☎ *817/451-2149*

*6230 Colleyville Boulevard*
*Colleyville, Texas 76034*
☎ *817/488-3525*
See complete listing on page 179.

## Stuart Nursery

*2317 Fort Worth Highway*
*Weatherford, Texas 76087*
☎ *817/596-0003*
   See complete listing on page 184.

## Weston Gardens In Bloom, Inc.

*8101 Anglin Drive*
*Fort Worth, Texas 76140*
☎ *817/572-0549*
   See complete listing on page 183.

# *Trinity Blacklands*

## Dallas Nature Center Nursery

*7171 Mountain Creek Parkway*
*Dallas, Texas 75249-1159*
☎ *972/296-2476*
**FAX** *972/296-2476*
**Hours** *Daylight year round*
**Accessible** *No*
   An incredible source for plants native to the Blackland Prairie, Grand Prairie and Cross Timber regions, this nursery/ educational organization also offers advice, seminars and special events. See additional listings on pages 47 and 245.

*Directions: From IH-20 between Dallas and Fort Worth, take the Mountain Creek Parkway exit. Go south 2.7 miles; located on the westside of the road.*

## Echols Farm Store

*107 South Interurban*
*Richardson, Texas 75081*
☎ *972/231-3116*
**Hours** *Mon-Fri 9-6, Sat 9-4*
**Accessible** *Yes*
   This small, family-owned and operated retail business specializes in animal feed. Because owners, Guy and Mike Echols, are recognized experts in attracting wild birds, they have become large-scale purveyors of wildflower seed. The store also carries extensive lines of soil amendments and pest and plant disease controls, as well as seasonal bedding plants and vegetable starts. "Our first principal is to give our customers honest, personal advice that works effectively and is cost efficient. We still believe in value and personal service," says Mike. " Our approach is to teach, not sell."

## The Greenhouse Nursery

*4402 West University Drive*
*McKinney, Texas 75070*
☎ *972/562-5895*
**FAX** *972/382-4941*
**Hours** *Daily 10-5:30*
**Accessible** *Yes*

The owners, Brad and Jennifer Stufflebeam, estimate that 80% of the trees, shrubs, grasses and perennials they stock are Texas natives. They market almost 100 varieties of salvia, a dozen varieties of cenizo and such unusual ground covers as horseherb and frogfruit. You'll find numerous wildflowers and rare cacti, including a yellow-blooming yucca available here. Also strong in perennials and culinary herbs, the Stufflebeams have recently purchased a plant farm where they will be growing their own ornamental grasses. The nursery is all-organic, and the company offers native garden design and installation service.

## Kings Creek Gardens

*813 Straus Road*
*Cedar Hill, Texas 75104*
☎ *214/291-7650*
See complete listing on page 185.

## Malzahn Landscape

*1911 Rhome Street*
*Dallas, Texas 75229*
☎ *972/556-1901*
**FAX** *972/556-1936*
**Hours** *By appointment*
**Accessible** *No*

Although Maltzhan is primarily a holding-yard for landscape contractors, the firm is happy to sell to retail customers. It carries large balled and burlapped trees and shrubs (no containerized plants). The tree selection varies, but usually includes red oak, cedar elms, and sweet gums. For large quantities, the company is willing place orders. Jerry Malzahn told us, "We're not fancy, but the prices and the quality are great."

## Nicholson-Hardie Garden Center

*5725 West Lovers Lane*                    *5060 West Lovers Lane*
*Dallas, Texas 75209*                        *Dallas, Texas 75209*
☎ *214/357-4348*                            ☎ *214/357-4674*

See complete listing on page 186.

## North Haven Gardens Inc.

*7700 Northaven Road*
*Dallas, Texas 75230*
☎ *214/363-5316*
See complete listing on page 187.

## Redenta's
*2001 Skillman Street*
*Dallas, Texas 75206*
☎ 214/823-9421
   See complete listing on page 179.

## Rohde's Nursery & Nature Store
*1651 Wall Street*
*Garland, Texas 75041*
☎ 972/864-1934
   Judging from the on-line plant list, this nursery stocks just about every native that will grow in North Texas. See complete listing on page 188.

## Southwest Landscape and Nursery Company
*2220 Sandy Lake Road*
*Carrollton, Texas 75006*
☎ 972/245-4557
   See complete listing on page 189.

# Piney Woods

## Country Connection Plants & Things
*8111 State Highway 31 East*
*Tyler, Texas 75705*
☎ 903/592-5893
   See complete listing on page 194.

## Ecotone Gardens
*806 Pine (Highway 69)*
*Kountze, Texas 77625*
☎ 409/246-3070
**Hours** *Mon-Sat 9-5, Sun 9-12*
**Accessible** *Yes*
   Located in the heart of the Big Thicket, Ecotone Gardens takes its name from the fact that four major plant zones meet here. The materials at this full-scale nursery range from tropicals to "all the trees native to East Texas" (in sizes from one- to 50-gallon containers) You'll find native azaleas, ferns and all types of shrubs and perennials suitable Gulf Coast, Central and East Texas gardens here. Owner Becky Wilder told us that the company carries garden supplies and offers design and contracting services that "emphasize the enhancement of the natural surroundings."
*Directions: Located in the heart of town, across from the Chamber of Commerce.*

## Lowrey Nursery

*407 North Liberty (Highway 149)*
*Montgomery, Texas 77356*
☎ *409/449-4040*
**FAX** *409/582-2874*
**Hours** *Mon-Sun 8-4:30*
**Accessible** *Yes*

Enthusiastic new owners, Martin Simonton and Patrick and Jana Campbell, have purchased this nursery, determined to "bring it back." Noting that four ecosystems come together here in southeast Texas, they're propagating native plants suitable for gardens in the Piney Woods, Gulf Coast, Blackland Prairie and Post Oak Savanna. As designers they advocate "the use of native plants that work well in the landscape, while keeping the old favorites."

*Directions: Located .8 mile north of downtown Montgomery.*

## Pope's Azalea Farm

*Route 2, Box 132*
*Canton, Texas 75103*
☎ *903/829-5921*

See complete listing on page 278.

## Senter's Nursery

*608 Railroad Avenue*
*Whitehouse, Texas 75791*
☎ *903/839-2626*
**FAX** *903/839-7399*
**Hours** *Mon-Fri 7:30-5*
**Accessible** *No*

"Although Senter's Nursery is primarily wholesale," says owner Gerald Senter, "we welcome retail customers! We've been in business since 1977 and try to do the best for our customers." The company must be doing something right! This nursery, located just a few miles south of Tyler, carries 82 kinds of container-grown native trees, shrubs and vines. The company collects its own seeds, ensuring that the trees will grow in the area.

*Directions: Take Highway 110 south to 346 east, and go left ¼ mile to the railroad track. The nursery is another mile, on the right.*

## Thompson-Hills Nursery

*11745 Highway 64 West*
*Tyler, Texas 75704*
☎ *903/597-9951*

See complete listing on page 194.

## *Coastal Marshes & Prairies*

### *Anderson Landscape & Nursery*

*2222 Pech*
*Houston, Texas 77055*
☎ *713/984-1342*
**FAX** *713/984-1388*
**Hours** *Mon-Fri 8-3; open Sat 10-4 in March & April*
**Accessible** *Yes*

   Mike and Patsy Anderson got a head start in natives. She is the daughter of the late Lynn Lowrey, whose name is synonymous with Texas native plants. The Andersons not only carry all the grasses, wildflowers, trees and shrubs her father collected and propagated, but also continue his commitment to natives as resources for a sustainable future. With its lovely little pathways and wealth of unusual plants, theirs counts as one of the most charming places we visited during our travels through the state. Spilling out of the flowerbeds in the different seasons you'll see columbines, turk's cap, dwarf ruellia, unusual strains of purple coneflower and oak leaf hydrangeas, to name a few. You'll find all the tried-and-true native shade trees here, plus the more rare understory trees including two-winged silverbell, fringetree, parsley hawthorn, scarlet buckeye, Louisiana crabapple and wax myrtle, so useful for small gardens. The company offers design and maintenance services. The Andersons also stock seasonal color and lots of container plants, as well as paving materials and soil amendments.

*Directions: From IH-10, take the Bingle Road exit. Go north on Bingle to the 4th light which is Hammerley, turn right and go to Pech Street and turn left on Pech.*

### *Bill Bownds Nursery*

*10519 FM 1464*
*Richmond, Texas 77469*
☎ *281/277-2033*
**FAX** *281/277-2035*
**Hours** *Mon-Sat 9-5:30, Sun 10-5:30*
**Accessible** *Yes*

   When we visited this nursery, we were wowed by the stock of specimen, field-grown native trees. You'll find oaks of all kinds (except post oaks), Drummond red maple, sweet gum, bald cypress, cedar elm, river birch, Mexican plum, yaupon, mayhaw, possumhaw and Texas mountain laurel along with such hardy adapted species as crepe myrtle. "No place in Texas can supply such large native trees," said Mr. Bownds. We saw no reason to dispute his claim.

### *Buchanan's Native Plants*

*611 East 11th*
*Houston, Texas 77008*
☎ *713/861-5702*
   See complete listing on page 199.

## Caldwell Nursery

2436 Band Road
Rosenberg, Texas 77471
☎ 281/342-4016
See complete listing on page 204.

## The Garden Shoppe

2345 Calder Avenue
Beaumont, Texas 77702
☎ 409/835-3266
See complete listing on page 375.

## Garden-Ville Square

2919 North Main
Stafford, Texas 77477
☎ 281/499-6995
**FAX** 281/261-2822
**Hours** Mon-Sat 8-5
**Accessible** Partially

Garden-Ville Square opened in the fall of 1995, and as president Donna Walk was quick to report, "We are definitely following in the Garden-Ville tradition." This nursery is an all-organic supplier, which offers natives, antique roses and herbs. You will also find soil mixes, compost, mulches, drip irrigation equipment, garden tools and books here. Located in an old building, it's a comfortable atmosphere for shopping, a "Mom and Pop" sort of place, with a wood stove, rocking chairs and plentiful garden advice. Donna's husband, Joe Scarpinato, operates Organic Services, an organic landscaping business, out of the premises.

## Glauser McNair Nursery

1707 Ojeman
Houston, Texas 77055
☎ 713/781-3841
See complete listing on page 201.

## Joshua's Native Plants & Garden Antiques

111 Heights Boulevard
Houston, Texas 77007
☎ 713/862-7444
**FAX** 713/862-7444
**Hours** Mon-Sun 10-6; Closed Jan
**Accessible** No

Says Joshua Kornegay, "Hardy, aggressive natives and old-fashioned perennials are our specialty...work less and enjoy more! Hard to find, yet easy to grow ornamentals, along with "old' fashioned advice" gets your garden just the way you've always wanted!" Bring pictures and measurements of your yard area, and they will help you design and plan with your color scheme. Sales are held November 15th — half off. Get on the mailing list for workshops, (most of them free), sales, parties, gardening tips, etc. See additional listing on page 375.

## Mark Fox Landscape Co. & Nursery

*4508 13th Street*
*Bacliff, Texas 77518*
☎ *281/339-3507*
**FAX** *281/559-2219*
**Hours** *Sat & Sun 9-5 (March, April, May, Oct and Nov) or by appointment*
**Accessible** *Partially (no access to restroom)*

Although this nursery is only open for retail trade on spring and fall weekends, it's worth visiting for the very good selection of natives, perennials, herbs, palms and the flowering and evergreen small trees. Says owner Mark Fox, "We experiment with new plants each year and carry the ones that survive our heat, humidity, abundant rain and summer dry spells. Bay and beach plants are our specialty." There is also a delightful demonstration garden for ideas, and locally made garden art is for sale. The staff offers advice and ensures that you know how to care for the plants you purchase. Sales are held in May and November.

*Directions: Take IH-45 south and go left of FM 646 (between League City and Dickenson). You'll cross Highways 3 and 146 before turning left on 13th Street in Bacliff.*

## RCW Nurseries Inc.

*15809 Tomball Parkway*
*Houston, Texas 77086*
☎ *281/440-5161*
See complete listing on page 202.

## Vaughan's Nursery and Gardens

*15647 Avenue C*
*Channelview, Texas 77530*
☎ *281/452-7369*
See complete listing on page 204.

# Coastal Bend

## Fox Tree & Landscape Nursery

*5902 South Staples Street*
*Corpus Christi, Texas 78413*
☎ *512/992-6928*
See complete listing on page 205.

## Gill Landscape Nursery

*2810 Airline Road*
*Corpus Christi, Texas 78414*
☎ *512/992-9674*
See complete listing on page 205.

# Valley

## Grimsell Seed Company

*213 West Monroe Avenue*
*Harlingen, Texas 78550*
☎ 956/423-0370
See complete listing on page 208.

## Heep's Nursery

*1711 Jason Street, #3*
*Edinburg, Texas 78539*
☎ 956/381-8813 *(leave message)*
**Hours** *By appointment*
  Biologist Mike Heep, who teaches at UT Pan American, operates this nursery as a labor of love. He grows a number of choice, hard-to-find plants suitable for Valley soils and climate. The four-page plant list includes shrubs from *Abutilon* (Indian mallow) to *Ziziphus* (lotebush), 25 tree species, and numerous perennials, ground covers and vines.

## Palm Gardens Nursery

*345 Galveston Street*
*Brownsville, Texas 78521*
☎ 956/546-1348
**Hours** *Mon- Sat 8-6, Sun 10-4*
**Accessible** *Partially*
  Morris Clint practices what he preaches. His own garden (across from the nursery and open to visitors) is a lush mixture of natives intermingled with hardy old-fashioned plants. "The natives are really shining," he told us in the midst of the heat and drought of the summer of '98. Among the familiar natives plants you'll find at the nursery are wild olive, Texas ebony, Texas mountain laurel, Barbados cherry and Texas persimmon, which is favored by eight species of birds. He has some rare plants too, including mountain torchwood (a member of the citrus family), la coma (a small evergreen tree with fragrant flowers) and brasil, which is attractive to birds.

## Rancho Lomitas Native Plants Nursery

*P.O. Box 442*
*Rio Grande City, Texas 78582*
☎ 956/486-2576
See complete listing on page 248.

## Stuart Place Nursery

*7701 West Business Highway 83*
*Harlingen, Texas 78552*
☎ 956/428-4439
See complete listing on page 208.

## Texas Natives

*Route 1, Box 214A*
*La Feria, Texas 78559*
☎ *956/797-2102*
**Hours** *By appointment*
**Accessible** *No*

Dr. Richard Hoverson and his wife Ruby (the CEO) began this "Mom & Pop backyard business" as a retirement project that has resulted in a new career for him as a wildlife habitat consultant. Texas Natives grows over 100 species of native chapparal ("all the Yankees call it thorn-scrub," he drawls, half-kidding). He's not only propagating these valuable plants, but also teaching others to do so. "We're running out of water," he says, observing that the Valley's lakes are at 21% capacity and "people are still planting St. Augustine lawns." He's a frequent contributor to *Texas Wildlife* magazine, profiling plants that serve as habitats for our bird and animal species.

*Directions: Take FM 2556 a little more than a mile south of Old Highway 83.*

# *Rio Grande Plain*

## The Antique Rose Emporium

*7561 East Evans Road*
*San Antonio, Texas 78226*
☎ *210/651-4565*
**FAX** *210/651-4569*
**Hours** *Mon-Sat 9-5:30, Sun 11-5:30*
**Accessible** *Yes*

New in 1998 is this branch of The Antique Rose Emporium in Brenham (also see page 276). The nursery shares a driveway with Garden-Ville, and manager Pam Paine says, "We swap customers back and forth." In and around the old Texas buildings here, you'll find lots of native trees and shrubs and display gardens brimming with roses and colorful "low water-no fuss" perennials. Pam reported that the gardens were "looking cheerful in the prolonged 100-degree weather." She also told us she is stocking lots of herbs, pots and giftware.

## Medina Valley Greenhouses

*Old River Road (CR 477)*
*Castroville, Texas 78009*
☎ *210/931-2298*
See complete listing on page 211.

## Shades of Green

*334 West Sunset Road*
*San Antonio, Texas 78209*
☎ *210/824-3772*
See complete listing on page 214.

# *Central Blacklands & Savannas*

## *Chaparral Estates Gardens*

*Route 1, Box 425*
*Killeen, Texas 76542*
☎ *254/526-3973*
**Hours** *Daily 8-6*
**Accessible** *Yes*

   This thriving little company began with a single greenhouse, which Ken Schoen bought for his German-born wife, Rita, "to get plants out of the living room." Thirty days later she had over 1,000 Texas plants in production. Now the Schoens grow natives on 3½ acres and are active in the Native Plant Society. Among her favorite perennials are big red sage, damianita, pink skullcap, turkscap, purple coneflower and columbine. A partial shrub list includes cenizo, mountain laurel and Mexican buckeye. Call for directions.

## *Contemporary Landscape Services*

*106 North Avenue*
*Bryan, Texas 77802*
☎ *409/846-1448*

   See complete listing on page 215.

## *Discount Trees of Brenham*

*2800 North Park Street*
*Brenham, Texas 77833*
☎ *409/836-7225*
**FAX** *409/830-8819*
**Hours** *Mon-Sat 8-5*
**Accessible** *Yes*

   While John and Verna Lammers publicize "quality container grown trees, shrubs and perennials at discount prices," the depth of their plant list provides a further incentive for visiting this nursery. Eight oak species, Montezuma and bald cypresses, Drummond red maple, sweetgum, Anacacho orchid tree, fringe tree, Eve's necklace, Texas persimmon, Texas pistachio, huisache, desert willow and escarpment cherry are among the trees listed here. You'll also find such shrubs as evergreen sumac, agarita, esperanza, coralberry, farkleberry and Virginia sweetspire. Desert plants, ground covers, herbs, fruit trees, tropicals and ornamental grasses complete the impressive plant list. The company also supplies Garden-Ville organic products, compost, mulch and books by Texas authors.

*Directions: One mile north of FM 577 on the eastside of Business 36 North.*

## Hill Country Cottage Gardens

*152 Blackberry*
*Salado, Texas 76571*
☎ *254/947-0416*
**Hours** *Wed-Sat 10-6, Sun 12-5*
**Accessible** *Yes*

Two-hundred varieties of native perennials bloom in the fabulous display garden at this out-of-the-way nursery. On the mild October day we visited, there were also at least seven varieties of butterflies flitting around the casually arranged array of shrubs, grasses and colorful herbaceous plants. Founded only three years ago by Les McCollum and Richard Teeler, this remarkable nursery has already evolved into an island of tranquillity. "As a child I saved my allowance to buy seeds and bulbs," said Les. He explained that the garden is the fulfillment of a life-long dream and noted that he and his partner had looked for years for just the right spot. More than a hundred of their hard-to-find heirloom and native plants are propagated on the premises. They also carry sophisticated pots, a few select pieces of furniture and numerous books on native plants and gardening with nature. While sometimes resorting to herbicide to control the johnsongrass that blows in from neighboring farmland, they are committed to organic gardening and take every opportunity to educate gardeners to the environmental benefits of growing a diverse selection of easy-care natives. The sheer beauty of their display areas speaks volumes, as well.

*Directions: From downtown Salado, follow Royal Street (as it twists and turns) in an easterly direction. Turn right on Blackberry. From IH-35N, take FM 2268 east 2.3 miles to Blackberry and turn left.*

## Organic + Nursery

*10568 North River Crossing*
*Waco, Texas 76712*
☎ *254/848-2103*
**FAX** *254/848-2104*
**Hours** *Mon-Sat 8:30-6, Sun 12:30-4:30*
**Accessible** *Yes*

Native trees, shrubs and perennials, herbs, vegetable starts, all-organic supplies and soil amendments share space at this nursery's new facility. When we spoke with owner Larry Walker just before going to press, he told us his company had just bought-out the native tree inventory of a large wholesale grower. And his shrub list includes such dependable favorites as beautyberry, wax myrtle, cenizo, rusty blackhaw viburnum, yellow bells and yaupon. This is a place that's well worth visiting even if you are not in the market for plants. The inventory of organics will be of interest to every gardener.

## Texian Country Nursery & Gift Shop

*Rt. 1, Box 243 Highway 23*
*Madisonville, Texas 77864*
☎ *409/348-5454*

See complete listing on page 219.

# *Hill Country*

## Amazing Texas Trees
*709 Clear Cove Road*
*Granite Shoals, Texas 78654*
☎ *830/598-2828*
**Hours** *Thurs-Sun noon to dark*
**Accessible** *Yes*

   Although Amazing Texas Trees is predominantly a wholesale supplier, owner Steve Muller (an Austin physician) is quick to say, "Retail customers are always welcome! This is a small single-owner nursery in its infancy, and I offer quality products, carefully grown." The trees are organically grown in local soil in containers that range from one gallon to fifteen gallons. The price list includes at least 34 varieties (when last we checked.) This selection ranges from ash, cherry laurel, redbud, sweet gum, elm, maple, pecan and several varieties of oaks to cypress and several varieties of pines. The low overhead at Amazing Texas Trees allows the owner to offer trees at discount prices throughout the year.

*Directions: Take Highway FM 1431 west of Marble Falls for six miles. So south on Phillips Ranch Road, east on Bluebriar and south on Clearview. The second left is Clear Cove.*

## Barton Springs Nursery
*3601 Bee Cave Road*
*Austin, Texas 78746*
☎ *512/328-6655*
   See complete listing on page 221.

## Deer Valley Nursery
*Route 16, Box 72*
*Medina, Texas 78055*
☎ *830/589-2230*
**FAX** *830/589-7756*
**Hours** *Mon-Fri 8-5 (call before coming)*
**Accessible** *No*

   As Deer Valley administrator Susan Seibert quickly assured us, "Although we are 95% wholesale, we are delighted to welcome retail customers! Even if they want just one tree, we are here to help them." Deer Valley carries from 5,000 to 8,000 trees. These are Central and South Texas natives and adapted ornamentals, and they're available both containerized and "ball and burlap." As Susan explains, "We are a xeriscape operation with trees ready-to-go. We don't 'juice them up' with water and fertilizer, so the trees don't suffer when planted." The prices are very competitive, and from time to time sales are held. Deer Valley is not easy to find, so your best bet is to call for directions. An availability list can be mailed or faxed at no cost.

## Dodds Family Tree Nursery
*515 Main*
*Fredericksburg, Texas 78624*
☎ *830/997-9571*
   See complete listing on page 226.

## Garden-Ville of Austin

8648 Old Bee Cave Road
Austin, Texas 78735
☎ 512/288-6113

See complete listing on page 222.

## Garden-Ville of San Marcos

2212 Ranch Road 12
San Marcos, Texas 78666
☎ 512/754-0060

See complete listing on page 229.

## Green 'n Growing

601 West Pecan
Pflugerville, Texas 78660
☎ 512/251-3262

See complete listing on page 226.

## Love Creek Nursery

Main Street (Highway 16)
Medina, Texas 78055
☎ 210/589-2588
**Hours** Mon-Sat 9-5, Sun 1-5
**Accessible** Partially
**Mail Order**
**Catalog** Free
**Mailing Address** P. O. Box 1401, Medina, Texas 78055

Love Creek Orchards is the retail outlet for this company's apples and dwarf apple trees. The firm also grows and sells big-tooth maples and chinquapin oaks from the Texas Hill Country, and it ships seedlings during the dormant season. There's a charming bakery here that specializes in "everything apple" — pies, cakes, jams, jellies and ice cream. Sales are held in January and February.

## Madrone Nursery

2318 Hilliard Road
San Marcos, Texas 78666
☎ 512/353-3944
**FAX** 512/353-3944
**Hours** Year-round, by appointment
**Accessible** No

Madrone Nursery grows trees, shrubs, grasses and wildflowers native to Texas, particularly the Trans-Pecos and Edwards Plateau regions of the state. All plants are propagated from seed or cutting and container-grown in a custom soil blend of nutrient-rich organic materials from the immediate central Texas area. Says owner Dan Hosage, "We specialize in rare and hard-to-find stock and are continually introducing promising species to the Southwest community. Recently we added an extensive selection of perennial native bunch grasses that offer a wide variety of colors and textures to complement trees, shrubs and perennial wildflowers in a natural landscape." Among other unusual plants, Dan has a patented weeping redbud (*Cercis canadensis* var. texensis 'Traveller'), which he propagates by tissue culture. Visitors are welcomed throughout the year to see the colorful demonstration gardens, pond and wild plant trail. He'll send a free catalog upon request: Call for directions to the nursery and "let the phone ring at least twelve times!"

## Main Street Garden Center

*500 Main Street (Highway 281)*
*Blanco, Texas 78606*
☎ *830/833-2199*
   See complete listing on page 225.

## Native Son Plant Nursery

*7400 McNeil Road*
*Austin, Texas 78729*
☎ *512/343-1448*
**FAX** *512/250-9707*
**Hours** *Mon-Fri 8-6, Sat by appointment*
**Accessible** *Yes*
   Sheryl McLaughlin and her partner Kevin Wood have re-opened this nursery to retail trade after several years as wholesale-only. This is good news because Sheryl has quite a collection of hard-to-find trees, shrubs, grasses and wildflowers. She was among the first to sing the praises of natives and is widely known for her broadcasts on KLBJ radio. (Nan bought her first native plants from Sheryl almost 20 years ago.) In addition to container plants, you'll discover some large, mature B&B stock — such trees as desert willow, red bud and cypress. The perennial collection includes white mist flower, snakeherb, pidgeonberry, native verbenas and 22 salvias. The company also sells soils, mulches, compost and rock. Ask to receive the nursery's newsletter.

## Natives of Texas

*6520 Medina Highway*
*Kerrville, Texas 78028*
☎ *830/896-2169*
   See complete listing on page 247.

## Park Place Gardens

*2710 Hancock Drive*
*Austin, Texas 78731*
☎ *512/458-5909*
   Members of the Native Plant Society of Texas can take a 10% discount here. See complete listing on page 223.

## Schumacher's Hill Country Gardens, Inc.

588 FM 1863
New Braunfels, Texas 78132
☎ 830/620-5149
**FAX** 830/608-0914
**Hours** Mon-Sat 8-5
**Accessible** Yes

The goal of Schumacher's Hill Country Gardens is "to introduce and provide exceptional quality landscape material, with special emphasis on Texas native perennials, old roses, and on plants for xeriscaping and naturalizing." The brochures the company has developed give naturalist gardeners easy-to-read information on plant size, sun and water requirements, bloom time and color. The owners publish, for example, long lists of plants that appeal to birds and butterflies. Here you'll find the most complete collection of salvias in the state: 77 varieties strong! The company's plant inventory includes 54 ornamental grasses, 81 plants that tolerate "wet feet" and scores of plants that resist drought and marauding deer. Chip Schumacher comments, "We feel that we are the only organization in Texas that provides the quality and variety of hard-to-find native plants to both landscapers and homeowners." The sales staff is extremely knowledgeable and qualified. Schumacher's often has sales promotions in fall and winter and holds seasonal seminars. And if you're buying more than the family car can hold, the firm offers delivery within the Austin-San Antonio corridor.

*Directions: Located on Highway 1863, west of New Braunfels off of Highway 46 to Boerne, Texas. (Take Loop 357 off IH-35.)*

## Texzen Gardens

4806 Burnet Road
Austin, Texas 78756
☎ 512/454-6471
**FAX** 512/454-1132
**Hours** Thurs-Sat 12-6 (Jan-Feb); Tues-Sat 9-6, Sun 12-5 (March-Dec)
**Accessible** Partially (most areas)

Texzen Gardens is in the heart of Austin, where it's only natural that a native Texan offers native plants for natural landscaping. It's a small garden in itself. Owner Glenn Cooper's philosophy is, "The right plant in the right place." Although Texzen can fill your shady courtyard with camellias and holly ferns, he generally recommends such combinations as Mexican buckeyes with carex as ground cover. Having worked with Glenn for many years, we know his dedication to organic, native gardening and to his clients. Mark-downs are rare, but he does offer lots of free advice. Seminars and special events are in the planning stages. Texzen is also connected with The Austin Groundskeeper, a lawn and garden maintenance service, which has served Austin for over ten years and prides itself on "responsible, prompt and personal service."

# Red Rolling Plains

## Native Ornamentals

110 South 6th
Mertzon, Texas 76941
☎ 915/835-2021
   For complete listing see page 246.

## The Rustic Wheelbarrow

416 West Avenue D
San Angelo, Texas 76903
☎ 915/659-2130
**FAX** 915/947-8407
**Hours** Mon-Sat 10-5:30
**Accessible** Partially

   Sammy and Belinda Armstrong report a "steadily growing demand" for the "more-than-a hundred" native plants they supply. Among the drought-tolerant trees they offer West Texas are bur oak, buckeye, desert willow, possumhaw, goldenball lead tree, flameleaf sumac and the beautiful Texas madrone. You'll find shrubs and antique roses here, plus a wide variety of perennials and grasses, including pavonia, heartleaf hibiscus, Mexican marigolds and Mexican feathergrass.

## Shade Tree Nursery & Landscaping

3122 Old Iowa Park Road
Wichita Falls, Texas 76305
☎ 817/322-9833
**FAX** 940/322-7275
**Hours** Mon-Sat 8-5:30; open Sundays March-May & Aug-Oct only (call for hours)
**Accessible** Partially

   Red oaks, live oaks, cedar elms and red buds are among the native trees this company grows alongside such hardy non-natives as Austrian, black and slash pines, and Chinese pistache, ranging in size from five-gallon to sizable 6-7" caliper specimen trees. Shade Tree Nursery also carries shrubs suitable for North Texas landscapes. With its 36-acre growing yard, this company offers a good selection of fruit trees, as well. It sells topsoil by the truckload and will install anything from a single tree to a complete landscape.

## Texas Star Gardens

P.O. Box 663
Abilene, Texas 79601
☎ 915/692-2733
**Hours** By appointment only
**Accessible** No

   Mary Buchanan caters to the wholesale market, but she's willing to accommodate retail customers. (While the place isn't wheelchair friendly, she brings plants to the customer's car.) All of the trees, shrubs and perennials here are grown in greenhouses on the premises and well hardened-off. Texas persimmon, big-tooth maple, Texas ash and two varieties of *Sophora* are among the trees you'll find. Native hibiscus and wild foxglove (*Penstemon cobaea*) are two of her most popular perennials. She even offers hanging baskets of native wildflowers.

## *Wichita Valley Landscape*

*5314 Southwest Parkway*
*Wichita Falls, Texas 76310*
☎ *817/696-3082*
See complete listing on page 233. This company offers a 10% discount to Native Plant Society of Texas members.

# *High Plains*

## *Coulter's*

*4200 South Coulter*
*Amarillo, Texas 79109*
☎ *806/359-7433*
See complete listing on page 233.

## *Tom's Tree Place*

*5104 34th Street*
*Lubbock, Texas 79410*
☎ *806/799-3677*
See complete listing on page 235.

# *Trans-Pecos*

## *Desertland Nursery*

*11306 Gateway Boulevard East*
*El Paso, Texas 79927*
☎ *915/858-1130*
**FAX** *915/858-1560*
**Hours** *Mon-Sat 8-6, Sun 10-6 (spring & summer); closes at 5 in fall & winter*
**Accessible** *Building and greenhouses only*
Specializing in cacti and other dry climate plants, Desertland is both a retail nursery and mail order company, Aztekakti (see page 269). It carries a nice variety of natives, including several acacias and shrub sages, desert willow, Mexican bird of paradise and numerous cacti. The cacti are also available as seeds.

# Gardening with Wildflowers

Lady Bird Johnson's book, *Wildflowers Across America*, co-authored by distinguished horticulturist Carlton B. Lees, includes numerous photographs of Texas wildflowers. Mrs. Johnson writes, "Often I am asked what my favorite wildflowers are. Since there are nearly five thousand species in Texas...that is a hard question to answer. Bluebonnets would certainly be on the list, although I am a little frustrated when people know only about bluebonnets and nothing at all about the vast panoply of others." She makes a convincing argument that these lovely little plants should be used not only for roadsides and parks, but also to make our home gardens.

The British and Europeans have been growing our wildflowers as garden flowers for 300 years, and many are now available as container plants at local nurseries. Used as a transition between the lawn and an unclipped shrub border, wildflowers make the landscape seem more relaxed and natural. As our water resources dwindle, we may want to take wildflower gardening a step further, replacing all or part of our lawns with meadows. In medieval times, before mechanical mowers, scythed meadows were known as "flowery medes" and were used for recreation. Now I'll admit that today's turf grass is more practical; it's hard to play touch football when you're knee-deep in bluebonnets. But how much grass do we really need? Certainly the parking strips and other sunny, seldom-used corners of our lawns are candidates for conversion to fields of flowers.

There are some obstacles to overcome when you attempt to get a wildflower meadow established, and there are some differences of opinion on how to garden with wildflowers. Mrs. Johnson describes wildflowers as "capricious." Certainly they have defied artists' ambitions of "painting with wildflowers." The most notable attempt took place about fifteen years ago when someone attempted to create colorful abstract designs adjoining the runways at DWF Airport. The patterns of color worked reasonably well the first year, and then the plants happily re-seeded themselves into a cheerful hodgepodge. John Thomas at Wildseed says people often call him asking to replicate the Texas flag in wildflowers. Good luck. Why do you think we call them "wild" flowers?

## Wildflowers that Welcome Butterflies

Butter Daisy (*Verbesina encelioides*)
Butterfly Weed (*Asclepias tuberosa*)
Candle Tree (*Cassia alata*)
Hummingbird Bush (*Anisacanthus wrightii*)
Lantana (*Lantana horrida*)
Passionflower Vine (*Passsiflora incarnata*)

Choose wildflowers native to your region of Texas. Many of the readily available, pre-packaged "wildflower mixes" contain a high percentage of commonly cultivated annuals that create a burst of color the first year, but do not re-seed the second year. Some may even contain potentially invasive non-native species that may create an ecological imbalance with other plants in the same habitat. Buy only from reputable regional seed producers, and don't expect to scatter the seed and let nature take its course.

You'll want to select a well-drained sunny site and clear it of non-native grasses and weeds before attempting to simulate a meadow or prairie. The Lady Bird Johnson Wildflower Center suggests using two applications of a non-residual, post emergent herbicide such as Roundup™ to remove existing vegetation. (Water the site for a week or two to promote germination of weed seeds and let the weeds grow for a couple of weeks before applying the herbicide. Repeat the process once more before planting.) The organization also recommends combining wildflowers with native grasses such as buffalo grass, little bluestem or sideoats grama to more closely simulate natural prairie conditions.

It takes time and patience to establish a wildflower meadow. The primary mistakes people make are planting and mowing at the wrong times. Follow the seed producers' instructions for planting times and techniques. Most mixes contain both annuals, which regenerate by setting seed, and perennials, which come back from the roots. Many of the perennial species will not even bloom until the second year. For the annuals to return the second year, you'll need to delay mowing until after the flowers have set seeds. While the annuals are going to seed, you can expect the foliage to look ragged for a few weeks. Therefore, if you're growing wildflowers in a small, highly visible area such as a parking strip, you may want to choose a mix of annual species. Simply cut them down after the blooming period and sow new seeds each year.

It is fair to say that the Texas Department of Transportation is the state's most energetic gardener. Its botanists distribute more than 60,000 pounds of wildflower seeds annually to more than 800,000 acres of highway right-of-way! With so much property to maintain, the Department has gained a wealth of experience in wildflower management. By trial and error over a sixty-year period, it has perfected mowing techniques that keep the native grasses healthy and the wildflowers blooming year after year. (These include less frequent mowing and leaving the native grasses taller to discourage invasive weeds.) In the process, the Department has also gained national recognition as a leader in highway beautification.

April is the prime time for enjoying wildflowers in bloom along Texas roadsides. There are several widely publicized Trails and Festivals during the month. If you want to strike out on your own, you can call Texas Tourism's Wildflower Hotline or the Lady Bird Johnson Wildflower Center's Hotline. (You'll find the numbers published in newspapers throughout the state.) Take a field guide such as Geyata Ajilvsgi's *Wildflowers of Texas*, and don't forget your camera!

The sources listed on pages 270-272 offer seeds specific to the Texas landscape. These companies can also be expected to provide you with planting information and cultural practices to ensure your success with wildflowers. There is an intellectual reward in the process that will far exceed planting a flat of pansies.

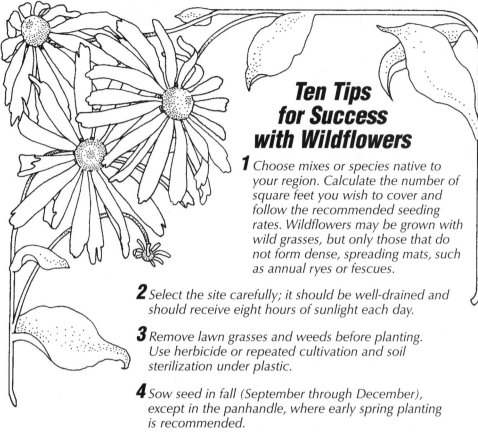

# Ten Tips for Success with Wildflowers

**1** Choose mixes or species native to your region. Calculate the number of square feet you wish to cover and follow the recommended seeding rates. Wildflowers may be grown with wild grasses, but only those that do not form dense, spreading mats, such as annual ryes or fescues.

**2** Select the site carefully; it should be well-drained and should receive eight hours of sunlight each day.

**3** Remove lawn grasses and weeds before planting. Use herbicide or repeated cultivation and soil sterilization under plastic.

**4** Sow seed in fall (September through December), except in the panhandle, where early spring planting is recommended.

**5** Because wildflower seed is very fine, mix it with masonry sand or potting soil at a ratio of four parts carrier to one part seed.

**6** Sow very shallowly and rake to barely cover the seed. Press the seed into the soil by walking or rolling over the newly planted area, and water it in.

**7** Keep the soil moist during the period the plants are becoming established, but don't soak it. Gradually reduce the water after the seedlings reach two inches in height.

**8** Avoid commercial fertilizers, pesticides or herbicides on or near wildflowers.

**9** For wildflowers to return year after year, they must be allowed to dry out and set seed. Mow or cut them down in fall after seed ripens (seedpods or seed heads turn brown and dry), or leave stalks standing to provide fall and winter food for birds. In either case, the annuals will re-seed themselves. If some of the wildflowers begin to re-seed too freely, remove the aggressors' seedpods and thin the unwanted seedlings.

**10** If you're growing wildflowers in highly visible areas, such as streetscapes, it's best to cut them down when they turn brown and replant seeds yearly.

# Mail-order Sources for Wildflower & Grass Seeds:

## Aztekakti

P.O. Box 26126
El Paso, Texas 79926
☎ 915/858-1130
**FAX** 915/858-1560
**Catalog** $1.00

Aztekakti, the mail-order arm of Desertland Nursery, specializes in seeds of cacti and succulents (both natives and non-natives collected from all over the world.)

## Browning Seed, Inc.

P.O. Box 1836
Plainview, Texas 79072
☎ 806/293-5271
**FAX** 806/293-9050
**Hours** Mon-Fri 8-5
**Accessible** Yes
**Catalog** Contact for quotes

This company carries all kinds of native plains grasses, and, from time-to-time, offers the harvested seeds of such wildflowers as Mexican hat, native sunflowers and purple and white varieties of clover.

## Earth Wildflowers

2520 Main Street
Woodward, Oklahoma 73801
☎ 580/254-2926 or 1-888/325-3995
**FAX** 580/256-2198
**Hours** Mon-Sat 8-5
**Catalog** $1.00 price sheet

Earth Wildflowers grows and conditions all types of wildflower seed. The company specializes in wildflower restoration, tree seed and bulk seed sales. It's also known for custom-designed seed packets and Christmas greeting cards complete with a wildflower packet. Rodney Guy says, "Simply tell us the square footage, location, soil type, what you are trying to accomplish, and we will formulate a mix for you. We provide seed by the pound or the packet along with advice about wildflower habitats." With a minimum order of 5,000 packets, the seeds can be packaged with your logo, colors or special design for fund-raising events. Smaller quantities are packaged in clear plastic bags and heat-sealed.

## Holland Wildflower Farm

P. O. Box 328
Elkins, Arkansas 72727
☎ 501/643-2622
**FAX** 501/643-2622
**Catalog** Guidebook $3.25; seed list free

This family business is operated from a 100-year-old farm in the White River Valley of the Ozark Mountains. Holland's offers over 65 different wildflower seed varieties as well as several mixes of flowers and native grasses. The "Little Bit Shady" Mix contains mainly species that are native to the eastern regions of the

United States, and therefore suitable for Piney Woods gardens. You'll also find several prairie mixes. As Julie Holland told us, "We have attractive seed displays of wildflowers and are extremely popular with botanical gardens, museums and national and state parks."

## J'Don Seeds International

*P.O. Box 10998*
*Austin, Texas 78766*
☎ *1-800/848-1641 (same # for FAX)*
**Hours** *Mon-Fri 7-6 (leave message)*
**Catalog** *Free*

This worldwide wholesaler markets a complete line of wildflowers and wildflower mixes to retail customers. Joycelyn Carlton explained that the company, which has been in business since 1985, works primarily on highway beautification projects. Its native seeds are collected from farms and ranches throughout the state. You can order 50 individual species or choose a very short mix (nothing over 8"), a butterfly mix, a red, white and blue mix or a custom blend (25-pound minimum). For large projects, staff members offer free consultation. The company does not carry grasses to mix with its wildflowers, but they'll direct you to an appropriate source.

## Native American Seed

*127 North 16th Street*
*Junction, Texas 76849*
☎ *915/446-3600 or 1-800/728-4043*
**FAX** *915/446-4537*
**Hours** *Mon-Fri 9-5 (answering machine after hours)*
**Catalog** *Free*

This business is a real labor of love that kindles enthusiasm and appreciation for Texas wildflowers and grasses. Talking with owners Jan and Bill Neiman about native wildflowers and grasses makes one want to join in the harvest! Perhaps a better idea is to call Native American Seed and request a catalog. These seeds are "locally harvested from the field to you!" The informative, full-color catalog is a visual treat. You'll find sections on butterfly havens, prairie gardens and wildlife habitats. In addition to a Native Texas Mix, shade-friendly mixes, prairie grasses and lawn grasses, the catalog also lists suggested books and gift items. According to Jan, "We have been in the plant business since 1975 and started to specialize in mail order, hard-to-find native seeds in 1985."

## Plants of the Southwest

*Agua Fria, Route 6, Box 11A*
*Santa Fe, New Mexico 87501*
☎ *505/471-2212 or 1-800/788-7333 (orders only)*

The company carries individual species and a Texas Prairie Mix. See page 247.

## Texas Seed Company, Inc.

P.O. Drawer 599
221 Airport Boulevard
Kenedy, Texas 78119-0599
☎ 830/583-9873
**FAX** 830/583-3363
**Hours** Mon-Fri 8-5
**Accessible** No

Texas Seed Company offers over twenty varieties of native grass seed suitable for South Texas meadows. Call or fax for availability.

## Turner Seed Company

211 CR 151
Breckenridge, Texas 76424
☎ 817/559-2065 or 1-800/722-8616
**FAX** 817/559-5024
**Hours** Mon-Fri 7-5, Sat 7-12
**Accessible** No

Turner Seed Company is a grower and conditioner of native and improved grasses, legumes, wildlife, field and wildflower seeds. It offers a fall and spring mix each year, plus a special xeriscape mix. There's no catalog, but the company can mail or fax you a very complete price list.

*Directions: Located 3 miles south of Breckenridge off Highway 183.*

## Wildseed Farms, Ltd.

425 Wildflower Hills
Fredericksburg, Texas 78624
☎ 830/990-8080 or 1-800/848-0078
**FAX** 830/990-8090
www.wildseedfarms.com
**Hours** Daily 9:30-6
**Accessible** Yes
**Mail Order**
**Catalog** Free
**Mailing Address** P.O. Box 3000, Fredericksburg, Texas, 78624-3000

Wildseed Farms is one of the worlds' largest growers of wildflowers! John Thomas began his company in 1983 when he was hired by the Houston Park Department to seed lawn grasses and discovered that there were no large-scale wildflower seed producers in the entire country. A farmer first, he now grows single-species wildflowers in rows, like crops, on several thousand acres. Small and large quantities are available, and there are over 70 species from which to choose. The new Market Center between Fredericksburg and Johnson City features an upscale gift shop and adjacent beer garden where the peach ice cream (in season) is as popular as the brew. Based on good advice alone, Wildseed's catalogs (both printed and on-line) are worth their weight in gold. In addition to single species, the company offers two mixes, a butterfly/hummingbird blend and a Texas/Oklahoma mix that may be especially appealing to urban dwellers with little space to plant.

*Directions: Located on Highway 290, seven miles east of Fredericksburg.*

Chapter Seven

# The Gardener's Garden

*"Don't hurry, don't worry.*
*You're only here for a short visit.*
*So be sure to stop*
*and smell the flowers."*
*....Walter C. Hagen*

# Beyond the Basics

Those of us who pore over magazines and books seeking ways to make our gardens special are always on the lookout for unusual plant varieties and new ideas in design. Perhaps you've become passionate about antique roses or want new, rare daylilies (no garden should be without several varieties). Maybe you plan to build an herb garden or introduce scrumptious berries and vegetables into your landscape. This chapter is for you! We've found sources that even the most avid gardeners may not know. These are growers who really know and love gardening. You'll enjoy meeting these people as well as exploring their nurseries and private display gardens, or, in some cases, their gorgeous color catalogs. Some specialize in flowering shrubs and others feature uncommon species of perennials. While a few sell primarily "to-the-trade," all are willing to deal with knowledgeable gardeners.

# A Tapestry of Trees & Shrubs

When you are attempting to transform a basic landscape into a refined garden, flowers come to mind first. Flower color, however, is relatively short-lived. For year-round interest, foliage-color and texture are the more important aspects of the plants you select. The garden's trees and shrubs are there to provide year-round structural interest.

To create more color in the planting scheme, look for variety in the shades of green. Add some gray, bronze, yellow, red or purple-leafed plants to serve as strong elements of contrast. The purple leaves of Japanese barberry and flowering plum, for example, can be as effective as flowers in a sophisticated garden. Don't overlook variegated shrubs and such silvery plants as artemisia and cenizo as opportunities to create subtle color harmonies (white and gray work as peacemakers in the garden and contribute a cooling effect). The plant materials should be woven together to create a rich tapestry.

After you have worked out your color scheme, consider the textures of the trees, shrubs and ground covers in your existing landscape. Repetition is used to unify the garden, but a landscape composed entirely of medium-textured plants, for example, would be boring. Variety is truly the spice. Any garden can be enlivened by interspersing such finely textured plants as yaupon or mesquite, and by adding a few plants with leaves as bold as those of loquats or magnolias.

Texture can even be used to fool the eye. If you are attempting to make an area of your garden look larger than it is, you can employ an old Japanese trick. Plant coarsely textured shrubs in the foreground, medium textures in the middle and fine textured plantings at the rear of the garden to increase the perception of depth. Worked in reverse, you can make a large space feel more intimate.

Remember, too, that sheen attracts the eye as much as color, so the introduction of such plants as Chinese hollies and Southern magnolias may be in order. There are even a few plants that produce splashes of fall color in Texas. For winter interest, look for shrubs and trees with attractive bark, sculptural forms and/or berries.

# Shrubs that Flower

Flowering shrubs make an impact in the garden, so I encourage my clients to first choose a flower color scheme and stick with it. I have never hesitated to remove or transplant existing shrubs that exhibit color clashes. One of my clients bought a home that boasted one of every variety of azaleas. In bloom, the garden looked like a gumball machine. We removed all the reds and oranges and grouped the remaining pink and purple varieties by color, using the white-blooming plants as "separators." To add color through the seasons, we augmented the landscape with such summer-blooming shrubs as old roses and althaea and planted perennials and ground covers to bring in the blues and yellows.

Roses are the best-loved shrubs in America. They may even surpass azaleas in popularity among Texas gardeners. I've rarely included hybrid roses in my designs for Texas landscapes unless the owner specifically asked for them. Few of my clients have the time that most hybrid varieties require in the way of expert pruning, regular feeding and spraying for black spot, powdery mildew and a variety of insects. And, in all fairness rose bushes cannot be termed the world's most wonderful landscape shrubs when out of season. But who can resist their blossoms?

The roses I appreciate most in Texas are found beside abandoned homesteads, in old cemeteries and along fence rows. Fortunately for Texans, a fellow named Mike Shoup saw the beauty in these neglected plants and started collecting cuttings to begin the Antique Rose Emporium in 1982. Any rose that will tolerate total neglect and Texas temperature extremes is worth its weight in gold. My kind of plant! The Texas Rose Rustlers is a non-profit organization dedicated to the promotion of old varieties. You'll find its Web site (**www**.texas-rose-rustlers.com) very informative.

There's renewed interest in older, hardier varieties of roses throughout North America. Old roses are best used as shrubs in a mixed border, where they flourish with sensible pruning and very little "doctoring." The downside to the old roses is that most of them bloom for only a brief period and produce less showy flowers than hybrids. Within the past decade nurseries have begun offering roses developed by crossing modern and old roses to produce extended periods of bloom, modern colors and wonderful fragrances. Rose fanciers report that the French Meidiland "shrub" roses and David Austin's English Roses, for example, are performing well in Texas gardens.

A few of my clients have wanted "a real rose garden." Because properly pruned hybrid teas will look ratty during the winter and because they prefer a bed all to themselves, I'll pick an out-of-the-way spot in the landscape. This will also allow the owner to plant varieties for cutting that may not complement the garden's overall color scheme. Choose only the most disease and pest-resistant hybrids (preferably budded onto hardy root stock) and find a garden location that will provide full sun and good air circulation to lessen the possibility of fungal diseases. Water with a drip irrigation system, prune off infected parts and attempt to keep the bushes happy with good soil and a clean growing environment.

Different categories of roses have different pruning requirements. Because all roses bloom on new growth, you'll want to master pruning techniques that promote strong plant development. The severe pruning practices your grandmother may have taught you have fallen out of favor.

☛**Money-saving tip: If you're investing money in hybrid roses, invest time in education.**

The American Rose Society has 19 local chapters in Texas. These groups offer tours, classes and demonstrations on the care and feeding of roses. Call the national headquarters in Shreveport (☎ 318/938-5402) for information. On-line (www.ars.org), you'll find eight consulting rosarians in Texas who can answer your questions. Even experienced rose growers say they never stop learning about roses and seeking better ways to deal with this very special plant!

# Mail-order Sources for Flowering Shrubs:

## *The Antique Rose Emporium*

*9300 Lueckemeyer Road*
*Brenham, Texas 77833*
☎ *409/836-5548 or 409/836-9051 (for mail order)*
*FAX 409/836-0928*
**Hours** *Mon-Sat 9-6, Sun 11-5:30; Mail Order Mon-Fri 8:30-5*
**Accessible** *Mostly*
**Catalog** *Free; Reference Guide $5.00*

Since its inception less than twenty years ago, The Antique Rose Emporium has become one of our "Texas Treasures." As Mike Shoup explains, "We offer old garden roses that are especially versatile for landscape use. Prior to the introduction of hybrid teas, which are predominately used for exhibition, were old roses; noteworthy not only because of their survival, but because they retain the characteristics of fragrance, disease resistance and diversity of form. Most were started from cuttings collected from old cemeteries and abandoned homesteads. These roses are garden-friendly. You plant them with perennials and companion plants, *not* in perfect rows."

While this is an excellent mail-order source for roses, do plan to visit The Antique Rose Emporium's retail stores. In Brenham you'll find eight-acres of roses, perennials and herbs for sale on an old Central Texas homestead. Mike and Jean Shoup have restored an 1850s salt box house, a turn-of-the-century Victorian home and an 1855 stone kitchen. The site, which is very popular for weddings and other special events, is exquisitely landscaped with old-fashioned cottage garden plants, a wildflower meadow and, of course, hundreds of colorful old roses. (The new store in San Antonio, which is listed on page 258, is landscaped with a more southwest flavor.) There's an Open House the third weekend in April and a Fall Festival the first weekend in November at the Brenham location. Its "Trellises and Treasures" shop is brimming year-round with art, gifts and books for gardeners. You can call to receive the company's newsletter.

*Directions: Located on FM 50 in the community of Independence, Texas, 12 miles north of Brenham.*

## Louisiana Nursery

Route 7, Box 43
Opelouses, Louisiana 70570
☎ 318/948-3696
**FAX** 318/942-6404
**Catalog** $3.00-$6.00, depending upon the catalog

Louisiana Nursery was founded in 1949 by landscape architect Ken Durio, who is still active in the company! Now he has been joined by sons trained in horticulture. This highly regarded mail order company hybridizes and grows a wide range of rare and choice species on a 56-acre site. The emphasis here is on quality and variety rather than quantity, and the nursery has become famous within the botanical world for its new introductions. Included among this firm's fine catalogs are 'Magnolias and Other Garden Aristocrats' ($6.00), 'Fruiting Trees, Shrubs and Vines' ($4.00), and 'Hydrangea Species and Cultivars' ($4.00). Also see page 287.

## Peaceful Habitations Rose Gardens

321 Craig Place (mailing address only)
San Antonio, Texas 78212
☎ 830/537-9177 or 210/736-2883
**FAX** 201/734-8665
**www.**ph-rose-gardens.com
**Hours** By appointment only
**Catalog** On-line

"We have just opened a new nursery and display garden where we presently have about 250 varieties of roses and about 100 varieties that we are actively propagating," says Joe Cooper. His passion for old roses began with a single cutting taken from his mother's house. It took him three years to find out that the bush was 'Bloomfield Abundant' and another few years to build his collection. He now has so many that he can bring his wife a freshly cut rose with her morning coffee "every day from February through Christmas!" With his background in the computer business, Joe began his on-line catalog to share his riches with others. He notes that he "never sprays, has done little amending to his soil and uses ladybugs to control the aphids."

He's busily preparing photos and descriptions of each rose for the Web site, but says that it's a daunting task. "Our hours of operation are a little irregular but there is usually someone at the gardens between 8 and 4:30 Monday through Friday, and we are open most Saturdays from 10 until 6. You are welcome to come by and see us when you are in the area, but it is best to call and make sure that someone is at the garden." The telephone number for the rose gardens, which are on a working ranch near Boerne, is listed above or you can call the office in San Antonio. Great tree houses, playhouses and garden furniture are made on the property. (See page 128.)

Directions: Located about 5½ miles north of Boerne FM 1376 Boerne and Sisterdale. From San Antonio drive north on IH-10 West. Take Exit 542 and go completely through Boerne on main street to the 5th stop light. Turn right at the Sisterdale Road Cutoff; go about ½-mile until it runs into Sisterdale Road. Turn right on FM 1376 and go about 5½-miles. Look for the sign for Peaceful Habitations Rose Gardens on the right just before a deep cut. Turn right on Seewald Road and go another half-mile.

## Pope's Azalea Farm

Route 2, Box 132
Canton, Texas 75103
☎ 903/829-5921
**FAX** 903/829-8022
**www.**growit.com/pope
**Hours** Mon-Fri 8-5; by appointment on weekends
**Accessible** Yes
**Catalog** Free brochure

As Chris Pope explained, "We specialize in growing only the finest azaleas by propagating our own cuttings and growing in a medium of peat moss and fine bark. We grow 65 varieties in our 60,000 square feet of greenhouses." Not only will you find the popular indica azaleas here, but also kurume, macrantha, pericat, Glendale hybrids and several varieties of native deciduous azaleas are among the inventory grown for the landscape trade as well as retail customers. While the majority of the azaleas are in one-gallon containers, you'll also find, under shade and sprinklers, plants in containers that range in size up to 20-gallons. Pope's takes advance bookings in the order in which they are received in late winter, so call or go by and place your orders early. In the spring of 1999, the Popes plan to increase their stock to include camellias and ground covers. The company also manufactures and distributes greenhouses (see page 125). Says Chris, "Come by and visit us in the spring — we're beautiful!" Advice (in person or by phone) is always available.

*Directions: Take IH-20 east of Canton to Exit 530. Stay on the feeder, passing 1255, and turn right on VZ (Van Zandt Country Road) 4125. It's on the left, about ½ mile.*

## Tate Rose Nursery

10306 FM 2767
Tyler, Texas 75708-9239
☎ 903/593-1020
**FAX** 903/593-2250
**Hours** Mon-Fri 8-5; other times by appointment.
**Accessible** Yes
**Catalog** Free

As far as we were able to tell, Tate Rose Nursery is the last remaining mail-order rose grower in Tyler. It's a small family operated business, with the second and third generations now involved. "We grow our own bushes (approximately 225,000 per year), and every family member has a working position," says Bobbie Tate. "We try to maintain a close contact with our customers. We think we are large enough to have quality, but small enough to have heart." The company supplies over 75 varieties of hybrid teas, grandifloras, florabundas climbers and shrub roses, all grown on hardy rootstock. The catalog is very informative. "If a customer has a question concerning roses, advice is freely given. From April through September everyone may be doing fieldwork, so call prior to coming. Basically we ship to our customers, but they can come for roses if they will call prior to the desired pickup date. We'll give instructions on how to find us."

*Teas Nursery Company Inc.*
4400 Bellaire Boulevard
Bellaire, Texas 77401
☎ 713/664-4400 or 1-800446-7723 (for catalog)
*www.teasnursery.com*
**Catalog** $1.00 Rose Selection List
   This well-respected Houston nursery ships bare root roses from February through April. Its 23-page catalog lists all the varieties the company offers, and it's impressive! On-line you'll find listing (by type), the company's recommendations for most fragrant, best shrubs, best climbers, etc. and lots of information on rose care.

# Ground Covers & Grasses: Ties that Bind

   Sophisticated gardeners use ground covers to create interesting patterns and textures in the landscape. Large swaths of vinca or Asian jasmine serve as an evergreen transition area between lawn and planting beds, keeping the garden livelier through the winter. Low-growing junipers are often employed as lawn substitutes in areas too difficult to mow, and ground-hugging ajuga is ideal for areas too shady for grass. Perennial ground covers such as sweet woodruff, lamium, violets and ferns may serve to tie together the many colors, forms and textures of a mixed shrub border. Ground covers act as living mulch, suppressing the weeds, conserving the soil moisture and shading the roots of valuable trees and shrubs.

   Lawn grass is the most common ground cover in Texas. I happen to think it's overused, but then I may be prejudiced by my years of watering St. Augustine lawns in sweltering heat without the benefit of an automated irrigation system. In Chapter Six, I suggested substituting wildflowers and native grasses for great expanses of lawn. More and more Texans are turning to native Buffalo grass as a replacement for the ubiquitous Bermuda grass that paves so many suburban tracts. In her book, *Native Texas Plants*, Sally Wasowski demonstrates that an entire garden can be effectively turned over to Buffalo and other ornamental native grasses.

   Ornamental grasses are getting a lot of attention in the gardening press. The category includes true grasses, sedges, reeds and some members of the lily family, including yucca, mondo grass (*Ophiopogon*) and the ever-popular monkey grass (*Liriope*). There's a lot to like about grasses. I particularly favor using grasses in big naturalistic drifts or ribbon-like shapes in the front of a shrub bed or perennial border, but I've also employed one big, showy clump as the focal point in a landscape.

   Played against the smooth texture of a lawn or the more rounded shapes of most shrubs and flowers, a grass's spiky foliage always stands as a refreshing point of contrast. The plume-like flowers of the true grasses contribute soft color to the autumn garden, and they are especially graceful in a water garden or an Oriental landscape. Grasses can be utilized as accent plants in containers, and they make wonderful additions to flower arrangements.

   Also in their favor is the fact that most grasses are tough and drought resistant. The downside is that some of the ornamental species being promoted by garden writers these days are potentially invasive foreigners. If you're wondering why I'm sounding an alarm, consider two very tenacious grasses that evolved elsewhere: bamboo and Johnsongrass. Tall running bamboos, which were widely planted as living fences in the 1950s, have been known to send shoots under a house foundation and come up on the other side. I've watched clients spend years trying to eradicate bamboo. And, Johnsongrass, which was never a garden plant but was brought to Texas for cattle feed, demonstrates how pervasive a grass can be. It now grows wild in every urban alley and vacant lot. When its seeds blow into your garden, you've got a problem!

Although a number of wholesale nurseries are testing new ornamental grasses for use in Texas gardens, the jury is still out. The *only* grasses I would allow in my garden are those that spread slowly outward from clumps and don't re-seed freely. Among the best of the exotic species is purple fountain grass (*Pennisetum setaceum* 'Rubrum'), which is winter-hardy in the southern portion of the state. Such native bunch grasses as Lindheimer muhly, switch grass and little bluestem are also getting play as accent plants. So, don't overlook the grasses (even some of the bamboos can be effectively contained), just use caution. Before you take home some cute little four-inch pot of grass, never forget that it could turn into a monster.

Actually, it's never wise to buy any plant without knowing its characteristics and cultural requirements. Take a horticultural reference guide such as the *Sunset National Garden Book* with you when you're window shopping. I know from experience that a dear little vine can grow up to consume an arbor, and that an innocuous-looking ground cover such as St. John's wort can out-compete everything in its path. As one of my friends put it, "Don't go home with strangers!"

# Mail-order Sources for Grasses & Ground Covers:

## *Bluestem Nursery*

*4101 Curry Road*
*Arlington, Texas 76001*
☎ *817/478-6202*
**FAX** *817/572-1289*
**Hours** *By appointment only*
**Accessible** *Partially*
**Catalog** *Free product list*

Bluestem Nursery specializes in containerized native ornamental grasses. Says owner John Snowden, "The best grass for the right job is a native! Whether it's for shade or sun, ground cover, specimen, drift or screen, we have a grass to fit your needs. Many are also excellent for erosion control. We can even beautify drainage ditches!" Wonderful in association with native perennials, these plants (tall or short) are tough and beautiful. The firm also grows a few "well-behaved" non-natives such as *Miscanthus*, *Pennisetum* species and weeping lovegrass, a very attractive African native that performs well throughout Texas. The company offers prairie reconstruction and landscape consultation. John participates in special events in concert with local nurseries and is available as a speaker for garden club events. If you call for an appointment, ask for driving directions.

## *Schomburg Ground Cover*

*Box 393*
*Brenham, Texas 77834-0393*
☎ *409/836-2136*

Doris Schomburg offers mondo grass at $8 per 100 and white- or purple-flowering liriope at $25 per hundred (plus UPS shipping). She explained that their small, family-run business grows only these two species, has no catalog, and sells only by mail-order.

# The Flower Garden

Texas gardeners would be well advised to study the pictures in English gardening books and then to studiously ignore the plant names listed in the text! Few of the species that grace England's gardens would survive the first season in our hot climate. Happily, Texas nurseries are making available our very own native perennials, plus a wider selection of hardy old-fashioned bulbs and annuals suitable for Texas gardens. Never has it been easier to sustain a lavish flower garden.

The factor that makes English gardens look so enchanting is that the beds are deep and layered. They are arranged in graduated heights, from tiny border plants at the front to lofty spires at the rear. Generally the billowing perennials are mixed with old roses and other deciduous shrubs and played against a wall or a richly textured screen of evergreens. Because perennials can't match the sustained blooming period of annuals, Texas gardeners who want a big summer show always tuck-in a few annuals, especially at the front of the bed.

In addition to the tried and true daisies, daylilies, iris, phlox and chrysanthemums our grandmothers grew, now we can pick from over thirty species of native salvias and readily find such gems as Lindheimer's butterflies (*Gaura*), white-blooming coneflowers and yellow pavonia. It's easy, however, to fall in love with every new perennial variety that comes on the market, and how tempting it is to buy one of every rare bulb you encounter. A good garden requires careful editing. Plant collecting is only a virtue if your garden is "established" and you're willing to remove an existing plant to replace it with something extra-special.

Another pitfall to avoid is concentrating all your efforts on a single season of the year. One of the best aspects of gardening in Texas is our long growing season, and with such a wealth of perennials, bulbs, grasses and flowering shrubs from which to choose, we can now extend the border's color throughout most of the year.

Be willing to correct your mistakes. No matter how much planning has gone into the garden, there are always a few surprises. One drift of plants grows taller than the species behind it or the color combination isn't just right. Unlike trees and shrubs, the elements of a flower garden are easily moved, and that's part of the fun. Don't get discouraged if it takes several years to get everything just as you want it.

## Perfecting the Art of the Perennial

The word "perennial" is not a synonym for "permanent." Establishing a perennial garden requires some advanced gardening skills followed by years of faithful care. Different perennials have different needs: some require staking, and most need to be deadheaded during the blooming season, cut down in fall, mulched and periodically divided.

The most sought-after characteristics in the perennial border today are fragrance, gentle color and resistance to pests and drought. Several generations of gardeners have taken inspiration from English cottage gardens in which Gertrude Jekyll painted year-round successions of "living pictures." It's hard to go wrong with the color schemes she orchestrated over a hundred years ago. I think the secret to her success was in the way she set-off vivid colors with soft drifts of white, gray and green.

I keep a notebook that lists all the perennials that thrive in Texas. I've organized the book with columns for height, color and season of bloom and sun/shade requirements. (Being a "lazy gardener," I put a big star by the varieties that require the least water, fertilizer and general TLC.) When I need a 24-inch-tall, pale-pink, summer-blooming sun-lover, I have a ready resource book that offers me several choices that fit the bill.

I plan the planting bed on ¼" grid paper, drawing in big overlapping oval shapes. I assign one plant per square, which allows me to estimate the number of plants I will need. (Particularly vigorous plants such as daylilies need more space to spread, so I plant them two-feet-on-center from the beginning.) I never plant fewer than five of a variety, usually nine or eleven. I lay out the bed on the ground with stakes and string to make a one-foot grid. This makes it simple to translate the plan-on-paper to the actual garden plot. No matter how carefully I've planned, I always end up making a few eye-pleasing changes as I do the planting.

The possibilities for beautiful combinations are unlimited. For example, one of my plans for a sunny spot might include purple coneflowers, white obedient plant, tall yellow yarrow and Louisiana iris at the rear. Large drifts of Shasta daisies, golden daylilies, purple salvia, artemisia and burgundy chrysanthemums could fill the middle ground. For the front, I might choose pink creeping phlox and daffodils for spring, with dwarf coreopsis to bloom until the first frost. I'd probably edge this bed with a ribbon of liriope for year-round foliage.

I'm especially fond of flower gardens that offer a wide variety of textures, so the garden of a dahlia collector or a chrysanthemum fancier is seldom appealing to me. But gardens are made to please the gardener, and if you want to "specialize" in a particular plant, it's still possible to create an attractive display using the same design principles and arranging the plants by color and height. I almost always include chrysanthemums in a perennial border, not only because I enjoy the late fall show, but also because chrysanthemums serve as a moisture meter! When they begin to wilt, you know it's time to water.

Perennials are normally sold in four-inch pots or one-gallon cans. If you are planting in the fall, purchase one-gallon plants so that the root systems are sufficiently developed to get the plant through the winter. When planting, inspect the root ball for matted or encircling roots. If you find a problem, you can cut half way

up the root ball and gently spread the roots. Plant in a hole up to twice the size of the diameter of the container. Amend the garden soil if it is low in organic matter, and backfill the planting hole with good soil. Water thoroughly. After the first freeze, cut perennials to the ground and mulch over the roots for winter protection.

It will take about three years for your perennials to become well established. By the third or fourth year, you'll need to start dividing them. Most perennials produce inferior blooms when crowded. Plant division not only serves to rejuvenate the plants, but also to keep the more vigorous growers from taking over. As you become an experienced perennial gardener, you'll get to know the individual needs of each species. In general, you'll divide spring and summer bloomers in late fall, and fall bloomers in spring.

We've found two exceptional mail-order sources for rare perennials. Also remember that most of the mail-order and local sources for native plants in Chapter Six supply a wide array of hard-to-find, Texas-bred perennials. Many of our herb sources (beginning on page 305) grow colorful perennials, as well.

# Mail-order Sources for Collector's Perennials:

## High Country Gardens

*2902 Rufina Street*
*Santa Fe, New Mexico 87505*
☎ *1-800/925-9387*
**FAX** *1-800/925-0097*
**Hours** *Mon-Fri 9-5 (M.S.T.) Jan-May and Sept-Nov*
**Catalog** *Free*

High Country Gardens, the catalog division of Sante Fe Greenhouses, grows a wide selection of top-performing perennials for southwestern gardens. In addition to providing such proven cultivars as 'Rosea' evening primrose, 'Moonshine' yarrow, 'May Night' salvia and 'Sunray' coreopsis, this company is a gold mine for unusual penstemon, salvia and lavender species. It's the first source in the country for hummingbird mint. The "Jumbo Water Wise Garden Collection" comes with a planting plan for a 100-square-foot perennial bed. "I've had many customers from Texas purchase plants from my retail garden center here in Santa Fe to take home with them," reports David Salman. "This has reinforced my feeling that gardeners in the West didn't have a source for really tough perennials (not the English and European imports that dominate the catalogs of many eastern nurseries!)" Additionally, you'll find a wealth of ground covers (including buffalo grass plugs), cold-hardy cacti and succulents and native xeric shrubs. The catalog is filled with helpful hints about the water requirements and other cultural needs of the plants. It even has a list of plants that are usually avoided by rabbits and deer.

## Yucca Do Nursery, Inc.

*Route 3, Box 104*
*Hempstead, Texas 77445*
☎ *409/826-4580*
**Catalog** *$4.00; $2.00 seasonal supplements*

Collectors will find a fabulous selection of rare perennials and bulbs at this nursery. Many of the species are not available from any other source in the world! Sea hollies, rosebud sage, an apricot-colored Mexican evening primrose, bee balms from the mountains of Mexico, fabulous salvias, and much more… See complete listing on page 248.

# All About Bulbs

From the first cheerful daffodils to the later spring iris and into the summer with daylilies, glads and dahlias and completing with fall-blooming lycoris, bulbs lend elegance to the flower garden. They combine beautifully with ferns, perennials and flowering shrubs. For the sake of simplicity, I'm calling a "bulb" any plant that stores its life-cycle underground. Actually, the group includes corms (gladiolus), rhizomes (agapanthus, cannas and most iris), tubers (begonia, anemone and caladiums), tuberous roots (daylilies and dahlias) and true bulbs (allium, amaryllis, crinum, daffodils, hyacinths, lycoris, some iris, tulips, etc.).

Bulbs are more effective en masse and most natural-looking when planted in soft, flowing drifts. It's tempting to order one of every variety. To make a big impact, however, buy at least two dozen bulbs of the same variety. Plant "minor" bulbs in groups of four dozen or more, lest they be lost is the landscape. Like all the garden's permanent plantings, bulbs should be orchestrated by color. Consult a bloom-sequence chart to prolong the joy and ensure pleasing color combinations of the varieties that bloom at the same time.

Since spring blooming bulbs begin showing color while the weather is still cool, I like to plant them where I can enjoy the display from a kitchen window or outside my living room. However, the best site for bulbs is where *they* will be happiest. Success begins with good-quality bulbs. All are easy to grow, but most prefer sun and well-drained soil. If your drainage is slow, plant bulbs over a sand or grit base.

The bulb's foliage shouldn't be cut down until it has begun to turn brown (the bulb rejuvenates itself by drawing down nutrients from the leaves). Therefore, to hide the foliage as it withers and dries, I usually interplant spring-flowering bulbs such as daffodils with deciduous ferns or set them behind a drift of later-blooming perennials.

Few garden centers carry a wide variety of bulbous plants. The iris and daylily selections seem especially *vin ordinaire* when compared to the array of varieties available from specialty nurseries. The American Hemerocallis Society has registered more than 20,000 named varieties of daylilies bred by amateur and professional growers. Moreover, it promotes display gardens throughout the country, where daylilies are grown with companion perennials! Daylilies are no longer the orange and yellow varieties I remember from my childhood. As Mabel Matthews, a large-scale daylily hybridizer, told us, "As the quality of daylilies has improved in form, substance and color variation, there is a noticeable trend toward wider segments, more corduroy texture and extremely ruffled segments. Deep, wide eyes, halos and picotee edges up to a ¼-inch-wide enhance the beauty of these cultivars. Colors now range from almost snow-white to a deep, black-red."

Likewise, hundreds of new iris hybrids are developed each year from the 300+ species that grow throughout the world. By acquiring several varieties, you can extend the blooming season well into the summer. Both iris and daylilies rank among the toughest, most trouble-free plants. Just give them plenty of sunlight, regular water and decent soil, and soon you'll be sharing divisions with your friends. We've included some of the biggest mail-order sources for bulbs here. You'll find additional mail-order sources, local retail nurseries that stock bulbs and The Garden Club of Houston's fabulous annual Bulb and Plant Mart listed under Regional Resources for the Flower Garden, beginning on page 289.

# Mail-order Sources for Daylilies, Iris & Other Great Bulbs:

## *Albert C. Faggard*

*3840 LeBleu Street*
*Beaumont, Texas 77707*
☎ *409/835-4322*
**Catalog** *$1.50 each for iris and daylilies*

The actual company name is Albert C. Faggard, Grower, Hybridizer and Distributor of Daylilies and Iris, but we shortened it here to include only this personable man's name! He offers 40 varieties of Louisiana iris, 35 to 40 varieties of crinum lilies and hundreds of daylilies. See complete listing on page 294.

## *Ater Nursery*

*3803 Greystone Drive*
*Austin, Texas 78731*
☎ *512/345-3225*
**Catalog** *$1*

Bill Ater is well-known in Texas gardening. In touch with all the hybridizers in the state, he offers over 300 of the best varieties. See page 300 for complete listing.

## *Bigbee Daylily Farm*

*16315 Channing Way*
*Cypress, Texas 77429-5013*
☎ *281/373-0682*
**Catalog** *Free*

The Bigbees carry over 1,200 named varieties of daylilies "in every color except blue, and no hybridizer has come up with that!" See complete listing on page 295.

## *Carolyn's Gardens*

*1616 Golden Valley Lane*
*La Grange, Texas 78945*
☎ *409/242-3713*
**Catalog** *Free*

Carolyn Mersiovsky not only offers a fine selection of daylilies, but also supplies such bulbs as cannas, iris and rain lilies, in limited quantities. See complete listing on page 299.

## Heartland Gardens

*Rt. 3, Box 3086*
*Cleveland, Texas 77327*
☎ *409/767-4705*
**Catalog** *$1*

From March through October, Sue and Zak Jackson offer a large selection of daylilies from leading hybridizers. They prefer not to risk shipping in the heat of summer. See complete listing on page 296.

## Hillcrest Iris and Daylily Garden

*3365 Northaven Road*
*Dallas, Texas 75229*
☎ *214/352-2191*
**Catalog** *Free iris and daylily lists*

Hooker and Bonnie Nichols offer bearded irises, plus some spuria, Louisiana and Siberian varieties. The couple's medley of daylilies runs from evergreen to dormant, with special emphasis on unusual new varieties. See complete listing on page 291.

## Hurst Park Daylily Garden

*P. O. Box 1404*
*Hurst, Texas 76053*
☎ *817/268-5189*
**Catalog** *$2.00*

While Mabel Matthews carries iris and other perennials, this American Hemerocallis Society national Display Garden specializes in daylilies hybridized from the latest cultivars throughout the U.S. See complete listing on page 290.

## The Lily Farm

*Route 4, Box 1465*
*Center, Texas 75935*
☎ *409/598-7556*
**Catalog** *Free price list*

J. B. Carpenter is known as a hybridizer of top-notch daylilies. His plants are all shipped bare-roo, so you can order by mail during March and April and again in September and October. See complete listing on page 293.

## Louisiana Nursery

*Route 7, Box 43*
*Opelouses, Louisiana 70570*
☎ *318/948-3696*
**FAX** *318/942-6404*

This mail order company offers fine catalogs for the flower garden. Included are *Daylillies, Louisiana Iris and Other Irises* ($.4.00), *Crinums and Other Rare Bulbs* ($4.00), *Bamboos and Ornamental Grasses* ($3.50) and *Clivia Species and Cultivars* ($3.00.) See additional listing on page 277.

## Mary's Garden

*Route 1, Box 348*
*Hico, Texas 76457*
☎ *254/796-4041*
**Catalog** *$2, refundable with first order*

"We offer approximately 1,600 varieties of bearded iris and some Louisiana and Spuria iris," says Mary L. Huggins. "We specialize in antique varieties and grow early, mid-season and late blooming iris and also dwarfs, intermediates and arilbred varieties to extend the season." Formerly known as Huggin's Farms Irises, this nursery accepts orders until the first of September. See complete listing on page 290.

## Nelson Garden

*326 Yorkshire Lane*
*Port Neches, Texas 77651*
☎ *409/724-1106*
**Catalog** *Send large stamped envelope*

As owner Mabel Nelson tells us, "My garden is a home garden, and I do the digging and the shipping myself." Nelson Garden sells only by mail-order and specializes in the latest daylilies and hand-pollinated seed. She ships in the fall.

## *Payne's in the Grass Daylily Farm*

*14103 Melanie Lane*
*Pearland, Texas 77581*
☎ *713/485-3821*
**Catalog** *Free*

"We offer many of the latest cultivars and our own introductions as well as those for the beginning collector or casual gardener," say Paula and Leon Payne. Theirs is an AHS Display Garden, which means that you'll find an exceptionally wide array of varieties here. See complete listing on page 296.

## *Pine Branch Daylily Garden*

*Route 1, Box 93*
*Brookston, Texas 75421*
☎ *903/785-0206*
**Catalog** *$1.00*

Aileen and Bobby Castlebury's catalog lists many of the 1,300 varieties this couple grows on their eight-acre AHS Display Garden near Paris. They've developed 32 registered hybrid varieties to date. See complete listing on page 292.

## *Pleasure Iris Gardens*

*425 Luna Azul Drive*
*Chaparral, New Mexico 88021*
☎ *505/824-4299*
**Catalog** *$1*

Since 1972 Luella Danielson has been busy breeding rare, prize-winning arilbreds and other interspecies hybrid iris at her place just north of El Paso. Because the species with their remarkably beautiful flowers originated in the semidesert regions of Central Asia and the Near East, they are especially well adapted to West Texas gardens. Iris fanciers will be impressed with her own introductions included among some 100 named varieties of arilbred iris, as well as the collection of oncocyclus and regeliocyclus hybrids. Her catalog also lists a number of intermediate bearded, standard dwarf bearded and spuria selections.

# Annuals Revisited

Annuals fell out of favor in the '80s as homeowners began thinking perennials would be easier to grow. (Many returned to annuals for the same reason!) Now rediscovered by the gardening press, annuals are suddenly back in vogue even among "serious" gardeners. Hundreds of old varieties are being resurrected by specialty growers as a new generation of gardeners has come to appreciate the long blooming season that only annuals can offer, plus the hues and fragrances these plants can contribute to  perennial borders and shrub  beds.

What's interesting is that many of today's trendy annuals were mainstays in turn-of-the-century gardens. (Fashion can be as heartless to flowers as to hemlines.) "Out" are the chromium marigolds and purple petunias. "In" are such mellow old favorites as cosmos, cleome and sweet peas. With the popularity of restoring old homesteads and creating "period" gardens for new traditional-styled houses, even biennials such as foxgloves and hollyhocks are back in demand. And, families are once again passing down seeds like heirlooms from generation to generation.

Annual vines are also finding new fans. I remember my mother planting morning glories to clamber up strings in front of west-facing windows when I was a child. Now gardeners seeking quick sunscreens can find a wide range of flowering vines that includes hyacinth bean, black-eyed Susan vine, passion vine, mandevilla and tender jasmines to perfume the summer night.

# Regional Resources for the Flower Garden:

We've listed a number of wonderful sources for the flower garden in the pages that follow. You'll notice that we've focused here on specialty nurseries with display gardens. We've also spotlighted several large wholesale/retail greenhouses, figuring that gourmet gardeners will be seeking both quantity and quality in their bedding plants and may be willing to drive some distances to visit large growers for flats of fabulous annuals and hanging baskets. We've also repeated here the names of a few native plant nurseries from Chapter Six that feature perennials and a couple of herb growers that use colorful perennials in "cottage garden" settings. (A Garden of Herbs begins on page 304.)

## *Cross Timbers & Grand Prairie*

### *Hughes Daylily Garden*
*2450 North Main Street*
*Mansfield, Texas 76063*
☎ *817/478-8144*
**Hours** *Mon-Sat 8-5*
**Accessible** *Yes*

According to Tom and Kirksey Hughes, "We grow and introduce our own hybridized cultivars of daylilies. We also grow several hundred varieties of daylilies introduced by other hybridizers." This small nursery is a genuine labor of love; it's best to phone before visiting. You can request the couple's free plant list in advance.
*Directions: Located on Highway 287 (North Main in Mansfield.)*

## Hurst Park Daylily Garden

*405 Crosstimber Drive*
*Hurst, Texas 76053*
☎ *817/268-5189*
**Hours** *Mon-Fri 9-5, Sat 9-12 (other times by appointment)*
**Accessible** *Yes*

Hurst Park Daylily Garden is an AHS Display Garden that features labeled daylilies and some iris and other perennials. "Growing and hybridizing daylilies has been a pleasure of mine for over 35 years," said Mabel Matthews. She carries over 700 named cultivars and approximately 10,000 seedlings from which the most distinctive ones are selected to introduce into the National AHS. There's a wide variety from which to choose — large flowered, small flowered and eyed in tall, medium and short, as well as doubles, spiders and spider variants. You will find *The Beginner's Handbook*, color slides and instruction sheets, all of which are helpful and informative. Special sales are held in March and October when the season is best for planting. "I like to have customers take time to sit and discuss their problems and my planting and growing procedures. I encourage everyone interested in growing daylilies to visit and relax in a quiet atmosphere where daylilies are queen!" Her catalog costs $2.00. (See page 286).

*Directions: From Highway Loop 820 at Precinct Line Road (near Northeast Mall), go east and exit at Precinct Line Road. Turn right (south) and go approximately 1/2 mile. Turn left on Rosebud and proceed several blocks to Crosstimber Drive. Turn right to the second corner of Crosstimber Drive.*

## Mary's Garden

*Route 1, Box 348*
*Hico, Texas 76457*
☎ *254/796-4041*
**Hours** *By appointment only*
**Accessible** *Yes*

With its 1,600 varieties of bearded iris (and some Louisiana and Spurias), Mary's Garden is wonderous sight. "Bloom season begins in mid-March and continues through mid-may when the daylilies take over the scene. Many irises bloom from time-to-time (whenever they feel like it) through the summer, and a large number have a second bloom season from August to the first hard freeze. We grow early, mid-season and late blooming iris and also dwarfs, intermediates and arilbred varieties, thereby extending the season," says Mary Huggins. She and her husband Pete accept catalog orders until September 1st (see page 287). Then they sell off surplus in September and October. "We welcome visitors to the garden and encourage them to bring a lunch (and a friend) and plan to stay awhile! I'm full of advice," she adds.

*Directions: Take Highway 281 five miles north of Hico. Turn right at FM 1824 (To Duffaw). Go about ¾ of a mile and turn right again on County Road 239. Third house on the right.*

## Weston Gardens In Bloom, Inc.

*8101 Anglin Drive*
*Fort Worth, Texas 76140*
☎ *817/572-0549*

See complete listing on page 183.

## *Trinity Blacklands*

## Amerson Daylily Garden

*13339 Castleton Circle*
*Dallas, Texas 75234*
☎ 972/241-1726
**Hours** *During late spring & early summer, by appointment only*
**Accessible** *Yes*

Binion Amerson's small garden will inspire any urban-dweller seeking to learn more about flower gardening. You'll find much more than a daylily collection (500 old and new varieties strong) at this AHS Display Garden. Mr. Amerson grows a wide range of perennials and seasonal annuals — iris, salvias of all kinds, Shasta daisies, coneflowers and hollyhocks, to name a few. He doesn't sell from his garden, but he's most willing to share his vast store of knowledge and very amenable to setting aside a day for artists and photographers to use his fabulous flowers as subject matter.

## Hillcrest Iris and Daylily Garden

*3365 Northaven Road*
*Dallas, Texas 75229*
☎ 214/352-2191
**Hours** *By appointment only*
**Accessible** *No*

Hooker and Bonnie Nichols began work on this AHS Display Garden only a decade ago, and already it's considered one of the loveliest in the state. They grow thousands of iris and daylilies in traditional raised beds that are accented with colorful annuals in containers. Hooker is an iris hybridizer. His collection focuses on bearded varieties, but also includes some spuria, Louisiana and Siberian irises. The couple's medley of daylilies runs from evergreen to dormant, with special emphasis on unusual new varieties. For catalog information see page 286.

## Jackson's Pottery & Garden Center

*6950 Lemmon Avenue*
*Dallas, Texas 75209*
☎ 214/350-9200
**FAX** *214/350-4253*
**Hours** *Mon-Sat 9-6, Sun 12-5*
**Accessible** *Yes*

Best-known for it's selection of containers, the nursery here offers every kind of plant material except trees. There's plenty of seasonal color from which to choose, with special emphasis on perennials. Jackson's is also well known for its large selection of herbs, and it carries a large assortment of wildflower seeds all year. See complete listing on page 371.

## Kings Creek Gardens

*813 Straus Road*
*Cedar Hill, Texas 75104*
☎ 972/291-7650

See complete listing on page 185.

## Nine-T Farms

*3364 East Highway 34*
*Ennis, Texas 75119*
☎ *972/875-8369 or 1-800/801-0083*
**FAX** *972/875-0231*
**Hours** *Mon & Wed-Sat 8-6, Sun 8-5*
**Accessible** *Partially*

There's no shortage of healthy plants, professional advice and friendly service at this seven-acre nursery between Ennis and Kaufman. Within its 30 greenhouses, Nine-T Farms grows most of the 80,000 hanging baskets the company sells annually. Seasonal color abounds in the bedding plants, herbs, vegetables, perennials, ground covers, shrubs and fruit trees on this family-owned farm. On staff are five Certified Nursery Professionals (two of whom are Master Certified) to help you with landscape design and installation.

## Pine Branch Daylily Garden

*Route 1, Box 93*
*Brookston, Texas 75421*
☎ *903/785-0206*
**Hours** *By appointment (mid May through mid-July only)*
**Accessible** *No*

Located just a couple of miles outside of Paris, Aileen and Bobby Castlebury's AHS Display Garden is considered one of the loveliest in the state. Its landscaped grounds back up to woodlands, and the planting beds are brimming with daylilies intermixed with other colorful perennials. You'll find a new hummingbird garden here, as well. Two lakes on the property not only serve as focal points, but also provide water for the gardens. In the adjacent growing fields, 1,300 varieties carpet eight acres of rich sandy loam soil. The couple has developed 32 registered hybrid varieties, "so far!" Call for directions or send for their catalog (see page 288.)

## Piney Woods

### Blue Moon Gardens

*Route 2, Box 2190*
*Chandler, Texas 75758*
☎ *903/852-3897*

See complete listing on page 305.

## Jordan's Plant Farm

*7523 State Highway 42 South*
*Henderson, Texas 75652*
☎ *903/854-2316*
**FAX** *903/854-4455*
**Hours** *Daily 8-5*
**Accessible** *Yes except for 2nd and 3rd floors in gift shop*

This is definitely a sight to behold! Not only was "The General Store" once part of a movie set, but also there are 400,000-square-feet of greenhouses on site. We were first impressed by the old-fashioned charm as we discovered a wooden building housing an old-time hotel complete with saloon, general store, post office, Grandma's kitchen, etc. Now comes the even better part, the plants. As Betty Gibson says, "It started as a hobby in 1976 with one greenhouse and became a family hobby that ran amuck." It is, of course, a wholesale business as well, but the retail customers (and garden book researchers) receive one-on-one attention and information. Jordan's offers a wide selection of bedding plants, vegetables, hanging baskets, perennials, bulbs, shrubs and trees. The prices are competitive, but the staff is quick to tell you that they won't sacrifice quality. Betty says, "We grow quality into every plant. Our staff goes that extra mile in TLC to furnish the customer with the healthiest and freshest plants." Christmas is a special time at Jordan's. The company grows over 40,000 poinsettias and furnishes every room with spectacularly designed Christmas trees. They were already hard at work when we were there in June!

*Directions: From Henderson, take Highway 79 South. At the traffic circle, go ten miles from the edge of town. Turn right on Highway 42. Go two miles and Jordan's will be on the right.*

---

## La Noria

*11174 Highway 80 West*
*Hallsville, Texas 75650*
☎ 903/668-2562
**Hours** *Daily 9-5 (March 15-Sept 15)*
**Accessible** *Partially (not in greenhouse)*

La Noria specializes in perennials, which is almost an understatement when you consider that Bill Lowry's nursery normally offers between 150 and 200 different varieties. Most are grown from seed, liners and cuttings in his test or demonstration gardens under extreme conditions, which ensure that they'll thrive in normal garden conditions. We were very impressed when we visited his garden in 1995, so we were sorry to hear that the drought had taken a toll on Bill's inventory and spirits when we called to chat in August of 1998. But he assured us that he'll be back next spring ready to share his enthusiasm for rare and beautiful perennials. "We try to introduce at least one new plant each year and provide natives, grasses and a few specialty shrubs and trees in addition to the perennials," he says. Sales are held in June, and advice is always available.

*Directions: Located three miles east of Hallsville.*

---

## The Lily Farm

*Route 4, Box 1465*
*Center, Texas 75935*
☎ 409/598-7556
**Accessible** *No*

Lilies may be purchased from the field during J. B. Carpenter'a annual "open house," which runs from the last week of May through the middle of June. Also see page 286.

*Directions: Located 19 miles northeast of Nacogdoches on state Highway 7. There's a sign on the highway during the open house.*

## May Lilley's Country Garden

*Route 1, Box 4990*
*Lufkin, Texas 75901*
☎ *409/824-2679*
**Hours** *By appointment only*
**Accessible** *Partially*

Janie Morrison, who owns May Lilley's Country Garden, is definitely one who loves the soil, the plants and the "critters!" As she tells her story, "My garden is very special because over 30 years ago my grandmother, May Lilley Smelley, started my collection of daylilies. Her expertise with flowers seemed to flow to my hands, and I still keep her memory alive in my gardens. She felt that a home was not a home without the blessing of the daylily." Birds, bunnies, deer and racoons share space with the 6,000 daylilies that now bloom in this serene country setting. Profits from the business go for care of the 54+ animals that call it home. "Expense for our critters is sometimes unbelievable, but we always manage. Sharing is a big word at this garden!" says Janie. Watch for sales in spring, early summer and October.

*Directions: Travel south on Highway 69 toward Huntington. Turn left on FM 326. The garden is located 1.2 miles on the right in a country gray cedar house on a hill.*

# Coastal Prairies & Marshes

## Albert C. Faggard

*3840 LeBleu Street*
*Beaumont, Texas 77707*
☎ *409/835-4322*
**Hours** *By appointment only*
**Accessible** *No*

Twenty-five years in the plant world, Albert C. Faggard is a master gardener, exhibition show judge and award-winning hybridizer with a large collection of daylilies, Louisiana iris and crinum lilies in his garden. He and his wife Anne welcome individuals and/or garden clubs. Directions are printed on the catalog. "The advantage to visiting during the blooming season is that you can select varieties for fall or spring delivery and get your beds prepared before the plants arrive," he says. For catalog information see page 285.

## Anderson Landscape & Nursery

*2222 Pech*
*Houston, Texas 77055*
☎ *713/984-1342*
See complete listing on page 254.

## Another Place in Time

*1102 Tulane Street*
*Houston, Texas 77008*
☎ *723/864-9717*
**FAX** *713/548-3002*
**Hours** *Tues-Sat 9-6, Sun 10-5*
**Accessible** *Partially*

For the past nine years Mike Lowry has been cultivating heirloom plants and collecting handcrafted garden accessories for an appreciative gardening audience. Ferns are a specialty here, along with unusual perennials, water plants, bonsai and tropicals, including orchids. Another Place in Time has been called, "a nurturing place," and the staff members who work out of this 1920s-vintage house in Houston's Heights are dedicated to personal service. Avid gardeners all, they're full of "old-fashioned" advice. The accessories here are especially nice. The selection of containers range from the dramatic to the whimsical.

## Bigbee Daylily Farm

*16315 Channing Way*
*Cypress, Texas 77429-5013*
☎ *281/373-0682*
**Hours** *Call for an appointment*
**Accessible** *Yes*

When asked the hours for the Bigbee Daylily Farm, Dorothy Bigbee replied, "Day and night...We live here and can't get away from it! They grow over 1,200 named varieties, so the farm is truly a glorious sight to behold in May and June. Many people make the trip just to enjoy the beauty of the blooms. See catalog info on page 285.

*Directions: From Houston, go northwest on Highway 290 and take the Barker Cypress exit to Woodworth Drive. You'll see the sign.*

## The Bulb and Plant Mart

*The Garden Club of Houston*
*5005 Woodway, suite 230 (office only)*
*Houston, Texas 77056*
☎ *713/626-7908*
**FAX** *713/626-7950*

A three-day annual event sponsored by The Garden Club of Houston for the past 57 years, this huge sale attracts gardeners from all over the state. It's always held in late September or early October. You'll find Dutch bulbs and rare Texas bulbs suitable for naturalizing, plus a wonderful collection of unusual plants from wholesale growers trroughout Texas. The sale is staffed by the club's members, and all proceeds go to garden-oriented community projects. Call, fax or write for dates, times, location and directions — this is not to be missed!

## Caldwell Nursery

*2436 Band Road*
*Rosenberg, Texas 77471*
☎ *281/342-4016*

See complete listing on page 204.

## Heartland Gardens

Rt. 3, Box 3086
Cleveland, Texas 77327
☎ 409/767-4705
**Hours** Garden open from end of April-Oct
**Accessible** No

From March through October, Sue and Zak Jackson offer a large selection of daylilies at Heartland Gardens. "We will also be introducing some of our own," says Sue, noting that she and her husband have one registered hybrid at this time and others "coming along." Her love of daylilies grew out of her parents' and grandparents' love of gardening, and she explained that she has moved her collection from place to place during her adult life. Sue invites visitors to the garden by appointment. "We are in the country with a relaxed garden setting, accent plants and an interesting fish pond," she adds. See page 286 for catalog info.
*Directions: From IH-45 or Highway 59, take FM 945 south. There is a sign on Eldridge Road. Follow the hearts posted on the trees to the garden.*

## Houston Flowery/ River Oaks Plant House

5920 Westheimer
Houston, Texas 77057
☎ 713/977-5350
FAX 713/977-5373
**Hours** Mon-Fri 7-8, Sat 8-8, Sun 9-7
**Accessible** Yes

3401 Westheimer
Houston, Texas 77027
☎ 713/622-5350

These stores are both retail nurseries and florists. Each carries an array of plant materials, with special emphasis on bedding plants by the flat and lavish hanging baskets. You'll also find houseplants, garden tools, soil and soil amendments, pest management supplies, and such accessories as pottery, statues and fountains. Manager Ben Shamoolian says, "Here we offer full service with the courtesy of a neighborhood garden center and florist. We are a family-owned and operated business that values the opinion of each and every person that walks through our garden." For information about wild and wonderful topiaries, see page 340.

## Payne's in the Grass Daylily Farm

14103 Melanie Lane
Pearland, Texas 77581
☎ 281/485-3821
**Hours** Thurs-Sun 9-5 during blooming time, by appointment at other times
**Accessible** No

"Our business evolved from our love of daylilies, and we take special interest in hybridizing," say Paula and Leon Payne. An AHS Display Garden, the Paynes' half-acre site presents daylilies in conjunction with other perennials, "to show how they work in the garden." Another two acres are devoted to fields, and all the varieties are labeled with the hybridizer's name and the year of introduction. You'll find everything from the old tried-and-true varieties to the most recent introductions. If you want a picture of some new variety, they'll send it to you. "Visitors are welcome!" At least once a year during the blooming season, the couple holds an "Open Garden" for the public. If you're unable to visit, request their free catalog. See page 288.
*Directions: Take 288 South to Lake Jackson. Exit at Pearland and go left under the freeway to the 5th light. Turn left on O'Day Road and go eight miles to the corner of Melanie Lane.*

## Pecan Hill Nursery

*34303 Pecan Hill Drive*
*Brookshire, Texas 77423*
☎ *281/346-2001 (same # for FAX)*
**Hours** *Wed-Sun 9-4 (Mar-May and Oct-Dec)*
**Accessible** *Yes*

As owners Michael and Marilyn Pawelek explain, "Pecan Hill, established in 1972, is a 'Mom and Pop' nursery with very personalized service, reasonable prices and 'in-house' advice from a degreed horticulturalist. Customers tell us they see plants here that are hard to find elsewhere, succulents, orchids and such." In the spring the focus is on four-, six- and ten-inch containers of annuals (tens of thousands, all over-sized and AAA quality) and 35-40 varieties of perennials. In the fall, the Paweleks feature pansies, flowering kale and garden mums. Hanging baskets abound during both seasons. At Christmas you'll find several thousand "Texas-size" poinsettias. (They're usually snapped up by mid-December.) Pecan Hill Nursery grows all of its plants and rotates the varieties to meet customer demands.

*Directions: Located between Brookshire and Fulshear off FM 359 at the deadend of Pecan Hill Drive behind the Pecan Hill subdivision.*

## Shimek Gardens

*Route1, Box 267*
*Alvin, Texas 77511-9308*
☎ *281/331-4395*
**Hours** *By appointment only*
**Accessible** *Yes*

Shimek Gardens, an AHS Display Garden, boasts 800 named daylilies plus thousands of seedlings. Here you will also see hundreds of other plants, including 110 roses. Harvey and Nell Shimek are serious collectors! Quotes Nell, "When one of our many visitors commented that we couldn't possibly want for another daylily, I just laughed and replied that my want-list of daylilies was probably longer than his!" Peak season for the daylilies is in May and June. The best time to buy the couple's overstock is October through February. Mrs. Shimek gives slide shows for a fee, and garden advice is freely offered.

*Directions: From State Highway 6, turn on 2nd Street. Go to the end and turn right on Sealy. Go exactly two miles and turn right onto County Road 283. The first left is County Road 237. Shimek Gardens is on the right, with the name on the mailbox.*

## Spring Creek Daylily Garden

*25150 Gosling*
*Spring, Texas 77389*
☎ *281/351-8827*
**Hours** *By appointment only*
**Accessible** *Partially*

Mary and Eddie Gage's half-acre of daylilies includes some 1,500 different varieties! Of course, not all are in the couple's free plant list, but "every year we eliminate some and add others." With four registered varieties of their own, they are continuing to hybridize, and they enjoy sharing both their wares and their storehouse of knowledge with other plantsmen.

## Sunshine Plant House

*3425 Concord*
*Beaumont, Texas 77703*
☎ *409/835-7007*
**Hours** *Mon-Sat 9-5 (spring and fall); call to confirm hours*
**Accessible** *Yes*

Richard Tinkle's three greenhouses are brimming with hanging baskets and seasonal bedding plants in spring and fall. All the plants are grown and carefully tended on-site. "I'm off the beaten path and I don't advertise," he says, but he has a loyal customer base that has grown by word of mouth. The company has been in business since 1958 (Richard has owned it for the past 18 years), so it must be doing all the right things. He also mentioned that he grows quite a few shrubs, including azaleas.

# Rio Grande Plain

## The Antique Rose Emporium

*7561 East Evans Road*
*San Antonio, Texas 78226*
☎ *210/651-4565*

See complete listing on page 258.

# Central Blacklands & Savannas

## Andrews Garden

*415 Walnut*
*Waller, Texas 77484*
☎ *409/931-3846*
**Hours** *By appointment only*
**Accessible** *Yes*

Four big pecan trees anchor the exuberant AHS Display Garden that Donald and Eddie Raye Andrews have created on two city lots in Waller. The daylilies reside in contoured, free-flowing beds with salvias, phlox, society garlic, Shasta daisies, coneflowers, stoksia, cleome and antique roses as companions. Lots of decorative surprises enliven the garden. Iron "creatures" peer out from the foliage; fragments of antique iron fences support an array of blooming vines; roses clamber over trellises and a water garden serves as a focal point. While the Andrews sometimes sell starts from their daylily collection, the garden exists primarily to stir your own imagination.

## The Antique Rose Emporium

*9300 Lueckemeyer Road*
*Brenham, Texas 77833*
☎ *409/836-5548*

The roses you can get by mail (See complete listing on page 276), but the display gardens and selection of perennials available here are worth a long day's drive!

## Carolyn's Gardens

1616 Golden Valley Lane
La Grange, Texas 78945
☎ 409/242-3713
**Hours** By appointment only
**Accessible** No

As Carolyn Mersiovsky describes her garden, "Visitors are welcome to stroll the growing fields as well as the garden where daylilies are interplanted among many other flowers. Or they might like to just sit under the trees and enjoy the peace and quiet." The specialty here is daylilies that perform well in the Central Texas area, and more are added each year. Carolyn's hybridizing program is focused on high bud count and immediate re-bloom as well as clear colors and unique patterns. She also offers cannas, iris and rain lilies. See page 286 for mail-order information.

*Directions: From La Grange, go one mile west on Highway 71. Turn right on Old Plum Road and go 1.3 miles to Golden Valley Lane. Turn right and go another half-mile to the sign on the gate.*

## Ellison's Greenhouses

1808 South Horton
Brenham, Texas 77833
☎ 409/836-0084
**FAX** 409/836-1455
**Hours** Mon-Fri 10-6, Sat 10:30-3:30
**Accessible** Yes

The gift shop of this huge wholesale nursery carries a selection of all the seasonal bedding plants that are available to retailers, except the trees and shrubs. You'll even find tropicals here. At Christmas the place is brimming with poinsettias. By appointment you can tour the company's five acres of greenhouses.

## Hill Country Cottage Gardens

152 Blackberry
Salado, Texas 76571
☎ 254/947-0416

See complete listing on page 260.

## Tanglewood Plants

Highway 77 North
Lexington, Texas 78947
☎ 512/446-2268
**FAX** 512/446-4293
**Hours** Mon-Sat 9-5, Sun 12:30-5 (summer); open until 7 in fall through the Christmas season; open until 6 in spring
**Accessible** Partially; some areas difficult on gravel paths

Hanging baskets and bedding plants are the big draws that bring city folks from as far away as Dallas and Houston to this country nursery. Owners Sue and Betty Smith (a mother and daughter-in-law team) began their business as a hobby, and they truly love their work. "It just grew and grew," says Betty. To keep up with demand, they not only grow, but also import from other growers their array of seasonal annuals and hanging baskets. "Quality plants at reasonable prices" is what they advertise, and the formula seems to be working for them. You'll also find lots of shrubs and trees on their seven-acre site, plus potting soils, fertilizers and the like.

# Hill Country

## Ater Nursery

*3803 Greystone Drive*
*Austin, Texas 78731*
☎ *512/345-3225*
**Hours** *By appointment only*
**Accessible** *No*

Mary Anne and Bill Ater's home garden is a daylily wonderland. Always brimming with enthusiasm, Bill stays in touch with all the hybridizers in the state and he's responsible for a wonderful new daylily display just inside the gates at Zilker Botanical Gardens. His own garden boasts about 300 varieties, with at least a hundred potted up and ready to plant. He'll happily share his wealth of knowledge with you, as he has shared it with so many grateful gardeners through the years. See page 146 for some of his growing tips and page 286 for mail order information.

## Barton Springs Nursery

*3601 Bee Cave Road*
*Austin, Texas 78746*
☎ *512/328-6655*

See complete listing on page 221.

## Breed & Company Garden Shop

*718 West 29th*
*Austin, Texas 78705*
☎ *512/474-6679*
**FAX** *512/474-6007*

*3663 Bee Cave Road*
*Austin, Texas 78746*
☎ *512/328-3960*
**FAX** *512/328-3486*

**Hours** *Mon-Fri 7:30-7, Sat 8-6, Sun 12-5*
**Accessible** *Yes*

Austin-natives quip that "You can find anything except a size-four dress at Breed's!" Gifts and garden accessories abound and there's certainly no problem finding tools and books at this combination hardware/housewares store and nursery. "We are special because we offer a wide range of gardening products and plants in combination with many other items," says Penny Adams. The seasonal color is a big draw and the emphasis is on xeriscaping. You'll discover such hard-to-find annuals and perennials as cuphea, chocolate plant and shrimp plant here. Breed's also carries some trees and shrubs, native grasses and wildflowers, culinary herbs and vegetable starts, water plants, bonsai, cacti and tropicals. The company offers seminars on bonsai, native plants and other topics. What would we do without it?

## Cornerstone Home and Hardware

*3801 Bee Caves Road*
*Austin, Texas 78746*
☎ *512/327-0404*
**FAX** *512/327-1054*
**Hours** *Mon-Fri 7:30-7, Sat 8-6, Sun 10-5*
**Accessible** *Yes*

"If gardening is your thing, and you're looking to jump-start your imagination, this is certainly a great place for you," co-owner Julie Thompson promised us. After our visit, we had to agree. Although this is not a large nursery, it is managed by a Texas Certified Nursery Professional. We found an enticing selection of annuals, perennials and herbs, including fern-leaf lavender, hibiscus tea plants and some lovely sedums. There were also espaliered hawthorn and jasmine plants, plus a lot of old-fashioned container gardens in tubs when we visited. Cornerstone stocks some garden furniture and a wide selection of accessories, plus pottery, wildlife supplies, bird feeders, soil and soil amendments, pest control supplies and garden books. The staff here is helpful and friendly, and shopping in this most attractive atmosphere offers a surprise around every "corner."

## Garden-Ville of Austin

*8648 Old Bee Cave Road*
*Austin, Texas 78735*
☎ *512/288-6113*
See complete listing on page 222.

## Garden-Ville of San Marcos

*2212 Ranch Road 12*
*San Marcos, Texas 78666*
☎ *512/754-0060*
See complete listing on page 229.

## It's About Thyme

*11726 Manchaca Road*
*Austin, Texas 78748*
☎ *512/280-1192*
See complete listing on page 308.

## Marbridge Farms

*1 Bliss Spillar Road*
*Manchaca, Texas 78652*
☎ *512/282-5504*
**FAX** *512/282-7147*
**Hours** *Daily 8-6*
**Accessible** *Yes*

Marbridge Farms is, to our knowledge, unlike any other nursery in the state. This organization was founded by Marge and Ben Bridges in 1953 as a non-profit foundation for developmentally disabled men and women, who successfully apply their skills in the greenhouses and craft shops on the property. Says Chris Winslow, "We employ and train about 25 clients in the basic skills of horticulture." Located 12 miles south of Austin, Marbridge is lovingly maintained, and it provides a comfortable, welcoming atmosphere for visitors. The prices are great; the plants are "TLC healthy;" and a very knowledgeable staff is there to assist you! Within 75,000-square-feet of greenhouse growing space, you can find almost anything your heart desires. Although the emphasis is on seasonal color, Marbridge Farms offers trees, shrubs, water plants and pond supplies, tropicals, cacti, herbs, roses and orchids...

*(Listing continued on next page)*

There are also lots of terra cotta pots (some glazed) from which to choose, summer sales, and advice is always gladly offered. Marbridge is a "must!" It makes you feel good just being there!

*Directions: Four miles west of IH-35. Take FM 1626 to Bliss Spillar Road.*

## Schumacher's Hill Country Gardens, Inc.

*588 FM 1863*
*New Braunfels, Texas 78132*
☎ *830/620-5149*
   See complete listing on page 264.

# Red Rolling Plains

## Magic Farm Greenhouses

*7678 Country Club Road*
*San Angelo, Texas 76904*
☎ *915/944-0617*
**Hours** *Daily 7-7 (closes at dark in winter)*
**Accessible** *Yes*

   Magic Farm Greenhouses has been serving the San Angelo area for 15 years. With 35,000 square feet under protective cover, the company is equipped to grow over 16,000 geraniums from cuttings each year! In spring you'll find all kinds of bedding plants, as well as a large selection of hanging baskets, some tropicals and bagged compost and fertilizer. By August, staff members are gearing up for fall with a huge selection of pansies, ornamental kale, snaps and mums. Meanwhile 10,000 poinsettias are coming on for the holiday season. Magic Farms holds end-of-the-season sales, and we were impressed to see four-inch geraniums marked at 89-cents!. The company also offers greenhouse construction.

*Directions: From San Angelo, take Highway 87 to the El Dorado exit and take the first right. Go 3 miles, take a sharp left on Country Club Road and go another ¼-mile. You will see the five greenhouses.*

## The Rustic Wheelbarrow

*416 West Avenue D*
*San Angelo, Texas 76903*
☎ *915/659-2130*
   See complete listing on page 265.

# High Plains

## The Garden Patch

*1311 Alcove Avenue*
*Lubbock, Texas 79416-6700*
☎ *806/793-0982*
   See complete listing on page 325.

## Ivey Gardens

*1318 Municipal Drive*
*Lubbock, Texas 79423*
☎ *806/744-4839*
**Hours** *Mon-Sat 9-6 (March-June); Mon-Fri 8-5 (July-Feb)*
**Accessible** *Yes*

This is a jewel! Upon entering Ivey Gardens, one is simply overwhelmed with seasonal color in flats and hanging baskets. It seems to go on and on… Each year the company sells 40,000 flats of bedding plants and 10,000 hanging baskets. It also offers ground covers, shrubs, tropicals, vegetable starts, herbs and natives among others. You can choose from 35,000 poinsettias for holiday season! Says Glen Ivey, "We carry plants that are homegrown and, therefore, acclimatized. We don't carry plants shipped in trucks, so they don't go through shock. People come back year after year because our plants do well for them." Texas Tech horticultural classes come by to look and learn, and advice is freely given to all customers.

*Directions: Near the airport off Loop 289 on Municipal Drive where it intersects Martin Luther King (formerly Quirt.)*

# A Garden of Herbs

Soft colors, interesting textures and wonderful fragrances are enough to recommend growing herbs in the garden. They're highly decorative in perennial borders and in containers on sunny terraces. A traditional herb garden, however, is the most interesting way to display your herbs. Hundreds of herbal books offer photographs and drawings of historical patterns for herb gardens — knots, stars, circles, cartwheels, diamonds and squares-within-a-square. Today, enthusiasts are even recreating "literary gardens" based on herbs mentioned in the Bible or the works of Shakespeare. An herb garden can easily become the focal point of your landscape.

Throughout the millennia, mankind has depended upon herbs for seasoning food and making dyes, cleaning products, cosmetics and medicine. Many of the earliest writings, on clay tablets and papyrus, were herbals that described useful plants — where they could be found and how they could be preserved. No home garden was without its herbs. Then, in the nineteenth century, commercial products replaced traditional herbal remedies, and herb gardens almost disappeared from the landscape.

When I set up housekeeping in the early '60s, the only culinary herbs I knew were those available on grocery shelves, dried and bottled. In the last few years there has been an explosion of interest in fresh cooking herbs that add exquisite flavors without salt or fat. These ancient, beneficial plants have also been rediscovered as sources for personal health and beauty products. And, there's new enthusiasm for herbs as decorative elements.

Herbs are rewarding in every way, and they're among the easiest plants to grow. They like lots of sunshine and fresh air, but they'll even tolerate living in a kitchen window — briefly. They grow best in raised beds filled with heavily composted soil. Most herbs tend to sprawl and spread, so give them plenty of growing room. And one more tip, label everything!

# Specialty Sources for Herbs:
## *Cross Timbers & Grand Prairie*

### *Hickory Hill Herbs & Antique Roses*
*307 West Ave E*
*Lampasas, Texas 76550*
☎ *512/556-8801*
**FAX** *512/556-8801 (call first)*
*www.n-link.com/~hillherb*
**Hours** *Mon-Sat 9-5*
**Accessible** *Partially*
**Mail Order**
**Catalog** *Free*

Although Hickory Hill Herbs & Antique Roses supplies plant material other than herbs, they are Paula and Don Hill's real passion. "Hickory Hill is a true cottage business. We started with just one basil plant in 1987, and now herbs, native plants, antique roses and scented geraniums are involved in every aspect of our lives!" says Paula. The Hills started the Texas Herb Society in 1990 and are big promoters of the annual Herb & Art Fest, which is held on the second Saturday of October in Lampasas! Classes are held in the fall on diverse aspects of herbs, and as Paula explains, "Our garden is ever-changing, and the thing that makes our business so unique is that we offer a chance to see, touch and smell the plants. Don and I give special attention to each customer. In our garden, love grows! Park on the Ridge Street side and enter through the back garden. We never hear the front door knockers!" You can enjoy their virtual garden on the Web — it's most inviting.

*Directions: Take Highway 183 North nearly through Lampasas. Turn left on Ave. E (west) and go up the hill to the old Victorian home at Ave. E. and Ridge Street.*

## *Trinity Blacklands*

### *The Greenhouse Nursery*
*4402 West University Drive*
*McKinney, Texas 75070*
☎ *972/562-5895*

In addition to native plants, the Stufflebeams grow over 200 varieties of herbs and host an annual Herb Fest. See complete listing on page 251.

# Piney Woods

## Blue Moon Gardens

*Route 2, Box 2190*
*Chandler, Texas 75758*
☎ *903/852-3897*
**Hours** *Mon-Sat 9-5:30, Sun 12-5*
**Accessible** *Partially (access to gardens, but not to shop)*

Nestled in the rolling hills and piney woods of East Texas, Blue Moon Gardens is an oasis of beauty and tranquillity. Here, an 80-year-old farmhouse is surrounded by display gardens filled with fragrant herbs and colorful perennials. As Sharon Lee Smith and Mary Wilhite explained, "Blue Moon started in 1984 as a wholesale herb growing operation, but now the propagation and production greenhouses are open during business hours for browsing and shopping." We suggest you set aside several hours to do just that. Their selection of herbs and cottage garden flowers is about as extensive as you can find in the entire state, and the setting is simply enchanting. The Herb and Gift Shop is brimming with herbal products, aromatherapy and essential oils, plus decorative accents for the home and garden. Blue Moon celebrates three annual events. A Spring Open House is held the last Saturday of April; a Fall Festival happens the third weekend of October, and the Christmas Open House is the weekend following Thanksgiving. The owners offer year round classes and workshops on herbs, gardening and crafting as well as a most informative, free newsletter on request.

*Directions: Located 15 miles east of Tyler, between Highways 64 and 31 on FM 279 (four and a half miles east of Edom.)*

# Coastal Prairies & Marshes

## Lucia's Garden

*2942 Virginia Street*
*Houston, Texas 77098*
☎ *713/523-6494*
**FAX** *713/521-9165*
**Hours** *Mon, Wed, Fri, Sat 10-6, Tues, Thurs 10-7*
**Accessible** *Partially*

In a charming little house in a residential area, you will find Lucia's Garden, the only garden shop in Houston that is exclusively dedicated to growing and using herbs. You'll find four-inch to five-gallon live plants (over 60 varieties, predominately culinary), plus a large selection of dried bulk herbs and the largest selection in Houston of gardening, crafting and personal health-use books on herbs and flowers. According to owners Michael and Lucia Bettler, "Our display garden is 25' by 22' with theme gardens. We hand out lots of free garden tip lists and frequently lecture and teach throughout the state." Their topics include growing herbs, cooking and crafting (potpourri, wreaths, tussie-mussies, etc) medicinal herbs and aromatherapy and a basic class in organic gardening practices. Don't miss Lucia's special theme festivals, which are held in May, June and August.

## Our Family's Herbs and Such

*702 Llano Street*
*Pasadena, Texas 77504*
☎ *713/943-1937 or 1-800/441-1230*
*FAX 713/943-1937*
*Hours Sat 10-6 (Mar-Oct); otherwise, by appointment*
*Accessible All except restroom*

With all the Sims participating, this licensed nursery and herb garden shop is definitely a family business! For nine years, they have specialized in on-site propagation and product sales. While most of the herbs are for culinary use, some are medicinal. As Lana Sims told us, "We have a third of an acre devoted to display gardens. There are at least 100 varieties growing all year, and we have a minimum of 40 varieties for sale in the greenhouse from May through October. You will also find dried herbs, jellies, teas, oils and fragrances, herbal flea collars and powders and many, many books. Lana and Bob Sims hold classes on growing and harvesting herbs as well as cooking and crafts using herbs. Be sure to sign up for the newsletter, which comes out in late February and early September, for more information on classes and the spring open house (refreshments, tours and demonstrations.) You can also make reservations for tours, which include a light lunch, featuring, of course, herbs from the garden! As Lana says, "At Our Family's Herbs and Such, we design gardens, offer instruction and provide the herbs. The rest is for you to enjoy!"

## Rosehill Herbs

*14914 Treichel*
*Tomball, Texas 77375*
☎ *281/351-2641*
*FAX 281/357-0099*
*Hours Mon-Sat 9-5, Sun 1-5*
*Accessible Partially*

Rosehill Herbs specializes in fresh herbs. In the fall, the nursery carries a line of unusual herbs including culinary and some medicinal herbs, and several times a year, Rosehill offers free seminars on the various uses of herbs. "All in all, we have a wonderful place to shop and learn," says Minnie Schultz.

*Directions: Located one mile west of Tomball at FM 2920 and Treichel Road.*

## Teas Herbs & Orchids, Inc.

*32920 Decker Prairie Road*
*Magnolia, Texas 77355*
☎ *281/356-2336 or 1-800/660-5735*
*FAX 281/356-2336*
*Hours Mon-Fri 7:30-4, weekends by appointment*
*Accessible Difficult (narrow aisles)*

Teas is a specialty wholesale/retail nursery and grows up to 175 species of herbs, orchids, vegetables and bedding plants. Says owner Janis Teas, "Our hours are limited, but we will make your trip worthwhile. In our 16,000-square-foot greenhouse, you will find unusual plant material at discount prices. You can choose from a whole crop instead of a few flats!" Since our visit, Janis has added a retail shop, offering pots, soaps, teas, oils, scented candles, teapots and other gift items.

For inspiration, there is also a lovely, display herb garden. You will find both culinary and medicinal herbs with the many varieties of basil being the "specialty of the house."

*Directions: Go three to four miles north of Tomball on state highway 249. Turn west on Decker Prairie/ Stagecoach Road. It is less than a mile on the right.*

# Rio Grande Plain

## Nature's Herb Farm

*7193 Old Talley Road #7*
*San Antonio, Texas 78253*
☎ *210/688-9421*
**FAX** *210/688-9042*
**Hours** *Mon-Sat 9-4*
**Accessible** *No*

    Natures Herb Farm offers a large variety of potted herbs from all over the country as well as edible flowers, peppers and native plants. Owner Mary Dunford says, "We farm naturally from potted to fresh-cut." She has been in business for more than 14 years, offering a large selection of high-quality plants, books about herbs and, in spring and fall, classes on herb growing and usage.

*Directions: From 1604 and Sea World, take 1604 to Old 471. At the four-way intersection, take the left onto Old Talley Road and follow the signs.*

# Central Blacklands & Savannas

## Steep Hollow Gardens

*7361 FM 1179*
*Bryan, Texas 77808*
☎ *409/776-5452*
**FAX** *409/776-6448*
**Hours** *Thurs-Sat 10-7 (March-Dec)*
**Accessible** *Yes*

    Carol Patterson-May's rustic gardens are nestled among oak trees and giant grapevines. There's a Bible garden, butterfly garden, edible flower garden, hummingbird garden, native garden and shade garden for your enjoyment. During the blooming season, you can even buy a bouquet from her 20 beds of cutting flowers. There are, of course, many varieties of culinary and medicinal herbs from which to choose.

*Directions: From Bryan, go east on Briarcrest, which becomes FM 1179. The gardens are located four miles past the Brazos Convention Center.*

## *Hill Country*

### *Fredericksburg Herb Farm*

*402 Whitney Street*
*Fredericksburg, Texas 78624*
☎ *830/997-8615 or 1-800/259-HERB*
**FAX** *830/997-5069*
*www.fredericksburgherbfarm.com*
**Hours** *Mon-Sat 9:30-5:30, Sun 1-4: closed Christmas, New Years, Easter & Thanksgiving; Tea Room lunch Tues-Sat 11-2 (reservations)*
**Accessible** *Yes*
**Mail Order**
**Catalog** *$2.00 (refundable with first order)*
**Mailing Address** *P.O. Drawer 927, Fredericksburg, Texas 78624*

Fredericksburg Herb Farm, located only six blocks from Main Street, is a treat for the senses! As Bill Varney explained, "We are an organic herb farm with 14 acres; we have display gardens, retail merchandise, a tea room, greenhouse, bed and breakfast and the newest addition, an aromatherapeutic day spa." We were a little late for the tearoom and a little early for the bed and breakfast, but we were most impressed with the display gardens, greenhouse and gift shop. Upon checking the web site (a really good one), we were charmed by the Gift Crates which are filled with items for the bath or kitchen. The Varney's first book, "Along the Garden Path," contains recipes which are used in the tea room, and their latest book, "Herbs: Growing and Using the Plants of Romance" will be out in the fall of '98. New to us was The Quiet Haus, a day spa offering massages, facials, wraps, etc. that feature herbal products. This spa "from a gardeners' point of view" sounds wonderful! It has been featured in both *Self* and *Victoria* magazines. It's open daily, so call for your reservation!

### *It's About Thyme*

*11726 Manchaca Road*
*Austin, Texas 78748*
☎ *512/280-1192*
**FAX** *512/280-6356*
**Hours** *Daily 9-5*
**Accessible** *Yes*
**Mail Order**
**Catalog** *Free*

In business for about 10 years, It's About Thyme specializes in medicinal, culinary and ornamental herbs. But as Lynne Estes was quick to add, "We also carry annuals, perennials, antique roses, trees such as crepe myrtle and oak as well as shrubs. We are partial to natives and can order items not displayed." The gift shop carries herbal oils, dried herbs, vinegars, candles, soaps and lots of pottery and books. One of the things we found most charming was the collection of birds in the greenhouse. The birds are not for sale, but they certainly enhance the bucolic atmosphere of this Hill Country nursery. We think you'll find it a most pleasant shopping experience!

*Directions: From Austin, go out Manchaca Road, past Slaughter Lane, almost to 1626.*

# The Edible Landscape

The latest trend in gardening circles is a landscape that both teases the eye and pleases the palate! Why not? There's nothing inherently homely about food plants. Who's to say that fig trees are less attractive than magnolias or that grapevines don't measure up to wisteria as a pergola cover? Have you ever tried parsley as a lacy border, strawberries as ground cover or 'Rhubarb' chard as a colorful filler in the autumn perennial bed? Attractive edibles not only make a landscape more interesting, but also they make better use of limited garden space.

Texas is one of the best places on earth to cultivate fruits, nuts and vegetables. Pears, peaches, persimmons and plums all make lovely shade trees for small gardens in Texas. Pecan and walnut trees can provide a canopy for larger landscapes. If your space is limited or you have a bare wall to cover, dwarf fruit trees can be grown in pots or espaliered. Pomegranates make attractive shrubs. Of course, not every fruit and nut producing plant is right for every region in the state. The apple trees that grow well in the cooler winter climes of West Texas would give way to citrus trees in the Rio Grande Valley. Your local county extension agent is your best source of information on varieties that thrive where you live.

Vegetables can be grown anywhere in the state, of course. They are easiest to tend in a conventional patch with raised rectangular beds, but if you don't have time or space to spare, veggies can be sown successfully amidst an ornamental landscape. Historically, farmer's wives mixed flowers in with their vegetables, so urban gardeners are picking up on an old idea when they tuck peppers or okra into the flower bed and run cucumbers or beans up a trellis.

☛**Money Saving Tip: Buy only the best varieties for your region.**

Having easy access to these wholesome plants in your garden allows you to harvest at the exact moment of ripeness. The produce is fresh, and the price is right. It may make sense to concentrate your efforts on herbs and vegetables such as arugula and exotic peppers that are expensive in supermarkets and to leave the carrots and corn for the farmers to grow. Most beginning gardeners make the mistake of thinking too big, anyway. One little plant can produce an incredible number of cherry tomatoes or summer squash!

Good soil is key to successful food crops. You'll need to add liberal amounts of organic compounds, which in turn will encourage worms and microorganisms to flourish. Microorganisms exist in a symbiotic relationship with plants, adding their own body secretions to the soil, enhancing and breaking down the compounds. Without microorganisms, air, water and nutrients become less available, and plants become more susceptible to disease and insects.

Remember, too, that you're making a commitment to managing without chemical pesticides. With the advent of new technologies, gardeners have more control over disease, pests, even the weather. Organic gardeners' secrets include choosing disease resistant varieties, using crop rotation and companion planting. In winter, they'll employ cover crops, which they dig back in to enrich the soil. Expecting some insect damage, they'll compensate with a few extra plants.

I am always tickled when I see gardeners grabbing tomato seedlings at the garden centers on the first warm day in February. Sure as the world, their plants will be zapped by one last hard freeze. You can get a head start on the season, however. Buy your vegetable starts a couple of weeks before your local extension agent says its time to set them out. Move them into larger pots and give the roots a stimulus with a dose of water-soluble houseplant fertilizer. Place the pots in a sunny spot outdoors and move them in at night. Meanwhile, you can be increasing the soil temperature in your planting areas by covering the soil with a layer of clear plastic. Experiment for the fun of it!

# Mail-order Sources for the Vegetable Garden:

## Dixondale Farms

P.O. Box 127
Carrizo Springs, Texas 78834
☎ 830/876-2430
**FAX** 1-888/876-9640
**Hours** Mon-Fri 8-5, Sat 9-12 (Oct 1-June1)
**Catalog** Free

Dixondale Farms is a fourth generation, family owned business which offers the finest onion plants available. According to Bruce Frasier, "Our personalized service and unconditional guarantee makes Dixondale Farms your best bet when ordering onion plants." Advice on growing is available by phone or letter, and planting guides are also offered.

## Plants of the Southwest

Agua Fria, Route 6, Box 11A
Santa Fe, New Mexico 87501
☎ 505/471-2212 or 1-800/788-7333 (orders only)
**FAX** 505/438-8800
**www.**plantsofthesouthwest.com
**Catalog** $3.50

Plants of the Southwest purveys drought tolerant, open pollinated traditional and adapted varieties of vegetables, herbs and chili peppers. The catalog urges customers to try some of the more unusual edibles such as purple amaranth, quinoa and tomatillos. "Allow some plants to go to seed, collect and store in a cool, dry place," says Gail Haggard, demonstrating that the company is not just out to sell a product. She talks of a "forest of food" with fruit and nut trees overhead and berries, grapes, herbs and vegetables on the land and beets and carrots underground, "all free of poisons and preservatives." Also see page 247.

## Seeds of Change

P.O. Box 15700
Santa Fe, New Mexico 87506-5700
☎ 1-888/762-7333
**Hours** Mon-Fri 8:30-5 (MST)
**Catalog** Free

"Seeds of Change is committed to providing 100% certified organic, open-pollinated seeds of the highest quality including many heirloom, traditional and unique Seeds of Change varieties. In so doing, we share with gardeners our commitment to sustainable agriculture and socially responsible food production systems. Seeds of Change contracts with certified organic family farmers across America to supply us with the seed we offer and works with various communities worldwide (Latin America, Africa, etc.) to spread the practices of sustainable agriculture." This company is strictly mail order and does not sell retail from the office. Its color catalog is outstanding. And inspiring! Beyond the array of gourmet vegetables one would expect, it offers annuals and perennials, books, tools and gift baskets, as well.

## Willhite Seed, Inc.

P.O. Box 23
Poolville, Texas 76487
☎ 817/599-8656 or 1-800/828-1840
**FAX** 817/599-5843
*www.willhiteseed.com*
**Hours** Mon-Fri 8-12 &1-5, Sat 8-12 ( mid-Jan to May); Mon-Fri 8-12 & 1-5 (June to mid-Jan)
**Catalog** Free

Willhite Seed Company carries all types of vegetable seed, from beans to tomatoes. But if you like melons, take a look in this catalog or check the Web site! The company sells many standard and open pollinated vegetable varieties, as well as hybrid varieties. All of the seeds are described in the catalog (many with color pictures), and Wilhite even offers unique varieties from France and India. "Our goal is the same as it has been for the past 78 years...to continue to provide the highest quality seed to our customers," said Carole Clark and Robyn Coffey. Their hearts seem to be in melons, given the many pages in the catalog devoted to cantaloupes and watermelons. Advice is freely offered!

*Directions: Should you care to visit, take Highway 199 west from Fort Worth. About 15 miles west of Springtown, take Highway 199 south (towards Weatherford) three miles to Poolville. Located next to the Post Office.*

# Mail-order Sources for Fruits, Nuts & Berries:

## Bob Wells Nursery

P.O. Box 606
Lindale, Texas 75771
☎ 903/882-3550
**FAX** 903/882-8030
**Hours** Mon-Sat 8-5 (call to confirm)
**Accessible** No
**Catalog** Free

This highly regarded, fourth-generation company specializes in fruits and berries. It's an excellent source for the best variety of blackberries, blueberries, boysenberries, raspberries and strawberries. You'll find grapes for the table and the vineyard here, as well. The firm also grows a large selection of shade and nut trees as well as crepe myrtles, roses and other flowering shrubs. It provides bare root trees and plants from November to May and container-grown varieties all year. According to owner Bob Wells, "We can sell you one tree or up into the hundreds and thousands." Bob, who works with horticulturists at Texas A&M and the University of Arkansas, is happy to visit with and advise retail customers. Occasionally there's a sale on shade or fruit trees.

*Directions: Located two miles east of Lindale on Highway 16.*

## Enoch Berry Farm

Route 2, Box 227
Fouke, Arkansas 71837
☎ 870/653-2806
**www.**berryfarm.com
**Hours** Mon-Fri 8-5
**Catalog** Price list

Enoch Berry Farm carries the newest blackberry cultivars from the University of Arkansas Experimental Station. Among the varieties offered are several patented ones such as the 'Navaho Thornless' and the 'Arapaho Thornless', both of which are erect and bear very high fruit. The 'Kiowa Thorny' is a "super size" with high quality fruit as well. Mr. Enoch ships plants from November through March.

## Highlander Nursery

P.O. Box 177
Pettigrew, Arkansas 72752
☎ 501/677-2300
**Hours** Daily 8-5
**Accessible** Yes
**Catalog** Free

Highlander Nursery is a specialized grower of blueberry plants. According to Lee and Louise McCoy, "We are a 'Mom and Pop' nursery with 20 years of experience propagating numerous northern and southern highbush blueberry cultivars." This nursery ships UPS with minimal root loss and nursery-to-field time. The McCoy's are happy to offer instructions and advice.

## Janak Nursery

*Highway 90 A*
*Shiner, Texas 77984*
☎ *512/798-3092*
**Catalog** *Free price list*

    Janak Nursery ships three varieties of the hardy jujube. See complete listing on page 218.

## Love Creek Orchards

*P. O. Box 1401*
*Medina, Texas 78055*
☎ *830/589-2588*
**Hours** *Mon-Sat 9-5, Sun 1-5*
**Accessible** *Partially*
**Catalog** *Free*

    Love Creek Orchards Cider Mill Store is a retail outlet for apples and dwarf apple trees. The owners also grow and sell several native trees from the Texas Hill Country.
*Directions: On Highway 16, on Main Street, Medina, between Kerrville and Bandera.*

## Pense Nursery

*16518 Matrie Lane*
*Mountainburg, Arkansas 72946*
☎ *501/369-2494*
*www.alcasoft.com\pense*
**Hours** *Mon-Fri 8-5*
**Catalog** *Free*

    For over 40 years, Pense Nursery has been family owned and operated, specializing in small fruit plants. Their 72 varieties include all of the new releases from the University of Arkansas, as well as leading varieties from around the world. Here you will find blackberry, raspberry, blueberry, strawberry, currants, gooseberry, elderberry, rhubarb, asparagus, seedless grapes and wine grapes. Pense Nursery also offers *The Backyard Berry Book* for people wanting to learn more about all areas of small fruit plants. As Phillip Pense reports, "We supply commercial growers, all the way down to home gardeners. Our plants are state inspected yearly and are premium quality plants, free of any known diseases." There are quantity price breaks (direct from the grower), and advice is freely given on small fruit growing... pruning, trellising, diseases and more.

## Severtson Farms

*4000 Highway 78 North*
*Wylie, Texas 75098*
☎ *972/442-1357 or 1-888/442-6846*
**FAX** *1-888/442-6846*
**Hours** *Flexible, so call first*
**Accessible** *Yes*
**Catalog** *Free information packet*

Kern and Mary Severtson operate a Certified Texas Nursery, selling (retail and worldwide mail-order) the patented Doyle Thornless Blackberry. Kern is more than enthusiastic in describing the product! As he says, "This blackberry yields between 10 and 20 gallons per plant, whereas the ordinary blackberry yields about one or two quarts. The berries grow in clumps, like grapes, and there are often 100 berries per clump! The fruit is delicious, and the plants don't 'take over' the way other blackberries do." And more good news. While a half-pint of blackberries may cost up to four dollars, the Doyle Thornless plant is a mere $14.95. As old "blackberry-pickers" ourselves, we find the "thornless" part most appealing! Severtson Farms also carries a fertilizer said to ensure great results, and the Severtsons have plenty of knowledge to share. They will have other unusual berry plants and fruiting trees by the spring of 1999. See the information packet for ordering their new blackberry cookbook, as well. Hummm, a cobbler sure sounds good right now!

## Womack's Nursery Co.

*Route 1, Box 80*
*De Leon, Texas 76444-9649*
☎ *254/893-6497*
**FAX** *254/893-3400*
**Hours** *Mon-Sat 8-12 & 1-5*
**Accessible** *No*
**Catalog** *Free*

Since 1937, Womack's has been a respected name in the Texas nursery business. From mid-December through mid-March, the company ships-out thousands and thousands of grapevines, berry plants, and fruit and nut trees adapted to Southern soils and climates. It's also a great source for propagation tools and supplies!

*Directions: Located on Highway 6 between De Leon & Gorman.*

## Chapter Eight

# Special Plants for Special Places

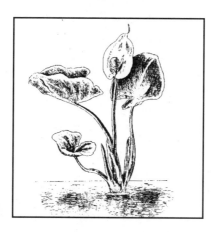

*"I know a bank whereon the
wild thyme blows,
Where oxslips and the nodding violet grows
Quite over-canopied with
luscious woodbine,
With sweet musk-roses, and
with eglantine…
….Shakespeare, A Midsummer-Night's Dream*

# Water Gardens

**W**ater is the elemental source of life and beauty. Quiet or dancing, no other substance adds such joy to a garden. The very words we use to describe its sights and sounds — bubbling, gurgling, rushing, trickling, shooting, spilling — suggest water's magical ability to play on our emotions. Flowing lazily along a natural stream, water is relaxing; tumbling down rocks, it has the power to excite. Be it wall fountain, fishpond, reflecting pool, bog or stream, indeed the smallest water feature and its attendant plants seem to cool the hottest summer day. Noisy running water can even be used to camouflage the sound of passing traffic.

A water feature may serve other utilitarian purposes. A naturally occurring depression, which could be a liability in the landscape, can be widened into a charming little bog. A rock-lined stream bed that channels water away from the house may suggest a pleasing creek, even when dry. Swimming pools and spas can be designed to appear as natural ponds or formal fountains, thus serving decorative as well as practical functions.

Fishponds, which were much in vogue early in this century, fell out of favor in the 1950s. People simply decided that the maintenance requirements were too great. Ponds are wildly popular again, partly because improved materials have made them less expensive to build and easier to maintain. Just how enthusiastically Texans have embraced water gardening became obvious to me when my Austin gardening friend Bill Ater mentioned that the Austin Pond Society has grown from a handful of members to the largest garden group in the city in the past five years!

Designed correctly, a garden pond can become self-sustaining. Plants will help keep the water clean, and a few colorful koi will eat any breeding mosquitoes. Today's pumps are energy-efficient, and new ultraviolet sterilizers make it easy to keep the pond free of algae without harming the fish. Traditional formal pools and naturalistic free-form ponds can now be made with flexible pond liners or pre-formed fiberglass and capped with brick or cut stone. Often the pond will incorporate a fountain or waterfall. Whatever form the water takes, the gardening possibilities in and around the pool include a range of delicate and colorful plants that would seem out-of-place in a dry landscape — luscious ferns, bog plants and water lilies. Add special-effects lighting, and you'll have a focal point to enjoy around the clock.

For maximum emotional effect, the water feature should be placed where it will reflect sky, trees and flowers by day. Visualize a pond from different sitting areas in the garden; picture a waterfall; layout various shapes with a garden hose. Let your imagination run free. You may even want a bridge to cross or an island to conquer. Observe carefully how nature builds her waterways; natural-looking streams and ponds are difficult to achieve. You may want to seek professional help. Talk to other people who have ponds and learn from their mistakes.

A few words of caution! Do not dam or alter a natural stream that runs through your property without a permit. Check the drainage around the area where you plan to build a pond (it may overflow during periods of heavy rain). Be sure to avoid underground utilities. Remember that children can drown in a few inches of water. Check regulations in your municipality before beginning construction and secure your pool or pond as soon as it is begun.

# Sources for Building Your Water Garden:

## Dunis Studios

23645 North Highway 281
San Antonio, Texas 78258
☎ 210-497-5787
**FAX** 210-497-8987
**Hours** Mon-Fri 8-12 & 1-5
**Accessible** Yes
**Mail Order**
**Catalog** Free brochures on request

This company makes gorgeous hand-painted tiles suitable for all kinds of exterior applications — fountain surrounds, pool liners, murals, signage and floor accents. The company has an extensive line of production pieces with floral and fish motifs. It also has the capability of making custom tiles or matching your color theme. Among its outstanding products is a line of tile with deep-sculpted flowers fabricated in several sizes from 2"x2" to 8"x8". The line includes ivy-patterned 2"x8" border tiles and a border depicting waving grasses.

## Firestone Building Products Company

☎ 1-800/428-4442, extension 3261 (Texas sales representative)

Firestone's *Pond Gard*® is absolutely the greatest for lining a pond! It's a black rubber material that's extremely durable, fish friendly and easy to install. It costs only pennies more per square foot than plastic products and will last for years. Call to get the name of a nearby retail source.

## Garden Accents

14907 Treichel Road
Tomball, Texas 77375
☎ 281/351-4804
**FAX** 281/255-9121
**Hours** Mon-Sat 8-5
**Accessible** Partially (outdoor display only)
**Mail Order**
**Catalog** Free

Bob Folger is what makes Garden Accents memorable. He creates a beautiful rock waterfall, then makes a mold of it and casts the piece in concrete. His products are sold all over Texas. Homeowners can call the factory for the nearest dealer or visit to find products not in the brochures. It will be an experience! Bob collects all sorts of concrete fountains and ornaments from his travels, but once he gets them, he doesn't want to let them go. In spite of that frustration, people usually leave with the trunk full. His wife Jeannine reports, "Bob adds his unique touch even to the business hours. He is usually here seven days a week until dark." And she jokes, "I'm fortunate because he is afraid of the dark. It's still best if you call first. Advice is given... sometimes without being asked!"

*Directions: From the intersection of 2920 and 249 in Tomball, go one mile west on 2920 to Treichel Road.*

## Lilypons Water Gardens

*839 FM 1489*
*Brookshire, Texas 77423-0188*
☎ *281/391-0076*
***FAX****281/934-2000*
*www.lilypons.com*
**Hours** *Mon-Sat 9:30-5:30, Sun 11-5:30 (March-Nov); Mon-Sat 9:30-4:30 (Dec-Feb); closed from Dec 24-Jan 3*
**Accessible** *Yes*
**Mail Order**
**Catalog** *$5.00*

Lilypons is a nationally known retail and mail-order nursery specializing in aquatic plants and an absolute delight to visit! Explains Leo vanPoppel, "We grow our own crop of water lilies and other aquatic plants and offer the ponds, pumps, fountains, sculpture and everything else needed to create a beautiful setting in your garden." The catalog is replete with color photographs of new, exclusive, fragrant, top-performing and night-blooming lily varieties in a multitude of hues and shapes. There are a dozen varieties of hardy lotus pictured here and almost as many choices in Louisiana iris. Other plants for the water's edge include both sun-loving and shade-tolerant species and a host of tropical bog plants. You can order koi, shubunkins and Japanese fantails, plus all the food and supplies to keep them healthy. More than just a catalog, it is packed with tips and ideas. The gift shop at the Brookshire store carries an array of accessories from wind chimes to frog candlesticks. Says Leo, "Call us any time. We will be happy to answer your questions and help you in any manner. Who knows? You may become immersed in the engaging, peaceful and tranquil hobby of water gardening." On-line you'll find seasonal tips, current specials, ordering information and a map.

## Materials Marketing

*120 West Josephine*
*San Antonio, Texas 78212*
☎ *210/731-8453*

*1801 North Lamar, suite 200*
*Austin, Texas 78701*
☎ *512/328-0225*

*3433 West Alabama*
*Houston, Texas 77027*
☎ *713/960-8601*

Materials Marketing is known for its wonderful array of stone fountains. It's also a great source for stone pool coping and several lines of decorative tile for the surrounds and liners. You'll also find compatible benches, birdbaths and decorative containers in the company's elegant showrooms. See complete listing on page 116.

## Villeroy & Boch Ceramic Tile Factory Outlet

2929 Longhorn Boulevard,
suites 101 & 102
Austin, Texas 78758
☎ 512/832-6694
FAX 512/832-9986

2230 LBJ Freeway, suite 100
Dallas, Texas 75229
☎ 972/488-2922
FAX 972/488-2969

**Hours** Mon-Fri 7:30-5, Sat 9-1
**Accessible** Yes
   Here we found great frost-proof decorative tile for fountains and walls, as well as handsome selections in slate and quarry tile for paving around pond or pool.

## Water Garden Gems, Inc.

3136 Bolton Road
Marion, Texas 78124
☎ 210/659-5841
FAX 210/659-1528
**Hours** Mon-Sat 9-5 (Nov-March), Mon-Sat 9-6 (April-Oct), Sun & holidays 11-4
**Accessible** Partially
**Mail Order**
**Catalog** Free
   Water Garden Gems offers complete water gardening supplies...plants, pumps, filters, pond liners, fountains, books, gifts, water quality products, fish (koi and goldfish), fish food, statuary, stepping stones, lighting (pond and outdoor), consultation and design. The catalog is complete, and Water Garden Gems carries the new, state-of-the-art *Bubble Bead Filter* for ornamental ponds. According to manager Burt Nichols, "This filter is manufactured in San Antonio and shipped around the world to Koi enthusiasts and aquaculture facilities."

# Regional Resources for Plants, Fish & Fountains:
## Cross Timbers & Grand Prairie

### Aqua-Tec Aquatic Farms

5916 Johnson County Road 402
Grandview, Texas 76050
☎ 817/996-1741
**Hours** By appointment only
**Accessible** Yes
**Mail Order**
**Catalog** Free price list
**Mailing Address** P.O. Box 817, Grandview, Texas 76050
   "We are water garden specialists at Aqua-Tec," owner Wiley Horton told us. "And you will find us on both the Texas Extension Service and the Neil Sperry Web site. We have been asked to provide a display at the Texas State Fair this year and plan to do so." Serving predominately the Metroplex area, this company sells, builds and installs water features. A certified Texas grown aquatic plant source, Aqua-Tec offers not only a large collection of plants, but also carries ponds, fish, supplies, equipment and books.

## Birdies' Backyard Habitats

*3300 Airport Freeway*
*Fort Worth, Texas 76111*
☎ *817/ 222-0558*
**FAX** *817/222-0578*
**Hours** *Tues-Sat 10-6, Sun 12-5*
**Accessible** *Yes*

"We strive to be in concert with nature and espouse organics as much as possible," said manager Andrew Spear. The company stocks pre-fabricated ponds and both butyl and pvc liners. You'll find aquatic plants and fish, plus all the supplies to keep your pond healthy and running. Also see page 384.

## Weston Gardens In Bloom, Inc.

*8101 Anglin Drive*
*Fort Worth, Texas 76140*
☎ *817/572-0549*
See complete listing on page 183.

# *Trinity Blacklands*

## Dickson Brothers, Inc.

*204 North Galloway*
*Mesquite, Texas 75149*
☎ *972/288-7537*
**FAX** *972/288-7536*
***www**.dicksonbrothers.com*
**Hours** *Mon-Fri 8-5:30, Sat 8-5*
**Accessible** *Yes*
**Mail Order**
**Catalog** *On-line*

As they proudly proclaim at Dickson Brothers, "For 25 years, we have been your water gardening headquarters!" In this company's 20,000-square-foot showroom and ½-acre outdoor site, you will find absolutely everything you need to enhance your water garden. Mary Traveland commented, "We only carry the best! All of our plants are Texas-grown." In the way of hard goods, Dickson Brothers has both flexible pond liners and green fiberglass pre-formed basins imported from England. You'll find *Cyprio* filtration systems, *Little Giant* pump systems and *Atlantis* pump and filtration systems, just to name a few of the major manufacturers represented. There are underwater lighting systems, waterfalls, floating fountains, decorative bridges and benches and, of course, fish and fish supplies. The water lilies are potted, established and ready to go. Also offered are marginal bog plants, oxygenators and aquatic fertilizer tabs. You will find informative books, brochures and hand-outs (we particularly liked the seasonal check lists), as well as a most helpful, informative staff. There's even more to see on the company's new Web site. Products can be shipped by UPS or common carrier.

## Powers Landscape Nursery

1150 Highway 205
Rockwall, Texas 75032
☎ 972/771-3738
*FAX* 972/771-6881
**Hours** By appointment
**Accessible** No

"Our water plants are potted, leafed out and ready to put in the pond," explains Johnny Mack Powers. His primarily wholesale nursery has four acres of water gardens, butterfly and hummingbird gardens, perennial gardens and wildflowers. "Powers is the largest grower of aquatic plants in North Texas," says Johnny Mack, who is always happy to share advice and information about water gardening. For embellishing the surrounding environment, he carries hard-to-find perennials, concentrating on those that do well in hot weather.

*Directions: Located 4½ miles south of IH-30 on Highway 205.*

## Ultrascapes Garden Gallery

404 Southwestern Blvd.
Coppell, Texas 75019
☎ 972/471-1271
*FAX* 972/393-7839
**Hours** Tues-Sat 9-5, Sun 12-5
**Accessible** Partially (no bathrooms)

Water lilies, koi, ponds, liners and a natural water garden kit with natural stone are all displayed at this specialty store. You'll also discover stone fountains, lanterns, sculpture and benches here. To complete your Japanese garden, the firm carries finished bonsai, pottery, tools and supplies, as well as landscape-size Japanese maples, pines and Japanese junipers.

## Water Gardens Galore

4236 West Lovers Lane
Dallas, Texas 75209
☎ 214/956-7382
*FAX* 214/351-5918
*www.*wggalore.com
**Hours** Tues-Sat 10-6; open Sun 1-4 in spring & summer
**Accessible** Partially (an inside ramp is planned)

As Steve Moeller explained, "We exist in a highly specialized niche. There is more to water gardening than digging a hole and dropping something in it. To be successful, you must have a clear goal in mind and get solid information and quality materials." The company provides any and all the help a client needs or wants. For the "do-it-yourselfer," Water Gardens Galore has all the materials including ponds, pumps, plants, fish and food, plus plenty of advice. For those who desire a hassle-free accent for their landscape, the company designs, installs and maintains a wide variety of features. According to Steve, "With the Texas Parks and Wildlife Department's Backyard Wildlife Habitat program, we plan on being among the first retail establishments to be certified as a 'Wildlife Habitat' and will become specialists in this endeavor." If there is an abundance of plants in October, you'll find items on sale. Seminars and special events are also offered at various times of the year. The Web site offers images of lovely ponds, instructions for winter care and an interesting Q & A.

## *Coastal Prairies & Marshes*

### Buchanan's Native Plants

*611 East 11th*
*Houston, Texas 77008*
☎ *713/861-5702*
See complete listing on page 199.

### Lilypons Water Gardens

*839 FM 1489*
*Brookshire, Texas 77423-0188*
☎ *281/391-0076*
Throughout the spring this nationally known water-garden center offers classes and demonstrations. Two festivals are held each year: the Water Garden Festival in June, when the gardens are at their peak, and the Koi Festival the third weekend in September. Groups may visit at any time for a self-guided tour, or you may schedule a guided tour simply by calling to set up an appointment. Even if you're not interested in water gardening, this is a fabulous place to visit! See page 318.
*Directions: Located 30 miles west of Houston, south of IH-10 on FM 1489.*

## *Coastal Bend*

### Adams Nursery

*1515 Highway 35 South*
*Rockport, Texas 78382*
☎ *512/729-7111*
See complete listing on page 206.

### Four Seasons Garden Center

*1209 East Salem Road*
*Victoria, Texas 77904*
☎ *512/575-8807*
See complete listing on page 207.

## *Valley*

### Allen's Garden Center

*1800 East Highway 83*
*Weslaco, Texas 78596*
☎ *956/973-1998*
See complete listing on page 209.

### Stuart Place Nursery

*7701 West Business Highway 83*
*Harlingen, Texas 78552*
☎ *956/428-4439*
See complete listing on page 208.

# Rio Grande Plain

## Rainbow Gardens

2585 Thousand Oaks
San Antonio, Texas 78232
☎ 210/494-6131

8516 Bandera Road
San Antonio, Texas 78250
☎ 210/680-2394

See complete listing on page 213.

## Water Garden Gems, Inc.

3136 Bolton Road
Marion, Texas 78124
☎ 210/659-5841

If you need it, this company has it! (See complete listing on page 319.) Water Garden Gems holds two seminars each year — the third week-end in May and the second weekend in October.

*Directions: Located on IH-10 east of San Antonio between exits 593 (Trainer Hale Road) and 595 (Zuehl Road).*

## Water Gardens of Texas

29110 Highway 281 North
Bulverde, Texas 78163
☎ 830/980-7663
**FAX** 830/980-7663
**Hours** *Wed-Sat 10-5; Sun 12-5 (call to confirm)*
**Accessible** *Partially (asphalt to main areas; wood shavings around ponds)*

Located a little north of San Antonio, the display ponds at Water Gardens of Texas are nestled under a canopy of live oaks. They're stocked with lovely aquatic plants and ornamental fish. "Water enthusiasts can see and learn how easily they'll be able to reproduce a similar effect in their own gardens," says Steve Cresswell. "Or, we can construct a natural stone waterfall and pond for you." The firm carries all the supplies and plants, as well as the fish. This company won the Water Features Award at the 1998 San Antonio Parade of Homes.

*Directions: Go nine miles north of 1604 on 281North to the southern outskirts of Bulverde.*

# Central Blacklands & Savannas

## Producers Cooperative

1800 North Texas Avenue
Bryan, Texas 77803
☎ 409/778-6000

See complete listing on page 217.

# Hill Country

## The Emerald Garden

*6910 Highway 71 West*
*Austin, Texas 78735*
☎ *512/288-5900*
*FAX 512/892-7272*
**Hours** *Mon-Sat 8-6, Sun 10-4 (daylight savings time); closes at 5:30 on standard time*
**Accessible** *Partially*

The Emerald Garden, a complete garden center, carries almost any type of plant material you might want... and much more! Says Jeff Yarbrough, "We are Central Texas' water garden specialists, offering plants, pumps, filters, fiberglass ponds, rubber liners, fish, snails, tub gardens, pond chemicals, fish food, fountains, water falls and all kinds of decorative rock, from river gravel to boulders." You will also find a bulk soil yard with over 20 different materials, four kinds of compost, special growing mixes, two kinds of sand, gravel in four sizes, mulches and flag stone. The Emerald Garden holds a water lily show and sale in June as well as seminars on ponds, herbs, perennials and soil amendments.

## Hill Country Nursery

*1398 FM 2673*
*Canyon Lake, Texas 78133*
☎ *210/964-3628*
See complete listing on page 228.

## Murffy's Nursery

*901 Sam Bass Road*
*Round Rock, Texas 78681*
☎ *512/255-3353*
See complete listing on page 227.

## Water Color Gardens

*4050 North Highway 183*
*Liberty Hill, Texas 78642*
☎ *512/515-5287*
*FAX 512/515-6486*
**Hours** *Call for hours and directions*
**Accessible** *No*
**Mail Order**
**Catalog** *Free price list*
**Mailing Address** *P.O. Box 358, Cedar Park, Texas 78630*

At Water Color Gardens, owner Kenneth Wilkerson carries only aquatic plants, with over 100 species (lilies, lotus and many others) in stock. He has recently expanded into the retail market and can both deliver and install the plants.

# Red Rolling Plains

## Olive's Nursery

*3402 Sherwood Way*
*San Angelo, Texas 76901*
☎ *915/949-3756*

When you visit San Angelo's international water lily display, you will certainly be motivated to visit Olive's Nursery where you will find well-known water lily hybridizer Ken Landon. As Debbie Olive told us, "We have been in the water gardening business for 30 years, long before it became so fashionable! We've had lots of experience selling, building and installing water features." This nursery carries not only plants, but also materials, equipment, fish, supplies and books. There are also many free informative pamphlets. See complete listing on page 231.

# High Plains

## The Garden Patch

*1311 Alcove Avenue*
*Lubbock, Texas 79416-6700*
☎ *806/793-0982*
**FAX** *806/785-3076*
**Hours** *Mon-Sat 9-5:30; Sun 1-5:30 (March 1-July 15); closed Jan & Feb, except by appt.*
**Accessible** *Yes*

Representing the third generation of her family in the nursery business, owner Roberta Davis is a Texas Master Certified Nursery Professional. The Garden Patch is a small nursery that emphasizes healthy plants and personal service. Explains Roberta, "Rather than trying to have some of everything, we put special emphasis on water gardening (including plants and supplies) and on perennials and drought tolerant plants." She has given the greenhouse and shop a country flavor with her collection of primitive antiques. We enjoyed seeing flowers planted in old buckets and hung from pulleys, plantings in old hog troughs, wash tubs, worn-out boots, hollow logs or other unusual containers. The staff will even plant containers that the customer brings in. Merchandise is usually marked down in July and August. There's an annual water lily seminar here, and this nursery contributes to Lubbock's water garden tour each year.

*Directions: Go 2½ miles west of Loop 289 on the Levelland Highway (W. 19th Street) and turn right on Alcove and go another ½-mile. Look for the sign by the road.*

## Midland Gardens

*4621 Sinclair*
*Midland, Texas 79707*
☎ *915/520-2012 (same # for FAX)*
**Hours** *Mon-Sat 10-7, Sun 12-6*
**Accessible** *Yes*

Family owned and operated, these old greenhouses have been serving the area since 1948, and they're still growing! On the drawing board is an extensive display garden with a 20,000 gallon pond, a garden train and children's classes. Midland Gardens specializes in natives, perennials and aquarium/ pond plants. "Our clientele base has leaned to the 'newcomers' in both the gardening and aquarium/pond hobbies, but we offer a large enough plant selection to also excite the 'old-timers.' Our goal is to give our customers more than enough knowledge to make their efforts a success. We want to be known as the Oasis of the Permian Basin," says Glenn Akin. Staff members hold monthly seminars on aquarium start-ups, pond building, West Texas gardening tips and more.

# Patios & Garden Rooms

Plants in handsome containers add significantly to the graciousness of any outdoor seating area. A single, elegant container plant can be used to serve as a focal point in the landscape. Paired, potted plants lend warmth to entrances and frame gateways. While distinctive specimen plants (such as a tree rose, a handsome cactus, an azalea or gardenia in full flower) can stand alone, I generally like plants displayed in groups, with a variety of textures and leaf shapes, especially when played against a bare wall.

Mixed plantings in a single container are also popular again. All the home magazines are featuring "how-to" articles on window boxes, Victorian-style hanging baskets and urns overflowing with multicolored flowers. Throughout the growing season my entrance courtyard and rear patio are brimming with tropical plants and seasonal annuals. One good decorator trick I've learned is to mass potted plants on both sides of a glass door or low window wall, doubling the impact inside and out.

In winter I turn my full attention to indoor gardening. My husband has always grumbled when asked to haul-in all the plants that decorate the outdoor living areas throughout the growing season, but even he is pleased with the effect when our sunny greenhouse/ breakfast room is filled with blooming hibiscus and bougainvillea on cold days. Especially in winter, a home is incomplete without houseplants to brighten bare walls, spill from bookshelves and bloom on tabletops.

The design ideas you use for the placement container plants on a deck or patio

apply equally well to houseplants. Big tropical plants are very useful for camouflaging architectural flaws. I've used plants to fill one end of a long narrow room, to divide space in an overly large room and always to soften the corners. I use fluffy ferns to fill the empty fireplace in summer (rotating them weekly between the garden and the house). In choosing houseplants, it's important to consider the scale of both the room and the plants. Too many small plants can make a room look "fussy." On the other hand, huge plants or plants with large leaves may look menacing in a small space.

I first learned the visual impact of indoor plants years ago when friends bought a house with a huge formal living room. Like most young couples, they couldn't afford much in the way of furnishings, so they invested in several large ficus trees. The "garden room" effect was so pleasing that they never did buy all the fine furniture they had originally envisioned.

Tropical plants are literally lifesavers for people who spend long hours confined indoors. Houseplants not only provide vital oxygen, but also raise a room's humidity level, which is a gift to anyone who suffers with dry skin. Used in large numbers, houseplants have even been shown to cleanse the air of noxious household chemicals.

A two-year study by NASA and the Associated Landscape Contractors of America proved that 'Janet Craig', 'Warneckii' and marginata dracaenas, peace lily, English ivy, mother-in-law's tongue, green spider plant, golden pothos and bamboo palm are among the best plants for removing concentrations of chemicals from the air. The researchers estimated that 15 to 20 potted plants of these species purify the interior of a typical 1,800-square-foot house. The other good news is that these common plants are easy to grow and among the most attractive for interior plantscaping.

It's important to know that most of the tropicals available in the United States are grown outdoors (in the Rio Grande Valley, California, Florida or Hawaii). Specialty shops and better garden centers know to acclimatize tropical plants for several weeks before offering them to the public. By gradually reducing light and moisture levels and withholding fertilizer, they prepare the plant for the drier conditions and lower light levels of a home environment. It's worth asking a nursery manager how the plants you buy have been grown and acclimatized.

Avoid plants that have brown edges on the leaves, which may indicate sun-scald or excessive fertilizer. Pale or yellow foliage may be a sign of improper watering. Sparse or leggy plants may have been subjected to abnormally forced growth. Roots growing above the soil surface or out the drainage hole are a sure sign of a plant that has become root-bound.

Inspect for insects on the undersides of leaves and at the junctions between the stem and the leaves. A "bargain" plant is certainly no bargain if it expires within a week or introduces an insect infestation to your existing plants.

☛**Money-saving tip: Inspect houseplants carefully before making your purchase.**

It's probably a good idea to place a new plant in quarantine in any case. To reduce the shock of moving it into a dry environment, mist the foliage every day with tepid water. It's also good practice to flood new plants with water to flush out salts that may have accumulated from heavy fertilizing by the grower. Run a slow stream of water through the soil for a full five minutes and let the plant drain thoroughly. (A bathtub or shower works well for this task.) Periodically, I run water through all of my house plants to prevent the build-up of salts.

It's normal for a few older leaves at the bottom to die as the plant adjusts to new conditions. Instead of pinching-off yellowed leaves, allow them to drop naturally; nature has a mechanism for sealing the wound. If the plant loses a lot of leaves, you're probably watering too much or have placed the plant where it isn't getting enough light. If it dies within the first month in spite of your TLC, take it back and ask for a replacement.

# Caring for Container Plants

Containerized plants of any kind require more attention than plants in the ground. Most of the houseplants you buy are grown in a potting soil, which contains no actual garden soil, but rather a blend of composted bark, sphagnum peat moss, vermiculite and other ingredients blended to provide good drainage, aeration and moisture retention. Because plants quickly use up the nutrients in the potting soil, they'll need regular doses of fertilizer. A professional grower we know keeps his hanging baskets gorgeous throughout the growing season with a single application of a twelve-month slow-release fertilizer.

Houseplants and containerized shrubs that remain outdoors through the year will require periodic re-potting. When the roots become too large for the pot, the plant can't store enough water to sustain itself. One can assume that if the plant has gotten bigger, the roots have grown as well. I generally re-pot most of my houseplants every year into a container that is an inch or two larger than the original. If the pot has been previously used, scrub it with an antibacterial soap. Gently shake-off the old potting soil and fill one-third of the new pot with a high-quality packaged soil mix. (Never use common garden soil, which will be too heavy for container plants and may contain weeds or pathogens.) Allow space for adding water; the root crown should be about an inch below the top of the pot.

In hot weather, the hanging baskets and container plants on your patio or porch may need watering twice each day. The upside to gardening in containers is that not a precious drop of water is wasted to surrounding soil. By adding biologically harmless polymers to the soil, you can further reduce the water needs of containerized plants by up to 75%.

Most garden centers maintain huge houseplant departments these days, and tropical plants have become almost ridiculously inexpensive. The ferns and potted palms favored in Victorian times are popular once again, but your options only begin there. With worldwide transportation, exotic species from tropical regions all over the world are available to the discriminating shopper. Never has there been such a vast array of colorful blossoms, fanciful leaf patterns, and marvelous plant-forms from which to choose. You'll find a wealth of especially wonderful tropicals available from the specialty nurseries listed on the following pages.

# Mail-order Sources for Tropicals & Exotics:

## Air Exposé

4703 Leffingwell Street
Houston, Texas 77026-3434
☎ 713/672-7017
**Catalog** $2.00 or self-addressed stamped business envelope
This company grows 400 varieties of hibiscus, seven varieties of althea and 14 varieties of bougainvillea. See complete listing on page 331.

## Palmer Orchids

P. O. Box 1143
Pasadena, Texas 77501
☎ 713/472-1364
*www.flash.net/~palmerr/*
**Catalog** On-line only
You'll find a selection of choice orchids on this Web site. See page 332 for complete listing.

## The Plumeria People

910 Leander Drive
Leander, Texas 78641
☎ 512/259-0807
**Catalog** $3.00
The Plumeria People offers fragrant, flowering plants — plumerias, bougainvilleas, bulbs, hibiscus, gingers, flowering vines and other rare tropical plants. This company also carries books and specialty fertilizers for tropicals. "We have the most beautiful catalog you've ever seen!" says Harry Leuzinger. One of the company's many happy customers wrote, "Wow! What a catalog! It was worth the wait. Many thanks for a stunning assortment of plants. I look forward eagerly to the arrival of the plumeria, whose fragrance I breathed over 20 years ago, but have never forgotten." The Summer Sale Spectacular is mailed to customers annually. To visit, see page 335.

## Rhapis Gardens

P.O. Box 287
Gregory, Texas 78359
☎ 512/643-2061
*www.rarepalms.com*
**Catalog** $2.00
Explains owner Lynn McKamey, "We specialize in four genera of the tropical plants. *Rhapis excelsa* (lady palm) is a low-light palm used mainly for interiors, although these plants will tolerate temperatures as low as twenty-five degrees. We grow 12 different varieties of lady palms, including variegated, in sizes ranging from 5" pots to 8' specimens in 17" pots. Our *Cissus Rhombifolia* (grape ivy) is an excellent interior/exterior container ivy, hardy to thirty-two degrees and available in 4", 6" and 10" baskets. We also grow 15 varieties of *Polyscias* (Ming aralia) in 4" and 6" pots; these are excellent interior container plants. And, the *Cycus revoluta* (king sago) can be used as a landscape or container plant in brightly lighted interiors. It is hardy to 15 degrees." Rhapis Gardens is not open to the public.

## Stokes Tropicals

P.O. Box 9868
New Iberia, Lousiana 70562-9868
☎ 1-800/624-9706
FAX 318/365-6991
www.stokestropicals.com
Catalog $4.00

This company's color catalog is filled with pictures of rare varieties of bananas, bromeliads, gingers, heliconias, plumerias and more. Just looking at it will make you drool! You can also order plants, books, specialty fertilizers and gardening garments from the on-line catalog. The site will link you to other sources of information, as well. If you want to view the stock "up-close and personal," Condon Gardens in Houston is a retail dealer for Stokes Tropicals. (See page 200.)

## Teas Nursery Company Inc.

4400 Bellaire Boulevard
Bellaire, Texas 77401
☎ 1-800/446-7723
www.teasnursery.com
Catalog $2.00

Teas' *Orchid and Plant Supply Catalog* offers orchids, of course, but also African violets, plumerias, tillandsias and tropical hibiscus, plus all the supplies and tools you could ever need to keep your topicals thriving. Now at 44 pages, the publication includes roses, books, gloves and general garden tools. It's really something special!

## Tropical Gardens at Southern Exposure

35 Minor at Rusk Street
Beaumont, Texas 77702
☎ 409/835-0644
FAX 409/835-5265
Catalog $5.00

"We offer the world's largest collection of the following plants: 142 varieties of *Platycerium* (staghorn ferns), 96 varieties of *Rhipsalis* (cacti) and over 800 varieties of *Cryptanthus* (bromeliads)," says Bob Whitman. The firm also offers an extensive collection of *Alocasia* and *Philodendron* varieties and many variegated plants for the serious collector. This mail-order-only nursery has been in business for 15 years, and its plants are shipped worldwide.

# Regional Resources for Tropical Plants:
## *Trinity Blacklands*

## Orchid Gardens

9748 Brockbank Drive
Dallas, Texas 75220
☎ 214/350-4985
Hours Mon-Sat 10-6
Accessible Yes (call ahead)

Owner Gene Boswell has been in the orchid business since 1977 and houses his numerous plants in a very large, state-of-the-art greenhouse. As he told us, "I've had customers from all over the world!" Orchid lovers will also find a selection of supplies.

## Texas Palm Trees & Plants

*2023 Cadiz Street*
*Dallas, Texas 75201*
☎ *214/741-2310*
**FAX** *214/741-2310*
**Hours** *Daily 8-7*
**Accessible** *Yes*

The cold-hardy palms and large selection of cacti really impressed us here, and we were surprised to discover such good selections of orchids, bromeliads, natives, trees and shrubs, perennials and bulbs at this shop in the Farmer's Market in downtown Dallas. We were also pleased by the array of terra cotta and white clay pots and pretty fountains. There are other vendors you should visit while you're in the market, but we're sure you'll find Texas Palm Trees and Plants a delight! In late summer and early fall, you will also find good mark-downs here. There's even a Texas Certified Nursery Professional to offer advice.

# Coastal Plains & Marshes

## Air Exposé

*4703 Leffingwell Street*
*Houston, Texas 77026-3434*
☎ *713/672-7017*
**Hours** *Daily 8-5*
**Accessible** *Yes*

Air Expose' is a family-owned landscape design firm that also grows 400 varieties of hibiscus, seven varieties of althea and 14 varieties of bougainvillea. Sales are held in September. See mail-order information on page 329.

## Garden House

*501 25th Street*
*Galveston, Texas 77550*
☎ *409/765-9819*
**FAX** *409/765-5144*
**Hours** *Mon-Sat 9-6*
**Accessible** *No*

Ben and Shawn Coleman have set up their floral and garden shop in a 120-year-old building in the Strand, where they are supplying rare plants for an increasingly sophisticated Gulf Coast gardening clientele. Their inventory is a treasure-trove of species for both interior and exterior uses. You'll find bananas, gingers and orchids in profusion, along with such tropical vines as Rangoon climber, allamanda, mandevilla, passionflower vine, bleeding heart vine, blue skyflower, rubber vine, coral bean and bougainvillea. They also carry hard-to-find fruits such as long-leaf figs and five varieties of true guava. A friend commented, "They've such good taste! This shop would be considered elegant anywhere in the world." Unusual Texas natives and the wind- and salt-tolerant landscape plants such as palms and grasses are, of course, staples here and vital to Ben's landscape design and installation business. There's no catalog, but the company will ship by UPS.

## Orchids & Ferns

*7802 Bellaire Boulevard*
*Houston, Texas 77036*
☎ *713/774-0949*
**FAX** *713/995-7320*
**Hours** *Tues-Sat 9-5*
**Accessible** *Yes*

This is one we "happened upon," and how glad we were! Bridgett Woods exclaimed, "Step into tropical paradise for the largest selection of locally grown, rare and fragrant orchids." We were enchanted with the beautiful plants and the unexpected, delightful experience! The firm also carries supplies, offers instructions and repotting services, and designs arrangements. Oh yes, and plant leases are available!

## Palmer Orchids

*1308 East Broadway*
*Pasadena, Texas 77506*
☎ *281/472-1364*
**FAX** *281/946-1749*
*www.flash.net/~palmerr/*
**Hours** *Mon-Sat 9:30-5:30*
**Accessible** *Yes*

Although Palmer Orchids carries other tropicals, the nursery definitely specializes in orchids, carrying 15,000 orchids and all orchid supplies. Says Terri Palmer, "We have the largest variety of orchids, blooming and green leaf, in the state of Texas! You will find plants at Palmer's that are not available elsewhere." Another really good deal is free delivery in the Houston area to residences, businesses, hospitals and funeral homes. Palmer's holds open house the last Friday and Saturday in May and offers programs for garden clubs, as well as field trips. Also see page 329.

*Directions: Located 20 minutes southeast of downtown Houston. Take the Red Bluff exit off Highway 225 and turn south to Broadway.*

## *Coastal Bend*

### Gulf Coast Floral

*1207 Salem Road*
*Victoria, Texas 77904*
☎ *512/573-3356*
**Hours** *Mon-Sat 9-5; Daily 9-5 March 1-Mother's Day; Daily 9-5 Thanksgiving- Christmas*
**Accessible** *Partially (one step up)*

This is a place " for all seasons!" In the spring, you'll find geraniums, hibiscus, impatiens (single, double and New Guinea), begonias (wax, angelwing and Rieger), coleus, petunias, hydrangeas, garden mums and a large variety of hanging baskets. "Our Christmas selection includes poinsettias (six- to ten-inch pots in red, white, pink marble and jingle bells, plus hanging baskets in red only) and Christmas cactus in baskets and pots," reports Michael Zeplin. Gulf Coast Floral has sales the week after Mother's Day and five days before Christmas. Advice is available any season!

*Directions: Located a little less than a mile down Salem Road off of Highway 77.*

# Valley

## Caldwell Jungle Nursery

*Route 2, Box 286*
*Raymondville, Texas 78580*
☎ *956/689-3432*
**Hours** *Mon-Fri 9-5, Sat 9-12*
**Accessible** *Yes*

You'll find a wealth of tropicals here — palms of all kinds, several varieties of ficus, bird of paradise, crotons, bougainvilla, plumbago and oleander, plus a variety of heat-tolerant ground covers and hedge materials.

*Directions: From Highway 77, take Highway 186 one mile west of town.*

# Rio Grande Plain

## E&E Orchids Nursery

*1803 S. E. Loop 410*
*San Antonio, Texas 78220*
☎ *210/648-5300*
**Hours** *Tues-Sat 9:30-5:30, 10-5:30 Sun (winter closing at 5)*
**Accessible** *Yes*

Part of the fun of visiting E&E Orchids Nursery is the owner Emil Wisakowski, who is a most charming gentleman! The plants are exotic and beautiful, and Mr. Wisakowski is knowledgeable, helpful and, did we mention, charming? As he told us, "I've been growing orchids for 35 years and have been in the business for 10 years. I have 20,000-square-feet of greenhouse space, which I take care of myself. I grow what I like!" A few of his favorites are plumeria, coconut palms and citrus. Of course the orchids are the "stars," and you will find all of the necessary supplies for growing and good advice for success at E&E Orchids Nursery.

*Directions: The nursery is located on the access road at exit 35 on Loop 410 and is visible from the Loop.*

## Gentry's Laredo Garden Center

*3020 Meadow Avenue*
*Laredo, Texas 78044*
☎ *956/722-0555*
See complete listing on page 211.

## Medina Valley Greenhouses

*Old River Road (CR 477)*
*Castroville, Texas 78009*
☎ *210/931-2298*
See complete listing on page 211.

## Central Blacklands & Savannas

### La Selva Orchids and Nursery

*3910 Harvey Road*
*College Station, Texas 77845*
☎ *409/774-4776*
**FAX** *409/822-4970*
**Hours** *Tues-Sat 9:30-5:30 or by appointment*
**Accessible** *Yes*

Eddie Ruth Chadbourne is another breeder/collector who has turned entrepreneur. This place is fabulous! Like a botanical garden inside, it's just filled with orchids (some very rare), bromeliads and other tropical plants. She also carries ferns, herbs, hanging baskets, bonsai and garden gifts. There are even some perennials and native plants available here. Mrs. Chadbourne tours with talks on orchids and gives expert advice on-site about their care and repotting requirements. "Orchid fanciers will find flasks, seedlings and mature flowering orchid plants here, and ordinary gardeners will appreciate cultural tips from our Texas Master Gardener." Call to get dates on the end-of-summer sale.

*Directions: From Highway 6 Bypass, exit Highway 30 (Harvey Road) and go about 1.3 miles.*

## Hill Country

### Hill Country African Violets & Nursery

*32005 IH-10 West*
*Boerne, Texas 78006*
☎ *830/249-2614*
**FAX** *830/249-8658*
**Hours** *Daily 8-6*
**Accessible** *Yes*

Explains owner Ken Froboese, "We started 27 years ago with just African violets and began our plant nursery about 12 years ago. From one small greenhouse, we have expanded to 11 greenhouses. Now there's even more emphasis on orchids than on violets. If you're looking for African violets, our selection is one of the largest in the state. Not only will you find hundreds of the best varieties, (both old and new), but also all types, from miniatures, semi-miniatures and trailers to standards." In addition, this nursery carries a few gesneriads (violet related plants) and a full line of violet supplies. "We also stock some of the best quality blooming plants, foliage plants and hanging baskets available, and we normally have about 150 varieties of herbs on hand year-round." You will also find bedding plants, shrubs and trees and clay pottery. "Visitors are always welcome!," says Ken. "At Hill Country, the staff is happy to offer advice on everything we sell."

*Directions: Take Exit 543 off IH-10. It's on the (two-way) west access road, 13 miles north of San Antonio's Outer Loop 1604 and two miles south of Boerne.*

## It's a Jungle

*907 Kramer Lane*
*Austin, Texas 78758*
☎ *512/837-1205*
**FAX** *512/339-7876*
**Hours** *Mon-Fri 12-6, Sat 9-5, Sun 1-5*
**Accessible** *Mostly*

When we visited this shop, we were almost put off by the appearance of the exterior. Don't be fooled! This place is a jewel in a plain wrapper. People come here from all over the state to select from some 500-600 varieties of the orchids that grow worldwide — *Phalaenopsis, Dendrobium, Cattaleya, Cymbidium, Oncidim.* In addition, Juanice Davis carries all sorts of bromeliads and other exotic plants, including the carnivorous ones. What began as a hobby keeps her and several employees busy delivering plants all over Central Texas and, periodically, as far away as Dallas. There's an annual winter sale, and she travels to several orchid shows each year. "People who grow orchids can't stop," observes this charming former banker!

## The Plumeria People

*910 Leander Drive*
*Leander, Texas 78641*
☎ *512/259-0807*
**FAX** *512/259-3210*
**Hours** *Tues-Sat 9-3 (open April-October)*
**Accessible** *Yes*

The Plumeria People's flowering plants can be seen in person and the owner is available to offer advice at this mail–order company's headquarters. See catalog information on page 329.

*Directions: From Austin, take Loop 1 north to Highway 183 West, turn right on CR 272, then take the next left to Leander Drive.*

# Living Sculpture in the Landscape

Some plants just grab your attention! Bonsai (the ultimate in restraint) and topiaries (on the opposite end of the scale) are hot items in the gardening press these days. And, cacti and succulents have never been more popular. We've lumped all of these kinds of plants together as "living sculpture" because they can be used as focal points on a patio or out in the garden, just as you might use sculpture made of steel or concrete. Several small nurseries in Texas specialize in these interesting plants. Those that practice the ancient art of bonsai not only sell plants, containers and tools, but also offer patient instruction for year-round maintenance.

## Sources for Bonsai:

### Cross Timbers & Grand Prairie

#### Artistic Plants Bonsai

608 Holly Drive
Burleson, Texas 76028
☎ 817/295-0802
**Hours** By appointment only
**Accessible** Partially (no ramp into shed where tools and pots are shown)
**Mail Order**
**Catalog** $1.00
**Mailing Address** 608 Holly Drive, Burleson, Texas 76028

Estella Flather is a founder and active member of the Fort Worth Bonsai Society and a past vice-president of the Lone Star Bonsai Federation. She specializes in miniature Japanese-style trees and carries pots, tools, soils and books. Advice and instruction are offered.

Directions: Take Renfro Street exit off IH-35 West and turn east. Go 2½ miles, and turn right on County Road 602. The fourth turn to the left is Holly Drive.

### Trinity Blacklands

#### Dallas Bonsai Garden

P.O. Box 551087
Dallas, Texas 75355
☎ 972/487-0130 or 1-800/982-1223
**FAX** 972/487/6978
www.dallasbonsai.com
**Hours** Mon-Fri 9-5
**Mail Order**
**Catalog** $4.00

4460 North Walnut Street, suite 218
Garland, Texas 75042
☎ 972/487-0213
**FAX** 972/487-6978
**Hours** Mon-Fri 12-5
**Accessible** No

This is the coolest Web site! Billed as "the most complete bonsai store in the Western Hemisphere," Dallas Bonsai Garden's Web site presents a complete line of imported and domestic bonsai, plus a large selection of containers, tools, books and supplies. What was especially exciting is that you can view pictures of actual specimen bonsai (plants that range from about $50 to $2,500 in cost) and select from a variety of glazed and unglazed pots. You'll find mail-order specials and advice on bonsai and related items. There's a $20 minimum on orders. The retail outlet for Dallas Bonsai Garden, which is located at the southeast corner of Plano Road and Walnut Street in Garland (not to be confused with Walnut Hill Lane in Dallas) carries a limited selection of plants and supplies.

## Ultrascapes Garden Gallery

404 Southwestern Boulevard
Coppell, Texas 75019
☎ 972/471-1271
See complete listing on page 321.

# Coastal Prairies & Marshes

## Minnetex Gardens

3102 Fuqua
Houston, Texas 77047
☎ 713/433-4981
**FAX** 713/433-4981
**Hours** Wed-Sun 9-5
**Accessible** No

Part of the fun of shopping at Minnetex Gardens is owner Harvey Shores, who is most charming! He has a delightful array of bonsai (imported, collected and grown) and is very helpful with selection and instruction. You will also find a complete line of tools, books, magazines and containers. Having been in business since 1985, Mr. Shores offers lectures, demonstrations and workshops. (Call for information.)

# Rio Grande Plain

## The Bonsai Farm

13827 Highway 87 South
Adkins, Texas 78101
☎ 210/649-2109
**Hours** Mon-Sat 9-4
**Accessible** Yes
**Mail Order**
**Catalog** Free

According to Jerry Sorge, "The Bonsai Farm, located just outside San Antonio, carries more than forty types of plants for bonsai, hundreds of bonsai containers, Kiku and Masakuni bonsai tools, and twenty-five bonsai books." There is a semi-annual newsletter for mail- order customers.

# Hill Country

## Lakeview Bonsai

Austin, Texas
☎ 512/266-2655
**Hours** By appointment only
**Accessible** Partially (gravel walks)

Explains Elaine White, "Since I do all the work and styling myself, each tree is very special to me. I want my customers to enjoy their bonsai as much as I do, and for a very long time, so I give extensive care instructions." You'll also find pots, soil, tools, and books here. Her bonsai are very moderately priced, and she holds classes for beginners in March. Lakeview Bonsai is located overlooking Lake Travis; call for directions.

## Vito's

P.O. Box 23644
Leander, Texas 78641
☎ 512/267-3319
FAX 512/267-3319
**Hours** By appointment
**Accessible** Yes

"If you are serious about bonsai, this is the place to come!" says owner Vito Megna. "We are the largest and most well-equipped retail outlet in the state. On his five acres, you will find four large greenhouses and a display studio. Vito's offers domestic, imported and collected bonsai here, as well as pots, wire, tools, soil and advice. Lectures and seminars are also available. When you call for an appointment, ask for directions!

# Sources for Cacti:
## *Piney Woods*

## The Cactus Farm

Route 5, Box 1610
Nacogdoches, Texas 75964
☎ 409/560-6406
**Hours** Call for appointment; open daily, daylight-dark (May-Sept)
**Accessible** Partially
**Mail Order**
**Catalog** Free

The Cactus Farm is the only cactus and succulent nursery in East Texas with both outdoor landscaping and greenhouse grown materials. Says Fred Bright, "We sell only seed grown and propagated material — nothing collected from the wild. The large outdoor plantings, which are carefully protected from winter freeze, make us unique. Covers are removed in spring, and you don't have to go to Southern California to see large cacti outside — plus, the surrounding pine forests make them extra exotic." Seasonal sales are usually held during October before the cold season. Staff members offer advice and host Cactus and Succulent Club groups.

*Directions: Go north on Highway 259 from Nacogdoches and then west on FM 698 about 4 miles at Central Heights. Turn right on CR 817, "Old Tyler Road" (dirt road) for three miles, and The Cactus Farm is on the left (Box 1610).*

## Coastal Prairies & Marshes

### Cactus King

*7800 IH-45 North*
*Houston, Texas 77037*
☎ *281/591-8833*
**Hours** *Mon-Sat 10-6, Sun 12-6*
**Accessible** *Partially*

Our visit to Cactus King (formerly Earth Star) was quite an "eclectic" experience! According to Lyn Rathburn, "We carry 3,000 varieties of cacti and succulents and 40 varieties of *Cycas*." We also found a wonder cache of books, garden accessories (stone, metal and wooden statues) and Mexican and African art. There's also pottery from Mexico and other countries, rocks, fossils, skulls, artifacts, pre-Columbian art and swords here, too. Cactus King holds August sales and offers advice and "plant identification" for "weird succulents."

## Valley

### Sunderland's Cactus Gardens

*North Alamo Road*
*Alamo, Texas 78516*
☎ *956/787-2040*
**Hours** *Tues-Fri 9-5 (May-Sept); Mon-Fri 9-5, Sun 2-5 (Oct-Apri)l*
**Accessible** *Yes*

Sunderland's *is* cacti and succulents. Many of the plants are very unusual ones that the company has hybridized and are for display purposes only. You will also find antiques hanging overhead and cases of mineral specimens. They maintain display rock and cactus gardens for inspiration. Harry Sunderland says, "We do not sell collected plants. They have to be grown from seed or cuttings. We grow about 99% of our plants." Sunderland's has five acres of cacti, many of which are very large specimens. The company does Southwest landscaping, and the owners are delighted to offer advice to customers. They run year-round specials.

*Directions: Located less than a mile off Expressway 83. Take exit 907. On crossroads FM 495 and FM 907.*

## Hill Country

### Living Desert Cactus Nursery

*12719 Highway 71 West*
*Austin, Texas 78736*
☎ *512/263-2428*
**Hours** *Daily 10-5:30*
**Accessible** *Partially*

Living Desert Cactus Nursery offers not only a wide selection of cacti, but also garden gifts and accessories such as pottery, wind chimes, birdhouses and feeders. As Darrell and Yvonna Dunten explain, "We specialize in the rugged, but romantic liveliness of the Southwest species of life, creating a flavor of sensual awareness." Texture, geometric designs, color and fragrances overwhelm in a nursery of desert landscapes. The store carries generic to artisan-designed vessels and crafts of Southwestern mythology along with cacti and succulents of the world's deserts. While they do not have a catalog, the Duntens are willing to ship merchandise to customers. They also offer xeriscaping advice.

*Directions: Located one block west of Bee Cave Road.*

## Sunrise Nursery

*13105 Canyon View*
*Leander, Texas 78641*
☎ *512/267-0023*
**Hours** *By appointment only*
**Accessible** *No*
**Mail Order**
**Catalog** *$1.00*

Sunrise Nursery is a major grower of cacti and succulents in Texas and the only mail order nursery for these plants in the state. Says Kathy Springer, "Most of the plants are grown from seed here at the nursery. I do not sell field-collected plants. People like my plants because they are reasonably priced and are labeled with the botanical name." Kathy is always willing to answer questions and offer suggestions. If you wish to visit, call for directions.

# A Source for Topiary:

## River Oaks Plant House

*3401 Westheimer*
*Houston, Texas 77027*
☎ *713/622-5350*
**FAX** *713/621-9662*
**Hours** *Mon-Fri 7-8, Sat 8-8, Sun 9-7 (all stores)*
**Accessible** *Yes*
**Mail Order**
**Catalog** *Free*

As one of the leading topiary makers in the nation, River Oaks Plant House revived the ancient art of shaping plants into decorative sculptures. Says owner Daniel Saparzaden, "Our firm is the largest manufacturer of topiaries in the world." Its artists have handcrafted a menagerie of deer, birds, elephants and many more animals, as well as other whimsical custom designs. To ensure quality control, each topiary is locally made in the company's studio greenhouse. The galvanized metal frames are designed, welded together and stuffed with sphagnum moss while being wrapped with monofilament, which brings out the detail. The frames are guaranteed to maintain their shape for at least 10 years under normal conditions. A sprinkler system, usually for larger pieces, is an optional feature and can be installed prior to filling the frame. The final step in creating a topiary is planting either fig ivy or Asian jasmine in the moss. The pieces are shipped to customers throughout the state. According to *Architectural Digest*, "River Oaks Plants represents the state of the art in topiary design." Gardeners also find a fine array of fountains, statuary and pots here. Also see Houston Flowery, page 296.

# Chapter Nine
# Garden Furniture

*"Sometimes I sits and thinks,
and sometimes I just sits."
....an old country saying*

# Please Be Seated

Just thinking about garden furniture revives happy memories. As a child I spent lazy afternoons watching the world go by from my grandmother's porch swing. I remember reclining in a sling-back canvas chair as my father pointed out the constellations on starry summer nights. I have faded photographs of family picnics and children's tea parties held around a big tile-topped table. And I often think about the old hammock where I loved to curl-up and read.

People have rediscovered such simple pleasures in the fast-paced '90s. Outdoor furniture is back in style, and it's better than ever. Visit a specialty furniture store or garden center today and you'll see sofas and chairs in a splendid array of materials and finishes. There will be dining tables and occasional tables, teacarts and etageres, bar stools and brightly colored market umbrellas — all reflecting new flair and elegance.

You'll still find the classical designs. Fanciful Victorian styles are in vogue again, but now the pieces may be fabricated of steel, cast aluminum and all-weather resin wicker, as well as traditional wrought iron and wood. Texans can find faithful reproductions of classic English-style garden benches and wonderful new versions of the Adirondack chair made here in the Lone Star State. To complement the country lifestyle, local craftsmen are creating new versions of the old picnic tables, chaise lounges, porch swings and gliders I remember from childhood. And national manufacturers are drawing on every stylistic trend from art deco to postmodern.

The choices in materials are equally wide, and manufacturers are emphasizing durability. Wood remains popular because it doesn't feel hot in the summer or cold in the winter. Since many of the exotic hardwood species once used for garden furniture come from ecologically sensitive areas of the world, manufacturers are increasingly fabricating their wares from domestic woods, which if properly selected and well-maintained will hold up as well as any tropical species. Responsible companies that do use woods such as teak certify that their material has been harvested from sustained-source plantations. Responsible consumers should demand the same.

Stone and concrete benches, the most durable of choices, have a tendency to collect water and are less user-friendly than other materials, but these, too, have their place in the garden. Furniture made from non-corrosive metals such as steel, aluminum (both cast and sturdy tubular forms) and welded wire-mesh are being offered with new anodized or baked-on, powder-coated paint finishes to provide a much longer life span than simple paint. And, furnishings made of high-tech plastics and resins treated with ultra-violet inhibitors have become popular alternatives.

Take a look at the colors available! White, greens and earth tones remain garden favorites, but today's site furnishings also come in wild and wonderful hues. In the right setting, pinks, purples and bright blues light up a garden. Cushions lend both pattern and color to seating areas, and here we are talking about a lot of choices. (If the furnishings will be visible from indoors, be sure the colors complement your interior design as well as the exterior setting.) All the national and regional manufacturers offer catalogs or brochures, and many are willing to customize orders to accommodate your special requests.

Your first priority should be comfort. Designers are responding to new consumer demands by studying human proportions and seeking the best fit for the widest possible range of human body types. While a garden bench need not be the ultimate in comfort, the chairs you use for dining and lounging should be as carefully selected as any that go into your home.

You'll also want to consider ease of maintenance and storage. If your furniture will be exposed to the elements, do not buy wood that has been sealed with a varnish or paint. Wood needs to breathe. An oil-based stain will protect the wood and allow it to expand and contract with changes in the weather. Wood furniture should be joined with brass, stainless steel or galvanized fasteners. In metal furniture, demand powder-coated finishes. If the pieces you are buying have webbed plastic seats, be sure the manufacturer offers replacement webbing. The metal parts can be kept sparkling with auto polish, but eventually the webbing will need to be replaced.

There are two ways to go. You can buy cheap, planning to discard the furniture when it falls apart. Or you can go for quality. It's hard to argue with the logic of stackable welded wire chairs that cost $4.95. (I've seen them at all the hardware stores, even the drugstore chains.) They're "knock-offs" of great looking Italian chairs that sell for about $89 apiece. Sure, if you leave them outdoors, the welds break and the paint peels, but at that price, who can complain? They are handy to pull out when you're entertaining large crowds. If you're willing to keep garden furniture in storage except when it's in use, you can get away with benches and chairs and tables of lesser quality. For the furnishings you are going see every day and plan to use year in and year out, buy the highest quality furniture you can afford.

☛**Money-saving tip: Buy off-season.**

Many of the sources we've listed markdown their products in late summer or early fall. It's hard to justify spending money on something you aren't going to use for several months, but you can save up to 50% just because a store needs to make room for other merchandise. Sometimes the sales begin as early as September, and this is usually about the time of year when we Texans venture back outdoors! During the season, check out such discount merchandisers as Home Depot and Lowes. If you've shopped around and know what to look for in quality, you may unearth some bargains.

We were surprised to discover that there are very few "outdoor furniture stores" in the state. It became apparent that folks in smaller towns may have to travel quite a distance to find high-quality garden furniture. We've begun this section with Texas manufacturers that ship their products. Under "Retail Sources" you'll also find several that offer catalogs and shipping services.

So, ladies and gentlemen, please be seated.

# Manufacturers & Importers of Garden Furniture:

## Adkins Reproduction Antique Lighting

IH-35
Georgetown, Texas 78626
☎ 512/869-1645
**FAX** 512/869-1645 *(call before sending)*
**Hours** *Mon-Sat 9-5:30, Sun 1-5:30*
**Accessible** *Yes*
**Mail Order**
**Catalog** *$6*
**Mailing Address** *108 Highview, Georgetown, Texas 78628*

The reproduction garden furnishings here are a real find. This company's 41-page catalog features many of the products offered, but visit if you can. Digging through the melange, you'll find old-fashioned mailboxes, street signs, a wide array of wrought iron garden furniture, new iron fencing that faithfully replicates old patterns, urns, fountains and more. Adkins shares property with Pecan Ridge Farms, where you may find garden antiques from time to time. Also refer to page 131.

*Directions: From the south, take exit 266, 4½ miles north of Georgetown. Coming from the north, take exit 268 and cross over; the company is on the east side of the Interstate.*

## B&H Wood Products

17244 FM 812
Del Valle, Texas 78617
☎ 512/243-2097 or 1-800/742-2542
**FAX** 512/243-2097
**Hours** *Mon-Fri 8-5*
**Accessible** *Yes*
**Mail Order**
**Catalog** *Free*

Says Fred Homesley, "Our furniture is hand-crafted, so if you want something different from our standard line, I will custom-make it for you. This is strong furniture that will take a lot of use. Rounded edges are sanded smooth to the touch, and there are no nails!" The pieces are all glued, screwed together and finished with a weather-resistant seal that makes them ready for use upon delivery. B & H carries a full line of tables, swings, gliders, chairs — even that hard-to-find Adirondack chair.

## Bush Wacker Handmade Furniture

1633 Hunter Road
Gruene, Texas 78130
☎ 210/620-4534
**Hours** *Open daily with no set hours; call ahead*
**Accessible** *No*
**Mail Order**
**Catalog** *Free brochure*

Since 1981 Steve Talley has been making high-quality benches, rocking chairs, porch swings, gliders and A-frame swings the old-fashioned way. Crafted from native and exotic woods, all pieces are available in the "Classic Design" or "Texas Star Back." He'll also take custom orders for indoor and outdoor furnishings. "If you have an idea, bring it to us," he says, "but please have an idea of the size, shape, wood and finish you want. A picture would help!" He'll ship his wares anywhere in the country. If you take the mail-order route, however, you'll miss visiting downtown Historic Gruene. (This charming little Hill Country town, which doesn't even appear on every Texas map, has been absorbed into New Braunfels.)

*Directions: From IH-35 take Highway 306 (Canyon Lake Exit). Turn left at the first light, which is Hunter Road and continue about ½ mile.*

## Cheyenne Cedar Unlimited

*3801 North Main*
*Victoria, Texas 77901*
☎ *512/572-4797*
**FAX** *512/572-4797*
**www.***cheyenne.selectric.net*
**Hours** *Mon-Sat 8-5*
**Accessible** *Partially*
**Mail Order**
**Catalog** *Free Brochure*

Cheyenne Cedar Unlimited manufactures free-standing and hanging porch swings, picnic tables, chairs, two styles of patio benches and chairs in durable red cedar. All products come with five coats of polyurethane unless otherwise specified by the customer. To see the furniture styles, visit the shop or write, phone or fax for a brochure. On the Web site, you will find not only pictures, but also a description of the process and a price list. These are "last-a-lifetime" pieces.

## Durham Trading & Design Co.

*1009 W. 6th Street*
*Austin, Texas 78703*
☎ *512/476-1216*
**FAX** *512/476-1611*
**Hours** *Mon-Sat 10-6, Sun 1-5*
**Accessible** *Yes*
**Mail Order**
**Catalog** *Free pamphlets and mailers*

Owner Charles Durham describes Durham Trading & Design Co. as "a combination of the old and the custom." This firm offers custom iron and wood furniture. The woods used are long leaf pine, walnut, mesquite, pecan, cypress and cedar and can be painted or stained. There are numerous styles, including Adirondack and "twig furniture." Also to be found are old ornamental architectural items such as gates, fences, window treatments and a large selection of benches. From time to time, there are antique (turn-of-the-century) wrought iron tables, chairs and day beds suitable for patio or poolside. Be sure to check the large selection of books. Next door, the antiques dealers at Whit Hanks may have some lovely accessories for the garden, as well.

## El Pueblito Iron Furniture

*10010 Montana*
*El Paso, Texas 79925*
☎ *915/591-7811*
**FAX** *915/591-0080*
**Hours** *Mon-Sat 9-7 (summer); Mon-Sat 10-6 (winter)*

*(Listing continued on next page)*

*Accessible* Yes
**Mail Order**
**Catalog** *Call to work with designer for custom pieces*

El Pueblito specializes in wrought iron furniture, both interior and exterior. With over 37 years of experience, this family-owned and operated company both designs and manufactures. Julio Carrillo has been well respected as a designer for over 52 years, and the showroom is filled with most attractive furnishings and accessories. As family members will proudly tell you, "We offer good service as well as the best quality in metal and paint finishing. As you might know, iron is not only one of the most durable materials, but it is also very versatile. This makes our designs limitless as well as elegant and distinctive. Since we are a direct area manufacturer, we can offer the best prices every day." Each piece this company makes is one-of-a-kind, so you'll never find your furniture at someone else's home. At the store, you'll also find a large selection of cushions, fabrics and other accessories from which to choose. If you are looking for wrought iron, pay El Pueblito a visit! Sales are held from April through August.

## Furniture by Design

*1131 Slocum Street*
*Dallas, Texas 75207*
☎ *214/760-2450*
**FAX** *214/760-2470*
**Hours** *Mon-Fri 9-5:30, Sat 10-1*
*Accessible* No
**Mail Order**
**Catalog** *Photographs on request*

You can commission unusual, high-end items here — "statement pieces" made of limestone, granite, marble and steel. Whether your look is Old World or contemporary, this custom-factory will help you with the design. In addition to benches, chaises and stone bases for glass-topped tables, the company fabricates handsome gates and fences ornamented with fanciful scrollwork. Furniture by Design ships wares all over the country.

## Hill Country Experience

*2608 Elm Street*
*Dallas, Texas 75226*
☎ *214/742-3400*
**FAX** *214/742-3407*
*www.hillcountryexp.com*
**Hours** *Tues-Sat 10-6, Sun 1-5*
*Accessible* No
**Mail Order**
**Catalog** *On-line*

Nationally profiled interior designer Maryneil Levatino has coined a new descriptive phrase — "Texas Country French!" Her shop and design center in Dallas' historic Deep Ellum district is steeped in Hill Country tradition and atmosphere. As she puts it, "You'll find 'down-home charm.' We specialize in furniture and accessories made in Texas by Texans!" For the patio and garden, Hill Country Experience offers treated-pine furniture; tables, chairs, benches, porch swings, rockers and gliders. You'll also find iron garden stakes with Texas animal motifs, wrought iron plant stands, a pretty limestone birdbath, tool sets, Mexican clay pots and other fun garden accessories.

## Jerald N. Bettes Company

*6105-A West 34th Street*
*Houston, Texas 77092*
☎ *713/682-7901*
**Hours** *Daily 7-5*
**Accessible** *Yes*
**Mail Order**
**Catalog** *Free brochure; include self-addressed, stamped envelope*

Jerald Bettes explained to us, "Because we couldn't buy any outdoor furniture that would last, our furniture was originally built for personal use, not to sell." Today his company produces all types of outdoor furniture — swings, gliders, park benches, picnic tables, planter boxes, trash receptacles and more. The company calls its product "lifetime outdoor furniture." Heavy materials (a steel framework and thick wood slats) are used to manufacture these high-quality, commercial-grade products, and you have a choice of available wood. At Jerald Bettes, there's a price range to fit everyone's budget. Swings and small pieces can be shipped by UPS.

## MF Industries

*6933 E. Lancaster, Suite A*
*Fort Worth, Texas 76112*
☎ *817/496-2116*
**FAX** *817/496-2130*
**Hours** *Mon-Fri 9-5, Sat 9-12*
**Accessible** *Yes*
**Mail Order**
**Catalog** *Free color brochure*

This wholesale-only import company offers swings, arbors, benches and top-of-the-line teak furniture. It's known for competitive prices and for furniture that's handsome, massive and very durable. "You could park a truck on the arms of our benches," says owner Michael Frank, only half joking. He has recently added a line of heavy-duty wrought iron furniture and chandeliers, plus children's benches and "lots of new things." Call to find a dealer near you; if they don't have what you need, the company will ship to you directly.

## Mind Over Metal

*11909 FM 2769*
*Austin, Texas 78726*
☎ *512/258-7000 or 1-800/320-1076*
**FAX** *512/219-1226*
***www.****mindovermetal.com*
**Hours** *By appointment only, Mon-Fri*
**Accessible** *Partially*
**Mail Order**
**Catalog** *Photos on-line; all items are custom-made (phone to order)*

As Richard Schultz told us, "Mind Over Metal has been in business since 1976. Primarily a wholesale business, we also do customized work for the retail customer." Among the items manufactured are furniture (handsome chairs, rockers and tables), garden gates, fountains, figurative and abstract sculpture, gazebo spires, railings and trellises. These pieces are available in bronze, copper, wrought iron and stainless steel. He also supplies glass and fossilized Texas limestone tops for the tables. Call Richard for an appointment and directions. He can make almost anything to meet

*(Listing continued on next page)*

your special needs! The Web site shows a multitude of creative items. We were especially impressed by the Squash Blossom fountain, the gazebo spire and the company's intricate architectural railings for walkways and balconies.

## Outback Outdoor Furniture

Route 2, Box 140C
Emory, Texas 75440
☎ 903/473-4213 or 1-800/ 982-6087
**Hours** Mon-Sat 9-5, Sun 12-6
**Accessible** Yes except gravel drive
**Mail Order**
**Catalog** Free brochure
    Here you'll find a very large yard display of pressure-treated pine furniture, including tables, chairs, gliders and benches. There's also a selection of metal swing frames and wind chimes. And, according to the folks at Outback Outdoor Furniture, "We carry the absolute best barbecues in the country, *Lyfe Time*, which are manufactured in Uvalde, Texas. The company is third generation owned and operated."
*Directions: Located three miles south of Emory on Highway 19 South; 20 miles north of Canton.*

## Salado Stone Company

P.O. Box 686
Salado, Texas 76571
☎ 254/947-8949
**Hours** By appointment only
**Accessible** No
    Artisan Wayne Phillips makes rustic limestone garden tables and benches that are billed as "Very Early American." Actually, they more evoke the Flintstones! These pieces are really quite charming. The antithesis of a commercial production company, Mr. Phillips' small enterprise has attracted a statewide following, not only for the furniture, but also for the roughhewn stone fountains and planters he makes.

## Woodscaping Company

2409 Commerce Street
Marble Falls, Texas 78654
☎ 830/693-6377
**FAX** 830/693-0134
**Hours** Mon-Fri 9-5, Sat 10-2; after-hours appointments are welcome
**Accessible** Yes
**Mail Order**
**Catalog** Free brochure
    This collection of tables, chairs, rockers, gliders, etc. is handcrafted for those who enjoy the relaxation and comfort of the outdoor environment. The basic structure of each piece of the company's furniture is specifically designed to follow the natural curvature of the body, hence "ergonomically designed." Non-corrosive screws, quality heart and clear grades of redwood, plus the addition of glue joints make each piece durable and weather resistant. As Rod Oberhaus says, "They are made one-at-a-time for a lifetime of pleasure."
*Directions: From Highway 281 on the north side of Marble Falls, Commerce Street is one block east of the highway across from Walmart.*

# Regional Resources for Garden Furniture:
## *Cross Timbers & Grand Prairie*

## *Coleman Bright Ideas*

*4820 S.E. Loop 820*
*Fort Worth, Texas 76140*
☎ *817/572-0004 or 1-800/880-4820*
**FAX** *817/572-2407*
**Hours** *Mon-Sat 10-6, Sun 1-5*
**Accessible** *Yes*

   Coleman specializes in "complete backyard living capability" with garden rooms (see page 124), swimming pools, *HotSpring* spas, outdoor/casual living furniture, tableware, outdoor clocks and thermometers. The garden furniture you'll find here is made by *Brown Jordan*, *Tropitone* and *Telescope*. As the manager told us, "Each of the specialty divisions operate with a staff of highly experienced professionals. Every Coleman customer benefits from our ability to bring complete backyard living together." Coleman showrooms in Dallas and Grapevine also carry the garden furniture.

## *Into the Garden*

*1615 South University Drive*
*Fort Worth, Texas 76107*
☎ *817/336-4686*
**FAX** *817/336-4687*
**Hours** *Mon-Thurs 10-8, Fri & Sat 10-9, Sun 12-5*
**Accessible** *Yes, both stores*

   See complete listing on page 369. Into the Garden specializes in elegant garden accessories. Both the Dallas and Fort Worth stores carry such quality garden furniture as *Kingsley-Bate* teak and *Summer Classics* in metal.

## *Southwest Teak & Unique*

*850 West Pipeline Road*
*Hurst, Texas 76053*
☎ *817/589-TEAK (8325)*
**FAX** *817/590-0680*
**www.**swteak.com
**Hours** *Mon-Sat 9-6, Sun 12-6*
**Accessible** *No*
**Mail Order**
**Catalog** *Free*

   As owner Rob Fisher told us, "We carry only teak outdoor furnishings manufactured in Indonesia. Our selection is large, and our prices are 20% to 50% lower than other stores. The great thing about teak is that it lasts forever and stays cool to the touch." The furnishings include tables (about five different designs), chairs (in about ten different styles), rockers for one or two, tree-stump benches, swings, benches (at least 20 designs), planters and outdoor bars and stools. Also available for purchase is oil for refurbishing teak. On-line, we found the company's Batavia and Monet benches, great looking rockers and an especially handsome steamer chair. You'll see ads for Southwest Teak & Unique in *Better Homes & Gardens* and *Neil Sperry's GARDENS*, as well as a very large display at Neil Sperry's show. This company is located in the Mid-Cities area, east of Fort Worth and west of DFW.

## Texas Patios

5742 Airport Freeway (Highway 121)
Fort Worth, Texas, 76117
☎ 817/831-2266
**FAX** 817/831-9753
**Hours** Mon-Fri 10-7, Sat 9-6, Sun 12-5 (spring and summer); Mon-Fri 9-6, Sat 9-5:30 (fall and winter)
**Accessible** Yes

Texas Patios was nominated for the Apollo Award for excellence in merchandising casual furniture in 1994. This nomination by the Summer & Casual Furniture Manufacturers Association makes Texas Patios one of the ten best casual furniture stores in the country. "Family owned and operated for over 20 years, Texas Patios believes in service and helping the customer with all their outdoor patio needs," reports owner Ken Mattoon. Here you will find tables, chairs, lounges, gliders, swings, arbors and standing plant holders made of wrought iron, cast aluminum, teak, extruded steel, concrete and outdoor weather wicker. Some of the lines represented are *O.W Lee, Lane/Venture, Weathercraft, Tropitone, Winston* and *Homecrest.* In addition to a huge display of concrete statuary, fountains, birdbaths, urns and planters, the company carries hammocks, umbrellas, replacement cushions and many other patio accessories. Advice and ideas on floating fountains for ponds or lakes as well as pond building referrals are available. Texas Patios stocks a vast inventory, and a warehouse clearance sale is held the last weekend in July.

## Yard Art

6407 Colleyville Boulevard (Hwy. 26)
Colleyville, Texas 76034
☎ 817/421-2414
**FAX** 817/421-2319
**Hours** Mon-Sat 9-6; open Sun 12-5 in summer
**Accessible** Yes
**Mail Order** Yes
**Catalog** Free brochures
**Mailing Address** P.O. Box 1011, Colleyville, Texas 76034

In the past four years this company has really made its mark in the business. Within his 6,000 square-foot showroom and half-acre outdoor display area, owner Butch Wallace features the country's most respected casual furniture manufacturers: *Woodard, Tropitone, Winston, Brown Jordan, Lloyd/Flanders, Lane/Venture, Lyon-Shaw, Cape Atlantic, Outdoor Lifestyles* and others. You'll find tubular and cast aluminum, wrought iron, all-weather wicker and teak in a multitude of styles and colors. Colorful tableware completes the scene. Outdoors, expect to find redwood swings by *Gym•N•I* and concrete statuary by *Henri Studios,* as well as lots of umbrellas and decorative accessories. Yard Art also offers high-end barbecue grills and fireplace equipment.

# *Trinity Blacklands*

## Elegant Casual

*1621 North Central Expressway*
*Richardson, Texas 75080*
☎ *972/669-9098 or 1-888/240-6936 (toll free)*
*FAX 972/669-8884*
*www.elegantcasual.com*
**Hours** *Mon-Sat 9:30-7, Sun 10-6; Closed Christmas Day and Thanksgiving*
**Accessible** *Yes*
**Mail Order** *Yes*
**Catalog** *Free*

Elegant Casual occupies a 25,000-square-foot showroom filled with patio furniture, rattan, wicker, casual dining tables and chairs and bar stools. You'll find garden accessories from *Henri*, clocks, thermometers, wind chimes, sisal rugs, glassware, *Olympia* outdoor lighting and replacement outdoor cushions. Patio lines include *Winston, Tropitone, Cast Classics, Homecrest, Lyon-Shaw, Woodard* and *Lane/Venture.* The company also carries *Weathermaster* outdoor wicker, which is featured in *House Beautiful* magazine. According to Darcie Grogan, "We have the largest selection in Texas!" Elegant Casual holds parking lot sales during major holiday weekends and has end-of-season sales in November and December.

*Directions: Located between the Campbell Road and Arapaho Road exits on the west side of the service road.*

## Inside Out Shop

*17390 Preston Road*
*Dallas, Texas 75252*
☎ *972/931-0626*
*FAX 972/931-0625*
**Hours** *Mon-Fri 9:30-7, Sat 9:30-6, Sun 12-6*
**Accessible** *Yes*

As manager Keith Kennington says, "Having been in business for 25 years, we pride ourselves on the highest quality merchandise and excellent customer service." At Inside Out, you will find most of the major casual furniture lines including *Winston, Lane/ Venture, Tropitone, Homecrest, Woddard, O.W. Lee, Kingsley-Bate, Meadowcraft, CFI* and *Outdoor Lifestyle.* These pieces are available in wrought iron, teak, cast aluminum and outdoor wicker. In addition, Inside Out carries animal statues, fountains, outdoor fireplaces, umbrellas, replacement cushions, wind chimes, bird feeders and houses and other accessories

## Into the Garden

*5370 West Lovers Lane*
*Dallas, Texas 75209*
☎ *214/351-5125*
*FAX 214/351-5212*
**Hours** *Mon-Sat 10-6, Sun 12-5*

See complete listing on page 369.

## Patio Fireplace Depot

*2625 Old Denton #326*
*Carrollton, Texas 75007*
☎ *972/245-7789*
**FAX** *972/245-7850*
**Hours** *Mon 9:30-8, Tues, Wed & Fri 9:30-7, Thurs 9:30-8, Sat 9:30-6, Sun 12-7*
**Accessible** *Yes*

Patio Fireplace Depot has been in business for six years and carries ourdoor tables, chairs, pool tables, benches, swings, gliders and picnic furniture. These pieces are made of cast aluminum, wrought iron, plastic, steel and outdoor wicker. Among the other items available are fountains, gas grills, planters, umbrellas, replacement cushions, glass tabletops, windchimes and birdhouses. You will often find great sales advertised in the local paper.

## Smith & Hawken

*3300 Knox Street*
*Dallas, Texas 75205*
☎ *214/522-6522*
**FAX** *214/522-2834*
**Hours** *Mon-Wed 10-6, Thurs & Fri 10-7, Sat 10-6, Sun 12-5*
**Accessible** *Yes*
**Mail Order** *Yes*
**Catalog** *Free (call 1-800/776-3336)*

Three retail stores in Texas personalize this company's famous catalog! Each displays lovely garden furniture of wrought iron and cast aluminum from Italy, but teak is the real star in the collection. These stores are just packed with metal and cast-stone ornaments and pots of every shape and size. You will also find tools, apparel (the complete line in the Houston store), antique roses, indoor color plants and organic herbs. "Every garden counts," says the manager's card, and it is hard to imagine a company more devoted to the garden's little pleasures. See pages 354 and 358 for other store locations.

## Weir's Furniture Village

*3219 Knox Street*
*Dallas, Texas 75205*
☎ *214/528-0321*
**FAX** *214/521-4302*
**Hours** *Mon-Fri 10-9, Sat 10-6*
**Accessible** *Yes*

The Weir family, celebrating a 50th anniversary, has long held a fine reputation for its furniture gallery in Highland Park Village. Although this handsome store does not specialize in patio furniture, it carries a very attractive selection of *Woodard*, *Brown Jordan*, *Meadow Craft*, *Kingsley-Bate*, and *Gloucester Teak*. You'll also find such accessories as mailboxes, weathervanes and birdhouses here.

# Piney Woods

## Murphy's Furniture Gallery

*1809 West S.W. Loop 323*
*Tyler, Texas 75701*
☎ *903/561-9900 or 1-800/256-4039*
**FAX** *903/581-8650*

*Hours* Mon-Sat 10-7
*Accessible* Yes

Family owned and operated for 19 years, Murphy's boasts of "the best service in East Texas!" The gallery carries a large selection of outdoor furniture year-round. You'll find *Homecrest* and *Birmingham* metal furniture and an outdoor wicker line in stock, and you can order *Meadowcraft* patio furniture. Check for year-round sales in the local paper and on TV and radio. Free delivery for 150 miles.

## Coastal Prairies & Marshes

### The Chair King

6393 Richmond
Houston, Texas 77057
☎ 713/781-7340
FAX 713/781-0498

11375 Fountain Lake Drive
Stafford, Texas 77477
☎ 281/240-8555
FAX 281/240-8996

5402 West FM 1960
Houston, Texas 77069
☎ 281/893-7130
FAX 281/893-6220

252 FM 1960 By-pass East
Humble, Texas 77338
☎ 281/446-8509
FAX 281/446-1536

14141 Gulf Freeway
Houston, Texas 77034
☎ 281/484-7489
FAX 281/484-0087

20061 Katy Freeway
Katy, Texas 77450
☎ 281/599-1818
FAX 281/599-7591

*Hours* Tues, Wed, Fri, Sat 10-6, Mon & Thurs 10-8, Sun 12-6
*Accessible* Yes
*Mail Order*
*Catalog* Free brochures

"We make it easy... to take it easy!" This has been the motto of this company for 45 years, and its stores continue to live up to that promise. The Chair King was purchased in 1973 by Marvin Barish, and, today his daughter, Jackie, and his son, David, have joined the business. Says Jackie Barish, "We all work side-by-side in a company that has grown from two stores into the largest specialty furniture retailer in the Southwest." The Chair King offers an extensive selection of fine casual furniture in wrought iron, aluminum, molded resins, traditional wicker, "perma-wicker" and teak. The manufacturers include *Brown Jordan*, *Woodard*, *Winston*, *Samsonite*, *Molla* and many more. You'll also find hammocks, swings, gliders and a variety of accessories including umbrellas, replacement cushions, furniture covers, torches, garden clocks and thermometers, plus a big selection of outdoor tableware. The Chair King prides itself on the large selection, warranty protection, professional, courteous personnel and prompt delivery. The company's brochures are especially helpful, not only for selection purposes, but also for maintenance instructions. Chair King is a Texas institution! Other locations on pages 355 and 357.

### Home & Patio

2525 FM 1960 West
Houston, Texas 77068
☎ 281/440-7667
FAX 281/440-7668

This Houston branch of a San Antonio-based company carries a comprehensive inventory of garden furnishings, plus all the accessories except barbecue grills. See complete listing on page 355.

## Patio One Furniture

5807 Richmond
Houston, Texas 77057
☎ 713/977-4455
FAX 713/783-2999

3105 FM 1960 West
Houston, Texas 77968
☎ 281/893-9700
FAX 281/893-3838

110 Highway 6 South
Houston, Texas 77079
☎ 281-531-0030
FAX 281/531-0330

2701 Chimney Rock
Houston, Texas 77056
☎ 713/961-1668
FAX 713/961-0057

7080 Southwest Freeway
Houston, Texas 77036
☎ 713/777-7080
FAX 713/777-8757

**Hours** Mon-Sat 10-7, Sun 12-6 (all stores)
**Accessible** Yes (all stores)

Having been in business since 1978, Patio One specializes in premium quality patio furniture. As founder and owner B. J. Mehrinfar proudly states, "We look all over the world for the newest in design and technology and offer traditional, classical and contemporary selections. Here, you can buy your 'last set first time!' With a central distribution center servicing five locations, we can suit any taste." This company manufactures furniture, cushions and umbrellas under the name *Sweet Life*. There is a five-year warranty on the exclusive "quick-dry" cushions. In addition to *Sweet Life*, other furniture lines are available in aluminum, cast aluminum, wrought iron, teak and other woods, resin and PVC. The customer may choose a frame from any furniture line and complete their purchase from the large and varied selection of *Sweet Life* cushions. The first four locations listed are called Patio One. The Sweet Life is the 20,000 sq. ft. "super store" on the Southwest Freeway. At this location, you will find all of the same merchandise offered at Patio One, plus indoor furniture, accessories and lighting. According to owner B. J. Mehrinfar, "We have the largest selection of bar stools in the city and much, much more."

## Smith & Hawken

3935 San Felipe Road
Houston, Texas 77027
☎ 713/621-9395

See complete listing on page 352.

# Coastal Bend

## Patio & Interiors

4130 South Padre Island Drive
Corpus Christi, Texas 78411
☎ 512/853-8493
FAX 512/853-8494
**Hours** Mon-Sat 9:30-5:30; open Sun 1-5 (Mar 15-Labor day)
**Accessible** Yes
**Mail Order**
**Catalog** Free

"We have twenty year's experience presenting outdoor products for use in the harsh South Texas climate. We are extremely careful to select only products that we know will endure," reports owner Art Babbitt. In addition to eight lines of lawn and patio furniture, the company offers ten lines of rattan and wicker furnishings for casual, indoor-outdoor relaxed styles of living. There are always sales at Patio & Interiors.

# Valley

## Arte en Cantera

2900 North McColl Road
McAllen, Texas 78501
☎ 956/682-1623
**FAX** 956/682-8252
**Hours** Mon-Fri 8-6, Sat 10-3
**Accessible** Yes

This shop, which imports Cantera stone columns, fountains and door surrounds, also brings in furniture from Mexico. The place is replete with imported Mexican pots and a large selection of other accessories, too. We loved its wares!

# Rio Grande Plain

## The Backyard Store

2108 N.W. Military Highway
San Antonio, Texas 78213
☎ 210/308-4762
**FAX** 210/308-4769
www.patiostore.com
**Hours** Mon-Thurs 10-7, Fri & Sat 10-6, Sun 12-4
**Accessible** Yes
**Mail Order**
**Catalog** Free

The Backyard Store carries as wide variety of casual furniture, including *Kettler, Telescope, Pride, Woodard, Lloyd/Flanders* and *Grosfillex* resin. But there's much, much more here — play equipment, gazebos, *Hatteras* hammocks, *Coleman* spas and garden accessories. This company's Web site is really impressive. And there are always sales, both on-line and in the store.

## The Chair King

6931 San Pedro
San Antonio, Texas 78216
☎ 210/349-3851
**FAX** 210/349-8860

See complete listing on page 353.

## Home & Patio

1047 N.E. Loop 410
San Antonio, Texas 78209
☎ 210/828-2807
**FAX** 210/828-2884
**Hours** Mon-Sat 10-5:30
**Accessible** Yes

*(Listing continued on next page)*

Explains Maxine Kelley, "Over thirty years ago my husband asked me (a garden-clubber) to help him (a builder) establish a casual patio store. Since then we have searched for special items to make a complete casual living atmosphere." Home & Patio now has many departments within its San Antonio and Houston stores. They are galleries for *Lane Venture's* all-weather wicker and rattan furniture. You'll also find *Brown Jordan, Winston, Lyon-Shaw, O.W. Lee* and *Samsonite* furniture for dining and seating. Among the array of products are outdoor wall sculptures, stone drinking fountains, outdoor thermometers with matching clocks, garden benches, umbrellas, statuary and signs. The *Ducane Gas Grilles* department features portable outdoor fireplaces. Home & Patio boasts a very large selection of fountains, and along with these are good choices in fountain pumps, pond liners and spray heads. There are always sales going on!

---

## Patio Haus

*2700 Lockhill-Selma Road*
*San Antonio, Texas 78230*
☎ *210/ 492-5559*
**FAX** *210/ 492-0402*
**Hours** *Mon-Sat 10-6, Sun 1-5*
**Accessible** *Yes*

Owner Earl Stein proudly told us, "Our company has been in business over 51 years, specializing in patio furniture since 1975. Patio Haus is family owned and operated...there are two generations of us working here now. We are an 'upper-middle to high-end' business, and we just keep growing!" With over 5,000 sq.ft. of space per store, each location offers a number of complete display areas. A great way to gather ideas! The furniture lines include *O.W. Lee, Meadowcraft, Brown Jordan, Winston, Homescrest, Kingsley-Bate* and several outdoor wicker lines. You may choose from teak, cast aluminum, tubular aluminum, wrought iron and jarrah wood. Stainless gas grills, wood smokers and umbrellas and matching replacement cushions are just a few of the accessories available. There are very high-quality imported fountains and statuary as well as ponds and pumps. We were impressed with the large selection and very friendly, knowledgeable personnel.

---

## Stowers Furniture

*210 Rector*
*San Antonio, Texas 78216*
☎ *210/342-9411*
**FAX** *210/342-2903*
**Hours** *Mon-Sat 10-6, open until 8 Mon & Thurs*
**Accessible** *Yes*

Founded 107 years ago, Stowers is the longest continually operating furniture store in Texas. Now owned by Spears Furniture of Lubbock, the 80,000-sq.-ft. showroom is located south of North Star Mall. The large second floor atrium area is modeled after the San Antonio River Walk, and outdoor furnishings are displayed in this very pleasant atmosphere. You will find the same quality furniture lines carried here as in Spears' Lubbock store, and the staff here emphasizes the same knowledgeable, helpful service. (See page 360).

## Central Blacklands & Savannas

### Furniture Center Casual Shop

*7407 Woodway Drive*
*Waco, Texas 76712*
☎ *254/772-7090*
*FAX 254/776-0857*
**Hours** *Mon & Thurs 9-8, other days (except Sun) 9-6*
**Accessible** *Yes*

This company is family owned and operated by the Brewers: Billy, Mary and son Robert, and it features a good selection of furniture and accessories for the patio and garden. According to manager Bob Abel, "We never have sales and do very little advertising. We've been in business for 36 years, and people know about our 'fair mark-up' policy and our 'almost anywhere' delivery policy!" The furniture lines include *Homecrest, Winston, Woodard, Telescope, Meadowcraft* and *Brown Jordan.* You will also find *Hattaras* hammocks, patio accessories, umbrellas, statuary and even citronella candleholders that snap onto umbrella poles. Replacement cushions of your choice in fabrics can be ordered.

## Hill Country

### The Chair King

*5335 Airport Boulevard*
*Austin, Texas 78751*
☎ *512/454-5464*
*FAX 512/454-7256*

See complete listing on page 353.

### Georgetown Fireplace & Patio

*2104 North Austin Avenue*
*Georgetown, Texas 78626*
☎ *512/863-8574*
*FAX 512/863-0687*
**Hours** *Mon-Fri 9-5:30, Sat 9-4*
**Accessible** *Yes*

As Ken Todd told us, "We have been in the fireplace business for 20 years as Georgetown Energy, but with the addition of furnishings for the patio, we are now Georgetown Fireplace & Patio. Our helpful staff is always ready to assist you, and, with our large inventory, we offer a very good outdoor selection." The furniture lines include *Tropitone, Woodard* and *Lloyd Flanders.* There are wide selections in wrought iron, cast aluminum and outdoor wicker. You will also find wooden swings and rockers, hammocks, umbrellas, replacement cushions and patio heaters and fireplaces. Check the numerous newspaper, TV and radio ad for sales!

### The Greenhouse Mall

*9900 Ranch Road 620 North*
*Austin, Texas 78726-2203*
☎ *512/250-0000*
*FAX 512/258-2146*
**Hours** *Mon-Sat 10-6, Sun 12-6 (summer); Mon-Sat 10-5, Sun 12-5 (winter)*
**Accessible** *Partially (carts available)*
**Mail Order**
**Catalog** *Free*

*(Listing continued on next page)*

The Greenhouse Mall is situated on eight acres and has golf carts available for customer use in viewing the extensive outdoor display. You may choose from aluminum, iron and steel, wicker and rattan, wood and resin outdoor furniture. The lines you'll discover here include *Brown-Jordan, Winston, Lyon-Shaw, Tropitone, Barlow Tyrie, Meadowcraft, Samsonite, Lane/ Venture, Lloyd/ Flanders, O.W. Lee* and *Telescope*. An indoor display area offers, among other things, replacement cushions and a large outdoor fabric selection for special order. You'll see *Pawley's Island* hammocks and swings, *Dayva* umbrellas and shade-brellas and countless accessories. Don't forget the comprehensive selection of gas and charcoal grills. The large inventory enables The Greenhouse Mall to offer same-day, free delivery most of the time, or the company will ship merchandise. Owner Matt Wiggers proudly states, "The Greenhouse Mall is Austin's largest and oldest (over 20 years) and only locally owned patio store. We have a very knowledgeable sales staff, and we guarantee that "our prices are the lowest in Texas! No ifs... no buts!" Also see page 124.

## Patio Haus

3702 IH-35 South
New Braunfels, Texas 78132
☎ 830/625-0221 or 830/606-0951
**FAX** 830/629-7333

12501 Highway 71 West
Austin, Texas 78733
☎ 512/ 263-1111
**FAX** 512/263-1119

507 West Liberty Street
Round Rock, Texas 78664
☎ 512/310-7222
**FAX** 512/310/7744

**Hours** Mon-Sat 10-6, Sun 1-5; Mon-Sat 8:30-5:30 (Round Rock location)
**Accessible** Yes, all stores
See complete listing on page 356.

## Smith & Hawken

9901 Capital of Texas Highway North
Austin, Texas 78759
☎ 512/345-8700
See complete listing on page 352.

# Red Rolling Plains

## Fielder Pools

3301 Southwest Boulevard
San Angelo, Texas 76904
☎ 915/944-9902
**FAX** 915/949-0390
**Hours** Mon-Fri 10-6, Sat 10-5
**Accessible** Yes, except restroom

Since our visit to Hot Spring Spas Plus in Midland (see page 360), the Fielder family has opened this location. As owner Shirley Fielder proudly told us, "We're your indoor/outdoor leisure center. Although furniture is not displayed, *Sun Coast* outdoor furniture can be ordered from company catalogs. The company sells saunas, builds arbors and gazebos to shelter spas, designs and builds decks, glass encloses existing patios, adds garden rooms, and builds and renovates swimming pools.

## S&S Iron Works

*2434 Industrial Boulevard*
*Abilene, Texas 79605*
☎ *915/698-3601*
**Hours** *Mon-Fri 8-5:30*
**Accessible** *No*

S & S Iron Works manufactures wrought iron tables, benches, arbors and gazebos in addition to custom garden gates and fences and decorative iron stairways and handrails.

## Waldrop Furniture

*201 Walnut Street*
*Abilene, Texas 97601*
☎ *915/677-5283*
**FAX** *915/677-5771*
**Hours** *Mon-Sat 9-5*
**Accessible** *Yes*

In talking with Sam Waldrop, Chairman of the Board, he told us, "Waldrop Furniture has been family owned and operated for 75 years. We're on our third generation now, and we're still located in downtown Abilene. We are definitely one of the oldest in Texas!" The showroom occupies 38,000 square feet, of which 2,000 are devoted to outdoor furniture. You will find teak, wrought iron (*Woodard*) and a handsome, heavy-duty aluminum (*Pompeii*). There are tables, chairs, gliders, benches and round rocking chairs from which to choose as well as iron fountains and statuary. Replacement cushions and umbrellas can be ordered, but as Mr. Waldrop reminded us, "Our stock has to be heavy-duty. Remember those bad West Texas winds!" Check the paper for fall sales on furniture and accessories especially geared to the West Texas climate.

# High Plains

## Fireplace Center & Patio Shop

*60-18 Canyon Expressway*
*Amarillo, Texas 79109*
☎ *806/352-2031 or 1-800/333-0317*
**FAX** *806/358-2254*
**Hours** *Mon-Sat 9-5:30*
**Accessible** *Yes*

The Fireplace Center & Patio Shop offers a wide range of very attractively displayed patio furniture and much more, including friendly and knowledgeable service. *Homecrest, Brown Jordan, Winston, O.W. Lee, Meadowcraft, Woodard, Lyon Shaw* and *Kingsley-Bate* are just some of the furniture lines represented. You will also find statuary, fountains, planters, barbecue equipment (wood and gas), bird feeders, cushions, umbrellas, baker's racks and other outdoor or garden room accessories. As the name suggests, this company is into year-round comfort!

## Hot Spring Spas Plus

*3303 North Midkiff Road*
*Midland, Texas 79705*
☎ *915/699-5904*
**FAX** *915/699-5904*
**Hours** *Mon-Sat 10-6*
**Accessible** *Partially*

Owner Shirley Fielder proudly promises "quality you can count on now and from now on!" She can order *Sun Coast* garden furniture out of Florida. From the company's name, you know to expect spas, but the "Plus" is that the company also stocks saunas and builds arbors and gazebos to shelter its spas. The company designs and builds decks, will glass-in an existing patio and can add a garden room and custom-build or renovate your swimming pool. Our favorite item here was a redwood spa cover with curved glass. It's a real beauty! Hot Spring Spas Plus holds close-out sales in March, a midsummer sale and a Christmas sale.

## Spears Furniture

*2710 Avenue Q*
*Lubbock, Texas 79405*
☎ *806/747-3401 or 1-800/677-3401*
**FAX** *806/747-5662*
**Hours** *Mon-Sat 10-6*
**Accessible** *Yes*

This store has been in business since 1950, and the main showroom occupies 32,000 sq. ft. During the spring and summer months, an additional 15,000-sq.-ft. building houses the outdoor furniture display. You will find *Woodard* wrought iron, *Carolina Forge* (a less-expensive division of *Woodard*), *Martin Smith* teak, *Kessler*, *Lexington* outdoor wicker, *Uwharrie Adirondack* and *Atlantic Beach & Leisure* look-alike teak. Mr. Spears was quick to emphasize, "We have very well trained staff members who really know their furniture and are of great assistance to every customer. We are happy to special order pieces at no additional charge. "Adding to the quality of life is the way we like to think of Spears!" Look for sales advertised in the local paper and on TV. Free delivery within 150 miles. Upon talking with David Spears, we learned that Stowers Furniture of San Antonio is also owned and operated by the Spears family.

# Trans-Pecos

## El Pueblito Iron Furniture

*10010 Montana*
*El Paso, Texas 79925*
☎ *915/591-7811*
See complete listing on page 345.

## Chapter Ten

# Finishing Touches

*"The Devil whispered behind the leaves,
'It's pretty, but is it Art?'"*
....Rudyard Kipling

# The Artful Garden

Exteriors are as thoughtfully accessorized as home interiors these days. Envision a rear garden or entry court as an outdoor room. A handsome piece of sculpture might be used to punctuate the space and draw the eye, just as a fireplace compels attention in the living room. An elegant water feature could serve the garden in the same way a landscape painting gives depth to a wall in the dining room. A pair of decorative pots holding sculptural trees might "finish" the outdoor space in the same way that good-looking lamps enrich a family room.

It's important to understand that exterior spaces are larger in scale than interiors. Even if an enclosed courtyard is the same size as an adjacent living room, the open sky makes the outdoor space seem larger. A small piece of art can easily become lost. To make an impact, garden accessories generally must be more substantial than interior furnishings.

Keep in mind the viewpoint from which a piece of garden art will be seen. Consider not only its size, but also its shape. Remember that works of garden art don't exist in isolation, but rather they compete with other elements in the landscape and with one another.

We've all giggled over front yards packed with pink flamingos, gnomes and whirly-gigs, but if these pieces bring pleasure to the owners, well... I have a friend (a fellow landscape architect) who owns a flock of plastic flamingos purchased when Woolworth's went out of business. About two hundred birds alight in his front yard for party occasions, and they are a hoot! However, I generally suggest restraint and caution clients against cluttering the landscape with too many decorative objects in view from one spot.

☛**Money-saving Tip: One nice piece of garden art may be all you need in the way of ornamentation.**

The placement of garden art is an art in itself. It affords the collector an opportunity to be creative with the artist. The idea is to make the piece appear effortless and permanent. It should be used to delight rather than to confront the viewer. Remember, too, that garden art will be seen in varying light conditions and changing seasons. Try the piece in several spots within the garden. Dare to be experimental.

Garden art is often used to create balance within the garden. For example, a large contemporary sculpture might be placed at the edge of a wooded area or on a rise within the lawn as a counterweight to the house and its more intensively landscaped environment. Formal gardens, on the other hand, call for symmetrical or rational placement of sculptural elements. A classical piece might be used as a central feature in the garden or placed in a niche at the end of a walkway. A pair of antique urns could set off a doorway or flank the head of a staircase.

A re-circulating fountain can serve as kinetic sculpture, with water tumbling down a rock waterfall, bubbling up from a pool like an underground spring or pouring out of a piece of classical statuary. A delicate wall fountain, a ceramic bowl filled with water lilies or a Japanese basin could be used to set the motif in a small garden. A plaque, clock or window box might brighten a bare wall. Whimsical pieces (a humorous garden sign or stone bunny peeking out of a planting bed) add elements of surprise. A birdhouse or wind chime can be used to attract the eye upward, while a sundial or birdbath may be placed to focus attention on the center of a formal garden.

☛**Money-saving tip: Look for craftsmanship and durability in outdoor accessories; avoid metals that rust and materials that deteriorate.**

A fine piece of garden art is a good investment if it will last a lifetime. It's no coincidence that stone and bronze have been the preferred materials of sculptors through the ages. Today, sculptors are also making wonderful works of garden art from aluminum, resins and concrete. In the pages that follow, I've listed a few Texas sculptors whose work I particularly admire.

If you're considering commissioning a piece of art for your garden, you might also want to contact a curator at your local art museum or the Art Department at a University. To better enable a third party to match you with an artist, be prepared to explain what you are seeking. Do you prefer a figurative piece or something more abstract? Where will the piece go? What is the size and shape of the space? What other elements will be involved, such as water, plants or a vista?

Unfortunately, security is a factor in the placement of art in the landscape. If its weight is not sufficient to deter a would-be thief, consider bolting, welding or mortaring the piece onto a base. A base may also serve to raise the piece, making it more "important" in the landscape. Of course, you must also secure the piece if it might fall over and hurt someone.

If you own a valuable piece of art, you'll need to consider its preservation, which is particularly challenging in an outdoor environment. Never apply a protective coating or cleaning solution or attempt a repair without consulting a qualified art conservator in your area. Contact the American Institute for the Conservation of Historic and Artistic Works (☎ 202/452-9545) for a referral. Non-professional attempts to preserve a sculpture may do more harm than good and can actually devalue the piece.

☞**Money-saving Tip: If you cannot afford garden art, one handsome potted tree or an arrangement of good-looking containers can function as sculpture.**

Big terra cotta pots can be used on a terrace to separate a seating area from the dining area. Out in the garden, urns might be used to break-up an overly large planting area. In working out an arrangement of plants in containers, remember that the plants will show to best advantage if they are played against a wall. When the grouping is played against foliage, the containers will predominate.

You'll find handsome terra cotta pots in every imaginable shape and size. A wide array of wood, stone, concrete and glazed ceramic containers are also available from Texas manufacturers and garden stores. The only word of caution I would interject here is to be sure that any clay container you buy is fired for outdoor use. Some of my favorite containers are glazed ceramics, which tend to deteriorate with cycles of freezing and thawing. I use these pots for the tropical plants I keep outdoors in summer, and I bring them inside for the winter.

Just as Texas is rich in plant materials, the selections in garden decorations are wondrous. Several Texas artists have received national acclaim for their outdoor sculpture. Regional artisans and craftspeople are making fabulous pots, planters and window boxes, birdhouses and banners, wind chimes and bells, topiary and fountains. (For more fountain sources, see Water Gardening, beginning on page 316.) There are fabulous garden emporiums and import shops that have quite literally brought the world to our doorsteps. Numerous antiques shops, galleries and botanical gardens' gift shops also seek out the highest-quality garden products on the market.

In the listings that follow, you'll discover varied and interesting sources. Don't just look within your own region; some of the companies listed will ship their wares. And keep these sources in mind as you travel. Shopping for unusual garden ornaments is often a "hit or miss" pursuit. The good pieces go quickly.

My daughter, who has an interest in the history of cemeteries, asked me to warn readers that stealing ornaments from grave sites and old churches has become a lucrative business. The only way to stop this heartless practice is for collectors to refuse to buy suspect pieces. Be particularly wary of weathered stone angels and other religious symbols. Never hesitate to ask dealers about their sources. A new piece will soon take on a patina in your garden, and you'll never have to wonder if it once marked the burial place of some other family's loved one.

# Artisans, Importers & Manufacturers of Garden Ornaments:

## Copper Falls

*1008 West Murphy Road*
*Colleyville, Texas 76034*
☎ *817/498-3386*
**FAX** *817/379-0889*
**Hours** *By appointment*

Since Shayla Clark began showing her works-in-copper at Neil Sperry's annual garden show, she has been too busy to catalog her work. Especially popular are the freestanding fountains ornamented with lily pads, grasses and cattails. The pieces range in size from small to large, and she makes handsome tables to display the smaller fountains. Patrons also quickly snap-up the whimsical copper jack o' lanterns and two-foot-long lizards designed to ornament a garden wall. This artist says she's willing to take-on commission work, and she has pictures to show you if you're interested in her work.

## Danville Chadbourne

*1002 West Summit*
*San Antonio, Texas 78201*
☎ *210/732-7303*
**Hours** *By appointment only*
**Accessible** *Difficult*

Working out of an old grocery store, artist Danville Chadbourne fabricates stacked vertical sculptures that have been described as "organic." His materials are clay, cast concrete, stone, bronze and wood. Human in scale (most pieces range between five and seven-feet in height), his primitive-flavored works stand in harmony with the natural environment. Mr. Chadbourne, who received his MFA from Texas Tech in the late '70s, shows his work in galleries throughout the country.

## French Wyres

*P.O. Box 131655*
*Tyler, Texas 75713*
☎ *903/597-8322*
**FAX** *903/597-9321*
**Hours** *By appointment only*
**Mail Order**
**Catalog** *$4.00*

Would you believe that exquisitely reproduced French wire garden furnishings are being made right here in Texas! Produced in limited quantity by a small group of artisans, each piece is of excellent construction and will provide a lifetime of use. They manufacture everything from chairs to urns, from trellises to pedestals, and much more. This is Victorian wire at its best! We encountered the product several times in nurseries and garden related shops in our travels. And we always said, "This has to be French Wyres!" The company's catalog is most comprehensive, containing pictures as well as written information. There's no retail store at this time, but there soon will be one in Tyler, welcoming customers by appointment. According to Terri and Paul Squyres, they took the admonition from *Field of Dreams*: "If you build it, they will come." And so they have!

## Kenneth Updike

P.O. Box 293
Lone Grove, Oklahoma 73443
☎ 580/657-3249 or 1-800/797-3249
FAX 580/657-3270
**Mail Order**
**Catalog** Free two-page brochure

As Kenneth Updike told us, "I started showing my birdhouses and feeders in Canton in 1989, and I've been going strong ever since." Made of western cedar, this delightful collection consists of a gazebo-style bird feeder (about $45) and 20-25 building-style birdhouses (about $12 to $20). There are churches, barns, schools, cottages, general stores, saloons and a number of patriotic buildings with flags (including, of course, a Texas flag!) You can write, phone or FAX Mr. Updike for a copy of his free brochure with pictures and order the perfect gift. Chances are, you will want one for your own garden! Shipping and freight are not included in the prices, but Mr.Updike does ship anywhere in the U.S.

## Lars Stanley — Architects & Artisans

2007 Kinney Avenue
Austin, Texas 78704
☎ 512/445-0444
FAX 512/445-3432
www.io.com/~stanarch/
**Hours** Mon-Sun 9-6
**Accessible** Yes
**Mail Order**
**Catalog** $5:00
**Mailing Address** P.O. Box 3095, Austin, Texas 78764

Mr. Stanley's firm designs and fabricates custom garden elements, which are handcrafted from forged steel, copper, brass and other metals. His portfolio includes elegant entry gates, gazebos, furniture, sundials, and lighting fixtures, and his work has been featured in several leading magazines. Each piece is unique. Staff architects help homeowners and designers elaborate their own ideas into well-detailed reality. The company holds studio tours in spring and fall.

## Marshall Pottery

4901 Elysian Fields Road
Marshall, Texas 75670
☎ 903/938-9201
FAX 930/938-8222
**Hours** Mon-Sat 9-6, Sun 10-6
**Accessible** Yes
**Mail Order**
**Catalog** Free
**Mailing Address** P.O. Box 1839, Marshall, Texas 75671

Marshall Pottery is the place to find red clay pots — all sizes from 1½" to 18½" standards, plus a multitude of shapes, round and square, plain or decorative. This company also carries oak swings and frames and a selection of concrete birdbaths. There's a year-round Christmas display.

## Music of the Spheres

*5003 East Caesar Chavez*
*Austin, Texas 78702*
☎ *512/385-0340*
*FAX 512/385-0420*
*www.monsterbit.com/mots/*
**Hours** *By appointment only*
**Accessible** *Partially*
**Mail Order**
**Catalog** *Free brochure*

In business since 1989, this company has become one of the country's leading manufacturers of fine windchimes. Designed by Larry Roark, who holds a degree in music theory from the University of North Texas, the chimes are tuned to orchestral pitch and available in soprano, alto, tenor or base. You can actually listen to the sounds on the web site and choose a pitch most pleasant to you! Finished in electrostatic powder-coated matte black, the aluminum alloy tubing is designed to withstand acid rain and salt air. The clapper slides on a central cord so that the chimes may be turned off. While most of the firm's business is mail order, people can visit the factory by appointment or see the products on display at the Texas Renaissance Festival.

## Phil Evett

*P.O. Box 1154*
*Blanco, Texas 78606*
☎ *830/833-4107*
**Hours** *By appointment only*
**Accessible** *Difficult*

Phil Evett retired as an art professor at Trinity University, moved to the country and found bliss carving abstracted human forms from wood. While his exquisitely finished, "table-top-size" works in wood are only suitable for indoor display, some of his pieces have now been cast in bronze. What a wonderful focal point for an outdoor living room!

## Smith Studio

*Route 5, Box 18*
*Caldwell, Texas 77836*
☎ *409/567-9620*
*FAX 409/567-0288*
**Hours** *By appointment*
**Catalog** *Free*

For more than a decade, sculptor Christopher Smith has been receiving national acclaim for his work in bronze. His elegant fountains and wildlife sculptures (all cast in the Old World lost wax method) are sold in exclusive limited editions to collectors throughout the country. As a place to live and work, this Montana-raised artist and his wife chose the Central Texas countryside for its inspirational diversity of wildlife.

## Stone Forest, Inc.

*213 St. Francis Drive*
*Santa Fe, New Mexico 87501*
☎ *505/986-8883*
*FAX 505/982-2712*
**Hours** *Mon Fri 9-5, Sat 10:30-5*

*(Listing continued on next page)*

*Accessible* Yes
*Mail Order*
*Catalog* $4.00
*Mailing Address* P.O. Box 2840, Santa Fe, New Mexico 78504

Stone Forest creates hand carved granite garden ornaments, which combine the elegant simplicity of Japanese style with contemporary design. "These are graceful, stunning garden sculptures, among the best we've seen," reports *San Diego Home & Garden* magazine. And we agree. Products include fountains, spheres, Japanese and contemporary lanterns, planters, birdbaths, benches and bridges. If you're in Santa Fe, you can visit the company.

## Wild Birds Unlimited

☎ 1-800/326-4928 *(national office)*

Call this interactive number to get the address and phone number of your nearest retail store. The company, which has been in business since 1981, now has 17 stores in Texas that carry an array of decorative fountains, sundials, birdbaths, and all the feeders, food and housing that goes with attracting birds to your garden. Ask to get on the store's mailing list.

## Williams' Sculpture Works

*223 East Quill Drive*
*San Antonio, Texas 78228*
☎ 210/434-7306
*http://lonestar.texas.net/~chilmer/WSW/wswidx.html*
*Hours* By appointment only
*Accessible* Yes

Don Williams' lyrical contemporary pieces can be viewed on his Web site, but like all works of sculpture, they need to be touched and seen from every angle to be fully appreciated. Working in bronze, welded steel and wood, this young but very experienced artist takes commissioned work and makes both limited-edition and one-of-a-kind pieces. After receiving a degree in religion from Trinity University, Don continued his love of sculpture as an apprentice at several foundries, where he not only mastered the technical aspects of casting, but also developed his uniquely spirited visual style.

## Wright Pottery

*Route 1, Box 42*
*Spicewood, Texas 78669*
☎ 512/264-1578
*Hours* By appointment
*Accessible* Partially
*Mail Order*
*Catalog* Free brochure

Bob and Debbie Wright make wonderful ceramic birdhouses, birdbaths, feeders and trays. They also produce hanging candle-holders and a pleasing variety of tableware and serving dishes suitable for outdoor entertaining. Their firing technique draws from the Asian tradition, but the pieces are made of Texas clay and the look is compatible with Southwest style. The couple holds kiln-opening parties the first weekend in May and December and a big yard sale on the 4th of July. They show in Austin's Barton Creek Mall during the Mothers Day and Christmas buying seasons. Order early if you're interested in their garden art as Christmas gifts.

# Regional Resources for Garden Accessories:

## *Cross Timbers & Grand Prairie*

### David's Patios

*3001 East Highway 199*
*Springtown, Texas 76082*
☎ *817/677-2759*
**FAX** *817/677-4921*
**Hours** *Mon-Fri 8-5, Sat 9-5, Sun 12-5 (best to call and check)*
**Accessible** *Partially (rough surfaces)*

As owners Cecelia and David Grimmett told us, "After 35 years in business, David's Patios is the largest on-site manufacturer of concrete garden products in Texas. We're a 'landmark' in this area!" True enough...you can't miss this one! There are at least 80 different fountains displayed, along with statuary, bird baths, table sets and benches, stepping stones and bed edging, planters and Japanese lanterns. The company also stocks wind chimes, sundials, terra cotta and ceramic pots, bird houses, bird feeders and wind socks. You will find no lack of selection here!

*Directions: From Fort Worth, David's Patios is northwest of Loop 820 about 18 miles.*

### Into the Garden

*1615 South University Drive*
*Fort Worth, Texas 76107*
☎ *817/336-4686*
**FAX** *817/336-4687*
**Hours** *Mon-Thurs 10-8, Fri & Sat 10-9, Sun 12-5*
**Accessible** *Yes, both stores*

"Anything you can find in a catalog, we have at Into the Garden. You can see it, touch it and take it home the same day!" notes design director Phillip Combs. This specialty garden store, which also has a Dallas branch, offers a broad selection of items for and from the garden. You'll find planters and statuary by *Stonecrafters* and *Campania*, plus trellises, fountains, wind chimes, birdhouses and birdbaths. The stores stock tropical plants, garden books, potting soils, very substantial garden tools and quality garden furniture.

Both locations have patios with a nice selection of perennials, herbs, topiaries, seasonal color and flowering shrubs. As owner Kevin Levy says "Into the Garden is solely organic and emphasizes organic gardening in its various symposia and in its newsletter." With a special array of garden-themed gifts and furnishings, this company "brings the garden indoors and takes the concept of interior decorating out into the garden." Markdowns occur occasionally after the end of a planting or holiday season. Into the Garden offers a series of seminars on organic gardening, perennials, bulbs and other topics. The stores sponsor book signings, lectures and open houses, so be sure you're on the mailing list. (See Dallas address on page 370.)

## Legacy

1715 East Lamar Boulevard
(**Antique Sampler**)
Arlington, Texas 76006
☎ 817/861-4747
**Hours** Mon-Sat 10-7, Sun 12-6
**Accessible** Yes

3708 Pioneer Parkway at Park Springs
(**Antiques & Moore**)
Arlington, Texas 76013
☎ 817/548-5931
**Hours** Mon-Sat 10-6, Sun 12-6
**Accessible** Yes

Shoppers can visit Legacy at four locations in the Dallas/Arlington area and be assured of finding the unusual! As owner Sharon Elmquist is quick to offer, " You never can tell what you will find at Legacy, but if you're looking for a particular item, call me at home (817/469-9801), and I can point you in the right direction. 'Shabby chic' is my favorite." Among the architectural offerings are fences, gates, columns, arbors and statuary. There are also garden benches, a number of unusual wind chimes and other garden accessories. One of the artists represented by Sharon makes birdhouses in the shape of a church, and another forges very imaginative wrought iron garden angels. Also popular are the planters made from ceiling tin and the wrought iron plant holders.

## Yard Art

6407 Colleyville Boulevard (Highway 26)
Colleyville, Texas 76034
☎ 817/421-2414
See complete listing on page 350.

# Trinity Blacklands

## Hill Country Experience

2608 Elm Street
Dallas, Texas 75226
☎ 214/742-3400
See complete listing on page 346.

## Into the Garden

5370 West Lovers Lane
Dallas, Texas 75209
☎ 214/351-5125
**Hours** Mon-Sat 10-6, Sun 12-5
See complete listing on page 369.

## J&J Antiques

15201 Midway Road
Addison, Texas 75244
☎ 972/490-4085
**Hours** Daily 10-6 except Thanksgiving and Christmas
**Accessible** Yes

J&J Antiques is located in Unlimited Limited, a big antique mall in, as the locals say, "North Dallas." Owners Joe and Judy Staser specialize in English antiques which include a large number of chimney pots, ceramic sundials, wrought iron gates, old watering cans and statuary. You never know what treasure you might find!

## Jackson's Pottery & Garden Center

*6950 Lemmon Avenue*
*Dallas, Texas 75209*
☎ *214/350-9200*
**FAX** *214/350-4253*
**Hours** *Mon-Sat 9-6, Sun 12-5*
**Accessible** *Yes*

Jackson's Pottery & Garden Center is housed in a lovely red brick Williamsburg-style building on a spacious site, with a waterfall on one side (the company is "big" on rock gardening and waterfalls). As owner Bob Jackson laughingly tells, "We occasionally have people come in because they think it's a restaurant. What most people call us, though, is the Neiman-Marcus of Gardening!" Whether you are decorating for Christmas, buying pottery or looking for gift ideas, there's something for you at Jackson's. Our pottery (the largest selection in the Southwest) is from Greece, Italy, China and Germany. It is personally chosen and of exceptional quality! You'll find gardening supplies, tools, barbecue smokers (including *Oklahoma Joe*), fountains, planters, statuary, books, gifts and accessories, materials for walks and patios and teak and wrought iron garden furniture. At Christmas, Jackson's really "decks the halls." Sales are held Memorial Day, July 4th, Labor Day and the "really big one" after Christmas. As reported in the *Park Cities News*, "Personalized service and satisfaction to the customer is guaranteed, and Mr. Jackson is in the store daily to answer any questions." You are bound to find something you "just have to have." The nursery part of the company is described on page 291.

## Legacy

*4908 West Lovers Lane*
**(Park Cities Antique Mall)**
*Dallas, Texas 75209*
☎ *214/369-4195*
**Hours** *Mon-Sat 10-6, Sun 12-6*
**Accessible** *Yes, in the garden area*

*3319 Knox Street*
**(Knox Street Antiques)**
*Dallas, Texas 75205*
☎ *214/521-8888*
**Hours** *Mon-Sat 10-6, Thurs 10-7, Sun 1-6*
**Accessible** *Yes*

See complete listing on page 370.

## The Little House

*514 South Pearl*
*Dallas, Texas 75201*
☎ *214/748-1443*
**FAX** *972/315-7395*
**Hours** *Wed-Fri 9-5, Sat & Sun 9-6*
**Accessible** *Partially*

The Little House is part of Landscape Systems of Texas and is located next door in the Farmer's Market in downtown Dallas. Having been in business for over five years, this company markets very heavy, good quality fountains and birdbaths as well as trellises, windchimes and bird feeders. You will find a large selection of stone and iron statuary, some of which can be planted. There are also iron benches, tables, chairs and baker's racks displayed. During the holiday season, The Little House carries Christmas trees and wreaths, and in the fall, decorative produce is available.

## North Haven Gardens Inc.

*7700 North Haven Road*
*Dallas, Texas 75230*
☎ 214/363-5316
See complete listing on page 187.

## Splendor in the Grass

*8626 Garland Road*
*Dallas, Texas 75218*
☎ *214/328-5011*
**FAX** *214/320-7859*
**Hours** *Mon-Sat 10-5:30, Sun 1-5*
**Accessible** *No*

In two little white houses across from the Dallas Arboretum you'll find a wealth of planters, sculptures, gazing balls and fountains. Billed as a garden boutique and wild bird center, the company sells houses and feeders and custom-blends birdseed mixes to attract specific birds. There are also lots of banners, hand-forged plant holders, planters made of terra cotta, cast-stone and concrete. Fountains are delivered free within a ten-mile radius.

## Texas Palm Trees & Plants

*2023 Cadiz Street*
*Dallas, Texas 75201*
☎ *214/741-2310*
See complete listing on page 331.

# Piney Woods

## Bloomies, Inc.

*1000 East Marshall Avenue*
*Longview, Texas 75601*
☎ *903/757-4313*
**Hours** *Mon-Fri 9-5, Sat 9-12*
**Accessible** *No*

To visit Bloomies is a visual treat! It's first and foremost a florist, providing beautiful arrangements in the unstructured European style and English garden baskets containing both blooming and green plants. Beyond that, Bloomies carries attractively displayed garden accessories that range from hose-holders to small pieces of furniture. You'll find fountains, unusual containers and topiaries, too. The indoor plants lean more to the unusual — bromeliads, anthuriums, orchids, etc. The staff, which includes a landscape architect, is friendly and knowledgeable. As Shelley Potter comments, "Customers come to Bloomies for 'that something different.'" Staff members host an in-store open house in November and an "after-Christmas" sale. They are frequently invited to speak to local groups. Find Bloomies and treat yourself to a lovely experience.

## Breedlove Nursery & Landscape

*11576 State Highway 64 West*
*Tyler, Texas 75704*
☎ *903/597-7421*
   See complete listing on page 194.

## Plantation Pottery

*3110 North Eastman Road*
*Longview, Texas 75605*
☎ *903/663-3387*
   See complete listing on page 192.

## Tankersley Gardens

*IH-30 at Loop 271*
*Mt. Pleasant, Texas 75455*
☎ *903/572-0567*
**Hours** *Tues-Sat 9-6*
**Accessible** *Yes*
   As Dana Havron told us, "The gift shop at Tankersley Gardens has a greenhouse filled with concrete statuary and fountains, and we are expanding into handcrafted items." You'll also find porcelain collectibles, pots, books and windchimes.

## Thompson-Hills Nursery

*11745 Highway 64 West*
*Tyler, Texas 75704*
☎ *903/597-9951*
   See complete listing on page 194.

# Coastal Prairies & Marshes

## Adkins Architectural Antiques

*3515 Fannin Street*
*Houston, Texas 77004*
☎ *713/522-6547 or 1-800/522-6547*
**FAX** *713/529-8253*
**Hours** *Mon-Sat 9:30-5:30, Sun 12-5*
**Accessible** *Partial*
**Mail Order** *Yes*
**Catalog** *Free*
   Adkins is known for period and reproduction garden decor, street lighting (in 40 styles), patio furniture, fountains, urns, benches, bronze/stone and concrete statuary, and wrought iron gates and fencing. Specializing in architectural antiques, its inventory is one of the largest in the Southwest. As Nancy O'Connor reports, "Adkins is frequently able to obtain large or unusual architectural embellishments or materials from landmark homes or buildings during renovation projects. The staff is experienced in working with home owners, decorators and architects to adapt these architectural treasures for use in restoration or new home and garden projects."
   *Directions: Located approximately eight blocks north of Highway 59 on Fannin, between downtown and the Medical Center.*

## Ann Gunnells Antiques

*635 Pine Creek*
*Seabrook, Texas 77586*
☎ *281/474-4544*
**FAX** *281/474-4544*
**Hours** *By appointment*
**Accessible** *Partially*

"We carry a number of items that can be transformed into something else. Customers come to us to get good ideas, find that perfect piece and have it modified to fit their needs," commented Ann Gunnells. This shop, in business for over 20 years, carries antique fountains, statuary, fragments, urns, planters and wrought iron gates, fences and window guards as well as arches, columns and capitals. You will find benches, tables and chairs, consoles and other garden furnishings. This is a great place to find that "one-of-a-kind" piece and let your imagination take over!

## Antiques & Eccentricities

*1921 Westheimer*
*Houston, Texas 77098*
☎ *713/523-1921*
**Hours** *Tues-Sat 11-5*
**Accessible** *No*

As Kay O'Toole explained, "Although I don't cater exclusively to the garden at Antiques & Eccentricities, I do carry a good selection of European antique garden furniture and accessories as well as architectural embellishments." In both the indoor and outdoor display areas, you will find antique chairs, tables, benches, plant stands and planters, fountains and statuary. There are also garden carts, stone bases for sinks, marble basins, terra cotta and stone wall hangings, concrete jardiniers, English stone balls and wrought iron garden surrounds. As Kay laughingly admits, "It seems like one buying trip after another, so the shop is always crowded with new treasures."

## Condon Gardens

*1214 Augusta Drive*
*Houston, Texas 77057*
☎ *713/782-3992*

See complete listing on page 200. The selections in accessories here are absolutely first rate!

## Cornelius Nurseries, Inc.

*2233 South Voss Road*
*Houston, Texas 77057*
☎ *713/782-8640*

Wait 'til you see the selection of pots! Complete listing on page 200.

## The Garden Gate

*5122 Morningside Drive*
*Houston, Texas 77005*
☎ *713/528-2654*
**FAX** *713/528-0074*
**Hours** *Mon-Sat 10-6, Sun 12-5*
**Accessible** *Yes*

You know you are going to love a place when you are met by "the two main guys," Milo and Otis, who just happen to be cats! They have their own calling cards and are available for consultation "only between catnaps." Beyond the lighter side, you will find a marvelous collection of accessories, plants and "people most helpful." We were astounded by The Garden Gate's array of planters, urns, statuary, fountains, benches and other garden antiques made from every imaginable material. You'll find tools, books, topiary, vines and seasonal color, all displayed in a charmingly casual manner. There are also water plants and equipment and possibly seminars on that subject coming soon. Says Donna Lokey, the owner, "One client referred to The Garden Gate as one giant garage sale... always something different!"

## The Garden Room

*2426 Mechanic*
*Galveston, Texas 77550*
**Hours** *Friday, Saturday & Sunday 11-4*

There's no phone at this little shop in the Strand, and the inventory comes and goes. It's almost always "bulging" with wrought iron antiques, but designers snap-up the garden urns, the fern-pattern iron benches and the French iron day beds almost as quickly as they come in. "You have to see it to believe it," says the owner Dan Kiestra, who scours the country for elegant and whimsical garden art. "Our manager Twyla Bagot *is* the shop. She'll help you find the perfect piece."

## The Garden Shoppe

*2345 Calder Avenue*
*Beaumont, Texas 77702*
☎ *409/835-3266*
**Hours** *Mon-Sat 9-5:30, Sun 1-5 (spring & holidays)*
**Accessible** *Yes*

Located in historic Olde Town, this renovated 1920's English-style house is "creatively packed" corner-to-corner with handmade products of local and recognized artists, herbs and herb related products and hard-to-find natives and perennials. You'll also find an extensive line of topiary, statues and fine garden ornaments. Additionally, staff members offer custom garden design and construction with "romantic gardening" as a mindset. As Rette Browning explains, "Our firm offers the unique for a discriminating garden clientele. We're inspired to use cobblestones, pergolas, antique roses and perennials, and we love fountains!" The Garden Shoppe holds an anniversary sale in the fall, another after Christmas and several special holiday events. Garden advice is freely dispensed.

## Joshua's Native Plants & Garden Antiques

*111 Heights Boulevard*
*Houston, Texas 77007*
☎ *713/862-7444*

Joshua hand-picks every item and plant for this shop — everything from the turn-of-the-century planters and birdbaths to funky '50s garden furniture. He imports fine European cast iron and garden benches, gates, statuary and old watering cans. For gardeners on a budget, there's a huge assortment of reproduction Victorian decor. The water features are particularly impressive. See nursery listing on page 255.

## Maas Nursery & Landscaping

*5511 Todville Road*
*Seabrook, Texas 77586*
☎ *281/474-2488*
    See complete listing on page 198.

## Tom's Thumb Nursery & Landscaping

*2014 45th Street*
*Galveston, Texas 77550*
☎ *409/763-4713*
    See complete listing on page 199.

# Coastal Bend

## Better Gardens & Landscape

*606 East Mockingbird*
*Victoria, Texas 77904*
☎ *512/573-7434*
    See complete listing on page 206.

## Fox Tree & Landscape Nursery

*5902 South Staples Street*
*Corpus Christi, Texas 78413*
☎ *512/992-6928*
    See complete listing on page 205.

## Gill Landscape Nursery

*2810 Airline Road*
*Corpus Christi, Texas 78414*
☎ *512/992-9674*
    See complete listing on page 205.

# Valley

## Arte en Cantera

*2900 North McColl Road*
*McAllen, Texas 78501*
☎ *956/682-1623*
    See complete listing on page 116.

## Bence Nursery

*West Expressway 83 at White Ranch Road*
*Harlingen, Texas 78551*
☎ *956/797-2021*
    See complete listing on page 207.

# Rio Grande Plain

## Accents, Inc.

*119 West Sunset*
*San Antonio, Texas 78209*
☎ *210/826-4500*
**FAX** *210/824-6089*
**Hours** *Mon-Sat 9-5*
**Accessible** *Yes*

   Accents is a charming shop that imports antique garden accessories from France and England. In the outdoor display area, you will find chimney pots, statuary, interesting planters, bird cages and furniture. Although this company emphasizes interior accessories, as customers comment, "There is always something wonderful and unusual here for both home and garden." Accents is a delightful place to visit!

## The Antique Rose Emporium

*7561 East Evans Road*
*San Antonio, Texas 78226*
☎ *210/651-4565*

   See complete listing on page 258.

## Rainbow Gardens

*2585 Thousand Oaks*
*San Antonio, Texas 78232*
☎ *210/494-6131*

*8516 Bandera Road*
*San Antonio, Texas 78250*
☎ *210/680-2394*

   See complete listing on page 213.

## Rooms and Gardens

*5405 Broadway*
*San Antonio, Texas 78209*
☎ *210/829-5511*
**Hours** *Mon-Fri 10-5:30, Sat 10-5*
**Accessible** *Yes*

   The antiques dealers and importers who share this space offer one-of-a-kind focal points for the garden and smaller exterior accessories, as well. When we visited we found the courtyard filled with hanging baskets, statuary, pots and planters, stone fountains and garden furniture. The Ivy Swan and Debbie McCullough's Plants Perfect have since closed (Debbie is showing her collection at such events as the Round Top Fair and the Tyler Junior League's annual Mistletoe and Magic). She plans to return to Rooms and Gardens with Christmas trees each year. Given the commitment of its owner, this ensemble of boutiques should continue to provide delightful shopping, and we look forward to visiting there again.

## *Central Blacklands & Savannas*

### The Antique Rose Emporium
*9300 Lueckemeyer Road*
*Brenham, Texas 77833*
☎ *409/836-5548*
  See complete listing on page 276.

### Earthscapes
*5317 Loop 205*
*Temple, Texas 76502*
☎ *254/773-4668*
  See complete listing on page 220.

### Frazier's
*Highway 290 East (Business 290)*
*Hempstead, Texas 77445*
☎ *409/826-6760*
**FAX** *409/826-4300*
**Hours** *Daily 9-6 (closed Wed)*
**Accessible** *Partially (gravel paths)*
  As Billy Frazier described this business, "It's two acres of 'Concrete Heaven' like you've never seen before! Family owned and operated for 44 years, Frazier's has been featured on *Eyes of Texas* twice and in *Texas Monthly* magazine." You'll be amazed by the selection of concrete garden accessories, locally manufactured and imported from around the world. Spread over the landscape are all manner of huge, elaborate custom fountains, birdbaths and houses, statuary (some of which is very large), hundreds of planters and arbors. There are chairs, tables and benches made of concrete, hand-carved stone, cast aluminum and wrought iron. Don't fail to notice the very attractively patterned stepping stones. "To find us, exit the new bypass at Hempstead and ask anyone," says Billy. This is an experience not to be missed!

### Margaret Shanks Garden Antiques and Ornaments
*901 Pecan street*
*Brenham, Texas 77833*
☎ *409/830-0606*
**Hours** *Thurs-Sat 11-4 (Call ahead)*
**Accessible** *No*
  Margaret Shanks Garden Antiques and Ornaments has been in business for eight years, and as Margaret told us, "As far as I know, I'm the first person in the area to specialize in old garden furniture and ornaments." This shop carries 18th, 19th and early 20th century antiques from France, England and America. Among her treasures are benches, tables, chairs, urns, sundials, old tools, hand lights, bell jars, old watering cans and rhubarb forcers. Plant climbers, woven willow fencing from England, birdbaths and small animal statuary for the garden are also displayed. As Margaret says, "I love to find just the right focal point for cottage gardens, and there is something in every price range."

# Hill Country

## Artisan Group, Inc.

*826 Water Street*
*Kerrville, Texas 78028*
☎ *830/896-4220*
**FAX** *830/896-4226*
**Hours** *Mon-Fri 8-5, Sat by appointment*
**Accessible** *Yes*

Artisan Group is an architecture/interior design/construction firm, or as Howell Ridout told us, "We design, build and furnish, and we find ourselves doing more and more landscape projects. In our retail gallery, we display handcrafted items and furniture, some of which are appropriate for the garden." There is an array of planters, urns, fountains, statuary and garden wall art, as well as patio furniture of wood, iron and stone from which to chose. Under any circumstances, it is a delightful shop to visit!

## Breed & Company Garden Shop

*718 West 29th*
*Austin, Texas 78705*
☎ *512/474-6679*
**FAX** *512/474-6007*

*3663 Bee Cave Road*
*Austin, Texas 78746*
☎ *512/328-3960*
**FAX** *512/328-3486*

Breed carries a wonderful selection of containers, as well as all the seasonal color you'll need to fill them. The Christmas Shop is sensational here, and the company holds an after-Christmas sale, as well as periodic sidewalk sales. See complete listing on page 300.

## Comfort Common

*717 High Street*
*Comfort, Texas 78013*
☎ *830/995-3030*
**Hours** *Daily 10:30-4:30*
**Accessible** *Yes*
**Mailing Address** *P.O. Box 969, Comfort, Texas 78013*

Comfort Common, formerly an old hotel, is now an antique mall where Bob and Diane Potter of Antiques on High (641 High Street) display their architectural embellishments. You will find such items as iron and wooden gates, fencing, benches, statuary, birdbaths and shutters. As Bob Potter told us, "With a constant turnover of merchandise, our inventory changes often. To find out what we have at any given time, you are welcome to call us at home (830/995-4180)." It's a great place to visit. You never know what you might find!

## Cornerstone Home and Hardware

*3801 Bee Caves Road*
*Austin, Texas 78746*
☎ *512/327-0404*

Everywhere you look there is a perfect garden accessory or an unusual garden tool (some of the best we found). See complete listing on page 300.

## Courtyard Shops

*5453 Burnet Road*
*Austin, Texas 78756*
☎ *512/451-8037* (**Halbert Antiques**)
☎ *419-1112* (**Robuck Antiques**)
☎ *451-3585* (**French Quarter Antiques**)
**Hours** *Generally, Tues-Sat 10-6*
**Accessible** *Mostly*

A new attraction for Austin gardeners is this self-described "eclectic collection of shops." Within the outdoor spaces adjacent to the above-named dealers' galleries, we discovered a plethora of garden ornaments, including handsome pots, fountains, statuary, wrought iron furniture, gates and trellises. We had no trouble finding several pieces that would fit quite happily into our own gardens! As we go to press with this book, landscape architect Bud Twilley is in the process of redesigning the environment adjacent to this funky assortment of metal buildings that once housed Stripling-Blake Lumber Company. We'll be watching its development.

## Edelweiss Markt

*239 East Main*
*Fredericksburg, Texas 78624*
☎ *830/997-3388*
**FAX** *830/990-8965*
**Hours** *Mon- Sat 10-6, Sun 11-5*
**Accessible** *Yes*

According to Nancy Durr, "Edelweiss Markt offers quite a selection of items to enhance your garden or patio." This charming shop carries forged steel hose holders, trellises and beautiful, ornate crosses. There are also stone recycling fountains and detailed stone garden statues with animal or angel motifs. Stone and resin sprinklers, key keepers, books, watering cans (some of which are made into fountains) and small pieces of logwood furniture are available.

## Gardens

*1818 West 35th Street*
*Austin, Texas 78703*
☎ *512/451-5490*

A visit to Gardens is, to say the least, a must. Its upscale gift shop includes unusual garden furniture and merchandise from around the world. Here you'll find elegant teak benches, terra cotta pots from Italy and England, one-of-a-kind Indonesian urns made of sandstone or lavastone, very impressive hand-carved Italian limestone urns and fountains. "We offer the best selection of pots in Texas, and, because we are direct importers, we offer very good prices on our pots," says Gary Peese. See complete nursery listing on page 222.

## Howard Nursery
111 East Koenig Lane
Austin, Texas 78751
☎ 512/453-3150
See complete listing on page 223.

## Idle Hours
233 East Main Street
Fredericksburg, Texas 78624
☎ 830/997-2908
**FAX** 830/997-9638
**Hours** Mon-Sat 10-5:30, Sun 1-5
**Accessible** Partially (through backdoor to garden only)

At Idle Hours, one of Fredericksburg's six homestead stores, you will find an absolutely charming, "tucked away" assortment of garden accessories! Among other things we found paintings of posies, rustic statuary, live topiaries, moss covered terra cotta pots, antique bird baths, candle lanterns and crosses from the 1800's. There were heads from old statuary adding graphic interest to the garden and concrete benches and accessories from the '30s that resembled trees. According to Carol Bolton, "Idle Hours is a store for armchair gardeners. Since opening our doors in 1993, we have earned a reputation for offering the unusual. Each item is chosen with a discerning eye, making Idle Hours a shop not only for gardeners, but one that offers something for those who may not have time, space, or even the inclination to become true gardeners."

## Pots & Plants
5902 Bee Cave Road
Austin, Texas 78746
☎ 512/327-4564
See complete listing on page 224.

## Star Antiques
301 River Road
Wimberly, Texas 78676
☎ 512/847-9970
**FAX** 512/847-7916
**Hours** Wed 10-2, Sat & Sun 11-5 (call for other appointments)
**Accessible** Partially (outdoor display area is accessible and items can be brought out)

Star Antiques carries trellises, topiaries, gates, fencing, window guards, arches, benches and holders for plant containers. Among the accessories you can expect to find are pots, birdbaths and urns decorated with river rocks or sea shells. A visit to Star Antiques can provide inspiration, as well an unusual selection for the garden. "My husband and I have specialized in 'fine vintage lighting' for 15 years," explained Lisa Kiefer. "In 1997, we moved our shop and now have an outdoor area in which to display the lights, architectural embellishments and garden accessories."

## Sunset Canyon Pottery

*4002 East Highway 290*
*Dripping Springs, Texas 78620*
☎ *512/894-0938*
**FAX** *512/858-2111*
**Hours** *Mon-Sat 10-6:30, Sun 11-5*
**Accessible** *Yes*

As Bill Hauser tells the story, "My wife, Bridget, grew up as a neighbor of the head of the ceramics department of the Chicago Art Institute. In exchange for babysitting, she received lessons and has been 'stuck in the mud' ever since!" The Hausers' studio made Clarksville pottery for 17 years, and they have been in Dripping Springs for the last year and a half. In addition to ceramics, you'll find decorative pieces made of concrete, glass and metal. There are planters, pots, birdfeeders, hummingbird feeders, metal sculpture called "garden sticks" and more. You can't miss the straw-bale building that is Sunset Canyon Pottery!

## Una Tierra Distante

*14211 Ranch Road 12 North*
*Wimberly, Texas 78676*
☎ *512/847-6544*
**FAX** *512/847-6544*
**Hours** *Mon-Sat 9:30-5:30, Sun 12-5, closed Tues*
**Accessible** *Outside only*

"We carry pottery and distinctive folk art from distant lands; thus the name, Una Tierra Distante," owner Kim Hunt explained. The merchandise is purchased throughout Mexico and is "hand-picked" to provide a most unusual selection. There are chimineas in abundance and a large collection of clay pots of all sizes, both plain and painted, including animal-shaped pots. You will find wrought iron benches and large wrought iron baskets for plants. These baskets can be hung or placed around the patio. Also on display are birdbaths and statues, some of which hold plants. Una Tierra Distante's spacious, shaded setting provides a very pleasant atmosphere in which to shop or browse.

# *Red Rolling Plains*

## The Gardens of the Southwest

*5250 South 14th Street*
*Abilene, Texas 79605*
☎ *915/692-1457*

The Gardens of the Southwest, a landscape architectural firm, carries outdoor ornamentation for the retail customer. You will find large, very handsome terra cotta containers, Italian urns and other planters made of brass, copper, ceramic and stone. There is also statuary by Austin Productions, metal fountains and furniture (mostly *Brown Jordan*) from which to choose. See complete listing on page 231.

## Star of Texas Forge

*FM 2125*
*Brownwood, Texas 76801*
☎ *915/646-4128*
**Hours** *By appointment*
**Accessible** *Partially*

Don and Debbie Morelock are building quite an interesting "cottage industry" on their property. Don, a blacksmith, is forging garden art — trellises and figurative forms, as well as such practical items as hose holders, finials and plant stakes. And, Debbie makes charming birdhouses and feeders from "found art" objects. They also produce handsome gates and iron fences. The garden shop/gallery displays their wares, but a lot of their work is custom, so if you have an idea, give these talented metalworkers a call. The Morelocks recently opened a B&B where guests are invited to enjoy their native plant landscape and extensive herb garden.

*Directions: Take Highway 279 West from town. Turn right on FM 2125 and go about 3½ miles. Look for a large stone with a star. Turn left onto the property and "follow the stars" for about another mile.*

# High Plains

## Alldredge Gardens

*3300 North Fairgrounds Road*
*Midland, Texas 79710*
☎ *915/682-4500*
See complete listing on page 236.

## The Gardens at Pete's Greenhouse

*7300 Canyon Drive*
*Amarillo, Texas 79109*
☎ *806/352-1664*
See complete listing on page 234.

# Trans-Pecos

## Casa Verde Nursery of El Paso

*77 Fountain Street*
*El Paso, Texas 79912*
☎ *915/584-1149*
See complete listing on page 237.

# Gifts for Fellow Gardeners

When it comes to finding a present for one of my gardening friends, I generally go for a rare plant, a particularly good garden tool or some fun piece of apparel that I might not buy for myself. Of course your neighborhood garden center will have a wealth of wonderful choices, but we thought it might be nice to consider some other especially appealing little shops. We've included in this section all of the public botanical gardens and nature centers that have gift shops because many of them offer nature-related items for the children and grandchildren in our lives. Like art museum gift shops, these stores are worth supporting, and the gifts you choose may spark a lifelong interest!

# Regional Resources for Garden Giftware:
## *Cross Timbers & Grand Prairie*

### *Birdies' Backyard Habitats*
*3300 Airport Freeway*
*Fort Worth, Texas 76111*
☎ *817/ 222-0558*
**FAX** *817/222-0578*
**Hours** *Tues-Sat 10-6, Sun 12-5*
**Accessible** *Yes*

"We strive to be in concert with nature and espouse organics as much as possible," said manager Andrew Spear. This water garden specialty store carries lots of birdhouses and bird feeders. There are tabletop fountains, books and gloves and boots for the aquatic gardener. Our favorite item was the bamboo restraining system which force the roots upward for trimming. What a great lifesaver for anyone plagued with the dreaded "bamboo takeover!" The company will ship its wares.

### *Fort Worth Japanese Garden*
*3220 Botanic Garden Drive*
*Fort Worth, Texas 76107*
☎ *817/871-7685*
**Hours** *Mon-Sat 10-4, Sun 1-4; closed on Mondays (Oct-March)*
**Accessible** *Yes*

The Fort Worth Japanese Garden gift shop carries windchimes, birdhouses, greeting cards, books (predominantly on water and Japanese gardening), toys and tee-shirts. For the garden's listing, see page 44.

## *Piney Woods*

### *Blue Moon Gardens*
*Route 2, Box 2190*
*Chandler, Texas 75758*
☎ *903/852-3897*

See complete listing on page 305.

## Jordan's Plant Farm

*7523 State Highway 42 South*
*Henderson, Texas 75652*
☎ *903/854-2316*
    See complete listing on page 292.

## Tyler Rose Museum Gift Shop

*420 Rose Park Drive*
*Tyler, Texas 75702*
☎ *903/597-3130*
**Hours** *Mon-Fri 9-4:30, Sat 10-4:30, Sun 1:30-4:30; closed Mon (Nov-Feb)*
**Accessible** *Yes*
    As Jennifer Bennett, Executive Director and Curator of the Tyler Rose Museum, proudly states, "We are Tyler's gift shop specializing in items that reflect the city's status as 'Rose Capital of the Nation.'" You will find a wide range of gifts and mementos from candles, lotions, stationary and Christmas ornaments to rose reference books, birdhouses and feeders, topiary, potpourri, sun catchers and wreaths made from Tyler roses." A great place to find a present for a friend or purchase a remembrance of your visit! For the garden's listing, see page 53.

# Coastal Prairies & Marshes

## Armand Bayou Nature Center

*8600 Bay Area Boulevard*
*Houston, Texas 77058*
☎ *281/474-3074*
**Hours** *Mon-Sat 9-5, Sun 12-dusk*
**Accessible** *Yes*
    The gift shop of the Armand Bayou Nature Center carries wind chimes, birdhouses and bird feeders, rocks, books, items for children, tee-shirts and totes. See page 58.

## Houston Arboretum and Nature Center

*4501 Woodway Drive*
*Houston, Texas 77024*
☎ *713/681-8433*
**Hours** *Daily 10-4*
**Accessible** *Yes*
    The gift shop here stocks lots of items with a wildflower or nature theme. Among the selections are books, tee shirts, wind chimes, birdhouses and feeders, things to please children as well as adults. See page 60.

## Lilypons Water Gardens

*839 FM 1489*
*Brookshire, Texas 77423-0188*
☎ *281/391-0076*
    See complete nursery listing on page 318.

## Mercer Arboretum and Botanic Gardens

*22306 Aldine Westfield Road*
*Humble, Texas 77338*
☎ *281/443-8731*
**Hours** *Call for information*
**Accessible** *Ramp, but very small*

You'll find a good collection of regional gardening books and "wild flower themed" merchandise at Mercer Gift Shop. There are also note cards and stationary, mesquite vases, jewelry, porcelain boxes, windchimes and hummingbird feeders. For the garden's listing, see page 61.

---

## Teas Herbs & Orchids, Inc.

*32920 Decker Prairie Road*
*Magnolia, Texas 77355*
☎ *281/356-2336 or 1-800/660-5735*

See complete listing on page 306.

## Coastal Bend

## Corpus Christi Botanical Gardens

*8545 South Staples Street*
*Corpus Christi, Texas 78413*
☎ *512/852-2100*
**FAX** *512/852-7875*
**Hours** *Tues-Sun 9-5*
**Accessible** *Yes*

The shop at the Corpus Christi Botanical Gardens carries "a little bit of everything." The turnover is great, so you never know what treasures await you. There are all-natural wreathes handcrafted from vines and dried flowers, garden angels, earth angels and pixies and mesquite Santas. You will find books, windchimes, birdhouses and bird feeders. The gift shop carries a variety of plants such as annuals, perennials, shrubs and even trees. For the garden's listing, see page 63.

---

## Michael's Fluttering Wings Butterfly Ranch

*Route 1, Box 447A*
*Mathis, Texas 78368*
☎ *512/547-5568*
*www.butterflyrelease.com*
**Hours** *Mon-Sat (call for hours)*
**Accessible** *Partial*
**Mail Order**
**Catalog** *Free*

We first heard of this unique shop and garden on "Good Morning America." Bethany Homeyer started the business as a butterfly breeder in memory of her son, Michael. As a Texas Certified Nursery Professional, Bethany not only raises butterflies but also butterfly-attracting plants, most of which are natives. She ships butterflies anywhere! Next year Bethany will open a one-acre garden and several buildings for tours. She has written a manual for butterfly breeders, is working on one for gardeners and presently holds seminars. Books, tee-shirts, butterfly hibernation houses and butterfly and caterpillar "crossing signs" are available now, and more gift items will be offered in the gift shop. You can even order live, hand-raised butterflies in origami packages to be released at weddings and other special events. This business is truly a "labor of love" for Bethany, and as she assures us, "Butterflies do have their own personalities!" A visit to Michael's Fluttering Wings is certainly not to be missed, whether you are looking for butterflies or plants or just a beautiful experience.

*Directions: From IH-37 South, take exit 47 which is Swinney Switch. Go south on FM 3024 until you come to a crossroad which is FM 3024 and FM 534 and go straight for 1.5 miles to Ranch Road. Turn right on Ranch Road, go another 1.5 miles, turn right and look for the sign.*

# Valley

## Sabal Palm Audubon Center and Sanctuary
*P.O. Box 5052*
*Brownsville, Texas 78523*
☎ *956/541-8034*
**Hours** *Tues -Sun 8:30-5*
**Accessible** *Yes*

Birding and native gardening books have been the focus at the Sabal Palm Audubon Center and Sanctuary's gift shop, but the inventory is being expanded to include a variety of gift items. For the Center's main listing, see page 66.

# Rio Grande Plain

## Big Red Nature Store
*5001 Broadway*
*San Antonio, Texas 78209*
☎ *210/822-2473*
**FAX** *210/824-3388*
**Hours** *Mon-Sat 10-7, Sun 11-5*
**Accessible** *Yes*
**Mail Order**
**Catalog** *Free*

If wild birds are "your thing," this is your store! Not only does it carry books, accessories, feeders, martin houses, birdseed, bat houses and birdbaths, but it also publishes a terrific newsletter. If you are having a problem or just want "to get started," there's always someone at Big Red Nature Store to offer friendly, knowledgeable assistance. Customers Jack and Sandra Kinslow wrote to the owners saying, "Entering your store is like walking into an enchanted place dedicated to enjoying nature and always full of wonderful surprises. You do the work to find the best in everything and offer your personal interest and help when needed."

## Garden Gate at San Antonio Botanical Gardens
*555 Funston Place*
*San Antonio, Texas 78209*
☎ *210/829-1227*
**Hours** *Daily 10-5:30 (summer), 9-5 (winter)*
**Accessible** *Yes*

The Garden Gate at the San Antonio Botanical Gardens is a charming place to shop for tools, gloves, seeds, pots and garden ornaments such as windchimes, birdhouses and feeders and books. For the garden's listing, see page 68.

## Schultz House Cottage Garden & Gifts

*514 Hemisfair Park*
*San Antonio, Texas 78205*
☎ *210/229-9161*
**Hours** *Tues-Sat 10-4*
**Accessible** *Yes*

The gift shop at Schultz House is also worth a visit! It carries a large variety of books and booklets as well as flowering plants and vegetable and wildflower seeds. Also displayed are such gift items as cards, tee shirts, birdhouses and feeders, a lovely selection of windchimes and all sizes of hand-painted clay pots. For the serious gardener, there are gloves, aprons, tools and kneeling benches. For the garden's listing, see page 69.

# Central Blacklands & Savannas

## Ellison's Greenhouses

*1808 South Horton*
*Brenham, Texas 77833*
☎ *409/836-0084*
**FAX** *409/830-1455*
**Hours** *Mon-Fri 10-6, Sat 10:30-3:30*
**Accessible** *Yes*

In the gift shop of this large wholesale grower, you'll find a large variety of pots, planters, apparel, birdhouses and feeders, windchimes, books and jewelry. There is also a selection of indoor and outdoor furniture including wooden benches. As manager, Lisa Oldson, explained, "Our gift shop greenhouse carries the same plants available to the wholesale market, with the exception of trees and shrubs." By appointment, you can tour the company's five acres of greenhouses, brimming with colorful seasonal plants and much, much more. See page 299.

## La Selva Orchids and Nursery

*3910 Harvey Road*
*College Station, Texas*
☎ *409/774-4776*

As if a blooming orchid alone would not make a perfect gift, the shop is filled with "pretties" to please your gardening friends. See complete listing on page 334.

# Hill Country

## Austin Area Garden Center/ Zilker Botanical Gardens

*2220 Barton Springs Road*
*Austin, Texas 78746-5737*
☎ *512/477-8672*

The gift shop here has wonderful custom-designed tee-shirts, as well as seeds, toys and note cards. See garden listing on page 75.

## Fredericksburg Herb Farm

*402 Whitney Street*
*Fredericksburg, Texas 78624*
☎ *830/997-8615 or 1-800/259-HERB*

Delicious scents available here! See complete listing on page 308.

## It's About Thyme

*11726 Manchaca Road*
*Austin, Texas 78748*
☎ *512/280-1192*
　　See complete listing on page 308.

## Living Desert Cactus Nursery

*12719 Highway 71 West*
*Austin, Texas 78736*
☎ *512/263-2428*
　　The containers here are as interesting as the plants. There are lots of little items in this store that would make inexpensive but thoughtful gifts. See complete listing on page 339.

## Mike Adams Household & Hardware

*3110 Windsor Road*
*Austin, Texas 78703*
☎ *512/478-2141*
**FAX** *512/478-2142*
**Hours** *Mon-Sat 8-6, Sun 12-4*
**Accessible** *Yes*
　　Mike Adams caters to the gardener in his stock of household items and gifts. You'll find yard tools, hand tools, garden gloves, metal watering cans, seeds and outdoor thermometers. The decorative accessories include birdhouses and feeders, candleholders, planters and wall plaques. Located in Tarrytown Center, Mike Adams Household & Hardware provides a friendly, neighborhood shopping atmosphere.

## Wild Ideas: The Store

*4801 La Crosse Avenue*
*Austin, Texas 78739*
☎ *512/292-4300*
**Hours** *Tues-Sat 9-5:30, Sun 1-4 (open Mon in April)*
**Accessible** *Yes*
**Mail Order** *Yes*
**Catalog** *Free*
　　You have read our raves about the Lady Bird Johnson Wildflower Center in preceding chapters. (See pages 21 and 76.) While you are at the Center, be sure to visit the newly enlarged gift shop, Wild Ideas. Here you will find a wide variety of books, including the largest selection of books on native plants in the country. Wild Ideas also carries seeds, "state fact packets", pots, tools, gloves, gardening apparel and accessories. This is a great place to buy a gift, especially one for yourself!

# High Plains

## The Lattice Shop at Amarillo Botanical Garden

*1400 Streit Drive*
*Amarillo, Texas 79106*
☎ *806/352-6513*
**FAX** *806/372-6667*
**Hours** *Tues-Fri 10-5, Sat & Sun 1-5*
**Accessible** *Yes*

*(Listing continued on next page)*

At the Lattice Shop, you will find garden tools, wind chimes, birdhouses and bird feeders, gardening gloves and aprons, books, tee-shirts and greeting cards. For the garden's listing, see page 85.

## Lubbock Memorial Arboretum

*4111 University Avenue*
*Lubbock, Texas 79413-3231*
☎ *806/797-4520*
    Currently staffed entirely by volunteers, the gift shop here is open only on weekends (Sat 10-1 and Sun 1-4). It's worth supporting. Items include tee-shirts, bird feeders and nature-related books and toys for children. See listing on page 86.

## Trans-Pecos

## Chihuahuan Desert Research Institute

*Texas Highway 118*
*Fort Davis, Texas 79734*
☎ *915/364-2499*
    The gift shop at the Chihuahuan Desert Research Institute (four miles south of Fort Davis) carries windchimes and bird feeders, as well as nature-related books, note cards, games and tee-shirts. For the garden's listing, see page 90.

# A Mail-order Source for the Art of the Barbecue:

## BBQ Pits by Klose

*2214½ West 34$^{th}$*
*Houston, Texas 77018*
☎ *713/686-8720 or 1-800/487-7487*
**FAX** *713/686-8793*
*www.bbqpits.com*
**Hours** *Mon-Fri 8-6, Sat 8-4*
**Catalog** *Free*
    David Klose founded this company in 1986 with the idea of maintaining the trail-drive style of cooking. His custom-made wood, charcoal and gas-fired barbecue grills and smokers range from a $69 drum to a half-million-dollar catering rig. In addition to standard, garden-variety pits, you'll find that chuck wagons, trains, old perambulators and automobiles have provided inspiration for his "usable art." Mr. Klose is a man who loves what he does. A great storyteller, he makes visiting the factory an experience. You'll find hundreds of sizes in stock, but if you can't get to Houston, he'll ship his products anywhere in the world. "Steel doesn't lie to you," he observes in a serious moment. "One welder makes each unit. Handmade all the way. These guys are really artists!" The catalog pictures David Klose, Dave Engel and Stan Hanek with the caption, "These men are considered dangerous with cooking utensils in their hands. Infamous for serving up road-kill recipes."

# Landscape Architects

The following landscape architectural firms and nurseries with landscape architects on staff have indicated to us that they design residential projects and/or advise clients on a consulting basis. Most work on an hourly fee. We've listed them in alphabetical order, by region.

## Cross Timbers & Grand Prairie

**Fuller Cotter Associates, Inc.**
1805 C West Park Row Drive
Arlington, Texas 76013
☎ 817/274-3955

**River Glen Studios**
303 Southwest Barnard Street
Glen Rose, Texas 76043
☎ 254/897-7364

**Sid Smith & Associates, Inc.**
5201 Mosson Road
Fort Worth, Texas 76119
☎ 817/478-7183

**Sunset Landscape**
P.O. Box 8173
Fort Worth, Texas 76124
☎ 817/451-3700

## Trinity Blacklands

**Armstrong Berger, Inc.**
4404 Ridge Road
Dallas, Texas 75229
☎ 214/871-0893

**Boyd-Heiderich & Associates, Inc.**
703 McKinney Avenue, suite 438
Dallas, Texas 75202
☎ 214/871-1530

**Doug Lang Landscape Architecture**
2148 Barberry
Dallas, Texas 75211
☎ 214/948-8809

**Herman Thompson Associates**
1345 Chemical Street
Dallas, Texas 75207
☎ 214/637-3545

**Julia Baltser Designs**
3616 Binkley
Dallas, Texas 75205
☎ 214/521-1338

**Lambert Landscape Company**
6333 Denton Drive
Dallas, Texas 75235
☎ 214/350-8350

**Mahlon B. Perry, Landscape Architects**
13129 Meandering Way
Dallas, Texas 75240
☎ 972/392-4413

## Trinity Blacklands *(continued)*

**Michael Parkey, Landscape Architect**
6254 Goliad Avenue
Dallas, Texas 75214
☎ 214/824-7067

**Naud Burnett and Partners**
5217 McKinney Avenue, suite 202
Dallas, Texas 75205
☎ 214/528-7600

**Puckett's Nursery**
811 East Main Street
Allen, Texas 75002
☎ 972/727-1145

**Thompson Landscape Architects**
702 North Bishop, suite 2
Dallas, Texas 75208
☎ 214/948-9256

## Piney Woods

**Breedlove Nursery & Landscape**
11576 State Highway 64 West
Tyler, Texas 75704
☎ 903/597-7421

**Diane Derebery, Landscape Architect**
18018 Silverleaf
Flint, Texas 75762
☎ 903/597-6615

**Wilhite Landscape**
13186 Highway 64 West
Tyler, Texas 75704
☎ 903/593-5975

## Coastal Marshes & Prairies

**Ben Lednicky & Associates**
10555 Westoffice
Houston, Texas 77042
☎ 713/977-9059

**Colorscape, Inc.**
16318 Pecan Drive
Richmond, Texas
☎ 713/277-6122

**Condon Gardens**
1214 Augusta Drive
Houston, Texas 77057
☎ 713/782-3992

## Coastal Marshes & Prairies

(continued)

**David Morello Garden Enterprises**
608 Peddie
Houston, Texas 77008
☎ 713/880-3244

**Duke Landscape Architecture + Planning**
1815 Avenue K
Galveston, Texas 77550
☎ 409/762-5193

**Kathleen M. Perilloux, Landscape Architects**
6440 Windsor Parkway
Beaumont, Texas 77706
☎ 409/866-9847

**Landesign of America**
17045 El Camino Real, suite 121
Houston, Texas 77058
☎ 281/486-1414

**McDugald-Steele**
849 West 26th Street
Houston, Texas 77008
☎ 713/868-8060

**McKinnon Associates**
1137 26th Street
Houston, Texas 77008
☎ 713/869-2797

**SLA Studio Land, Inc.**
10260 Westheimer Boulevard, suite 770
Houston, Texas 77042
☎ 713/787-0719

**Teas Nursery Company, Inc.**
4400 Bellaire Boulevard
Bellaire, Texas 77401
☎ 713/664-4400

**Thompson + Hanson**
2770 Edloe
Houston, Texas 77027
☎ 713/622-3722

## Coastal Bend

**Doug Wade, ASLA Landscape Architect**
537 Chamberlain
Corpus Christi, Texas 78404
☎ 512/855-1951

## Valley

**Hewlett-White, Inc.**
212 North Main Street
McAllen, Texas 78501
☎ 956/687-5242

**Stuart Place Nursery**
7701 West Business Highway 83
Harlingen, Texas 78552
☎ 956/428-3411

## Rio Grande Plain

**Jeff Taenzeler Landscape Architect**
4810 Wesleyan
an Antonio, Texas 78249
☎ 210/558-9192

**John S. Troy Landscape Architect**
122 Lewis Street, suite 1
San Antonio, Texas 78212
☎ 210/222-1355

**L.H. Bell Landscape Architecture/Planning**
1107 White Pine
San Antonio, Texas 78232
☎ 210/496-7139

**John Meister Landscape Architect**
520 Alta
San Antonio, Texas 78209
☎ 210/821-6504

**Rialto Studio, Inc.**
4901 Broadway, suite 211
San Antonio, Texas 78209
☎ 210/828-1155

**Terry Lewis Landscape Architects**
5108 Broadway, suite 221
San Antonio, Texas 78209
☎ 210/826-5544

## Central Blacklands & Savannas

**Contemporary Landscape Services, Inc.**
106 North Avenue
Bryan, Texas 77801
☎ 409/846-1448

**Earthscapes**
5317 Loop 205
Temple, Texas 76502
☎ 254/773-4668

**Hal E. Stringer & Associates**
510 North Valley Mills Drive
Waco Texas 76710
☎ 817/776-6440

**Westview Nursery & Landscape Company**
1136 North Valley Mills Drive
Waco, Texas 76710
☎ 254/772-7890

# Hill Country

**Carolyn Kelly Landscape Architect**
2905 Oak Crest Avenue
Austin, Texas 78704
☎ 512/445-0431

**Dan Becnel Landscape Architects**
1716 Pecos Valley Cove
Round Rock, Texas 78664
☎ 512/218-1481

**Gardens**
1818 West 35th Street
Austin, Texas 78703
☎ 512/451-5490

**Inge Marie Carmel Landscape Architect**
209 West 39th Street
Austin, Texas 78751
☎ 512/371-1895

**J. Robert Anderson Landscape Architect**
1715 S. Capital of Texas Highway
Austin, Texas 78746
☎ 512/329-8882

**Russ Bragg Landscape Architect**
3930 Bee Cave, suite F
Austin, Texas 78746
☎ 512/327-3388

**TexaScapes, Inc.**
1603 Manor Road
Austin, Texas 78722
☎ 512/472-0207

# High Plains

**Alldredge Gardens**
3300 North Fairgrounds Road
Midland, Texas 79710
☎ 915/682-4500

**KDC Landscape Architecture**
306 West Wall, suite 1025
Midland, Texas 79701
☎ 915/686-8001

**Love & Son, Inc.**
1103 South Ross
Amarillo, Texas 79102
☎ 806/373-9563

**Paul D. Nash Landscape Architects**
3806 50th, suite 102
Lubbock, Texas 79413
☎ 806/793-0047

**Oliver Landscape Company, Inc.**
P.O. Box 15409
Lubbock, Texas 79490
☎ 806/788-1883

**Tom's Tree Place**
5104 34th
Lubbock, Texas 79410
☎ 806/799-3677

**Turner LandArchitecture**
724 South Polk Street, suite 250
Amarillo, Texas 79101
☎ 806/342-9400

# Red Rolling Plains

**Gardens of the Southwest**
5250 South 14th Street
Abilene, Texas 79605
☎ 915-692-1457

**John C. Shinn III, Landscape Architect**
2228 Valley View, suite 1106
San Angelo, Texas 76904
☎ 915/947-9236

**Paul Harrison & Associates**
901 Indiana, suite 550
Wichita Falls, Texas 76301
☎ 940/723-4926

**Scherz Landscape Co.**
2225 Knickerbocker
San Angelo, Texas 76904
☎ 915/944-0511

# Trans-Pecos

**Landscape Architectural Services**
3400 Doniphan Drive
El Paso, Texas 79922
☎ 915/581-2676

# Shopping by Mail

Today's busy life-styles have made catalog shopping more popular than ever. It's comforting to know that many garden products are as close as your phone, fax or internet connection! Before you place an order, however, here are 25 tips that could save you some grief.

## Catalog Shopping Tips:

**1.** Be sure you're ordering from a catalog that is current.

**2.** Read catalog descriptions carefully.

**3.** If you're ordering a plant, make sure that it is suitable for your growing conditions.

**4.** Consider whether it is of sufficient size to give you the kind of garden results you expect in your lifetime.

**5.** Read between the lines, and don't be misled by hype. The word "vigorous" may be a euphemism for a vine that can smother your fence in a single season Assume that inexpensive "collections" are the most common plants the company grows. A collection may contain a hodgepodge of hues that won't complement your color scheme.

**6.** Be sure the shipping and handling charges aren't excessive in relation to the order.

**7.** Order early in the season.

**8.** Specify exactly what you are ordering; list the name of the item, item number, flower color, size of pot, etc.

**9.** If you require a specific delivery date, state it clearly.

**10.** If you don't want a substitute, say so.

11. Be careful about timing when the products are to shipped. While most companies are attentive to the proper time for shipment, the company can't be expected to know when you'll be away on vacation.

12. If there's a toll-free number, don't hesitate to use it, but be sure you communicate all pertinent information (see previous tips).

13. If the order blank is too small for you to write all the information you wish to convey, photocopy the blank on a larger sheet of paper and use the bottom to write additional information. If the blank is too small to write legibly, look for a copier with enlarging capability.

14. Provide clear, complete shipping instructions. Include your phone number, even if it's not requested. Remember that private shipping companies such as UPS cannot deliver to a post office box.

15. Don't send cash through the mail. Paying by credit card gives you some recourse. Otherwise; send a check or money order.

16. Read the catalog to be sure your preferred method of payment is acceptable to the company.

17. Don't forget to add in shipping, handling and taxes if applicable.

18. Keep a copy of your order. If you're ordering by phone, make notes.

19. Read the company's guarantee policy to see if it will replace plants that die in shipment or fail to thrive in your garden.

20. Open and inspect the package as soon as it arrives.

21. If you have ordered live plants, get them in the ground as soon as possible. If any item fails to thrive, notify the nursery.

22. If you find items missing, notify the company at once.

23. If you need to return or exchange an item, do it immediately.

24. If you put the order on your credit card, check to make sure you were billed the correct amount. If the company offered to refund the price of the catalog with the first order, be sure that amount was actually deducted.

25. Save a tree. Don't order a catalog you don't need. Catalogs are costly to produce. If you regularly receive a catalog that doesn't meet your gardening needs, ask to be dropped from the list.

# Glossary

Here is a short vocabulary of terms used in this book and phrases gardeners will encounter in plant catalogs:

**Annual**. A plant that grows, flowers, sets seeds or fruits and dies within a year.

**Award Winner**. Generally a new cultivar (variety) of a plant that has received an award from a plant society for its special characteristics such as bloom color, ability to withstand drought, disease resistance, etc. (Because these plants are judged by professionals in test gardens located throughout the country, such plants may or may not be suitable for Texas gardens.)

**Balled-and-burlapped (B&B)**. Plants grown in the ground, then dug with the root ball intact, and wrapped in burlap for shipping and storage.

**Bare-root**: Stock that is shipped while dormant without any soil around the roots. Berry plants, fruit trees, perennials and roses are often sold in this form.

**Berm**. A man-made mound or bank of soil used to create topographical variety, to muffle sound or to channel wind or water.

**Biennial**. A plant that grows, flowers, produces seeds or fruits and dies in two years. Generally a biennial produces foliage the first year and flowers the next.

**Border**. A long, wide planting bed filled with perennials and flowering shrubs.

**Botanical name**. Every plant has a two-part scientific name: 1) the name of the genus and 2) the name of the species. For example, the complete botanical name of a post oak is *Quercus stellata*. (The genus is always written with a capital letter and the species name, which is often descriptive of the plant, is never capitalized.) *Quercus* is, thus, the botanical name for all oaks; *stellata* is specifically a post oak.

**Bud**. An unexpanded flower or shoot.

**Cation exchange capacity**. The capacity of organic matter to absorb nutrients and release them for plant use.

**Climate Zones**. A designation often seen on plant tags and in catalogs that was created to help gardeners select plants that are suitable for a certain region. The United States Department of Agriculture has established "winter hardiness zones" (Zones 1-10) that address average minimum winter temperatures as a way of predicting whether a plant can be expected to survive in the different areas of the country. (See pages 168-171 for a more complete discussion of Climate Zones.)

**Climber**. A plant that seeks support by tendrils, twining or aerial roots.

**Compost**. (*n.*) Material derived from the biological (aerobic or anaerobic) decomposition of organic matter. (*v.*) To convert matter into compost.

**Common name**. A plant's popular, non-botanical name. Common names vary from region-to-region, which is why horticulturists use internationally accepted botanical nomenclature to differentiate between plants.

**Conifer**. A cone-bearing plant.

**Cultivar**. A man-made variation of a species. In modern horticulture, people have selected out individuals from a species, and bred plants to be different from the parent species. In print, cultivar names follow the species name. Cultivars are always capitalized and in single quotes. For example, *Ilex vomitoria* 'Nana' is a dwarf selection of the large shrub/ small tree that is commonly called yaupon holly. Cultivars used in the landscape trade have generally been bred for improved size, hardiness and/or color. (Also see **Variety**.)

**Days to maturity**. Approximate time it takes for a variety to produce harvestable fruits or vegetables. Because local climate and soils factor into the equation, gardeners most often use the number as a way of comparing one variety with another.

**Deciduous**. A plant that sheds all of its leaves each year.

**Disease resistant** or **Disease tolerant**. Plant description that indicates a variety's ability to withstand common plant diseases. Resistant is the stronger of the two terms.

**Division**. A method of propagating plants (usually perennials or bulbs) by digging and splitting the root-ball into two or more pieces.

**Dormant**. A state of reduced metabolic activity in which plant tissues remain alive but do not grow.

**Drip irrigation**. The process of slowly applying water directly to the plant's roots via perforated hose or tube emitters.

**Dripline**. An imaginary circle one could draw on the ground directly beneath the outermost branches of a tree or shrub.

**Ecology**. The science dealing with plants in relation to their environment.

**Espalier**. (*n.*) 1) A frame or trellis on which plants are trained to grow flat. 2) A plant so trained. (*v.*) To train a plant to grow along a supporting trellis, wired wall or fence railing.

**Evergreen**. A plant that retains all or most of its foliage throughout the year.

**Exotic plant**. Any plant introduced from another region.

**Fertilizer**. A material that provides nutrients that plants convert into proteins, enzymes, vitamins and other elements essential for plant growth. Fertilizers may be organic or inorganic, liquid or dry, and may be formulated in different ways.

**Genus**. A classification of plants with common distinguishing characteristics; a subdivision of plant families. Each genus includes one or more species.

**Germination**. The sprouting of seeds.

**Graft**. The uniting of a stem or bud of one plant to the stem or root of another, usually for the purpose of improving the viability of a desirable plant form.

**Growing season**. The period between the last freeze in spring until the first frost in the fall.

**Growth habit**. General aspect of form and size of a plant.

**Habitat**. The natural locality of a plant or animal. In nature, plants share complex, interrelated habitats with other organisms in "communities" or "ecosystems."

**Herbaceous**. Plants that produce little or no woody tissue.

**Herbicide**. A chemical that kills or retards plant growth.

**Hybrid**. A cross between two species. Hybridization may occur in nature or result from deliberate crossing to produce a plant that is different from and more attractive or disease-resistant plant than either of its parents.

**Indigenous species**. A plant natural to a region. Generally, a species is considered indigenous to North America if it was here before European settlement. The term is used interchangeably with "native plant."

**Insecticide**. A chemical that kills insects.

**Invasive**. Any plant that crowds out other species in a habitat.

**Microclimate**. A small geographic location with very specific climatic conditions, such as a south-facing enclosed courtyard that would benefit in winter from reflected heat and lack of wind.

**Mulch**. A layer of organic or organic material placed on the soil surface to moderate soil temperature, reduce moisture loss and suppress weed growth.

**Native Plant**. Any plant that evolved in any given region without human intervention.

**Naturalize**. The ability of a bulb or perennial to multiply in the garden with no special tending. In landscape design, naturalized plantings create the look of a wildflower meadow.

**Organic matter**. A substance derived from plant or animal material.

**Pathogen**. Disease-producing organisms such as bacteria, fungi and viruses.

**Percolation**. The downward movement of water through the soil.

**Perennial**. A plant that lives more than two years.

**Pesticide**. Any chemical used to kill insects, weeds, etc. See **Toxicity**.

**pH**. A measure of the acidity or alkalinity of the soil on a scale of 1 to 10.

**Photosynthesis**. The process by which plants use the sun's light to produce food.

**Potting soil**. Material suitable for growing plants in containers. Generally made without natural soil, it may contain compost and such additives as perlite, vermiculite, sand, peat moss and charcoal.

**Propagation**. Reproducing plants by seeds, cuttings, budding, grafting or cloning.

**Solubility**. The degree to which a plant nutrient will dissolve in water.

**Species**. A single distinct kind of plant (or animal). Plants of the same species are similar in structures to each other, but sufficiently dissimilar to other plants in the genus to require a separate classification, as post oaks (*Quercus stellata*) are different from bur oaks (*Quercus macrocarpa*).

**Tender**. A plant that cannot withstand freezing temperatures.

**Topsoil**. The upper layer of the soil, suitable for growing outdoor plants. Packaged topsoil may contain natural soils, bark, compost and/or manure.

**Toxicity**. By law, pesticides must be labeled with one of three warning words regarding toxicity. **1**: Danger (or Poison) indicates the highest level of toxicity (a taste could kill a human). **2**: Warning indicates moderate toxicity (from a teaspoon to a tablespoon could cause death). **3**: Caution indicates relatively low toxicity (an ounce to a pint could cause death.) All pesticides, both organic and chemical, should be used with extreme caution.

**Transpiration**. Evaporation of water from plant tissue to the surrounding air.

**Variety**. A natural subdivision of a species, varying from the type in one or more characteristics such as plant size, foliage variation and flower color or form. The term "variety" is often interchanged in common speech with the term "cultivar."

**Weed**. Any plant that is growing where a gardener does not want it or a plant that out-competes or overruns it's neighbors (Bishop's Weed, for example, is not a misnomer.)

**Wildflower**. A flowering plant that grows in open meadows and woodlands without cultivation. All cultivated flowering plants began as wildflowers somewhere. Wildflowers may or may not be indigenous to the area where they are found. Many common plants that grow wild in North America are "adapted" species that were introduced by settlers from other continents.

**Wildflower Mix**. Seed mixes that may include species that did not evolve in the area where they are to be grown (non-native).

**Xeriscape**. A landscape designed to survive periods of drought with very little supplemental water.

# Geographical Index

# General Index

*Notes & Observations:*

*Notes & Observations:*

*Notes & Observations:*

# Nomination Form

*Based upon my personal experience, I wish to nominate the following garden resource for inclusion in the next edition of* **Great Garden Sources for Texans.**

Please include the source's name, address, phone number and your comments or observations in the space provided below, on a photocopy of this page, or on a separate sheet of paper. Mail, e-mail or FAX the forms to the address given below.

_____
*Source Name*

_____
*Address*

_____

_____
*City, State/Province & ZIP/Postal Coce*

_____
*Phone, FAX and/or e-mail*

## Comments & Observations

_____

_____

_____

_____

_____

_____

_____

_____

Please include your name, address and phone number below

_____
*Your Name*

_____
*Address*

_____

_____
*City, State/Province & ZIP/Postal Coce*

_____
*Your Phone, FAX and/or e-mail*

May we telephone you for more information about your nominee?

☐ YES

☐ NO

Please mail or FAX your nomination to:
**Great Garden Sources for Texans**
Post Office Box 50506
Austin, Texas 78763-0506 U.S.A.
**FAX** 512/476-8419
**e-mail** Pat@ddc.net

First printing January, 1999